Leonardo the Florentine

Cartoon for Saint Anne and the Virgin.
by Leonardo da Vinci.
(Burlington House.)

Leonardo the Florentine

A Study in Personality

By

Rachel Annand Taylor

With a Note on the Author's Work by
Gilbert Murray

Blue Ribbon Books, Inc.

New York

Twelfth Printing

PRINTED IN THE UNITED STATES OF AMERICA
BY THE POLYGRAPHIC COMPANY OF AMERICA, N.Y.

To

Dr Percival S. Connellan

from whose skill as a physician and a psychologist
this book has drawn what vitality
it may possess

Contents

Part iii.—*continued*

Part iv
The Hostel of Francis

Part v
Leonardo da Vinci

Contents

Part i
The City of Lorenzo

Part ii
The Court of Lodovico

Part iii
The Wandering Years

Note

RACHEL ANNAND TAYLOR'S verse became known to me first in the year 1909, through a very remarkable volume of poetry, *Rose and Vine*. It was poetry of intense imagination and exquisite craftsmanship, never simple, never commonplace, never easy, defiantly and mockingly anti-modern, and instinct with a rich and dreamlike beauty of phrase. It seemed almost impossible that such a book should attain any degree of popular success, yet it went almost immediately into a second edition, and was followed quickly by another volume of similar quality, *The Hours of Fiammetta* (1910). Critics who waited eagerly for Mrs Taylor's next work had to wait some thirteen years, and then received a learned, brilliant, wayward and fascinating treatise in prose on *Aspects of the Italian Renaissance*, of which I wrote at the time : " Certainly I cannot promise that a reader will find in this volume the white light of impersonal judgment, or that the right man will always be hanged. Every sentence has passed through the medium of a strong and sensitive personality, which some-times may distort, as it undoubtedly penetrates and reveals. . . . The book is through and through the work of a poet and has to be judged, like a poem or a Platonic rhapsody, by the beauty which it discovers and creates." The same year saw another volume of verse, *The End of Fiammetta*, which seemed both in style and outlook to show the effects of experience and disillusion ; and I now hear of the approaching publication of a profound esoteric study of Leonardo da Vinci.

I am told that unprincipled critics in disturbed states of society have been known to write reviews of books which they have not read. If I were to follow that criminal example I should say that Mrs Taylor's *Leonardo* will offend many readers and bewilder more ; that it will be strange and perhaps morbid, and at times startling ; that it is sure to be written with wide knowledge, sincere feeling, and exact scholarship, but that such qualities will almost be forgotten, for good or ill, in an exotic and riotous luxury of imagination and phrasing, and a power of poetic interpretation which at times acts like a flashlight. Altogether a book dangerous in its power of illusion, as Chaucer is dangerous to a weak speller: dangerous to students who cannot pick and choose

Note

among its highly personal pronouncements, and particularly to those young writers who are already too prone to be intoxicated by beautiful language and strange doctrine, but full of value and new light to sober persons who care about style and art and human personality and nevertheless know how to keep their heads.

GILBERT MURRAY.

21st June 1927.

Author's Note

IF, in describing one side of the psychical history of Leonardo, I have contemplated the full tide of Renaissance energy as it sweeps around his art, have tried to restore the cities in which he dwelt, and to reanimate the people who decided his movements, it is because only this kind of indirect approach seemed to offer any novel angle from which to consider his unique and baffling figure. The array of books, treatises, and studies concerning the amazing Florentine is overpowering in its serried numbers. Exhaustive and minute research has been spent on the details of his work and his existence, especially in France and Italy, comparatively little having been done in this country, though the volumes of Dr J. P. Richter remain invaluable, and the briefer essays of Mr Edward MacCurdy are lucid and scholarly. But nearly all the extensive accounts of Leonardo seem to present him as too isolated a personage, more unaffected by time and place than could possibly be even the most detached of mortals. Certainly Leonardo was not easily impressionable; but the vivid cities and the startling contacts of his period did become part of the consciousness that expressed itself in the *Cavallo*, *The Last Supper*, and *Mona Lisa*.

I have not tried to determine controversial dates or to decide the authenticities of debatable pictures and drawings; but have, on the whole, accepted the conclusions of authorities whose competence has been reinforced by large opportunity. When they differ, I venture to trust my own impression, for a searching though reverent attention to the imaginative phases behind the acknowledged masterpieces naturally develops criteria of its own. Not being a trained scientist, I have done little more for the analytic and experimental side of Leonardo's genius than keep its existence steadily in mind as balancing and disciplining the ambiguous spiritual mood behind his art.

But, while Leonardo walks a little apart, communing with truth and beauty in his absolute way, I have done my best to irradiate his mystery with such exploring rays as may proceed from the luminous morning of Florence, the rosy glow of Milan, the evening sky of Amboise; and to bring him to speech with Lorenzo, Lodovico, Cesare, Francis, and the rest, so that, frankly, he may regain rather than farther lose that fabulous air which he wore for his own and for the next generation, and which our modern biographers, in their sad manner, are so sedulous

Author's Note

to dissipate. Writers like Vasari, the Anonimo, Lomazzo, Cellini even, really did know more of Leonardo as a person than any twentieth-century critic can, and the fable at least was a report, if a magnifying report, of the truth.

Though I have devoted much space to the reconstruction of Florence and Milan, the two cities that chiefly affected Leonardo, in neither case do I consider the picture complete, for I have not dwelt on matters that appear entirely outside his interest. If, on the other hand, I seem to have lost sight of him occasionally, in no sentence have I really forgotten him as the reason for divagation. The study of Milan is perhaps overlong; but some analysis of the genius of that city is a necessary justification of the theory that it wrought considerable change in the great painter's psychology.

Of course, in forging some kind of imaginative logic for the progress of Leonardo's art, I have not flattered myself that long-sustained attention and much collateral study can discover more than vestigial truth. If I see him at times posing like a Cyrenaic philosopher, with ironic doubt and satire of established doctrine defending the unsuspected heresies of a mystical art, sometimes almost like a late lone primate of the race, concentrating in himself one of those species which Nature seems to elaborate only to lose, sometimes as an idealist intent on expressing an impossible desire not to be patterned in the world of matter he has so mightily ransacked, there are many other ways of regarding a spirit that will be for ever interpreted as variously as a sunset or a symphony. But the more one realizes the agitation of the Renaissance around Leonardo's composure, the closer the approach to the intellectual prince of the period.

I may have told some truth about Leonardo that many minds may refuse as unpalatable, though this is an age that, with all its failings, has certainly acquired a fairly liberal and honest attitude towards unusual psychical states. But, while attempting to suggest, probably with some excess of symbolism natural to a mind more at ease in verse, the cause of the disquiet in the beauty of Leonardo's art, I have said nothing to the denigration of his serene and restrained existence. I have remembered his own comment: "Falsehood is so contemptible that, if she said the noblest things of God, she would plunder the grace from his divinity, while Truth is of such surpassing potency that, if she praised infinitesimal things, she would lift them into matters of glory." And again: "The truth of things is a perfect food for fine intelligences; but it is not for wandering wits."

It grieves me that space does not permit me to give my complete bibliography; and that I have had to omit from the Appendix various

xii

Author's Note

pieces of information that should have found a place there. But I have left out nothing essential; and I have authority for even my glittering details.

The publication of this volume has been long delayed by many accidents of fortune. I should like to express my sincere regret that the book does not bear the name of Mr Grant Richards, who suggested the theme, endured with patience and courtesy the frequent dismay of the author, and finally brought the work to press with a lively sympathy surely unusual in the race of publishers.

RACHEL ANNAND TAYLOR.

Introduction

i

LEONARDO the Florentine! So he wrote himself wherever fortune drew him, however estranged and exiled he might seem from the bright city that bred him. As Leonardo the Florentine was he known by those alien places that gave him hospitality, however richly they might flatter him. For, sceptic and mystic, various artist and savant of all the sciences, cavalier and student, sweet with an ironic sweetness, strong with a serenity of grace, armoured in pride, with the Medusa on his breastplate, splendid but reticent, supple with courtesy, love-compelling, with some cruelty, beautiful in spirit and in body, fitted alike for the symposia or the sacred games of Hellas, a natural heir to the Greek tradition rather than the Roman, this great Renaissance figure inevitably proceeds from that supremely Renaissance City for whose midsummer festival he suddenly sighed in the quiet French castle of his closing years, remembering her, doubtless, in the resentful Dantesque regret with which all her exiles remained loyal to Florence. He was not Milanese, nor Roman, nor French. He seemed indifferent to the destiny of his city as to other mortal circumstances; he even served her enemies, as if suavely unaware of her danger. But the great exemplar of " l'uomo universale " was a Florentine; and he allowed it.

There are magical names in the history of humanity—names that are like shaken lights or sudden chords of music. They are properly to be called magical because they make an indescribable stir in the mind and provoke excited responses, and awake the sense of wonder. They are not often the names of the good, for Aristides is not a magical name, though Saint Francis is; they are rarely the names of the wise, for Confucius is not, though Plato is. They are only sometimes the names of the mighty, for even Constantine is not, though Charlemagne is. They are the names of the beautiful, the strange, the kindred of the gods, of the people who pass easily into legend because we do not question them as to what they achieved while we ponder what they were. It does not much matter what they have done. What they have not done, what they might have done, has usually a rarer quality of rainbow-like radiance. They had enchanting and vibrating personality; and so, though their eyes and hands have long been blown dust in the windy

Introduction

ways of Time, their glances and gestures are caught and carried thrilling down the besetting waves of the immortal ether.

ii

Few of us have not known some person or persons so by nature lavishly endowed as to seem doomed to conquest, whose words were so witty and exciting, whose voices had such a moving intonation, whose glances were so captivating, whose smile had such a promise of felicity, whose hands were so adept in beautiful and fortunate gestures, that they moved like the deeply plighted bridegrooms of fame, irrevocably destined to superb consummations. Yet, if they achieved anything at all, it was accidentally and by the way, as a courteous concession to friends, or a disarming apologia for enemies, and only as if human action were a second-best mode of expression. Their works in art, or in philosophy, or statecraft, appeared mere works of supererogation, beautiful though unnecessary in those that are justified by grace. For, born under some cryptic star, sealed to the orders of an Unknown God, they were as if busied upon some secret service, actually dispensed by their lord from the ordinary traffic of mortal affairs as they went on a heavenlier embassy. And the age may be unfavourable to them, or death may seize their young beauty untimely for a trophy like a great rose-white bough of may, or some dæmon of unholy desire, more potent for angelic hurt because of like essence, may destroy them. Madness or accidia may waste them; caprice may shatter their perfect crystal to a sparkle of dust. Whatever they do or leave undone, they live like a kindling of stars at the borders of mortality, like a faëry music prevailing against the crushing claims of reality. And whether theirs be a false enchantment or not, even the fanatics of truth hardly care to inquire. The common imagination is so taken in the toils of their charm, so subdued by a certain incomparable ease and grace of bearing, that it is moved as if to strange tears. Because they have transcended the limitations and leaden duties of their kind, because they live poetry, and are bondsmen only to beauty, it will love them as it loves the people in a great play. It will exalt their charm to a fable, and shape their cloudy glory into a glittering myth.

At least, so the racial imagination did once conspire with its heroes. A period that cannot create a Leonardo expresses itself mostly in depreciation.

iii

So Leonardo became a legend and a fable even to his contemporaries. Unlike many shining apostles of divine charm, he created much, though

Introduction

a strange fatality of destruction dogged, shadow-like, his bright traces. For picture and statue, for builded and graven and painted thing, he was praised extravagantly. But it was because he seemed to reconcile in himself all the contrary qualities of humanity, because he was intent on knowing and being rather than doing, because he was lovely in his person and exquisite in his ways and enchanting in his speech, because those delicate and sinister hands could master stallions, and torture steel like a ribbon, as well as wake a silver lute, because he could be painter, sculptor, architect, philosopher, and all the rest, and yet be a great personage with a leisurely air and a love of conversation, that he passed into legend, "l'uomo universale." *La Gioconda* might be lost indeed, as some of her strange sisters have incredibly vanished ; the meditation of Saint Anne and the sophisticated invitation of Saint John might be unwoven from our tapestry of reverie ; the uncongenial refectory-wall might refuse to keep even a ghost of *The Last Supper* ; that great softly-lighted vision of *Epiphany* in Florence might be darkened, and those manuscripts, that have been the spoil of armies and the envy of lesser thieves, might never have revealed the processes of the interstellar adventures, of his spirit. Leonardo would still walk in noble rose-colour through the twilit Florentine streets, with music and lights and other beautiful faces. Artists of all orders have their fame, but few have acquired the mythic kind—their personalities have been consumed by their works. The young Sophocles, crowned with roses, is choragus after Salamis : Sappho bends her strange head, softly smiling and violet-crowned : Virgil becomes a mediæval sorcerer and a philosopher. But even in the Renaissance, when artists might become princes among princes, only Leonardo keeps the attitude of a king. Michelangelo was jealously coveted, but only as an artist. Raphael was exploited and popular, but rather as a spoilt favourite than an equal. Leonardo, more than any other of the artists and thinkers, was of one temper with the despots of the time. Like a Medici, a Visconti, or a Sforza, a d'Este, a Malatesta, a Baglioni, or a Borgia, he obeyed the passion of the period, and developed his own qualities to the uttermost. Their way lay through burning cities and flagrant excesses and violated treaties and unstable magnificences, and all the creative paradoxes of conduct caused by a blind worship of Greek and beauty. His way led through forsaken masterpieces, the wrack of a thousand dreams, the shattered locks of a thousand curiosities ; his intimacies and alliances were with the Protean elements and the dæmonic forces of nature.

But their way went also and of necessity through love and hate ; while Leonardo might tread the wind and water but not the burning marl of that extreme suffering. He did not need his kind ; he was at heart

Introduction

indifferent to it, though he was patient and considerate with those who wore his spiritual livery, and courteous to such as bought his versatile services. This lord of bright companions was essentially lonely at heart. He painted to please himself, whatever opportunities came ; he experimented to satisfy his own insatiable curiosity, which was almost an intellectual lust. He never loved a woman, so a great area of dark-bright, quivering, and infinitely strange experience was unknown to him. He may have been a wonderful friend, but not to any equal. He knew the brilliant Lorenzo and Lorenzo's brilliant friends ; he knew Lodovico Sforza and all the vivid agitated figures of his Court ; he knew French captains and princes ; he knew the gentle reluctant Duke, Giuliano de' Medici, and the inflexible Cesare Borgia, and Pope Leo, cynical and luxurious, and King Francis, eager and young, still a squire of Bayard. They seem hardly to have interested him except as the givers of opportunity. Murder might flash a deadly dagger in the choir of Santa Croce, the Duchess Beatrice might lie dead in her golden robe amid torchlight and great lamentation, Astorre Manfredi might sink violated and poignarded in the Tiber by Valentino's will, Savonarola might burn and the Borgia corrupt, armies might come and go, France and Italy might interlock mortally in a duel the fiercer because there was love in it. He was indifferent, preoccupied with the great processes behind those sumptuous shifting patterns they traced in the driven dust. He squared his circles, and slid his interpenetrating scalpel in the light of burning Milan, seeking for some absolute truth.

Sometimes the blurred pages of the manuscript unconsciously betray exasperated nerves, but hardly a wounded heart. He considered love, but he was not subdued by it. As the years go on, he becomes lonelier and lonelier ; for those who possess and reconcile the qualities of their period to the highest degree are supermen, and doomed to some kind of solitude. Though it is no longer fashionable to call him " the Italian brother of Faust," and speak of him as the hierophant of some secret hermetic knowledge, those who accused him of traffic with forbidden arts were crudely expressing their sense of something sinister and paralysing in that enchanting spirituality. They felt that all great knowledge is gained only by unlawful sacrifice ; and probably they were right in thinking that Leonardo had surrendered too much. To gain his intellectual apotheosis he conceded his humanity ; and it did not struggle overmuch upon his cold altar.

More often than any other artist is Leonardo called " divine " ; and divinity of an unchristian kind did run sidereal through his veins. He was more and less than human. He had the serene and fascinating beauty one ascribes to an Olympian in exile ; he was capricious, a little

Introduction

cruel, adorable, excelling, a creature of fire and grace, with an exotic air, as if he were a princely changeling from another planet. One does think sometimes that the spirit of the Renaissance almost consciously cast him as the apostle of the new Olympos to which it aspired. But he comes from its burning creative centre of passion like a beautiful bronze from its furnace, almost passionless—not like Michelangelo whom the breath of the flame has scarred. Pure, puissant, he seems to wear a couchant beast for diadem on his head, and to carry a lyre like a Greek who has become orientalized in an Asian city. For there is just a touch of the monstrous about Leonardo, as about all gods. They are made of the sun and the moon and the stars and the dark holy fury of the natural earth which considers man no more than the bird or the panther, who are indeed less removed from her. So much must go to the making of a god that some wistful and evasive qualities proper to mortality are lost in the great process. Even in these days it is not too much to say that Leonardo's powers were godlike. But that still means he was not completely human. It also means that he lived in a duality of light and dark, in the perpetual conflict which the god maintains with his other self, the dragon. He seems to have kept the dragon at his feet with sensitive equipoise; but the need of vigilance absorbed some energy, and inhibited him in some ways from his art. This is a parable; but it explains something.

So it is wonder, it is fascination rather than love, that the " divine Leonardo " awakes in his contemporaries. But this kind of personal magic is as mighty as it is rare. Francesco Melzi lived under it; and was articulate for once in describing its extinction. Yet the stormy Michelangelo, faring better, has a comprehending Condivi to write his biography, because he is fierce and tender. Still better, he has a Tommaso Cavalieri for whom he can experience the true ecstasy of Platonic love. But yet again even Vasari, jealously possessed as he is by that same melancholy genius, is so overcome by the legend of his more mysterious rival that he rises into literature in recording it.

It all comes back to this. If you consider Leonardo as an artist, it is open to anyone to say, " Moi, je préfère Botticelli "—or another. If you consider him as a savant, you may think he is only a remarkably patient experimenter, with brilliant intuitions. But not one of the great Renaissance figures—Alberti, Lorenzo the Magnificent, Pico della Mirandola, Michelangelo, Erasmus, Montaigne—was so nearly " l'uomo universale." Not one so combined the creative and the critical intellect, not one was at once so great an artist and so great a pioneer of science; above all not one had so enigmatic a personality.

The idolatry he awoke, and still awakens, which causes the face of

Introduction

Mona Lisa to be considered like a mask of magic, and sacredly keeps all his works like reliquaries wherein you may see the liquefaction of some crystal blood, some ichor, has in later times provoked considerable revenges on his fame. His faction to-day talks of him too freely as " sage " and " mage "—a dull way of describing one who never pontificated, and who particularly disliked all dabblers in the dubious occult. So there is a fierce reaction against the " legend." Mr Berenson's last utterance on Leonardo has a recreant's violence, and breaks all his own æsthetic canons in its fury. The official moralists, again, darkly suggest that he evades their rules, the more annoyed because they cannot be precise in their charges. Leonardo's life was without observable sensual violence of any kind, a record remarkable in his period. His ethic was serene and indifferently pagan in the loftier sense. He belonged to a difficult æsthetic tradition and wore it like a distinction ; but, so far as we may know, he had " sublimated " his strangeness, an attitude, a " perversity " almost normal to Renaissance psychology, without much conflict. He probably corrupted his young men as much as Socrates corrupted Athenian youth, and no more.

It is true, however, that no overture to the description of Leonardo would be sincere if your nerves did not detect among the rare concerts of wood and wind instruments, trumpets and flutes and hautboys and organs and viole d'amore, the faint sinister throbbing of barbaric tympani. Among his flowering perfections there creeps that suggestion not only of the bizarre but of the monstrous. At one or two disconcerting moments one feels that Leonardo, indifferent at heart as the " Nature " of his devotion, is, like her, capable of communicating a horror incomprehensible to those who love humanity, the species that is at once her prince and her irrevocable enemy. It is as if his all-regarding ethos could permit itself the serene insensate glory that lies behind the earthquake, the flood, the gorgeous beast of prey—a mood not more wicked than lightning or leopards, but terrible and inimical to his kind. But, if the soul of Leonardo had phases in which, pardlike, it found the jungle, his disciplined reason so swiftly followed to cover the track that no slot could ever be found. Altogether, he contains his cruel and grotesque elements as imperturbably as Nature and as triumphantly as Art ; and the incalculable range of his winged and starry interests justify one who needed his kind so little. And whether his destructive principle ever escaped, shattering and shocking, into the physical realm, we can have only an impression, conveyed in terms of mere sensibility, and therefore unfair.

Whatever the emotional impression, the vague *arrière-pensée*, we must allow that a man cannot make himself into a legend by his own

Introduction

will ; it takes an immense conspiracy of believers to do that, and some divine quality is certainly necessary to excite such a devotion. When the name of one long perished still provokes flashing reactions of delight or anger, when his mind is still as differently translated as a sunset or a landscape is described by diverse gazers, there is a power in him not lightly to be dismissed, even by a period that belittles all the dead. This is an age of iconoclasts, but Leonardo does not reside in his images. It takes more dynamic force to begin a legend than to discover a star or a new element.

Modern critics incline to keep all the praise for Leonardo the scientist ; and it is true that, by unifying patience with imaginative interest, he attained a cosmic vision amazing for his time. But it is still most in his strange and dreamlike painting that his mysterious personality prevails, for there the less conscious part of him is revealed and allures. All his passion for shifting light and shadow, all his cunning perspective, all his pyramidal design, all his cool, deep, blue-green colours, are but meant to lay snares for a beauty from some remote and ecstatic shore —the beauty that knows what song the sirens sang, and what magic Helen learned in dead-golden Egypt, and how Dionysos fared in Hades. It is the beauty of sidereal flame and jasper twilights and spellbound waters. It is neither good nor evil ; and it traffics not in mortal desires or tears.

Some say Leonardo was not affected by the antique merely because he was not friendly with the grammarians. He was more antique than any, for he brought back the temper of the gods, being one of them. Gods that have been in exile, and have become amused, ironic, half compassionate in Gothic cathedrals and Hollow Hills!

But, serene as ever, they know their only duty is to disturb and disconcert humanity with their difference. Darkened and spoiled as Leonardo's canvas may be, any passer-by is arrested by that strange gaze which only this intimate skill can snare in its plots of light and shadow. He pauses, and has the æsthetic moment. He assents or revolts : he is troubled. And, if he be one of Leonardo's people, he is also soothed. He accepts the invitation and dissolves into the enchantment.

For it is true that Leonardo is not for everybody. He has his elect, his chosen. He always had his secret sept ; he is something of a sacred prince. He always has his enemies ; for many distrust the genius who has a dæmon. His lovers are aristocrats, like himself. Every artist has his clan ; but Leonardo's is a sodality. Let us admit that his initiates desire sophistications and subtleties for an ethereal food. Those who wish Leonardo to be simple may follow his scientific ways. For that is required only some mathematics. To apprehend him as an artist demands

Introduction

a temperament. Botticelli will give you more fantasy and more poetic rhythm, as well as more intricate and lovely patterns; Michelangelo will sound greater chords of a superb melancholia, and bring angels and men out of the dark like a demiurge. But Leonardo has troubled some arrogant eyes, and thrilled some difficult hearts, and altered the seed of the generations.

We look and speak differently to-day because Leonardo imagined his type. He knows the mysterious annihilations where all extremes are as one, and all fanatics lay down their startling spears of love and hate, where achievement becomes a folly, and the over-refined spirit recoils from the blunted and debased actions, the soiling contacts necessary to a triumph, where fastidious hands wearily refuse that defaced currency of deeds wherewith the vulgar buy their expression. They have passed beyond the extremities of love and are done with the physical; their great wisdom is silent like mere exhaustion. They have stayed so long in the House of Ecstasy, they have gazed so unwaveringly in the Mirror of God, that there is nothing they care to write even on the Emerald Tablet. Leonardo the artist uses Leonardo the scientist to fix his design, to mix his cool colours, to dart his true perspectives, to build his pyramids, to imprison light like Ariel in a web. But what he gives as a painter, like a suspension of pale rose-colour in the clear æsthetic pleasure, is a mystical experience of the contemplative kind in the higher and wider sense; and he did not give the key to it because he knew the only key was the immediate apprehension of his gazer.

There are phases and adventures in the mere attentive meditation of Leonardo, even for a disciple. For, when the first enchantment becomes no more amazing, there is a continual surprise in considering the incessant variations of that intellect as prismatic and as sudden and unwearying as a fountain. Then follows an odd sense of intense labour in icy caverns where the only things that glow are furnaces and retorts, and the only outlook is through crevices to the inevitable and august motions of the infinite sea, and the preordained march of those legionaries of necessity, the suns and stars. There is doubt if the enchantment be not one with the Medusa's, that once had power over the master, and one longs for roses and the sound of weeping and laughter. Till the cavern dissolves in smoke, and the evocations of the drawings begin, and you see musing women with spindles and fruit, and young men with vines in their curls, and children playing with kittens, and angels dancing in a ring—and the travesty of these again in faces grotesque and terrible. So you understand that all things indeed are gathered in his gaze, and that all created things are equal to his pleasure in creation, his pleasure in that faint floral foam he sees cresting the

Introduction

falling waves of time. And he seems a god again, with a god's defects. Inhuman as well as superhuman !

You knew the Olympians, it was said, when they moved among mortals because of their unwavering eyes. So Leonardo bends over his corpses and crucibles, and gazes at the universe with unflickering lids. And when he is young he is like Apollo, and when he is mature he is like that bust of Dionysos that is often called Plato ; when he is old, for all his wisdom the chain of his humanity drags more heavily upon him, and he looks like Tiresias—with a touch of Tithonus. Perhaps he would be greater if his eyes had been shaken oftener with the tears that are in the mortal things he knew too well. Almost we wish that the serene exponent of the Renaissance knew something of its extremes—of the rare enthusiasm of a Pico della Mirandola, of the rage of a Malatesta, something of the tortured sweetness that wreathes the brows of certain of those princely heads on the triumphant medals of the time. Shakespeare was not divine, and his vision seems more desirable than the divine Leonardo's. Even Michelangelo is more moving because he greatly loved in diverse ways. But Leonardo's may be the higher mode. The divine way of beholding the universe has its authority, and may have its compassions. The invitation of his Saint John is to some mystery of beauty we do not altogether understand. For with all his inquiries and all his manuscripts he left his last secret unexplored and untold. He was in exile after all, and mortality lay on him in the form of fear. Moreover he was too much a hybrid. Realist and idealist met in him, and the antinomies of the Renaissance found their intellectual reconciliations ; the conscious life subjugated too steadily and completely the unconscious life that feeds great art. The soul of Leonardo is androgyne like that Saint John, beautiful and sterile like a white flame in the dark. It is an undying flame, however, and can still communicate its great unrest.

It is true that he did not render to beauty all that he owed, that his devotion to science might have been more valuable if it had been less selfish and solitary, that, though he was kind to persons, he was indifferent to humanity. But his was yet an endowment so great that no possible set of circumstances could have sufficed to its pomp of display, no single mortal life have given time enough for its exhibition. His record seems but one phase of an existence begun and continued in eternity : he did behave as if he were immortal, and probably was right. Perhaps the mere exercise of transcendent powers enriches the traditions of the race. Whether such rare beings exist as a portent of warning or of promise, as part of the inexorable economy or the stupendous waste of nature, is still an insoluble

Introduction

problem. Though he comprehended all the august elements that made the great Italian Renaissance, and all the qualities and defects that undid it, part of him was not of any period, and so is of every period. Leonardo is never forgotten—he has some lure for all the centuries.

Yet let him live not as Leonardo the Universal but as Leonardo the Florentine. Leonardo da Vinci is a victorious name, but Leonardo the Florentine has a sound as of lovers' lutes. For "Florentine" has to most votaries of art and history a peculiar connotation, pictorial and musical, yet ethical in its way. It is a drift of images a cloud of perfume swirling into lovely shapes. It means waters lapsing by ancient walls, moonlight on the cypresses, narrow streets between high palaces, a slender white boy in violet, a slender white girl in gold brocade, a stricken viol, a silken night and a sun-drenched day, scholars in black velvet, a group of iris-flowers, a branch of jasmine, a crystal cup with gilt acanthus and lions' feet, the flash of a dagger, the call of a carnival song, a white statue clasped by a trailing vine, a sunken garden of roses, a sudden fire for sweet vanities, and for the Preacher who calls them vain, a line from Dante, a wreath of wreathed heads from the *Decameron*, a breath of incense for Christ murmuring Greek, or for Plato as the apostle of Divine Love, the Virgin and her lilies, Cybele and her lions, Aphrodite among pale roses, a golden pageant and a siege of steel, a dome, a campanile, and an angry tower—the pride and passion of a City, acting, choosing, fighting, dreaming, praying, loving and hating, a City like a Greek flute-player in a rose-red robe, a City like a young herald shod like Hermes, a City like a queen-warrior on a champing steed, a City sweet, cruel, capricious in her moods, but steadily intent on splendid things, a City in the end like Michelangelo's *Dawn*, a beautiful Despair.

So was she romance to Leonardo, though less consciously. His pride was in her intellectual primacy, her place as the first Republic in the world of thought, as a paradoxical democracy of spiritual aristocrats, the great Academy where scholars and artists must go to school. She was the City of the tower of Giotto, the gates of Ghiberti, the dome of Brunellesco, the City of certitude, of clean satisfying achievements, great captures of beautiful vision within delicate indestructible lines, the City that disdained the second-best, and would not trade in spurious things, the City where intellect did not quarrel with emotion, and the religion of beauty achieved its noblest synthesis. The intelligence of Florence was finer, clearer, more fastidious than that of Rome or Venice or Milan or Naples. When Leonardo called himself Florentine, he drew the old distinction between Greek and Barbarian.

Introduction

And, though he had been vexed in that City of his, it was also, even for Leonardo, the one place where the Arno flowed jade-green in the evening, and the midsummer moon hung over the red-hung festival and the heathen fires of the Precursor. Even for Leonardo one peculiar city was the City of Youth; and so a sweet and sad note of nostalgia comes rarely through the foreign twilight round the quiet castle of Cloux.

The Prologue

AWAY beyond Empoli, not far from Florence, a little village
lies asleep round its old fortress-tower. And, beyond Vinci
again, on the sun-steeped slopes of Monte Albano, is a lovely
lonely place where the seas of olive fluctuate grey and green
and silver, and the vines are trained in odd-shaped pyramidal terraces,
or garlanded from tree to tree. The suave and gracious ranges of the
Tuscan hills make a serenely dying harmony in the distance, pricked
here and there in the nearer movements by the poignant note of some
solitary cypress. Overhead the great pure light of the Tuscan evening
soothes the skies like a benediction. The small sweet Tuscan roses are
sweet in the air. On the lonely road a peasant sometimes absently
follows his calm white oxen. A procession of Silenus would seem as
natural. The secret half-smiling hills, the sleepy woody places, are
haunted by spirits not unaware of mortals, and the caverns and lakes
murmur of that strange Sybilla who sometimes becomes in Italy a
Venus of the Hollow Hill. It is a " pagan " country in the true Latin
sense of the word, ungrieving and unchristened. The pipes of Pan
sound in the brake as unconcernedly as the larks in the sky. Lake and
river in the distance keep the wonder of hidden water.

The blood-red poppies are lavishly spilt everywhere, as if some
strange Cupbearer had passed that way. But it is not the Iniquity of
Oblivion, for here a young man caught and held a girl among the
vines, wild satyr and Mænad in the triumphal Renaissance day—and
the love-child of their fortunate moment was Leonardo da Vinci.

It was only a momentary illumination. The young man presently
remembered that he was a notary, and the son and grandson of notaries,
playing at an idyll with a hill-girl while his family dwelt in their country
casa. So he did as he was told. In the year of his child's birth he
married the bride chosen for him, the first of four; and his farther
recorded history suggests that he henceforth trod a bourgeois path of
safe domestic sensuality. As for Caterina, she submitted to a peasant
bridegroom with an uncouth name, and surrendered the child already
beautiful and rare enough for his father to desire him—too rare and
beautiful for her to keep.

The record tells no more of Leonardo's mother, nor suggests with what weariness of weeping or agony of fatalism she ended her chapter of high tragedy, and sank heavily to a dullard lot. The only bond of woman to which her son seems sensitive is that of the mother and her unborn infant. When he searches so absorbedly into the anatomy of life he recurs again and again to the idea that the dim prenatal months can shape immutably the destiny of the child, compact of the agitations and quietudes of the blood and nerves that feed it. Perhaps he thought his own secret unanalysable fear, that shackled his pride, estranged him from the dangerous drama of action, turned the keys upon the dangerous drama of thought, and at the end paralysed one beautiful hand, was born twin with him from the frightened soul of a brooding mother.

If he meditated thus, it was long afterwards, and otherwise was probably somewhat pleased that he was no legitimate offspring. For the word " love-child " is a pretty phrase, telling of an embrace that at least was hardly compulsory. The Renaissance period was a great age of love-children. In Ferrara and in Rimini, in Urbino, Naples and Milan, they were heirs of the house, and sometimes took precedence of their lawful brethren. In Milan the dukes bought alliances and sealed treaties with the weddings of their natural daughters. In Rome, the popes and cardinals openly exalted their children. In Florence, Leonardo's great predecessor, Alberti, was a love-child, immediately adopted into a family whose gracious and noble manners were proverbial. Carlo de' Medici was the son of a lovely Circassian slave. Giuliano de' Medici's natural son was gladly received into the family as a remembrance of his early-slain father. Love-children were popes, princes, captains, cardinals, poets, artists like Giorgione. Leonardo, considering his heavier stepbrothers, might have joined with Shakespeare's Edmund in his characteristically Renaissance cry :

> " Base ?
> Who, in the lusty stealth of nature, take
> More composition and fierce quality,
> Than doth, within a dull, stale, tirèd bed,
> Go to the creating a whole tribe of fops,
> Got 'tween asleep and wake ? "

The Renaissance put a great value on intensity. "Fierce quality " was all it asked, recognizing that the children of the passionate moment might have more " virtù " than those of the arranged marriage, if they were delicately bred.

Caterina was a peasant, says one account ; " di bon sangue " says the Anonimo. She may have been both. In the Italy of that day princely

The Prologue

conquerors went recklessly about, and where they loved they took. From the beginning Leonardo moved like an aristocrat by birth as well as temper ; and some superb ancestry may have stirred in his blood. Notaries, though a respected guild in Florence, do not bear themselves so proudly. They are incurably middle-class, by nature obsequious to the propertied. But genius is always inexplicable by the pedigree of parents. There is an element of divinity in all birth, as if a god had at one moment sent his strange essence through the mortal, changing and quickening the seed. When the intellectual prince of the Renaissance was born, Dionysos, serene giver of ecstasy, intervened. Leonardo, like Alexander the Great, had a weakness for a fabulous infancy, as his odd story of the prophetic vulture shows, and, if he could have eliminated a parent, it would have been the notary. Among the vines he was born and among the vines he grew. They paid him with a vineyard in Florence ; they paid him with a vineyard in Milan. The monks sent him wine as a bribe for their picture. Like that of a kylix was the design and decortion of his earlier life, as he sate at communion and lyre-playing with his wreathed and beautiful young men. His existence would have been like a curious and exalted ritual if the inevitable disturbance of what seemed to him vast caprices of circumstance, like great wars, had not marred its choric ceremonies. He died meditating Saint John the Forerunner as a subtly-inviting twy-souled Dionysos.

But the olives also were his friends, those trees of wisdom and great melancholy, since among them the gods have suffered. Leonardo has his own melancholy, interlacing the glittering intrecciamenta of his life with a sable strand. For all his beguiling conversation and the plaintive gestures of appeal he seems to make occasionally to the young people in whom he takes pleasure, the loneliness darkens around him as he pursues the long quest for some absolute truth, some extreme beauty. The departure for France is not a triumph but a defeat.

The château of Cloux was a long spiralled way from the country villa near Vinci, where the beautiful and distracting child grew startling in the household of quiet elders, whose attention and diversion he must have plundered greatly for some while—a grandfather and grandmother, an uncle and an aunt, a father, and a languid young stepmother, soon to be succeeded by a second, childless too. His own mother vanishes from his history ; the speculation connecting her with a servant to whom in late years he showed some kindness being very idle, one authority arguing that she was identical with his mother because he paid so much for the funeral, another, because he paid so little.

She may have waylaid him with a longing look as he went brightly among the vine-dressers and olive-growers, a tranquil folk whose quaint

The Prologue

heathen stories were figured shards of antiquity as potent in suggestion as the grammarian's brown scripts. His fine mind seized quickly on all that was given to it, and early showed its pleasure in versatility. Leonardo, attentive to his own myth, tells that, as he lay in his cradle, a vulture descended and struck his mouth several times with his tail. The strong birds nested in the ruined robber-keep of Anchiano, not far away from him; but it sounds like a lonely leonardesque joke—of which Professor Freud has taken an elaborate and surprisingly ingenious advantage. But it is certain that some odd incident drew his childish eyes with passionate sympathy to throbbing wings, and that he gazed long at the beauty of pinions patterning the stainless sky.

From his infancy, what he saw he drew, even while he learned the simple things his guardians could teach him. Also he could ride very soon, and became intimate with the ways of horses. He was wonderfully lithe, and ambidextrous.

He was indeed a child of great spaces; and, though he was formed by the splendid cities through which his progress of necessity lay, he maintained a nostalgia for the far horizons and the mountain slopes, so that in courts and camps he kept in his mind august solitudes and the processions of the heavenly tides, while his miraculous eyes habitually recorded the ways of bird and beast and flower in delicate detail. Even when he devises glittering masques for Lodovico, the great wings of the spirits of wood and wind and water seem lifted behind him, and mingle their cool inviolable shadows with the feverish lights and the gaudy raiment. When he absorbedly draws circles and cones and pyramids, his deeplier-dreaming self will seize his hand and evoke faëry violets and colombines among the inexorable arrays of geometrical figures.

For all imaginative children, the countryside—especially a woody countryside—is an experience of fascination and terror. They live as in a fable, with wide retentive eyes; but the woods of Westermain do have their panic even for the fearless. And there is a hesitation and a sense of shock about Leonardo's later actions, as if his great courage often failed. The orange-tree grew, and the figs ripened round his homestead, but the wild things stirred in the upper woods and the hills. Perhaps, like Marius the Epicurean, he lifted the leaves and found a coil of snakes and became suddenly sick with the apprehension of evil. At least, the idea of the Medusa seems to haunt him. There was some horror among the vines, some crucifixion among the olives when, in a little flicker of wind, their turning leaves clothed the slopes with sudden silk of silver. It was a dark and obscure apprehension for that imperious child, early unafraid of the great trampling horses. But certainly to his infinite curiosity was added a withholding fear most unexpected in his

The Prologue

temperament, in which courage is no obvious ornament, but a condition, a steady implication, a merely axiomatic quality. Probably the vague distress of a unique mind, realizing soon that it is definitely condemned to a solitude in which it must contemplate the things of good and evil from an unusual angle and so without sympathy, was reinforced by some childish panic in his Pan-haunted birthplace.

Yet the woods have secrets of beauty as well as terror. Leonardo's mythopœic mind is, in the true sense of the word, nympholept, nymph-stricken, nymph-enchanted. His are the eyes of one who, having seen one flash of moon-white immortality in the brake, looks coldly on all womanhood thereafter, since mortal experience cannot yield the quality of oread or naiad. Pan-stricken, nymph-stricken, he seems, for good or ill.

He learned what formal knowledge they taught him, learned it quickly and impatiently. It was simple enough, probably. He acquired more Latin later on. Meanwhile, like the grave fair boy in Luca della Robbia's *Grammar* in the Campanile, he studied the primary matters of reading and arithmetic, and despised them a little. He sang sweetly and drew constantly. At last his father, proud enough, took his drawings to his friend Verrocchio, and Verrocchio received the astonishing pupil who was to find his tradition such an admirable school for his temperament as well as his powers.

The woods, the waters on the way to Florence, the skies, the spirals of the birds in the skies, the smiling of the lonely women that watched his infancy and which was all of woman he desired to know—these he took from Vinci, and the blood of the vine. From the undulations of the dreamy Tuscan earth, gracious with its symbolic fruits, he drew space and freedom, so that even among the crowds that waited on princes he moved with a sense of space and solitude about him. And he learned the illimitable ways of light, and the mysterious ways of the shadow, and brooded thereafter on that eternal opposition in union which is at the core of all mythologies, till it became his supreme artistic pleasure to imprison the concentrated and exquisite spirit of brightness in the caves and grottos of the dark.

Part i
The City of Lorenzo
(1452-1483)

Chapter i

The Aspect of Florence in Leonardo's Time

i

THE Tuscan woods and waters bore him, great cities bred him, and Florence most of all. In 1469 Leonardo's family moved entirely into the town, and when he was seventeen he was altogether his own master in the crucial city of the new Hellenistic civilization.

Florence was then a sweet and dangerous capital of ideas, lions in her courts, lilies on her banners, working out the finer, franker, more Athenian qualities of the middle Renaissance under the proud guise of a Republic, with all the encouragements of a politic and sympathetic tyranny in that Medicean rule which broke into gold with the Magnificent Lorenzo. For, as other artists made pictures or music or books or palaces for God or man, so he loved to compose a city. Therefore he carved and gilded and crowned the noble place, decorating alike her cloisters and her carnivals, ravishing Greek scripts for her libraries, fostering her scholars and artists, sending Italian songs to break in high-flung foam against the dark façades of her palaces. If he fitted the haggard falcon of Florence with gilded jesses he flew her at the prey of her own desire ; and the lure with which he drew her from her bright skies was beauty.

To the imperious City of the Red Lily, still shaken from time to time by the feverish changes and strifes that enraged Dante, her denunciant incurable lover, to Florence, emotional, reasonable, severe, sumptuous, sceptical, mystical, libertine, idealist, steadily demanding the hard, bright outline for the darkly burning symbol, Leonardo early carried his own resolution of that conflicting period. He brought an incredulous curiosity, a mystery of emotion subtilized by the intellect, a new kind of craft for the things of art, a new method for the things of knowledge, and a character that raised all the Florentine qualities to their highest power, even while it rarefied and enriched them with a baffling mood of heavenly serenity. He was to capture his vision of beauty with a novel technique, while his unresting mind steadily drove the share of reason through all the world of fact that was not inexplicable but merely unexplained. So in Florence he early set his amazing parallelism, that never could find coincidence and

3

contradiction in time, since the lines ran true in different atmospheres, one in the physical air, one in the spiritual ether. The scepticism of Florence edged the questioning brain of the thinker, the mysticism of Florence sank through the reverie of the artist. A wisdom won by many refusals, a beauty set about with swords and ordeals, these were the desires of all the great Florentines, and they were Leonardo's desires.

"Lo spirito bizarro fiorentino" was as original and exciting as the City's own peculiar dye of crimson. It had included and fused spirits so diverse as those of Dante, Cavalcanti, Petrarch, Boccaccio, Giotto, Arnolfo, the Medici. It was a city made in the past by hunters and weavers. It was subtle in every sense, created by the meditations of folk that wove thought as well as silk and wool on their looms, by the dyers that plunged their tissues in vats of noble colour, by the descendants of the aristocratic riders, the swift, fierce hunters of the mountains, by witty chafferers in the wares of these. The lilies were red, the saints were the Baptist and the Magdalene. It meant steel and silk, it meant lions and lilies, it meant lute and trumpet ; it was made of love and war, by Ares and his lover. Under its brightness it hid a dark mystery, the sombre temper of the unknown Etruscans of the hills whose chimæra ambiguously abode within its gates. A disquieting vanished people these, with obscure earth-gods of a menacing kind and an art with something hostile and sinister in its queerly-smiling images. But wonderful goldsmiths, beside whose thin chains, dropping beaten flowers and vaselets, a Cellini jewel, even, looks a little heavy !

ii

Florence was then a clear and lovely city. Vasari and the Duke Cosimo, Jesuitry and the baroque were as yet far-off enemies to her beauty. There is something to be said for the baroque in Milan, in Naples, in Rome, and in Venice, for elements of ostentation have always existed in the temper of these cities; and, when the sincerity and passion of the Renaissance perished away, the pomp passed easily into the pompous. But turgid line and tumid form and impotent gesture were never in the mood of Florence : now she is like a great picture over-scrawled by an idiot. The twentieth century cannot spoil her as the seventeenth has done. She was Florence most when she shone new-coined from that Renaissance mint, where the masters and followers of Arnolfo and Giotto were Brunellesco, Michelozzo, Alberti, Ghiberti, Donatello.

In Leonardo's day she lay beautiful by her green-yellow river, still gripped by her strong walls and locked by her ancient gates, though the cool villas climbed the slopes of her serene and reasonable hills, and in peace the portals were open to the gardens and vineyards where the

Florence in Leonardo's Time

grapes swang between the fruit-trees. In the great light of the sunset she rested, laved by that clear, thrilling air that quickened and stressed all the senses, that strung to concert-pitch Leonardo's tunable nerves. The suave and harmonious lines of the hills around her were composed by God remembering that He is an artist. From the heights she seemed an arrangement in plaques of ivory, softly stained red and green and topaz, richly blurred at the edges. White spaces showed her many piazzas, green spaces her many gardens. Her beautiful bridges went with graceful steps across her river. The mighty palaces were walled like keeps. Hundreds of towers, long since erased, stood subject only to the dominion of the terrible Tower of the People. The Dome had risen moon-wise to its perfection. The Campanile sang wonder into the lyric sky.

The Duomo, the Baptistery, and the Campanile stood amazingly together, a superb and delicate bulk of building, divinely and idly at ease among the everyday hurry of mundane life, splendidly matter-of-course to the crowd that had passionately willed it to be, and to be superlative, since " it was the noble city's soul, which is the soul of all her citizens." Life eddied around as it eddies to-day. It is daily bread, and its Italian God is indulgent to this world's affairs.

Created patiently by Arnolfo, Giotto, Brunellesco, Michelozzo, Ghiberti, the Duomo was still the proud concern of the exacting citizens, who critically took toll of their artists for its farther decoration. The colour of the completed part was not so faint then as now, when it is cream and green and ghostly-rose under the moon, its exquisite arcading climbing nearly as far as the lightly-supported dome of Brunellesco, doors and windows beautifully inset, carven and storied and frescoed, with delicate Madonnas over its least portal, and the two Cantoria rapturous within— wrought like an embroidery, arrogant as an army with banners. The round Baptistery, still brooding over the ancient gods, black and white, built with irregular tender eurythmies, glorious within, with stories written in gold mosaic and noble tombs, kept the graven treasure of that Silver Altar which was the City's Palladium, with the Cross containing the fragment of the True Tree of Suffering—Charlemagne's love-gift to Florence. (The Baptistery? Leonardo would have raised it, and inserted the basement of the plan.) The Campanile, carven toy of the angels, sudden and sweet and perfect, perfect like the pillars of Pæstum, or a spire of rose-white gladiolus, perfect in itself and its unisons, sent its carillons of melody through the great symphony of the triple group. Leonardo, learning the three by heart as part of his education, will remember always, even as he meditates a treatise on cupolas amid the more restless and petulant buildings of Milan, the easily-borne dome of Santa

5

Leonardo the Florentine

Maria del Fiore, the calming round temple of the Baptistery, the singing campanile of Giotto, the delighting gates of Ghiberti.

Statues, doors, broideries, crucifixes, vessels, were still a-making for this trinity. And so for Or San Michele, the church of the guilds, lifted and squared, riveted strongly from a grain-market to house a miraculous Madonna, a great cube pierced by arrows of beauty, its smooth mass decorated with medallions and saints in carved tabernacles, its painted roof covering the glittering pinnacles of Orcagna's triumphal shrine, a jewelled jewel, yet a builded jewel, a pride to both goldsmith and architect. Courageous and splendid without on those high walls stood Donatello's young St George, like a captain of Florentine youth ; and the sceptical beautiful St Thomas, Florentine too in his exquisite dubiety, would come with the gracious Christ from Verrocchio's studio, while his wonderful pupil quickened his imagination.

Other churches were written on that pupil's meditative eyes, especially those touched by the great genius of Brunellesco, who so well understood the spirit of the Florentine Renaissance, providing mass, dignity, beautiful proportion, grave perspectives, serene basilicas, domes of reconciliation and comprehension—sweetly and nobly composed spaces where the spirit of decoration might play happily without embarrassing the tranquillity of the whole. San Lorenzo, beloved by the Medici, he knew well, for Verrocchio, with other artists, was in its rich service. He was familiar with that satisfying composition, with all the adjustments, spacings, fortunately-placed doors and windows striking muted chords of harmony from the unconsciously quieted senses. There, again, lay the long, grave aisles of San Spirito, arising after the Holy Dove had burned the old church during the festival in honour of the Milanese duke. There brooded the sombre, soothing spaces of half-Gothic Santa Croce, temple of holy traditions, all the floor rich with lovely memorials of the dead, where he might see the tombs of the early humanists sepulchred as Florentine citizens. Rossellino's Leonardo Bruni lay nobly at rest, with laureate brows, the Renaissance foaming softly over the base of his couch. But Desiderio's Marsuppini, a serene king of learning, his book on his breast, had the new Rapture exulting in acanthus over his great sarcophagus with the puissant lion's feet, the sweet assenting Madonna above. Verrocchio and Leonardo were well aware of this exultant and rhythmic monument, with its living interplay of delicate stresses and tenderly conspiring images, the dead scholar afloat in perfect rest under the sheltering arch, the honeysuckle yearning up to him, a dream of beautiful boys with ropes of fruit, immortal leaves, and soft-winged harpies supporting him—just such a dream as might indeed be softly woven through that scholar's sleep. Santa Croce could also tell of the greatness of Giotto, of Donatello's unexpected romantic idyll of a

Florence in Leonardo's Time

high-bred gilded Virgin arrested in her shy and courteous movement towards the kneeling angel. Beyond the painted cloisters, too, the exquisitely shaped and decorated Pazzi chapel murmured sweetly of eternity with all its lovely shells, gracious and light, a little temple made of the power of Brunellesco and the grace of Luca della Robbia, whose grave, lovely and innocent spirit was known and approved by Leonardo.

Santa Maria Novella, to be hailed thereafter by Michelangelo as his bride among the churches, was wedded also to the fancy of the older artist, for he drew the faintly triumphal swirling lines of the façade long after, when he was planning façades of his own. He should have had great sympathy for Leo Battista Alberti, his true forerunner, who seems to have infused into that smiling frontage, with the easy grace of its volutes, a little mystical with signs of the zodiac, patterned and scrolled, mondaine and gracious, as if done for a Madonna who is yet a great lady, some of the tradition of romantic courtesy peculiar to his House. Black and white cloisters, armorial shields of ancient families, the Spanish Chapel behind the cypresses and roses, Cimabue, Orcagna, Dante, a memory of Decameronian ladies in the portal, Ghirlandajo painting Florentine beauties in the choir, dreamy long vistas to the altar !—Santa Maria Novella was as dear to Florence as the Annunziata, where the lilies were cast in heaps before the miraculous picture of Our Lady.

There was many another hallowed place, hallowed even for Leonardo by the tribute gathered from the artists his kin. He must have been intimate with San Marco, kind with dispensations of calm retreat, tender with ethereal colour, where Fra Angelico still painted Annunciations rosy-pale and dawn-thrilled like any virgin's dreams, paradises of dancing angels, and hushed Crucifixions against a red sky. Did he have a studio in the gardens of San Marco, where the white splinters of antiquity hid among the hallowed leaves ? One story says Lorenzo granted it. If Leonardo brooded among the sacred roses of San Marco it was as if some unbaptized knight had surprisingly found himself alone " under a rose-tree in the field Sarras."

For he was naturally unchristian. The " Divine Leonardo," unlike most artists, had no idolatrous strain in his temper. He had the mind of an Archimedes, and the soul of a Praxiteles, and occasionally the temper of a Voltaire. Nothing in him swooned into dark ecstasy when the monstrance went by among the censing acolytes, and he made a cold riddle of the burning thuribles. His questing intelligence hunted the monks and friars, and hailed God as the inscrutable Necessity behind the forces of the Universe. His artistic religion desired a lord of invincible beauty with uncrucified hands. The Sacred Plays still made part of the Florentine succession of festivals ; and, as he went his way along the streets,

7

he might see the stable, the magi, and the golden censers. He gazed at the Epiphany, but when he encountered the Stations of the Cross he averted his eyes. He could not understand a suffering God. So when in time he drew his own many-domed churches, they do not seem hallowed for either Christian or Paynim, or for any child of adoration. They have a strange air of being sometimes wonderful problems in construction, sometimes symbols of his less conscious reverie, like the irrelevant flowers and faces that also interrupt his mathematical demonstrations, at best fabulous palaces for some Persian prince. No High Mass will sanctify his choirs, no mourner kneel solitary in one of his chapels.

iii

But there were throbbing centres of life in Florence besides those of God and the Virgin and the saints. To the calling bells of the holy Campanile the boding Martinella of the Palazzo Vecchio often gave an iron and dominant reply. For the Palazzo Vecchio was the other valve of the heart of Florence, the obdurate challenging centre of its liberties, the house of the captains of its freedom, built awry by the relentless spirit of disdain, the fierce tower and proud walls not yet dreaming that they were doomed to shelter a Grand Duke. Near by was the Bargello, the Palace of the Podestà, with its decorated court, where Leonardo was to stand, carefully drawing the hanged conspirator in his furry robes. Round these fast-nesses of civic pride the conversation leapt and fell, as it does yet, while fascist and communist renew the ancient dispute between Guelf and Ghibelline, Black and White. They talked in the great Piazza, and on the steps of the Loggia de' Priori, where the images of the City's genius were to gather—David, Perseus, Judith—figures of youth, freedom, daring. They talked in the Mercato Vecchio by Donatello's totem of bronze, the Marzocco, specially mocking at the befooled in the Florentine manner, a lively and motley crowd, while Lorenzo's giraffe pushed its head in a basket or stole an apple from a child, going its way to delight the nuns of the different convents, a beloved beast, desired of queens. They talked on the bridges also, particularly at the ancient bridgehead where Buondelmonte the beautiful died for love in his red and white bridal raiment by the old statue of Ares, and began the long vendetta.

And Leonardo talked with them, especially with the young men resting on the steps of the Loggia in the evening. But to the storm-bell of the Palazzo Vecchio, as to the call of the Campanile, he was philosophically indifferent ; and in the passing of the great red *carroccio*, with its red-clad steeds and its red antennæ and its red banners, he took but an æsthetic interest. Men had died round it in desperate agony to

Florence in Leonardo's Time

keep its crimson bright, resolving calmly, even in the bitter hour of Montaperto, that " by no means must they bring shame upon the haughty name of Florence, and that to survive were infamy." For Leonardo, Florence was a great city because she was curious, beautiful, fastidious and supreme in art, not because she had a dream of God or a dream of liberty, or, as on that day of her defeat by Siena, a dream of pride. He was not a Renaissance pacifist or an internationalist : though he considered war irrational and brutal he was always ready to sell more destruction to the combatants. He was merely the first of the " léonardistes."

iv

With the eyes of a connoisseur he considered the palaces. They were palaces that must still be fortresses, palaces made for a siege, but with their cyclopean blocks of Etruscan stone massed mightily so that their squared strength might be a satisfaction to the eyes, while their windows, entrances and loggie gave sweet earnest of the sweetness within, the honey in the lion's mouth—the beautifully spaced cortile with its fountains or carven well-heads, the friezes, the statuary, the medallions, the noble rooms with broidered doors, the terra-cotta lunettes, the coffered roofs, the cupboards whose panels were inlaid with delicate wreaths of flowers, the tapestries and painted cassoni, the Eastern carpets and cloths smouldering rose and emerald, the treasures of past and present art. With the light they made a great treaty to secure a rich and variable beauty. Their deep cornices cast lanes of cool darkness in the sunlight ; and they wore like springing wallflowers their wrought lanterns and torchholders, the golden lions rampant holding bright iris stems that did duty for weathercocks, while the cunning carving about their portals, the roundels or demilunes of Della Robbia ware, showed dewy as suddenly-seen hyacinth. Their proportions were planned for defence, yet remembered grace : their happy doors and windows were so fortunately set that they still strike calm chords of harmony. Brunellesco had raised the gigantic sombre masses of the Pitti Palace, quarried from the antiquity of Fiesole, satisfying as a pyramid is satisfying, planned like the lower storeys of a Babylonian ziggurat. Not until his return from Milan did Leonardo see the Strozzi Palace rise, a great house that was still a citadel, and put on like Etruscan goldwork the gilded rings and lanterns of Caparra. But his predecessor, Alberti, had gone gravely and graciously about Florence before him, drawing his classic lines ; and the Palazzo Rucellai, smooth-built with many charming windows, bore the impress of that smiling and urbane humanism of his which had so

9

strangely served the apotheosis of the Malatesta. Michelozzo, close friend of Cosimo and colleague of Donatello, had built the Medicean castle with its lovely cortile, and its garden under glass—no threatening military stronghold, but a neighbourly, though a puissant dwelling. Many another proud house held its own. Beauty knelt, or danced, or stole with soft feet through all the great spaces. Oratories, fountains, chimneypieces, doors, were harmonious in quality. Pattern was not patter yet, but a living language. A Florentine architect of this period could have made a palace down to the lampada, the locks and the linkholders. Leonardo could have done that, amongst other things.

Within these dwellings the least object was carved, enamelled, painted with imagery. The spirit of the Renaissance was liberal for all the senses, but blindingly prodigal for the eye, considered by Leonardo as the lord of them all. The people of that time lived in a maze of images ; they loved, sang, felt, ate, drank, and were clothed with images. It seems occasionally as if their air is thick with golden birds and their way is through a thicket of gold-thorn set with roses. But in Florence there is always a sense of the restful spaces behind the minute decoration, so that, however sumptuous, it lies in separate and sparse definition against its background like the lovely pattern of the olive branches. Away in courtly Milan, in the heavier damper air, in the more jealous closes of a despotic Court, the excesses of super-imposed imagery will become confused and run together in a disturbing intoxicating smoke of colour through the city of pleasure.

V

But the Florence beyond the walls, the Florentine garden-land, was known to Leonardo, the debonair companion, the natural lord of woodland and water-meadow. By the ancient Way of the Cross he reached the heights where lay Samminiato, rare citadel of death, where the cypresses stood round a temple embroidered, inlaid with the pale colours of an Elysian sorrow, carved and painted as with a concentrated passion of tenderness. There the sumptuous chapel of the Cardinal of Portugal, beautiful and pure, suddenly seized by death in passing through Florence, keeps his chaste memory sympathetically with a fantasy of angels and unicorns and great swags of ornament, all quiring to Our Lady above, the sweeter Virgin of the dedicated Renaissance Hippolytus " who lived in the flesh as if he were freed from it, an angel rather than a man." Rossellino spends lavish and innocent treasures of beauty over the unique Cardinal, like the caresses of a child. Yonder, opposite, were the lighted heights of Fiesole, down whose winding ways

Florence in Leonardo's Time

the Three Kings had come glittering, past the little smooth hills and the fantastical trees, with faëry cavalcades, golden bridles and brocaded coats, elfin pages, camelopards, monkeys and philosophers, through meadows of wild iris and roses, to be spellbound for ever by Benozzo Gozzoli in the dark Chapel of the Medicean House. There, too, when the night minted a strange new moon and secret stars, the witches met in their grottos in the great ruined amphitheatre, and the woods were shaken by the spells of Thessaly. But, though Leonardo was tall and beautiful and golden like Lucius Apuleius, he scorned both the spells of the witches and the redemption by roses and by prayer.

In the daylight Marsilio Ficino, from his simple dwelling among the waters, Poliziano from his canonry, and Pico from his oakwoods, drew to each other to compare their lore and their wine. Or one might climb to Settignano, that nurse of sculptors, or where Vallombrosa murmured through all its autumn-dropping woods, or where Camaldoli, cool and high among the firs and beeches, had heard the grave disputations by the Abbot's leave since the early days of Alberti, where even the bright young reveller, Giuliano, laid wisdom like the cooling garland of ivy leaves around his brows of festival.

The great villas and gardens were known to all the artists—squared and pillared houses of summer pleasure with terraces sloping to water-meadows of iris and meadowsweet and lily-floats. There was Careggi, turned dreamily towards the west, the house that Michelozzo exalted into a castle with battlements and covered galleries, where the philosophers of the cult of Plato particularly gathered in the frescoed loggia looking over the dark pinewoods to the crimson-flaming sunset, and where Lorenzo walked alone one April evening thinking of the dying Simonetta, and saw the white wistful star, and the sad sunflower still gazing into the fading light. There was Poggio a Cajano that Sangallo made for Lorenzo, with its great gardens and its islet of exotic flowers ; and there was Cafaggiuolo with a procession of great cypresses, and Petraja with its roses and carnations vivid among the ilex, and the Villa di Castello with its cacti and fountains, where the other young Lorenzo, Lorenzo di Piero Francesco Medici, would shrine the beauty of the Botticellian *Masque of Spring* and the *Advent of Aphrodite*. There was the Villa Palmieri, and the Villa Salviati, and the Medicean Fiesole Villa, and many more. With a vision of antique Tuscan pleasure-places were they wrought. They had tall towers, and loggie and dark cypress walks, and marble sedia in cool semicircles at the end of the fragrant flagged paths, and great espaliers of rose and jasmine and white lilies in bevies against the dark cypresses ; and orange-trees hung their glowing globes overhead, and great sunflowers were ranged on the terraces.

Leonardo the Florentine

Apple-blossom and lemon-flower were sweet in their seasons; violets and carnations gave up their perfumes. Rich pots of marble and terra-cotta stood overflowing with massed scarlet, and the sweet broken gesture of a white nymph or satyr from ancient time gleamed here and there among the branches.

It was not yet the day of Colonna's *Hypnerotomachia*, with its cut and carved garden-world as solid and as constructed as its temples: but Alberti had had some pleasure in designing gardens, so they paused at present between nature and art. There were chambers of ilex and box, and lawns of lovely green, and niches of cypress, with copper vases bound with branches on the arms of the decorated seats. Tunnels of pleached and knotted trees hid fugitives from the too lavish sunlight; everywhere was the rumour and plash of fanciful fountains like that for which Verrocchio made the *Boy with the Dolphin*, and here slept lilied pools, and there " went wandering water ever weltering." From the loggia one saw vast prospects of hill and valley drowsing or sparkling in the light. Great flights of easy stairs led to the intimate " guardino segreto," the little garden with its sunny paths and its sunken parterre of blood-red roses. Rose and oleander, they sent soft and sumptuous clouds of reverie through all the cypresses; by night it was always full moon on the terraces, and the lovers came to the secret garden.—Cypresses, orange-flower scent, murmur of nightingales, fireflies innumerable, and lutes lamenting away up by the white colonnades !

vi

Round Florence lay many little cities, linked with her strangely by hatred of her power and love of her artists. San Gimignano, with its girdling towers, remembered Dante. Leonardo climbed the ways to Siena, the beautiful suffering hill-phœnix, invincible, made of earthly violence and heavenly sweetness. He knew the desolation round Monte Oliveto, the blighted mutable land of startling ravines and friable rocks. He was aware of maltreated and agonizing Pisa whom pride devoured, clasping her incomparable ivory caskets of beauty under her veils of despair against her wounded breast. Lucca, elegant and vain, once a king's capital, yet kept a wonderful princess asleep in marble. Prato, early withdrawn from the desperate strife, friendly town to Donatello and to Lippo Lippi, was the kindliest subject of imperious Florence. There went a lady, dressed in crimson, white-throated, golden-haired, dark-eyed, the lady Ippolita, sung by Poliziano. Keen Arezzo guarded much of the clear illumination of Piero della Francesca, towards which all artists turned thoughtful eyes. (Arezzo, whence the

Florence in Leonardo's Time

golden Pico once rode away with a lady, betrayed by his own courtesy, and so caused a scandal in Florence—for Pico was an angel !)   And there was delicate Pistoja, where Leonardo listened to his heart a little, among the clear air and windy skies.

But Leonardo, as we shall presently realize, also passed into the wilderness like Saint John the Baptist.   He went farther and went alone.   He often took the road between Florence and his birthplace, watching how the River Arno sifted her coloured sands, moulding and remoulding the face of the earth.   And once, lonely in a region of desolate rocks, he came to a great cave whereby he stooped long gazing, his hand covering his eyes, torn between desire and fear, unconsciously creating the parable of his life, of the consuming desire to know, and of the unforsaking dread that stopped him on the threshold of the last discoveries.   Perhaps it was Cybele he followed to her caves ; and recoiled from the disturbance of her orgiastic rites.   He refused the complete initiation.

" Unable to resist my eager desire, and longing to see . . . the various and strange shapes made by formative nature, and having wandered some distance among gloomy rocks, I came to the entrance of a great cavern in front of which I stood some time, astonished and unaware of such a thing.   Bending my back into an arch, I rested my left hand on my knee, and held my right hand over my downcast and contracted eyebrows, often bending first one way and then the other, to see whether I could discover anything inside, and this being forbidden by the deep darkness within, and after having remained there some time, two contrary conditions arose in me, fear and desire—fear of the threatening dark cavern, desire to see whether there were any marvellous thing within it."   So runs Leonardo's confession.

He desired to be a priest of Mithra, god of the air, whose mysteries also were locked in deep caverns, and whose priests were forced into reluctant alliance with the acolytes of the earth-goddess.   Whether the cave he considered covered the ritual of Mithra or of that Cybele who is not always the friend of light, he never did know, being afraid.   The story of the sombre hillside is Leonardo's version of how

" Childe Roland to the Dark Tower came "

—and did not blow the slughorn.

Chapter ii

Lorenzo and his Friends

i

WHEN Leonardo was in the pride of his youth, Lorenzo de' Medici, in the pride of his, was magnificent in Florence. It is impossible to know what these two contemporaries, almost of one age, thought of each other; and no imaginary conversation could be more desirable than one between the most competent and the most "modern" of Renaissance rulers, and the most synthetic and the most modern of Renaissance painters. One biographer says that Lorenzo gave Leonardo an atelier in those gardens of San Marco of which the Florentine painters had such freedom ; and at least " il nostro Leonardo " and his ways were familiar to the Medicean group then and afterwards. But there is no such record of close patronage and friendly intercourse as animates the story of Medicean relations with Signorelli, Lippo Lippi, Botticelli, Filippino, Pollaiuolo, Verrocchio, the alien Mantegna even, and, later, Michelangelo. Yet both loved lute-playing, riding, fencing, and beautiful persons, and both believed that an artist should be a gentleman. Leonardo probably found the Platonic Academy slightly airy and unconvincing, though the distinctive grace of Marsilio and Pico della Mirandola must have touched him closely. Still, Lorenzo did not require an artist to be a professed Platonist—and Leonardo was platonic enough in some ways. Nor is it likely, as has been suggested, that his attitude was affected by the legal accusation brought against the painter, for it was an accusation often thrown at Poliziano and others of the platonizing fraternity, as well as at Leonardo's master, Verrocchio.

Lorenzo's supreme game was his play with people, and he understood them. With that ironic comprehension written so strongly on his dark strangely-set features he must have looked at Leonardo, tricked with the charming affectations of his age, gracious in his short tunic of aristocratic rose-colour, and smiled faintly, discerning in him a certain taste for princelier princes, a certain distaste for any criticism from his fellows. So, according to one story, he sent him as an ambassador of Florentine culture, carrying a novel cithara of silver, to his shifting friend, Lodovico Sforza, that he might find a more splendid tyrant and a more Lydian court, a sovereignty among artists, a singular and opulent opportunity for all his talents. Contemplating the reserves and reluctances of the serene and luxurious young man, as he dissembled his insatiable curiosity, his amazing conviction of power, under the masks of music and gay conversation, so he may have pondered the needs of Leonardo.

What Leonardo thought of Lorenzo is still as incalculable as what he thought, in after times, of Lodovico, or Cesare Borgia, or King Francis. Lorenzo had what the great genius had not—what great genius rarely has—an imaginative sympathy with his kind. Yet he and the Florence he created became part of Leonardo; the atmosphere of his evoking settled in rich dews of impregnation through the artist's spirit.

ii

Swarthy, ungainly by nature, yet disciplined into grace and attractiveness by sheer intelligence and spiritual vivacity, quite as paradoxical as more violent Renaissance rulers, with the melancholy Medicean eyes of the mystical voluptuary and the cynical mouth of the sceptic, the first citizen of Florence kept his court of Platonists, scholars, artists, gallants lettered and decorative, with subtle dreamy ladies "fit for verse." Accepted as a prince among the dynastic princes, he was content not to be called one. If he had captured his Florence, he would not break her wings. Connoisseur in all rare qualities, he could not, if only because of high æsthetic pleasure, deprive her of that energy and rarity of temper natural only to a city whose true *carroccio* was at least the proud and rosy dream of freedom. It may be that all the freedom possible to the sons or the cities of mortality is the freedom to choose their own bondage. But even that is a superb privilege; and every true Florentine, possessing it, went haughtily, no dark slave of annihilation and night, inalterably a sharer in his city's bright inheritance. It was part of Leonardo's mistake that he, in a way, sold his birthright. He was too much of an individualist and an immortal to be a good citizen; but, unconsciously or not, he regretted it. When he calls himself "the Florentine" in Milan, that natural appanage of a despot, he is like Paul, exclaiming passionately: "But I was free-born!"

So Lorenzo himself writes wisely, thinking both of Florence and of Italy: "It does not please me that the ultramontanes and the barbarians interfere with the business of Italy." And again, courteously reproving his mutable friend and ally: "Milan and the lord Lodovico seem to forget that this City calls herself a City of freedom." When Louis XI. wrote " mon cousin," " Lorenzo, Citizen of Florence " replied. Florence, after long tossing on her unquiet bed, found her " liberties " safer with Lorenzo than she did later under the black theocracy of Savonarola, whose bigotry was his undoing. The Medici had been the Gonfalonieri of the City, and they took long to forget it. It is an ever-recurring and exciting historic paradox that only a living republic can create an admirable tyrant. Florence made her Lorenzo, and Lorenzo lavished love's labour on his Florence. When Pope Sixtus obviously stabbed at the subtle dictator as at a personal enemy, the City turned to a tigress and tore his assailants to pieces, and even dared an interdict for her beloved.

iii

Lorenzo was something of a Voltaire, yet in his heart much of a heavenly dreamer like his rare mother, who wrote her hymns of God while remaining fast friends with mocking poets and scholars like Pulci and Poliziano. He was the complete appreciator, the *arbiter elegantiarum* of Italy, with a passion for perfection in many things that Petronius never knew. He was the sincere and tender friend whose lovers did not cease to " chide the world-without-end hour " while they watched the clock for him. He was the dear playfellow of those children, so charming in their early days, with their Botticellian heads and their frankly engaging ways, that it seems a pity that they solidified into popes and dukes. The pensive Giuliano, indeed, destined to a sweet immortality in the lovely pages of *The Courtier*, and also to be Leonardo's friend, does keep some of his childish grace, though after death, by Michelangelo's decree, he is to find a sombre apotheosis as one of the dark archangels that watch the coffers of doom in the sacristy of San Lorenzo.

And Lorenzo is also the romantic who was fain to ransom the dust of Dante from Ravenna. He is the poet who made his sweet Italian sweeter, for all his devotion to the antique tongues, with love-songs appealing as those of the *Vita Nuova*, with carnival-songs dancing in the madness of spring, with liquid stories of the rare amber water that welled about his villa, and a tale of Nencia, fresh as clotted cream. He was the idealist who talked of Platonic love in the woods of Camaldoli and the loggie of Careggi. He was the statesman whose wits were equal to the spoliating greeds of Rome, and Venice, and Naples. His was the courage to ride alone to Alfonso's camp, and his the wit and charm to make of that magnificent gesture a spell to capture his enemy.

Lorenzo and his Friends

(Doubtless it was a studied piece of magnanimity, a conscious effect of picturesque risk, but no other could have so justified it with brilliant success.) He was wise enough to throw the golden net of his peace over all the troubled states of Italy : his life became a hostage for tranquillity.

iv

Meanwhile he was the lord of a palace and a garden of art that existed not merely for himself but for all enthusiasts, for he was a superb spendthrift in beauty's cause only that he might scatter the largess of the lovely mercy that is more than twice blessed. He gave, as princes rarely gave, even in a period when they were capable of excesses in generosity as in other matters, and as collectors never give in any period at all. He was the cherishing and splendid miser of all perfect things so that other ecstatics might have of them an exquisite usufruct, since he "considered all money well spent that was spent in decorating his city, and his house which was also the city's."

Lorenzo can receive Milan, sounding with gold, and scarlet with trumpeters, into a dwelling of so much dignity and such delicate supplication of lovely art that the barbaric splendours tarnish discomfited ; and Galeazzo Sforza is like a Lydian king coming to Athens. Even the Crown Princess of Naples sends him perfumes, desiring in her inimical Court to be his ally. But it is among his artists and humanists that he is happy. They are indeed his friends, and hold with him the dear converse of equals. There is a note of emotional sadness, a half-ironic tenderness, in the man who was chivalrous to Lucrezia Donati, patient with his limited Roman Clarice, pensively, sweetly sorrowful over Simonetta, beauty's doomed vassal ; but his spirit glows best in mere amity. "Do not treat me as if I were old iron," wrote Luigi Pulci, that mocking and courageous man of letters, "for I shall soon be well if thou carest for me." "I wish," said the dying Magnifico to Politian and Pico, "that Death had spared me till I had completed your libraries." Nevertheless death took him, though Lodovico Sforza sent him his own physician with a miraculous medicine of dissolved gold and pearls such as had greatly comforted the mighty condottiere his father. And he died at peace. It is time that the confused story of an intolerant monk should be repeated no more.

When the wars were stilled the Florentines "lived in great felicity," says Machiavelli. The whole city was Lorenzo's vivacious Court ; and his ambassadors were artists and humanists. He had a tolerance even for Savonarola, for the fierce prophet had a Hebraic kind of frenzy, a fiery-figured denunciation, a throbbing and crashing music of a peculiar æsthetic value. He was so humane that the sack which sent Volterra to witness bloodily with Siena and Pisa against Florentine cruelty remains a scarlet blot on his memory, though he did not ordain it, as any other Renaissance despot might have done, and yet had it uncounted in the great sum of his violences. Lorenzo's robes of state were the Renaissance magnificence and the Aristotelian magnanimity.

v

He had the " appetito di bellezza " both in his spirit and in his senses; and he avowed it. So the artists as well as the humanists delighted to serve him. Antonio Pollaiuolo struck his medals and drew him wonderful nudes. Signorelli remained his friend as he had been his father's. Verrocchio made helmets and statues and tombs. Lippo Lippi was buried nobly by his decree. The great Mantegna was glad of him. Michelangelo was bred in his house. Legions of goldsmiths, jewellers, enamellers, and ivory-workers did his will.

Botticelli was the preferred Medicean painter; but Leonardo should have created something for Lorenzo. Botticelli captivated with a new poignant sweetness, a wild regret, a peculiar dream of paganism held in a mesh of rhythmic hieratic lines, a liturgic dance of creatures beautiful enough to be spring-sacrifices. But Leonardo also should have painted great myths, he who was himself a mythical figure already. If Botticelli expressed the emotional condition of Florentine dreamers, Leonardo once at least conveyed their intellectual state, the temper that had prevailed since the Council of the East and West, fading inconclusively as councils will, had dusted from its anthers the pollen of Alexandrian Platonism, and caused Marsilio Ficino to be dedicated from his infancy to the service of the divine philosopher. His version of *The Adoration of the Magi*, the theme that served so many painters for a comprehending vision of humanity, is no more merely a pageant of splendours and a crowd of portraits, but a conciliation of spiritual types, a great synthesis of all magian quests and human pilgrimages towards the light of the world.

Yes; he should have painted a great myth at this period of free and harmonious composition, for the bright clear paganism of Florence was lost from his spiritual spectrum at imperial Milan. Lorenzo and his kinsman and namesake at Castello possessed between them Signorelli's musical dewy picture of the dreaming Pan under the crescent moon, with his mysterious lovely companions, and Pollaiuolo's strong graceful tapestry of naked figures, and the Botticellian evocations of wistful divinities. Piero di Cosimo, too, could sometimes make a piece of tender sorrow

melt into a pitiful landscape because of an old Greek story. Why did
not Lorenzo ask Leonardo for some " nude gods " ? So might he have
obtained a divine Symposium with a wreathed cupbearing Ganymede,
a too-pensive Narcissus among the woods and waters and flowers he
loved, Castor and Pollux riding their immortal steeds through battle,
Apollo singing to the sumptuous brows of Hyacinthus, Hylas, white girlish
boy, drawn through the lilies of the amber wood-pools by naiades as
slim as he. Or Leda, the lover of strong white plumes moving through
mysterious air, might have passed earlier upon the canvas with a more
candid grace. But probably Lorenzo liked his pictures finished.

vi

Round the dictator went diverse animated figures. More amusing
to Leonardo's eyes Giuliano, the beloved young brother, in whom the
bizarre Medicean type heightened to physical beauty, a beauty snatched
from conflicts and surprises. He too was a lover of art and letters,
but more a lover of radiant hours. Moving really like the Mercury in
the Botticellian *Spring*, a lord of youth and gaiety, a Discobolus with
much of the dreamy grace of a Diadumenos, the king of the revels, with
his tossed forelock of dark hair, riding easily at the head of the jousters
and the masquers, leading through the city his dukedoms of beautiful
folly, the playfellow of colour and music, his eyes darker at times with
graver dreams, since he, too, had been the pupil of Alberti, and was the
friend of Ficino and the servant of Simonetta with the suffering air,
Giuliano was the tune to his brother's song. The two were naturally
the starry sons of Leda to their poets as they saw them ride in love
together down the Renaissance skies. They were easily the best of the
princes of the time, temperate, frank and brotherly—not tigers burning
bright like the Baglioni or the Malatesti, not moody dynasts driven
by hereditary furies like the Estensi or the Visconti or the House of
Naples, not faithless condottieri like the Gonzaga, not ruthless plunderers
like the Papal nipoti.

vii

There were other Medici kinsmen, like the sons of Piero Francesco, all
with equivocal handsome heads, with slightly ironic airs and arrogant
bearing and a glance of suppressed passion, all ready for a tournament,
a carnival, a discussion on Platonic love or Palmieri's doctrine of angels,
all ready with the lute or the sword. You see their bodies and habits
in Botticelli's paintings and in Benozzo Gozzoli's, their naked souls in

some of the figures of Leonardo's *Adoration*. They were platonizing, adonizing young creatures, with a springlike grace we shall hardly find in the more languorous Milanese.

Among their companions were fastidious Rucellai, wealthy, glittering Strozzi, ruffling Pazzi, elegant Albizzi. Bartolommeo Benci, another marshal of masques, rode as Lord Love on a horse with rainbow wings outside his lady's window. And Lorenzo Tornabuoni, typical of the noblest young Florentines, a flower of *gentilezza*, handsome, suave, sweetly serious, moved quietly in his red robe to receive the wisdoms and the arts, as you see him in Botticelli's fresco, turning his fair destined head amusedly, as you see him in Ghirlandajo's. He had a great marriage festival composed like a picture by Lorenzo himself, when he wedded a lady lovely and rare, his equal. But both were doomed to early and tragic death, so that they seem to move softly and somewhat mournfully in the shadow of doom. Accomplished and beautiful Domenico Acciajuoli is a golden gonfalonier and a noble ambassador ; he wears his chastity proudly like a great pearl in a mesh of silver. One pale, heavy-curled child slips past, dying because he has plighted himself to Artemis, for the swift sister of Apollo has also her cult and her green altars. Blithely go the sons of Lorenzo, Botticellian angels—Giovanni, cardinal at thirteen ; Piero, " with the profile of an angel and rather long hair, which stands out a little and is charming to see," and Giuliano, the sweetest, " smooth, clear, bright as a mirror, joyous, and with those contemplative eyes." So Matteo Franco reveals them, across the centuries.

viii

With the gallants the scholars of Florence mingled freely, thinking of Greek olive-trees sprung again in Tuscany, and of the Athenian philosophies which they had dyed the colour of young roses in the vat of Alexandria. The humanists were a gentler company than in most cities. Scala, for instance, fought fiercely enough ; but Lorenzo imposed a harmony on those near him, and their quarrels were usually of that dialectical " flyting " kind, dear to the Chaucerian poets of Scotland. The flower of them all was a noble himself, Pico della Mirandola, that " great lord out of Italy," whose esoteric and ingenious philosophy and queer recondite learning, brought from China, Crim Tartary, Chaldæa, Syria, Araby, as well as Athens and Alexandria, had their best justification in his sweet and sincere personality, in that intimate daydream of his that curled softly his gold hair and deepened his great eyes. He was " the Phœnix who nested in the Laurel," fair visionary and saint of the

Lorenzo and his Friends

New Learning. He was blond, slender, beautiful, beloved; and even Machiavelli seems to regard him as a " hero," a quasi-divine creature, whose own existence justified his discourse on " The Dignity of Man," man created by God so that he may choose to rise or fall, man who may be "twice-born" like a god. Almost as lovable, Marsilio Ficino went musing, the dedicated priest of the strange Christian Platonism of the time and place, that trustful reconciliation of the more mystical Dialogues and the more mystical Gospel. He was contemplative and kind and simple, a lover of music, a tender friend. When he sang, a fine enthusiast, the lays of the pseudo-Orpheus, men felt that by some pure white magic they might indeed become initiates of a new peace, wherein Platonism and the Logos of Saint John might kiss each other. His grace and wisdom and the delicate quality of feeling in his interpretation became a kind of mysterious violet-colour in the minds of many, a sense of the purple and incense and music of adoration more kindling to the imagination than dogma and doctrine.

From the philosophy of Pico, for all his lovely manners and eloquent lips, Leonardo probably dissented. Among the astonishing challenges which Pico desired to throw to all comers to his intellectual tourney were the contentions that "mathematicæ non sunt vera scientiæ," and also " si felicitas sit in speculativa perfectione, mathematicæ non faciunt ad felicitatem." And Lorenzo agreed with him, for the poetic mind does not willingly accept mathematics as the one condition of all knowledge, the only strait gate to the truth. It prefers a more flagrant and even more difficult portal. Probably it was Leonardo's passion for mathematics that made him averse from literature, and disdainful of all poets except Dante, the circles and pyramids of his unearthly universe commending his story. On the whole, Leonardo's attitude to the Platonic Academy must have been conflicting, and was probably marked by a shrug of amused impatience. In some ways their idol was sympathetic to him; but the idolaters were vague, and he detested vagueness. Still, he liked Marsilio Ficino well enough to possess his book on the immortality of the soul.

They sincerely loved each other, this Neo-Platonic family of Fiesole and Careggi—Lorenzo, Marsilio, Pico, Poliziano. True, they did not sufficiently distinguish Platonism from Plotinism, the emerald from the chrysoprase: the colour was entrancing in each. They loved each other with a pure, sensitive, slightly feverish intensity, those who preferred the Fourth Gospel, and made of Plato the dearest of Christ's apostles. They used love's language; they gave each other gifts of doves, lilies, baskets of roses, and verses. Yet though Lorenzo and Poliziano at least had a sensual side, the harmonies of the Platonic chapel are innocent as well as beautiful; and by their glad excitement they quickened while they coloured a great and lovely tradition. All Florence was affected by their pulsations—even Leonardo, though he did not belong to that cult. Perhaps only a thin web divided its incandescence from sentimentality. This was of asbestos, however, and sufficient. The group was saved indeed by its fire. But for Neo-Platonism Leonardo's mind was too lucid, and his heart was too hard.

Probably he went also to hear Landino, as he sought Plato everywhere, especially in the haunting Virgilian cadence. This Platonist was also an ardent expositor of Dante, the great mediæval master now become a Renaissance prince, partly because of that magnificent sin of Superbià which made him, as well as his own unconquerable heresiarch in the tomb of fire, talk as an equal of his God, partly because a people enamoured of language became enchanted by that lamenting, accusing, exultant, marvellous music of his. Matteo Palmieri again, brooding in his lovely villa on the transmigration of souls and a sweet heresy stolen from Origen, thinking, in his Renaissance passion for all forms of existence, that even the rebel angels must be ransomed in the end to their original felicity, was an attractive dealer in fantastical doctrine. The Inquisition disliked his theories of errant angels and the Cumæan Sibyl; but when he died his friends laid his poem on his breast, a heretical manuscript, adorned with the signs of the zodiac. Leonardo, who allowed that it was logical to consider spiritual things so long as it was clearly understood that spirits could not violate universal law by invading the realms of matter, and who had a distinct taste for the fantastic, probably had some interest in Matteo Palmieri, for he loved angels, if only for their wings and their equivocal fair faces, and he detested any inquisition but his own.

ix

Among the poets and poetasters he surely talked with Luigi Pulci, intelligent, entertaining, sceptical, of three poet-brothers the one destined to a little fame. No academician, the writer had yet a great tenderness for Lorenzo, not always responsive to the over-importunate affection of the elder man, who complained that his friend cared more for his verse and his wild wit than for himself. Yet Luigi, struggling lifelong with debts and poverty, watching kindly over his younger brother, has a bitter-sweet value in his personality. "I am not much of a poet, though I go through the wood flute in hand," he says charmingly. If his complimentary verse concerning the Giostra has faded, and the mock-virulent strambotti about Matteo Franco have no bite for the

Lorenzo and his Friends

modern palate, the *Morgante Maggiore*, partly improvised at Lorenzo's table, with its wild alternations between jest and earnest, and its brilliant creation of Astarotte, gives some foretaste of the pungent, ever-varying pleasures of *Don Juan*. The Vatican condemned it as atheistical, and Savonarola burned it as libertine, so Leonardo must have found Pulci amusing. And the surprising flash of geographical knowledge in Astarotte's prediction about another hemisphere on the round earth, where also are castles and cities and empires, has suggested that Pulci had learned from the famous Toscanelli, so that Leonardo, who did read the *Morgante*, must also have conversed with the poet as a geographer. Luigi Pulci's poem was much of a burlesque ; but the mediæval romances were eagerly heard in earnest, and Ogier the Dane and the paladins of Charlemagne were still dear to people who were loth to let go the silver-mailed slim knights of the Middle Ages even though they had won white adolescents from Hellas. In Milan, too, Leonardo will find the Court, in full Renaissance noon, debating learnedly the rival merits of Rinaldo and Orlando. But Florence had the stronger Provençal note, the true tradition of troubadours. The austere fine scene of Tuscany insisted on a crystalline and rarefied kind of sweetness, that arrowy attack which is found somewhere in the art of all periods, but which especially pierces and quivers in the heart of the Middle Ages. Florentine taste had an instinctive justness : it could detain the " Gothic " fantasy for its literature while refusing it, for the most part, as inappropriate to the architecture that grew from its Latin landscape.

Dearest of all scholars for Lorenzo was Angelo Ambrogini, the ugly Poliziano with the golden voice, with the black hair and sensual lips, versatile and dulcet poet, delicate latinist, enthusiastic teacher, a king among the scholars of his time, a friend who could not long outlive him. Poliziano's sweetest verses have a Herrick flavour, all hawthorn and golden colours, and a ringing of lovely words. But Leonardo did not approve those poets, though he made his own songs for his lute.

With Poliziano, Pico, and Marsilio, Lorenzo could pass in great happiness an evening divided among Saint Augustine, Plato, and Dante, and go from lute-playing and dancing to hear Mass, as the mood swayed him. For Lorenzo, like many a man of a sceptic mind, had a religious temperament ; and, though Pope Sixtus was an evil old man, that did not prevent him from drinking deeply of the great symbolism of the Mass. But Leonardo had not a religious temperament : he had his own mysticism, but it was not Christian. His imagination had " never bathed in the red flood that flows from the side of the Crucified," even in a dream. So these two sceptics understood each other little : Lorenzo was *simpatico* and Leonardo was not.

Leonardo the Florentine

Lorenzo, who rose from his dying bed, and dragged himself to the door to meet the Eucharist, saying, "I will not suffer that my Lord and my God should come to me," confessed himself a Christian mystic who had more in common with Savonarola than with Leonardo. With Pico, Marsilio, Botticelli, even Poliziano, he had longed to make a tender conquest of Hellas for Christendom ; but he could not have lost Mount Calvary for Mount Olympos. Leonardo, serene recusant, was excited over neither. He knew himself an Olympian in exile, and accepted, not without irony, the customs of his alien state. The grave Alberti was moved to tears by the music in the Duomo ; such æsthetic tears are not recorded of Leonardo's intolerable eyes. If he were capable of worship he worshipped the sun, and like a true eagle could look at it with unflickering eyelids.

Chapter iii

Daily Life in Florence

i

THE Florentine day was blithe with amenities, and in time of peace life ran like a round of festival. There was a community of pleasure under Lorenzo, and Leonardo was a participant, though always a little preoccupied. In holiday and music, however, he gladly dipped his youth.

The devotional year in Florence went gaily, for the City was, and is, much at home with God and His saints, as if they are really akin to the old Tuscan deities of place and home—had at least taken over their duties. The Duomo and the other churches were places where idolaters and lovers might meet. The gallants moved in the choir, the little acolytes like angels jostled and dipped their candles in the processions even when a great red cardinal was carrying the pyx. At vesper-tide a coloured crowd watched the sacred plays, and criticized the last invention in moving things. While the sacred girdle of the Virgin was being shown to the throng in the Cathedral piazza, Fra Lippo Lippi could steal his pretty nuns from the Carmine. When the *soave-austero* Tuscan landscape was purfled with flushing blossom, when Florence lay like a carved jade-white jewel in the lap of Spring, herself a precious Adonis-basket of almond and peach branches, anemones and carnations, under the matinal turkis-coloured sky, when the thrilling air was rarer with the sense of the Passion Play, then Leonardo might meet, among the little hills round the City, processions bearing the image of the dead Christ, with slow deep-sighing lamentations that have been borne from Egypt and Syria. Then he would look on at the shadowy toneless Mass in the Duomo and go home to write that : " On this day all the world is in mourning because once one man died in the Orient." A shallow statement for a Leonardo—with the undying Linus-song still dreamy in his ears ! He must have known it was because God had been slain many times in the East.

ii

At Easter, at the door of Santa Reparata, the New Fire is struck from the stones that came from the Holy Sepulchre, and the Burning Dove

25

hangs mysteriously in the centre of the Cathedral; and Leonardo likes the spectacle. The fire-bird goes down the nave to communicate the flame, virgin flame from the holy stones, to the antique chariot in the Square; which breaks into ardent flowers, and passes to present the new-hallowed symbol at the doors of the palace of the Pazzi, whose iniquities could never quite cancel their forefather's ecstatic service, while the Dove returns to the altar, scattering its flakes of sacred and flagrant luck. Again, there is an Ascension in the Carmine. Or the vestments glitter at the mystic marriage of the Abbess of San Piero Maggiore with the Lord Bishop; and the litanies are soft and strange, as if underneath there faintly throbbed the liturgical double-flutes of the worshippers of the Cyprian Aphrodite.

Green boughs are hung on the column where the miraculously-flowering elm-tree stood, for an ancient worship has been christened by Saint Zenobius. The Day of Saint Anne is " kept like Easter," for on that festival the hated Duke of Athens was driven from the City. But full summer brings the supreme Florentine festival, the festival that devoured minor gaudy-days as fuel for its bonfires, the day branded deeply in Leonardo's nerves, tangled hard with his imagination. The Florentines are true sun-worshippers; and Leonardo might in some incarnation have worn the purple robes of the Syrian sun-priest in Emesa. It is the ancient heathen ritual, the triumph of Midsummer, when all the gods of life and death, all the immortal faëry host, the borderers that are not subject to heaven or hell, awake and have power in the charmed hour of the solstice. It is the day of the recognition and the propitiation of nature, whereon Christianity, by strange processes of disguise, suppression and contradiction, has converted the sun-life and flame-life to the ambiguous figure of Saint John the Baptist. Extreme denial is as frank as avowal. The eyes of the ascetic are excited by the images of the mythic luxury that possesses his imagination, he carries in his burning veins the beautiful plague he cannot exorcise by fast or prayer. The Baptist was a Syrian ascetic; and the Syrian ascetic was as much a victim of sensual rapture as the voluptuary. So the secret heathen soul of Florence wrought out her patron-saint, regarding him sometimes as a wasted wild witness in savage weeds, sometimes as a lost prince of beauty, delicate, sad, perverse as the Syrian Atys, lovely zealot of that Cybele who had laid her dread on Leonardo. The City feasted Saint John and the ambiguous paganism that invested him with flames and sweet odours, feasted him who recreated that mysterious myth of meeting extremes which dwells in the tale of every true god, and who began in the desert a decorated legend of sadist love, troubling the sensual trance of Herodias and waking the panther in the Herodiad. Dear to Florence

Daily Life in Florence

her Saint the Precursor, opening a new Way of Life, for she felt herself a precursor among Renaissance cities. Dear to Leonardo, who early felt himself the first of a new order of illuminati. The day of Saint John, at least, was understood by that dionysiac soul; and the image of the midsummer god was the last he evoked from the darkness. There are artists who carry in their work the spirit of the seasons. Botticelli has the sharp sweetness, the gracile gods, the exquisite pattern of the spring; Giorgione has the rich melancholy, the romantic regret, the heavily-haunted golden air of autumn; Michelangelo is austere and naked and a lord of storms and spaces like winter, with winter's hidden hours of hived honey rarer than any. Leonardo is midsummer, though his palette is cool. He knows the faëry solstice, the moment of nature's fulfilment, and the heathen sacrifice.

They feasted Saint John the Baptist with great music and living trees of light, heavenly hills of altar-candles burning slim and steady, plumed with delicate feathers of flame, with red raiment and pageants and great expense of incense and torches. They feasted him with sacred games like an antique god indeed, for the whole town was shaken by the *palio* of Saint John. The beautiful riders passed first through a straight street full of flowers and bright Florentine ladies wearing their garlands and fanciful jewels. The gorgeous golden *palio*, woven for two months by chosen craftsmen, was borne on a sacred *carroccio* in the piazza of the saint. The holy car had four great wheels decorated with four carved lions, and the horses were clothed in blazing heraldries; the piazza was hung with blue hangings embroidered with golden lilies. The reckless course was run from east to west through the Mercato Vecchio. In the evening, while the pagan bonfires blazed, fierce baleful patterns on the black velvet summer night, remembering yet the solemn propitiations of old and the tale of human sacrifice, the great black steeds brought home the brocade of honour, and so ended the Day of Saint John. Leonardo went within, and pensively sketched the horses he loved and understood.

In the year 1476 he drew a strange image of the Saint, slim, sensuous, with cloudy soft hair, carrying a thin cross and pointing downward. One critic thinks the model was Jacopo Saltarelli. It is a penetrating surmise.

Once a great princess, Eleanora of Aragon, was in Florence on that day, pausing in her wedding journey. Then the " companies " of boys went about, dressed like many kinds of angels; and the banners were larger and brighter, and the tapers were immense painted things. Those reprieved from death carried their piteous olive branches. The racing horses reared more haughtily in the procession. The end of that day

27

was like a dream indeed, a dream of dances in the sunset air to the sound of viols and lutes till the music passed into the faces, " sad with the whole of pleasure." When Leonardo, long afterwards, drew his ring of three ethereal dancers in their strange atmosphere, he may have remembered that evening, with its moving haloed figures seen like immortals through the mingling motes of powdered gold and music.

iii

There were other *palios*. There was even a grotesque *palio*, the dyers', after which the little book he carried with him had pages of caricature, pathetic or terrible.

Other games of an almost ritual character engaged his sympathies as athlete and as artist. The different forms of ball-games were popular everywhere; and Florence possessed, besides, its peculiar Giucco del Calcio. The people were passionately greedy for shows, so this game was a pageant of splendid youth as well as a trial of endurance and energy. The players were chosen for physical perfection and honourable birth, disdainful graceful boys able and willing to pose as Davids. Two by two they went round the great piazza, sheathed in their satin, the red and the green cunningly interwoven, colour by colour, hand in hand, the banner-bearers walking beside them before the frantic play began ; and the ball bounded towards the wall attacked by feet and hands.

iv

" Then shalt thou speak of banqueting delights,
    Of jousts and triumphs that sweet youth did make,
    Of tourneys and great challenges of knights
    And all these honours for thy beauty's sake."

These were part of the mediæval heritage that Florence would not lose, though she translated them into terms of such complicated decoration that the cloth-of-gold somewhat muffled the shocks of conflict. The desire of the eyes was almost a mania with Renaissance folk. They made a pageant of everything—birth, baptism, marriage, death—hanging these elemental events with gorgeous cloths, bringing great cups and fair monstrous jewels and storied plates for gifts, robing the actors in gold-flowered raiment, summoning a chorus of taborers and violers. Is it a wedding ? Under a canopy of blue cloths, on a triangular dais, the guests feast in the open air ; or they look at the rose-strewn table and play with the fruits in a painted loggia. Branches of olive are thrust graciously through the torchholders. If it be Lorenzo's

Daily Life in Florence

wedding, the Roman bride in white and gold is feasting with fifty Florentine girls on the balcony, while different companies of fifties banquet in the lower halls, and in the medallioned loggia looking on the cortile where the *David* of Donatello stands. Or is it a wedding of lilies? Donato Acciajuoli, the beautiful gonfalonier and enchanting ambassador, goes virgin to his bride. Is it a birth? The mother reclines on her painted bed, perfumed and dressed, while her friends come, carrying her gifts, and her attendants offer her delicacies on precious platters fired with the Judgment of Paris or the lives of the gods. Is it a death? Medicean princes in the habit of the Misericorde will carry the tapers after the softly-borne Simonetta, beautiful as when she sighed her life away. Or is it a death of lilies? A scholar lies dead at eighteen of his own chastity, they fancy; so with dirges, like epithalamies, that white jonquil is surrendered to the dark Nympholept.

The Florentines delighted in dramatic gestures. Even a young professor could not go to his University chair without a troop of enthusiastic young nobles to enthrone him. If it were May Day the dancers gathered before Lorenzo's house to give him fresh garlands, and sing his songs. These were the spontaneous processions of daily accident. But they had an appetite also for set pageants of every kind, which were only sublimations of the more magnificent moments of that actual existence, not the laborious lifeless efforts of a period and a people really ashamed of public expression. Those insatiate eyes had an organic craving for elaborate shifting patterns of sight and sound, and the sumptuous solidities of pomp in the sun and air, like the physical craving for food and love. Those Greece-drunken minds at any moment threw mythic apologues, rose and white friezes, against the purple evening. Leonardo, like all Florentines, loved the glittering and the miming. Triumphs delighted them, triumphs of love, of death, of Dionysos, the true Renaissance god, with his horned head-dress, in a chariot hung with heavy vines. They desired the masquerades because they were solutions of colour, music, sweet lighted faces, rainbow wings and gilt armour, sweet fading words. The purist may quarrel with their taste for these wasteful evanescent marriages of sound and colour; but they were logical in their passion for synthesis, burningly alive in their call for confounding delights. Such frail and lovely evocations, perfect pictures lasting a gilded hour, were ravishing to Leonardo's mood. He loved them excessively to the end, always glad to compose a masque, a momentary rich plot of crossing vibrations, sight and sound, vanishing softly into eternity. They fed that distinctive love of waste and extravagance in beauty which is part of his " divine " temper. He was reckless with it.

Leonardo the Florentine

So, when Verrocchio was pageant-master for the Medicean jousts he had a fanciful helper—who probably thought he should have ridden in the lists himself. Lorenzo had his tournament in honour of one lady who had given him a wreath of violets, Lucrezia Donati, his Beatrice, before he coldly received his Gemma, in the person of the Roman Clarice Orsini. He rode with all his trumpeters and taborers and fifers into the great Square of Santa Croce, whose sombre undecorated frontage was embroidered enough by the revels for which it was a continual background. He and his horse were clothed in red and white silk, with hems of pearl, his famous scarf was of flowering and fading roses, and his device : " Le temps revient." On his shield blazed " Il Libro," the kingly diamond. Giuliano went in silver and pearl. He had his own joust later ; and Poliziano made a sweet song of it, in honour of the wistful lady who throned it in tender moon-soft veils, dreamily divining what dark Love would ravish her soon. " White she is and white her robe, embroidered with roses and grass and flowers."

Another time the Florentine night was painted with a lovely living fresco for an hour, when Bartolommeo Benci, lord of his company, clothed in jewelled colours, came on a horse plumed with gold and rose and green, followed by his friends as torchbearers in emerald, violet and crimson, falcons broidered on back and breast, silver falcon's feathers scattering down their raiment, to the window of the lady Marietta Strozzi. When she appeared like a Madonna between four lit flambeaux, the cavaliers, riding upright in their saddles, fought with flying gilded darts and lances. These masquers of love, coming and going, returned gently at last with the music of serenade. Again, when Florence lay hushed and softly excited under an unusual mask of snow, the same cavalier brought his company to the window of the same lady for a siege with elfin artillery. But she happily discomfited them with the same weapons, for she was lively as well as lovely.

v

Hospitalities in Florence were the charge of the Medici and the delight of the citizens. In 1469 the exotic embassy from the Sultan of Egypt came like an Arabian tale, bearing sovran and surprising gifts, including a lion and the popular giraffe, coloured fleeces, horns of civet and great vases of porcelain, striped tents and fine muslins. Leonardo, ever curious of the East, listened, inquired, contemplated.

In 1472 splendour met splendour, when Galeazzo Maria Sforza and his French princess on her golden palfrey, led by golden pages, came to the house of Lorenzo with the colours and trumpets of the sunset ;

Daily Life in Florence

and not all the cavaliers and huntsmen and falconers of the luxurious Milanese, and all the slim gilt pages with their curled bright heads, and all the great war-horses in glittering cloths and silk-broidered bridles, and all the least menials in inappropriate velvet, could drown the serene silver harmonies of Lorenzo's great dwelling in the Via Larga, where there was nothing that was not beautiful, and the soul drank what the eyes received. Then there were indeed pageants and miracle plays, the lilies and low music of the Annunciation in San Felice, the joy of the Ascension in the Carmine, the blazing Descent of the Holy Ghost in San Spirito, where the flame caught and burnt too well. Two young Sforza princesses in the company of this cruel and gorgeous dynast brought the smooth Lombard beauty among the reticent Florentine women. One of them, a slender and secret child with fiery thoughts, awake already to great ambition and its price, was Caterina Sforza, looking for the first time at the City that enchanted her, where at last, after clangorous, passionate years, she was to die in peace.

So the proud ambassadors and princes came and went through the storms of pearl that seem to rain miraculously over Renaissance festivals. Sometimes there was an interlude of soft silver-grey, as when the tired Danish King went simply through the City on his way to Jerusalem, travelling much on foot. But the grave King Christian was released from his vow in Rome, and returned to his land with the Golden Rose instead of the Palmer's Branch.

vi

Nevertheless at times Florence suddenly heard her lions roar, and seized her daggers; and the coloured gay tenor of her days was terribly interrupted. When Pope Sixtus IV., humanist and tyrant, vicious, greedy, doting on his nipoti, set Pietro Riario, the luxurious, evil young cardinal, in the archbishopric of Florence, his desire for some sovereignty in the Tuscan region seemed to creep nearer, and though Pietro died of excess, Girolamo, more vigorous, remained. The Pazzi, discontented and jealous, had their rankling grievances; Salviati, the Archbishop of Pisa, was enraged at the material losses caused by Florentine disapproval. The plot was laid carefully. Though the Pope verbally dissociated himself with bloodshed, it was evident that blood only could dye the conspiracy with success. Yet even in that time of cynical conspiracies the Pazzi affair became infamous. It was not a " beautiful treason "; it was no cold masterpiece of Borgian strategy against inconvenient or inimical people: it was a crude attack on elemental rights. That a Pope should be cognizant of so much treachery, and connive at the murder

31

of hospitality; that his princes of the Church should desire to stab at the High Altar; that friend should embrace friend to prove the absence of the protecting mail-coat—guest-right, sanctuary-right, friendship-right, Church-right, all so flagrantly flouted—seemed so monstrous a violation of the most necessary pacts between mortals that the City rose for Lorenzo, and Lorenzo was the City's honour. When Giuliano went down in the cruel amazement of the Pazzi dagger, and Lorenzo was driven by his poets and his devoted pages into the Sacristy, so fierce was that knot of conflict and death suddenly involved at the climax of the Mass, that the young Cardinal Raffaelle Riario, whose unsuspecting presence had given the plotters their opportunity, went pale in his red robes for ever after, through his life of elegant dissipation and futile intrigue, his white hand nervously feeling the imaginary rope at his throat.

Leonardo, lover of distorted and terrified expressions, must have reaped a rich harvest then. Has he not vividly seen "Anger"? "An angry figure should be represented seizing someone by the hair and twisting his head down to the ground, with one knee on his ribs, and with the right arm and fist raised high up; let him have his hair dishevelled, his eyebrows low and knit together, his teeth clenched, the two corners of his mouth arched, and his neck, which is all swollen and extended as he bends over the foe, should be full of furrows." And he has closely contemplated "Despair." "A man who is in despair you should make turning his knife against himself, and rending his garments with his hands, and one of his hands should be in the act of tearing open his wound. Make him with his feet apart, his legs somewhat bent, and the whole body likewise bending to the ground, and with his hair torn and streaming."

He could have watched Lorenzo walk with Poliziano in the choir, and Giuliano enter, led embraced by his traitor friends, sure now that there was no armour under the blue velvet. He could have seen Montesecco, the bought captain, lowering darkly, for he was afraid to strike "where Christ could see him"; and the two sinister priests who were not afraid. And Jacopo Pazzi, accomplished gentleman with unquiet gambler's eyes, suddenly stricken when his vague admissions and agreements are mortally translated into blood, when Francesco Pazzi, frizzed and powdered and bitter invert, in the evil ecstasy of his blood-lust, strikes the victim so often and so at random that he plunges the blade in his own thigh. He might have seen Lorenzo desperately defending, drawn by his desperate pages at last through the graven bronze doors of Luca della Robbia into the New Sacristy, to breathe hard among the indifferent calm images of kneeling angels, till the tumult died in the

voices of friends, dissuading away the wounded man from the sight of the fair dead brother.

Giuliano the beloved was ruthlessly avenged. He was young, he was sweet, he was kind, he was daring and a poet ; and both Lorenzo and Florence loved him. So Leonardo saw the Bargello hung with mortal fruit ; and that macabre scene, fit for a Dantean Inferno, when the robed Archbishop turned in his death agony to bite his writhing fellow, Francesco Pazzi, in the shoulder. He saw faces convulsed with fury and torment, and Jacopo Pazzi's mortal remnant twice dragged from the grave because the corn would not grow, and thrown shockingly about the streets by those demoniacal children, and cast in the river at last, since Florence was possessed and insane with an uncontrollable rage.

For Leonardo could always watch the writhings of human torment with those inscrutable eyes. He would go with the condemned to the scaffold, like Saint Catherine of Siena, but in no similar passion of heavenly tenderness—rather like a serene Mephistopheles. His devouring gaze noted the miserably betraying nerves about the mouth, the twitching eyelid, the unspeakable spasm in which suffering abandons human shape to become a mere horrible brute breathing from a clot of blood and nerves. He could regard the last extremity. For all his unusual humanitarianism to the inarticulate beasts, he never shrank from the anguish of his kind. He contemplated that, though he fastidiously refrained from provoking it, so slaking the repressed sadism of his strange heart while assuaging the ruthless curiosity of his mind. Now, when it was all over, he wandered back to the bottega, and found Verrocchio making an ex-voto wax effigy of Lorenzo, holding sacrificial candles in his hand.

To the Pazzi drama there were two epilogues, both true to the Florentine mood. Leonardo certainly stood under the Bargello, drawing that hanged conspirator Bernardo Bandini, who had miserably found that not even under the alien Crescent was he safe, not even under the golden shield of the Soldan, in the alien ways of Constantinople, could he hide from the patient implacable hounds of Lorenzo's justice. So Leonardo, impassible, drew him, most dejectedly, absolutely hanged from the window, with limp feet that have a kind of hopeless pathos about them, Leonardo industrious under the Bargello in the sharp January day. Then he carefully noted beside the sketch the colours of the furred foreign raiment of the dead man : " Small tan-coloured cap, black satin doublet, lined black jerkin, blue cloak lined with fur of foxes' breasts, and the collar of the cloak covered with velvet speckled with black and red. Bernardo di Bandino Baroncelli. Black hose." Botticelli had

painted the other sufferers on the Bargello at the command of the Signoria, "hanging by the feet in strange attitudes." It is not really likely that Leonardo had any intention of performing a similar commission. He did this kind of thing only for his own amusement.

He had looked more tenderly at the Hellenic epilogue, when Giuliano was carried to his grave in San Lorenzo by his lamenting companions. Then Lorenzo, instead of moulding graceful lekythi, bade Antonio Pollaiuolo strike great medals, precious coins that buy from posterity remembrance of past wrath, and pride, and sorrow. And Botticelli painted a mournful fair Pallas, all wreathed with sweet-patterned olive, beside a conquered Centaur, to transmute the whole fierce story to rhythms of peace.

Before that peace fell, like a merciful golden evening, there were times of interdict, plague and war. Leonardo mused apart, and thought of the waste and wrong of processes that brutishly arrest and undo the wonderful work of nature. But he began to draw beautiful and deadly weapons of destruction, some being merely exquisite tools for a diabolic fantasy, some being ingeniously and practically destructive. For, if men would senselessly fight, he saw no reason why he should not assist their efficiency. Besides, it relieved the dim pressure of cruelty in his soul to draw these things. He was cruel as God is ; but, being human in his tissue, he was also humane enough to take that out on paper.

vii

Even the ordinary days, unconvulsed by special festival, war, or dreadful justice, were varied enough for one who danced and fenced and rode and mastered horses, and had much conversation, besides work in the bottega and study in solitude. The atmosphere of Renaissance Florence vibrates with crossing waves of imaginative excitement. There are flowers before the pure Della Robbia Madonnas ; somewhere the lamp of Plato burns, and a vision comes to Marsilio Ficino. The young men are talking on the steps of the loggia ; the sand-sifters with movements of rhythmic grace harrow the waves of the Arno. The girls are dancing in the street to win the prize of a silver garland. The revels go through the summer night. The gallants dismount round their leader and tie their horses to the rings, while the torches burn in the holders. They are beautiful and alert : their fashions are fantastic and variable. Leonardo wears his short tunic of rose-colour in a fashion all his own. At this period, to the careless observer, he seems a little like what Oscar Wilde would fain have been.

So clad, you may see him go look at the lions, those lions which

Daily Life in Florence

delighted Charles VIII. more than anything else in Florence. " In our city of Firenze there are always twenty-five or thirty of them, and there they bear young." So says Leonardo. With a few strokes of the tongue one tears away a lamb's fleece. The lion has an interesting kind of tongue. He wanders on and pauses by the bird-sellers, and watches that peculiar agony of caged wings so like the perturbation of the soul. He ransoms some of the wildest, with softly soothing hands releases them gently, and considers them throbbing away across their recovered skies. There is no Franciscan pity in his heart ; but he hates to see imprisoned wings. His own archangelic plumes are fretted already.

The great ball of gilded copper from Verrocchio's studio swings over the lantern on Brunellesco's dome on a radiant festival day of May. A year later the cross, carrying the sacred relics in its arms, surmounts the ball while the *Te Deum* surges exultantly. When he tires of crowds, he goes wandering in the Val d'Arno, and draws a vision of rocks and water, or loiters on a high lonely road watching the hawk. Or he lives for a day among the flowers he has known all his life, drawing them with exquisite fidelity, yet with such keen sweetness of line that they become Elysian fioretti, marsh-marigold and wood-anemone of unearthly meadows, and arclike branches of bramble, paradisal enough for the King of Portugal's tapestry.

There are graver moods. One may hearken to the limpid perfected music in the Baptistery. Or Landino is lecturing in the Duomo on Dante. Or Marsilio Ficino, Canon of Fiesole, preaches on the " Timæus " in the Church of the Angels, for " We would contemplate Divine truth in this abode of the Angels."

Leonardo is a Dante scholar like the rest. There seems little in common between these haughty spirits except that great haughtiness of theirs, and their individual power of resuming all the knowledge of their time. Like Leonardo, Dante desired an ordered universe ; unlike Leonardo, but very like Michelangelo, his other great enthusiast, he made ready a universe to satisfy his aching love and his hatred, which is only a malady and perversion of love. It was love that moved the earth and the other stars for Dante : he would have struck and carved with fiery images Leonardo's cold First Cause into a Rose of Flame.

There is conversation with artists, travellers, scholars. There is, too, Antonio Segni, that handsome art-loving young man, friend also to Botticelli, who lives near Santa Croce with his widowed mother, doing nothing much. In a charming casual way he " repairs at times to a bank." Later, perhaps, Leonardo makes a *Triumph of Poseidon* for him, a marvel of beautiful curving and spiral lines, now, alas ! as vanished

Leonardo the Florentine

as Antonio. Queerer and wilder companions often divert him. Zoroastro da Pertola is an odd charlatan, something of a painter, mingling some ingenious mechanical devices with his absurd magical pretensions. The reputed child of Bernardo Rucellai, he is a person with " humours," and a vegetarian in his clothes, wearing steadily a vest of gall-nuts, Leonardo's gift. He causes his brilliant friend a faintly interested amusement. Indeed, Zoroastro is full of practical jokes as well as devotion, and lord Leonardo, taking pleasure in the grotesque, is not loth to have his fool like any mere material duke. Atalante is his musician. The young lord, the lutanist, and the fool were not loth to *épater* the Florentine bourgeoisie. It is an alliance of three love-children against sober society. Beauty, music, mirth—as garlanded and beautiful anarchists they often play their parts. Then there are the lost, incalculable gipsy people, who may keep secrets of Egypt or Babylon occult in an amulet or an incomprehensible phrase. There are the gay jesters too, who help him to gather the peasants whom he makes drunk with wine and mirth till they laugh their heads off while he draws them. He plays tricks on people in a puckish way, disguising both his arts and sciences like startling tumblers in a ring sometimes, in moods not wholly kind, stung rather with an elvish or divine mirth at grotesque human capers, like a royal child, or a god in exile, or a young leopard quite surprised if his inhuman gambols bewilder or hurt.

A series of names in the Codex Atlanticus reveals abstruse interests and calm company, names of Giovanni Argiropoulus, the Hellenist, who was in Florence from 1456 to 1472 ; Benedetto dell' Abbaco (Benedetto Aritmetico), the great Florentine mathematician ; Maestro Paolo Medico (Paolo del Pozzo Toscanelli, the distinguished mathematician and geographer, adviser of Columbus) ; Carlo Marmocchio the astronomer ; Filarete the architect, to be encountered again, in later years, on the commission concerning the site of Michelangelo's *David* ; " il Calvo degli Alberti," one of the noble Alberti family and a great Grecian, and other scholars.

So versatile must have been Leonardo's conversation in Florence, so diverse the speakers in those changeable colloquies—courtiers, scholars, artists, lutanists, free companions—that it is easy to comprehend his rueful comment on the wastefulness of much intercourse for the artist, who divides himself into as many selves as he has visitants. Every reflective being has a sense of multiple personality when he splits his attention amongst the dramatis personæ of his social scene ; and Leonardo, while dividing himself like an inexhaustible light, yet felt some loss in diffusion. It seems one of his problems always, how to maintain this converse with his friends which stimulated his wits like light and wine, while

36

Daily Life in Florence

keeping inviolate behind the trellis of his jasmine-decorated speech that solitude in which the lotos of the creative imagination mysteriously restores its leaves, feeding on the honeydew of silence, striking its roots deeper in the waters of Eternity, and folding more closely its petals around its mysterious jewel.

Chapter iv

The " Legend " of Leonardo

i

SO he often goes alone about the streets when the violet veils of twilight are soft, and the too-bright Florentine day becomes tenderly tired. Or, when the light is blurred with rain, and merciful to wearied faces, he follows those that attract him till they give up their essential qualities, as flowers exhale their peculiar souls to the healing kisses of the dusk. And, at those uncanny hours when sleep is coming or going, when the strange process of reminiscence has its way like a subterranean river that becomes articulate in white cascades and dark-eddying pools, when all images can be sealed hard in the half-hypnotized brain, softened, sated and drugged with rest, he earnestly remembers the faces he is conjuring into his imaginative processions. (But sometimes the dark and cruel part that lies chained in him demands its food, and with a like interest, even with a morbid craving, he registers the bestial and ravaged countenances, wronged, defaced, mutilated, contorted and caricatured by time, accident, disease, and vice, into crétins, and apes, and wolves, their cousins.)

Or he goes, alone again, in the breathless, hot summer night among the roses and cypresses of Fiesole, while the innumerable fireflies softly and fluently stitch the dark earth and air with green-and-silver fire, and the nightingales murmur their contented after-song, the rhapsodies over, and the orange-flowers are heady, and the great moon floats overhead. But already the moon is more than a lover's lamp or a goddess' chariot. It is another world to be conquered.

For, while he gazes with those devouring eyes that never know satiety with the shapes and forms and shifting phase of visible things, his brain is intent on the great play of those in the genii of that inscrutable Necessity that brings in universe by processes of complicated in now very dimly aware. Alone in his clue that will take him to the labyri Becoming. He calls his Ariadne Trut

38

The " Legend " of Leonardo

responding desire, as they bent listening to the intimate plangent crying of their plucked strings.

Leonardo was the most brilliant of the improvisatori. For this is the paradox of great genius with its patient and secret complications. It demands for its achievements all the disciplines and preparations that are possible—or none at all. Leonardo desired years for the accomplishment of a piece of perfection—or only one instant, for a drawing or a song.

Music remains, of all the arts, the rare sympathetic sister of his mind, a dear art kept for mere love and pleasure and relief, never exploited for wage or fame or curiosity, though his lyre incidentally did commend him to the lute-loving Court of Milan. For him it was the art that came at the mere sounding of a string to marry the mood of the moment, not exacting long labour and expense of spirit. He could confide his emotional secret to the inviolable cipher of the sweet vanishing notes, whether or not he used the masking words as well. Music was the delicate Ariel who went with Prospero the Dream-Duke of Milan, while Lodovico bought the imperial investiture of the material throne with gold and plot and battle and shame and great unrest.

iv

It is in this Early Florentine period that the *légende* of Leonardo radiantly begins. In his youth, when body and soul were aflame and aflower with their day of perfection, he must have seemed much of a miracle to a time and place so enamoured of dazzling personality. And, if the selective memory of his admirers heightened the colours and double-petalled the qualities, the myth was rooted deep enough in rich realities.

In this coloured, vibrating Florence, with Platonic dreams and luted love-songs drifting down the ways like white and purple butterflies, through the clear excited morning-gold went Leonardo in a music of his own making, creating his own legend by the sweetness of his voice, the grace of his bearing, the beauty of his curled and perfumed self. It was the union of so much strength with so much grace that first seduced the Renaissance folk—strength of an Olympic athlete, grace of a daffodil or a mediæval donzellon. Flown fair in the thrilling air of Florence, strength and grace were as banners behind him, broidered with her lions and lilies.

It was a virtue of the various temper of the city that it could especially display that power of remembering the last wave under the crescent wave, the shoaling of the green and blue, the mother-of-pearl iridescence of mood that shimmers through the alluring Earlier Renaissance, when the more exquisite qualities of mediævalism linger through the ecstatic recognition of a new age. Florence, lover of Charlemagne, had been intimate with France, who had, in her castles, her cathedrals, her knights, her saints, her poets, her ivories, and her tapestries, made most visible the passionate disturbing beauty of the Middle Ages. She had borrowed from the love-poets of Provence a *dolce stil nuova*, and stamped it her own with splendid names. So Leonardo is in his outward aspect, as well as in his subtle mind, something of a troubadour, dressed in rose-colour, with bright long curls and eyes of vair, playing on his silver lute, riming his own verses. In the city where Dante had met Beatrice and suffered the wasting imaginative love of the *Vita Nuova*, where Cavalcanti had mused among the graves, he is, among his Protean aspects, the last great descendant of these. He resumes the old beauty while he promises all the new. And, if he meet no flame-clad " lord of terrible aspect," it may be that he is Love himself, with his soft curled hair and strangely-smiling mouth, an enchanting, faintly-cruel Eros-Narcissus, the true Renaissance love-god. Again, in a way, he goes among the graves like Cavalcanti ; but it is because those fine hands, so subtle in stealing the hearts of the lutes, are as apt in rifling the hearts of the piteous dead of whatever secrets the dead may keep. Many motives go to make a great anatomist, but when a fastidious artist devotes his nights to it, insupportable nights such as Leonardo himself describes, the disconcerting artistic zest in what may be macabre, and is at least bizarre, can certainly be no deterrent. He has a betraying dark exultation in the mortuary horrors of that kind of toil.

v

But the whisper of forbidden things then merely added to the fascination of one who wore the triple tiara of youth, beauty and genius, who was vindicated by the double justification of grace invincible and works incalculable. Golden and gracious in his rose-colour, the hue of Florentine nobility, riding and taming his beloved horses, chevalier, and so the more aristocrat, he goes cherishing his secret hope that one day he will ride the evening air on great wings like Zeus and be as a god. Meanwhile, he will take the universe to pieces, and extort from Nature her secrets, and beguile into nonpareil pictures the beauty that burns on the strange islands beyond the ultimate Verge of Eternity. His beautiful hands can persuade music, or twist a horseshoe, or trace on paper such signs, magical indeed, as might create great buildings and raze impregnable fortresses, can flatter or insult humanity by drawing its image angelic or obscene. His

The " Legend " of Leonardo

amazing mind, while searching for the august laws of Necessity, will strew its track with inventions of " practicable and beautiful things," for it is magnificent to tame the elements as well as horses. He has drawn his own young soul in that drawing at Windsor of the delightful squire, all air and fire, a proud and eager boy with flying sleeves, swiftly moving on a rare adventure, his poignant lance in hand, enigmatic but decided in his imperious quest, looking back in smiling teasing defiance, not reluctant to break a heart or two as he goes. He wears an audacious romantic garment, with the fanciful sleeves flying into points like a girl's, and his bush of rebel hair is capped with fluttering ribbons and a plume. There is a suggestion of hidden wings about him. He is a Renaissance Hermes, a lightfoot god, acquainted with the ways of mere mischief as well as with ethereal embassies. Critics may decide that he belongs to the drawings for the Milanese pageants, and place him with those lax Amazonian figures in breastplates and smoke-soft raiment. But the languor of the Milanese courtier is not his : he is the spirit of Leonardo's Florentine youth.

" If liberty is dear to you, may you never discover that my face is love's prison." So runs the sudden mysterious line widdershins across the manuscript. When he sang " flower-songs " with his companions it was to " Fior de Narciso " that his stornello found the rimes.

vi

Some say he was painted as the Archangel Michael. So they should have painted him, for he had his conflict with the dragon, which was his more destructive self, though he kept it underfoot. (The form of the symbolic dragon which was one with him, dazzling and destroying, that prince of the air made of like heavenly stuff with Michael, pre-occupied him. Steadily he drew it, in deadly embrace with his name-sake the lion, his ally the horse.) But his spiritual armour was light and decorated, chiselled with muses and graces and courtesies ; and his Medusa-symbol was visible only as a lovely quiver of lines on his breast-plate. His defence against inquisition was of the eloquent kind, more baffling than silence, for it distracted by sweet words and blinded by brilliance. He was witty ; he was dancing and beguiling in conversation. He was more. One so powerful evidently had the hypnotic spell, an effect disengaged from some still unravelled union of psychical qualities like any other effect of personality. " With the splendour of his countenance, which was most beautiful, he made serene every broken spirit, and with his words he turned to yea or nay every violent intention." That sentence is enough to make a myth. Whatever his admirations,

Leonardo the Florentine

Vasari did not speak of other artists in that wondering key. But he had had speech with Francesco Melzi, who still radiated some of the light that dwelt starry in Leonardo, even when, grown old and weary in the twilight of the Renaissance gods, he was passing from life with the fragrant manners of his youth.

" Beauty, grace, and ability being beyond measure united in a single person, in a manner that, whatever such an one turns to do, his every action is so divine, surpassing all other men, it is plainly recognized as a thing bestowed by God, and not acquired by human art." " He was so perfected in mind and body that, to whatever difficult things he turned his mind, he solved them with ease." He was royal and magnanimous. " Truly marvellous and celestial was Leonardo, son of Ser Piero da Vinci."

vii

The note of divinity is stressed in all the earlier tributes. He moves not like a mortal. He is more than an artist. His idolaters delight even in that assumption of caprice with which, like a gilded pennon, the young Leonardo seems to ride the lists, challenging the arts and sciences. They like even that touch of superfine ostentation, the dilettante air, with which he turns from deed to deed. They like the long slim fingers bending the horseshoe, without realizing the iron purpose dictating the airy motions of the seductive young man, who is brooding unsuspected on the intricate inevitable logic behind the rainbow, the fountain, the changing lute, the lovers' smiling lips. They like to see him so, shaking the white and red leaves of his youth down the winds of Time, as other potentates, spiritual or temporal, have lavished their early years in the sumptuous dissimulation of a great intention. Such sweet extravagance, such happy confidence in the conquest of Time, humanity has ever found endearing.

Indeed, Leonardo's great intention was a star in his brain that drove him through the arts and sciences, seeking his own imperial seat and his unprecedented coronation. Sometimes he seems in all ways merely the most magnificent of the amateurs ; and the secret, one occasionally doubts, may be that even to himself that intention is not altogether revealed. Sciences and arts are his conquests by the way to some ultimate victory. For, as I have already said, in some spirits God sets a purpose so original and haughty that there is no possible plot for its adventure within the silly dimensions of time and space. There is no stadium on earth for the chariot with the heavenly steeds : the hooves of those horses can beat only ethereal matter into flame. Their amazing riders are incompatible with the limitations of humanity.

The " Legend " of Leonardo

By some Olympian negligence or some incomprehensible irony He has set them on the wrong star, so that their most innocent gestures create something of a planetary disturbance. Even their ways of loving, though angelic, are alien ; and, natural to the seraphim or the gods, are disconcerting to mortality.

viii

If Leonardo looked at the Florentine ladies, it was merely to see their slow smiling, for his master had already observed how their secret rose up to their lips and eyes. As reflected by Ghirlandajo in his honest mirror, stately in their brocades, as exalted by Botticelli in his troubled reverie, with swirling hair and dream-laden eyes and floating motion, as, most clearly perhaps, captured by Verrocchio and the sculptors in their chastely moulding vision, high-bred reticent women with severe fair faces and flowerlike hands, too intelligent, too nervously alert to be sensuously beautiful, they are yet charming enough. They seem proud and delicate and pure, with their high brows and complicated masses of yellow hair, and wide-set considering eyes. They have long graceful necks and little mediæval breasts. When they are young they are like white iris or swan-children.

The lady that haunted Botticelli's mind, the lady who was a beautiful idea to the poetic minds of the two Medici, was a Genovese. But Simonetta alive might go by with that sweet suffering air, and that enchanting way of hers, in her rose-flowered white raiment, or Simonetta dead be carried through the soft April to her grave, with her fantastic face uncovered, princes for her mourners in the hoods of the Misericorde. Lucrezia Donati might sit in gold at Lorenzo's tournament, Lorenzo's mother might look on, her amused wise eyes lighting a worn fine face. Alessandra Scala, lovely and learned, changing violets and Greek verses with Poliziano, might recall " softly smiling Sappho " replying to Alcæus ; or, with the lyric Greek on her lips, make all men in love with Antigone. Giovanna Tornabuoni, immortal in art, might move through her brilliant marriage festival, beautiful bride to beautiful bridegroom, lilylike, her pale face faintly flushed among her soft puffs of bright hair. Marietta Strozzi, the defiant Queen of Hearts who " lived where she liked and did what she liked," a wreathed bright lady whose ancestress must have walked with Fiammetta, Pampinea, Philomena and Emilia among the flowers and the fountains, might come to her window between the lighted torches to watch love's masquerade break gilded lances for her. The sharp-medalled face of the ascetic Camilla Rucellai might be white and tense like Cassandra's with her abiding second-sight of the loved Lord of Mirandola dead among

45

the new-blown lilies. Nannina de' Medici, the Rucellai bride, might wrap her bizarre dark beauty in white velvet and white fur. Leonardo was serenely indifferent to them. The only lady whose face could hold him long was still folded " in shady leaves of destiny " at Naples. Sometimes he draws the clear still profile of a young girl, inviolate, her soul as yet withholden. If he designs a Madonna she is quiet and cold and apart, locked with her Child in a remote cloister of light, like her of the Adoration.

Florence, the city of Dante, Petrarch, Cavalcanti, and their kind, had been, more than other Italian cities, a centre of the mediæval and chivalrous poetry of woman-worship. But she had caught that dangerous doctrine from the troubadours ; and it remained an exotic kind of canonization, though her greatest poet had carried it into the realms of God and His beatitude. The ecstatic creed of romantic love was one of the ineffably beautiful consequences, like the Arthurian legend and Gothic architecture, of the marriage of Celtic and Frankish qualities. It is not native to the Latin or Greek temper, though the Platonic ideal, now superseding it in Florence with soft Alexandrian degradations of colour, had with it a certain affinity. The Renaissance people educated their well-born daughters like their sons, and esteemed their women for courage, wisdom, learning, courtly grace, the great air, beauty— for the qualities the men themselves exhibited, and which they could not sufficiently admire. The Hellenistic age naturally found its ideal type of beauty in the adolescent youth. The Renaissance had not, Florence, whom Poliziano saw as a return of "Athens as she was," had not, the passionless Leonardo most of all had not, any need of the complementary kind of experience and beauty that women can subtly supply. They thirsted no more for her Ionian sweetness, her Asiatic subconscious, sacred reverie of immemorial ritual and blind ecstasy, her heritage of the great emotional wisdom which is behind all the philosophies. (Leonardo had the instinctive as well as the reasoned knowledge himself. He did not require it from another.) They accepted the hetæra, wedded or unwedded, as the recognized, even the dedicated, priestess of pleasure. They demanded the great lady to reign over and to decorate their regal and decorated courts. They had some desire of woman as the Cnidian Venus, though many considered Adonis more beautiful. They liked her well enough as Hebe ; but the sweeter sonnets were written to Ganymede. They did not worship her as Artemis ; but they built rare tombs to the green-garlanded white Hippolytus. If they had found the grave inviolable head of the Lemnian Athena they would have called it Ion, Charmides, or Critias. Florence particularly delighted in the reticent unwounded lines of the ephebus. The old song numbering the best things of every country speaks of " le jouvenceau de Toscane " as its loveliest flower.   If Saint John the Baptist was the City's patron saint, David the deliverer was her " genius," a shepherd as enchanting to their Hellenic fancy as Phrygian Paris on the woody slopes of Ida.   He was beauty militant and prevailing : he was the lover of Jonathan as well as the slayer of Goliath, the friend of all friends who loved with a love " passing the love of woman."   Donatello carved him, romantic and triumphal ; Verrocchio made him slim, a little perverse, enchanting, like a young Renaissance prince ; Pollaiuolo painted him like a faintly-melancholy Florentine noble ; Michelangelo was yet to turn him into a boyish Titan as a *tour de force*.

Other lovely youths in stone and bronze were to be of his company —champions, torchbearers, angels, paladin figures of Saint George, the youthful Saint John, Perseus.   Florence, like Athens, was friezed with beautiful pages and knights.   They were smooth and fair in the gates of Ghiberti ; they sang earnest alleluia in the cantoria of Luca della Robbia ; like gladiolus they brightened the niches among prophets and evangelists ; they stood as saints and angels in the pictures ; they sprang free, to exult in the cortile and the loggia.   Where a Greek would have said Discobolus or Diadumenos, a Renaissance artist often said Saint Sebastian, Saint Thomas, Saint George, Saint Louis, Saint Martin, Saint Maurice, Saint Michael.   The names did not trouble him.   The Madonna brooded still over them all, for they knew she kept a secret irrevocable beauty and a magic of suffering that could not be despoiled, a beauty for whom no procession of filleted maidens brought the Panathenaic veil, nor gifts of doves and roses.   They dreamed of surrendering no beauty.   But hers was seven times wounded.

ix

As for Leonardo, he gazed at the masque of Florentine youth with a pleasure as intricate as it was serene.   Woman, he thinks, is necessary to the great adventure of birth.   He is not concerned with the mystery of her heart but with the mystery of the uterus ; he will consider even her emotional state if it affects the child in its pre-natal chamber.   But otherwise women could give his complete nature nothing he had not already, except a disintegrating anguish he did not desire.   He had seen in the house of the Medici a gem where the fair secret son of Hermes and Aphrodite lay intagliate in red jasper, tended by wistful amorini ; and he mused on the veiled paradox of a love so perfect that it is sterile.

In Florence, where Niccolo Niccoli had sorrowed so sincerely over a beautiful boy untouched by learning, thinking him a flower without

Leonardo the Florentine

perfume if he had no dream of Greece, that this fair young listener, a young man earnestly desiring these greater possessions, straightway left his gay companions to become a scholar and a noble citizen, the Socratic attitude to youth was fashionable enough, though the children who posed for the Davids were less modest than the young Athenians who blushed and lowered their eyes. The Leonardesque attitude was at once less intellectual and even more æsthetic. He did not love people for their wisdom, for he had no lack of wisdom. He loved them for their beauty, of which he never had enough. He did love them evidently because they had luxurious soft hair, and broad sweet eyelids that seemed burdened with a secret of the gods. But it is possible to love physical things with a psychical pleasure. And Leonardo loved Florentine youth as he loved flowers, and red wine, and soaring wings, and lapsing water, and rare perfumes, and his horses, and his lutes. A little more anxiously perhaps, since human things can hurt. Why did he write so musingly upon that page of drawings: " Fioravante, the son of Domenico, who is *amantissimo* towards me as any maid, I could love " ? Adoring eyes of Fioravante, were they blinded by Leonardo's strange love ? It is hard to say what stirred in that masked soul, as he painted some of its troubles in the lost ambiguous head of the Medusa, frozen beauty among tormenting snakes.

Whatever flickered in his soul, whatever psychical experiments he made in strange permutations of emotion—and an intelligence so fiery and so insatiable could hardly have left the problems of human affinity unprobed and untried, especially at a period when the rage of curiosity and the passion for experience were so reckless that the differences of sex and age were often ignored as futile barriers to be consumed by the rapture of power—Leonardo was doomed to a shock of a real kind, sounding like a throb of sinister drums through the lute-music of his legend. Dreamstuff is a soft violet medium for the subtle stealths and evasions, the glowing fading ways of a unique spirit seeking rarefied emotional pleasures ; and imaginative caresses are lovely that become horribly degraded when translated into the inappropriate terms of the flesh, with its crude reactions and animal consequences. Fancies wreaked beautifully in aëry images may be astoundingly confused with the brutalities of lust by those who are not adepts in æsthetic lore. In love, at least, only the aristocrats understand each other ; and there is a laity that knows nothing but physical desire. The distinction is not worldly nor intellectual. It is a matter of spiritual texture ; and in the aristocracy of love the simplest soul meets the most sophisticated.

The " Legend " of Leonardo

None could be so conspicuous a creature as Leonardo without rousing some desire to throw mud at his rose-coloured raiment. Therefore this sudden interruption in the music and the dancing, the mote of darkness in the sunlight, the evil young face of Jacopo Saltarelli, the malevolent blackmailers behind him, and the anonymous accusation dropped in the *tamburatione*. It is an accusation for a Francesco Pazzi, say, not for a Leonardo.

Leonardo and others were summoned to answer the following charge : " Notifico a voi, padri officiale, con egli è vera cosa che Jacopo Saltarelli, fratello carnale di Giovanni Saltarelli (sta con lui all 'orafo, in Vacchereccie dirempetto al buco, veste nero, d'eta d'anni 170 circa) il quale Jacopo dietro a molte miserie, et consente compiacere a quelle persone lo richieggano di simili tristazi. A questo modo ha avuto a fare di molte cose, cioè servire parecchie dozzino di persone delle quarli ne so buona data. Tal parte diro d'alcuni Bartheo di Pasquino orafo, sta in, Vacchereccia Leonardo de ser Piero da Vinci, sta con Andrea del Verrocchio. Baccino farsettaio, sta in Orto San Michele, Leonardo Tornabuoni dicto il Tere, veste nero."

This accusation was repeated on the seventh of June ; but the Council found the charge unproven, and dismissed it entirely, doubtless none too pleased with a dubious arraignment aimed at a psychical fashion, an artistic affectation paraded in Medicean circles more innocently and more gracefully than in Rome or Naples or Perugia.

There is no record of how this event affected Leonardo or the opinions of others. The Council and the Church offered him commissions soon afterwards, so that his reputation did not suffer. In those days Council and Church practically ignored the idiosyncrasies of artists. But probably the incident deeply shocked his pride, and embittered him against his City. And the memory rankled and inhibited, so that his nervous fear became reinforced, and his dislike of overt expression stronger. He had had his conflict. He had been Perseus with Medusa, Saint Michael with his Dragon. He had been the lion wrestling with the pterodactyl that was winged and kin to the Ancient of Days, and kin to some part of himself, and yet inimical. He had had his peculiar victory, and it had been mistaken.

To casual onlookers he had seemed splendid, somewhat spendthrift, dissipating his days rather carelessly. Long after, he alludes in the manuscripts to the idle reed-beds of Tuscany, and their wanton mornings plundered from labour, with a certain note of regret, so probably even Leonardo was wise enough to waste some time in the Castle of Indolence.

Moreover, he was supposed to fear no God. He was young, so he said so. Vasari says doubtfully in his earlier version of Leonardo's biography that he was of " so heretical a cast of mind that he conformed to no religion whatever, accounting it perchance much better to be a philosopher." (But the only complaint that the monks had against the enchanting heretic was that they could not hold him long enough to finish their pictures.)

xi

He was probably deeply angry at being trapped into the pillory for a moment. When popes and princes were openly bisexual, when the Florentine artists, including Verrocchio, continually praised the beauty of the adolescent, when Lorenzo's Academy thought tenderly of the sensitive sweet boys with downcast eyes who listened to Socrates and Plato, when even the gracious Marsilio Ficino sang this love to the lute, why should he be singled out for base accusation? Benivieni, the sacred poet, might allude to Sodom; but it was his trade to draw rhetorical images from the Bible. Scholars and artists had the great Greek way—so they were convinced. Leonardo had worn his Greek preferences as haughtily as Marsilio or Poliziano, though he talked less pedantically about it, having, indeed, a serene conviction that he belonged to that holy Apostolic Succession whose representatives can do no wrong because their grace makes all things gracious. He had believed in the integrity of his *virtù* : to his crystal mind all thoughts were good if he thought them. With a sense of outrage, shock, and bewilderment, he found his psychic attitudes and his Athenian loves reduced to mere ugliness, and himself denounced as merely a seeker of *capilliti* instead of courtesans. He, who with expense of spirit had converted all wayward and excessive fancies to a clear flame of intellectual ardour that illumined his days and consumed his nights ! He who had been that rarest of ascetics, the spiritual æsthete whose fastidiousness cannot tolerate bodily appetites at all, so that he has a sincerer and much more disdainful loathing of carnality than any monk ! Indeed, therein is more truly Leonardo's sin, his excess, and his outlawry. He refused to see that beauty can enter into human passion, even as God enters into the Holy Bread. He believed in transubstantiation in no way whatever.

The incident cannot have been without psychical consequences. He was left with a suppressed sense of wrong against a social ethic naturally incomprehensible to him, who never would have sacrificed individual variations to the general conspiracy for the perpetuation of the race, and with a greater uncertainty concerning all reactions to his self-

The " Legend " of Leonardo

expression. Long afterwards he writes to his fellow-citizens with
bitterness : " Quando io feci Domeniddio putto voi me mettisti in
prigione, ora s'io lo fo grande voi me farate peggio." It is a mysterious
sentence, and translators differ. But it is as if at this time he had at
least put his secret soul in prison and thrown away the key.

Chapter v

The Bottega of Verrocchio

i

IN the "city like a garden," all garlanded vine and olive, and lute songs and sunset dances, and clear bright colours, and restless Athenian people, undisturbed by their sudden spasms of flashing daggers and shaken bells, and murder crying from the choirs and the parapets, art seemed to grow as easily as the flowers, and clave as naturally as their shadows to the churches and the palaces. In other Renaissance cities, like the passionate enemy Siena, art dwells as a wasting sweet fever of the soul. In some, like Assisi, it is an act of devotion. In some, like Milan, it is a personal decoration and luxury. In Rome it is a commanded pomp. In so different Venice, art again seems indissolubly one with nature; but there it comes fulfilled and slowly splendid like the sunsets and the autumns. Early Florentine art has a sudden and thrilling air like the spring and the morning "with dewy fingers cold." Like Athens indeed, the City possessed a sense of spiritual liberty and much marble. So, for the earlier Tuscan sculptors, the stone seems to flower with angels as with lilies, and the low relief flickers on the surface as if responsive to the mere breath of desire, as if fair figures and twining raiment and trophies were arrested on the borders of sight by a passing chord of music. It is a lyrical response that first hails the new Annunciation Angel, coming so swiftly with a serpentine charming-rod, wearing petasus and talaria; and the more unconscious Renaissance art is the sweeter, its native originalities just excited and enriched by the apprehension of rare Hellenic images and the fragrance of liberation. While the peculiarly mediæval intensity and sincerity lingered on through the new sense of conquest and freedom and inspiration caught from the recovered and adored images of Hellenic antiquity, the painters and sculptors of Italy smote the eyes with the piercing sweetness of a song sung all alone for the sake of its mere delight.

But Leonardo's lot was to appear when Italian art was passing from the first enthusiasm of its half-conscious pleasure to the phase of deliberate experiment; and he was destined to be one of the three

The Bottega of Verrocchio

artists who carried painting, sculpture and architecture as far as intellectual processes could take imaginative conception. After Leonardo, Michelangelo, and Raphael in easier, more popularized fashion, painting could do nothing but specialize in one or other of their characteristics till it might discover and break new fields of vision altogether.

ii

Leonardo was about fourteen or fifteen when his father brought him to the house and bottega of Verrocchio, the " true-eyed " artist, where he grew and learned and discussed his art. Whatever Leonardo's mode of existence, he seems flamingo-like in the house and circle of Verrocchio, for whom, nevertheless, he entertained an affection strong enough to keep him a considerable time in this dwelling, for he is not described as being " in casa propria " till 1476. Whether he kept open house then, with a retinue of servants and horses, as Vasari says, remains a vaguely golden matter. His amusements were expensive, he did little paid work, he did not execute his commissions. It is improbable that his father, though his income increased with his family, helped him much after the earlier years. As a successful notary, however, in touch with religious communities and with the Medici, he may have done something to procure his son those unfulfilled orders. Still, there is no evidence to destroy the powerful implication that he lived like a Renaissance gentleman. He never seems to have worn the irritating cilice of poverty. Servants and horses were necessary to him, and servants and horses he always had. All the reports and references of his time or near his time maintain a tone regarding him which differs from that used for other artists. Princes write of him more plaintively than imperiously ; ambassadors speak of him with respect ; Isabella d'Este, Castiglione, Bandello, all more or less reveal him as a personage and an equal. In Florence his finances seem to be variable. At times he lives gaily and " nobody knows where the money comes from " ; at others, evidently straitened, he will gild a clock for the monks, or get another to do it. He was luxurious in his raiment ; he loved riding, music, festival, perfumes, fine friends ; and he gave freely what he had. His physical appetites were temperate and fastidious. Good wine, bread, fruit, salad, chicken, a little meat, sometimes, not always, served his needs. He had an odd psychological trick of writing down small sporadic accounts when vexed by persons or circumstances. But discussion of his social position belongs rather to his life in Milan.

There was evident sympathy between pupil and master during those restless experimental years. Every phase in Leonardo's development is disputed by critical experts, and the interaction of the two artists is a theme for endless discussion. Some will have it that Verrocchio acquired all his merit from his pupil, and some none at all. It seems as if there had been a rare and fortunate understanding between them. Leonardo's exciting, exploring spirit came as a stimulant to the somewhat grave and tired master, square, thoughtful, kind—paralysed by such difficult circumstances and responsibilities as Leonardo never knew nor accepted, for the bitter constraint of long-endured want, which is no high discipline, but mere waste and misery and deadly depression for any artist, was never really familiar to the younger, though he had a financial crisis occasionally when his patrons came to grief. He, however, happily discovered in his elder a master that accorded with his imaginative temper, a sensitive mind that had already struck out many motives which he instantly accepted, grafting, cherishing, and caressing, drenching with emotional magic the crude buds left untended on Verrocchio's overtasked tree of art. Though he was but fourteen or fifteen years old when he first came to the bottega, Renaissance youth began early, and his was a personality vivid and compelling from his childhood.

iii

Verrocchio certainly had greater power over metal and stone than paint. Much employed by Lorenzo, he made Piero de' Medici's beautiful tomb in San Lorenzo, red porphyry and green marble on great lions' paws, with twisted thorny bronze foliage. He had wrought on the Forteguerra tomb. He lifted the ball of gilded copper on the Dome ; and set the Cross over the ball. In 1476 his bronze *David*, an enchanting and perverse prince, passed from Lorenzo to guard the staircase of the Palazzo Vecchio. Next year he was exquisitely labouring on the great Silver Altar of the Baptistery. In 1478 the daring dreamy group of the Christ and the suave dubitative Thomas went to its decorated niche on Or San Michele. For the Medici he was always at work—tombs, statues, armour, pageantry, ex-votos, busts of both brothers, Giuliano and Lorenzo—Lorenzo with graven harpies on his breast. He did many things cheerfully, for, oppressed by poverty and duty to his kin, he had known himself so thwarted that he could not even ply for want of metals the trade of goldsmith. He fashioned the silver hind for Giuliano's helmet ; he had made breastplates for Galeazzo Maria Sforza ; he painted standards and devised gilded steel for the tournaments ; he cast a church-bell for the monks at Vallombrosa. In an inspired and radiant mood he charmed from some garden-nursery of Olympos

The Bottega of Verrocchio

that inimitable *putto* with the dolphin for Careggi, and he restored the antique red marble bust of Marsyas, using the white veins in the stone for the sinews. He made clasps and cups with devices of foliage and fabulous beasts, acanthus and pinions alive and lovely, but with that hint of natural malice in them which becomes a conscious threat of danger in Leonardo's spined wings and leaves. Even when he laboured on his great Rider he was under promise to make a marble well for the King of Hungary ; but he died, so no far-off princess out of a ballad gazed in that great cup. He had much of his pupil's versatility, but none of his disdains, for he was goldsmith, and intaglio-maker, even bell-caster, as well as painter, musician, geometrician. When, long afterwards, Leonardo, grown supercilious among princely patrons, wrote to the citizens of Piacenza, "This one is a potter, that one a maker of cuirasses, a bell-founder, a bell-ringer," he chose to forget some customs of the artists in that City of the Florentines whose beautiful bronze gates he was even then praising.

Leonardo came, brightly perturbing, a strange bird of paradise for Verrocchio's strait grey house, to discover there the themes for which he had immediate appreciation, and which he readily stamped with the flamelike seal of his perfection. At no time could Leonardo have been easily impressionable, but it is characteristic of the greatest genius to be in its early hours a little uncertain, a little dubious as to the occasion, the hint, the formal device which will precipitate its marvellous fine suspension of beauty into crystals of novel colour and shape ; and it seizes instantly with a divine plagiarism on any existing specks of artistic matter that may serve. Why should it trouble to invent the excuses for its mysteries of colour and sound ? It does not care to begin creating in a void ; even when it is revolutionary, new-born it shivers a little in the unfamiliar universe and sensitively attaches itself to whatever more or less congenial mote of tradition may sustain it awhile. Leonardo, more fortunate than many, found in Verrocchio's painting and sculpture, faint and chill, the adumbration of the jasper landscapes, the winding water and distant wood, the dreamily-inclining heads with broad lids and convoluted hair, the expressive hands, that have already been clearing into shape within the cloudy mirror of his young fancy. Delighted, he deepened the jasper twilights, charmed the strange waters into more mysterious pools, concentrated the woods into some solitary brooding tree of life or death, twined richer, rarer spirals in the curling hair, made heavier the lids, more subtly promising the mouth, affined the nervous hands, with sensitive fingers drew raiment of silkier kind into softer folds, suppled the limbs, sent a new audacity into the grouping—and cast over all the unearthly transfiguring light of his own singular fantasy. "Tristo e quel discepolo che non avanza il suo maestro," says Leonardo himself, whose own disciples were to turn to such a strengthless grace the great example of their master.

He found in Verrocchio even some tentative gleams from the unearthly emotional states in which he was to plunge his imagery. He found also a sceptical, curious intelligence, anxious, like his own, to pry into anatomy and the laws of movement, as well as a kindred love of geometry and music. There was an elective affinity between master and pupil ; all the suggestions of Verrocchio were to become eloquent in Leonardo, confused with his own strengthening, original vision like milk-white stars in the kindling dawn. But they struck responses from each other. Leonardo gave—or merely radiated—the imaginative sympathy, the contagion of bright vitality, his master's laborious, thirsting life required, so that Verrocchio's age is his most brilliant period. The studio is illuminated with the graces of youth, and dartles with sensations of wonder and danger, as if Apollo had taken service again with a mortal. There is a snatch of song, a chord from a lute, a dropped fine glove, a waft of foreign fragrance, a branch of blossom, a dead lizard lost from the noxious spoil in the chamber of horrors upstairs where, with a god's indifference, the bright disciple composes a dragon—a trail of beauty with a hint of malice. The marble heads of the calm chaste Florentine girls smile faintly, the *David* becomes more sweetly insolent, the winged griffins and Medusa heads quicken, the lion's paws are terribly alert, acanthus, fruit and flower come alive like scorpions and basilisks, with that fierce intention so acute in the spinous leaves and wings of the lavabo of San Lorenzo. The tortured head of the antique Marsyas flinches and flushes deeper, remembering that the flute is heard no more in the Phrygian mountains. The horses in the drawings pace more proudly, rear magnificently. But Verrocchio was wise and tolerant, and still splendid in achievement, a fitter lord than Admetus to entertain a god. It is a great artist indeed who makes the *Boy with the Dolphin*, the arrogant slim *David*, the suave *Thomas*, a king of his kind who sends Colleone riding on his bronze steed after Gattamelata.

It is easy to undervalue him. He sank like steel into the richer, younger genius, imparting a trenchant and chiselled quality of his own. He uses even the minor Leonardo notes, for the fantastic monsters, gorgons and dragons, drawn with scintillating line, in which Leonardo, with insouciant grace, yet reveals a certain psychic distress, are the haughtier descendants of heraldic beasts in Verrocchio's masterpieces in metal. All the supreme victors have their preluders ; and sometimes the prelude has a kind of harsh sweetness, a tang of sharp surprise

The Bottega of Verrocchio

missing from the smooth harmony to come. Though Verrocchio's personality is reticent, inassertive, his drawings are powerful in their own way, his crafts are exquisite in their own way. A brilliant apparition came and caught his devices into a richer, more composite art ; he retains his identity. Leonardo could not have carved that wise pure lady with the primroses in her most lovely hands : she is too humanly kind and sweet ; she is Verrocchio's. The silver relief of the *Decollation of Saint John* is forcible and elaborate at once to a marvellous degree, and the dreamy compassionate youth with the boars' heads on his greaves is like an armoured lily. And the *David*, that dainty stripling in the ethereally-broidered armour, with the lifted lips and sideways eyes, is also his own. Though there be a touch of Leonardo's youth about him, he has a pointed reedy charm, an awkward princeliness, something of a piercing Gothic grace that Leonardo might have softened away into ambiguity. Verrocchio's earnest blunt-nosed angels, with their clustered curls, have an honest, anxious-to-please as well as a wistful air, which is most appealing. Leonardo's, more beautiful, more mystical, sometimes have more than a touch of the mignon. If Verrocchio's beauty be " hard-won," it is never oversweet. Still, what Leonardo was, as well as what he did in his art, the beauty and enchantment of his presence, must have been kindling to his senior's imagination. It was not Leonardo who was impressionable ; and all Verrocchio's work has a new flame playing over it after the arrival of his kindling pupil.

Dying at fifty-three, wasted by the fever of the lagoons while labouring at his great riding statue, Verrocchio perished too early, since he was still in the pride and ease of his final development.

iv

Verrocchio's bottega was well crowded, for his influence, strong and quiet, stole into others who did not call themselves pupils, the Pollaiuoli, for example, whose strenuous house was in the same street, and the dreaming Botticelli. If Leonardo was the strange angel within his gates, the most loyal of the pupils was Lorenzo di Credi, one of those gentle souls whose clear candour can render true echoes, and whose sweet sensibility can receive and multiply charming impressions so long as it may live in the presence of a master. There is little room for an " Alunno di Verrocchio " while Lorenzo is there, obediently transposing both his master and his fellow-pupil into his milder mood. In his drawing he often proves himself worthy of his company, though Mr Berenson's remark that his heads are sometimes like those of Burne-Jones angels is evidently not intended as a compliment. If he drew the silverpoint of the reclining Venus attended by a love he was capable of ravishing things. But I think it is Verrocchio's. His light went out when he had faithfully fulfilled the desires of his dead master ; and his latter pictures are dull and sentimental, though the return of Leonardo brightened him awhile. Now, however, at the bottega he is young, kind, sweet, with the flushed, eager look of a boy interested in matters a little beyond him.

Within that bottega the discussion was strong. Conversation was at once an art and an education in those days, conversation of courts, conversation of the piazza, conversation of the campagna, conversation of the workshop. In Florence, especially, the social and specialist barriers that became bastions when the exultant enthusiasms of the Renaissance died away, that always are erected by the jealousies of sciences and arts in their petrifying periods, when they have become self-sufficing, and therefore purblind cenobites, were dissolved in one molten mood. Princes, scholars, courtiers, artists, jesters, merchants, peasants, citizens, threw their shuttles in the loom of speech, and wove an iridescent tapestry. From Campanile, Duomo and Baptistery, from palaces and chapels, from portal and loggia and window-frame, the flags of beauty triumphant sent delicate vibrations through the air. So they talked and were excited. The interchange of vivid minds, duelling, embracing, searching, criticizing, inquiring together, electrifying their common knowledge with their individual reactions, reflexes and comparisons, suppled and enriched the communicants.

Leonardo, notably a conversationalist, whose circles of acquaintance intersected in a most complicated " fantasia dei vinci," found himself, through most of his existence, in a dilemma. He knew that solitude is necessary to the artist, that his work exacts a concentration of mind and soul not possible to many except within the clear cloisters of silence. As he says, the painter eloquent must divide himself into as many selves as there are persons in his colloquies, which means diffusion and exhaustion and waste of time and energy in re-establishing the creative quietude. But he also knew that, to the sheer anchorites of art, the air of their cells will become unbreathably strange, their visions, over-excited, take on chimerical and extravagant shapes, their hands go numb and silly over the imponderable stuff they handle. So that conversation is necessary to dispel the dreadful doubt, the queer ghastly apprehension whispering to the solitary worker in immaterial things that he may be merely the prey of a vampirish delusion. Conversation, said Leonardo, critical conversation is necessary while the work is in progress. His own mind made a solitude round itself ; but, with his sure instinct for equilibrium, he did seek society, which normalizes the artistic experience just enough to keep it sane. It will sometimes do more, for there are stray moods on which some accident of listened words will drop like burning oil, running wildfire along the creative track, touching the fuse of the unconscious train of the imaginative logic, whose coruscating conclusion is a *rose-de-joie*. There are coloured changes of speech; there are silver chances and crystal accents falling through the white nights of silence. Leonardo, all desirous, knew both.

v

They talked in the bottega, and were excited, for discoveries, long since become commonplaces, were new to them. They were romantics, returning to realism as the just proof of their passion for Greece— romantic adventurers sailing for Athens in a new-built caravel of their own, with a brown palimpsest for a chart, setting up a thousand novel shrines in their endless track. "Naturalism" was the strange new beauty. In Florence they were tired of gold backgrounds and the "calm cold beautiful regard," and the hieratic rigidity. They had discovered with delight that the human body is beautiful, veiled or unveiled. Donatello had even discovered the paradox we make so much fuss over, that it may be beautiful even when it is ugly. They were intoxicated with the pride of their intellectual freedom; they were carried by a sense of power into the "insolence" that infuriates the gods. They were enchanted to see figures from their own flashing world move and sit at ease with ravishing play of muscle in the wonderful light and air now most astonishingly lured within the canvas. And, being Florentines, they were as exalted in their love of "pure form" as any Cubist or worshipper of Cézanne. Agate exactitudes, diamond perfections—these they would chisel out of any medium, marble or jewel or paint or words.

vi

Little they said, one thinks, of neighbouring schools: Florence was the first city in Art. They might sometimes discuss the painting of their angry sister, high Siena, that citadel of Virgin-worship, from whose essential fierceness of mood her painters had secreted a gilded hieratic art of an extreme dreamy sweetness, an excessively decorated mysticism, such as often strangely dwells in the heart of violence, a fragile wonder stolen in a reliquary ark from perishing Constantinople. Duccio was the faint perfect blossom of that precious Byzantine tree of jewels, the last refinement of that sacerdotal pattern of pale roses on a ground of

59

heavenly gold. But though Duccio's lovely etiolated figures might keep their hush and chastity of holy beauty within a mesh of lines as beautiful and unerring as any Florentine could make, he was not doomed to enter into the Renaissance tradition. Pure beauty will make a man immortal, will make him count for all time, but not necessarily for his own time, for even a great artist is not inevitably in contemporary mood.

So Duccio might affect an ecstatic monk like Fra Angelico ; and an inheritor as fine and sumptuous as Simone Martini might cherish his jewelled flame awhile ; the tender Lorenzetti might put their personal passion into his formula, and the romantic Matteo di Giovanni and Neruccio bring their strange flowers into the Renaissance light. But his city's next adventure in art would be to call for Signorelli and Perugino, and to betray his tradition to the secular trumpets and banners of Sodoma's capture of its cloisters. Nevertheless this exquisite art of the passionate hill-city, delicate as a white porphyrogenita princess in convents of Byzantine gold, quivering with rare sensibility like the wings of a marvellous butterfly, did send its fine vibration to meet and mingle with the Gothic intensity of Sandro Botticelli, while the purely decorative beauty of its Byzantine line, almost like the Chinese, was caught by him into a pattern charged with a strange new fever.

Meanwhile, the Florentines themselves remembered, as Leonardo himself always remembered, that Giotto who, not so fascinating to many as Duccio, yet, after Cimabue, freed the holy figures from the frigidities and the archaic melancholies. " Giotto of Florence appeared," said Leonardo ; and, as a solitary goatherd among the mountains, " drew what he saw." He had dissolved the Byzantine prison, the painted golden shadow of the golden mosaic, and had linked his figures composedly in a world of clear colours and rhythmical lines, at peace within an atmosphere of stilled and tender emotion. The innovators felt their debt, though they had wearied a little of those quiet attitudes ; and, after Masolino had made life more visible and audible, the greatly gifted, early dead Masaccio had, in the Brancacci Chapel of the Carmine, disengaged the coloured Florentines themselves to move about naturally as well as beautifully in bright breathable air. The old miracle-play had become the mere pretext for imitating the new thrilling drama of their own day, and bringing it into the eternity of art. " Masaccio," thought Leonardo, " showed by perfect works that those who are led by any guide except Nature, the supreme mistress, are consumed by sterile labour."

Gentile da Fabriano, that courtly Umbrian, had made a hectic lovely procession of kings, with rarely illuminated landscapes in the predella ; and Pisanello had brought real animals and fruits, and fresh country sights, into his vivid adventurous pictures, with clear far skies.

The Bottega of Verrocchio

He could set his delectable fantastic people in a wooded landscape with rare perspectives. But these strangers had not counted strongly in Florence ; and Jacopo Bellini, Gentile's brilliant helper, had reason to quit the jealous town. With all painters and sculptors the talk was still of the great Donatello, who, a gentle and generous old man, still moved about his native city till 1466, living his happy communistic life. He had suffered privations in his quest for ancient beauty, and had greatly loved the Greeks with a Gothic intensity ; but, like all true Renaissance idolaters of the antique, had merely learned from them that it was right to consider reality with unprejudiced eyes, and that it was easy to alter the Christian traditions of formal art while still serving the traditional themes. But the world had indeed known that Christian fever, that martyrdom of the body, that malady of the Orient, that wild sense of perdition or of redemption, which is involved with the idea of an agonizing human God. The many inhibitions of the Pauline religion had driven the senses inward to crucify the soul, which there-after would keep incurably the stigmata of the Five Wounds, whatever its adventures. Donatello brought an electricity into sculpture ; but, using his eyes as the Greeks did, he saw, not the bright worshipped bodies of the palæstra and the stadium, true images of the inviolable shapes of immortals, but creatures wasted, tortured, strung, excited, transfigured sometimes by their psychical trouble, and by the conflict between soul and body, whom no man may join again since they were sundered by a god out of Asia. His figures are not clothed with mere muscles ; they wear a cilice of nerves. No longer locked in the sweet catalepsy of the queens and saints of Rheims or Amiens, they all are aware of their trances and fevers, some of their brutalities, some of their state of grace. They are elated, possessed, quivering with emotion. The Gothic fever runs amazingly into the Hellenistic rapture.

Donatello had more notes than even Michelangelo his great successor, though the Titan was not monotonous. He could be *naïf*, pitiful, fantastic, realistic, excitable, serene. He had set a sad and splendid tomb for a despoiled Pope in the Baptistery. Or San Michele wore his tabernacles and medallioned stemmas, especially keeping, poised like a lance in rest, the patrician *Saint George* that "moved itself within the stone." His genius is written in bronze in San Lorenzo. The Campanile and the Duomo possessed his saints, his haggard, humorous, or pathetic prophets and evangelists. The Baptistery had his famous *Magdalene*, disengaging a heart-breaking beauty from the tragedy of her ruined age, like Rodin's less contrite *Vieille Heaulmière*. He carved the story of the patron saint of Florence, from the dreamy and excitable childhood to the delirious vision of the desert, the drama of a *nèvrose* told in images. In a mood of rare quality he created that high-born Virgin in Santa Croce within her exquisite cloison of gilded stone, shy and proud, softly inclining in delicate courtesy, half recoiling from the sweet angel, half welcoming. His romantic figure of David, lightly bent and boyish, a charming demigod-shepherd in hat and boots, began the line of beautiful youths that act as the " genius " of Florence. His uncertain delicate Judith, the Florentine feminine parallel for the *David*, stood lifting her fine-fashioned sword over the limp Holofernes. He drew a riot of genii, lovely satyr-children, in a frenzy of rapturous sound about a singing-loft, the clashing cymbals of their masque of misrule almost drowning the christened musicians and singers of Luca's opposed to them. Busts of great people, graven plaques, subtly vanishing pictures in metal, expressed the versatility of his genius. He could make of a Cupid something movingly absurd and delicious, and he had sent out the first great Rider of the Renaissance in bronze. He had been in Rome and in Prato as well as in Padua, where he left much of his great imagery, like that great Byzantine *Madonna*, throned between sphinxes, though he had deliberately quitted its adulations for his beloved Florence, because he missed the zest of the ironical comment which Leonardo resented.

Donatello's imaginative daring and his triumphant skill in casting the figures of his versatile mood still fascinated all the painters and sculptors of Florence. Verrocchio had been much affected by Donatello, had received some of his dynamic energy, and had especially studied his Condottiere at Padua. The bitter and taut emotion of the great sculptor was painful to Leonardo's nerves ; but he could find in many of his figures the elusive faunlike glance he needed as one element of the mysterious expression he was mingling for his own. And he also admired Donatello, as he admired Ghiberti, for those wonderful bronzes with their vanishing effects as aerial as paint could give.

Certainly the artists of the time did love merely technical bravura too well. But the triumph over matter had gone to their heads ; and, when all the arts were choiring together, it was sometimes amusing as well as brilliant to make one art do the work of another, a kind of virtuosity justified by consequences while great genius prevailed, though a dangerous precedent for days to come when listless talent could merely play with the tools of the giants.

Ghiberti painted in bronze already, and Ghiberti had talked of the *Canon* of Polycleitus, and of the passionately alluring quality of antique fragments. Ghiberti, who counted time by olympiads, and whose gates were dear to Leonardo as to Michelaneglo, was still quoted in the studios. After Donatello, the artistic tradition of Florence perhaps

The Bottega of Verrocchio

still favoured the sculptors. The city with a sense of marble and of freedom instinctively preferred the perdurable and definite lines of stone and of irretrievable bronze to the fluidities of paint. The citizens were *gardiens du contour pur*. If a people thinks nobly of its own humanity it does incline to sculpture, which is the art of free cities. The ineluctable quality in Leonardo's *chatoyant* personality, chafing at the more rigorous material like Ariel in his tree, made him prefer the deliquescence of his palette; and there was much sincerity in his confessed pleasure in a charming studio, for his exaltation of the painter's lot is not childish, but merely candid. Still, the Florentines loved and used their sculptors, who rival the picture makers too well, perhaps, in a quivering emotion and a penetrating sweetness, as of the leaves of beauty trembling from their pure sheaths of stone. With faint and musical modalities they entreat their angels and virgins into sight with an effect not merely of white lilies but of soft white roses. Desiderio da Settignano, Antonio Rossellino, Benedetto da Majano, Mino da Fiesole, makers of beautiful tombs, and pulpits, and reliefs, and busts, moulding marble like clay, just breathing it into form, were creating from the sweet soil of Tuscany its peculiar yet classic art. Agostino di Duccio, maker of rare romantic figures with swirling and fluted raiment, also came to Florence now and then; and had some trouble with the great block of marble where Michelangelo's *David* still lay in formless slumber.

Verrocchio was a sculptor first; and all sculptors must have been discussed in his bottega. Leonardo himself was making his models in clay and wax, and thinking, as time went on, of the great horse desired in proud Milan. And it was well for him that he was trained in a sculptor's bottega, for all his later love of rich chiaroscuro and soft dissolution of colour never affects the unerring trick of pencil or silverpoint, drawing its triumphal line, the sculptor's irrevocable line, that cannot know uncertainty.

Of all the sculptors Luca della Robbia was the most esteemed, for Leonardo remembers him more than once in later times, the only contemporary artist he mentions except Botticelli. The endearing vernacular of Luca's blue and white makes us forget the beauty of his singing marble and his deep-toned bronze. The tondos and the lunettes of that lovely ware, with its wonderful ivory glazes, brought the early Renaissance running like an azure convolvulus through Florence, sent its dews and its lilies, its sense of dawn and the birth of flowers in the darkling air through all the Tuscan lands. This art, that seems so effortless and so happy, that blossoms over the garden-well under the cypress as easily as above the door of a palace chamber or the altar of a preciously-recessed chapel, is more Greek in its spirit of grace and ease than much of the more ambitious Renaissance sculpture. It is indeed a little comparable with the Tanagra terra-cottas. But, at least in Luca's time, each piece is a personal expression of the artist's, and keeps a rare gravity with its innocence, a seriousness in its sweetness, for it is chiefly concerned with merciful immortalities, not with the exquisite pleading mimicry of life which drenches a Tanagra figure with heart-breaking charm, the mere coquetry and elegance of childish, wanton and gracile gestures that would piteously placate the unheeding disdains of Death.

Luca had been in the service of the Duomo. His lovely reliefs were on the Campanile. His cantoria, opposite Donatello's, was a miracle of sculptured sound—drum and trumpet, lute and viol and singing voice : his earnest fair musicians, wholly captivated by their harmonious duty, carved by a spirit with much of antique and tender, lost, many of them, in a pure ecstasy, proved that unheard melodies are the sweetest with a holier restraint than the satyr-children opposite. His carven bronze sacristy doors had locked Lorenzo into safety once. The sleep of the Cardinal of Portugal in Samminiato had clear colours because of Luca's Madonna. The ceiling of the Pazzi Chapel was a radiant bell-flower ; and happy was the added frieze of cherubim. On Antonio Pazzi's villa was the great blare of the stemma of King Réné, all the emblems and romantic kingdoms in the air, Hungary, Sicily, Jerusalem, Anjou, Bar Aragon, making a symphony of brave devices, *dardant désir*. Later, Andrea, with his aid, stars the Ospedale with those "innocents" of perfect pathos. The Renaissance discovered children in art. Donatello saw the little faun in them ; Verrocchio caught the flying elf in them, and gave it a dolphin for plaything. Leonardo looked at them attentively, a prince with princes, and drew them intent on their own slightly enigmatic, indifferent affairs, shrinking shyly from the stranger. Luca's were earnest, beautifully good children, rapt in enthusiasm.

A sense of intent angels with pots of lilies, really like young-eyed cherubim, and of those lovely children, their kin, Leonardo would take from Luca's fragrant grove of blue and white lilac—that, and of a Madonna of the Lilacs fine as well as frank. For, among these garlands gathered from the flowery felicity of Samminiato and Fiesole, the candid are as delicate as the subtle. And they have this in common with Leonardo's own people, different as they are : they do not affect the habits of joy and sorrow, but keep the clear unchanging air of their own region.

vii

They would discuss architecture too, in the bottega, for most of them could have been builders, and all of them had to consider building

The Bottega of Verrocchio

in relation to most of their works, speaking of Brunellesco's way of decorating his façades with changing light and shadow instead of the pale polychrome of inlaid marble, and the modes of the airy suspension of his domes, or Michelozzo's last frieze of ribbons and garlands nailed by the heads of cherubim.

They would argue the principles of Leon Battista Alberti, Leonardo's stately precursor, a love-child like himself, though of a nobler house, like him an athlete and a horseman, so passionately given to all the sciences that he wasted under them, and took to " repose " in physics, literature, art, and medicine ; a lettered and an harmonious person, definitely considering architecture as visible music. He was already thinking in terms of Vitruvius touched by emotion ; and, in the Temple builded for the Tyrant of Rimini, and in his Church of Saint Andrew at Mantua, had remarkably set a reminiscence of Roman triumphal arches. He did not die till 1472, and his architectural work seriously intrigued with the mind of Leonardo.

They would also savour the little arts—arguing how Ghiberti once mounted a cornelian on the wings of a gold dragon, what spinous gryphon should couch on the next tournament-helmet, or what gold miracle should oppress the great graven morse of the broidered cope for the Baptistery. But they were chiefly painters, and spoke of painting. Leonardo and the young Lorenzo di Credi and a crowd of other pupils were there, and Perugino, older, was strengthening his talent in Verrocchio's bottega. And Botticelli would come, and the young Filippino. And Piero di Cosimo would steal some of Leonardo's light, and his blue-green colour, for his myths, Greekish and grotesque. And Paolo Doni Uccello, grown old, would still murmur of the sweetness of perspective. Ghirlandajo would wish for the walls of Florence to paint ; and be heard without much enthusiasm. Antonio Pollaiuolo, eager for all the new realism, a little acrid in his effect, who could make a decorative pergola out of startling opposing nudes, would come with his brother from the noisier bottega in the same street. Signorelli was in Florence sometimes, and Piero della Francesca had been there in the earlier part of the fifteenth century. Hugo van der Goes came from Flanders in 1481 ; and there was much talk of oils, and tempera glazes that could give the effect of oils.

It was a great group of experimentalists, and they debated new effects in perspective and form and positions, as our moderns excite themselves over Cézanne, Picasso, and Matisse. Some of their immediate predecessors were already *démodé*. Fra Angelico, they would say kindly, lingering with mediæval meditations in the cloister, painting with his pure heart as well as with gold and the three Giottesque vases of carnation and with precious ultramarine, had been justified by his ecstasy. For even he had charged the sweet rigid Giottesque people with a new sensibility. His Madonnas bow down with a rare astonishment, his music-making angels are glad enthusiasts, all the rose-pale faces are flushed like wild roses. There is a quivering beatitude in those ethereal Annunciations on the white walls; there is a joy in the rings of Paradise; the figures in the Crucifixion mourn actually detached against the red unfinished sky. Even to the cloister went the vine-wreathed spirit of the time; and the angels danced to a new measure in the rose-gardens of heaven:

> " A quel Sposo van davanti
> Tutti danzan per amore. . . ."

Fra Angelico is no mere maker of jewelled iconographies. His glad saints are alive within their stoles coloured like jonquil and iris, though wasted by fast and prayer. He has seen his bright trumpets and fine pages on earth before he caught them to heaven. He draws his arcades and his vistas of blue sky and dark ilex with care for true linear perspective, and his roses and carnations, marguerites and wild orchids have patterned the meadows of Fiesole before they are imparadised. So they said he at least had beautiful line, and that his colours were daring and pure, and approved him, especially at San Marco.

Benozzo Gozzoli had painted an Earthly Paradise with equal rapture, and told his Florentine romance of the Three Kings with the gilded cavaliers, the fanciful pages, the Medicean princes and rose-bearing angels, in the dark chapel of the house in the Via Larga, the pomps of this world enchanted by a spiritual quest, though the seekers have almost forgotten it in their morning pleasure. But the joyous Fra Lippo Lippi, privileged thief of nuns, carried the strictly religious tradition yet farther into this world, bringing the mood of a Florentine song into paint, boldly pressing the burden of the Madonna on the candid beauty of a real Florentine girl, hushed and lovely, simply adoring her baby among delighted angels that embower her like a flowering apple-tree, altering Nativities and Epiphanies into happy idylls, coloured and fragrant as flowers and fruits, painted in powder-blues, clear roses. His was the " naturalism " of romance. His son, the young Filippino, gentle and kind, a friend of Leonardo's, Botticelli's pupil, shyly combined his father's lyrical moods with some plaintive cadence caught from his master, and created pictures more delicately tender in quality though less radiant in their energy.

But it was the experimenters who caused the discussions; and they were many—those who did not fear to surprise the secrets of the uncovered muscles, and to hunt through geometrical tangles and

The Bottega of Verrocchio

triangles the cunning plots of optical deception. *The Book of the Art of Cennino Cennini* is closed. No longer does the painter begin his work with a prayer to "that delightful advocate of all sinners, the Virgin Mary," and complete it with a commendation to the Heavenly Powers. The sweet plainsong of the clear colours, sinopia, cinnabar, amatisto, lovely verderame tempered with wine, ultramarine—the "ethereal colour," the "colour noble, beautiful and perfect beyond all other colours," thieved by the covetous from the heavy initials of sumptuous manuscripts, given by princes to monasteries in magian jars, as the Queen of Cyprus gave it to Assisi—is drowned by the gathering orchestration of the new gods. Tempera may hold its own awhile ; but oil is the new fusing, enriching, glowing medium in which the strange half-heathen new colours will run together in harmony. Yet the Florentines' genius for line kept many of them true to tempera. The problems of drawing engrossed them so much. Verrocchio's bottega was a kind of laboratory : they gathered there. Paolo Uccello was an elder among them ; but the infatuated lover of "that sweet thing perspective" was still uncloyed over his pleasure, and his heraldic battlepieces, at once so decorative, with their lances and their orange-trees, and their occasional unhelmed boy-warriors like youth incarnate going to war, and so full of sweet absurdities, had novel characteristics for his contemporaries. His pictures were a strange mixture of old and new notions, not interfused, but interlocking like a captivating puzzle. His conceptions were almost infantile, his manner experimental. An admirable designer, he achieved almost modern simplification ; his linear perspective is often brilliant ; his imagination is innocent and frank like a child's. Sometimes he captures a figure that excites with a new energy, like the drawing of the knight charging blue-green through the green dusk of the paper.

One early "realist" and experimenter was Andrea Del Castagno, a painter of great ability and no allure, though it is hard to deny some tribute to a portrait like that of Pippo Spini, swaggering in the Duomo, a true soldier of fortune. He had been "Andrea of the hanged men," for he had painted executed conspirators for the state with gruesome power. Leonardo must have gazed at his *Cenacolo*, powerful and charmless, with capable uninteresting figures, responding, nevertheless, with dramatic earnestness to the accusation of their Lord. Earnest and forcible as his manner is, there is something savage in his attack on a subject which almost accounts for the legend of murder that haunts his name.

Luca Signorelli, one of the first to delight in the play of muscles, and to anatomize for painting's sake, came sometimes to Florence, where he had given away his mysterious, enchanted *School of Pan*. And there he found something too; for, later, the faces of his calm women and strong angels are now and then just touched by the Leonardesque look.

There was Ghirlandajo, clear, competent, and honest, like a good mirror, his bright true colours and safe satisfactory arrangements and quiet gestures hardly lifting into the key of delight, though reflecting most pleasurably the demeanour of great families, and ladies beautiful in their brocade. Ghirlandajo's hour of illumination was to befall him in San Gimignano, where his orderly mind, translating into an idyll of flowers the dreadful physical distress of the story of poor Santa Fina, rose into mystical grace at last when he composed the young acolytes round the glorified dead girl. Ghirlandajo, on the whole, represents the culture of an enlightened bourgeoisie, and the æsthetic pleasure of the average man when the average understanding is unusually high. The journeymen artists of our modern day would have been spurned by the Florentine merchant; but when there was a general taste for magnificence any journeyman artist could do well. Ghirlandajo was the mere recorder of Renaissance Florence, but his was a gorgeous and vibrating time.

For the experimentalists, of more vivid interest was the elder Pollaiuolo, Antonio, who, with the feebler Piero, kept his clamorous bottega in the same street as Verrocchio. He also, with laborious ardour, loved to " remove the skin from many corpses and be fascinated by the play of muscles." He was likewise Antonio the goldsmith, who had carved on the bronze doors of Ghiberti, who could turn from making a reliquary as light as a flower cherishing a holy thing in its closed corolla, from enriching the Silver Altar and making his Cross of Angels and Sphinxes in green, blue and red enamel and silver, or from his designs for the wonderful canonicals of Saint John, to consider the Tombs of the Popes. Enchanted by new discoveries he learned to delight overmuch in violent movement, strung sinew and bent bow, the planted foot and the vibrating arm. But the beautiful nudes he painted and engraved for Lorenzo, his figures of Herakles in heroic tension, arrays of young warriors with high heads, Saint Sebastians like severe young Tuscans, realistic bodies caught into grace by the romantic Florentine mood, and by a true genius for decoration, Leonardo found exciting and worthy of study. They showed how muscle could ripple, and with what natural joy art could lay hold on matter. The Virtues the two Pollaiuoli had carved for the Palace of the Mercantazia were noble as well as powerful; the faces, a little *camus* but charming, revealed a debt to Verrocchio. Antonio was also drawing horses and thinking of the steed desired by Milan's Duke, little dreaming how that shadowy charger was with insubstantial paces to echo through the ways of the elegant and ambiguous

The Bottega of Verrocchio

youth in his neighbour's studio. Too strenuously imitating *les enèrgumes* was Baldovinetti, who was not content with the delicately detailed landscapes in which he could set his Nativities, and who merely puffed and distorted a naturally gentle style with a false emphasis.

Perugino, that cynical exploiter of sweet sentiment, who would have been a very great painter if he had had any artistic conscience, frequented the bottega for some time, considering matters of technique. Leonardo and he were to encounter again and again, in Lombardy, in Florence, about 1500, when he had a bottega of his own in the city. There was a certain ironic sympathy between Leonardo and his friend, painting his too-acquiescent Madonnas without conviction. But at his best Perugino can overarch Saint Sebastian with such a triumphant Umbrian sky that martyrdom is music, and the little feathered trees with minor pathos quiver the inconscient sympathy of inconscient things. He is a lord of great blue spaces ; his martyrdoms are lost and healed in the reconciling light of a radiant heaven. His mood also, dulcet, a little morbid like sick violets, drowsy and dovelike, has an element that Leonardo found not altogether unfamiliar.

The most eagerly-discussed master was still Piero dei' Franceschi, Florentine in temper, though merely Tuscan by birth, who had worked in the city with Domenico in the forties of the fifteenth century. Problems of chemistry and geometry were dear to the artist who could set a group of grave angels, with their close crowns of pale quiet roses and their clear straight robes, so actually in four dimensions, in such free air and open sky, that they seem real apparitions in a clarified world. It is as if some sudden panel is withdrawn from sight, as from the sight of the shepherds on the halcyon morning of Nativity. Some similar shutter is slid from the last cell of hearing, for the sensitive throats tell if they sing high or low. The fame of those participant angels, making their chill pure April music as if charmed fast for ever within the crystal of an inviolable indissoluble dawn, of the great dignity wherewith the painter had set Sigismondo before his Saint against spaces of a sacred muted blue at Rimini, of the groups of grave magian women about the Holy Wisdom he calls the Queen of Sheba, of the mystic light and shadow so hung about the sleep of Constantine that it becomes an august moment in time and the wardens of his rest seem spirits in mortal disguises, of the power of that startling Risen Christ in Borgo San Sepolcro whose authority and conviction of completed suffering makes of physical beauty no more than a useless cast-off ornament, passed serenely about Northern Italy. It carried his fellows into curiosity concerning his cool soft tones, his aerial qualities and sweet rectitudes of pale colour, virginal azures, hushed roses, elusive lilacs, ashen violets, and cool lavenders, vanishing away towards white. They all had to learn from the severe and delicate originalities of this painter.

But the greatest artist who was at the same time most Leonardo's contemporary, and the most kindred with him in imaginative temper, was Sandro Botticelli, for he also perplexed a mystery of strange expression, and evoked the gods of old, though his were rather the gods who had changed into faery people during the Middle Ages, riding on the silver marches of life, hiding their beautiful vanishing courts and orchards in the hills and the woods, serving the Secret Rose of the World, pale with sweet desire and apprehension of mortality. Leonardo's gods and angels are of rare magic stuff, they are People of the Sidhe indeed, in the language of the West. But Botticelli's are changelings, in the counter-sense. They have loved themselves into a soul. And, again, Botticelli's is the feminine principle in painting, troubling and troubled, sad, desirous and desired. He still clings to the mediæval woman-worship, to a goddess whom Love wounds like a victim. Both Leonardo and he loved that Secret Rose of the mystic; but, while Botticelli found it in the garden of the Sepulchre, Leonardo gathered it on some lost ultimate island whereof only his own Saint John was aware, for Botticelli sought the beauty of love, and Leonardo beauty only.

When, on his return to Florence, he saw the *Primavera* and the *Birth of Venus*, strange and beautiful creations of a paganism with tears in it, wistful divinities more melancholy than mortals, sad roses, flickering seas, groves of love and death, ravishing patterns and entoiling lines, Leonardo must have gazed, regretting somewhat that he had not painted his own *Triumph of Poseidon* in a great light of aquamarine foaming into mother-of-pearl, for the heads of the sea-gods were enchanting. Well! Antonio Segni had his drawing—and Botticelli's quivering *Calumny*, observing which, Leonardo may have winced, for the theme wounded. And, though faintly deprecating Botticelli's tired Fortitudes and despairing Truths, he may have sighed once, knowing that this painter, whose soul had been freely touched to fine issues by Plato and Dante and Olympian myth, had dipped his art in a sunken dream of romantic love, earthly and heavenly, and won a gliding shot-effect such as the Renaissance people loved in their textures, impalpable or actual. That was a strange colour he dared not use. Meanwhile the treatment of the hair, the hieratic efforts of drapery and attitude, the fantastic dream-laden faces, the subtleties of expression, were things to his liking. And if he afterwards deprecates Botticelli's supposed notion of landscape in the *Treatise on Painting* he is evidently confused, or badly reported; however, he refers, as if affectionately, to " il nostro Botticelli." As for the older artist, when he paints his *Spring*, the

The Bottega of Verrocchio

twisted hair of the Graces, the silhouetted myrtles, the feverish startling face of the Flora with the mouth of immortal desire and the challenging eyes, have some remote kinships with things seen and imagined in Verrocchio's bottega.

Among the younger people Piero di Cosimo would come, to learn how to set a blue-green landscape behind his Grecian fairy tales, so sweetly gauche and attractive. Perseus rescuing Andromeda, Peleus wedding Thetis, but never anything so tender as the stricken nymph of Cephalus ! His pupil was to be Andrea del Sarto, a thwarted and richly-endowed painter, doomed, according to a tradition that seems truth, to damn his genius for a softly-moulded soulless face, and to become the painter of a dulcet sensuous melancholy, the last of the Florentine artists to draw some of Leonardo's suavity into the sad nonchalance that serves his Madonnas for a soul.

Distant painters did not greatly affect the haughty Florentines. They were ware of an austere and mighty genius with a plangent quality as of stricken bronze, first from learned Padua, and then from palaced Mantua, where a great artist solidified his personal images of Roman antiquity. In his quarried world, in his pillared places, where great garlands were hung, or in his gravely-builded bowers where orange and citron glowed like lamps in a temple, Madonnas were guarded by saints and angels like beautiful legionaries. In 1466 he had brought his proud challenging head to Florence, and Lorenzo visited him in Mantua, as friend with friend, so they remembered him as an artist whom the antique had frozen, but into a strange nobility. Now they spoke of the startling foreshortening of the frescoes of the Eremitani in Padua, to be carried further in his later picture of *The Dead Christ*. He was also arraying splendidly the Gonzaga princes on their castle walls over the lake of reeds. It was not yet the time when the great Mantegna must translate a lady's classic fancies into brilliant visions fit for a blue-and-gold studiolo. And it was far from the dark day when Isabella would tear from his dying clasp his marble love, his " dear Faustina," after intolerable experience of the " steep stairs and bitter bread."

In Venice, Vivarini, Carpaccio, and especially the Bellini, were working out their humane conceptions in terms of absolute light and colour —colour intense and flamboyant, too sure of its primacy to be entirely welcome to the Florentine lovers of line. Giorgione had not even begun to melt into art like a vague golden music. Gentile Bellini was away in Constantinople, painting aphrodisiac pictures for his terrible protector, the Sultan Mohammed II., whose oblique and cruel eyes and fierce nose he has recorded with fidelity. He would return in 1481 to paint the vivacity of Greek horses and Oriental costumes in his canvases. His brother Giovanni was still somewhat Paduan, steadily becoming more lucent in atmosphere and dreamier of mood.

And away in the Marches of Ancona, one of those singular painters whose mind has been caught by some strange angle of vision, an unusual sudden mode of sincerity like the flash of a kingfisher, made beauty like a white peacock, a swan crowned with rubies, roses under snow, or a white child with rainbow wings, a gilded masquer pierced with love, or anything at once exotic, pure and sumptuous, yet with a lyric cry in it. Carlo Crivelli created fabulous gold chambers of a mystical Byzantium in the wild morning of a Japanese fairyland, and set marvellously tender and fragile figures, clothed in great embroideries of fantasy, to their sweet slavery of perpetual adoration there. But his decorated casket of spikenard, orientally sweet as the Magdalene's, whose pointed fingers are so dear to him, had no savour for the Florentine. So Crivelli went on painting *The Annunciation* as it might have been in some lost Eastern city, some Spiritual Place in Trebizond.

viii

The treasure-houses of Florence have much to say of Michelangelo, of his creative might, his magnificent melancholia, his passionate evocation of Olympian men and women, bound and unbound, of grieving or dreaming Madonnas sweet as Antigone, of immortal indictments and lamentations. Of all her other artists she keeps priceless pledges. Of Leonardo, all that her walls can tell is that he once began a great picture.

There are no records of fumbling and tentative things. His earliest drawing, so far as we can know, leaps from an unerring pencil ; his first authentic picture, we recognize, unfinished is a masterpiece. He moves into his art as easily and superbly as a noble ship sliding from the slips into her natural sovereignty of illimitable waters. Probably his hand is in much of Verrocchio's work, both sculpture and painting. From the beginning he loves blue-green landscapes and still waters, and Eastern enigmatic angels with strong wings and smiling eyes and lips. From the beginning he treats curling hair and long hands with a kind of superfine fetishism. And his early drawings reveal that, also from the beginning, he divides his interest between two kinds of humanity. There are creatures of frenzy, of illimitable destructive rage—like those who will fight for the Standard when he plots *The Battle of Anghiari*, the terrible tribes of the Dragon. And there are reticent smiling people with the slight significant gestures and sweetly deprecating manners of a great dynasty of princes—brethren of Apollo or Monseigneur Saint Michael, as you please.

The Bottega of Verrocchio

The first story of his apprenticeship tells that Verrocchio paints a *Baptism*. It is angular and harsh, though once it had miracles of novelty in it, and set a fashion. The Christ and Saint John were not beautiful, but they were modelled like real people using real gestures in a new bewitching landscape. Did Leonardo draw the too-famous kneeling angel —that angel so seductive that Verrocchio left off painting, " disdaining that a child should know more than he "? For all Vasari's story it is most unlikely. Verrocchio did not abandon painting after this picture ; it was not in his serious, steadfast temper to behave with irritated vanity ; and, finally, the angel is no great credit to anybody. The same hand might have drawn both angels, some may think. But the more Verrocchio-like angel, with the frank, lit boy's face, is much more attractive than his simpering operatic fellow in the affected attitude, not at all in the key of the laborious astringent picture, the historic value of which lay in its original harmonizing of figures and landscape. Half-suggested dolomites of dreamland, winding water, firs, strange cliffs—Leonardo is present in this picture as a mood behind it. With the Uffizi *Annunciation* he may have had more to do, though the bland fixed expressions, the goldsmith's reading-desk, rich with classical ornament, above all, the heavy, obtuse-angled draperies and the enamelled surface, speak far more of the interposition of Lorenzo di Credi than of Leonardo, though the deepening jasper landscape might be his. I do not find the Leonardo study for the angel's sleeve convincing evidence. He was not secretive with his drawings as with his writings : and would draw a sleeve to help a fellow-pupil with great graciousness. The *Annunciation* of the Louvre, however, is probably Leonardo's early work, with its angel stayed in strong flight, the air yet thrilling his strong pinions. Before he began the *Adoration* he might have seen the matter so—a sad fair lady with a mighty angel, a crouching Eastern angel, a prince of the air, and a blue distance filled with afterglow. Mystery and magic and strange faces ! It may be.

But of the early original work described by Vasari little remains. The story of the rondache is probably true, Leonardo's diablerie, the notary's prudence and the peasant's *naïveté* making a vivid little story. But it is gone. And certainly he drew a *Medusa*, for the theme intrigued him. Despite his studies in realism, it would have been a face of frozen beauty among serpent-plaits woven into a labyrinthine pattern, much nearer the Rondanini masque than to the sorry daub that usurps his name : when he was in a Baudelairean mood for a subject he invariably had a Baudelairean surety of style. The lost terra-cotta heads of women smiling, and of boys, do also vainly entice the imagination.

It is with an extreme regret that we remember the cartoon for the

73

Leonardo the Florentine

King of Portugal's tapestry that was to be wrought in silk and gold, of Adam and Eve " in the Earthly Paradise at the moment of sinning," under the fig and the palm, turning to embrace with the kindling gesture of terror and ecstasy that is the invitation to the sempiternal history of lovers, while the meadows at their feet are starred with exultant and conspiring flowers. An uncle of his had the cartoon, which he sold to " The Duke of Florence "; then " suddenly, as rare things will, it vanished."

On the day of Saint Mary of the Snow, on the fifth day of August 1473, while walking in the Val d'Arno, Leonardo deftly drew a landscape of rocks and heights and dim hills, cascades and winding water, and lightly indicated trees, that had charmed his dreaming eyes, all space and light and atmosphere and ethereal distances ; and added a note in that famous sinistral script, so early revealing how reluctantly his mind recorded itself in writing, for already he knew himself different from others and solitary at heart, and had been wounded by that difference.

When he was twenty-five the State recognized his powers by asking him to paint an altarpiece for the Chapel of Saint Bernard in the Florentine Council House. Different drawings seem to show that he possibly meditated an *Adoration of the Shepherds*, the gentle instinctive souls who pipe round all the gods—Pan, Apollo, Mithra, Christ—whose blind listening emotions hear the angels singing, who, needing no star, come to the birthplace of God before the subtle and meditative Magi have concentrated their starry reasoning on the bright intruder in the heavens. But, in the beginning as in the end, the thing was not done, so no press of soft and dreamy faces, like that drawing of Philip, made long after, is suffused with the divine light ; there is no concourse of a folk innocent, tender as their crooks and flutes and lambs. The groups of the young men for this Arcadian *Adoration* stand devotional and hushed with wonder. One figure clasps his hands in rapt worship. They seem to gather like a ring of daffodils round the sweet Mystery. If Leonardo had painted this picture he would have done as Michelangelo did thereafter, and used his nude youths at once as acolytes and decorations, luring his young fauns within the sacred idyll.

Ghirlandajo was to supply this defection : Filippino did in the end. Later, the monks of San Scopeto, a wealthy fraternity, bound Leonardo with an intricate covenant to make them an altarpiece ; and many details convince us that the great design of *The Adoration of the Magi* was intended to adorn their chapel. But perhaps the conditions annoyed him, though they seemed fair enough ; perhaps the quaint notion of providing the dowry of an orphan girl irked his mind as an absurd irrelevance. (There's a sardonic reference later to the dowries of maidens in the MSS.) But remonstrances and gifts of wine were vain ; and the gentle Filippino provided the adoring Magi for the brotherhood.

Still, the great cartoon for the *Adoration of the Magi* is perhaps the sovran masterpiece of Leonardo's that time has left us. It is merely a complete design coloured in an amber monochrome which the afternoon sun can transmute to a powdering gold ; but so satisfying are its charmed and breathless groups, all turned towards the bright avatar by miraculous compulsion, so dreamily beautiful its enchanted perspectives of faery ruin and fantastic rock and symbolic tree, where the mere phantom of the world outside the spell makes an unreal show of bravery with great steeds and contention, that the gazer can but feel that here even the sweet trumpets of colour would be excess and intrusion. Completion, indeed, might have meant a harmony of beryl and chrysocolla and faint gold ; but the amber tone sufficiently warms that wonder of composition, while paralysing so impalpably, so fortunately, and so effectively, the rash hand of the restorer, which has crudely flayed the sensitive surfaces of all the other Leonardo pictures we know. In a world of visionary landscape and ruined palace, before a dark Tree of Life and its shadowy companion, the Virgin and Child sit in a pyramid of light as in a chambered silence and beautiful benediction, while the crowd of seekers, in every mood of rapture, doubt, wistfulness, adoration—and one as in sad negation (did he draw himself among the rest, Leonardo at twenty-five ?)—are arrested in the great illumination at the end of the Way. Enough to say here that the magnificent pattern of the design, which expresses the coming of all the intellectual dreamers and seekers to the Light which is the God of all, imposes itself on the attentive eyes and mind with that sudden vitality of peace which attends supreme æsthetic pleasure. Why such patterns imply delight no kind of critic can clearly explain. They fit some intricate mood of vision which belongs to a highly-tuned state ; and which is not so much an obscure as an ultra-violet kind of experience. But never again shall Leonardo throw such a rhythmic design of fluctuating figures on the canvas, for never again will he accept a theme so close to human and catholic sympathy. And in all his pursuit of light never again will he accept the vastidity of glory that irradiates the hush of the *Adoration*.

Since by considered steps he approached this final vision, he drew many and beautiful studies for the great picture he inexplicably abandoned—riders, conversations, agitated discussions, resumed again for *The Last Supper*, attitudes, Madonnas, fragments of ruined palaces with visionary stairs. There is a version in the Louvre where the Madonna is more girlish, less hieratic and mysterious than in the finished design, and the Child is more excited amid the throng of intent faces. In a

Leonardo the Florentine

study of broken dream-architecture in the Uffizi, the shattered palace of tetrarch or satrap, the flight of steps vanishes in the antique airs, a miracle of ethereal perspective. The notions for the background of the great picture will serve him henceforth for his greatest work. The tilting motive begins his studies for the great Cavallo, the " argument " drawings he will use again when he comes to prepare his *Cenacolo*. He would put into this great theme of the pageant of the spiritual powers all that he knew, his pyramids of light and his far perspectives, his love of chiaroscuro, his knowledge of horses, his sense of living air, his fetishisms even, his mastery of certain types of humanity old and young, his power of weaving all these interests into a great composition, his worship of the dual magnificence of art and nature. He designs it, draws it, spaces it, illuminates it, so that you see it through a thin shard of old amber, with greenish glints. Then he leaves it, for he has vanquished all the problems of it and the rest is too easy. He has had his vision of all things in God, and has laid his marvellous plot of lines to snare the winglike tremor of the presence of the Paraclete. It is the harmony of some sacred place and time beyond frustration, some Sarras of Renaissance souls. The colonnades vanish in the distance ; under the dark oak-tree and the pavilion of the light sits the faint mysterious Virgin with her princely Child, suffused with her own mystery of illumination. The beauty-stricken people press around, rapturous, craving, incredulous, receiving, adoring, meditative, yearning, all arrested in great astonishment, as in *The Last Supper*. But how ethereally soft and rich the garlanded rhythm of emotion that is tossed and flung about these seekers, compared with the heavy cadences of the tragic masterpiece ! Outlined forms appear dimly in the recessionals of amber, so that the picture seems to enclose a throng. The exultant theme of those that seek and find soars smooth and golden : it is pricked by lyric and poignant cadenzas like the upflung arm of the passionate youth beyond the dreamer. All the wavering excitement is steadied by two figures, one on either side, upright and calm, like variants of the ambiguous supporters that for ever watch the Tree of Life. Leonardo the Philosopher is one perhaps, merely meditative. Leonardo the Dark Knight is another, turning away, serene and sardonic. Far off, lost in the distance, faint figures are seen on the palace steps, riders on beautiful horses tilt —as if, just without the golden crystal, the life uncharmed went on.

When the afternoon sun invests the Uffizi and falls on the great picture of Leonardo's youth, the canvas glows deep topaz, gold and amber, with shadows of emerald, and all there is of light and dark seems fused in that superb illumination. Doubt, aspiration, acceptance, refusal itself, meet as rapt witnesses to the reconciling power of the mystic core of Light. It is a great composition from a technical point of view, easily enduring a geometrical analysis ; its greatness is not lessened by the fact that here Leonardo's imagination does not refuse the sense of compassionate humanity which dwells through all supreme art. It is beauty and only beauty that here passes within our souls by the gates of vision ; but beauty that comes with a heavenly kindness and the silence of a sacrament. Whatever unearthly images of loveliness the spirit of Leonardo hereafter leaves on his strange track on the verges of mortality, with whatever discoveries his wisdom may amaze, in *The Adoration of the Magi* his genius offered something henceforward lost or withholden. You will not find it again. No ; not in *The Last Supper* !

Something of an æsthetic shock is communicated by the violently-drawn cartoon of the penitence of Saint Jerome : the strange, rocky and watery landscape and the beautiful swirl and sweep of the untamed and unconverted-looking lion in the foreground. But Jerome himself is a cruel study in mere attitude and chiaroscuro. This gaunt melodramatic penitent is hardly the saint who was scourged in heaven for the love of Plato. The desert ascetic was merely a kind of madman to the ascetic of art ; and, though the picture has its power, its key is harsh and jarring. Its discovery by Cardinal Fesch in the nineteenth century was odd enough : he found the torso serving as a box-cover in a Roman shop, and the rest in a shoemaker's.

Some have suggested that the Leichtenstein lady, with the startling pale face in the romantic setting of juniper-trees, belongs to this period, and is by Leonardo. I have not seen this picture ; and photographs of it are very variable. The chief reason for imputing it to Leonardo seems to be that it is difficult to attribute it certainly to anybody. The type of the lady is not Florentine : her long narrow eyes and high cheekbones have a Slavonic effect. In some photographs the vigilant gaze and locked mouth seem wickedly at odds with the little curls round the brow. In others the delicacy of the modelling is more visible, and gives a kind of wasted and inwardly-suffering quality to the cryptic face. Does she show the emotional density of the cold criminal to whom slow poisoning might be a silent pleasure ? Does she look out as if she were in burning torture behind that ivory mask ? Who disposed those juniper boughs behind her so enigmatically and decoratively, and evoked the blue-green perspectives of strange light and water ? From Verrocchio's studio, at least, she came ; and Leonardo may have meddled with her secret.

The *Madonna Litta* at Petrograd may be a copy of an original. She looks too smooth and insipid for even an early *Madonna* of Leonardo's. The drawing in the Louvre which resembles her, though more naïvely

sweet than usual, is alive and engaging, as the picture is not. As for
the Benoist *Madonna*—the imbecile creature with the ear in the wrong
place and the gaping mouth—not all the restoration in the world
could have altered that from a Leonardesque intention ; and though
Mr Berenson can accept it, it is only when he loses his delicate tact in
the rage of the recreant.

ix

Leonardo's chief artistic work in his early period resides in his
drawing. With pencil, pen, and silverpoint, he is constantly at work ;
and, indeed, perfection lies like a seal on his every knot of lines, whether
it be an intent and intense gesture for the *Adoration*, or a mere graph of
his scientific interest. He is following masques of beauty or of terror,
learning by heart lovely limbs and betraying motions, before sleeping
and at waking remembering them ; enclosing a world of children, women,
warriors, adolescents, angels, rearing steeds, and "the beautiful heads
of the sea-gods," in a broken arabesque of flowers and birds and beasts.
He is "ringed round with a ring of fair faces" ; but often the ring
dissolves, and there is a vision of furious fabulous gryphons in conflict,
and the mop and mow of evil.

One page contains a fierce and splendid fight between a dragon and
a lion, with shadowy Madonna heads in the corner. Since now the
Madonna is the great symbol of beauty, as other goddesses before her,
he works at a new type, remote, smiling, enchanting, a principle in the
Universe, and the mother, or the stepmother, of Love. He draws Our Lady
with a dreaming smile, archaic, archaistic, tender and yet withdrawn.
In 1478 he writes on a sketch : " Having begun the two Madonnas . . ."
We do not know them. They were Madonnas in the open, Madonnas with
fruits, drenched, glittering flowers, babies and cats—delicately amused
Madonnas, not yet the strange enchantresses he will create in Milan,
though the Uffizi drawing of *The Madonna with a Cat* has much
of the later Circean irony. Once he takes a bowed Verrocchio head,
weighs down the broad eyelids, knots and curls the fallen hair, and
sets the winged Egyptian symbol on the brow, making a beautiful
supersensitive thing of it.

But most of the first Florentine drawings form a procession of youth—
boys and girls, with the equivocal intercrossing grace of those who have
not yet recoiled and been cleft asunder by the sudden dagger of sex.
Giovanotta and giovanotto, " whose young sex is yet within their soul,"
they are trembling slightly at the cross-roads, lilies themselves, among
the plot of betraying, unfolding lilies with pollen in their passionate

The Bottega of Verrocchio

hearts. The young men are distinctly of the hyacinthine and fantastic kind, often of Praxitelean grace; but though they already have the short upper-lip, straight nose, rounded chin, broad lids, softly curled hair and great gazing eyes of the type he prefers, his young Florentines, riding or walking swiftly, earnestly discussing sometimes, are more alert and eager than the languorous faintly-sullen types of the Milanese. The rapturous face of one young man in the *Adoration*, which is also the face of the refusing knight in armour, occurs frequently. It may be his own: it is sharp with sensibility. But the *Adoration* studies cover a fervent delicate throng of young men, all quivering with ecstatic attention, unstrung as if with lassitude, or tense as if to speed an arrowy soul, while their spent elders muse among them. One fascinating page in an attitude of affected grace is of a feminine equivocal type; but even he has the lithe limbs and the sparkling air of the Florentine boys who posed as Davids, or decorated the processions of Saint John. Another youth with uplifted arm has the profound passion of a Bound Captive by Michelangelo. Some are gazing, hand on hip, with shaded eyes. Some are stripped as if ready for a great initiation, or, "without spot or blemish," for a glad sacrifice. Others with blown hair seem driven by the rising wind of an irresistible power. Some are hard, with the great intolerance of youth; some are soft and sweet with the great spring-weariness of youth.

Beautiful bending heads, of girls and boys in Florence, the grace of each united in the angel! So he makes a frieze of Florentine knights and maidens, for the Dionysiac Apollo—not for Athena!

You see a nymphlike figure wafted on an ethereal path like that of Beatrice. There are Virgins with their doting Unicorns. There is a delicate evocation of Mary and Elizabeth with their children, and a lovely little arabesque of birds. The old man and the youth face each other, interlocked in thought, the old man wise and sombre with the wisdom of age, the young man secure and inaccessible in the wisdom of his youth, a "conversation" frankly recurrent. In Windsor there is a page of kittens and cats, turning characteristically into little dragons. There are great dragons, terribly embracing wild horses and lions. The lion and the dragon seem a definite piece of symbolism, an anagram of the soul. Probably at this time the magnificent condottiere head, with its exquisitely, dangerously wrought helmet and breastplate, was drawn, in the bottega famous for fanciful crests, where the fierce armed figure of Colleone was conceived. The Florentine period is the most human period of his drawing. Women, children, boys, old men, beasts, flowers— he sketches them all, as yet without too obvious preferences.

He is moulding his waxen heads of women smiling, he is drawing,

drawing all the things that amuse him, he is planning Adorations and Nativities, he is playing tricks, he is analysing landscape, he is coaxing fine linen folds dipped in plaster to fall as sweetly as a snatch of verse on his clay models, he is luting, he is talking, he is plotting to raise the Baptistery, he would like to change the course of rivers. He would pierce the mountains and scoop the harbours, would alter the world like a god indeed. Æsthetic dream, insatiate intelligence, he sustains both wasting splendours. "I can conduct water from one place to another," he says, already with the ease of divinity. So, like an artist, a scholar and a lord of revel, Leonardo comes with music to the confrontation of his thirtieth year. There is much talk of the great new Duke in Milan. suborning his enemies in such a glorious way that they almost forget his title has a flaw. He dreams of a mythic steed, it is said, on which his strong father will ride for ever as he once rode conqueror through the great cathedral doors. Leonardo takes his deep-toned lyre, fashioned like the head of a charger of Helios, calls for his companion in song, and for his jester, and so fares to the city of sumptuous pleasure.

Whether Lorenzo sent him and his lute as a compliment to Lodovico we do not know. Probably he accredited them with some letters of praise. Whether, as one story goes, Leonardo was the victor in a Milanese contest of song, and with the charm of his discourse concluded the triumph of his lute, is again debatable. What seems clear is that music swept him into the music-mad Court which he was to serve as architect, engineer, sculptor, and painter.

x

He left the City of the red lilies and the girdling hills, he left the clear air and the ironic sweetness, and the eager rivalries and the quickening intercourse of equals, the democratic city of spiritual equalities that made all its patricians matriculate into one of the guilds, for the Lombard plains and the coloured caprices of a despotic Court. He was to come again to Florence, but only to encounter a rivalry grown too strong, with ways not unspoilt by the service of princes. He had seen the last of the golden age of Florence.

He had seen the last bright jousting of the Florentine youth ; he had seen the great ball swing into place in the Duomo, and watched the ladies begin to appear in the frescoes of Santa Maria Novella. He had seen Simonetta dead, and such as Lorenzo Tornabuoni take their brides by the hand. He had seen Giuliano, young as he was young, fall stricken in his beauty, slain in dreadful violation of hospitality in the holiest place at the holiest moment. He had seen the Bargello hung with

The Bottega of Verrocchio

tormented forms, and the devil-possessed children playing with terrible shreds of the dead. He had heard the divine services quicken and tremble with fever while Florence dared the ghostly terrors of an Interdict. He had seen Lorenzo ride simply away to the jealous and treacherous camp of his enemy Naples, and return triumphant. He had seen the *carroccio* drawn, decorated red and white, with a great banner flying from the red-lilied staves, the red-clad moving City Militant. He had seen the bright bridal pageant of Leonora of Aragon, and the golden falconers of Gian Galeazzo Sforza. He had heard the great bell calling war with Naples, Rome, Venice, Ferrara or Sicily. He had felt plague go creeping with soft loathsome feet through the silent streets of his town. And with every May he listened the refrains of the ballate sing love and longing through the streets, nor knew it was the month which in distant lands would yet come soft with death.

Carrying that silver lute, shaped like the head of the steed of Apollo, he went with Atalante from a free city to the Court of a tyrant—a humane and enlightened tyrant, but no First Citizen like Lorenzo. "Be happy, be Florentine," said Marsilio, writing to Pico, before his brilliant friend came to rest in Fiesole ; and there certainly was an ease and brightness of intercourse in Lorenzo's city that made for intellectual felicity.

To the end Leonardo's attitude to Florence, and the attitude of Florence to Leonardo, is ambiguous ; but the touch of bitterness betrays the reality of the bond. There is a quarrel ; but it is a lovers' quarrel. He, too, was part of the " noble city's soul " ; and, in his strange inhuman way, felt himself soldered in that fair federation of forces. In no other city could he have captured the bright illusion of freedom, freedom to be himself, freedom for the mind to wreak its excess of energy on honourable deeds.

Like all great cities Florence is as Cybele of the Towers, goddess and mother, with a touch of the wanton. She has the greatest roll of sons, perhaps, that any city has had : but if she gave them much, much she required. Therefore, perhaps, he went. He had better have stayed. The something excessive in him needed the Florentine disciplines. It was well for him to be a prince among princes, open to the criticisms of his peers. The proud City was written in his eyes and on his brain : when he drew his buildings he remembered her Dome and her Campanile, and long afterwards, almost passionately, he vaunted her primacy in beauty, as part of his own ·dominance, to the citizens of Piacenza.

For even the great, the universal Leonardo, who seemed to serve impartially any host that would provide him with his servants and his horses, had his latent patriotism, even as had his enemy, Michelangelo, stolen to serve Rome—patriotism of the City-State, intense, concentrated, full of flavour, locked within ramparts. Italy was not yet, but the Italies were. And patriotism is an organic quality, like love or hunger or a mere sense of beauty, not arguable, not to be bled to death by war, not to be babbled to folly by peace, for love of country is axiomatic to all noble souls that have their kindly roots in earth. It is one of the primary enchantments; and, if it be an illusion, it throbs with every generous heart, and is a fibre of every original mind. Artists are of their country; and, though their art be for every nation, its peculiar and most valuable quality is derived from their native hills or lowlands. There are no international artists, though every art that offers a grail of beauty brings a golden loving-cup—like a saint with her symbol—that seals it a sacred and fragile hostager of the peace that lies within understanding. Patriotism is not a blind belief that one's country is the best, wisest, sanest, strongest, the only standard of absolute right and wrong. Though it be sweet and comely to die for her when her conduct accords with a chivalric ideal, it may be a bitter necessity to abstain if she crave cruelly for gold or oppression. She may be silly like a mother: she may be wayward like a lover. The intelligence may smile ironically at her, or suffer ignominiously because of her. Not the best, not the wisest, but the dearest! All her antinomies are resolved in the tenderness of her breast and the caress of her speech, when, " wearied with a world of woe," her exiles come back to mingle with her dust.

She has qualities no other place possesses—a sweetness like wild honey, like a little lonely tune within a glade. In foreign lands, however fair, we have a blind craving, a tyrannical nostalgia for the rhythm of her hills, the timbre of her twilight, the unique time and colour of her throbbing stars, the keynote of her sunsets, orange or green or scarlet, the salts and sweets of her own history, the tang of her ballads, the cry of her songs, the sweet idiom of her " little language," the banked, rosy fires of her romantic tradition, the inseparable incorporation with her secreted from our mothers' milk. She is the food we thrive upon, and must not be poisoned: she is the flesh we wear, and must not be wounded. She is indeed incarnate in the haughtiest of us, for she has grown us with her fruits and flowers; and the secret, ever-virginal, beautifully fantastic notion that we call honour finds it intolerable that she be hurt. We cannot bear it, unless we are perverted to the unnatural asceticism of self-torture. We are shamed in her shame, glorified in her beauty. Where the rivers have run through the morning of wonder, where the trees have caught the sunset, entreating it to linger with the white young stars over the first love,

The Bottega of Verrocchio

where the birds have called and cried through the first passionate desolation, where the springs and the autumns have built silver and gold pavilions for those impossible heartshaking hopes of youth that keep the world alive, is a region that has subdued the constant soul to an endless fidelity, and the recreant to everlasting regret.

Whether it be the cypresses and iris of Italy, or the poplars and meadows of France, or the sombre dream-drift of the Volga, or the violet capes of Greece, or the proud bastions and faery wild edges of Scotland—whatever kindred beauty of scene lie intagliate in the sard of the mind, it is different from all others, and it is the difference that is dear. Every country has her genius, moulding all interlopers to her own likeness, subduing them to her proper race in a few generations. If all men and women were miserably enslaved to one curst ethic, and all cities subjugated in a grey amphictyony of similarities, the varying skies and seas would instantly shatter the mould of monotonous likeness, the distinctive contours of their hills and the matchless moods of their rivers impose again upon their children a passionate imitation suddenly reclothing human existence with purple and silver differences.

> " Heureux ceux qui sont morts pour des cités charnelles
> Car elles sont le corps de la cité de Dieu ;
> Heureux ceux qui sont morts pour leur âtre et leur feu
> Et les pauvres honneurs des maisons paternelles."

Sophocles is a Greek and so is Phidias. Lucretius is a Roman and so is Catullus. Racine and Villon are French. Santa Teresa and Cervantes are Spanish. The greatest ballad-makers are Scots. Dostoevsky and Tchekoff are Russian. Shakespeare and Shelley, amazingly, are English. The artist wanders spiritually if not actually through many lands, being the pilgrim and the evangelist of beauty ; yet, as he wanders, not merely his tongue but the accent of his spirit bewrayeth him.

So Leonardo is not only Italian but Florentine. Not enough to keep him inexpediently loyal, but enough to make him troubled, dissatisfied, enough to touch his departure for Milan with something of apostasy. The doubt turned him moody and almost morbid in that city, it vexed him in the camp with Cæsar, it paralysed him in Rome, and his tired heart refused at the end to renew its pulsations for an alien king. For all her caprices Florence was always loved like a great romantic lady. The history of Milan had been too much that of a splendid sacred harlot in an Eastern temple—desired, violated, despised, by kings, emperors, and popes. Even Leonardo dimly realized that the glancing imperious ways of the great romantic Lady of Italian Cities were better for his diamond mind.

Part ii
The Court of Lodovico
(1483-1499)

Chapter i

The Spirit of Milan

i

LEONARDO came to Milan as an Athenian might have gone to a city like Miletus, or perhaps Antioch. He passed from a lively polity dreaming of Hellas in its own ironic and lovely fashion, and seeking for the Academe by way of Alexandria, to one that, more ancient in its civic history, had been shaped by the powers of Rome and Byzantium and Ravenna, and by the ever-burning creatures of the four-winged winds of the world, into something at once too deeply sophisticated and too frequently wounded to reply to the pagan pentecost of the Renaissance with a truly Hellenistic reaction. Magnificence and music, these were the things brought by Milan to the new altar served by the five great city-states of Italy. Magnificence and music, these had invested with amethyst all the great hours of her long history.

Whatever Milan had been, she was barbaric and splendid when Leonardo sought her courts like a new Citharœdus, barbaric in her excess of pearl and gold, in her clouds of perfume, her rose-drift cupid-broidered palaces, her snowdrift incredible cathedral, her mythic pageantry of pleasure and power, barbaric like Grecian cities of old richly corrupting into strange colours in Asia and in Egypt, through sweet, spendthrift, luxurious moods. So his secret pulses lost the rhythm of the Dorian mode, and, for all his intellectual resistances, subsided dreamily to the Lydian measure—even at times replying suddenly to an ominous beat more insistent. For, unrecognized by any, the throbbing of the Phrygian drums and flutes prevailed over the dear-bought music of the ducal chapel, and the rare inviolate liturgy of the Ambrosian basilica, when the devotees carried that image of the Virgin, Idæa, from church to church on Purification Day, and in the darkness of their souls remembered the shadowy lion-drawn chariot of Cybele, the goddess whom Leonardo adored and dreaded, with his reason trying to prove her reasonable, with his imagination revealing her as antinomian, dangerous, enchanting, almost as if, indeed, he had by some elfin shift escaped the fate of spring-sacrifice, and knew too much, but dreaded to tell.

87

Leonardo the Florentine

ii

The history of Milan lay heavily upon her. When the Lombards came down on her over the Alps she was already ancient in her tale of cæsarian glories and monstrous rapes. Through the ages called "dark," Milan remains, a dim flame of rose, a rumour of litanies and a tumult of spears and eagles. She had great traffic with kings and popes and emperors; she had spoken haughtily in the gate with many powers and principalities, and she had felt the clash of armies from all the ways of the world shiver in her beautiful breast. Within her walls the last Emperors of the West had kept their solemn, excessive court, throbbing under all its golden etiquette with a luxurious fever. Ambrose, "the royal priest," had been her bishop; Augustine, the darkly-burning lover among the saints, had been her rhetorician.

Milan is part of the agony of the most famous of earth's empires; one of the red wounds in her dying breast, one of the last rubies in her spoilt diadem. In the great amber-lighted hollow of time that lies between Constantine and Charlemagne the mighty cities of old lie signalling each to each as with tossing torches; and across all the hurtling and lightning of glories comes the breathing of their double-flutes. Carthage, Rome, Ravenna, Byzantium, Milan, Antioch, Alexandria, pulse like the Pleiades through this great Twilight of the Gods. The torchlight is refracted and splintered into spectral blurs and comets and asteroids of colour—for colour is the communication of life: the melody is muted and distorted into an inaudible moaning that clears, articulate and sweet, into the crying of the litanies—for music is the art that rises with unbroken wings over the dissolution of mortal magnificences, lamenting, reconciling, prevailing.

Through this opaque twilight the adventurers ride headlong, wild horsemen of flamboyant chance. In desperate pride, lost fragments of the imperial cohorts gleam and vanish. Imperial children, pale ivory automata with painted eyes and gold-powdered hair, loosen a tall Easter lily with crimson stamens, when their tired hands remember some great last gesture. Wild circles of blue-and-green charioteers sweep cæsars and augustas dethroned within their fiery eddies. Strange eunuchs, impassible and ironic, endure terrible victories and defeats. Barbarians, shaggy and horned with gold, appear on the walls of the sacred cities, half afraid of the beauty they ravish. Puissant figures uplift bright crosiers that flash terror like sceptres, while the shepherd's stole hardens into a mail of gems. Basilicas dimly mound themselves, couchant as sacred lions, in the dusk. Monasteries hide by the still waters, hostels for the sensitive and the weary and the god-stricken;

with unconscious hands the monks lay the beautiful images of pagan
philosophy and poetry to sleep in coffins of cypress and cedar. Canticles
and liturgies arise on the wings of the morning to importune the Musician
of the Spheres.

iii

The terrible bow of the Alps lay to the north of the Plain of Lombardy,
the terrible bow that loosed the maddened arrow of an invasion, time
and again, for the god of those awful, indifferent peaks had no compassion for either side of his dreadful defiles when, in huntsman's mood,
he wound his starry taunting bugle. The far Apennines closed the
east : on the west the Plain ran fair and fruitful to the Adriatic.

Of all the cities of the Plain, Milan stood first in power, in riches
and in place of danger, to the assault of the eager and furious enemy.
She was the Imperial City, sister to Rome, sister to Ravenna, watching
the icy and phantasmal passes, the lifted Alpine gates of fear whose
terrible pure indifference sent, not help, like human hills, but any spoiler
strong enough to conquer. Because of these distant Alps she was the
anvil of iron whereon great swords and superb armour were fashioned.
But, because she was so far away, sunk in her fertile plains, she knew
herself also as Mediolanum, in whose rich, persuasive earth all invaders
were subdued sooner or later into her peculiar mood of the Latin soul,
Mediolanum, where roads of east and west converged, for whom the
rivers were persuaded to be taken in the net of her orchards, rare
market of silk and spices, rare temple of good and evil, city of Venus
rather than Ceres ; and the threatening Alps seemed often merely
faint fantasy of clouds on the uttermost horizon. Because only when
her soft humidities became crystal-clear could she see the lyric peak
of Monte Rosa calling the Morning Star, she was also the may-city
in the mayland—an amphora of delectable odours for gods and men.
Drowsing in her great campagna, stretching westward to the Adriatic,
built on a responsive moist earth that offered easily the rosy matter of
her building and compassed her with a ravishing world of rich orchards
and clear waters, she forgot how doubly desirable she seemed to the
barbarians of the North, sweet spoil herself, sweet earnest of excessive
sweetness. She was the key of Italy—and never key more beautifully
wrought, like an iron flower : hers was the orchard of Italy, an orchard
rare with the undersong of running water—and never orchard more red
and golden, more soliciting with Hesperidean closes.

Being bound by her honour and her necessity to keep those Alpine
passes, she made strong her towers, and kept wrought armour of gold

and steel. But, being beautiful and delightful in the dance of Earth, she was dear to the gods, and her heart was sacred. She had been a holy temple-harlot in dove-murmurous courts before Ambrose, proud prefect and ecstatic scholar in virginity, drew her immaculate through the fountain of Christ, and poured her heart of molten tears into his liturgy. She had something stranger, at least, in her seething soul than Florence, whose mysticism was captured in a stringent symbolism of art, and intellectualized into bright parable by the imitation of the luminous myths of Plato. Milan had a vanishing reverie of Celtic romance coloured like white peacocks, of Roman rituals, Byzantine traditions stiff with purple gems, wild Gothic wonders white with wings, Saracenic legends, subtle spells from Araby, Egypt, and Syria, fierce moon-worships from water-gleaming Carthage, dark-bright Manichæan heresies from magical Madaura, city of Apuleius, dear to Augustine, Latin intensities of love and death, a complex of images, a conflict of colours, a spiral of diverse incense rising from the thuribles of strangely coifed and mitred censer-collets.

Powers, spiritual and temporal, for ever rending her asunder, seemed to disengage a forbidden sweetness. She had been the Magic Cauldron before she was the Very Rich and Holy Grail of Ambrose; she had been the loving-cup of a commune, the crowning-chalice of kings. She belonged to Our Lady of the Graces and to Our Lady of Life. Like all Lombardy, she had been specially given to the mysterious Syrian god, Saint John the Baptist, and she was his Herodiad. She was the most mediæval of the great cities of Italy—and the most imperial. She was pagan and Christian, sweet, immoral, furious, extreme in pleasure and penance. Emperors, prince-bishops, dukes, and leaders of revolt—all had changed rings with her.

Because of her heavy charge of perilous passes and roads that wound towards all the other great cities of Italy, in her secret heart that was passive and wanton and narcotic with pleasure, she fell in love with a dream of painted horsemen on her wall, and took a duke of armies to defend her. And sometimes he was archbishop as well as prince, for something irrationally sacred, as of the king-priest, clung to the worst tyrants of Milan, blunting, even in full Renaissance, the bright edge of a superb piece of tyrannicide, while fading from Lodovico, who had not the courage of his superstitions. For Galeazzo and Lodovico had their drifting destinies, because, after enduring a procession of fantastic, moody, and violent cavaliers, her people carried the great new Horseman on his steed through the cathedral doors to the very altar. So Francesco Sforza rode down the aisle, it seems, to many ends—one being that Leonardo the Florentine should weary his haughty heart and his fine

The Spirit of Milan

hand in labouring ten years to deify him in an unparalleled bronze image—and all in vain.

iv

What are the pictures in her history? Her very name, "Mediolanum," is " sweet bastard Latin "—Latin turned dreamy by the Celt. Race on race kneaded out her Etruscan core—Insubri, Roman, Carthaginian, Goth, Lombard, Saxon, Hun, Frank, Saracen, tribes that claimed descent from Asgard, tribes that claimed descent from Troy, tribes that claimed descent from a dagger in the desert. See the shadow of Hannibal, first conqueror of the Alps, pressing desperately for Rome. See the strong Diocletian, who neatly squared the circle of the world, fixed his capitals as Milan, Rome, Antioch, Carthage, and crowned his two Augusti, his two Cæsars, only to watch in the end, from his carven palace in Spoleto, his scheme dissolve in gold and scarlet, and many rival emperors raised up on the shields of the legions. In his reign, also, is born in Milan the beautiful Sebastian, white captain of cohorts, doomed to be the prey of the archers, to be the victim of imperial love and wrath at Rome, and strangely to impose on Christian art the image of Adonis. Diocletian's Milan was a serenely domed and concentric vision of baths, aqueducts, temples and amphitheatres, all vanishing in smoke and fire, leaving only a line of disdainful pale pillars to be its lovely enigma and lone remembrancer. Constantine's mean face, hidden in the golden hood of a Christian legend, flashes into sight at moments, as he signs an edict that alters the world, though none comprehend that the true Galilean dies as well as the Olympian when the emperor lifts the labarum with a side-thought of Mithra. Again, the soldiers clash their shields against their knees to salute Julian as their emperor—Julian, a reluctant young scholar from Athens, new to the dress of war—Julian, most sincere and courageous of all apostates, whose ironic shade may walk again in the sun-worship of the Renaissance.

The first Valentinian, cruel though just, irritably strikes his sword through the magic of magic-loving places, Antioch and Byzantium as well as Milan, useless material weapon for the spidery stuff that closes up over the wounds, with soft obstinacy spinning itself strong again. His two bears live in his palace chambers, as horrible immediate justiciaries, even as in later days a Visconti shall use his hounds for executioners, for the soft masochistic air of the fair city breeds a lust of cruelty in her possessors.

Gratian, the beloved, is hunting too wildly in the parks, wrapped in Scythian furs, among his proud guard of Amal princes. In Milan, now a great capital of luxury and culture, that beautiful Arian, Justina, with her pretty child-emperor, the second Valentinian, tries to wrest a basilica from the superb Ambrose, who keeps it inviolate from her heresy, as easily as with one fine gesture, while his impassioned people sing their canticles, and her own Gothic tribunes refuse to break sanctuary, and her Levantine eunuchs carry threats and entreaties in vain. Gervasus and Protinus, the young martyrs, miraculously found in their graves, bleed to glorify the cause of Ambrose. Augustine, come from magical Madaura, and beautiful Carthage, and haughty Rome, is living in a house by the wall with his friend, the chaste Alypius, whose one weakness is that, like many another Christian, he overloves the gladiators in the circus, with Monica, who takes her little African love-feasts to the doors of the basilicas till she is shocked to find them banned as pagan, and with others, including one woman who has no name, and who yet burns more sweetly and sadly in the *Confessions* than Monica herself—the mother of the rare child Adeodatus, whom God took at his name. That passionate Augustine, afraid of yielding to the Highest a soul merely " caught up to God by his beauty," amid the lapsing waters and dreamy leaves of Cassisiacum incidentally concludes the Socratic tradition, while walking there under the chestnuts with his gay heathen pupil, Licentius, yet submits his soul to searching disciplines, till with great expense of tears, and lovely amatisto-coloured Latin, he comes to that crisis in the Milan garden when the child's voice sings ethereal, " Tolle, lege," and he moves at last to the Easter baptism of Ambrose. But in this same Milan, that most pagan Christian Ausonius had pondered the " mira omnia " of the city's delicious luxury, and, musing in a flowery orchard, had seen Love crucified in a garden.

Theodosius, the magnificent and courtly emperor, does public penance at the basilica gates for blind brute massacre at Thessalonica. The last Emperors of the West live on behind the purple veil, while the thirty bright-helmed Silentiarii, like figures charmed to silver, guard the " eternity " of these idols, served by pages and eunuchs. The pale child, Honorius, with painted eyes, indifferently plays with his doves as the mocking sumptuous wedding song of Claudian breathes through his flower-strewn palace chambers. Stilicho goes forth to grapple with Alaric, and the last of the Western emperors flees to Ravenna. The great Belisarius rides through, wrapt already in an incorruptible cloak of glory and grief, but his wake is disaster for Milan, for the enemies that hang behind him burn the city. Ataulphus, King of the Goths, dies here, and leaves the most imperial Galla Placidia to more of the violent chances and changes that work out her life in purple and scarlet. Alboin and his bearded Lombards, in their linen garments striped with colour, pass through to fair Pavia ; and the sombre eyes of Rosamond

The Spirit of Milan

behold Milan. Theodolinda, slim, sweet, golden, whom Love has given a sceptre to give again, with ecstatic eyes presses on her brows the Iron Crown, the Sacred Nail beaten and bound with gold. The monstrous rage of Attila crushes the city's pride in his path, and his grotesque image is painted on its palace walls. Charlemagne's half-mystical redemption ebbs over it. Emperor and Pope snatch at it; the prince-bishops, backed by the people, defy both, till the commune they have wrought turns on these, grown despots also. The Iron Crown is a magnet for the mighty. Otto the Great comes for the talisman and redeems the captive princess who sits spinning in the keep by Lake Garda. Otto the Third, too, will be crowned King of the Lombards, romantic Italy-drunken dreamer, sweetest and least fortunate of her northern lovers. An archbishop like Aribert is king-maker for Italy, till the folk break him they have adored. Princes and priests, Guelfs and Ghibellines, are grappling in many-crested confusion. But the dream of a Republic is in the heart's core of every great city. Milan remembers Ambrose, who led a commune against imperial powers, and the Car of the City moves red through the dark, bearing the Standard of the Saint, bearing the Cross and the Altar. Her republican coins are stamped with beauty, silver *fiorini*, golden *ambrogini*. But that paradoxical doom of nature which compels any free thing to feed on the freedom of others makes her a bitter neighbour to Pavia and Lodi, Monza, Verona, and Brescia; till the terrible Barbarossa over-powers her at last, and blinds and maims and crucifies her, shameful and abject, all but obliterated from the companionship of cities. For he broke her Standard, seized her relics, and extorted her life-symbol, her dear *carroccio*. That mortal pageant of surrender was indeed a passion-tide for Milan. The Iron Crown the conqueror took to Monza, and stole the magian dust in Saint Eustorgio for Cologne. And though the very sister-cities that had helped to destroy gathered round to restore, till she, still half-blinded, arose and led the famous Lombard League, and redeemed her *carroccio* with a Company of Death, the dream of the Commune had been mixed with despair. There are great passages still. The Saracen troops of Frederic II. besiege her; his golden son, King Enzo, beautiful among his beautiful, exotic brethren, is taken in desperate single combat. The dreadful riders of the pale devil, Ezzelin, hover near. Henry of Luxemburg is crowned and betrayed here. But Milan, weary, turned to her dukes again, and not till the Risorgimento did she once more loosen her banners for liberty. The first perpetual lord of Milan appears in a crusading Visconti, archbishop and noble, who has taken the device of a slain Saracen for his own; and, with the burning serpent of the East, what magical bale and accursed power ! With these perpetual lords the city renews its wealth and luxury, its merchandise of Venice and the Orient ; and the Humiliati, who had vowed themselves to penitence and the protection of God, become proud and luxurious.

The Visconti made a dynasty of violence, passion, madness, and the twin strange cunning that with cold hands holds the hot palm of madness, and some flashing, disconcerting genius—a fantastic race under a Saracenic curse. They are lords of most gilded festival, great bridals and superb dowries. Some have wreaths of roses in their yellow hair, some are dark and heavy like monstrous spiders. They hunt with leopards ; and carry an Ave like a crazy chime of heaven in their terrible names. There is sullen Bernabo, who literally gave his people to the " power of the dog." Famous in the annals of pomp was the wedding of Violante to the English Lionel of Clarence, though the fabled wedding feast and wedding gifts preluded the early death of the bridegroom. And not only Petrarch, but Chaucer, knew the mayland. Surely the smiling may-poet went happily here on his diplomatic business, gazing at the dreamy tender women, so like his own Criseyde. There is the puissant Gian Galeazzo, fine dissembler, who dreamed of a crown, a great duke who imagined rich building, and loved scholars, and wrestled with rivers as well as with rivals, and who watched his foes go out before him, like a calm crowned basilisk, till the plague touched him unawares. Petrarch read his Cicero under the leaves beside his growing Certosa. His daughter, Valentina, *cette Lombarde grâce*, the pale witch, goes with legendary clothes all stitched with jewels, and a golden retinue, to her delicate dissolute love of Orleans, a fatal wedding for Italy. Giovanni Maria, the blood-maniac, for ten terrible years gluts his horrible fancies, till in blood he perishes ; and his grave has the strange pathos of such roses as were laid on Nero's. Filippo Maria, astute, indifferent, fearful, is a little like Louis XI. with his astrologers and his hidden life in his keep. A master-plotter, a " duke of fantastical dark corners," he spun his strong webs in his occult chambers, creeping hooded over the canals at night ; murdered one wife and imprisoned another ; bought, sold and betrayed, till at last, after long plot and counter-plot, he died of supreme ennui, refusing to acknowledge an heir. Yet he had loved one woman ; and her daughter, Bianca, beautiful and spirited, could read her Greek and Latin as well as wear her cuirass and helmet when the moment called for them ; and her great bridal of Cremona grafted a fierce new shoot on the tired dynasty. When the last Visconti perished, the confused city made a somnambulistic motion to become the Golden Republic of San Ambrogio again. She had remembered the royal priest, for it took a superb person like Ambrose to recognize even dimly the inevitable

The Spirit of Milan

communism of the Gospel of Christ, the rare and ethereal anarchy implicit in a commandment of pure love and sacrifice ; and he had moulded her, first to the community of sorrow with those antiphonies in which all the people, not the priests alone, on one wave rose and fell about the mercy-seat, and thereafter into a community of purpose that could defeat emperors. But those who have lived long in the ergastulum cannot remember the gestures of freedom in an hour. The armies march and counter-march. Encompassed with foes, she seeks a new Captain ; and Francesco Sforza is rapt riding to the altar.

It is the strange, viper-bitten Visconti blood that prevails in Francesco's children, for all the wisdom and force of the great con-dottiere, all the gallantry and nobility of Bianca. What careful and splendid education could do to moderate the desires of Gian Galeazzo, to antidote Lodovico's stealth of fear, was done indeed ; but the sons were at once princelier and more morbid than their father. Galeazzo Maria, all a Visconti, in splendour, craft, cruelty, superstition, with amazing moments of sweet miracle thrusting themselves through the red fantasy of his mind, dies by the daggers he invites ; his son is a mere sickly child with a silly mother ; and his brother, Lodovico, Duke of Bari, is the only duke that matters when Leonardo comes to Milan.

v

So much for Milan as a fortress-city. But it is the strange duality of her history that is most important to her impression. Not only was she a fortress-city, but from of old a sumptuous pleasure-city, lying like a rose among her streams and meadows, a little as Naucratis of old dwelt like a great flushed nymphæa on her Nile-green delta. Like that she was famous for perfumes, colours, flowers, beautiful women and strange gods. Like her and other cities of fame she trafficked in "merchandise of gold and silver and precious stones, and ivory, and cinnamon and spice, and frankincense and wine, and wheat, and mer-chandise of horses and chariots and slaves and the souls of men." Milan is so rare and so helpless to the keepers of her enchanted castle that they wreak a sadist passion on her, and bruise her soft limbs with steel. The dubiety of her temper captures, disables and confuses, yet enriches, all those who dwell long within her walls. Their courage is sapped by strange terror, their will is relaxed or divided, their humanity is cankered with cruelty, their love is blinded with desire, their religion becomes a magical superstition. Her tyrants are of those who develop a cæsarian madness. They invent the Quarisema, by which a man's death agony may last for forty days ; but they imagine glorious building,

95

and they have seized a great mastery of the waters even before Leonardo's advent. But there is a certain rich and dewy pathos in all the moods of this city that crystals naturally from the watered plain, from her orchards and her gardens, the kind of inconscient innocence deep-dwelling within all natural things, that redeems with strange turns her sinful ways. She had the gift of tears.

> " Pardonnez-moi comme a l'Egyptienne !
> Si, si, je suis heureuse, mais je suis triste.
> Elle va pleurer aussi, j'ai pitié d'elle."

vi

So the dooms of emperors, prelates and dukes and furious invaders fall in solemn cadence on either side Lodovico's gilded stage, when Leonardo brings his starry figures there, a masque within a masque ; and cast a pallor and a shadow sometimes upon the brocaded courtiers.

The great Captains had taken Milan and branded the keys on her soft breast, and built a castle to hold their odalisque. Remembering an ancient way of pleasure, she painted her eyes, and, like a temple-wanton, clothed with emeralds and twined with lotos, like a rose-pale unconscious Herodiad, she danced before them. But she was confused as she danced among tapers like great lilies, and music liturgical, for Ambrose had taught her the beauty of virginity, and Augustine dead had wandered back to lie near Pavia with a king at his feet, and Theodolinda had pressed the holy iron garland burning on her temples, and given her with all Lombardy to her strange lord and Leonardo's, Saint John the Baptist. Catharists, patarini and Umiliati had done penance within her walls, perfetti had given the " consolation " of the Spirit, fraticelli had perished for strange doctrines of love in the name of the Paraclete, and flagellants had broken moaning at her gates. So she was also a great Penitent, because she forgot the passes and the roads, and she forgot the voice of Ambrose.

> " But evermore
> She had the same red sin to purge.
> Poor passionate keeper of the door."

For all that Ambrose, Dominic, Saint Peter Martyr and, in later times, Saint Carlo Borromeo could do, the sweet Manichæan despairing heart of Milan remained mystically confounded between good and evil. The great Captain, the Herodiad who could also be the Penitent, these had become the mythic forces in the spirit of Renaissance Milan—the Celtic, Byzantine, Latin, Syrian, Gothic spirit. Leonardo recognized her

The Spirit of Milan

myth. With heroic wrestling he was to evoke the Apocalyptic Rider, the Arch-Captain, the great Duke, the ideal Lord of Armies adored by distracted communes in Renaissance Italy. He watched the Herodiad, from her creating type and antitype of the unearthly beauty that is dangerous, ecstatic and alone, whom only the strong, like himself, can endure through the Dance of the Seven Veils without losing a soul within the bright eddy of her mystery. He paints that beauty, stilled and dreaming, in the Virgin, in Saint Anne, in Saint John, in Dionysos, in Leda. Even last year the knot of throbbing Manichæan love came alive in the so-altered city of Milan. Not long since, Ida Rubenstein danced there the sacred dance of the Herodiad in the guise of the beautiful Sebastian who perished by Milan's Diocletian, and who is but a shift of the form of the god of the solstice, Saint John.

But the Gothic anguish of the Penitent, Leonardo cannot satisfy. He made the final pattern of *The Last Supper* in a place where the passing of miracle demanded it, but there is no poignancy in this chorale of betrayal. When the great picture lay unique on the corroding wall, the impression seems to have been almost as serene as that of a Sophoclean tragedy. He had never seen " Christ's blood stream in the firmament." He did not believe that it could. The starry image of Berenice's hair was more actual to him, and more life-giving to his mind. And yet it is in science, perhaps, that the piercing mediæval note is heard, when he unmasks the pathos of the human body, and stresses the macabre note sometimes, though even then he has, pagan, more to say of its beauty.

No ! The lamenting and religious note of Milan he does not know. Her penitent voice he never heard, for he was tone-deaf to that, though she " made sweet moan." Beatrice kneeling at Bianca's tomb for hours on her own death-day ; Lodovico mourning alone in his black-hung room, vibrated with its agony. But Leonardo could not hear.

The unearthly child's voice again, that often smote pure through the history of Milan, with miraculous interposition calling Ambrose to his ivory Chair and Augustine to the Kiss of peace, sounding in the amazed soul of the commune, and, as if overheard like a fluting angel, answered by some of the tyrants, also he did not hear. This note of heavenly candour seems almost to lift again from the parted lips of the young Bianca, who died while all her plotting kin loved her for love's sake only. Hoarsened with dread, the same warning, as from some other sphere, came on the lips of the mad friar who cried on the Piazza to Lodovico before Charles of France came stumbling : " Prince, prince, show him not the way." Leonardo was too busy—and he had lost the innocence of his ear to more subtle melodies.

G

Leonardo the Florentine

Again, with those who helmed and mounted the Warrior, who clotted with gold the rubies on the Dancer's breast, and wrought the little stars of iron on the scourge of the Visconti princess who was a Penitent, whose labour and bitter dues built the immense fabric of pride, with the suppressed and overtaxed commune, in fact, Leonardo had no sympathy at all.

Tne Manichæan metaphysic that lay implicit in the red meshes of the city, all beating heart and flickering crimson wings, soft, fluctuating, inarticulate, involved with natural things, Leonardo tried to analyse out, with his other experiments. But the sob in the heart of Milan, the waft of litanies and lilies, the sombre eyes of the Herodiad, the sacred iron within the golden ring, were problems in a kind of dynamic not to be solved by the most exquisitely drawn problems of the scientist, though they dwelt like dyes in the secret soul of the artist. Julian also had reasoned in this city, and reasoned his way back to the sun-god. Leonardo's multiform speculations helped to maintain the beautiful equilibrium of his brain; but they did little more than lead him to the same radiant conclusion. It is in his painting, of which so much has been lost and destroyed, that the rich trouble of Milan softly dissembles, though not destroys, the Florentine line of beauty.

Chapter ii

The Renaissance Mood in Milan

i

WHEN the wave of the Renaissance was crescent in Italy the powers were five—Florence, Naples, Venice, Rome and Milan—all jealous and splendid.

Milan was still an Imperial City, with dukes the better-pleased if they wore the faint halo of an investiture. She was still the key-city to the conquest of Italy, the warden of the roads and passes. Still her prelates were warriors and hunters, and still her tyrants had something of a sacerdotal impunity. Deacons in red dalmatics, dukes in crimson and white, they carried on the tradition of Milan, the red may-tree in the blood-soaked mayland. The Holy Emperor was now but a picturesque and uncertain condottiere, the Roman Pope a certain enemy.

But still she was the dual city of strength and luxury, of armourers and dancers. Still she lay in the path of Northern invaders, among her waters and her meadows, soft as a lotos behind impregnable castles. Still she was the Gate of Italy, therefore the Gate of Dreams; still the Golden Orchard of the Hesperides, held by a dragon and a wall. The perfumes floated from her brasiers, her colours ran into the nights of the barbarians beyond the Alps. She was become the centre of a duchy of delight. Flushed like a thicket of azaleas at their moment of perfection, her image possessed their covetous minds. They saw her thus, glowing softly through the gleaming rivulets and the white apple-closes, and the great hunting forests, where the Renaissance stole about with soft fauns' laughter. They thirsted for her roses and her rose-coloured fruits; in a fever of desire they saw her fabulously fair. Over a way beset with perils, over passes haunted by the ghosts of heroic and tragic imperators, down the ruthless icy slopes, into the lovely nativities of spring, they would come, to find a Rocca strong with star-fast magic and a cathedral like the filigree Babylon of some exotic elves, and red palaces amazing and glittering with plunder. They would foul the lucid streams, and defile the pavilions, and trick the great castle, and kill its enchanted swans, and rend the violet

99

pages of its book of antique story, and glut their senses in all its wondrous pleasure, and force it to conjure up more.

So the French dreamed often, and dreamed the more, after, through Lodovico's folly, they had indeed gazed greedily on his dukedom, though his guile diverted them awhile to Naples.

ii

The red pillars of porphyry, rent from Zeus to Christ, in the baldacchino of Saint Ambrose' altar within its marvellous paillotto of gold, the fair cryptic colonnade of San Lorenzo, strange sun-symbols in cathedral windows, and wild heathen images hid in cloistral carving, like the bacchante riding her goat in the traceries round the door of Saint Aquilino's chapel, the great red font that was a pagan sarcophagus before it was a saintly tomb, were all signs and tokens that antiquity was ready to leap alive again when the mood that was at once the reaction from, and the inevitable calm consequence of, the Middle Ages, sounded its flutes and timbrels. The towering albero, as at the Duomo, branching like a Tree of Life, had dragons and vines and magi among its well-wrought tales of Christ. That Eastern Tree of Life was strong in all Milanese decoration, and the mystic supporters took many shapes.

In Milan only some dreamers tasted the Hellenistic rapture of Florence. Even the great insolence and pomp of Rome, remembering her own ancient glory, were not in the romantic key of sumptuous Mediolanum. Through Ravenna, she went back rather to the purple chambers of Byzantium, and farther, to Antioch, Alexandria, Persia. Like Rome, indeed, she translated her Renaissance into sheer magnificence; but not, like Rome, into a material ostentation, grandiose but shapeless. Hers ran into a great Court that should satiate fastidious senses with every kind of perfection possible to sound, touch, sight and hearing.

For Milan was at present the most mingled city in all mingled Italy. The Celt, the Carthaginian, the Goth, the Latin, the Frank, the Saracen, had left in Lombardy that deposit of peculiar dreams inherent in their spilt blood, the extreme racial secrets that do so often " amazèd meet." There were too many diverse qualities in Milan, from East and West, North and South. She might have said:

> " I am a place where music music meets,
>   Putting it out."

Her vision was kaleidoscopic; she was not single-hearted. Florence was a unity—a thing of art herself. Milan could not have the Florentine joy as of waking in a clear Athenian morning. Florence is like the en-

The Renaissance Mood in Milan

chanted flute-player on the Lodovisi throne pouring her dream through the reeds for her sole and flawless delight in an exquisite lonely ritual. Though Milan is not unaware of the precious spoil of Hellas, she takes it like other sacred relics, adoringly, uncomprehendingly, as a sweet barbarian city might.

The East prevails in Milan. The Renaissance did not so much create new elements as quicken and rarefy all elements that already were. Milan under Lodovico has the air of a great satrapy, something Asian. The chants that sobbed and cried in her churches were of the Oriental kind. The bones of the Magian kings had rested in San Eustorgio. And there was something Iranic indeed in the very domes and plans of many of her churches, kindred to temples in soft Cilicia. Persian textures, Persian hues, silkily invested Milan even more than other cities, by way of Venice, by way of Constantinople. Persian red was the rich subtle colour that under-smouldered all her turquoise and emerald and pearly crossing colours. Persian odours hung in the chambers of her children of luxury. Persian patterns flowered in her looms, communicating roses and pomegranates and pineapple fruits and blossoming boughs to her tapestries and her robes. Persian carpets themselves, dreaming of unearthly tints—carpets like " white roses," white peacocks, lay on the floors. The definitely " Saracenic " note, magical and aerial, frequently excited and thrilled the brooding splendour of her Byzantine tradition, throwing it up into rainbow fountains and bubbles, dropping brilliant pendentives into her building, suddenly shifting the gemmed pageant into mirage. Some of the scenes of Beatrice's maying pleasures and the groups of her music-makers and verse-readers, in the open loggie or by the lilied pools, are like the diversions of the charming affected lovers on Persian illuminations. Sometimes, when the processions rode out under the skies of dim amethyst and emerald, when a wild light and tender from the far mountains and the lakes dwelt within the drifts of swan-soft ethereal cloud, the picture married the romance of East and West.

And sometimes, in their chambers hung and perfumed with the East, they sang the Frankish song of Roncesvalles, and remembered the Celtic stories of Lancelot and Tristan, so mingled were they.

East may be East and West, West ; but farthest East and farthest West do meet like all extremes. It is only the Saxon that is confounded in the East. The early Celtic strain did not perish out of Milan, and it was strengthened strangely now and then. The astonishing Wilhelmina, inexplicable " princess of Bohemia," who lived like a saint, and was buried in Chiaravalle, who preached strange doctrines of Love in the name of the Holy Ghost, that winged Asiatic principle of Ecstasy

round which all love-heresies flicker, saying that God would next come
in the form of a woman, and that she was sent to preach Christ to
Saracens and Jews and the outcast, reminds one of a like tradition that
lingers in lost western islands, and of the divining and strange story of
Saint Bride who, virgin of the West, dreaming among dove-coloured waters,
is mystically drawn to succour the Virgin of the East under the sumptuous Oriental stars in the stable hung with the lotos-woven cloths of the
Magi.   There are spirals on the episcopal seat of Ambrose, and Celtic
enamels hang from the Golden Altar.   And from the cells of the Irish
Rule at Bobbio came illuminated books with great enamelled capitals
and woven borders of labyrinthine work, kindred to some cryptic stone
now standing lone with its holy brede of laced serpents and lovely
symbolic apples in a vast bleak field under the northern sky, while
sometimes the kine browse round it.

In Leonardo's work, as we shall see, there is a strange quality, a faëry
glimmer within the " fire and grace," such as we are used to call Celtic.
And no other Italian artist has it, except, to a less degree, Botticelli and
the very dissimilar Crivelli.   Admitting that it is probably a temperamental rather than a racial quality, undeniably it became more powerful
in Leonardo's art after he had been long steeped in Milan, and had
fingered the Gordian richness of her knotted soul.

But the crossing strains exceed her consciousness, and Milan bears
splendours and splendid people for the time instead of great artists.
Gracious obedient builders and craftsmen to serve the Court, she had ;
but great artists are free-born, and they require some one besetting
vision of unconfused pattern, one dominant rhythm that overrules the
rest.

iii

Not only was cinquecento Milan too composite to express herself in
definite forms of art, but the whole fine fiery matter of the Renaissance
was here left to the despots.   It was a family affair of the Visconti and
the Sforza, a point of honour in their conception of the magnificence
with which they dazed the eyes of others.   The city merely connived.
She was wearier than Florence.   She had known the worst violations,
and had had her holy communal heart torn out by alien powers while
Florence was battling for pride of place in Tuscany.   She had made
and unmade gods with Constantine and Julian and Ambrose.   She had
been victor and victim in Imperial duels ; she had slowly forced her
sacred standard through the interlocked steel of Imperial vicars and
prince-bishops, and with wailing trumpets had surrendered her *carroccio*.
She had lived fantastically with the fantastic Visconti, and surrendered

The Renaissance Mood in Milan

to the great Rider through languor of heart. Too often had her spirit been wronged. A broken man is a more horrible sight than a dead man. His brethren dare not look at him, they are so involved in his shame. So, better a dead city than a humbled city. The sense of freedom within her seems to have perished of fatigue ; and the Republic ideal is fallen on sleep for centuries, to awaken restored for the wars of the Risorgimento. The eyes of Milan are closed ; only the eternal foison of her mayland keeps her alive. The commune lies buried in the red, rich earth, unhastily revitalizing herself from that soil against the time to come. The redemptions of the earth are drowsy and deathlike, mysteriously mixed with narcotic seeds. But the citadel with its court remains, a superb *moles* that is also a palace-fortress. And there the Visconti and the Sforza receive the Genius of the Renaissance, and become the most sumptuous, if not the most comprehending, of its companions.

From the Medicean house in Florence Music and Masque ran gliding and glittering through the City as if constraining her willing soul with chains of lilies to the Renaissance festival. Florence herself was Lorenzo's Court. His imagination vibrated through the streets and accosted the souls of all his folk. What he dreamed settled through the minds of the burghers. What he sang eddied in the lighted air and overflowed the walls of the City, and literally set all Italy dancing. If he went versing of love and death and the flying feet of spring, and the ancient mirth inextricably confused with the ancient terror in the obscure worship of life, he sang of eternal things and set his measures to a creative music. He was a poet, and the walls of Florence, like those of Thebes and Troy, were fortified by the sound of the lyre. He sang to corrupt his people, said the suspicious Machiavelli, too insistent on finding a deep-coiled motive for even spontaneous actions. Hardly ! He rather wanted a people in his own image—ironic, tender, voluptuous. So his tournaments were Florentine pleasures, his pageants of hospitality for the folk as well as the guests, his collections for the City's use and honour. His table was set for any scholar, his gardens free to any artist. He was the First Citizen, and the stemmas of the guilds, flowered so richly upon Or San Michele, had a proud authority he did not deface.

Lodovico, mild and merciful as a ruler, romantic, subtle, and emotional in his mood, generous to all artists, dazed almost by a vision of historic magnificence, is an Italian despot of the most accomplished kind, yet undone by lack of one quality almost every other Italian despot wore like a plume, the bright amoral virtue of courage. It was a matter of nerve, part hereditary, part personal. Though he had not Lorenzo's great intelligence, he had imagination, ambition, an attractive and princely bearing. But, as is readily perceived, he was not unlike

Macbeth. He had more sensibility than most of his kind. He knew his title doubly weak, weak because of his father's ill-supported claim, weak because of the ailing prince, his brother's child. So his nerves shuddered at the blind brute-people outside his gates who might rise and kill any day ; as it had killed before. His work for the Renaissance was the composition of a Court, and not of a city. All the builded rose-colours, all the mayings and masquings and dances and jousts were shut up in the caskets of his castles and villas and chosen churches, his parks and his gardens.

The Milanese were patient while the largesses and the splendours ran over in bridal pageants and processions, while snatches of the glory were thrown to them. The overflow sufficed them : the Visconti also had been a jealous and secret folk. And the luxury trades and traffics created armies of craftsmen and opulent merchants who carried on an adequate bourgeois imitation of the Court in the way of ostentation. But Renaissance Milan existed only to serve and nourish and guard the most sumptuous Court in Italy ; and the people who, after Lodovico's first flight, welcomed and rejected conqueror after conqueror, were not those that, with blind agony of will and with a Company of Death, had redeemed the honour of their lost *carroccio*. Milan had had an agony to endure from each new lord, and was no more an identity like Florence— mutable, ironical, accusing, assenting, refusing, crying " Ad leones ! " Its folk were slaves who had lived with their master's hounds, punished slaves whose flesh had felt the fangs of the beasts. They are pleased all the same with the hurry in their streets, the new waters stealing through the lands. They like the sense of the East, and the return of the mythic luxury that once dwelt in their town as a sacred city, again making softer the very air. It is now a market of Venetian and Oriental merchants, of goldsmiths who make wonderful dishes for God in His chapels and Lodovico in his palaces, who decorate every day for Beatrice, " amantissima del lusso," with chains of jewels and gorgets of gold, and fabrics of fantasy. The craftsmen express the double temper of their Iron Crown, in which the bitter steel is covered by the fine-wrought circle of gold. Goldsmiths make astonishing crosses where Christ is crucified in magnificence, and with equal cunning the pearled hoods and imaged bells for the peregrine falcons ; ironworkers create gates like trellises of flowers, and clasp every door with hinges and locks of finely foliated adamant. Woodcarvers cover with like broidery of fabulous beasts and pointed leaves the choral sedilia of the Certosa and the window-seats of courtly lovers. Famed Milanese ricamatori weave rare thread with rarer thread, the precious on the precious ; the lute-devisers set ebony and ivory lovingly together, and lay in pearl a tale of Orpheus

The Renaissance Mood in Milan

on their caskets of music; the armourers are intent on beautiful blades and gilded breastplates and wyvern-gripped helmets—they clothe with angry beauty all the great lords of both Christendom and Heathenesse. The enamellers, embroiderers, perfumers, tapestry-weavers, potters, makers of painted glass, mosaicists, artists in playing cards, ply their coloured crafts. And there is a very populace of the servants of the falcons, horses, hounds, swans, apes and peacocks, all the human meinie attending the winged, racing, gliding things, the symbols and totems that please the mighty.

The merchants and the craftsmen thrive. While the glory endures the people are acquiescent, and faintly aware of the Renaissance as a cloud of perfume, a sense of deepening rose-colour, a great new picture hid on a cloister wall, a shadow of a kingly steed—and a stealthy quickening of ancient magical practices. They are content enough, and when Olgiati and his friends deliver them from a glittering irrational prince, a strange devil with insane angelical flashes, they howl with horror and rage. Yet the blind and beautiful motions of the unconscious life of Milan struck out in that deed a more typical episode of the conflicting traditions in Renaissance scarlet than any other city could show. For the conspirators make their pure pathetic orisons to pagan and Christian saints; with their noble classic intention of tyrannicide, their dream of Harmodius and Aristogeiton, mingle the sudden sweetness and ominous wistful gestures of their victim, walking in red damask to his doom, his unanswerable cry of dolour, the stricken moment when death seems to change him from a vicious duke to a king-priest stabbed at the altar by those fair young men in their short crimson coats of satin, whose expiations are crowned by the ecstatic anæsthesia of Olgiati, dreadfully, slowly, killed for his idealist faith. Galeazzo Maria, descendant of some late Cæsar, Olgiati fostered by Brutus, both are born from the very core of the Renaissance, though in drowsy Milan.

Drowsy Milan! For a certain passive sweetness as of the sacred courtesan, the innocence of unconscious things like flowers and fauns, astonished at the fates that befall them, dwells through the streets of the fair barbarian city. What was common to all men—Lodovico, Leonardo, burgher, craftsman, peasant without—was the soothing mansuetude of tender, rainy lights and lapsing waters outside the city walls. And still for rich and poor was offered the comfort of great lights, of burning incense, of significant ingressæ, of romantic litanies and the pomp of slowly changing pontifical robes. Still the holy images could gleam with supernatural lights, and miracle burned about the city in days of doom and stress, and reconciling music harmonized all conflicts in the churches, the castles and the streets.

Leonardo the Florentine

Leonardo definitely preferred the delicate ostentation of a Court to the critical applause of a free city, for this intense egoist required a princely patron whose extravagant desires would make possible his extravagant dreams. Lorenzo, Lodovico, Louis XI., Cesare Borgia, Ippolito d'Este, Giuliano de' Medici, Francis the First, these were definitely friends of his, and he liked to work for them. He was a despot himself in his intellectual worlds : he was ruthless, unscrupulous, cruel, luxurious, like them. They had high qualities ; he also had that superbia of attitude which is a matter of beauty, not of goodness. He understood them : and they did appreciate him, though Lodovico once or twice nearly quarrelled with his too dilatory prince of artists.

Leonardo was a courtier; it was one of his phases. Though the present-day writers try to leave out the courtier, they cannot so deny all the early testimonies. He was capable of planning a town so that all the lower ways of service should be definitely separated from the gracious seigneurial existence in its guarded paths of splendour. He had his chosen pupils, beautiful, graceful, brightly clothed, well-born ; he had his scientific friends, a group who, like himself, made something of a mystery of their knowledge. He was also deeply involved with the castle-pageantry, and used to the dancing debate of the versing and romantic young nobles. It did not concern him that the cathedral was no great gorgeous adumbration of the City in God, as it should have been, the mighty Ark of its Covenant with Time, served by the singers, the dreamers, the imagers, the lovers, the idolaters, the philosophers, calling the greatest and the least to the Adorations of the High Altar and the infinite Compassions of the Mass. His mind did not march with the German Gothic mass of the cathedral, not because it was the caprice of a despot or two, however, but because his own preference was for architecture that rose inevitably into domes and semi-domes. He liked the proud falconries, he loved the Sicilian stallions and willingly planned their stables, he was charmed by the rarefied music of the ducal chapel, he had an æsthetic delight in the delicate preposterous pages that glittered over all the chambers and bridges of the castello. For the rest, he remembered that he was a Florentine, as did everybody else ; and heard his own pure Tuscan go silvery among the softly blurred and hoarser confusions of the Lombard speech. But Lodovico was his complement, the subtle, craving, magnificent Duke, desiring great things of the artist for his own glory. The snakes of his secret Medusa were kin to the crowned Vipers of Milan ; and Leonardo could forgive Lodovico's failure all the less because the inhibitions and the

The Renaissance Mood in Milan

paralysing fears that caused the Duke's overthrow were the corroding guests of his own bosom.

While it lasted, Lodovico's was a Court where Leonardo could be most of all an autocrat among artists, as the after-tale of Milanese art, with its iteration of Leonardesque themes, often charming at first, fading finally into a grimace and a mutter, was to reveal. He had no rivals in quality, no predecessors mighty enough to impress him, no contemporaries enchanting enough to dispute his novel and exciting powers, no pupils cool and intelligent enough to steal a little of his genius to heighten a synthetic talent, as Raphael quietly did in the later Florentine years.

Milan had some timid, not ungracious minor artists, but she had no great tradition of art. As with most imperial cities, as with Rome, whom she had rivalled, the artists who served her had rarely been of her own soil. Preoccupied with the conflicts of the past, intoxicated with strange libations, she had little tranquillity to develop schools of imagery. She had been Milan of the Iron Crown, Milan with the Standard of Ambrose, Milan with the Eastern Viper for a garland, Milan who sang Exsultet and Crept to the Cross, Milan the pride of the Lombards, famous for armourers and lovers. Without her portals emperors had waited, and, when she endured a siege, to her every gate her enemy assigned a prince. Architecture? Let strangers build and plan and engineer. Painting? For her largess would any great painter come. Decoration? Well, her children could always make her friezes; it is natural for artists with sweet names like Amadeo and Dolcebuone to work her soft rich substance into endless wreaths of dreamy delight. But heroic sculpture of the supreme idea of the Italian superman and overlord? Let the Florentine come.

V

If I have spent many words in analysing the history and temper of Milan, in discovering what desires and dreams were heavy in the trance of golden pleasure with which Lodovico at his supreme hour invested her, it is because Leonardo the impassible was deeply affected by his long residence in the city, and his amazing powers were altered, not in kind, indeed, but in correlation and disposition. His Florentine clarity of vision remained: his Florentine irony protested in diverse ways against the insidious luxuries and the magical traffics. But, as by osmosis, the sensuous atmosphere drenched him, and stole through his labyrinthine soul, sundering with the sweetness of a philtre. The duality of the city pressed close to the duality of his pagan divinity.

Leonardo the Florentine

At thirty years he came to Milan with his imagination iridescent, chatoyant, his curiosity and his fantasy interchangeable and at one, in the give and take of true lovers. In Florence the music of his unconscious self had kept time with the song of the conscious. He was variety in unison. But in Milan the unconscious part sank from its lit penumbra into a purple darkness. In the fertile soil, the rainy lights, the suffusion of soft colours incarnadine, the atmosphere of music and of dreamy dancing, the clouds of amber and violet perfume, the trancelike, feverish pattern of existence, the two selves were delicately divided by some inarticulate distrust. The negative reactions of the illuminated reason, and the positive reactions of the other blind, listening and feeling self in the bosom, became so strong and so contrary that they almost separated. Milan, with her dreamy conflicts of mood, vision, sex, coincided with his own conflicts too well. She cleft with silk and decided with kisses—she laid roses on the aching difference.

In Florence the shaping, unresting imagination kept working the underdrift of emotion into wreaths of sweet images. The mind was perhaps more excited in that eager air than the heart, and the senses, like young singers, served the soul as Leonardo definitely said they should. But in Milan the lucid Florentine intellect seems to think it can save its clarity only by separating itself away from the heavy colours and perfumes, the rich musiques and the glittering images that with soft golden siren-feathers caress the passionate dreamer in the breast. The pure reason withdraws itself, monklike, to discover the universe with the icy abstract processes of mathematics. All these bright beginnings of "treatises," on light, and cupolas, and mechanics, and perspective, are splinters from the crystalline hard protest of that reason. But the unconscious self, suppressed, ascetically denied, like a twin Cæsar thrust out by an arrogant brother, sinks into its dark chamber to feed on the witless wisdom of the spices and the sounds, to create a kind of mysticism of the senses, and with white poppy and mandragora to evoke a vision of ambiguous hermaphroditic shapes. This Herodiad of a city, devoted with her Lombardy to Saint John, the myth of the unity of god and devil, whose Duchess, even before Leonardo's eyes, danced for the pleasure of kings, and danced herself to piteous death, with her traditions of love and hate, her sadisms, masochisms, perversities, her extremes of adoration and hatred, seduced the spirit that had already considered too deeply the great Florentine festivals of midsummer.

Henceforth Leonardo is like the Paduan student who lost his shadow. It does not walk abroad now—his dreaming self, the shadow that followed fast the aery knight who went with winged feet in the

The Renaissance Mood in Milan

light of Florence. But the shadow is not vanished to infinity; it lives in the underworld, absorbed in its own magic, black or white.

This division of his interests is not altogether strengthening to his art. Often he falters and fails in his scientific problems when some spring of the instinctive logic would have carried him over the border into a new truth; while his art, like his personality, loses some of its miraculous polarity. The *Adoration* of Florence is candid as well as beautiful. *The Last Supper*, if the whole truth were told, has always excited wonder rather than delight. It is full of problems worked out in intricate lines in his study-chamber; it is composed and observed with all his intellectual attention—but he dares not now admit his entire personality into any picture. Yet the baffled and denied secret soul, sorrowfully remembering its nobler companionship of old, rose up to paint the head of Philip like the dream-fast boy in the *Adoration*, to bow the head of the Beloved Disciple, and to veil the face of the Christ.

And the Olympian arrogance which is one of the assumptions of his art was strengthened by the survival in Milan of the uncritical Early Christian temper that accepted sweetly and confusedly the new names of saints for ancient gods and continued to annoy the Pauline mind by eating communion food from unhallowed altars, not yet realizing that Pan is dead, and that of all the shepherds who come fluting out of Asia they must hearken only to one, steadily preferring the lilies, the rare emotions, the passion-flowers and the great vines of the Ephesian Gospel. Milan was a Thaïs whose converted eyes unconsciously kept some of the purple images of her pagan hours. She had heard Christ play His lute like Orpheus, and felt Him pass through the underworld like Dionysos, and seen Him fold His sheep like Apollo, and tasted Him in the bread and wine like Mithra; so she thrilled to the mingled mythos of Leonardo, enchanted by the suavity, aware of the irony only as a rare flavour called " sottigliezza." Milan had a kind of heathen innocence, and his artistic libertinism throve upon it.

Because Milan was pagan and Christian, because she kept her ancient magic, because she was paradoxically virgin and harlot, because she was sophisticated in love imperial, mediæval, Renaissance, because she was of double sex, he painted the face of Saint Anne like the face of Dionysos and Saint John, and ultimately made Madonna Lisa look like Anaït of Carthage, whom the Christians continued to worship as the Virgin. He in whose consciousness all strains met came to a city that all races had made. To double and triple the flower, to sift over it from a rare tissue some exotic fertilizing pollen-dust, was always his desire. Florence was complete already; a great seeding iris-lily, rose-ivory, rose-golden. Milan was a crucifer with many a mystery dusted over its anthers, a passion-flower for more than one passion, a passion-flower crimson with its confusions. But Leonardo remained Florentine enough to transmute it to the true colours of the gods, and the spirit of Milan flowers in his later pictures, amethyst and pale emerald, with only some sweet stain of her carnation.

What is a dream of Renaissance Milan? Toppling columns and dissolving circles of Roman palaces, thermæ, aqueducts, amphitheatres, frenzied priests of Cybele, proud mailed initiates of Mithra, roses—roses dark and deeply scented, roses desired by emperors, roses of Aphrodite—the labarum of Constantine, the sun-song of Julian, monstrous shapes of terror, Alaric, Attila, litanies rising like white birds among virgin-lilies, passionate Latin of Augustine, darkly sweet like violets, the mystical Dove in the sun-symbol, dreadful violations and the cry of an outraged people, crowned vipers in the rose-gardens, frenzied flagellants at the gates, burning heretics and dancing spring-masquers alternate in the squares, helmeted conquerors riding up to the altar, brocades fit for the Queen of Sheba, clouds of perfume and music dissolved in carnation-colour, crystal voices in a choir, a may-city in a mayland, a labyrinth of bright waters, lovers leaning from pierced galleries, a castle like a looming fable, a cathedral like an unshepherded alp, a drift of carnival people afraid of Lent, golden ladies laughing at an ape, rose-white ladies with their Nubian slaves, a duchess dancing her pain to death, Lodovico's sweet suppliant eyes, Leonardo's rarefied profile sharply detached among the contesting splendours as a face in painted glass disengages itself pearl-white among the emerald, mauve, and rose—all these, and a sombre sleeping commune awaiting the Risorgimento.

Chapter iii

The Aspect of Milan

i

RENAISSANCE Florence is still easily to be seen. Walk over the Ponte Vecchio and along the Arno at the sunset hour, or pass from the beautiful trinity of the Baptistery, the Duomo and the Campanile to the Piazza della Signoria, or seek shelter from the sun under the enormous eaves of her palaces, or hear the mandolin insist upon the summer air—you slip lightly away from the modern noises, and bring a branch of quattrocento may before the clear house of Lorenzo. The stones of mediæval and Renaissance Florence still dominate the city. But Lodovico's Milan, like that of Diocletian, Ambrose, Ansperto, Gian Galeazzo, Visconti, of Stendhal even, is a vanished story. She has been seized again at her place of meeting ways by new captains, those that call themselves " of industry " ; and they have disfigured her more than Spaniard or Austrian could. Her passive red soul is beaten hard by the heavy feet of the toilers in factories, and she is roofed with hideous glass and steel, she who once carved milky visions in rare crystal, and wrought her iron as delicate and wonderful as gold.

Lodovico's Milan, steadily enriching its churches and castles, and extending itself in lovely garden-houses along the streams and canals, looked like a city made by the splendid wealth and the great will of successive tyrants. Her ancient Duomo was gone, her palace of liberty was no more ; her old market-place was a trivial corner. Her aspect and configuration had been fixed by the Roman prefects, the prince-bishops, the vicars of the Empire, the dukes and the counts, by the cæsarian passion for exotic, excessive building, by the terrors and desires of the Visconti race. Where Florence had a Duomo and a Palazzo Vecchio builded from her civic soul, Milan had a Cathedral and a Castello, alike dictated by her lords, who repeated their splendour and pride in the Certosa and Keep of Pavia. It was a fair city, for Lodovico was widening the ways, and inviting light and air to pass through the new streets that strove to make amends for the unholy devastation of the Plague, while he drew the rivers and the canals in silver links through the lovely mayland, even like that great Visconti predecessor who also dreamed of being King of Liguria, King of Lombardy, King of Italy perhaps. This was not merely the personal caprice of a ruler who still had something to spare from his pageants, his jewels, his falconries, his stables and his armies. Lodovico's mind was varicoloured, and he meant well by the city he was too unnerved to solder to his rule. Besides, he evidently was stimulated by his helper, for to command water, light, and air, none so potent as Leonardo, who loved the puissant mastery of the elements.

But the greatest buildings were the gorgeous appanages of an absolute ruler. They had some hybrid, artful surprises of beauty, betraying the bright violences and flashes of fantastic will that startled them into being. Strangers had been busy all over the city, masters of Como, Germans, of late mostly Tuscans—Filarete, Brunellesco, Michelozzo, San Gallo, Bramante, with Leonardo himself to abet in castle and cathedral—all working, especially Bramante, in admirable humour, more fancifully than usual, in the moist, strange air, in the wilful picturesque tradition, with the facile, coloured material of brick and terra-cotta and cream-coloured stone. Meanwhile the Romanesque churches, domed and quiet, with the larvæ and batwings of the night held in the heavy foliage of the capitals of their massive pillars, and, with precious traces of indestructible mosaic hid in low-vaulted dark chapels, kept the remembrance of a simpler and sincerer faith.

ii

Cities that are set by sacred hills and rivers have their lovely contours determined from the beginning of earthly times. Milan grew from long roots in the water-meadows where the great roads decided her place in the vast Plain of Lombardy ; and no necessity of immediate ranges, no caprice of the led waters that united the Ticino and the Adda around her, absolutely defined her configuration. With the Naviglio wound about her edges, she lay round her castello and her cathedral like the may-branch she was, mingling her petals with her orchards beyond her gates, a theme for painted symphonies and nocturnes, in soft tones of rose-colour and chrysoprase. When Louis XII. rode from Vigevano to the capital, the French courtiers gazed enraptured at the smiling " paradise on earth," stretching on either side the canal. Great guelder-roses hung their rich white moons among their bowering leaves. The little brooks ran crystal through the meadow-orchards. The pleasure-houses and villas rose cool and fair from the brink of the water, with charming drawbridges and sanded paths among the pale green trees.

The Aspect of Milan

And ladies in golden robes and rosy jewels were dancing on the greensward, though Lodovico would look on dancing ladies no more.

Orchard on orchard, wheatfield on wheatfield, vineyard on vineyard, marshes and woodlands, waters on waters, meadows on meadows, the great Plain of Lombardy rolled round Milan and the smaller cities, rolled to the Alps, the Apennines and the sea. On a clear day Mont Blanc, the Matterhorn and Monte Rosa hung like faint, serrated clouds on the far edges of the amethystine ether. There were no gracious friendly hills about her. Far away these green and violet and crystal peaks seemed to be the ramparts of a world not human. But among their foothills lay those enchanted lakes sunk in their luminous airs, with their sweet fables of sybillic ladies in green-glowing caves, of sirens in grots of lapis, their pagan insolence of oleander, their faëry islands with names liquid as their waters, whence the moist winds came cooling and dreaming.

" Day by day
New pollen on the lily petal grows,
And still more labyrinthine buds the rose."

Spring came suddenly over the plain ; the buds that are the very colour of miracle breded the almond-trees ; between dusk and dawn the white flower woke softly and suddenly on the blackthorn ; peach and apple and pomegranate blossom paled and flushed and kindled on their branches. The " white trees," the tall poplars, took on their air of pricking adventure, and the sea of mulberry leaves sighed and swayed. The skies seemed illimitable, whether by day the cloudy galleons moved with sails of silk across the violet-blue, or the sunset spread golden vans over the green-turquoise skies of a rainy land, or the landscape went azure, as the light withdrew tenderly to its western lavers from the vast hollowed jewel of the afterglow, or by night there marched and wheeled the processional planets and the flame-fraught constellations, from the gemmy hunter Orion to the tender-pulsing Pleiades. Many a dark hour Leonardo went lone through these infinite spaces, trying to measure the light of dead or dying stars, lost from the overcrowded and overcoloured life of the city below.

iii

" You will draw Milan," Leonardo admonishes himself, evidently anxious to grasp the city. So he drew a map, showing irregular walled Milan with the ways leading from the Broletto Nuove to her different ancient gates and the Naviglio as the centre of her mesh of waters. Otherwise Milan did not lend herself to drawing, like Florence. For Florence was a pattern of clear enchanting lines with washes of pure, pale colour, intent heads of people sharply detached on the golden air, precious things so delicately isolated that they could sing out their rare cadenzas inviolate in their own little silences. But Milan, built in her soft brick and terra-cotta, among her facile bountiful plains, where mortality had fertilized the fruits, was like a picture in some thick modern impasto. She was colour and mass and richness. Extravagant white surprise of a cathedral, insolent impregnable towers of a castello that in itself was a city, romantic apses and arcaded, rising roofs of Sante Maria delle Grazie, mounded old Lombard churches, palaces not like the great compositions of Florentine palaces, but engaging with red-broidered doors and windows, and carved and twisted chimneys—it was all fantastic, dreamlike, interfused by the moist airs into one impression, as if seen through a smoke of rose. The soft sun and the soft rain made a kind of physical dreaminess, breathed a soothing haze over all things like the bloom on perfect peaches, and charged the senses with drowsy, heavily-pulsing emotion. Leonardo, who sometimes found the clarified air of Florence a little ruthless, and her hot nights breathless, who loved the wet lights and the quivering haloes round beauty, and the unearthly colours of the rainbow, took pleasure in an atmosphere where all the red turned rose, and the innumerable pomp of jewels was transmuted into " one faint eternal eventide of gems." It was in Milan that he discovered the delicious artistic mystery of sfumato. Clear colours of tempera and patterned line for Florence! Milan amid her orchards and waters is a red city of pleasure, softly obscuring her beauty with rich veils, flushed at the dawn like red hawthorn, flushed when the sunset burns in precious clots through the branches, for she is as leafy as Ferrara. She is a cluster of rubies caught in iron and gold. Stained-ivory Florence is delicately powdered with little roses ; Milan is all one rose before its fall. Every note of red sings in Milan and its hectic, breathless life. It is like red apples, red coral, gladiolus, cinnabar, red agate ; like azaleas, pale carnations, jacinths, cornelians, autumn linden leaves : it seems founded on sard and red jasper ; it is wine-red, lover-red, sunset-red ; and the Castello hides reds even more concentrated and brilliant, reds as of fire-opals, deep almandines, great rubies, crimson enamels and painted glass. The *carroccio* of its freedom had been coloured like red and white roses. Even the princes went clothed in red and white : and Lodovico's red ducal raiment, as well as his kingly bearing, betrayed him at last to his captors. Four heathen pillars of red porphyry raised the baldacchino over the Golden Altar ; a heathen hollow of red porphyry was the cathedral's great christening bowl. But the green evening skies of a rainy world soothed the eyes of Leonardo.

Hemicycles of golden ivory seen from a sacred hill ! That was the symbolic dream of Florence that visited sometimes Leonardo's musing, exiled mind. A drift of fallen rose leaves round an amazing lost avalanche of a cathedral—that image might have tortured the darkening mind of Lodovico, dying by cruel degrees in the dungeon of Loches. Snow among roses ! Symbol of the rare luxury of festival Milan, symbol desired by Elagabalus, prince of luxury, and considered by Leonardo for Lodovico.

iv

How strangely must Leonardo's gaze have rested on this alien vision of a cathedral, Gian Galeazzo's " Folly," the marble hallucination of an obstinate wizard of power whose desire, like its image, certainly could not " leave the ground to find itself in the sky." Given labour of men, given jewels of women had built the ancient Duomo which it superseded. But that had been the house of the Sacred Car ; and its portico had covered the Parliament of Milan. The caprice of a despot and the pride of his successors had raised this. German Gothic architects and Italian engineers made it—a Teutonic thing embarrassed, not inspired, by its Latinity, and further distracted by an insidious Orientalism. For all its pinnacles and towers, this monstrous swan will never fly ; it has not even folded wings. Not by this are you " caught up to God by his beauty," as with the thrusting wings and spears of the true Gothic. At its best it is a semi-northern embroidery, a guipure of silver, fantastic, not flamelike. It is only an immense reliquary, that should have been fashioned fragile in alabaster, silver, and vermeil, only an exquisite toy grown gigantic. What Italy could take from the decorated Gothic is seen in Orvieto, in the Ça d'Oro of Venice, even in the overwrought Certosa—gracious, pointed and pierced ornament, translated sweetly from French to Italian, kindred tongues.

The cathedral is unequal, wrong, preposterous ; it has been vulgarized by later ages. It is unpardonable as mere architecture ; it violates the sense of proportion ; it is a clangour of unresolved discords ; it is sometimes even like a heraldic white porcupine *hérissé*. It is a perverse fantasia composed by one with no sense of music, groping confusedly amid the recollections of a subtle Italian traveller who has been surprised out of his subtlety in ultramontane lands. There is no rest or sovran calm in its aspect. All these things are true. It is a mistake. Nevertheless it is at once a superb and a naïve mistake. It is touchingly wrong. It captures and keeps the sense of true childish wonder ; for it is partly the architecture of a fairy tale—a German fairy tale, absurd, sentimental and charming. You can have adventures among the roofs and spirelets, surprises of Asmodeus on its pinnacled slopes. There are marble grottos among the frost-fine stalagmites. There is a flowery forest and a garden of fantasy. There are ramparts as of faëry with clear bugles blowing. Many of those little peaks are as delicately wrought as if a legion of cave-dwarfs or elves had been carried up there to a giddier task than metal-working. The eyes are entangled among its broideries and idly smiling buttresses. And by Amadeo's ravishing turret no purist even could be cold enough to refuse praise.

Yet the Duomo is more than a German fairy tale, lightened by some Eastern caprices. Though it vanishes before such names as Chartres, for example, and fades before the true Italian shapes in Florence, Pisa, Venice, even its eager excess has a kind of sincerity; and it is at least alive because it is so full of conflicts. It is not vacuous like a Baroque church; its very feverishness justified its place in Renaissance Milan.

And the beauty of the fabric, quarried from the siren caves of Maggiore, flattered by the moist air and changeable light, spiritualizes the effect of the whole. It seems a fantastic, tattered cloud of sunset, an insubstantial galleon of glory, frayed at the edges, drifting across the green-blue sky. In the clear, unearthly afterglow it is ghostly fair. In a soft twilight it is coloured like a white peacock, and in a weeping twilight like smoked mother-of-pearl, while it is a kind of faëry city of Saint Michel by moonlight. And within there is no feverishness; within, there is space, peace, quiet, for multitudes. Majestic, mighty, solemnizing, broken only by shifting radiances of light, the great nave sails to the gleaming High Altar, and the lateral naves take their serenely parallel ways in a dark, cool world—five great naves altogether, like a final chord of Mass music.

And that sincerity in excess ends by moving you. If this be the irrelevant dream of a despot, he was Milanese all the same, and a human sorrow of the city's had ebbed to his own heart. For all the men-children were dying out of Milan, and this cathedral was built to Maria Nascenti, who had mercy on all, even on the despots, so that her sweet name was mingled with their violent names thereafter. Presently, therefore, the contemplative mind, slowly aware of a pathos flickering about these ways, as of some beauty from beyond the Alps, lost in the white forest, singing crazed romaunts, thinks of the ghost of a beautiful dead woman calling to her unborn son. Singular and sumptuous the great cathedral stands, not altogether Christian, for all that it pierces like the spear, the reed, the thorns, the nails. It is pricked, not pointed. There are beautiful windows with sun-symbols in them. It is " part pagan, part papistical," though the pagans for once have come from the wild northern heath, not from the valleys of Sicilian asphodel.

Like the other architects of the Duke, Leonardo had considerable dealings with this cathedral, which he probably regarded with some astonishment and some distaste. Lodovico gave it an octagonal dome, for which Leonardo, with others, made a model, perhaps two models. But his design was too calm for the restless thing, though he did not refuse it some decoration in its own temper. The cathedral needed a puissant high-winged, wild-spined beast of a dome that could grip, not without fierceness, the scattering effects into some unity. Amadeo's cupola rose up instead, as true to the distracted sentiment as a dome might be, but too small for that wilderness of pinnacles.

And when the great relic, the Sacred Nail, bitter brother to that of the Iron Crown, has to go up to its high place, Leonardo draws the design for the pulleys and ropes. You see him standing by as the hallowed piece of metal swings into place, with his amused and interested eyes. He has made a beautiful drawing of the mechanism, with triumphant slant lines that look adventurous as a ship's riggings; and he has confided a sardonic riddle about relics to the ciphers of his manuscript book.

Yet, as he carried all countries in his mind, so he carried all ages, and the distorted Gothic of the Duomo, seen like a broken mirage, unconsciously strengthened the mediæval strain of his thinking. In Milan he began to read those German scholars of the Middle Ages who searched into the ways of the earth's mechanism—Albertus Magnus and his kind. The ravening great gargoyles and fragile queens on perilous ledges, the caricatures of kings and priests and cats, diverted this prince of the air. And the grotesque and fanciful element that nests like bats in the hid capitals of the great pillars is often busy like a little devil about his notebooks. He draws many sketches of the cathedral interior. The pressures of Milanese life gave him a kind of claustrophobia; and he felt relieved in the vastness of the place.

v

" You will buy a book treating of Milan and its churches," Leonardo further reminds himself, evidently determined to understand. And he was perfectly right in especially contemplating and drawing the churches, where still the more ancient Milan lay acquiescent and brooding, sacred in its essence, while Renaissance Milan came and went in all its agitations of love and hate. Churches, especially in Milan, were not then mere elected places for definite acts of worship; they were part of the scene of daily life, where people met, gazed, saw their shows, and heard their music. Love and death made assignation there, and the saints heard prayers as conscienceless as ever did the gods; and dukes in red and white came at their peril, to be courteous to Christ even if the dagger lurked within. For in Milan the ancient instinct to regard the elect and sacred figure not only as king and priest, but as sacrifice, seemed strong as other ancient urgencies ; and Lodovico, like some of his predecessors, hardly escaped the assassins that felt the churches apt as well as convenient for tyrannicide.

So Leonardo draws the churches, and seems to sketch plans for their benefit. But it is difficult now to tell where he has touched them. Amadeo and Dolcebuone were at their suave, smiling work. Brunellesco and Michelozzo had done proud and gracious things. Bramante was the architect of the moment. He had been active in Milan for the last quarter of the fifteenth century ; and the Bramante of Milan is at once vigorous and pictorial, as if, charmed by its plastic material and picturesque tradition, he were enjoying some princedom of fancy before being called to his severe lordship in Rome. Glad pupil of Laurana, he here accepts the gifts of the earth, terra-cotta, rosy brick, red tiles, a little creamy marble from the lakes, some almond-coloured marble from Verona ; and gives you lidded cupolas, and picturesque slant roofs, walls pierced with ocelli, galleried arcades, surfaces covered with fresco, smiling places at fanciful play with their shadows. But, though Leonardo seems to have assented to Bramante, and worked with him amiably in several matters, it was the ancient, more Eastern churches that engaged his eyes most deeply, and mingled with his memories of Brunellesco's and Alberti's work. Long naves and solemn choirs, such had been the early basilicas wherein the young Augustine had kept his love-trysts. These were the churches, Romanesque and Lombard, still reminiscent of Barnaby, Paul, and Cilicia—bearing an impress of East-bred emperors and a time when Constantine was doming the Holy Sepulchre, and sending the Holy Wisdom afloat on a bubble of golden moons—mounded into cupolas, arcaded with round arches borne by thick pillars in whose capitals hid the flora and fauna of the night that dreamed of the *Dies Iræ*, larvæ and succubæ changing by stress of the Italian spirit into dragons, angels, sirens and sphinxes. Leonardo did not dislike these endlessly interlacing beasts that express so well the primeval fears and terrors that lurk still in the most civilized state. He did grotesques himself ; and his were more dreadful.

San Ambrogio was the true duomo of Milan. Massed brick and stone, it lay glorious in colour. Before the great door was the beautiful atrium, the covered walk round the three sides, where the white catechumens once gathered at Easter and Pentecost, to gaze from afar at the altar mystery for which their souls were preparing ; and the assured nave on its round, strong arches, with strange beasts in the pillars, moved darkly up to where the lantern shed light on the wonderful Holy

The Aspect of Milan

of Holies, where the four heathen pillars of red porphyry upheld the baldacchino, and the inestimable palliotto clothed the altar, telling the story of Christ in Carlovingian gold and of Ambrose in Carlovingian silver, while great Celtic enamels and strange, uncut stones, rubies, opals, cats' eyes, betrayed the wonder and adoration of hearts for whom these tales were moving things, as of yester-eve. All the smouldering riches of the church were so gathered into the Altar-place. And away in the dark lay Ambrose himself, beside the skeletons of the saints he found, Gervasius and Protasius, with duly cloven heads; while from the choir, in passionate monotone, persisted the pure Ambrosian liturgy, even as he had decreed it. But, ancient and equivocal, two great symbols were lifted on isolated pillars, the Cross, and the spiral bronze Serpent, with its traditions of the wilderness, to whom mothers brought their sick children. Also the great church of the bishop covered a Temple of Dionysos, and if Leonardo often haunts the place, he seems drawn by the wine-hallowed stones.

Here, in the chapel of Saint Satiro, that lovable brother of Ambrogio, who is a little like Sir Palomydes the Unchristened Knight, as also here and there in older churches like Saint Lorenzo, comes glowing through the dark the peacock-blue iridescence, the burning gold of Byzantine mosaic, fragments that promise the imperial cloisters of flame in the sepulchre of the Eastern Empire at Saint Vitale of Ravenna, where colour fiercer than fire sounds soft, dreadful trumpets round the white and rigid Theodora with her eyes of immoderate desire, offering as to an equal a golden cup to her God.

Ancient! But Bramante built for the pile a Renaissance canonica, thinking of Rimini, and Mantua, and the superb tricks of Alberti, whom, like Leonardo, he reverenced; and touched it with fantasy in the twisted chimneys. And he disturbed the dust of two lovers,

> " Who in this way
> Had thought by this device to make some stay,"

so that the court-poets spoke tenderly to their lutes of this piteous matter.

It is San Lorenzo, most antique building in Milan, that haunts the minds of the new builders. Leonardo, San Gallo, Bramante, all draw the cupola, as if desiring to surprise a forgotten secret of noble stresses. Strangely standing, interlocked with it, ending on a Gothic arch and a flower-garlanded shrine, are the sixteen columns of white marble in the midst of the Corso da Porte, left lone from the Thermæ of Heracles, perhaps, communing with the cypresses, expressing with the poignancy of all beautiful fragments, like some lines from a great lost ode, the legend of Imperial Rome. Rome here at least—not Byzantium! But Byzantium grips San Lorenzo beside the lucid pillars, San Lorenzo coeval with San Vitale, built of the wreckage of Roman temples, cousin to the ancient basilicas of Asia Minor, quatrefoil within quatrefoil, an octagonal church with a dome, the four main sides closed by semi-cupolas, borne by two colonnades of four columns each. Its peristyle is Corinthian, but it has lost its inner robe of mosaic and gold, save in the old and older chapel of San Aquilino, where Ataulphus, King of the Goths, lies in his great stone tomb, his dust remembering the secret of Alaric's monstrous burial, when rivers were turned aside, and massacre kept the tomb inviolate; dreaming too of the thrice imperial Galla Placidia, his idolized lady. But Galla Placidia is not here. In Leonardo's time, at least, she still sat on her chair of carven cypress wood in the blue night of mosaic within an alabaster shrine at Ravenna.

So you see Leonardo often by San Lorenzo, drawing the dome, for he was deeply attracted by a cupola. It is one of his symbols even, with its reconciling, peace-imposing, evening-star effect, harmonizing all dialects, all religions, all conflicts. He builds little domes along his scientific page sometimes, just as he scatters violets or fair faces, automatically, as if his emotional self desperately seized the tired hand of the scientist.

Then San Eustorgio drew him, San Eustorgio in delicate brick-work, still fragrant from its lost magian dust. It was not the Gothic shrine of Saint Peter Martyr, nor the slender pointed windows, that charmed his mind; but the proud grace of the little Portinari chapel, crying itself Florentine beside the strange campanile, its ocelli, turrets and cornices all exquisitely wrought and sweetly spaced, a ballata in terra-cotta, crushed-rose brick, and almond-pale stone. Within, under the cupola painted in reds and blues, was Michelozzo's famous frieze of dancing angels, svelte and morbid, rose and fair, linked by a chain whence hang bells of fruit and flowers, while the putti swing the same bright tassels in the pilasters, all in blithe pure colours of carnation and blue and green, sending the lyrical Tuscan note of high romance ringing rarely through the drowsy richness of Milanese decoration, like a young voice following its own clear song over a chanting multitude.

Yet did he not linger by that Gothic shrine within, after all, not so much puzzling out the overcrowded sculptured panels as gazing at the supporting figures that wear the secret archaic smile of mediævalism (that secret archaic smile not so unlike his own), whose nobler kindred stood in Amiens and Rheims, queens and saints, and taking pleasure in the engaging contrast between the great Gothic shrine and the arch where Michelozzo's amorini rang the Renaissance elfin music from the bells?

But on most days his feet went, sometimes pensively, sometimes swiftly, like the feet of one who has received some intimation he fears to lose, where Santa Maria degli Grazie stood lovely and kind. Sincere and natural and fanciful rose the church loved by Lodovico and served by Leonardo. Lombard in her soul, with just a Gothic spring in her, yet accepting as a happy gift the new classic kind of grace, she was of true Milanese soil and temper. The Duomo might be to the ruling family a kind of exotic mistress ; Santa Maria was, to Lodovico particularly, as a dear wedded wife. It was a long low church with a triple Lombard nave leading to a radiant choir, and with three apses. Choir, cupola and lovely central apse all are Bramante's, in his most lyrical and gladly decorative mood. The view of the dome and the apse is one of the blithest romantic things in Milan—the flat cupola, the tiers of arcading, the medallions and the ocelli devised as finely as snow-crystals, the broken surfaces of the red lids of the apse patterning fantastic shade. There is much joyous ornament about, of children, musicians, dancers, fruit-gatherers. Lodovico gave his church Il Gobbo for a sculptor ; he filled its sacristy with brocaded and coloured and jewelled treasures, and every stone proclaimed him Duke and Mæcenas ; while the convent garden and pergola, delicately wreathed with vine and set with flowers by his care, breathed him Lodovico, lover of fragile and tender things. In the refectory, on the treacherous wall, Leonardo was daily painting *The Last Supper* as it had never been painted before.

And there was San Stefano, where the Duke Galeazzo Maria, stabbed in the atrium, said, " O Nostra Donna ! " and died. The campanile of San Gotthardo was enchanting, all ruddy with arcading and shafting of marble, by a shrine where another had perished, the mad Gian Maria. This was the most delicate torch-lily among all the campanili, steepled with slender grace, more poignant than the others, more fancifully broidered at the edges of its degrees. San Celso was Lombard, with surprised monsters on the portal, beautiful and simple with star-shaped windows. Bramante had joyously modelled San Satiro, and added chapels and sacristies elsewhere. Sta Maria di San Satiro had " shifted lifted steeps " and a short flat cupola, with outbuilt chapels and many ocelli, and painted pillars within. In the octagonal chamber of low-built San Nazaro were the lordly tombs of the great Trivulzio family so fatal to Il Moro. San Vincenzo was painted with early symbols— alberos, candelabra, lambs. San Simpliciano had a door lively with squat animated figures.

The incense seems heavy in some of the churches, as if no formula could hallow them altogether. For when they mask the sites of imperial theatre, circus, compitum, arena, vividarium and capitol, strange visions of chariot and gladiator and heathen hunt will come through the sacred smoke.

Leonardo the Florentine

The Palazzo del Podesta in the Piazza dei Mercanti was the last fragment of free Milan. Of subject Milan, the dominant adamantine Castello, with the Rocchetta for its uncrushable core, the most sumptuous palace and the most invincible keep in all Italy, was the marvellous ostentation. From the old defence of the Porta Giovia, from the ashes of its predecessor, had grown this city enclosed, this great and gorgeous domain of tyrants. Filarete had planned the Entrance Tower. Giant curtains of masonry now closed piazza within piazza ; it was a majestic quadrant of the earth, formidably willed to be one vast security of pleasure. Its spacious quadrangles were strengthened by four strong towers ; the walls sloped imperturbably solid and smooth and strong. Sometimes Leonardo, whose genius also went into those immense ramparts and circumvallations, draws some great corner of the arrogant bastions : rendered by that vitalizing pencil, it seems aware of its own superb menace. But the Castello was rosy-coloured and many-gated. There were inner courts, there were double cloisters, there were colonnades. There were groves, lawns, pavilions, parks—great spaces to make the dwellers forget the walls. There were streets, squares, gardens, rivers and lakes within the mighty terrain. When Leonardo came to Milan Lodovico kept state in the Rocchetta ; the young nephew Gian, for whom he ruled, had his listless Court in the beautiful Corte Ducale. And until Lodovico was near his end the Castello grew stronger without, and more flowered within. Bramante and Leonardo were always at work on it, strengthening and decorating. In the immense main piazza Leonardo tried trajectile experiments. " This was done by Leone in the piazza of the Castle with a chain and arrow."—While Galeazzo Sanseverino reined up his white stallion to gaze, one thinks, and Lodovico smiled, and Salaino, with the gleaming mass of curls, looking more like San Sebastian than usual, went to find the arrow.

It was a legend, this puissant place. French and Italians dreamed of the great wicked castle as if it were the key-plot of a necromantic history. It was a star-charmed magic citadel, and Merlin might have built it—as the Merlin of the age did help to build it. It was wondrous fair and soft within, they said. It had windows with Arabian-wrought recesses ; vast rooms where beauty danced or played at ball, where fabulous banquets were served by masquers from Olympus, where the blue skies and the green trees had been conjured within and laced together with gilded cords by an enchanter against the hot weather, carven oratories with great crucifixes flowering into jewels, libraries of precious blazoned books, where astrolabes stood on graven stands,

The Aspect of Milan

supported by sphinxes. There, a painted Argus kept a treasury like
the Lydian king's in a figured tower behind gilded webs of gates woven
of iron ; there, the sacristies of beauty held robes from mythic looms ;
there, Lodovico and Beatrice lay in gold and sardonyx ; and the younger
Bianca in a " white chamber sewn with gladiolus " ; there, steeds
could ride up a wide winding stair ; there, in cedar cloisters imagined
with cupids, rare ladies waited for their lovers ; there, in meditated
and plotted waters, deep in the gardens lay, luxurious as Egypt,
the large rose-coloured water-lilies ; there, in a chapel of intarsiatura
rose a clear sound like the sinless voices of angels ; there, the walls
wore tapestries fair as the Sidonian wefts that hung the chambers of
Paris ; there, a ponticella sprang over a lucid moat, strangely and
delightedly bearing a set of painted chambers opening into an enchanted
loggia, the outer wall made of stones faceted like cabochon diamonds ;
there, knights went in white with shoes fit for Venus, and drank of
the cup of Tristan and Lancelot. Swans on the water of the moat,
peacocks on the sunny walls, doves by the traceried windows, and
apes in the rosery ! It was a dwelling created for dukes with dark,
alluring faces and delicate hands, clothed in crimson and white, with
great rubies on their breasts, whose slim, white hounds, collared with
their golden devices, pressed close to them, while on their wrists the
velvet-hooded peregrines shook their gold and silver bells. The last
frenzied duke had made the cunning artists decorate his castle by day
and by night. But now was a greater duke than any ; and the stars
moved singing in miraculous masqué of light and sound at Leonardo's
bidding for Lodovico's glory.

So said the legend, and the legend was true enough. The castle
had an inner rose-robe of wonderful terra-cotta, recessing tenderly the
lovely windows, framing with festival garlands the doors, swinging
cherubim and cornucopias round the courts, brocading chimeras and
volutes on the walls. Arcading and indentation everywhere, the
columns and arches and patterns created another flickering faëry world
in light and shadow. All the great groined and carven place was
softened with silken cushions and carpets from the East, and rose
and turkis arras-cloths. In lovelier niches, where the walls were more
minutely flowered, heavy lions' heads through rich garlands spilt their
crystal in immense basins stamped with imprese. In some of the cor-
ridors a zigzag or waving application of pure colours struck again the
Saracenic note. There was the Hall of Lancelot, where a Visconti lady
had died for love like Guenevere's, for love went softly on panther's
feet about the castle. There was the Sala d'Asse, which Leonardo
had made into a phantom bower, masses of green leaves against which

bright figures shone all golden. There was the beautiful Room of the Doves. And all the halls and chambers were filled with things that every craft had accomplished, chairs, benches, chimneypieces, and bridal chests covered with proud brocades and clasped with floriated iron. The whole place was broidered over with the devices and imprese of the castle folk—Viper, Imperial Eagle, French lily, armed axe-bearing hand, dog and pine, the Scopetta (Lodovico's most decorative broom), the three interlaced rings, the caduceus, waves, lions, doves, flames, the Savoy Cross, the double towers. Il Moro's symbols were everywhere upon this rich casket so nobly locked. And all was in rare order, and fastidiously kept, till the French came.

And Lodovico had caused a fresco to be painted of coloured dancers in the sunlight with a thundercloud in the distance, the device being: " Post Tenebras, ecco spero lusem." Leonardo makes a note of it, without comment. Lodovico thought his picture was of the past. What Leonardo thought he leaves clear enough by his uncommented statement. The Duke's uneasy mind, ever-strengthening his fortress, provided underground passages from wall to counterscarp ; but he rode away out of its gates in the end, leaving the proudest fortress in Italy to be lightly surrendered by a traitor.

The Castello brought Leonardo and Bramante much together. Whether he was strengthening the great walls, or painting the great salas, or decorating the camerini on the bridge which Bramante made strong and fair without, he worked much with the vivacious Tuscan who found life so glad a field for energy. In many pages of his manuscripts Leonardo, I suspect, tries to prepare a little conversation in Bramantesque vein. But in this, at least, he hardly succeeds.

vii

Like much Renaissance architecture, the building of Milan was too often of the nature of *décor*, a matter of erecting splendid but sometimes mendacious façades for the masquerade without, setting the piazzas for the scene, in fantastic points of the cathedral, bastions of the Castello, broidered frontages of the palaces, astonishing encounters of the Certosa. Or rather it would have been too like stage-craft at any other time. For those who lived as in a pageant it was appropriate.

The building materials in Milan were brick that weathered into the colour of pale roses, baked earth like rose-attar that easily captivated the shapes of cupids and garlands, tiles that overlapped like dahlia petals on the sloped roofs, a little creamy stone, far-fetched, that melted dulcet into the harmony of glowing hues. There was also sweet sympathy in the *mandorlato* of Verona, the almond-blossom marble that varied from rose to ivory, and with soft lustre heightened the terra-cotta. Startling glimpses of the Duomo, caught white between the quick-rose and dead-rose fabrics, heightened the fervent setting that waited for its vivid actors.

But Leonardo missed certainly the great compositions of the Florentine palaces, with the enormous eaves that gave a cool hush of darkness to the sunlit strip of street, and invested with a fatal import any mote of humanity that moved on the borders of their shadows. Missed them as values in reminiscence! For pleasure-houses it is possible that the original château of Chambord, whether he devised it or not, was nearer his peculiar notion of a palace. Still, he had a sense of the spirit of place—and Florentine things were best in Florence, as he indicated afterwards to the lord of Mantua. Here was no need for rival strongholds. The Castello was insuperable. Other palaces could imitate only, and could imitate merely its amenities and graces, with their fountained and friezed courtyards and imaged façades, not its flawless fortitudes of towers and bastions. They were but bright pools, reflecting the splendour that overflowed the castle walls. The homes of the Belgiojosi, the Pallavicini, the Melzi, the Sanseverini, of other Visconti and Sforza lords, were worthy of their prince. Bramante had been at work among the palaces also, with his Tuscan sense of proportion arranging right spaces for the happy decoration so natural to the soil. This is the time when he plays with pillars, tempiettos, colonnaded courts and many-angled shapes in singing mood. But Filarete and Michelozzo had also been in Milan. The Medici Bank in the Via de' Brorsi, altered and decorated for Cosimo, decorated again for Galeazzo di Sanseverino, still has some rare tatters of its beauty left. Michelozzo's lovely door of delightful ornament opened on the most enchanting house in Milan, it was said, with its inner court and the three loggie all swung with wrought wreaths and set with terra-cotta medallions. Beautiful enough for Lodovico to refuse Lorenzo's desire to buy it back, since he would give it for a bridal pavilion to the beloved Galeazzo Sanseverino, the spoilt Prince Charming, when he also gave him his exquisite child, Bianca. So there they dwelt; and Leonardo planned lofty stables for Galeazzo's haughty steeds of Sicily and Araby, with columned aisles and chivalric frescoes. The Villa Borromeo, the walls richly roughened with Eastern patterns, an intensively decorated palace, loggia over loggia, with lines of splendid shields between, had frescoes in the great rooms of mediæval ladies at pretty traditional pastimes still sweet to the play of the Milanese women.

Few of the great buildings were yet finished. The façades, being most desired, were frequently completed before the chambers were: they often seduced like shows, as bright settings for the masque. But frescoed and garlanded, cooled with bright waters and green leaves were all those dwellings—Castello and palaces recalling the elegiac music of Shakespeare's Duke of Milan. Luxury lay coiled in them all like that Saracenic serpent, insidious, dangerous, forbidden; and even in the villa gardens without the walls beauty went with gilded shoes, exotic and conscious. Hung with French arras and Persian cloths, twined with roses, couched among white magnolia, rose oleander, and purple, tender bell-flowers, they were expectant of all the Triumphs of Life. The great chestnuts lifted their fragrant rosy candles around them, altars of the spring. The bees drifted heavily across their gardens, drunk from the fields of blood-red clover.

viii

Nevertheless in Milan rose a great building that justified her more than cathedral, keep, or palace, and proffered one noble excuse to heaven for the frenzied luxury of her despots and all those that served them. For, begun by Francesco Sforza and continued by his heirs, planned by the Florentine Filarete, the Ospedale Maggiore stood virile and beautiful. It was not the first hospital in Italy, but it was the first to say: " Come in and be healed, whatever your creed, wherever you were born. Come in if you have a franchise in the kingdom of suffering." This was a more superb monument to Francesco Sforza than Leonardo's proud Cavallo. For it was a recognition that the alleviation and abolition of human misery was not an affair of personal compassion for special cases, but a form of justice due from a state. This great hostel of pain was begun by a despot, dimly urged, perhaps, by some blind half-remorse for the reawakening commune he had subverted, some confused kindness that dwelt in the Sforza blood, even when it was distraught (for mercy would sometimes come like madness on such as Galeazzo Maria), some sweet compulsion from his duchess, a true Visconti of the finer kind, who lived her life between cloth-of-gold and penitential cilice. It was not a mere concession to the human travail he lived by, but a reconciling gesture towards the divine rights of suffering—divine in the dæmonic sense, not because it is a way to Paradise, but because this kind may alter Earth to very Hell.

In the wind of the Renaissance Pentecost all the human qualities flamed together, not only these mysterious and fierily beautiful energies men dreamed they had caught from the tombs of Greece and Rome, but also those wistful and tender emotions that drifted from the lilies of the fields of Galilee to take strange and pathetic shapes in the catacombs,

The Aspect of Milan

the deserts and the cloisters, where in uncherished stone they often broke into miraculous red flowers. Even these mediæval sweetnesses, though they sometimes survived as if sun-blinded into magical superstitions, could be changed and charged by the new illumination of energy. The dim pressure of the past pities of saints, interpenetrated by the flamelike vitality of the Renaissance, began to work out a kind of social as distinguished from a religious mercy. Ruthless as were many of the glowing and terrible tyrants of the time, they now and then considered ruth as a part of statecraft; and admitted the idea of justice, not so paradoxically, because they were more interested in Greek authors than in the Gospels. Pity was less a heavenly miracle in the Renaissance days; but from antiquity the Greek-learned tyrants apprehended that there might be some respect for this justice, a superb concept more valued in Plato's *Republic* than in Christendom. The people begin to count for more. They do not exist merely to be exploited by those who require of them a religious adoration. In Italy they make and unmake their tyrants, they suffer them long for quaint reasons, for superstitions obscurely wise, for their magnificence, their courage, their strange pathos of astonishment at their dying moments, above all for their beauty, their singular achievement. And, indeed, out of the divine and brutal energies of the folk many of the despots themselves rode through spears to splendour. They are of one flesh with them, and are exalted in their magnificence.

In the Renaissance, with all its wars and cruelty, the social conscience awoke uneasily as never before, even in the time of the guilds. The glittering pyramid of mediævalism was beautiful in its way; but the theory of the overlord's responsibility asked too much from crude human nature. It was founded on false values. The education of a knight was a lovely lyrical thing, but it was based on an artificial privilege, since many a youth with " the gentle soul " could be for ever debarred from sword and lyre by a mere accident of birth. The serf could but accept serfdom as a divine dispensation, equal with his brother in Christ perhaps, but never this side of eternity, whatever his loyalty. Pity was a holy mystery, and mercy came like an exquisite passion of love from one person to another. Something was lost, indeed, when that mediæval rapture of divine pity no longer flowered miraculous as the almond-rod; but that there is too much risk about a miracle is a conclusion with which long-suffering is familiar. Now the sound idea spreads that there is something wrong, something accusing about intolerable pain. It is reasonable of Montmorency in France to say that the Wars of the Barons are bitter for " the poor people " who know nothing of their causes. It is reasonable of Cesare Borgia to govern his Romagna carefully. It is reasonable of Machiavelli to write his *Prince*, not for the sake of the prince, but for the sake of the distracted people for whom the vision of a republic is still too incredibly fair, he thinks. It is reasonable of Francesco Sforza to build his great hospital for any sick person whatever his creed or nationality. Emotions certainly become nobler when they pass over the dubious sills of personal thought into the world of great ideas ; and compassion is a higher state than pity. This dim stir of a social conscience, begun even in the cruel Renaissance, was stifled again when Reformation and counter-Reformation, after locking in labyrinthine byways slippery with blood, forked out awhile into two great bigotries whereof one, at least, kept some immortal sweetness with her ungrudging communism of the Bread and Wine. But the reactions of Spain and Austria strangled for long the natural tolerances of Italy, and starved the soul of France ; and social compassion had become insane with tortured suppression before it broke bleeding through the Revolution.

Meanwhile, the Ospedale Maggiore had risen in the Sforza city, acknowledging the terrible authority of suffering, the extremity of pain which purifies the victim from blame, and cancels all indictments. It had been a Visconti palace, with some additions ; but Filarete remade it. So the house of mercy grows from the very cruelty of Milan ; the building went on when Olgiati was dying through eternities of torture.

The vast Lazaretto also, glowing in deep-red brick and terra-cotta, was made by Lodovico and by Ascanio, for the subtle priest had the great way also. The whole moist plain, alas ! was fretted with fever and haunted by plague. These maladies were endemic, and Lodovico from his keep denied not the darkness as well as the felicity of his duchy. It is one deadly visitation of plague, indeed, that makes him dream of wider streets and regulated ways. He accepted his responsibilities.

Leonardo's interest in the Ospedale and the Lazaretto was merely scientific. One finds no gleam of social conscience in him, even when he is planning roads and waterways. They are merely novel problems for his ingenious mind. For in his diamond perfection he knows no attraction towards the rich dark quarry of humanity. He seems himself a casual wonder, a great firebird in a bright lone Araby of the soul, and, when he passes to Heliopolis, his Phœnix-tree will perish. He often designs architectural fancies, absentmindedly, on his mathematical pages, as a kind of relief, Oriental temples and vast palaces. So with a shock of surprise one finds he suddenly draws a lupanar—but never a lazaret. The other constructive problem amused him more at the moment.

But he would go to the great hospital, as to that of Florence, to watch the processes of slow decay, and to observe with what intolerable spasms and slipping gasps and grips of reluctant farewell the soul leaves the body—while the invincible magnetism of his eyes and hands effortlessly soothed the last pangs, perhaps. Or, with the terrible clairvoyance of the dying, did they divine the cold indifferent curiosity of the soul behind, and relapse with a shuddering foretaste of the unimagined chill of death ?

Think of him more amicably, recognizing his Florence in the noble façade of the Ospedale, just touched with the pointed Gothic, where the architect remembers the arcades of the Bigallo, and the cornice of the Rucellai palace. The archivolts of the window bays are divided by gracious colonnettes ; consoling decorations of fruits and flowers and volutes and children assuage the eyes. These are perfectly contained in their given spaces ; and the medallions in bold relief obey the law of measure. Whatever gift the Renaissance gave was given with beauty ; and hospitality for penniless patients meant carven windows and flower-set cortile.

ix

But what was the may-city without its mayland, the region that was one orchard everywhere, with the rumour and undersong of running water, sweet and chill and pure, sometimes drowsy as a charm, sometimes softly hesitant, as when it lapped through the insomnia of Augustine at Cassisiacum ? As in all fertile regions of soft rain and rich earth, the ageless spell of sympathetic magic coiled round the roots of things. Magic in the city, heathenism in the campagna ! So said the Inquisition. A bacchante rode a goat on the door-border of San Aquilino's chapel. Witches were often young in the Renaissance time, when the old gods came again, and women young and beautiful perished by fire, because, naked and wreathed with vervain, they had seen the goat-foot god, or worshipped Diana in the guise of silver-veiled Hecate. Or under the crescent moon, while the grain-shaped fireflies communicated light and strength to the glittering wheat, they had sought the herbs for Thessalian potions, like Mandragore that gives ecstatic sleep, or called on her strange daughter, Aradia, as she went past in the air, that they might know the voice of the wind, or alter water into wine, or give beauty to the beautyless and love to the loveless, and tell the secrets of the hands, or learn the dread incantations that put " ligature " on those they hated. For Leonardo, the Herodiad, incarnation of Lilith, was the principle of lone ecstasy ; without the walls she was Aradia, queen of the witches, daughter of Hecate, the virgin-harlot, who could fly through the darkling air as he desired to do.

As well as Milan did Leonardo know Pavia, where rivers ran together among the woods, once the rival city of empire in Lombardy, now but a beautiful pendant to Milan, a minor pleasure capital for the dukes, where a Visconti had fulfilled a vow to build there a palace for a dwelling, a garden for a pleasure, a chapel for devotion. The chapel was also to be a tomb for his pride ; and the Certosa was long a-building. One day Leonardo rode, in some state, with the distinguished architect, Francesco di Giorgio Martini of Siena, to consider the plans for the Duomo of Pavia, with which Ascanio Sforza was much concerned. Finding a great library in the Castello, and a university full of ardent experimenters in the new sciences, the artist was loth to come away, and tarried and tarried, indulging " the worst voluptuousness, which is an hydroptic and immoderate desire of human learning and languages."

The Certosa, the church-sepulchre of the lords of Milan, was now steadily becoming the most sumptuous thing in Pavia. For the proud have ever demanded a palace or a pyramid even for their dust. Bernard of Venice had worked on it, and Lombard masons, and the Campionesi from the lakes, who had also laboured on Galeazzo's cathedral. But the Northern influence did not here prevail over the Lombard. There was an hour when the Certosa was to be made in the likeness of the Duomo of Milan ; then it changed back to the Romanesque mood, and at last found even a " classic " inspiration. The variation of design only causes a light dissonance of style, a little hesitation in the rhythm which really qualifies pleasurably the excessive sweetness of the decoration. Amadeo and Dolcebuone and Borgognone had impulsively massed and composed, not so much as imaginative architects as instinctive builders, with a kin and kind feeling for their materials ; and Boseo and his successors maintained a harmony of happy faith, a tradition of soft fervour which lasted till about 1507, when a cold wave of doubt and melancholy seems to sweep over this decorated bower of death ; and the chisels and brains become weary, insincere, and mechanical.

But rather than a bower of death it still stands like a palace of love, at least for considering eyes. As seen from the Cloister of the Fountain it is a world of covered arcades, on round broidered arches ; bright figures, indeed, might lean and listen to the water from these pierced galleries, while behind them the fantastic cupola rises on pillared degrees to its charming lantern. The façade was simply designed by Solari ; the main design is pure and clear. That simplicity became a fortunate background on which Amadeo and Borgognone let loose the revel of a fancy both delicate and gorgeous. No cold Carthusian place is here ! It is covered as in a rapture with princes, saints, sirens, angels, loves, shields and fruits, all caught in revelling vine and acanthus.

The Certosa has perhaps the most brocaded stones of all the brocaded Milanese places, for it is the most hybrid, and Lombard, Gothic, Venetian, and Classic visions are all confounded in this one startling page

The Aspect of Milan

of illumination. The least door, the least window is perfected for the bygone and luxurious tyrants whose violent heads appear in roundels above the portals. It is loaded and overloaded with delightful imagery, with patterns like that of the children rhythmically climbing a grape stem, grafted on from an ancient vine. There are bas-reliefs of angels turning the leaves of a great book amid the flowers; there are ocelli of lucid pierced marble, medallions on low relief as on ivory; there are windows that recede within border on border of differing broidery. There are wonderful lavabos, antique vases; there is a lovely frieze in the sacristy. Pillars vanish upward in acanthus harbouring the heraldic Viper. The arcades of the Little Cloister have circles looped by garlands wherein swing the little loves. But the Little Cloister in itself is serene and classic as a lovesong by Meleager, though it is all arcaded and turreted and set with lampada. The receding storeys of the Certosa are flowered with ornament, softening the bold mass and coffered arches. It is carved and embroidered to the last lavabo. This prodigality of decoration has a kind of refreshing zest. It is the blithe and delicious genius of Amadeo that lifts the whole thing into a rapture. Rich, sweet, voluptuous, he retains a wild lyricism that dissolves all the ducal arrogances into a motet well sung by cupid-children.

Within, the strong pillars rise into semi-ogival arches on arches; but there are coloured friezes and rich pendentives and capricious chapels. The Certosa glowed in all the rosy tones of brick, tile, and terra-cotta, except where it was inlaid with creamy marble from Lake Maggiore. And it was set in a fragrant hush, for Gian Galeazzo, an accomplished æsthete, had decreed that only twenty monks should live in his foundation, since a sumptuous work of art should be set in a crystal solitude. In those days the great Certosa lay lone in its gardens and pools, so it must have seemed at times a kind of Pavilion for the Sleeping Beauty, lost in a music of *Soir des Roses*.

It was in 1497 that the church was consecrated by a cardinal in his glory, with processions of bishops, protonotaries apostolic, abbots and ambassadors, among specially woven hangings of blazoned heraldries. Leonardo must have gazed at all this flowering of Milanese fancy, effortless as the opening of the blooms on a great camellia-tree, with an indulgent smile, thinking how strange and arduous must seem to these folk his disciplines and preparations for the great Steed. Then probably he turned to the quivering reflections in the pools, thinking, as always, how much more beautiful were all things in the mirror of Narcissus.

The Castello of Pavia stood in a wild and immense hunting-park, destined to become a tragic scene for the chivalry of France on the day that its king, captured in his brocades and jewels, so strangely imagined that he had not lost his honour. It was another Sforza monument, another great space of towers and courts and sweet waters, with merlato crenellations attractive with terra-cotta, frescoed with pictures of the chase and of rest from the chase. There was a noble armoury in it, filled with elaborated breastplates, greaves and swords ; and also a precious library of illuminated books, some of them brilliantly plotted by Fra Antonio de' Monza, who could lure the Leonardesque quality which permeated the arts of Milan like a strange new dye within even that altered but persistent mediæval art of illumination. Both armoury and library were pastures for the curious artist.

The old, old university was an amicable place for Leonardo, as it had been for Petrarch, that very different Florentine. Columbus had been studying there in 1477 ; but if Leonardo was interested in Columbus we have no sign of it, though, after all, we have no complete record of his sympathies. It was not over-peaceful, the university : the students were so lively that the Duke had to interfere. In the great shrine of Saint Pietro in Ciel d'Oro lay the rare chaffered dust of Saint Augustine, with the Lombard king who ransomed it devotedly mouldering at the coffin foot. That certainly annoyed Leonardo rather than otherwise, for he has bitter sayings about the relics of saints. At the corners of the pointed, crocketed, gabled shrine of Saint Peter enchanting figures bow their heads and smile over secret violences and provocations. But the steadfast antique riding statue, called *Il Regisole*, was still erect in Pavia, and with deep attention he considered it, and drew its paces within that arena of amazing steeds which his pencil was creating for the good of the great Cavallo.

Not so far was Monza, where dove-led Theodolinda, blonde and lovely, had with her slight, sceptral hands assured all Lombardy beauty and peace awhile, and given it to Leonardo's Baptist ; and built a fair great church here. Still she lay in her cloister of death with her fan, her comb and her golden holy book, for a bitter saint had not yet cast her out because the Pope who gave her the Iron Crown of the Sacred Nail had forgotten to canonize her.

But dear to Beatrice, Lodovico, and also to Leonardo, was Vigevano of the vines, where the courtiers went to breathe the wilder air, and to forget the world's game in pastorals set in gardens, woods and welling waters, pastorals and idylls rich as double rainbows. Galeazzo Sanseverino also had a palace there ; and Beatrice went maying with all her ladies and her squires, clothed in deep emerald against the pale emerald and the rose-purfled branches and the immaterial violet of the spring. Or her coloured people lost themselves in the very cunning labyrinth in her garden, to meet again where the bright dome of the Eastern pavilion, designed by Leonardo, marked the centre of the maze. They lingered by the garden-pools and watched the collared swans; and drowned their eyes in the sunset as they sat in the Ladies' Loggia, while the Duchess' singers, fair and young, made a clear requiem for the dying day; and in the morning they sent to the great falconry of Bramante for their splendid hunting-birds. Leonardo as well as Bramante had also worked at the Sforzesca of Vigevano, and all the delights of the Milanese Castello were repeated here, less ornately, more blithely perhaps, since the slim-shafted windows opened on Arcady.

> " I know a little garden-close
> Set thick with lily and red rose
> Where I would wander if I might,
> From dewy dawn to dewy night,
> And have one with me wandering."

That was the burthen of Vigevano, for the squires and ladies.

Vigevano was serious as well as lovely in its existence. The Duke had his model farms, where the beasts of the field were so fairly housed that the French were lost in amazement thereat, and Vigevano was like a vast nursery for the waters and the wines and the silks that charmed the cities of the plain. Experimental science was here at work to ease and fertilize yet more that facile and bounteous earth. About 1498 Leonardo was chief engineer, and Vigevano, with its great aqueducts, was the centre of his canal work, one of his engrossing activities, for he was the most illustrious of the quiet dynasty who governed the waters of Lombardy. Also that his eyes were attentive to the growing vines and the golden cocoons there is testimony. Water, wine and silk were all close friends of his.

x

To other retreats Leonardo followed the Court. To Cusago, the Duchess' own playing-place, given to her with the most beautiful love-deed ever blazoned with spendthrift ecstasy, so strangely given again to the child of another, she being dead, Cusago, a long, low, coloured house, an old Visconti dwelling with a storied marble door and a romantic cortile, all Romanesque arches and fretting ornament, whence they especially rode out to fly the great proud falcons, conscious of their pride of place as any duke, and where they wound the hunting-horn thinking of Roncesvalles! To Abbiategrasso sometimes, plain, ancient, peaceful, where Lodovico had learned to make Latin orations and sing

French songs. Sometimes to Chiaravalle, the abbey-church, with its great dim-rosy campanile rising oddly stepwise with flashes of white, couched among flowery fields, camped in luminous air, sometimes remembering soft ways heretical, a Cisterican cloister that once had nearly lapsed into the sweet freedom of Thelema, because it befriended a strange Bohemian lady who certainly lived kind and pure, and who at worst had her dream of the Holy Dove. In the marshlands near flew the stork, and the lone white heron meditated precious against the sunset. Farther away was Saronno, Cecilia's domain now, where the Duke had been used to make his retreat, by the little church of miracle. In that undulating and smiling country of knolls, and woods, and lisping streams, vineyards and fields, broken by tender intercessory Ways of the Cross, villas and castles lay happily everywhere, built square and low round their courtyards with one tall tower. In the tales of Bandello one is constantly aware of the rare cool villa-land, where ladies and their courtiers and poets talk in dim adorned loggie, among the flowery gardens, with water welling and plashing and laving the brinks of summer, sighing a little in the soft rose-taken airs of felicity. "Few gentlemen but have some castle or other in the champaign country or hills or villages," says the canonical novelist. And no ladies but had their summer pavilions, evidently. It is a different villa-land from the Tuscan retreats of philosophers, where women pass pale among the distances of cypress and olive, merely like remote Ideas of beauty. The Platonism here is not Marsilio's and Pico's, but Bembo's lovely depravation of the doctrine, so touchingly apt to that wistful sense of women which is "with their senses all mixed in."

Leonardo knew the villas before Bandello began to tell stories in them—especially one, soothing and leafy, and tempered to his rest, at Vaprio, between Milan and Bergamo, on the Martesana, where the sweet eyes of the child Francesco Melzo promised a farther fidelity of adoration. And he went to talk with other artists and gentlemen at Marchesino Stanga's embroidered house at Bellaggio, which he had helped to decorate. Also he fared far north to Chiavenna and the Valsossina, evidently bent on tasks of fortification on the edge of the duchy, where he gazed on precipices and cascades falling like bridal veils, and knew that nothing seems so unearthly soft and sumptuous as the faëry smoke of foam on black rock. There the mountains stood at watch among the pines and larches, and the campanili sprang to piercing stars like heavenly spearsmen. And at this time, or another, he ventured on some alp of eternal ice where the sky was "dark overhead, as I saw it."

The Aspect of Milan

But it was in the magical lakeland that much Lombard beauty invaded his art. Como he knew, a stage-city, where rich classic ornament is Gothically used, a place of masking façades and terraces, where a happy cathedral was growing, easily, guiltlessly, charmed with its own dionysiac and faunlike imagery. He went south and east also, to other cities of the plain. For fossil shells he sought on the hills of Bergamo, where the warrior, Colleone, had lived his life among the brown walls flowered with wild red valerian, amid a little court of scholars, secure from the dangerous great city he served, and where he had so beautifully sepulchred his flowerlike Medea, slender, pure and vivid, with long throat and fine faun's ears under her crownlike hair. He knew Crema with its daffodil tower. He knew Cremona, that ancient Roman town, pale-rose among the white-blossoming mulberry-trees, where in the fantastic cathedral the great bridal of Francesco had shaken the bells at last, where the martens gathered round the towers in the pure carrying air, and where the sweet viols of the Renaissance were to grow into amazing carven cotes of rare sound under the hands of men whose very names are amber harmonies. He knew the lonely Abbey of Bobbio, where long ago Saint Columban, beautiful, beloved and pensive, had escaped from Burgundy to found the Irish Rule, and leave an intensive library from which the Celtic serpent of the illuminations might escape to intercoil with the Lombard and the Saracenic snakes, and Leonardo take infinite diversion in slipping his own peculiar spiral into the symbolic twist. Lodi and Parma must have seen him. Even to Mantua, gazing at red sails on the green lagoons, its palace rising from the sedges, he went once at least, for he brought viol-strings to Isabella. Grave and sweet Verona, proud in red marble behind the cypresses, drew him sometimes. To Piacenza the pleasant, with its great town hall, half-Moorish, half-Gothic, Leonardo wrote one of his most arrogant epistles, pitying it somewhat for desiring great figured gates when no artist was at once fit and free to undertake them.

The distant lakes were—too much almost—a secret paradise for the gods of flowers. There lay sickle-shaped Lugano, and noble Maggiore, and Lydian Garda which Catullus had beset with the sound of mourning flutes. The islands sent fantastic peaks above the waters and those meads of Proserpine, for they were still unlevelled and untamed, but he saw citron, and orange, and jasmine flower impossibly sweet, and magnolia and camellia drowse like the bride-chambers of Eastern queens ; and divined Daphne couched rose-white among the inordinate rose pavilions of the oleander. And here he heard stories kindling like

ancient moon-fire in the track of an immortal wonder, the sibyl of
the caves, the loreley of the lake, the singing siren in the jasper twilight,
the Madonna of the Rocks, who charms the soul, soul of Hylas, soul
of Narcissus, to her enchanted floor, and locks it in her trance, the
queen of an ultimate secret not known to philosophers, set by the still
pools and the lapsing rivers, and the shining meres and the sea-edges,
and the rare ethereal springs in the forest, to draw men away from
their heady mortality to a delicate death of dreams. All Italy is enthralled by the siren in the waters, the queen-sibyl in the hollow hill,
Fata Morgana, Morgan Le Fay, the Lady of mere Wonder. But in blue
and green worlds Leonardo found her, the dancing Herodiad fallen still
in her ecstasy by the waters, and with Florentine irony and passion he
charged her Lombard face.

xii

Be it again admitted that the Milanese architecture of the Renaissance
is decorated, kind, smiling, excessively sweet, temperamentally romantic.
It is not aware of the pure canons of any ideal of beauty ; but it is
sincere to the emotional, changeable soul of its city. It does what it
likes ; but its caprices are lovable. And the traditional Lombard
dignity, as well as the borrowed measures of the Florentine masters,
kept these in harmony. The " soave-austero " note was not in Milan,
nor in the rich landscape around it ; and its architecture grew truly
from the soil. It was lush and disarranged like its meadows. The
matter of which it was built was not crystallized, and its organic fer-
tilities had not been baked out of it in the kilns : it seemed to go on
putting forth a radiant folly of flowers and fruits and little fauns after
it had been shaped into churches and palaces. There was a natural
sympathy and a natural magic that seemed indestructible once in Milan.
Florence appears almost to have fitted her hills about her, and laid the
pressure of her æsthetic will on the delicate austere landscape of her
Tuscany. Or Nature at least seems there to have imagined a harmony
with her children. But Milan accepted her place in the natural world
with submission : she struck her roots deeply in the Lombard earth
and drank its moisture with the wheat and the fruits. Soft furry things
like the little rabbits that scuttle about the pages of Bona's *Book of Hours*
seem at home in the painted scenes of splendour. In the carved pulpit
of San Ambrogio the bambino lies between the ass and the ox, quite
alone and content with his companions. There are correspondences and
sympathies in Milan. The walls of the Duchess' garden fall down on
the night she dies. That seems appropriate to the story in such a place.
Lodovico set his wide new streets ; but Lodovico's son saw the grass grow

free between the stones. The city had to lapse but a short time into a fit of anguish and despair: the genius of her earth hastily set to weaving over her a shroud of emerald and red again, green grass and red poppies.

So its Renaissance architecture grew too many sunflowers and torch-lilies. There were too many gadgets about it, lifted cups and candelabra, and little towers and rondels ; but they were lovely gadgets, most intricately wrought, for the carvers' concentrated passion was faithful and unfailing. Milan had no building incorrupt and absolute like a star, such as the Campanile of Florence, the Mangia Tower of Siena, the Baptistery of Pisa. There was no page so tenderly illuminated as the façade at Orvieto. Nothing so strangely combined an inward singing of individual passion with an exterior of Roman severity as the Temple of Rimini. But the Castello, the cathedral, the domed churches, and the palaces of the Beautiful Way of Milan composed a singular, soft symphony of pleasure. These vanishing arcades, these open galleries, these lidded roofs composed of dahlia petals, these pierced ocelli, often delicately enclosed in squares of airy design, these lifted lampada and glad campanili, like gladiolus in a red August, the polygonal flattened Eastern cupolas, with the wrought lanterns, the great bastions of the Castello, the charming falsified façades, all the rosy ornaments and flushed sweetness, with the carved ivory glints of the cathedral, were wholly transfused in the humid blues and greens and dove-coloured glamours of the atmosphere, till the flowery, leafy place was as rich as a frieze of Persian peacocks, a city set for the gold-shod feet of Amor in red raiment, a capital of Aphrodite, even as it was seen by the adoring doom-dreading eyes of the historian Corio.

xiii

Leonardo's mind refreshed itself with memory of the pure spaces and the restrained embroidery of Florence, which, however exquisite, never seemed more than the patterned hem of her fair-fluted tunic. He remembered the Florentine economy of grace, as of an angel delicately drooping with closed feet on quietly burning pinions through the evening air. He remembered the singing note through the City, the wild sweet lyricism of Tuscany that made the sacred Imitation of Hellas a live new kind of beauty, so that the sense of far clear pillars of perfection, the breath of Athenian violets, stole into the spirits of all artists, making them more than artists.

But the drowsy rosy beauty of Milan suffused his senses. There was no absolute perfection in Milan : but there was matter for perfection. He was happy there. His unconscious and more dæmonic part might go wandering in a dripping sea-world of reverie among the cool water-flowers, seeking Our Lady of Wonder, a Uranian Aphrodite that kept her caves like the bowers of the moon. And all the multiple activities of his unparalleled intellect had room in Milan, so much more ductile and docile a city than Florence, with needs so manifold, and with a sovereign so " magnificent " in the true Renaissance way.

In that over-moist, too-fertile country, fever, plague and leprosy crept hooded within the city, and Lodovico, one repeats, accepted the responsibilities of his duchy, whether or not he had thieved it. His lands owned him as he them. He was destined for his place. It is a pity that his weakness of title unnerved him, and strangely invalidated by lack of courage the natural right which was so much the prouder authority. He could think regally ; his ailing and dissolute young nephew could not. That would have been enough in Ferrara, Rome, Naples, Bologna ; but Lodovico had the scruples which a tyrant cannot afford. Still, while he ruled, he shaped his duchy well. Round the cathedral still clung the webs of the narrow streets of the traffickers in precious things, the embroiderers, the goldsmiths, the workers in blue and scarlet, all those intent on the suppliance of the " luxury for God," and the implied luxury of sacred princes. But many of the streets were wide and stately ; and the place was leafy as Ferrara, and the tall white lilies grew along the way from the gates to the Duomo.

Lodovico intended greatly by all his cities ; and, even more than his predecessors, he recognized his lordship of the waters of the plain so well that his neglect of the Alpine gates might easily be forgiven him. The dukes before him had instinctively recognized the task that the mere vision of their territory imposed upon them. Theirs to inter-marry the bright tributaries of the Po, and send them limpidly and gaily through the responsive land. Even the French who overthrew Lodovico, after they had muddied the lucid streams and defiled the castle in the first brutalities of invasion, took up the inheritance of the canals, and Leonardo's water-wizardry with it. But Lodovico and Leonardo together had begun an immense work, with the Naviglio and the Martesana.

One of the layers of the primeval earth under Milan is the great coralline-reef that runs across Lombardy. Leonardo, who sometimes beheld the whole plain " in the dim backward and abysm of time " as a vast inland sea, with the Alps and the Apennines chasing the brim of its cup, may have gazed across the moist sunken land, all lakes and lakelets and rivers, and caves remembering something of their old sea-magic, and found it change back mysteriously in his gazing, as all things shift and dissolve and re-create before the eyes of trance, to a green water-world, with Milan branching like a pattern of rose-coral through the dense.

The Aspect of Milan

rich aquamarine, while a rare sound of siren-singing grew unearthly, inaudibly, without vibrations, into a charm in his brain :

> " Christ keep the Hollow Land
> Through the sweet spring-tide
> When the apple-blossoms bless
> The lowly bent hill-side.
>
> Christ keep the Hollow Land
> All the summer-tide !
> Still we cannot understand
> Where the waters glide ;
>
> Only dimly seeing them,
> Coldly slipping through
> Many green-lipped caverned mouths
> Where the hills are blue."

The god who kept that Hollow Land, however, was painted long after by Leonardo himself, and his brow had never been pierced with thorns.

Leonardo made his own projection of his Milanese scene like another who never saw Milan, but to whom, as to all Italy-drunken Elizabethans, it shone incredibly romantic. Like a rosy may-tree, indeed, against emerald skies did it beguile the distant eyes. Like that image of fragile rose-coral branching through dense beryl did it seem to the drowned men in *The Tempest* as they rose to life. We can see " fair Milan " like a radiant mirage of domes and towers on the far horizons of chrysoprase, over the green and purple seas, from the smooth yellow sands, immaterial as the other masques of the enchanted island. Rocks and seas and enchanted lutes of Shakespeare ! Rocks and seas and enchanted lutes of Leonardo ! Exquisite magical projections of water-garlanded sea-forgotten Milan ! Shakespeare was Prospero. So in a way was Leonardo, masque-master, lord of the elements, lover of Ariel and his music. Both knew usurping dukes and gracious princes, awakening girls, ruffling lords and heedless jesters ; both were impatient of Caliban. And Leonardo would have consented with all his imagination and all his scientific certitude to that defunctive music of Prospero's dirge of the visible world :

> " The cloud-capped towers and gorgeous palaces,
> The solemn temples, the great globe itself,
> Yea, all which it inherit, shall dissolve,
> And, like this insubstantial pageant faded,
> Leave not a wrack behind."

This was after a masque of Ceres and Iris, altogether true to the Lombard world of foison and rainbows, for the heedless divination of the poets tells the essential truth that often eludes the cold inquiries of the geographers.

Chapter iv

Lodovico and his Friends (1)

i

MANY of the "léonardistes" of to-day would fain disperse the vision of Leonardo the companion of courtiers. But the testimony of his own time is strongly and unanimously to the effect that his personality was pleasing to great lords, and that his conversation was delectable to them. Indeed, he was regarded emphatically as the divine and the unique Leonardo, because he could so ally distinguished manners with a marvellous artistic capacity. The absorbed savant of the manuscripts was hardly suspected by any; and these dishevelled notes, various as they are, were not intended to be in any sense diaries of his crowded existence. Many are said to live a double life: Leonardo's was multiple. He was a kind of revel-marshal at the Court and yet an anatomist at Pavia. He was lost in mechanics, "the paradise of the sciences," and also in the hollow paradise of the Queen of the Sibyls, in the Court of Venus which was Lodovico's.

"Durant toute sa vie, il plut étrangement à tous les princes," says Jovius. It would be no compliment in these times to record this of a painter. His art and his conversation would instantly fall under suspicion of banality. But Renaissance despots kept their eminence, regrettable if you like, by passion of spirit and sheer exercise of *virtù*. They were personalities of the most diverse and cultivated kind, used to Latin and Greek from childhood, versed in ancient philosophy, whose devotion to the arts was no ignorant fashion. In mere intelligence they were the equals of their artists; and, like them, they often destroyed to create. Lorenzo, Lodovico Sforza, Chaumont, Louis XII., Cesare Borgia, Giuliano de' Medici, Isabella d' Este, the Cardinal Ippolito, her brother, Francis the First, were some of the princes who were friends of Leonardo; and they were worthy of the honour. Splendour and intelligence were Leonardo's exactions; splendid and intelligent these people were. Even Louis XII. had a bright hour in Italy.

Lodovico Sforza was the ideal prince for a Leonardo, for he was the most magnificent and spendthrift tyrant in Italy, one who dreamed of a crown, and who certainly had regal dispositions towards his duchy.

Lodovico and his Friends

Painting, architecture, engineering, sculpture, masquerade, music—he wanted them all; and Leonardo's aptitudes were as versatile as his needs. True that Leonardo once drafted a letter explaining that his salary was in arrears, that the two once nearly quarrelled concerning Leonardo's long delay over the Cavallo, that the artist's comment on the Duke's tragedy is bitter-brief. But the manuscripts are not intended to be a record of Leonardo's emotions and psychical reactions; and, though he had a straitened period when Lodovico was driven to exhaust his revenues for the Swiss mercenaries, he lived in Milan with some state and luxury; he did not leave it without provision, though he had no gift for economy, and he found no other illustrissimo to use him so variously and so tunably again.

Constantly occupied with castle-work, cathedral-work, and with irrigation, collaborating with Bramante in the masques and shows of the Court, finding imprese for the crests and sleeves of cavaliers and ladies, designing their tourney raiment, their girdles, their sword-hilts, discussing horses and birds with the owners of the noblest steeds and falcons in Italy, matching silver lyres with chivalrous musicians, painting beautiful amorous ladies, Leonardo was in constant contact with the Court, even when he was at that part of his labour which, according to himself, most needed solitude, for Bandello's bright account of Leonardo's method of painting *The Last Supper* has the vivacity of the eye-witness. Besides, he lived like a courtier. He, too, had his horses, musicians, his curled pages in rose-and-green slashed with silver, his embroidered gloves and boots of fine Turkish leather, his perfumes, his furred and silken raiment, his city and villa life. His young pupils were chiefly of good birth and of personal grace and beauty. It was this delicate ostentation people saw and admired, though Michelangelo loathed him for it. Like many another artist, like the hapless Balzac, who considered " a certain regal luxury the natural right of a man of genius," he did take fine contacts as his due. (Corroding contacts he accepted with a macerating zest when he sought them, as in the dissecting-room, not otherwise.) Indeed, there must be a certain nervous craving for subtle flavours and soft touches in a body disturbed and wasted by the desire for beauty, and by the absorbing creation of *phantasmata splendida*, which considerably explains why many artists of lower degree endure poverty only by drugging themselves into insensibility. They should be content with bread and shelter no doubt; but genius heavily refuses a grudged existence. The wine-coloured, the silken-feeling, the rose-smelling, the lute-sounding things of life are organically necessary; they warm the chilled imagination. They are psychical food. So Leonardo would have his wine, his silk, his rose-and-green colours, his chalcedony ring, his pretty

141

pages, his lutes and his sensitive horses. It was only that he required a measure of grace from life. In nothing was he libertine save in expense of time.

So his mind reflected this coloured world of Lodovico's like that fascinating toy in which both he and Alberti, who first invented it, took pleasure, the camera obscura. In its illumined pool it received the images of rare princesses and fine lords, with a world of roses and peacock skies behind them, though softened and rarefied till it was transubstantiated into precious smokes and clouds of pale carnation and dulled lapis and faint emerald. But his nerves, steeped in the fragrance of this luxurious world, became rich and heavy, and drowsily dripped their secret honey into the dark cells of his heart. Quite clearly Milan was pleasurable to him, and Duke Lodovico generous. He could be much an autocrat in this passive city where no strong personality had set precedent or authority in art. He could create his tradition—and end it. Milan was indeed a nest of herbs and spices, the phœnix-tree for his strange imagination.

ii

Lodovico Sforza with a whole desire and a dubious mind had pressed subtly into the dukedom. Half-heartedly, because he had enough conscience to feel that his brother's child had a true claim on himself, even more than on the dukedom, which was only doubtfully any Sforza's, after all. Lodovico could plot and evade and betray in diplomacy like any other; but, for an Italian tyrant, his nerves were hesitant. He was the kindest as well as the subtlest of Milanese dukes; he had imagination, mercy, generosity. Like a poet he dreamed of mythic crowns, crowns of rare dream-conquest, Liguria, Lombardy, Italy. So had Gian Galeazzo meditated when that craftier assassin, the Plague, slid a sickening hand within his breast. So was Cesare Borgia about to meditate. But Lodovico had neither Gian Galeazzo's basilisk concentration nor Cesare's inflexible will. He was hampered by his emotions.

The Sforza family had a romantic strain, and a sort of human kindness rare in that period. Even the founder, the great soldier Muzio-Attenduolo, who leaped mightily from that fierce family of poor land-owners that lived by fighting, to capture the heart of the fickle Queen of Naples, and earn a fiery-forcible surname from her, tempered the severe discipline of his men with stories of the paladins, and tales from Greek and Latin historians, and died all armed in the rushing river vainly trying to save a drowning page. Some wild innocence redeems

Lodovico and his Friends

these desperate people : every now and then their story is crossed by quivering lights like happy children's tears, sudden irradiances of sacrificial tenderness.

His son Francesco married Bianca Visconti, the natural daughter of the reluctant Filippo. Desire for a crown was in the Sforza blood ; it had been in the Visconti mood for centuries. After he had saved the Golden Republic of San Ambrogio, by defeating the Venetians as its Captain-General, he was borne riding to the High Altar as its lord. Domination ripened his kingly qualities ; and not alone did the great Ospedale testify that he was magnanimous, pitiful, and courteous. Violent as he could be when his patience broke, he was, for a con-dottiere and a despot, really humane. His wife, Bianca, loved him, fought for him, ruled for him. With her white jewelled hands she soothed the soul of the city ; and her alternations between penitential cilice and cloth-of-gold were in the Milanese as well as the Visconti mood.

Her sons were educated by great scholars, Filelfo in particular, at Abbiategrasso, in history, the humanities, princecraft, with a passionate care for body and soul. When they stood round King René of Anjou, singing their French songs to him, these dark lithe children with the stars caught between their lashes, they seemed to come carolling from a Milan that might indeed be Miraflores.

Yet the eldest broke her heart, drove her to Cremona, and made it easy to die. For Galeazzo proved that the Visconti madness was stronger than education and Sforza sagacity. Indeed the virus seemed fiercer in the fresh Sforza blood. Perhaps he was spoiled by excessive compliment : perhaps that attractive cynic, Duke Borso, who sent the boy home " satiate with Ferrarese pleasure," was much to blame. Sensual, vainglorious, cruel, with the terrible Visconti cruelty, he yet had his peculiar dream of splendour, and a distorted kind of imagination. A " fantastic," an " extravagant," a " névrose," a decadent was Galeazzo, with his hawk nose and his great black feverish eyes, with the white hands so excessively cared for ! He composed a masque of inordinate magnificence, and, calling it his retinue, led it to the treasurable house of Lorenzo in Florence. Quick enough in many ways, he may have felt some rebuke from the more nobly ordered beauty to his gilt and coloured meinie ; but the dust of gold shed from that legendary procession infected the veins of Florence with the passion for luxury, some grave critics said.

For Galeazzo artists wrought in fear of death, and the Castello swiftly took on decoration. He offered his people abundance, and many festivals ; but he was an insane oppressor, and the mania of his desire struck like lightning, leaped like a tiger about the city. So, with classic orisons, Lampugnano, Olgiati and another Visconti slew him. But the people raved and wept for Galeazzo Maria, lying in the cathedral in the golden shroud given by his blindly adoring wife : and the conspirators died in torments.

They did not rave and weep for Lodovico, who widened their ways, and watered their fields, who could not bear to see an execution, whose loves at worst were amourettes, at best irrepressible indulgences of a romantic tenderness, whose record was clear of rapes and sodomies. But Galeazzo Maria played the extravagant in all men's sight : he had the confidence of the sacred prince. The populace liked those hands, kept like carved ivory, liked his revulsions of pity and tenderness, loved his great excess of splendour, had a sort of compassion for his madness. The perverse logic of some of his acts of justice had a dramatic quality. So irrational is human nature, in dealing with which nothing is ever reformed except possibly the reformers! Rénan's instinct was right in supposing that Prospero was a failure when he returned to his dukedom. In the " mood of the people " the feminine note disconcertingly predominates. It indulges the spoilt princes of splendour if they can smile sweetly and carry themselves with an air, and it stones the too logical prophets who cannot.

Lodovico smiled sweetly and carried himself with an air, but Lodovico kept his dream to himself. He had the reticence of Gian Galeazzo ; he had his brain for great plots, but not his nerve nor his quiet diabolic patience. His brother's debile and witless boy was alive and loved him : he had deposed the silly Bona, that " dame de petit sens," and ended the able Simonetta. He ruled as Regent, the Duke of Bari ; he might have so continued if he had not married Beatrice. He was a Visconti too, as fine and insolent an autocrat as any. His excessive magnificence is not a trait of the parvenu : the Visconti all had the cæsarian splendours. But he dreamed too much of the assassin's dagger ; he never moved without an elaborately-arranged bodyguard ; he hid himself in his glory, and never cried out in pride or anguish to the Milan he loved. So he seemed only a stranger.

He was not born the sacred prince in fact, and that shook his imagination and his nerve. Galeazzo Maria, said his daughter Caterina, who resembled him, " did not know fear." But Lodovico, sensitive, delicate, had a morbid and pathological fear which to his enemies seemed cowardice. Like Macbeth indeed, he could not " trammel up the consequence." He needed the confidence of some outside sanction. " Homme très sage, mais fort craintif, et bien souple lorsqu'il avait peur." So Commines described him. Usurpation was an easy and

Lodovico and his Friends

common trade in Renaissance Italy. The bold did not reason about it ;
Lodovico did. He was not the sacred prince : but he proved he was.
He said he was the first born after Francesco assumed the dukedom.
He said he was at least mystically elect by the heavens, the fortunate
favourite of the mysterious stars. He said he had the Imperial In-
vestiture ; he said he was called by the people. He said his nephew's
little child was not fitted to succeed his father in such a troubled time.
He should have argued nothing, like those who held Naples, Ferrara,
Rimini, and the cities of the Romagna.

Nevertheless he had a sovran mind. He had " very rare perfection,
and was not unworthy of the name of mild and merciful," and broken
lights of idealism played round his vexed purposes ever since, as a boy
of thirteen, he had been chosen to lead the Milanese to the crusade
of Pius II. But not only fear trammelled him ; so did affection. His
quivering sensibility outdid his scheming brain. Like a modern he said
to the great Trivulzio, whom he had alienated to such deadly purpose :
" Who can tell why he loves one man and hates another ? "

Because Galeazzo Sanseverino was young and beautiful, and beautifully dressed, and as brave a soldier as he was a debonair gallant, Lodovico
concluded that he had the mind of a general. Lodovico, who had himself the quality called " charm," also exquisitely loved that rare glamour
in others, and readily believed that the charming would do all that the
powerful could. His cool brain surrendered entirely to personalities
picturesque and enchanting, not realizing that, to those who dream in
the webs of their own fine spinning, far-off battles and sieges are only
a sound in the distance, and that a dramatic lance-thrust, or a death
like a gallant song when the dream is shattered, is all the devoir of
the decorative. Lodovico's own mind could move outside his personal
charm : he supposed the minds of others did likewise. So he had a
useless though valiant general, and a traitor castellan, and ambassadors
more effective at jousts than at councils.

Most of all he was betrayed by his own psychic inhibition and
weakness, like a modern neuropath. His diplomacy with France, Venice,
Florence, is full of shifts and evasions. He breaks treaties, and changes
alliances, though indeed not more notably than any diplomatist in any
country at any time. IIis allies and enemies alike considered him
perfidious. It was not so much that he planned deception and confusion,
as that he was at the mercy of the fits and starts of his fears. Of a
planned slaughter, like the " bell' inganno " of Sinigaglia, he was quite
incapable. He fluctuates with the need of the moment ; he is uneasy
and confused like a sensitive child who has stolen a toy ; he knows
himself naturally a great duke, and is fretful at having had to cheat

K   145

over a title. And his very horror of blood urges him into more ruses and defeats.

So, like all who are afflicted with spiritual confusion and quivering nerves, he puts on the armour of fatalism, and depends on a mysterious power outside himself that cannot be affected by the mortal contagion of fear. He had omens and superstitions in the blood ; all the ancient magic of Milan, persecuted and harried in the woodland, stole in bright raiment round the castle. Ambrogio da Rosate, physician and astrologer, regulates the moments of Lodovico's life more carefully than his pulses. When Leonardo confides to paper his extreme dislike of both physicians and astrologers, it is certainly his devious way of expressing an opinion of Ambrogio, who must have crossed him frequently. A journey could not be begun, nor an embassy received, nor a marriage consummated, without the augur. It is the stars that make and mar Lodovico to a degree unimaginable to us, who find them at once so much more familiar and so much less intimate. Life has perhaps become a less brilliant business since we have shaken " the yoke of inauspicious stars " from our flesh so world-wearied in a duller way, and realized that no gods set our horoscopes because we are not worthy to have stellar fire in our veins.

Lodovico was strong in the faith of astrology. He was the beloved of his Star, a rosy sumptuous Star ; he was bathed in that rare influence ; he was the darling of the heavens, and he followed his radiant guide till, grown " fey " and insolent to the gods, it betrayed him to all disaster. He could not recover pride or faith after the first shock of doom.

As a human being he was paradoxical, fine, corrupt—a sensualist, but a delicate one, no maniac in the matter. Lodovico illustrates the famous paradox of Burke that vice loses half its evil in losing all its grossness. He is a sweet and subtle satrap, something barbaric, something sophisticated ; and the look of the faun that glides about the Milanese lovers of this date hides behind his eyelashes. His princely head on medals, medallions, manuscripts is easily recognizable and attractive. The hood of hair hangs heavily over a definite profile, and the eyes are set in a dreamy importunate manner, regal eyes of soft fire that condescend to burn imploring incense.

He looks charming in the votive picture of the Poldi-Pezzoli Museum, sitting up in bed, his artist hands clasped for the healing Madonna, with the expression of a good child. Even when the chin becomes heavier with age his features keep the beseeching sad Italian sweetness. He could combine a princely bearing with manners seductive, solicitous, caressing ; and the jealous Beatrice found it more bitter to have rivals than did any great lady in Italy, while the rivals found it

Lodovico and his Friends

sweeter to surrender to Lodovico than to any other great lord. Within a wonderful border of gryphons, sphinxes, lions and loves, on one page of the *Sforziada*, an exquisite angel holds the medallion of Lodovico. The deep cap of hair is arranged in three smooth waves, the eyes are those of a dreamer, the nose is finely aquiline, the lips are sensuous and suppliant, the proud chin is masked with flesh. He is idealist and voluptuary, the Lodovico that can adore a pictured Madonna whose child blesses a rose, and who is Cecilia. His is the mood behind Keats' *Ode to Melancholy*. If Lodovico asked for pardon in his musical voice, he was not often denied.

But if he loved women overmuch, he did love them kindly, if not constantly; and cared for them when passion was over. He was a finished artist in love-attitudes, a seeker for elusive sensations. His was not the mad desire of a Malatesta or a d'Este, not the cruel mania of his brother. The ladies who moved him were lovely, and troubling to the imagination. They were bowered in beauty; they had lyric eyes and singing lips and dreaming looks. There was something of the chase of the well-beloved in his mood; and when Beatrice came, enchanting by her youth, her laughter, her wonderful zest for experience, and the splendid courage which was as natural to her as breathing, she certainly conquered his heart. He delighted in the fiery d'Este princess, but the dreamlike grace of his Lombards had become a sweet opiate his anxious nerves could not altogether surrender. He was faithful to her " in his fashion." But that sweetly sensuous temperament of his had too much of the Orientalism of Milan in it. He needed other types—he would gather the camellias. It was wrong, but natural; and the camellia-tree grew sumptuous within his golden castle. He loved much and often, and was penitent, like his city.

His glowing sensibility is of a piece with the gorgeous fantasy of the Court he made; it is indeed the peculiar rose-golden glitter that intertextures the picture. He may be distinctly eclectic in his tastes, and show a disposition towards the *outré*, the bizarre, the Asiatic. He wished to send to the King of Hungary a statue of Dionysos, some gleaming Indian pheasants, and the goldsmith Caradosso, a characteristic gift. Nevertheless the insolent ostentation of his brother became soft splendour in him, for he had a fine enthusiasm for beauty. With his emotional flux and reflux, his chills and hesitations, his dreamy senses, his impulses of love and revulsions of dismay, Lodovico had more of the artistic " temperament " than Leonardo himself. The feminine side of him was strong. In his gliding shifts, his astute instincts, the shudder in his soul, his appetite for personal luxury, his propitiations and contradictions, his sympathy with mere coloured play, his infatuation for his Star, the maddening way in which his considered policies were wrecked by a momentary impulse, Lodovico was feminine. Like a woman's too, his longing to create hours of such perfection in visual and audible and tactile beauty, such symphonies in colour and music and love, such miracles and harmonies of quivering gold, that they might storm and flame over the pale borders of time and ravish immortality by sheer intensity, their vibrations of viol and violer and violet, hautboy and clavichord, crossing from excited air to imperishable ether !

But the poetic temper of this dreamer of crowns had its masculine power. He could think like a king. The Castello was only the bright core of his ambitions. Aware of the jar and folly, the disunion of the warring cities, he could imagine Lombardy, Liguria, Italy, at peace under one lord, the diverse communities bringing their separate magian offerings to the altar of beauty. Of cities he dreamed, and of their waterways, and of imperishable buildings. He saw himself sometimes as the Egyptian Hermes leading his people to some perfect peace of magnificence; and altered the Visconti Vipers to the Snakes of the Caduceus.

This bizarre, subtly conflicting tyrant was lord of many things, including Leonardo's energies. Lord and artist were well matched. Leonardo, when he came to Court with his great and slightly mysterious reputation, looked a little like a golden magician with a lyre—smiling lips and ironic eyes. The dark and mobile face of the Duke flashed often in appreciation of the fair Tuscan's wit in snatching profits of power and pleasure from the chancy world of things. Poets and scholars were not so dazzling as at Florence, maybe. In other arts and sciences, at least, he was well served.

Lodovico's temperament was Milanese in its love of dreamy pleasure, though his intellectual grasp and great range of vision made him the rightful successor of the less lovable but mighty Gian Galeazzo Visconti. How much the personality of the prince counted in the communication of the Lombard mood to Leonardo it is hard to say. The Duke's passion for gay and amorous imagery, as well as his nervous need of impregnable fortifications, naturally affected the work of his architects and his decorators. Lodovico's superstition, Lodovico's love-affairs, Lodovico's extension of his delight to the very shows and baubles of joy, could but give Leonardo a tolerant amusement. But he painted the Duke's ladies for him, most lovely daughters of Herodias ; and from Cecilia at least he may have drawn some imaginative pleasure. He made rare masques for his splendid hours, and designed fantastic raiment for his friends, and painted cupids in the Castello when he decided to bring home a bride. And I do not believe that he did or said anything to annoy the Duke's faith in astrology, and alchemy, and the like. His own exasperated

Lodovico and his Friends

opinion he confided to his manuscripts ; but all his patrons were interested in magic, and he himself was popularly regarded as something of a wizard. The borders of natural science and magic were not yet fixed ; and Leonardo, always ready to fit his austere scientific knowledge with a fool's cap and bells, and amuse his friends with mystifications, seems to have been on quite friendly terms with professional wizards and soothsayers. He was not minded to be a chill martyr for scientific truth, and probably thought, and thought rightly, that no human soul has ever been convinced by argument, but only the more confirmed in his own opinion.

For the Lodovico who was building or continuing the Cathedral, the Castello, Santa Maria delle Grazie, San Celso, the cloister of San Ambrogio, the Ospedale Maggiore, the archiepiscopal palace, the university, the Duomo and the Certosa and the Sforzesca of Pavia, he was most serviceable. For the Lodovico who linked the canals and the tributaries he was enthusiastic. With the Lodovico who wanted the Cavallo he was almost on terms of emotional strain, so much did their desire for absolute perfection in this matter at once conflict and agree. For the Lodovico who was for a time the most splendid tyrant in Italy he had admiration, for his own golden opportunities were part of that splendour.

Both, besides, were sick of the same malady ; both were inhibited by a nervous fear, much better corrected in Leonardo's case by a great self-confidence. But a weakness that, in the world of art and science, suddenly unravels great tissues of impalpable labour, and creates heartbreaking tragedies of negation, in the world of material gestures, and those the gestures of a Renaissance city, must become evident in fire and blood and irreparable loss. Leonardo was not sympathetic. Lodovico and all his passion of glory, his feverish hours of love and music, his beautiful feats of magnificence, and his crafts of wisdom or folly, in the end meant nothing to him but a unique opportunity that had failed him. There were many who thought it unseemly that the French should bury alive in the oubliettes of Loches the quick soul and the gracious body of a prince who had let the knightly Bayard go so freely, when that courteous enemy overrode into his camp. But Leonardo was making friends with the conquerors. The spoils to the victor, said he.

iii

Renaissance Milan was one of the great capitals of pleasure, and celebrated by its chroniclers as a City of Love. It was like a rosy-sailed bucentaur moving from Paphos to Naucratis, with riotous myrtle garlanding and starring the masts, as in the ancient story.

spendthrift lilies along the streets, golden women like the lilies on the balconies ! It was a city of dedicated amorists. Theirs was love desirous and pagan, as at Naples and Venice ; but from the northern cycles of Charlemagne and Arthur, from the emotional Virgin-worship of its mediæval history, it had caught and kept a romantic sweetness of mood, foreign to the bright animalism of the sister-cities. The lovely ladies of Milan were famous for their grace and dulcet skill in loving. It was not Dante's terrible flame-clad Love they knew, though, like Lodovico himself, they often read the story of Francesca in the rare sad afterglow of sunset ; nor was it Leonardo's white Eros brooding apart in the ambiguous cloister of his own great folded emerald wings. It was Love the delicately shod, the lover-loving, the dreamy, gracious god of soft kisses and sighing surrenders and tears of delight, who goes where shed roses and murmuring waters are, and sits plucking chords from a lute in the Duchess' pavilion while the lovers are drawn through the labyrinth. Or, with curled hair and a jewel on his brow, he dances the torch-dance in the Castello, clothed like the peacock, till the music and the lights are as one, and at his own moment he inverts the flambeau.

> " da me basia mille, deinde centum,
> dein milla altera, dein secunda centum,
> deinde usque altera mille, deinde centum.
> dein, cum milia multa fecerimus
> conturbabimus illa, ne sciamus."

That was the mood of Lodovico's Milan at its moment of exaltation. In the Plain of Lombardy, Virgil and Catullus had sung sweet and bitter ; and still the witches, like the witches under Thessalian crescent-moons, brewed potions for luckless lovers and wasted waxen images for the frenzied. When Roman Emperors called for redder roses they meant Milanese roses, darker and more fragrant than all the other roses of Italy. And in Milan, as in Ravenna, the dead lovers still called from their graves in Catullus' own Latin for their tithe of such summer roses. There was still a trace of the great epithalamies of old in the ritual that brought the virgin to the white-hung bride chambers of the Milanese. Even that Augustine who had once wept for Dido dead of love had his true-love with him in Milan, and parted loth at heart from her dear company. Even Ambrose etherealized passion into mysticism when he sang of the Beloved feeding among the lilies :

> " Jesu, corona virginum
> Qui pascis inter ilia
> Septus Choreis virginum . . ."

Lodovico and his Friends

Bramante, devising his new Canonica in the great Church of the Bishop, disturbs the hallowed dust of two lovers, and sets the court-poets singing. Even priests, unchidden by Ambrose, had claimed love as their right in Milan, let Rome do as it would. From such a marriage indeed sprang the bizarre and impassioned heresiarch, Dolcino, and all his daring apostolate, and his mystic marriage with the incomparable Margarita, and the triumph of their terrible end. For all those sweet and serious heresies that too earnestly concentrate on the immemorial Asiatic mystery of the Holy Ghost, moving dovelike round the Dove, fervent doctrines of grace, flown here from Southern France, some of them, found a covert in Milan, though drawn by all the questing hounds of Dominic.

Now with Lodovico, a lord of lovers, for a Duke, with life keyed to the drums and flutes of an invasion of beauty, at once barbaric and Hellenistic, the dreamy Lombard ladies and their decorated gallants, meeting in the dance of life, with longing, lyric eyes, caught hands and kissed, as it is natural to do at the love-feast of a god, and that god Dionysos, lord of ecstasy. Dionysos—Greece and Asia ! The city was flushed like a sunset, and within the sunset all the sirens were singing.

In 1495, the chronicler Corio tells us, Milan was the most beautiful Court of Cupid. It was thronged with lovely youths. But—" fathers gave their daughters, husbands their wives, brothers their sisters," and all ran heedlessly to " the amorous hall." Yet Love never quite lost his great ways in Lodovico's " excelling Court ": he never can lose them while he keeps those romantic manners we now despise, with such a rage of regret.

iv

There was an ape, actually, in the rosary ; and a smiling, innocent young satyr in every gilded squire who still used the phrases of chivalric love, as they did in Milan. Yet here the women counted for more in creating the atmosphere than in any other Renaissance city. In Florence they either earned admiration by qualities like those of men, or they had some strange symbolic value as if derived from Diotima. In Florence the only woman that counted greatly was the City herself; her Court and Council were of men. In Ferrara, Mantua, and Urbino great ladies shone like sovereigns and enchanted as queens ; but their courts were masculine in character, and they carried themselves like elegant cavaliers. In Venice they were a part of the golden pomp ; but their soft murmuring lives smelled of sandalwood chambers like the lives of odalisques. In Rome, cardinals sighed sometimes for a " court of ladies," because cardinals wanted every kind of social pleasure. But Lodovico depended on beautiful women for the decoration and enchantment of his Court and City ; and, though he liked them gracefully intelligent, even more he desired them as vessels of the Circean charm, spell-weavers of an imaginative art in which only rarefied and exquisite senses floated like moonflowers.

The feminine principle had been strong in the shaping of Milan. Aphrodite had been mighty as Ares and Mithra. The chalices of Monza had been made from a precious idol. It seems as if some of the bells of Milan had been molten from bronze images of Venus to ring a dubious vespers through the green eventide. The Virgin had kept the doves and soft roses and sweet complaisances of the goddess. The cathedral had arisen to Maria Nascentis, and the processional cross kept the green-flaming emeralds of Aphrodite buried in its gold. The loveliest of the churches grew for Our Lady of the Graces. She was sung as the Shade of Paradise, the Fountain of Living Water in the Secret Garden, the Green Branch of the Dove, the Close of Lilies. And behind rare forms of rose-red Aphrodite and rose-white Mary moved the great car of the Mighty Mother herself, claiming the city as she claimed it of old, tolerantly sharing its moods with Mithra, shaking it with her dark ecstasy and entrancing the features of the youths to the sweet Syrian mould of Atthis in a mystery of violets.

The names of Drusilla and Agrippina, fair and sinister sisters of Caligula, accomplices of his mad hierogamies, are written on its stones. The violent beauty of the Empress Justina was fixed in the annals of Milan with that of her petulant young Adonis of a son, as in an ivory diptych. Thrice imperial Galla Placidia, rarely white in the purple of a dying dynasty, hatefully beloved by a brother, ravished and throned by turns, had moved, a goddess, by the noble barbarian husband whom she did love. Amalasuntha, delicate, pale-gold sovran of the Ostrogoths, who, for her fine affectation of arts and letters and the perversion of her boy's heart to imaginative delights unfit for a warrior, had lost son, crown, and life, had dreamed in Milan. Lombard queens had held it like a cup in their tapered hands between their long jewel-plaited hair. Theodolinda had crowned it with burning iron ; Rosamond's brooding eyes had carried covered fires of death through its gates. Not far off was a strange tale of a Papessa, and a Gospel of sheer love to Saracens and all heretics, sealed with a flaming end, avenging Abélard on Bernard in an Italian Clairvaux. The Visconti women were warriors as well as lovers ; one had died for love in the Hall of Lancelot, that great lord who has a train of desperate lovers to follow him, white leaves flying through the red drift of hell. Valentina, white and strange, whose robes were a legend, rode on her broidered palfrey with a rich host into France, to work Italian magic on a mad king, and to cry vengeance for a fantastic dissolute husband; and, so riding, took with her, unconscious, the luck of Milan. Another Valentina took arms for her brother. There was the beautiful dauntless princess called Regina for her pride. Bianca fought for her armed lord, and prayed away his sins. Fierce flower of Visconti and Sforza too was the famous Caterina, when she sat in white brocade on her tall cathedra at Forli, talking to her golden lover in the window-seat, her fair madonna-face forgetful of the blood-lust that had seized her victorious, and would seize her again.

But Caterina was not typically Milanese, though she was pure Renaissance, the kind of beautiful young Amazon, the Bradamante, the gallant rider in silver cuirass and casque they admired, as a variant on their Greekish figures of David and Perseus. The Milanese ladies were not exactly mediæval now; but, if the new Hellenism could be found in them, it would be the sought Asian Hellenism of Miletus and Lesbos. They were famous for their dreamy grace, their *air d'aisance*, the liquid tenderness with which their silence faded into speech. They were not over-facile like the blanched and gilded Venetians, nor over-difficult like the composed Florentines. Their faces were shaped from the running waters of a sweet melancholy by the moon-goddess, the Artemis out of Asia, the virgin-harlot who loved Endymion in secret silver ecstasy. They went " with the moon's beauty and the moon's soft pace." They were " sad with the whole of pleasure." The humid air keeps the pure oval of their faces smooth and soft, in the dissolvent wet twilights the hair curls and quickens and springs and thickens like a precious waterweed—as if all for Leonardo's pleasure, since he had an obsession, almost, for luxurious curls.

Still the women steadily fingered the doom of Milan, with more of Lilith, more of the unchanging feminine, slipping like a bright snake in their souls, than in their sisters', brilliant and armoured in the restless bright cities of Platonism. They were for centuries perfect in the art of being women, sophisticated in offering rare moments of rapture like flowers from their secret rose-tree, white magicians in a city of magic. The Florentine had her roses; they were small, pale and exquisite—like Botticelli's, " small, but roses." The lines were indestructible as the iris-lily's. Flowers in Florence were enchanted into the eternal shape of a symbol. But Milan's were mortal—dark and heavy, with a subsidence of delicious petals into a divine abandon of colour, perfume and dew.

> " Roseleaves when their bloom is shed
> Are heaped for the Beloved's bed."

The Milanese are sensuous but not sensual. True, Bandello's stories are often of some hapless " possessed " creatures, children of a dangerous ecstasy perverted to mania, ladies like the Countess of Cellant, of Greek blood and fatal flesh, of the terrible Pandora. The emotionals have their *âmes damnées*, of course. Besides, Bandello wrote when Milan was a broken city, thrown about among enemies, and when the fine folk, as usual, went to sensual extremes, possessed by the one cynical notion that the time for pleasure was brief. But the beautiful women of Lodovico's great years moved, most of them, in gracious ways. Their beauty was so dreamy that it came tenderly about the soul like the music of their clavichords. It was like the given perfumes of those roses, it was like great wines. It had a flavour rather than a substance, and a bouquet rather than a flavour. And the bouquet might be a soul. Under those heavy lids, burthened with their own sweetness, sunken like drowned stars in the pellucid eyes, hidden like vervain in those soft breasts, was a mystery made of the stories of saints and tyrants, the litanies, the dances, the Persian odours, the dead lovers who craved the live summer's roses, all the passional part of Milan. Within the pure oval of their faces was harmonized the beauty dreamed of by north and south, east and west, in the orchards of the snow, and the oases of Araby, in the pale-rose pavilions of China, and under the wild swans' flight over Celtic islands lost in emerald-violet seas.

So Lodovico had an æsthete's pleasure in different types of beauty. Beatrice his wife, and her famous sister Isabella, charmed both his eyes and his thinking heart with their imperious bearing and their fiery Estensian ways, their edged sweet wits like the diamonds and daggers of their house. But Lucia—Cecilia—Lucrezia, beautiful Lombard camellias with their suborning sweetness, " gracious silences " or low-fluting speakers at his will, with their antinomian innocent gaze of antimonied eyes, were the true daughters of Herodias, whose heavy lids and secret lips were irresistible to Lodovico, and who were recognized even by Leonardo as priestesses to whom he might confide, like a mysterious votive gift, like the *baiser de paix* of an appreciative enemy, the irony of that riddling smile. He found and elaborated the type he needed for his symbol long before he saw La Gioconda, and finely smoothed her destined head into his ideal masque of grace.

Generations afterwards, a descendant of these ladies passes into literature. In Milan does Stendhal's most ravishing woman sparkle in the formalism of the Austrian Court, looking " like a Herodiad by Leonardo da Vinci," and playing with Fabrizio before he is old enough to hurt, a Fabrizio mignon and sweetly pagan as the boys that gaze from the pictures of Boltraffio.

But, when love lives in chambers of luxury, beauty sometimes takes on the strange air of a procuress, and Leonardo perhaps nearly assumes

Lodovico and his Friends

the surprising vizard of Sir Pandar of Troy when he paints the young Cecilia as the Virgin in an odour of roses for Lodovico's cedarn oratory. The artist merely took some æsthetic pleasure in the half-sensuous imaginative confusion. To him Cecilia was a beautiful thing giving alms of her beauty to the desirous, of whom he was not, though he always preferred her to the Duchess, it is evident. Besides, in the new evangel, the perfection of beauty was its own chastity.

V

The first lady in the Court had few smiles for Leonardo, when she was brought, without hurry, to her destined place. Yet the Estensian vitality of Beatrice quickened the whole Milanese languor of pleasure: her true Renaissance zest in living wrought up the coloured days into dramatic moods, wild jest and tragic earnest. Of a haughty and violent blood, of a city early aware of the new humanism and the new irradiance, in many ways the fiercest and finest, and the most poetic city in Italy, all swords and flowers, Beatrice, though not so glittering in wit, so perfect in poise, as her famous sister, being younger, more passionate, more fitful, yet moved so frankly enraptured, as with parted lips lifted at the corners, a Renaissance Erigone in vine-broidered brocades with her grapes turned into rubies, down the lanes of gold and over the lilied meadows, with such a rare enthusiasm in her dancing and singing and hunting and mirth, that others smiled to see her play, and called her " the sweetest lady in Italy."

It was through bitter weather and swollen floods that she came from the red towers of Ferrara, to halls of music, masque and banquet, and the dark bridegroom who betrothed her in her cradle. Like a child she came in her great golden raiment, a pretty child in a play, to a husband not young indeed, but handsome, princely, debonair, loverlike. She was like a dark clove-carnation to be crushed on Milanese armour; but she had a will of steel to find the joints in that armour. Spice-flower and dagger—it was Beatrice's way! Lodovico, a little pleasure-weary, was touched, charmed, amused by her flashing spirit of delight; then captivated by the audacity of her courage. Isabella, whom he would have wedded had she not as a child been promised to Mantua, could not have so moved his heart, though she might have been better for his head. Isabella would have understood more wisely how to hold Milan: she would have orchestrated the colours and crossing musiques of the Court into a more stately, less feverish symphony: she would have ignored Lodovico's amourettes as she did the flagrant infidelities of her swart little Gonzaga. As for Leonardo, he would certainly have been still more busily employed ; there would have been more pictures and fewer manuscript notes.

Lodovico had Beatrice, and loved her in that divided way of his. The Estenian princesses are both beyond reproach as wives. But, while Isabella loved herself, Beatrice surprisingly loved her husband, and loved him with the passion of her terrible and splendid dynasty. As a child she had been captivated by a romantic figure, and her wedding was consummated with the sweetness of an artistic seduction. Being a Renaissance lady, she forgave the past of a husband much older than herself, and gladly accepted his beloved natural daughter Bianca for her dearest playmate. But, unlike most Renaissance ladies, unlike her sister Isabella, and Vittoria Colonna, who differently defended themselves by a deliberate blindness, having once seized her bridegroom's heart she refused to share it. The counterpart of Cecilia's vest of woven gold she would not wear. Cecilia, rare enchantress, still hidden, against promise, in the vast Castello, had to go, richly dowered, with the ducal ciphers on her marriage coffers, to an aged bridegroom, having no mind for the alternative of an elegant convent, since Lodovico's child lay under her heart. The Duke, cloyed with dulcet compliances, loved the bitter-sweet for a change, loved Beatrice too much to anger her, loved her as no other Renaissance lord loved his lady ; and with passionate penitences laved his incurable infidelities. The allure of her soft, irregular, babyish face, her infantile absurdities and wild games, alternating with splendid courage and steady companionship in troubled times, her passionate ways of being child, lover and mother, playmate and ambassador, with equal fervour, never ceased to hold his attention. Even her gaucheries, her girlish ways of sulking, her fierce hereditary jealousies, her candour in dislike, amused his sophisticated mind. She was a girl, and she was in love ; she was a d'Este, so she was all fire and flower. She was soft as a dove, fierce as a haggard falcon.

She was his mascot, his fortune, his prestige ; she seemed to have taken from heaven his sumptuous red Star, like his best-beloved ruby, to carry in her little hands so stiff with rings. She had courage, mirth, pride, vanity, love ; and she had a sweet voice. Whether she rode a-maying with an emerald company, or hunted the boar so recklessly that she faced her wild quarry alone, or went flushed and in her greatest brocades to make Latin orations, with a quiver of sweet cadences, to the courteous inimical patricians of Venice, or danced all the dances of France and Italy with a ritual passion before the King, she did it " with her whole heart," and bewitched the throng with her airs of young privilege.

Lodovico and his Friends

She was a great lady all the same. Dusky and rose-coloured, a soft plump child looking best in her curls, she spoke with Kaiser, King and Doge, and she spoke well. Hers to ride through the angry city when the people growled and Lodovico's nerves were in panic : hers to dance her heavy heart to death. For though Lodovico loved her dearly, he loved all fair things too well, so he went murmuring like Saint Augustine : " Give me chastity, but not yet.'

Did she too much desire to be the first Duchess in Milan ? Young Gian Galeazzo was a rather dissolute boy, pretty and gracile till sickness faded him, loving his hounds and horses, unfit to rule, pathetically adoring his uncle. Lodovico had wedded him with extreme pomp to a proud and lovely princess, Isabella of Aragon—a folly if he intended darkly by his nephew. But Beatrice and Isabella were cousins, and so the deadlier rivals. At first, indeed, all the young people were happy together, and Beatrice hung over Isabella's baby, declaring she wanted no other. The charming merry-making lasted till Beatrice's own son, born in a room hung with silver brocade, and couched in a golden cradle, was hailed with ringing festivals and large amnesties fit only for an heir to the duchy. Then Beatrice found it a moody matter that her dark splendid lord should give even a nominal precedence to a debile boy, and that she in her glory should yield to a girl too haughty or too witless even to make a power of her beautiful face. Gian Galeazzo died, grieving for his uncle, away riding in jewelled mail with the King of France. There was a demonstration, and Lodovico was asked to be Duke in title now, of Milan as of Bari, the times being too troubled for the reign of a minor, the infant son of the dead prince. Lodovico had it not in him to be a direct murderer, one feels. Whether, irresistibly held by the will of his Duchess, he simply allowed his nephew to die, or refused to admit to himself that others might help the patient deathward, or whether, as is quite possible, the young prince perished of his malady, remains a matter for speculation. It was at least convenient for Lodovico that he should die. Situations that seem unthinkable at first to suggestible minds become conceivable, and then possible, and at last quite natural, if they be steadily presented by veiled eyes and caressing lips ; and even monstrous things seem sometimes to be normalized when they are irreparably things done. So there was a doubt as to Lodovico's innocence, and the shadow of accusation fell across the flowers.

Well ! Beatrice danced too much, desired too much. But she seems always a high-spirited child, astonished that people are wounding and wounded when she wants their ducal caps, more astonished still that she herself should be wounded in the soft stealthy pressures of the love-game in Milan. There is a constriction at her heart: the Viper has bitten it. Not all her pride of place and her unmitigated queenship will console her when Lodovico's eyes have looked tenderly into the love-locked face of her maid-of-honour. So she keeps her sad vigil in the Chapel of Santa Maria delle Grazie by her playfellow's grave; and the tears of her suffering soul fall through to the dead sweet breast of Bianca, who never hurt anybody; and then she is clad in her brocade of flying white doves on a red ground and her cuirass of jewels for the evening, and dances herself into agonizing death. Little avail Lodovico's long days in the black chamber of lamentation, and the hundred tapers burning silver in the darkness where she lies in her most golden camorra, and the hundred masses sung to quiet her restless soul, little the lovely tomb where she shall be sculptured her sweetest.

Beatrice as the lady of splendour was what mattered to the Court. Isabella Gonzaga had to make her Mantua exquisite rather than dazzling, because economies and even avarices were necessary to her effects. But for Beatrice, to be " amantissima del lusso " was to find, as in a fairy tale, that every fanciful desire came true. She was ingenious in marvellous raiment, "novarum vestrium inventrix." The gold and silver threads were burdened with milky pearls for her: preciousness with preciousness wove her bright sheaths; there was a rich romantic contest of gems about her; she glowed ardent among the glittering fires. Her wardrobes at Milan and Vigevano were like the sacristies of great cathedrals, filled with chasubles of velvet flowers, dalmatics of cloth-of-gold, jewels like the rose-violet balas-ruby, jewels with names and histories. Her stanze were golden and perfumed; her horses were clothed in blazonries; her chalices were crystal flowers; her dishes were fired with bright fables; her embroiderers were the most skilled in their craft. Her singers and violers were coaxed and stolen from all Italy, and fetched from Flemish lands. They were beautiful as doves and lyric as larks; they stood singing and violing round the pools when she feasted out-of-doors like young Narcissi. Jacopo da San Secondo was her chief violer, he who was yet to sit enthroned on Parnassus as Apollo by Raphael's art. She had a woven marvel of a robe that tortured Isabella her sister, and a perfect clavichord that cost that lady sleepless nights of craving. She had a court-fool like a Feste, and a delicate monster of a drawf clothed in gold like a princess. She had three splendid cavaliers to make her verses, and a company of pearl-broidered ladies only less gorgeous than herself. She had the " elegantissimo " Calmeta for a secretary, who lamented her as a lost felicity, and the gentle courtly Cristoforo Romano not only to carve for her but to sing for her. She could give an Emperor a litter of woven gold. And when she was in a mocking mood she would ask the debonair Messer Leonardo Fiorentino to devise a new "fantasia dei vinci" for her sleeve or her girdle.

For, though she evidently refused Leonardo as a painter, even as she refused that vest of pure gold that was too like Cecilia's, she would allow him to build that pavilion in the midst of her labyrinth in her Vigevano gardens ; and she takes those patterns of linked chains, and shares them with Isabella. These "fantasie dei vinci" may not have been entirely due to Leonardo ; yet he spends so many pages of his manuscripts in drawing novel and elaborate pieces of chain-work that they evidently did find their way to sleeve, girdle and sword. But he did not paint her, except perhaps in one ceremonial picture with Lodovico and their children. Apart from the Cecilia affair, Beatrice was a candid thing, and would naturally distrust the Florentine's green-gleaming eyes, be his manners never so courteous. Besides, she knew he did not like to paint ladies in brocades and monstrous jewels. He was all for soft-falling raiment of no time or fashion, with only some fairy twine or glister of symbolic ornament at the green edges. So her soft clove-carnation irregular face never submitted to Leonardo's masque of dreams, for she had no desire to become a dim-robed immortal in Elysian caves, far from her roseate duchy. She loved the jewelled chains of her mortality. Leonardo would have dissuaded the poor eager child from her splendid gauds, unlike the compassionate sculptor of her dead state, who left her so pathetic and lovely in her love-knots and trinkets that we forgive her anything. Of course she loved her brocades and her dances, her lutes and her jewels, and to be first lady in Milan, and that fine Duke of hers. She was only fourteen when she wedded. twenty-one when she died, stricken in her passion and magnificence. Dusk-thorny rose, she had " lived, a rose, for the space of a morning."

vi

Sometimes her wonderful sister, " regina delle cose adorne," appeared from her precious enamel cloisons of azure in the proud old Castello of Mantua, dipped among the reeds in the green lakes whereon passed red sails and white swans. Golden-haired, dark-eyed, exquisite in profile, with mysterious musical motives, to heighten the enigma of her personality, impearled and gilded on her great sleeves, Isabella came in mingled mood ; but, as she approached all novel and luxurious places, with a delicate rapacity for unusual impressions. She was a little blinded by all that " barbaric pearl and gold," a little dazed by those soft clouds of perfume, faintly aghast at a world so gemmed and gemlike that it was not unlike an Arabian tale. And this faëry Court might have been hers; her brilliant fancies had to stint sometimes at Mantua! But it was Isabella's policy to be friendly with everybody, for who might not pluck from a feast, or a siege, or a conclave, some precious æsthetic toy for her—a clavichord, an Eros, a brocade, a painted panel, an ermine fur, a rosary in black amber and gold, white herons' plumes, an antique agate cup with dragon's wings for a stand, an ancient script, a virgin scroll of verse for her eyes to deflower, or, it might be, a cardinal's hat or a marshal's baton or a wealthy unwed prince for the needs of her House?

Probably nobody experienced more of the Renaissance than Isabella, who collected strange places and unique moments more avidly than anything. A diamond disk indeed, her spirit writes her name on the great Venetian mirror of the time wherever the lights cluster most thickly, wherever the colours are most opalescent, wherever the cardinals and the kings forgather among masques and dances. The lights and the colours cry like trumpets from Milan; and Isabella, still young like her sister, answers their invitation with gaiety and zest. She liked the company, she liked the fanciful young nobles, she liked the brother-in-law who might have been her husband, she liked her sister, who was generous, equally she liked Cecilia, and, later, Lucrezia. She corresponded with them all when she was at home at Mantua; and carried on debates of courtesy with Lodovico over baskets of peaches, golden tissues, wine, carp, swans. The swans in the waters of Mantua and Ferrara had charmed Lodovico's romantic eyes, so some of the white birds came to ruffle their pure plumes in his castle moat also, while Leonardo gazed above, dreaming of Leda.

She liked, not loved. She was hard, much harder than Beatrice. She might be finely tempered, this amateur of the Renaissance: evidently her dancing wit and considered grace, her delicate pampered beauty captivated all her acquaintance. She was either temperamentally cold, or had early adopted repression as a mode of heightening her æsthetic values, and arming herself against pain, as with silk-fine mail of woven gold. Love was too much a gleaming beast of prey in the House of Este; but passion sank no talon in Isabella's heart, closed up like a white flicker in a hollowed gem. Queen of diamonds, with an exquisite famine for all material beauty, a dazzling lust of the eyes, she sent all the violence of her Estensian blood into an æsthetic ecstasy. There may be something of a betrayal in this craving appetite for the flowers and essences of matter. She centres her desire like an emerald salamander in the scorchless flame of beautiful things, " cose adorne," and builds herself a cool cloister of azure, set with lovely devices like springes to seize such birds-of-paradise, such exquisite images, as the music of

Lodovico and his Friends

her importunity may lure to drop within that bright aviary. But she was not love-breathing. Lucrezia Borgia, whatever her tale, emanated that strange atmosphere of desire which some unconscious daughters of beauty can communicate, themselves immune. When Lucrezia bound her emerald upon her white brow between the swathes of great pure gold, Isabella's poets and knights were suddenly faithless. The so different Vittoria Colonna, half-sainted in her widow's weeds, is a heavenly lover whose melancholy eyes can illumine with a mystical tenderness the darkness of Michelangelo. Elisabetta of Urbino had an enchanting gentleness of courtesy that is remembered as with tears in the pure lament of Castiglione. Even Beatrice the Duchess shook soft petals from her flowering moods: she could be as sweet as a cleft pomegranate. Isabella glittered and was wonderful. She was a spectacle and an entertainment. She was a masque of the arts and the graces in her sole personality. The Queen of Diamonds, certainly, but not the Queen of Hearts! An amateur of unique experiences, herself at the centre of none!

Leonardo should have sympathized with her ruthless æstheticism. He was to draw her intelligent and delicate profile later, in Mantua ; and she was to implore his attention more graciously, more persistently, more meekly, more unconditionally than was her way with artists. She was to plead as friend with friend. But even when he watched her move about the Castello now, he dismissed her vivid ways, her bright greeds, and dancing movements, as disturbing. She had a frenzy of the mind: she was immoderate in her intellectual pleasures, she was the delighting libertine of the arts rather than their lover. She was too restless. Diamond-bright, diamond-cold, she lacked atmosphere and she lacked rhythm, for all those gowns provocatively sewn with pearly music. Surely she was more beautiful than Mona Lisa, we think, gazing at Leonardo's drawing of her. Yes. But she was not the type he had chosen—the strange goddess, quiet at the heart of the labyrinthine sea-paven world, the Herodiad stilled from the Dance of Matter, whose smile can wean away the soul of man from all vain fancies and noises of mortality.

Nevertheless, when Isabella adorns the Court, the music is gayer and the colours are yet deeper, for she is one of the most accomplished dancers in Italy and the mistress of " ravishing divisions on the lute." She is " la prima donna del mondo " ; and the sparkle and penetrative art of her gestures do chide the dreamy Milanese graces. She amuses Lodovico so that he will even go with her in her *caretta*, which is considered almost unmanly of him. She likes him for a playmate, and is as entertaining for him as possible. But her duty and her interest are with her ugly little husband, who may be serving the French any moment. So she cares for Lodovico no more than does the marble Leda that Caradosso found for him. She will snatch what she covets from the rape of his castle, and tread a measure with the King of France while he, suddenly obsolete in her glittering hours, agonizes in a dungeon. She, remaining for ever young and courted, has no time for sad anachronisms like obliterated princes.

vii

Dolorous among the duchesses was Isabella d'Aragona, " madonna infeliccissima, unica in disgrazia," as she came to describe herself in that melodious language which melts even bitterness into melody. Her soul was pride, and when her dark beauty came to wed the fragile young Gian Galeazzo, the nominal duke, a slender boy with wreathed hair and a vague sweet face, her husband's uncle did not fail in a magnificence that promised her pride should have its way. Dark and fair, they sat at the famous bridal-feast when the bright Olympians brought the courses, and the planets of Leonardo's masque sang wonder to the bride. But the time came when the boy, her bridegroom, lay sick in Pavia, among the hounds he loved with hereditary passion, and the French went on to sack her Naples. Her retinues and her trumpeters and her brocades were nothing to her, for they were all overpassed by those of Beatrice ; and it was the little Maximilian who was reared like the prince, not her pretty ducchetto. Hapless lady ! She could not melt her beauty into an appeal, as even the French king observed ; and her grief became a grievance because she had not true tragic quality. It was evidently for her that Leonardo planned the bathing pavilion in the Park of Pavia so carefully that he arranged how much water the eels' heads would pour, three parts hot to four of cold. Since Duchess Beatrice did not like him, Duchess Isabella could.

There are many other ladies interwoven with the Court. Lodovico had a gift for varied emotional attitudes, for chivalric friendships as well as fine sensualities ; for he was of a rich, romantic and generous temper. When Leonardo came to Milan, Cecilia Gallerani, seventeen years old, was almost its queen, for Lodovico thought her rare enough to be his duchess. Policy, however, strangled that thought ; and Cecilia would not exact marriage as her price. Even after Beatrice drives her from the Castello she is still young and beautiful, wedded to an elderly count, moving discreetly, receiving poets, artists, scholars and gallant lords in her villa and her palace, a great lady who has been much loved, and who keeps the remembrance like a perfume of roses

Lodovico and his Friends

in her breast, and like ashes of violet in her eyes. Besides, there is her fair son Cæsar, beloved by Il Moro, used like a brother by Maximilian the little prince. She of Este may now wear her lover with an aching, jealous love. Cecilia, " regal, graceful and pleasant as roses," keeps her court of scholars and poets, and makes her pensive soft sonnets. She has Saronno, with its Way of the Cross ; and the great Palazzo Carmagnola, and a villa by the water. She still has the power of communicating happiness. They call her Aspasia, with a glance at a more faithless Pericles. She is Greek enough to like the name. They call her Sappho, and she looks sidelong and softly-smiling, like Leonardo's Saint Anne. Hers was that enchanting art of conversation, perishing as the ear that receives the falling intonations, and the nerves that thrill to the violin pauses, as the eye that captures the faint gestures and the suddenly irised look. All her visitors spoke their best to her, speaking of their best. Warriors made no secret of their affairs, musicians sang and played, poets murmured their verses, painters and builders drew their figures. She was *simpatica*, and people flowered in her sympathy. So did Leonardo, who painted her young, *giovanetta*, a rosy-gold gladiolus within a green sheath. Where is the portrait that Isabella borrowed, and of which Cecilia, softly complying, wrote that, if it no more resembled her, that was no fault of the surpassing master's, but because she was so young, so young when it was painted ? I would rather have that picture than a thousand new pages of diagrams on perspective and mechanics. It should have been a kind of *Virgin of the Rocks*, with a touch of the young Dionysos.

" Madonna Cecilia—Amantissima mia Diva—Lecte la tua suaviss."

So runs the broken line on the page of the Codex Atlanticus. Over against it, practising Latin phrases, he has written " Amor vincit omnia et nos cedamus amori." The image of Cecilia may have presented itself one moment as a thing for love, though, if he was about to draft a letter to any great lady, he would not fail in dulcet words. The verse-makers about the Court were much moved by the beautiful portrait of the beautiful Cecilia. Bellincioni, the official poet, wrote a sonnet upon it, and, though it is not much of a sonnet, it is a curiosity, since nowhere so closely in verse or prose is Leonardo's great name linked with the sweet name of an Italian lady :

" *Poeta*. Di qui t' adiri ? a che invidia ha natura ?
Natura. Al Vinci che ha ritratto una tua stella ;
Cecilia ! si bellissima hoggi è quella
Che a' suoi begli occhi el sol par umbra oscura.
Poeta. L'honor è tuo, se ben con sua pictura

163

Leonardo the Florentine

La fa che par che ascolti e non favella
Pensa ; quanto sarà più viva e bella,
Piu a te sia gloria in ogni età futura.
Ringratiar dunque Lodovico or puoi
Et l'ingegno e la man di Leonardo
Chi lei vedrà, così ben che sie tardo
Vederla viva, dirà : basti ad noi
Comprender or qual che è natura et arte."

Later, Leonardo is called to paint Lucrezia Crivelli. It is nearing the end of the sumptuous Duke's way of passion, splendour, and regal dreams, and it is with some irony that Leonardo charges his palette for Lucrezia, moving with that arrested look of swift intelligence which caught the Moor away from the difficult interviews with ambassadors, away from plot and counterplot with Venice, Mantua, Maximilian, Florence, Rome, away from his ardent Duchess—who was too much part and parcel of his ambition, too instant a nerve in his vexing coil of misery—to a bower of quiet dreams and the *pax rosarum* of the senses. Lucrezia's secret flashes like the jewel on her smooth brow, though she is the Duchess' own lady, and there is something of a guilty silence in the Court. If she be " La Belle Ferronnière," she looks as if, startled in passing, she unconsciously sprang to defence. How could she refuse the starry bistred eyes, the perfumed hands of Lodovico, that subtle casuist who could persuade himself even in her arms that he was faithful to Beatrice ? The remarkable thing about the Duke was that he really had the sense of sin, as his Renaissance brethren had not. It was mediæval and Milanese of him ; and, from a Machiavellian point of view, part of his weakness. Some say Leonardo painted Lucrezia when he was quarrelling with the Servite Friars, and that there is something of her in the Virgin who is secluded among the rocks, cold and strange among the dwarf oaks, irises, and cyclamen, from far high places :

" Mother of grace, the pass is difficult."

But I fancy the face that most persuasively haunted Leonardo's Lombard Virgins was Cecilia's ; a conviction which, though not provable, is arguable. Of Lucrezia, too, however, the history is : " Amavit Ludovicus : pinxit Leonardus."

Crowds of rare ladies, softly glowing like fireflies, come and go. Sforza, Visconti, Sanseverino, Trivulzio, Borromeo, and other great names are theirs. Anna Sforza is a gentle princess who is destined to be a bride in Ferrara, and to die there. Fragile and tender, she moves apart, often clothed in white on Saturdays, because of a votive promise made in sickness, and she was "most beautiful, most gracious, and little else can be written about her for she lived but a short while." Caterina, who quartered her Vipers with the cruel Rose of Riario, will not come to Milan without her jewels. But, as she holds her high castle at Forli with pride, glory and cruelty, she is a friend of her uncle's, who lends her soldiers and money, though he regards this she-panther of his race with some misgiving. There is Madonna Fiordelisa, another Sforza love-child, fair as her name. There is Lucia Marliani, Countess of Melzo, so amazingly beloved by the last Duke for the "purity and honesty of her life" that he bound her to inviolable chastity and to himself even after his death. Ippolita Sforza, married to a Bentivoglio, a patron of art and letters, goes brilliant in gold sleeves powdered with love-knots. That other Beatrice d'Este, who was once called the Queen of Feasts, wearing a dream of past adorations like Eastern kohl round her lids, and veiled with rare pathos as with frayed gauze of gold, would gaze at her son, Niccolo de' Correggio, that complete courtier, repeating her triumphs of grace to a knightly tune. Chiara Gonzaga, Countess of Montpensier, had a soft sentimental lustre. She worried Lodovico a little about passports for her extravagant journeys to France, and once had to be consoled with a precious *baiser de paix* because a Mantuan doctor began a story that Lodovico, widowed, might wed her. The French called her *folle*, and she certainly was extravagant, but she was a friend to Lodovico who did not desert him when he fell, this slight gay mother for a tragic and brilliant son, the Constable of Bourbon.

Duchess Bona went aggrieved in the background, grown too heavily handsome, in habits besprinkled with fleurs-de-lis, wearing a jewelled cap. They found her not dangerous, but tiresome, with the old old stories of her wrongs. She was always a lady *de petit sens*, as Commines unkindly said. "Of tendre wittes," is the sweeter Chaucerian phrase of her kind; but the sweet silliness quite attractive in youth is wearisome in age. They have all forgotten that she had her wonderful hours, when she was "the first Madonna in Italy," because of the great amnesty she coaxed from her violent bridegroom, when she rode in that legendary procession to Florence with fifty palfreys barded in gold, when she ruled in Milan with the crafty Cecco Simonetta and her popinjay lover Tassino. Now of all that splendour she must console herself with a gorgeous *Book of Hours*, still a-making, and a daughter who at least will have an august title. Bianca Maria moves lazily about. She has large eyes that darken only for her Violante, a short upper lip, and an infantile soft face that will match oddly on medals with the tired fantastic profile of Maximilian. She loves food and finery and other women—too lazy to entertain the men. Her great moment is when the imperial convoy comes to celebrate her bridal in the ringing town, decorated with blazoned vipers and eagles, and when, ultimate symbol of the pride of Milan, Leonardo's long-meditated model of the great Cavallo and its Rider surges like a cloudy shape of wonder in the Piazza before the Castello. As Queen of the Romans, sold with a great dowry to buy an obsolete investiture, she writes to her uncle babbling letters, demanding pearls, perfumes and white herons' plumes. Lodovico sends them : she is affectionate and even weakly helpful in the end, and willing to be more.

But one innocent piece of beauty grew fragrant and dewy like lily of the valley in her moist green cloisters, and rang faint bells of wonder, a guiltless thing of love among the delicate wanton people in gold and red. Such was the sweet younger Bianca, Lodovico's daughter, almost of an age with the Duchess, but tenderly childish. "On ni faisait pas grand différence entre les bâtards et les femmes légitimes," says Commines of such bright intruders. Leonardo saw her grow, and be wedded to the great lord his friend, and be loved and dazzled to death ; he, who took pleasure in flowers and children, surely saw her gracile and pure. If he did not paint her portrait, he must have urged Ambrogio da Predis to do his best, if Ambrogio did that picture of the little Princess, who is not Beatrice, nor Cecilia, nor the other Bianca. The sweet irregular profile is in a halter of jewels ; the heavy green robe has a fantasia de' vinci embroidered upon it. She is behaving like a great lady, and does what she is told in a charming patient way. The lips childishly ask for kisses the candid eyes do not comprehend. The little tricks of her eyebrows, the quaint crooked smiles invite her friends to innocent mirth. A child she is indeed, with that faintly smiling look, as if amused by some golden secret her elders cannot share. But she is content, delighted with their caresses, their gifts, their marvellous shows. She is sweet as running water, sweet as wild briar, sweet as windflowers, sweet as a white bird, accepting her gorgeous cages and jewelled jesses with a pretty fatalism as if it were all a great gilt game. Everybody is kind to her, who is so lovely and so guileless. Her splendid father calls her his "most priceless thing on earth." The impetuous, imperious Duchess embraces her, lays her hurt spirit under Bianca's cool palms, softens to her tricks of subtle unconscious charm—like Lodovico's become sinless. The pale Aragonese with the angry eyes laughs with Bianca, and welcomes her to her nurseries. Even the lazy fair woman who will be Queen of the Romans catches her hand as she passes. The tall and beautiful cavalier with the sweet voice and the silver armour, so like

Lodovico and his Friends

a prince in a fairy tale, who wedded her when she was eight, and who carried her away, still a child, to her sumptuous carven palace, is intolerably grieved when a thing so flowerlike lies dead among all the jewels, like wood-anemones or " fast-fading violets covered up with leaves "—leaves of gold. She is over-cherished in gold.

Leonardo, friend and abettor in magnificence of her superb lord, so dear to Lodovico, saw her flit about the splendid house, once the Medicean palace in Milan, a serene dwelling with beauty-wreathed doors, painted with radiant figures, steeped in cool gardens. Leonardo designed Galeazzo Sanseverino's raiment for joust and festival; set his pageants; planned the vast stables for his proud horses, frescoed with great chargers as if to please Semiramis, and lingered often there, drawing the sons of speed and fire he loved so well, creating his Platonic idea of a Cavallo. Let those unwavering eyes softly relent for the young bride of the superfine sophisticated Galeazzo. But she also lived in the Castello with her household, and had place and part in all proud ceremonies. Her shy smiles are not absent from the greeting of the Duchess; she sits high at the tournament when Galeazzo, with that band of Scythians who cost Leonardo some trouble, comes brilliantly to take the prize, while her father, dark and princely in his cloth-of-gold, rides on his mighty destrier among the trumpets. After the Imperial wedding, in white satin and pearls she separates with lily sweetness the splendours of the rival duchesses. When the King of France is at Asti she dances with Beatrice the French and Italian dances, all pearls again. When her husband is ill with fever she receives the Venetian ambassadors at Vigevano, with an engaging deprecation uttering the great Latinities of welcome, capturing them with her dryad air, trembling like a white doe in a snare of gems and silk.

She is a delicate disarming thing, a strain of virginal-music, diffident and fragrant indeed like that spire of rich white valley lilies.

> " The naiad-like lily of the vale
> Whom youth makes so fair and passion so pale."

They felt her so, tried to dress her so, with her green and white satins and pearls. She gathers garden-flowers at the Castello in the morning; she dances, plays palle, runs races, goes haymaking with Gian Galeazzo and his wife. With all the dukes and duchesses she receives the first flowers of May, in green again, with long silken veils. All situations are natural to her. She is worn like a favoured flower on every gilded or arcadian occasion. Nobody denies her, or asks who she is. Love made her, love gave her to the gorgeous, dreamily iniquitous Court

167

that its decadent beauty might not lack something rare and tender and limpid, like a hidden spring set with narcissus and maidenhair, like the sound of the pure child's voice singing innocence through all the somnambulist sins of Milan's long history from the days of Ambrose and Augustine.

But, after Galeazzo claims his fragile wife, though she is happy, yet she begins to die. The felicity they have put on her is too heavily burdened with gems; and her rare virginity is too much amazed by the fiercer claims of love. Her greenish eyes grew larger and brighter with her ingenuous surprises; her reddish hair burned deeper; her satin cheek now flushed, now paled its carnations. She was tethered to earth by her own mere ethereal colour and a net of pearls. Herself she was as frail and fine as a drift of silken gossamer on summer air. But it was winter:

> " How with his rage shall beauty hold a plea
> Whose action is no stronger than a flower ? "

She fainted and died one November day. Like a flower she exhaled her soul, held by hands too feverish. And they all wept and suffered over their perished pleasure. Lodovico cried, with all his quivering sensibility : " I do not wish Bianca to be buried in a place where I can see her grave." (And so he might suffer ! For if Beatrice was his golden mascot, Bianca had been his miracle, his bribe to the angels.) The splendid husband, so implacably and almost ironically destined for golden hours, whether Italy or France might possess him, had many black days for Bianca. The Duchess was shaken by a subtle searching sorrow for the girl who preceded her in death, as if she were the lost gage of some profound innocence and sincerity in Lodovico's treasonable soul. She had anguish " because of the place she held in my heart." She is dead, the little princess, but the purity of the tears shed over her seem to keep her elusive image closed up as in a charm of incorruptible crystal and amber. Unbetrayed and unbetraying, she lay in Santa Maria delle Grazie; and Beatrice, betrayed in love by her lord, went to weep there for hours before she died herself, and Lodovico, clothed in black, betrayed by his City, and more to be betrayed by his Castellan, came to pray in agony and remorse in his turn—in Santa Maria delle Grazie, the church of his heart, where Leonardo was still painting the great mythos and ultimate symbolism of Betrayal as accepted by Christendom.

Bianca was not important ? She danced with the wind like a sweet Guelder rose, like a golden feather, like a sweet idea. The historic method may deny her; and be wrong. She was spiritually and symbolically important. She was the keeper of the mysterious sweetness that does not perish from the heart of a sacred city. When she dies there is a pause and a silence. The picture fades out before the fifth Act begins. The curtain is a dead-green evening sky with loops of the small bells called bleeding-heart festooned dark red above the horizon, ringing a lonely faëry peal for Bianca, whose little white ghost will go smiling and naked among the asphodel, escaped from the burden of gems, from the breaking plot of splendour and guilt she never under-stood. All the seductions of Milan laid siege to the heart of Leonardo ; the seduction of a mystical sweetness was not missing, like that of a young-eyed cherubin violing apart among the coloured lovers from the Hollow Hill.

From the Hollow Hill ? Crowds and crowds of them—fair ladies and their lords, appealing and ravishing ladies of Milan, some with long swathes of ribbon-bound hair, some with soft smooth curls exultant under the thin line of gold that held the enigmatic jewel of the ferron-nière. You see them in the portraits of Ambrogio da Predis, Gian-pietrino, Boltraffio, Luini, of Leonardo's imitators. All softly smiling, their dreamy senses imagining fastidious pleasures, children of amorous rather than erotic fantasy ! It was a wistful love-game they often played, " charmes, chutes, offrandes, et les surprises, et les oui et les non, et les pas tristement perdus." Not often " tristement perdus," for the women of Milan were more tender than chaste, and, when the stars were throbbing and " sfumato," soft-blurred silver, came lovers with voices of masked music, " powdered finely with sundry sighs," pleading under the casement, not in vain. With a little cry the white child Bianca had slipped stainless away.

viii

In this court of women, created by Lodovico who loved them overmuch, Leonardo, who loved them too little, equably adapts himself to their needs, as at no other period. True, he was Leonardo the scientist all the time, of which more presently ; but he was Leonardo the gracious courtier none the less. He must paint the rarest of them, he must give them music and masque, and even twine patterns for them. Since his amazing zest for trifles as well as great things has not diminished yet, he lets his own feminine part accord with such services ; and the spirit of the woman softly encroaches and invades his imagination by invisible stealths and inaudible vibrations.

He talks with these camellia-coloured women, of whom he never consciously thinks, unless he spend a glance on the golden curls of

Leonardo the Florentine

Cecilia or the immature grace of Bianca. The Serpent was a part of Leonardo, so he knew how to talk to Eve.

> ". . . dore-lui les
> Plus doux des dits que tu connaisses
> Allusions, fables, finesses,
> Mille silences ciselés."

And the fact that Milan is so much a city of women alters his painting and curiously changes the chemistry of his nerves. In the perfumed atmosphere of their creating, his own peculiar tenderness stirs and searches. Platonism of a kind is talked here as in every Renaissance court; but it is not the platonism or plotinism of Florence. It has suffered a further dulcet degradation, for it must charm the ears of fine ladies as well as of beautiful youths and philosophic elders. It is the platonism of Asolo, and Urbino, and Ferrara, the pseudo-platonism which will find its rarest rhapsodist in Bembo, uttering the "rapture" in *The Courtier*, and which Cecilia and Isabelle d'Este will murmur together when Lodovico and Leonardo are passed away.

The Florentine ladies were bitter-sweet: they were quick and proud and witty, and they were of the line of Beatrice Portinari. But they had made no sweet assassin-stroke through the bright armour of his youth. The Milanese fetched effortless magic from the isles of Circe. They were sorcerers, and, for all his too-anxious disclaimer, in some ways so was he. As an æsthete he loved the smooth oval of those Lombard faces. Sometimes they looked like liturgical lilies, sometimes like the sumptuous bells of white digitalis, drowsy with vespers of death. The morbidezza might be a physical quality; but it invited to strange psychical fancies. The dreamy trance had a luminism, as of light within alabaster; and he could quicken it into that high imaginative irony which sends a rare aurora through ethereal pleasures, and saves desire from scattered haloes, broken wings, and limèd pits of sad satiety. Within the calyx of this Lombard beauty, within eyes so deep and lips so subtly curved he can pour his own mysterious spell. To hands so finely articulated he commits his cup of strange immortality. Theirs are faces moulded by the beauty of murmuring sound; and they have the far gaze of dwellers by great spaces. The law of the waves has moulded like pearly smooth shells those faces that murmur, unconscious like shells, of Eternity. The spirals of water, air, and fire are germane to the spirals of their soft hair. They are one with the elements, as the Florentine women deliberately refuse, with their sharp differences, to be. Their kindred gaze dreamily over leonardesque rocks by Hebridean seas. The smiling of women and the motion of

Lodovico and his Friends

great waters haunted his earliest years. In Milan both delights ran together in his profound attention. With *The Virgin of the Rocks* he not only brought a new type into the world of art but created a new quality in the tradition of human emotion, the most " divine " thing he did.

He was friendly with these women ; he attended to their baths, their lute-strings, their pavilions, their amorini, their lutes, their broidered imprese. Such beauty, such strength, such fiery grace as his must have attracted those Milanese masochists, long accustomed to suborn with sweetness the spirits of their lords. He knew their special decorative values ; like them he loved perfumes, music, silken ways. His masculine part was absorbed in scientific play ; his imaginative self was left undefended. Its fantasia became more deeply and richly irised by all the divinations and obscure wisdoms that certain women seem to communicate by breathing and feeling. He knew those sacred ibis-wings just vanishing over green horizons, those impossible angelic desires that pass in a smile or a sigh, those evasions as of the perfumes of unearthly jasmine, those cloudy dreams that linger only as faint violet shapes from which no distress will wring their images of agonized import.

The more sternly his masculine mind cleaves to pure science, the more softly the feminine principle almost swoons into his art ; and the mystery of sex that asceticism, intellectual or spiritual, can deny but not destroy, cloistered as in the heart of an orchid, prevails in sublimated power over each leaf and petal of his art, and even in his science the pistons and parts of his great levers are called male and female.

And he becomes at this time most intensely Leonardo the anatomist. If the feminine part of him becomes more emotional, that vibration shows itself in a keener sensibility towards his beautiful young men, who hurt his nerves and his pride sometimes, as various blurred pages of the manuscripts betray, and in a larger indulgence for pretty popin-jays like Salaino. His indestructible poise saved him, doubtless, from the illogical revulsions and sudden insane cruelties with which his kind suddenly destroy their friendships with such women as awaken in them at least admiration. But, while he went meditating the rare Lombard faces, with their beauty-stricken eyes and sacred looks from ancient temples, and mystic lips that invited to more than a sensual bed—to some couch of unrealizable embrace among the asphodel, even while he noted the faint and fine pulse at the base of the lovely throat, confessing the ethereal pathos of the wondering heart, he would suddenly stiffen with mockery, and think that all those lissom ladies with their dreamy airs as of waiting for Eastern angels of dubious annunciation, with their soft satins of gracious flesh, were at one in the dreadful democracy of their entrails. He would think of some sorrowful *écorchée* yielding to the inquisition of the knives her last intolerable secrets, or the sexless cynical ultimatum of some finely articulated bones that no longer support the breast of desire or the womb of life. "To this favour must ye all come at last," saith Leonardo the Florentine, like Hamlet the Dane.

And then the " great Etrurian Lord," sickened with the suffocating roses of Milan, might, with exquisite pencil and devilish malignity, draw that annihilating Anatomy of Love.

Chapter v

Lodovico and his Friends (2)

i

THE king of the tourneys and the prime squire of ladies in Renaissance Milan was Galeazzo di Sanseverino, son of the famous condottiere, who had helped Lodovico back from his exile. Galeazzo was loved by Lodovico with that excessive tenderness which he spent on all his personal relationships, and which, like a light flame, suddenly undid many of his anxious webs of policy. Most Italian tyrants of the day regarded some attractive young man with an ambiguous romantic idolatry which was more or less a symbol of their æsthetic passion for rare beauty manifest in mortality. In Lodovico, the feminist, this Græco-Roman attitude was innocent enough, though imprudent. Trivulzio, the great noble, the wise statesman and the skilled general, was worth far more to his dukedom than Galeazzo. But: " Who among us can tell the reason why we love one man and hate another ? " said Lodovico to Trivulzio in his unanswerable manner. So he lost the proud commander to the French, and laid up treachery from the jealous brothers of his favourite.

But Galeazzo had that personal glamour for which fascinated friends pay away recklessly their power, their riches and their hearts. He was a chivalrous person, and the great ladies of Italy called him friend. His inimitable grace and his rare paladinesque ways caught the sated fancy of great princes, so that not only Lodovico, but Lodovico's foes, were glad of his existence. Fortune has her minions, of whom she exacts nothing but charm. Though Galeazzo di Sanseverino, to be fair, was also a gallant soldier and something of a diplomatist.

In Milan his chief use in time of peace was to be Beauty's feudatory. Lodovico was a much-occupied prince. What with tortuous diplomacy, financial affairs, and an intelligent interest in matters of architecture, irrigation, and painting, Lodovico was a hard-working Duke, for all his court of pleasure. He could not always attend the Duchess and her friends at their diversions, so he assigned Galeazzo to her as the chief cavalier of those picturesque games, in which the young Bianca, his wife, was usually also a reveller. This brilliant personage was an irresistible victor in the jousts, an artist in masquerade, a musician, a poet, a lover of those great stories of Charlemagne and Arthur that had set their seal upon his gracious attitudes. When he went clothed in white, with a great plume flying, and fanciful gilded shoes " fitter for Venus than for Ares," some jealous courtiers mocked a little ; but, like many exquisite dandies, Galeazzo had a dangerous sword. Nevertheless, his mind, astray in the hunting woods and fantastic challenges and personal devoirs of too-mediæval adventure, was bewildered by the cool and complicated task of generalship. He was loyal while there was any hope for Lodovico. Then he resigned himself to the allurements of his foe. That " sweet enemy " caressed him richly.

For four years he worked for Lodovico in vain. He came back as Grand Ecuyer of France, in the train of King Louis, jousting as of old, but surely like a somnambulist in his graven silver Milanese armour, riding his noble Milanese horse, dancing as of old, with the collar of Saint Michael on his breast, and bowing to Isabella d'Este when she could spare a look from the new sovereign. Galeazzo remembered better than Isabella, one imagines, for Lodovico was then quite cancelled from her brilliant life, wherein to be ruined was always to be forgotten. He was slain on the stricken field of Pavia, very bravely defending King Francis. Dying in the very scene where he had so often followed the flying feather of Beatrice, reckless in the chase, near the home of the little Bianca, he was forgetful in the last darkness surely of the gilded favours of the stranger, remembering the ringing lists of his great romantic days, the rose-white branches of the maying, the faint fragrance of the little lady, set like a posy of white violets in his golden casque, and the generous eyes of his friend, long filled with dust in Loches.

Of all the nobles he was the most friendly with Leonardo, who took pleasure in his air, his splendid gestures, and still more in his horses. Both would meet once and again, with some long look of remembrance, in the Court of France.

They were all slightly effeminate, like Galeazzo, the young lords of the Court. For in Milan they were formed by women, and devoted to women.

Gaspare Visconti was a cavalier as precious as Galeazzo, and even more sympathetic. Poetic and exquisite in his mood, he was " cavalier grande per lo splendore della nascita e per la stima che del suo signalato merito era fatte." When he gave his sonnets to Beatrice they were written in golden letters on red parchment. Those Petrarchan verses sang of love and the beauty of the ladies he served. The aristocratic amateur had a more lyrical spring in his song than the Florentine court-poet Bellincioni, facile as he was to every occasion. But all the young

Lodovico and his Friends

nobles rimed to their lutes in sweet Italian, for, somewhat belated among the Renaissance arts, poetry was gathering strength in the allied Court of Ferrara, where Ariosto would follow Boiardo in the ways of princely adventure and Eastern magic.

A third brilliant cavalier was Niccolo da Correggio, son of the Queen of Feasts, who divided his devotion among Milan, Ferrara, and somewhat jealous Mantua, for Isabella spared him to Beatrice with reluctance. He moved amid a glitter of lutes and a rumour of golden colour, for he had been the victor in a great tourney in honour of the love-god, and the fine fabulous distinction made him whimsically sweet. At Lodovico's wedding he went kinglike in golden brocade, and he was among the readiest of Beatrice's lutanists and deployers of fine arguments concerning

> ". . . beauty making beautiful old rime
> In praise of ladies dead and lovely knights."

But this bird-of-paradise, fair son of a fair mother, that dropped so soft and so benvenuto into the intimate chambers of the great courts, dropped into darkness and dust at last in Ferrara, haughtiest, fiercest, deadliest of all Renaissance cities ; and pitying Fate seems to overbroider the felicity of this complete Renaissance knight, dreaming to the end his dream of fair women, of whom the last is the golden Lucrezia, while he is still in his gracious prime, safe yet from the spites of spoiling time.

Ercole Strozza, too, coming often from Ferrara, with fair young head thrown high, limping and perfumed, another lord of dandies, was dauntlessly singing down a path of love and music to where an assassin would lurk among the flowers, and the cry of a poet-lover would ring true for him in the sincerest sonnet of the Renaissance. Antonio Tebaldeo, beautiful and sinister and witty, close friend of Cardinal Ippolito, pauses here awhile, to be the celebrant of the honour of Ippolito's sister. They all made verses, these young people, fantastical lyrics and sonnets, much moved by the example of Poliziano and Lorenzo. They were too artificial to find an original music, too engrossed with compliment and ceremonial love-making ; but it was in the sweet vernacular that they were heard :

> " C'est une idylle rose ou le flot bleu soupire,
> Ou l'art mièvre zézaie en vers adonisés."

Only Il Pistoja, needy and a figure of jest, bitter jest sometimes, moved by a sudden pang of prophecy, occasionally swings into true poetry with a sombre bell of doom.

The young cavaliers were as lovely as the ladies, for whom they look fit acolytes with their splendid extravagant raiment, their rippled hair,

175

their beautiful hands. Even the young Duca, Gian Galeazzo, till his maladies tarnished him too much, looked like a girl, delicate and perverse, his long fair hair clasped with a ring of gems, though he loved little but his slim hounds, his great horses and his uncle. They are most attractive, these courtly adolescents, with the curled lips of pleasure, and their long agate eyes, burning deeply, yet coolly, like the limpid eyes of Persian cats, and their locks waving under their birettas. Others look more moody in their hoods of hair ; or wear it turned in long curls, or, more bizarre, frizzed in a golden bush like a chrysanthemum. As they pose dreamily in fine attitudes, with brief bright mantles flaring into godets of fur, or go slim in silken doublets and fine lawn vests, they seem very flowery—sprigs of jasmine set about their rare palace-world. With drowsily enthusiastic faces, with their long tresses, their jewels, their slender limbs, are they girls or boys ? When Leonardo draws their casqued fair heads for his masquerades they do indeed " confound and multiply the beauty of the sexes." The young Florentines who posed for the Davids, though delicate and svelte, were true sword-lilies, shepherds of Olympos or even of Ida, quick to spring to their light broidered armour. These are the crimson and purple anemones that woke from the shed blood of the knight of Venus, they are brethren of the adoniasts of ancient Milan. But their overwrought and morbid grace has something of the French mediæval intensity, and with their lutes and love-songs they are not so remote from Aucassin and Amis and Pharamond, and Parthenopex of Blois, as the youth of the more Hellenized cities.

Boltraffio, a gifted though limited disciple of Leonardo's, himself a beautiful young noble, paints these palace-children of luxury as lovely youths whose smile is the faint effluence of their beauty. As Sebastian, as Dionysos, as Narcissus, frankly as Casio his friend, crowned poet and cavalier, he paints them, their dreamy lives concentrated in their lips, eyes, rich hair bound with gems and flowers, creatures whose duty seems to be that of genii or angels, to alternate with the great vases of the swung decorative garlands of Milan. The wreathed heads dream against the green-blue skies, with the arrested gaze of youth charmed by its own perfume of pathos and delight. There is nothing corrupt in Boltraffio. He loves the tender brotherhood of joy, celebrants of beauty as natural as the lilies, and he sets a jewel on the brow of his rare silken friend, as he twines the ivy-wreath round the head of his Narcissus-Christ.

Sometimes they stand pensive, pure, in straight doublet like Borgognone's young scholar-saint. Then they have the more austere and poignant beauty of a Lycidas. Such graver suavities are preferred by one fine pupil of Court and university alike, who will some day strike a preluding note to the great Miltonic lament. Years later, this singularly gentle youth, a distinguished person in black velvet, now sweetly attentive both to the famous coloured Court and to the cherished learning of the university, will hive the secret honey of many spirits we would otherwise know only by their violences, in a noble book. Baldassare Castiglione, flower of courtiers, is studying the ways of magnificence in cosmopolitan and opulent Milan. He learns to latinize from Giorgio Merula, "the sun of Alexandria," and finds Greek come rarely to his mind from the Athenian Demetrius Chalcondylas. He is Lombard and Mantuan, though the home of his heart will be the delicious little duchy of Urbino, where Elisabetta will create her harmonies of felicity by the grace of a really beautiful soul. Now he is one of the young gentlemen who gather to watch Leonardo in the refectory of Santa Maria delle Grazie. His intercourse with the painter is evident from the intimate references in the pages of his book. And it is also evident that Castiglione, who had frequented so many glorious courts, thought of Lodovico's Milan with a romantic regret. He remembers Beatrice the vivid Duchess, and Sanseverino the enchanting king of knights, Leonardo the divine chimerical painter, and all the shimmering sumptuous Court that shed its petals of roses and music and Greek over his gracious youth. For Milan was learned in her great and easy way. She did not talk so much of her scholarship because all her worldly affairs were so important. But the scholars seethed round the gorge of Bobbio, when they found what texts the quiet copyist had preserved. The Duke and the Duchess could make their Latin orations, and the beautiful ladies drank the verse of Virgil and Tibullus like a rare antique wine to make more musical their faces. Milan was "the School of the Master of those that know," said Isabella d'Este, though none too willing to praise. In that assembly of accomplished people, dedicated most of them to mournful ends, whose discourses form the dewy sweet interlude of peace called *Il Cortegiano*, many of the speakers had been bred in Lodovico's Milan awhile—Gonzaga young men, Fregoso young men, and even the Magnifico Giuliano, an exile from Florence. Another child of the Castiglione house watches Leonardo with interest. Fra Sabba will soon be an eager young Knight of Saint John of Jerusalem, bound to languish awhile on the island of Rhodes, where he will search for fragments of antique gods for Isabella d'Este.

ii

More imperious figures sharply define themselves, as dominants in the come and go. There went Ascanio Sforza, his eager subtle face cut as in a sardonyx, a cardinal who was hunter and warrior and intriguer, gorgeous as his brother in his ways, moving dangerous pieces against the Borgia, himself meditating the Tiara. He was one of those cardinals, early given to the Church, whose passion was for the sword ; and he had a natural friendship for the other warrior-prince of the Church, Giuliano delle Rovere. " Monseigneur, pardon me if I do not trust you though you are my brother," wrote Lodovico with sardonic courtesy. He did surpass Lodovico in his stratagems, and nearly equalled him in his splendours. He followed his ducal brother's interests closely, however ; and struggled hard for the restoration of his sons. His life was a succession of chapters in astonishing intrigue ; but, when Leonardo in the end came to Rome, Sansovino had already built him that florid tomb where he lies uneasily, as if still troubled by mundane affairs, and still regretting that he had yielded the dream of the Tiara for one of the Borgia's most superb and most shameless simonies. " The Nimrod of the Sacred College," they called him, as he hunted, like Gratian before him, in the great parks about Milan and Vigevano ; and all the people ran to see him. But in the city he led a princely life, was a lord of artists, musicians, and scholars, helped his brother with hospital and lazaret, and had for his peculiar interest the Cathedral of Pavia, with which Leonardo had much business, till he lost himself in the libraries. Amazing he was when he forgot his Cardinal's red, and rode out in his armour inlaid with amorous myths, arrogant plumes floating from his casque and from his great destrier, the lance within his hand. Yet in quiet hours his spirit's festival was music, and he had a book concerning that art which was one of Fra Antonio's loveliest achievements in illumination, a blazonry of loves, branches, medallions, with, it is said, a picture of Leonardo himself playing the lyre.

Fregoso of Genoa, Bentivoglio, Pallavacino, Visconti, Sforza, Borromeo, Melzo, by name, the great nobles thronged luxurious. Marchesino Stanga, Lodovico's devoted Cremonese secretary, had many dealings with Leonardo. Artists and gentlemen gathered at his bright villa at Bellaggio. Landriani was the treasurer, at whom they laughed a little, though not so much as at Trotti, the bewildered Ferrarese ambassador. Cristoforo da Calabria was the ducal captain. Bernardino da Conte was the charming and dearly caressed friend who was to end as the worst Judas in Renaissance Italy. Nor did the great Trivulzio leave Milan altogether till he definitely took service with France. With unusual acerbity, Lodovico had him painted upside down on the walls of the city, till the remonstrances of the French King, still his ally, brought the two into a reluctant civility again for a time.

Lodovico and his Friends

Moving with their stately tyrants, sumptuous courts meet and mingle, shoaling currents of amethyst, emerald, and peacock-blue. Milan, Urbino, Mantua, Ferrara, and even Venice, with superb visitations astonish one another, and exchange their flowery essences of wonder in myrrhine caskets. The rival trains meet in battles of silver and gold, contests of glittering gems, emulations of ingenious wit in rare and fair devices, and in learned amusements like Plautine comedy. The young Ariosto was among the company of graceful youths brought by Ercole d'Este to play Plautus at Pavia in 1493.

Frequent among the guests were the princes of the House of Este, steeled and brocaded persons, collared with jewels, before whom all uncovered when they dipped their long hands in the rose-water at a feast. They were surrounded by their Ferrarese gallants, noticeable by their point-device elegance, and a certain slim insolence of bearing. With one of these, most beautiful and dangerous, Leonardo had that thrilling natural affinity with which he welcomed the splendid devastating forces of nature, lightning, flood, the power of wild horses, the rush of the winged dragons. Ippolito d'Este, the famous Cardinal-Archbishop of Milan, was ruthless, strong, and graceful like a "tiger, burning bright," and he went attended by athletes, slingers, wrestlers, acrobats from many lands, and retinues of magnificent pages, chosen for their beauty. He had "the most vigorous body with the fiercest mind." A lord all pride and fire, descended from Bradamante, as Ariosto vainly fabled! With him came the poet Tebaldeo, a handsome, witty and restless person, who devoted himself awhile to be a celebrant of the honour of Beatrice. As yet Ippolito was young, and had not blinded his brother because Angela Borgia liked his eyes better than his own. This damascened sword of a sacred prince, who listened with languor to Ariosto's stories, was a friend of Leonardo's, and continued to befriend him. A cardinal who decorated his life with beautiful people as if they were things of *virtù* was much to his liking. A great way and an imperial he kept, this arrogant cardinal, who mocked at despot, father, and Pope, who ordered white armour in which to fight for his friend Lodovico, nor desisted till all was lost.

One notable visitor was Maximilian, King of the Romans, a mediæval figure smitten by the Renaissance, ambitious and able, sensitive and ironic, dreaming of great crusades while entangled in little wars, living like a condottiere, desirous of Constantinople and the title of Emperor in some lost dazzling style, a romantic astray, a paladin *manqué*. Once he had had a great moment when, after long delay, he came to succour the beautiful Princess Mary of Burgundy, like Lohengrin in silver armour, with a crown of pearls on his head. But, since death the kestrel struck her as she hawked in the meadows of Bruges, he had lost his heart and his head, and frittered away his days on mercenaries he could not pay, books he could not write, tongues he could not speak, forbidden distinctions and frustrate wars. Now he came penniless to treat with Lodovico and to sell the trivial investiture desired by the restless conscience of the Duke, for an undesired bride who seemed to him but a pretty parvenue with an enormous dowry. Italy was always a siren luring Northern emperors to her enchanted shores. Across all their policies and lusts of conquests, hardly disguised by some paltry diplomatic excuse, came the secret desire to seize a principality in the fabulous land, and inherit a supreme civilization. Did Maximilian dream for a moment as " Romanorum Imperator semper Augustus," he who could even preposterously imagine himself as a pope ? If, through assuring Lodovico's affairs, he had vanquished the French and settled the peace of Italy, his disappointed mind might have seized on some visionary throne to its liking. But he had too many troubles north of the Alps ; and, when Lodovico needed him, his armies were lacking.

Still, universally interested, half romantic, half cynic, the fitful Maximilian came to hunt at Vigevano. Did he meet there Leonardo, whose long shining hair and beautiful hands he would see again, Germanized, in Albrecht Dürer ? A light extravagant, a lost, disconsolate knight looks the Emperor now, joined in the shock of nations, crushed between the blind thrusts of new forces. Yet, chaste and delicate in his manners, clothed always in black velvet because of his unfulfilled crusader's vow, with only the Collar of the Golden Fleece for splendour's sake, with wilful wits and wistful carving his ironical profile, he moves a melancholy and sometimes august figure among the avid over-coloured Italian princes, not without some aura of mystical authority. Some say he had a *Nativity* of Leonardo's given him by Lodovico. Well ! He had a trick of losing things.

A more portentous guest was Charles the Eighth, King of France. Why did Lodovico bring Charles to Italy ? Lorenzo was dead in Florence, the Pope was antagonistic, Venice meant enmity. He wanted an army between him and Naples, and did not realize how desirable looked his own duchy to invaders, nor how obstinately a French prince thought that he had inherited Valentina Visconti's title to Milan, as well as a claim to Naples. Amid these rival city-states, France was often considered an arbitrator. The fantastic politic of Italy still remembered Charlemagne. Cosimo de' Medici and Francesco Sforza

Lodovico and his Friends

had meditated on French intervention. Savonarola called aloud for the New Cyrus. Ferrara consented, and Mantua. The future Pope Julius and the cardinals desired the coming of French armies, though Julius would cry in the end : " Fuori gli barbari ! " Yet the odium lies on Lodovico, because it was obscurely felt to be Milan's destiny to refuse the stranger. " Prince, prince, show him not the way," called the friar in the Piazza, called the dying King of Naples.

Charles came, ugly, ridiculous, so silly that God seemed to take care of him as He guides imbeciles. Yet he saw himself as a great paladin, and he is touched with pathos by his gawky romanticism—a real Don Quixote betrayed by the tastes of Sancho Panza, redeemed by a royal gesture or two. He was disproportionate, and open-mouthed, and stammering, with twitching hands, heavy nose and lips. Yet he loved perfumes like a courtesan, and slept on a rose-scented bed like a fairy princess. He had a horrible disease in his body and a crusader's fantasy in his mind. Lodovico's great courtesies and persuasive manners alarmed him ; but he had seen Sanseverino riding at the jousts, and he loved him. He had used this noble like a prince of the blood, had made him free of his gross pleasures. Galeazzo was what he desired to be ; he wanted to own him like a fair picture. Charles is seen in Pavia, Vigevano, Milan, distrustful, but admiring. The Duchess in her most regal brocades with all her flowery ladies danced the dreamy twining dances. She had a choir of musicians, and singers; and eight sweet herodiads danced before the King in emerald colours. Beatrice and he, she in a loose gown of green satin, are like Beauty and the Beast, and he feels her too consciously alluring. Indeed the French had a kind of sacred terror of the pagan delight of Italy, and had already made a mystery play of the golden Borgian knot of Egyptian iniquity. Nevertheless they press on Naples, most heathenishly lovely of all ; and there, indeed, as if they were indeed people in a miracle play, a Plague finds them in their siren beds.

The Duchess Isabella at Pavia had wept when Charles visited her dying husband, and pleaded for kindred at Naples. He had been moved, uneasy. But the Prince dies while Lodovico is riding splendidly at the King's side, dies wondering if his uncle is sorry. That uncle, after a deprecating scene with the Milanese, goes in cloth-of-gold to the cathedral, Duke of Milan now in name as well as fact. When Charles, after blundering on and off the thrones of Italy, comes clumsily back like a pitiful great fly clogged with sweet poison-honey of Naples, Lodovico no more conceals his cold disgust. The invaders have been too gross and unmannerly : they are repugnant to all, and the Duke is now at the head of a League which includes Venice and the Pope.

But Charles most undeservedly gets home again, after the confused battle of Fornovo which should have defeated him hopelessly. It is necessary to observe the advent of Charles in speaking of Milanese matters. This coming of the French was the prologue to the destruction of Lodovico and his greatly composed Court. And, strangely enough, it decided that Leonardo should die an exile at Cloux.

iv

So much for courtiers and great visitors and poets !

In Milan the scholars were not so powerful to create new terms of thought and feeling as in Florence. There was no Platonic Academy, no poetic vision of a Hellenic past, no lives dedicated to a dreamy, musical, Alexandrian philosophy. For Lodovico, the Duke, had never the leisure and the security to affect the half-ironic, half-tender detachment of the Magnificent Lorenzo, even if his temperament had cared to dally with an intimate, unfeminine little court of philosophers. There was no grave and beautiful mystic like Pico della Mirandola, no sweet-souled acolyte of Plato like Marsilio Ficino, no live lover of antiquity like Poliziano to write ballets for the girls dancing in the spring-lit Square, or make a poem like *La Giostra*, a cloudy glitter of myths not easily forgotten, as well as rival all other humanists with his fine Latinities. But there had been great scholars in Milan since Filelfo fled there from Florence with his Greek wife, his manuscripts, his reputation for Hellenic learning and illimitable abusiveness. Merula, "the sun of Alexandria," Barbaro, Simonetta, Antiquario, Lascaris, Chalcondylas were all great names in Milan. They came from Venice, Calabria, Florence, Perugia, Greece itself. Milan wore Greek and Latin with her other graces, but did not mould a scholar all her own, though the first Greek book was printed here in 1476. The humanists were of the more pedantic and quarrelsome kind, which probably causes not only Leonardo but Bramante to claim to be "illiterate," evidently in moods of sarcasm and reaction. Lodovico was filling the chairs of Milan and Pavia in earnest mood. Fra Luca Pacioli was the chief mathematician: he was fast friends with Leonardo, who was more willing than ever to turn his mind and senses away from the over-excited murmurous capital, and soothe them, crystalline, in the scentless, hueless, soundless, touchless, emotionless concepts of pure form. Corio and Calco went about observingly, being chroniclers.

The great library at Pavia is open to Court historians, and to all true scholars. In the Castello a Jewish scholar, Salomone Ebreo, glides deprecatingly about, caring for the documents. Caradosso, the famous goldsmith, is also Lodovico's agent for finding him beautiful antique fragments. There is a new school of music established in the music-loving city. The printing-press becomes a centre of passionate interest. The first chair of history, as is fitting to a city with a history so long and various, is established in Pavia and Milan. The Duke tries to foster a chair of Hebrew in Pavia ; Merula and Chalcondylas between them draw distant students to both universities of Milan and Pavia, fair Northerners and dark Spaniards. The scholars' furred robes are never omitted from the great pageants of solemn occasions ; and Renaissance pleasure in Milan would have been counted a poor fallen creature if she had had no taste for grave interludes and no ear for the idolized accents of antiquity. The courtiers laid, for cooling dark ivy-leaves about their flushed revellers' brows, antique philosophy and the marvellous histories of Greek cities.

Once Lodovico held a great duello or congress of scholars, evidently a loose kind of British Association Meeting, in which Leonardo was concerned ; but that the result of the conferences was a permanent academy of arts and sciences is very doubtful. The council included alchemists and astrologists ; and Ambrogio da Rosate played a leading part, so it seems incredible that Leonardo did more than move through it in his most courteous and his most inscrutable way.

v

How did those sophisticated yet fiery people pass their days when affairs of state or the more ornate celebrations did not employ them ? Whatever the amusements and violences of the courtly life of Milan, there were many pauses of orison in their ritual of beauty. Sometimes it was crested tide of music and gold and ecstatic suspension of High Mass ; but sometimes it was as if they slipped softly into an æsthetic Prime or Vespers, tired of the heat of the day. There was a fine sensibility in these people, and a sincere devotion for lovely things. They were more highly trained æsthetes than had been since the days of Pericles. Such were the gentlemen who would go of a Sunday to sit still in the refectory of the Grazie, subjugated and satisfied by the noble rhythms, the unearthly colours, the profound and accusing symbolism of the Last Supper.

When the Court company sat still in the more intimate camerini, they talked of the " matters " of France and Britain. They had intricate debates on the qualities of the rival paladins. And Lancelot and Tristram, the great lovers of the woodlands and the meres, still rode singing through their lives and keyed their courtesies to a finer pitch ; while the mighty horn of Roncesvalles, that peals lonely through Christendom for ever, sent broken echoes of dying splendour and starry challenge through their charmed minds, as it still sounds immortal-clear to-day for the lost lovers of romance, bringing splendour of the West against splendour of the East. Or they discussed curiously some point of chivalry, or in gold-leaf speech beat out some sweet syllogism while a rare melancholy dropped its plumes beside them like a white peacock sleeping in the dusk. For Ferrara the piercing mingled well with soft Milan, and one of her nobles had already made a new poem, mingling things of Arthur with things of Charlemagne, and creating that Renaissance witch, the white Angelica. Or at the sunset hour they sat still in the loggia, and the low-voiced Dante reader chanted the marvellous passion of Francesca, and the long heartbreak of La Pia, and Piccarda, still lingering in the silver meads of the moon. Or they changed the key, and another told once more how Psyche was brought amazed to the bridal-bed of Love himself, and they wondered again over that golden romance, that exotic symbolism of the baffling Apuleius.

They talked much concerning points of honour, finesses of conduct, and loved verbal quibbles, for which we have lost patience. The conversation was both subtle and gross, for when they were merry they were frank and, we would say, shameless. Isabella d'Este had *The Golden Ass* as well as the *Miserere* of Savonarola in her library ; Mariolo, the fool, was a various buffoon. Bramante was a gay talker ; and if he debated with Gaspare Visconti the comparative merits of Petrarch and Dante, the argument might end in mirth. But they were all so candid in tossing their branch of tribute to the garden-god, and so gaily aware of other altars requiring more splendid sacrifices, that they would have been surprised as well as shocked to hear a group of young people in this year of grace moodily discussing their " complexes." They were out for verbal fun. Emilia Pia, the witty, bright lady in *The Courtier*, dying, forgot the last Sacraments in her eagerness to take a point in Montaigne.

Serafino d'Aquila would extemporize seraphically ; he sang strambotti to the lute. Gian Cristoforo Romano, who had sculptured Beatrice before she wedded Lodovico, goldsmith, medallist, architect, carver of crystal too, was often with the company. He was fragile and an invalid, but his voice was of such beauty that the Duchess carried him with her from place to place. You hear him gently urged to speak, long after, in the Urbino Palace ; his is a silvery, crystalline presence. The craving Isabella tried to steal him, but he preferred the Milanese Court till Lodovico's distresses sent him sadly away to Genoa. Sometimes, when the talk is all of imprese, motives, fables, allegories, Messer Leonardo

may be among them. But if he tell them a story of talking beasts
and trees they will taste something tart in the anecdotes, an astringent
note after the dulcet, "some satire keen and critical" in this suave
Ysopet, however musical his voice. Was there, as Lomazzo states, a
special book written for the Duke of Milan by Leonardo to prove the
superiority of the painter among all artists? Possibly. It was a theme
dear to Leonardo, and the kind of subject courtiers liked for the debates
in which they kept their wits keen. They toss about the argument
in *The Courtier*. Leonardo may have worked up his part of some such
discussion into a treatise. It does not exist now; but we know the drift
of it.

They would walk in the Room of the Doves, while the ladies who
wore the sbernia held up their great gold sleeves "in the peacock's way."
They played at games of ball, pallette and pallone in the high halls or
in the gardens. They had sweet, dreamy games like "batter le palme
in cadenza." They sat in circles, passing a clove-carnation or a rose,
and murmured sweet enigmatic words. They idled in tender games like
"J'ai perdu mon cœur." They had sudden little round dances like an
acted verse in Love's liturgy They played scartino; and the Duchess,
alas! was lucky at cards. With more intent and mysterious look they
gathered their bright jewelled heads like a frieze of precious sunflowers,
between the pillars of the loggia, against the pale-gleaming beryl sky,
over the exquisite tarocco cards painted with figures, and dipped in
myth and magic of dead-golden Egypt, and dead-rose Babylon, and
smiled against the darkening background, till some faint red-ringed hand
let fall the lovely lover's card. Or two by two they sat at amazing
chessboards where, rose and ivory, the small symbolic armies of beauty
were set, and began the immemorial moves of the game known by
Persian and Arabian lovers as by Celtic Deirdre and Naois in the West.

Enchanting things, the tarocco cards! Cardinal Ascanio's pack of
these fragile riddles of fortune survives with a lovely pathos all that
wrack of gorgeous things. Images of swords, cups, denarii, bastone, of
Greek Hermes and mysterious Thoth, his Egyptian identity, a papessa
with peacocks, queens, kings, hierophants, lovers, virtues, Osiris, Death,
devil's castles, Sirius, Star of Isis, moons and suns—these bright superstitious toys carry some coloured dust of divination from Greece and
Araby and Egypt.

But most of the dreamier moments fell dewy from the clepsydra
under the spell of music. The knights had their viole d'amore; the
ladies bowed over their psalteries like angels in a gilded ancona.
Beatrice had a sweet voice: her organs and clavichords were perfect
pieces from the hands of Lorenzo de Pavia, who delighted to lay "these

dear companions, ebony and ivory," lovingly together. It was chamber-music when the cypress-wood burned clearly in the immense chimney-pieces like heraldic altars, clasped and guarded by Milanese springing ironwork. It was flower-music when the spring sent them laughing or musing to the garlanded loggia, set with orange-trees in great jars of Gubbio ware.

Even when the life was *intime* they danced—danced gracefully with lifted hands, and reticent faces, and swaying figures, and low reverences. Harpers and lutanists made their music as they danced, and some-times the pastoral cornamusa. In those measured and lovely patterns, cardinals could move with dignity. In the " Petit Rose " ballet, in " Love's Combat," in " Burning Sun," and the ghirlandetta known to Dante, lovers separated silently, to come again ; imploring hands were lifted and caught. One circular dance went fluently and more swiftly. " The water runs on the slope ; the grape is in the Vine," was its motto. More feverish dances troubled the festival nights, like " La Gaillarde " and the " Branle," the torch dance, when, late, the last masquer reversed the flambeau with the mournful sweet gesture of some genius of Death.

Often the duchesses go to play with the children. It is not only in the art of the Renaissance that children come alive. The letters of the great Italian princes at this time are often wonderfully charming and tender in their pride and solicitude concerning their infants. Education was one of the arts in the Renaissance ; and children were found more delightful and amusing than they had been before or would be again for a long time. The Renaissance did not mature to its natural conclusion ; it was an Italian affair, and when Italy was wounded to death her Renaissance perished with her.

vi

With all this ceremonial and high courtesy, these singers and dancers have time and appetite for the open air and the maytide. The great spring festival was especially glorious, and even sacramental, in Milan, aware of the old gods, towards whom some drowsy undertow still drew in the litanies. So maytide was really something of an Anthesteria, a special ritual of ghosts and flowers. They sit in state to " receive the may." They ride out singing to meet the morning, shy with wet lilies in her hands, since " in her lids hung the rich tears of May." They are three princesses in pearl and emerald, with their knights ; but their knights are only their bright shadows, for Milan is not Florence, it is mayland. In green camorras they ride their white horses, and their donzelle are in green samite and green sendal. So they pass through branches variously set with the hearts and diamonds and cloven flames and little feathers and slim arrows of pale viridis and deep viridis that are the leaf-patterns of Ascension-tide ; and the air is a wash of soft chrysoprase and silver. The seed-pearl is set on the ebony branches ; the black almond-rods are enchanted with rare rose-pardon and the myrtle-wands are creamily, dreamily offering stars of fragrance. It is an Arthurian idyll, suffused with the richer airs of Italy :

" Cras amet qui nunque amavit : quique amavit cras amet."

Or Duke Lodovico is thoughtfully watching the work at the great Certosa. He is suddenly encompassed by a band of Turkish ladies, Beatrice and her friends—she has worked all night devising the dresses. Lodovico is ravished by the flushed laughing faces emerging from the dark veils, soft vivid flowers among the new-shaped cupids of the Certosa and the cypresses, for he is as charmed by a sudden picture of this kind as by the great diamond of Charles the Bold. As for Beatrice, who would think she could make Latin orations, and listen as closely as he to ambassadors of intricate, maybe deadly, import ? Next morning she will be leader of a hunting company that breaks out of the green glades of Vigevano like an explosion of gems, a woodland scene by Monticelli ; and, recklessly overriding, will face her wild quarry alone. In a habit of rose, with a priceless jewel in her silk hat, she is like an Eastern bird on her great black horse. But she rides straight as a man, they say, even if her plumes are wanton with the wind ; and sometimes she seems to charge in air, as high as the length of a lance.

There is a water-festival on the Ticino. The ducal Bucentaur is covered with Persian lotos-cloths, and hung with great banners rosy and green, wavering rarefied in the pools. Music with her faint fine viol is moving unearthly upon the water ; and the amaranthine dusk blurs the rose and the jasper and the profound soft blue about the golden figures, till the scene confuses sight and sound like the beautiful arrogant corruptions of colour in one of Turner's splendidly perishing canvases. It is the Renaissance version, rich and deep and impassioned, of *Embarquant pour la Cythère*.

The knights and poets, coming to read their verses, tease Isabella d'Este, who sits in her blue-hung guest-chamber, while Teodora and Beatrice and Violante, her maidens, comb out and curl her long swathes of honey-golden hair. Her dark and darkened eyes laugh at them, with her lovely art as of giving some unique and inviolate look to each. She is like a lady in a Rossetti picture or a Swinburne ballad.

" The queen's mouth was most fair,
 She spake a word of God's mother
 As the combs went in her hair."

Leonardo the Florentine

God's mother, with Isabella, is as likely to have been Aphrodite or Leda, though in her own camerini she affects the Triumph of Chastity. Meanwhile, the Duchess, singing to her clavichord with a new feather of rubies darkling and dartling in her black tresses, is red as a rose with delight, for soon she will be dancing, and Lodovico has never looked princelier than in the suit of ethereal stuff, the white Lyons velvet presented for the investiture of Genoa. When Beatrice is friends with felicity, she is ready to clash her soul like kissing silver cymbals.

Anna Sforza goes like a lovely pale Pascall candle, robed all in white for Saturday, for she has been ill, and keeps her wistful vow. The little Bianca has taken off her hood of pearls, and strings white violets. Her great lord, passing from changing songs with the Duchess, looks down at her with a movement of strange desire and compassion, and kisses her little hands. Pearls and white violets lie together in her lap, and she gazes with a faint smile into a vision of asphodel, not knowing what she sees—only that she is too happy.

And Cecilia Gallerani sits still in her broidered villa, while all the artists and poets and witty gentlemen throng about her. Here, most probably, is Leonardo da Vinci playing, for a little diversion, on his own silver lyre, with its curious stops and strings, while Fra Antonio da Monza draws him for the book of music he is illuminating for Cardinal Ascanio. Atalante the singer is here, explaining that he has given another silver lyre to their friend Gaspare Visconti, and that Isabella of Mantua has taken one of her fierce fits of æsthetic covetize for this shining piece of sound-craft.

vii

Sometimes the whole company goes mad for a moment, and rushes away to play a practical joke. It is not always in the best of taste, according to our notions ; but a practical joke never is a delicate form of fun. When the two duchesses in their mirth take to wrestling, and " she of Bari hath knocked down her of Milan," you feel that there is a touch of hysteria in the matter, struck out from the long constraint of elaborate public courtesy put on two women who are at deadly odds. The tomboy fun with which both duchesses in disguise try " flyting " with the crowd, and the mystifications practised on poor Trotti the ambassador, and the delegated mirth of those buffoons on whom such a surprising value was set, seem odd lapses from a life so sincere in its " magnificence." But Antony and Cleopatra went hooded to mix with the crowds at night, and " disguise is the spice of life." Yet some of these fools have the quality of Shakespeare's Feste ; and there are fashions in humour, though the most primitive form of practical joking

appears to delight all the centuries. Because ours is a tired and disillusioned age, distrustful of great passions and enthusiasms, it seems to
have achieved great conquests in the world of humour, and sets its aching
heart very divertingly to all the modalities of mirth. Extraordinary
qualities and flavours of irony, derisive gestures, mimicry, finesses of
absurdity, singing Pierrot fantasies that slide from the moon to a thin
ice of sorrow, sardonic graces, dancing stars of elusive innuendo, daring
somersaults of paradox, macabre surprises, ethereal and exquisite *mots*
like those exchanged by Watteau ghosts, dancing gaieties of the dying,
mad sallies that shake the angels, all the expressions that ultimately
but disguise hidden daggers or unshed tears—we have all these, and
they are all precious gains, with dangerous edges. But great ages and
great people are apt to be simple in their mirth. "Laughter holding both
its sides" is perhaps most beloved by persons relaxing from a great
intensity of living. Subtle and various mirth is one of the arts of the
decadence. Ours is, on the whole, the grace of delicate Sadducees.
For, after all, our exquisite stained-ivory Chinese puzzles of intellectual
mirth are only for the spiritual aristocrats who have somehow stolen or
ravished enough leisure to complicate their thoughts. For the mass,
and more especially for the rich, I expect a Renaissance clown could be as
amusing as some of our famous comedians.

Leonardo, somewhat unexpectedly for those who forget the diablerie
which played like summer lightning about his scientific studios when
visitors came to wonder, seems to have loved a practical joke or a
mystification as well as any young emperor of the fading Empire,
like Elagabalus, for instance. The delight in startling was the airier
expression of his more sinister self. So he even writes down a recipe,
"To make fire in a hall without injury. It is a good trick to play."
The fire-makers would think so. Leonardo would have agreed with
Hobbes that laughter is "a passion of sudden glory."

viii

But most of all they danced. The Estensian princesses had, as
children, been trained by the best masters in Italy; and dancing was
the very soul of Milan. All Renaissance Italy danced indeed, as in the
sacramental dance round the garlanded altar in her great Easter of
the Risen God, who was wreathed with vine, the white Pascall whence
all the world caught light, by whatever name they called him. And
Florence was more the lute-player, for Lorenzo set his tunes for all
the cities when the young men and girls of Florence danced through
the streets. In the other great cities the dancing went on like a ritual.

Lucrezia, incomparable, danced with Cesare ; Isabella, exquisite, danced
with kings and cardinals, with whoever was mightiest at the moment :
Beatrice, mænad, danced with Joy. The dances of Italy were more
ceremonial than the dances of France ; but in this art the nations of the
West gave and took their gracious rhythms, like flowers from the dancers'
hands. There was the beautiful pavane, where the bowed heads of the
lutanists accorded dreamily with the sweet sadness that passes into
the faces of all dancers, caught unwitting into an immemorial sacrament, an august and pathetic mimicry of life and death. There was
the Venetian, the Bergamask, the Florentine, the Roman, the Sicilian,
the Spanish, the French way. And as Isabella said, there was " il mio
modo." There are figures like sacred dancers in Leonardo's drawings,
wafted with wavy fine raiment to their place in the heavenly measure.

All this dancing continually passed over into masques and shows.
There never was such an extravagance of colours and sounds for the
artist in ephemeral pictures. " The best in this kind are but shadows."
Not shadows in sumptuous Milan ! Life itself so easily and even
sincerely fell into drama. That weeping encounter of the two duchesses
outside Milan, the one in black veils and mean cloth, the other in all
her gemmed and brocaded pride, is a true picture of Milan. The one
has lost her all ; the other has much and yet will take that all. But
the strain of the desirous life is terrible, and the sudden moment unmasks
them : glory and grief are confounded in the innocence and community
of tears.

It is a different human masque when Beatrice lies in state, with her
new-born heir in a golden cradle, and she in a great bed golden and
sard-coloured, while through the silver-hung room the curled pages in
silver brocade bring her moon-coloured fruits and roses on vessels of
gold and silver, and the gilt-broidered guests come and go, not without
soft sound of trumpets.

The whole Court was a *Masque of Comus* ; but when, as on great
occasions of hospitality, or bridal, or investiture, the dancers were controlled, selected, by minds so shaping and sensitive as those of Bramante
and Leonardo, the figures were etherealized into images of Olympos,
and the momentary pageant became something ideal ; the excess of
colour and jewels fell away, and the rhythmic paces took on the gravity
and gorgeousness of timeless measures, the mimers looked what the gazers
felt, gods and bridegrooms of immortals. Leonardo forgets his crucibles
and his scalpels, and takes the wand of revel-master. But he does not
forget his paradisal " mechanics " ; his engineering devices are welcome,
while Bramante too assists in the " insubstantial fabric of the vision."
In a fit of remorse Leonardo once wrote : " Shun those studies in which

the work that results dies with the worker." But, in his wasteful way, he loved the shifting pictures where he had real human beauty, wistfully breathing attitudes, for his pieces. He could casque a Paris, or set little wings on the brow of a Hermes, or give a lyre to Orpheus, that figure sent violing from Florence through the whole Renaissance, with the sense of fragrant Sicily and fallen flowers and death the snake, and Hades half-yielding the Greek Eurydice, and sequels of Thracian blood-communion and immortal mystery. These compositions had a dreamlike and vanishing effect he could hardly find in line and colour. He could lay gold on gold, and scatter rains of pearls. He lifted them upon the altar of beauty for an hour, and perhaps that hour for ever included them in her crystal eternity.

His most famous masque was woven around a splendid and luckless bridal. It seems to have adorned the bridal-feast made for young Gian Galeazzo and Isabella of Aragon, in a room set with immense jars of branching flower-trees, while Persian cloths muted, with soft rose spaces, the golden background. The princely banquet was in itself an amazing pageant, when the gods brought the food and wine—Apollo, Atalanta, Diana, Isis, Jason, Thetis, Pomona, Hebe. When the golden guests were weary with the rainbows and the roasted peacocks, Leonardo's great *Paradiso* must have come like a soothing benediction, with the dewy scintillating effects of the æsthetic peace, great silver archangels moving solemnly with the stars between their hands, ethereal music as from heavenly distances, sweet planetary cadences of song transfusing Bellincioni's rimes into that soft white surge of epithalamia which should from all time betray the mystic figure of the Bride to the ultimate adventure where the pride of virginity will be paid, for love—for hate. Some such unique enchantment, made of unearthly colours of auroras and silver stars, some still ravishment of sound like the falling of white roses or breaking of white foam, or singing of Elysian nightingales, something altogether rare and unexpected, must have so consoled the eyes, exceeded with gold and bright colour and vivid images and Neapolitan dances, to make this masque of Leonardo's, among all his masques, most memorable. What mattered Bellincioni's words ? Leonardo made it a marvel of waving rhythm—rhythmical motion and music. He could be dazzling too. At one time he is much preoccupied with a masquer who must wear a great peacock on a golden globe for a helmet, while the rest of the apparel is all peacock feathers on a gold ground. Evidently the palace birds of Milan will not let fall enough of their glorious plumes to please him, so he invents a way of creating bright substitutes. He has a passion for peacock feathers, naturally ; all lovely unlucky things are harmless for those who have a strain of the divine.

Leonardo the Florentine

But there was also the ballet of Medea and the Argonauts, with Jason, another Renaissance hero seeking the Golden Fleece of Wonder, and the fair mythic host of his friends, with Atalanta among them, and the outraged Medea on her dragon-car, magician and moon-goddess, and kin to the queen of the witches.

Another famed pageant of this time was that of Hippolytus and Theseus, at the lovely house of Niccolo da Correggio. Hippolytus was a cherished theme to the Renaissance ; for the Grecian philosophers had their cult of chastity as much as the mediæval monks, however strangely they wove it into other worships. Green-garlanded Hippolytus, tamer of horses, was dear and beautiful, and dazzlingly white in their evocation of gods and demigods.

Then, there were great giostra, where always Galeazzo Sanseverino moved superb and victorious on a conscious steed, richly panoplied— romantic giostra, where the victor won prizes like a golden pallium, or a crystal cup, enamelled green and crimson with the love of Tristram and Iseult, glowing on a silver-gilt stand. At Lodovico's wedding there was a great tourney, where the knights of Mantua rode in green and gold, and those of Bologna wore for device the silver unicorn, Gaspare Sanseverino had a troop of seeming Moors in black and gold, with white doves on their black armour. Galeazzo won the prize with a band of Scythians on wild Barbary horses whose savage dress Leonardo arranged in Galeazzo's house, while his little curly-haired page Jacopo crept to the cast-off purses of the squires and stole some money for sweets. And for Sanseverino himself Leonardo designed the raiment for the victory he had won with a golden lance, for Galeazzo was also one of his pictures. And the young Duke's nephew was wild with joy over it all.

The most amazing show of all was Bianca Sforza's, where the bride, on a triumphal car drawn by four white horses, like the charioted Chastity or Beauty of some allegorical triumph, attended by all the duchesses, with counts to hold her great winged sleeves of gold and her enormous train, went to be proxy-married, not to a man, but to a ghost of magnificence, a lord of mystic authority, while the streets were hung with garlands of golden apples and blazoned with vipers and eagles. It was a flaming, rejoicing, singing and dancing city, for the dukedom had allied itself to a title of such mysterious prestige that the very echo of it could sound august in the soul of Europe even till yesterday. It was Lodovico's own Triumph, for he had revived the fainting myth of the Holy Roman Empire so that he might become its feudatory and claim a vassal's privilege. The city became as May in November ; the streets were hung with satin and frescoed ; the priests were clothed in great vestments of mightier brocades than the women's ; the altar bore those vessels of perfect craft that the Duke reserved for God's state occasions, and the Mass was said with trumpets, flutes and organs. Firing of guns, ringing of bells, flourish of trumpets—colour and sound seemed to have gone mad together. So Bianca went with floods of violet, green, and cramoisie, and the labours of goldsmiths and silver-smiths locked in her bridal caskets, on caparisoned steeds, in painted boats and gilded, to shudder in storms and faint on mountain-tracks and wait long in Innsbruck for her sacerdotal lord, who will have neither money nor men when Lodovico's fall is near.

There were triumphal arches and miracle plays and masquerades for Charles VIII., who, when he went to Florence, wanted to see nothing but the lions. There were lions here for him, beautiful African lions. There were investitures in cloth-of-gold, or precious white Lyons velvet, as when Lodovico went to Genoa, and his womenfolk envied the weft he wore. For Isabella there must always be classical comedies, in Lodovico's portable theatre copied from Ferrara's. There are shows and jousts for Sanseverino, jousts and shows and banquets of music for Cardinal Ascanio. And at all great festivals the houses were hung with webs of Persia and Araby, garlanded with juniper and oranges, or stretched with satin, or painted with bright pictures.

There were festivals by the water, where amid sophisticated and splendid settings the dewy and simple shepherd stories gave the double delight of their intrinsic freshness and the piquant contrast with their luxurious " emplacement." Scenes of Arcady on the banks of the Ticino, where satyr, shepherd and nymph fluted and sang in tender desire, alarm, reassurance ! Galeazzo Sanseverino does not have it all his own way in shows. His condottiere brother, the Conte di Caiazzo, gives Bellincioni the argument for a pastoral in which the shepherds debate on love, only to appeal for a decision to the Genoese lady he loves. Dances and songs, pipes and timbrels ! So far the soothing shepherd-play !

ix

Always about the Castello there is a great press of people. Beatrice's retinue, the Duchess Isabella's retinue, Lodovico's retinue, Ascanio's, Galeazzo's, Ippolito d'Este's, the young Duke's, and many more. Lords, ladies, musicians, readers, chaplains, jesters, astrologers, falconers, dwarfs, soothsayers, pages, music-makers of every kind, perfume-sellers, Levantines with things of the East, white Circassians and Nubians carved in ebony, are among the coloured crowd. The women drive in the famous carette of Milan, all blazoned and slashed with silk and gold. A great lady like the Countess of Cellant had four white horses to draw her ; and two were clothed in gold and two in scarlet. Before Ambrogio da Rosate, court physician and astrologer, all cleared a way, for he was wrapt in his cloak and his reverie, deciding a date for a wedding festival, a foundation stone, a voyage, a reception of ambassadors, a consummation of marriage. Leonardo was courteous with him, discreetly expressing his opinion of physicians and star-gazers only to his manuscripts. The fencing-masters went by with springing steps. These he saluted, for he still loved parry and thrust, swords and swordsmen. Camillo Agrippa was a famed Milanese sword-master. Pietro Monte, jouster, fencer, wrestler, vaulter, who had for pupil the famous Galeazzo Sanseverino himself, fascinated Leonardo by his skill in throwing darts. His swift unerring pencil followed with zest the swift unerring trajectory. Captains in brocades with gemmed spurs, parti-coloured soldiers of many bodyguards, stamped with haughty badges, scholars in black gowns or in scarlet, like the elder Cardano, proud armourers, the aristocrats of Milanese craftsmen, who marshalled their lines of knightly panoply down their street at Lodovico's wedding like a motionless army, the varletry of the great war-horses, the great horses themselves, from Araby, Sicily, Barbary, wild coursers from furious Thrace, hollow-eyed feverish inventors of " some new thing," young poets with fresh scrolls, young singers with tried lutes, are all woven into the curves of the blazon of the Viper. Falconers rode on great white stallions, holding on their wrists those precious birds of race that have, according to Leonardo, fastidious and magnanimous ways of their own in their hunting, princes of the upper air. Huntsmen went in green doublets broidered with silver herons. Wandering minstrels sang songs of Roland with such fire and pathos that even simple burghers went weeping home, though the knight " has been dead seven hundred years." But if Leonardo stayed to listen, it was to a minstrel who chanted " the matter of Troy " and the still smile of unravishable Helen.

And everywhere there are coveys and swarms of pages, with serried curls and fantastic boots, and young and earnest faces or young and evil faces, mingling with surprising little dwarfs, loud little dogs, rare Persian cats. They are as if scattered like red and white and golden leaves all over the Castello. The Duchess' pages, the Duke's, Ascanio's, Cardinal Ippolito's meinie of superlatively elegant, wanton and lovely pages ! Lawn vests and velvet coats and kittens' eyes and bright curls, you may see them in the illuminated books like a flight of dragonflies and butterflies just alighted on the galleries and the gardens.

It was a world of mazes, " mazes of heat and sound." Leonardo's feet tread delicately and fluently like his moon-led waters in wavering

music. He seems to be shod with silence, a smiling apparition where
and when he is remembered and desired.

X

All the populace of the Palace moved on inlaid pavements ; their light
fell through painted glass, blazoned with stories or chased with the concentrated legends of arrogant heraldries. They sat on cushions broidered
with amorini and darting suns ; their gryphoned and sphinxen and
siren-toiled seats were also rich with intarsia or gilded leather. At their
feet were Persian carpets spread there softly like ghostly ineffable roses
and pale ethereal violets ; on the walls were tapestries telling of Troy and
antique Rome.

They ate from plates fired with Olympian love tales, dishes of Rhodes
all tulips and roses, brilliant dishes of Faenza in the key of blue, lustrous
dishes of Gubbio, romantic with dolphins and wreaths and loves ; their
fruits glowed in glowing Murano glass, and they drank from goblets
of silver-gilt, shaped like ships and conchs, or semilunes with covers of
agate. Cypress-wood burned rarely amid its floriated ironwork in its
own great alcove, large as a *chapelle ardente,* charged with masks and
volutes. Their tapers rose from tall lampada, great candelabra flowering into silver flame. Or light lay in such pure arks as the great lantern
of rock-crystal and silver which Venice once gave to Lodovico as a false
baiser de paix, or in miraculous Arabian lamps thieved from Moorish
mosques.

Their chamber-music woke from cloisters of pearl and amber, ebony
and ivory. Their pierced perfume balls were foliated with marvellous
delicacy. The caskets were wrought ivory and lucid enamel ; the cassoni
were of gilt leather, or stamped velvet fitted into scrolls of acanthus, or
set on wyverns' feet, or covered with centaurs of bronze. Their rosaries
were black amber and gold ; there were baroque pearls even on the necks
of their swans. Their bridal beds had golden columns ; the clocks that
warned them of the death of the roses slipped their sands, or dripped their
waters, or swung their tongues within apologia of lovely devices. They
looked in mirrors of gilded walnut-wood where dragons crouched either
side a classic vase (strange variant of the Tree of Life above the gazer's
lovely head), while the dolphins were caught by the cupids in the leafage
on either side. They had their own little collections of superfine things,
to handle for love of some organically pure texture, moulded by craft
with an amorous pleasure, like Beatrice's own camerino of toys. Things
of ivory, crystal, and majolica, and Murano glass, exotic perfumes, and
fairy hunting-horns !

Leonardo the Florentine

In their great libraries they turned the painted books on lecterns like winged dragons, and the astrolabes solicited their curious eyes from serpent-graven stands. A book of sonnets might be written in silver and gold letters on ivory vellum, with tondos like blue and green gems, with silver-gilt boards enamelled with flowers. They were gorgeous, those painted books of Milan, as if illuminated with jewels powdered and infused into layers of rich and smooth, too smooth, enamel, so lively with images recalling the secular life, even in the *Book of Hours*, that surely Anna Sforza, for instance, forgot the words of her psalter in the rounds of sweet young figures of luting gallants that captivated her eyes. Antonio do Monza was the master of a whole world of psaltery-playing angels and kissing birds, singing or violing children with thick curls, peacocks spilling kindled moons of emerald down the page. Copies of Virgil, Epithalamia, Acts of Donation, all have their lovely branches and great candelabra bearing vipers and eagles. Harpy turns to angel, angel to volute. The architectural motives are repeated here with concentrated intensity. The absorbing Protean vitality of the Renaissance, with its curious sense of shift and change, of alterations and successions in spirit and things, turns the fountains into candelabra and the candelabra into Trees of Life. The Tree of Life is indeed an endless theme, as vine, as acanthus, as lotos, with equally varying supporters, dragons, angels, amorini, sirens. It triumphs everywhere, especially in the choral sedilia of the Certosa and San Ambrogio. Leonardo's mind in itself is this Renaissance masque of Proteus ; you will find him drawing such moments of metamorphosis, siren disappearing into acanthus, and the like, Daphne vanishing in the poet's laurel, Syrinx flying in music into the reeds—the fugitive thrilling moment of change, the infinite shift and drift of the universe, the flux of beauty, one beauty vanishing into another—in decoration, at least, this dim sweet excitement reveals a philosophy.

So the handles of the swords, and the crooks of the crosiers even, were illumined by this rapture of desire to seize flying things. The swords of Milan were astonishing. Their blades were damascened with vines ; and they spoke with sinister silver mottoes. They were poignant iris-lilies of death, and Leonardo draws them page on page. The helmets are gripped or hooded with fabled silver-winged beasts fit for the proud sullen brows of the Seleucid. Their breast-pieces are lily-calyxes, their knee-pieces are medusas. They had " greaves, beautiful, fastened with silver ankle-clasps."

Even keys and locks are caught by the running mirth of ornament. The very tools are carved by other tools. The pression and torsion of the decorative spirit falls upon every object of use and delight. For this is the Court of Luxury, as never since the time of Ausonius. It is the House of Bliss where Acrasia spins her spell, a spell like a web and a dew of imagery over the yielding substance of the city. This is the Triumph of Adorned Things. Not since the Lord God of Israel dictated the details of His carven Ark of acacia-wood to Moses with such zest and precision that the bored multitude showed a similar appreciation of the graven images He wished to reserve for Himself, by making a golden calf, has there been such joy in ornament. "Of beaten work shall the candlestick be made, his shafts, and his branches; his bowls, his knops, and his flowers shall be of one piece with it." The "pure candlestick," with its furniture of knops and almond-blossom bowls, had many true descendants in Milan.

A certain irony in the Florentine mood kept the pagan patterns of Tuscany in a rhythm more reticent. The vine of ornament runs wild in Milan; and clambers over all that the hand may adore, caress, or kill. over all with which the hand may adore, caress, or kill.

xi

The women of Milan were always luxurious. Even saintly Theodolinda took her golden comb, her fine fan, her sapphire cup, her cross of crystal, and her gold-shut missal to her last bed with her, like any heathen Egyptian queen, like a Mycenæan princess, all faring to the grey ferry with their lovely vanities. They were naturally the chief acolytes of the great brocades of their city, and Beatrice was the high priestess. Books were written about them, laws were made concerning them, feuds were created by them, they were gifts between princes, offerings for God—they were sacerdotal stuffs. The symbols of love and life and religion, the wilful passions of personality, were woven within them. They were a psychological expression of Renaissance Milan.

White, green, cornelian, violet, black—and always intertextured with gold! Green-and-gold with silver grapes; green, cramoisie, and violet, like lunar rainbows; black-gold brocade and white-gold brocade! Heraldic, symbolic, musical, amorous, chimerical devices! Beatrice goes to Venice in golden brocade broidered with crimson doves, wearing chains of red and white jewels, a great ruby burning on her breast. Her brocade of the double towers, with their waves, was considered the most dazzling. But at the Imperial wedding she went wonderful in violet velvet, charged with that great " fantasia dei vinci " pattern she implored from Isabella, wrought in white and gold and green enamel. (Gaspare Visconti gave the Marchesa the device: he possibly had it from Leonardo.) Anna Sforza has letters of gold on black—Gothic letters, probably. The ancient and perfect motives of the lotos, the pomegranate, the pineapple are implicated in gold and crimson and green. Eagles, and unicorns, and Lucca's lions learn silken ways. Blue satin is strewn with flickering flames and flying butterflies for some very feverish lady.

The ducal garments and the seigneurial also demand the brocaders. A luxurious clergy with an Oriental tradition needs red vine and the red lotos and the rose-seraphim sacredly and perfectly laid upon the white. Dalmatics and chasubles, stoles and orphreys, in heavy brocades and pure satins, for ladies and for priests ! The sacristy of Sta Maria delle Grazie and the Duchess' wardrobes at Vigevano and the Castello were not so much unlike. Dalmatics and copes and chasubles and golden orphreys of beauty, they needed a sacristy in palace or cathedral. Stuff on stuff, grace on grace, precious on precious, beaten gold and silver threads fatigued by the weight of the jewels, the famous ricamatori of Milan wove their marvellous masterpieces.

But Leonardo's eyes of vair, considering, accepting, refusing, declined for his art the great brocades that distracted the gazer from the face and hands, the symbols of the soul. It is possible to catch a new æsthetic excitement from the vision of a rare slight lady rising frail and haughty from the robes of her coronation and magnificence. Even Raphael did that once, inspired by the beauty of Joanna. But Leonardo, who had himself first achieved the thing more subtly in the drawing of Isabella, would hardly have considered that peculiar exaggerated effect as any but a borrowed, and for him unlawful, pathos. His women must be clothed in cadences of pure colour unbroken by pattern, with fall of faint veils as he would clothe the immortals, like people in the Parthenon frieze. He is painting Saint Anne and the Virgin ; he wants thin fine stuff, as might have come from the looms of the Phæacian Islands, or heavy rich fabrics with sombre falls, fit for Clytemnestra. If his women arise in strange landscapes they must wear timeless raiment, with perhaps a faint gilded twine of filigree, a broider of unearthly fingers to hint of some occult tenderness. The Duke's mistresses would resign while he painted them their brocades and ornaments for the sake of the mystery wherewith he veiled and enchanted them, and because he could so provoke the faint sweet challenge of eyes and lips. But Beatrice loved her brocades and her knots of rose ribbon and her gems with an organic craving ; and she was much too proud, and a little too stupid, to deal in mystery and faint challenges. Well ! Zenale and others could paint brocades ; and Cristoforo Solari the sculptor makes her preferences lovely in death. Isabella had better wit. Veiled hair and timeless raiment, she is mysterious for once in

Lodovico and his Friends

Leonardo's drawing, though all her sweet speeches could not charm the sketch into a picture. Like Madonna Lisa, she wears fine stuffs just indicating a certain pomp. In his drawings, however, he seems to desire the raiment of nymphs and angels and goddesses ; rare veils from the craft of Cos. He accepts even the ribbons and points and flying sleeves if they float and sing into serpentine lines for his pleasure. The obliterating rigid robes of brocade, that turned the wearer to a kind of idol, were too pontifical for his taste.

xii

But the jewels that married the brocades had a still statelier life of their own. They had names and histories like the swords of mediæval romance. (Horses, brocades, jewels, swords are all firmly chained into Renaissance psychology ; and I cannot understand the jaded minds who do not realize the Renaissance Hamlet unless they strip him of the "inky suit" which is so involved with the cause of the play.) They had a ritual and a worship. They were ransoms, gages, triumphs. Love, hope, pride, delight, desire, victory and defeat fed their crystal fires. Lodovico had the great Sancy diamond of Charles the Bold. El Spigo was the priceless ruby ; Il Lupo was a diamond with three rare pearls ; Il Marone was another proud crimson gem. He had a great arrow of diamonds, and his caduceus wrought in pearls. The Moraglia lay glittering in emeralds, diamonds, pearls. King-emeralds, male-rubies, rose-diamonds, queen-pearls, star-sapphires, they blazed on the brocaded figures till the faces seemed moon-pale amid the glow and glitter. Pendants of enamel and heavy stones, shaped into fabled beasts or ivory nymphs and satyrs, of faëry ships in mother-of-pearl, lay taken in wonders of arachnean gold. Brow-jewels, breast-jewels, are the most intimate of these ornaments, bright fantastic ciphers of personality. The women seem to wear coats of coloured stones. Beatrice is like a dark carnation thrust within a gilt filigree of gems. Her finest girdle is the cord of Saint Francis clasped with a clear-cut ruby—true symbol of Milan, penitence inextricably linked with luxury, blood and tears crystallized into jewels.

Amadeo di Milano belongs to a famous family of jewellers and enamellers. Gian Cristoforo Romano's carved crystals, delicate milky visions, charmed within lucid spheres, gleamed like the dew. Caradosso is an artist and a scholar, who could make gold figures that Cellini envied. He creates tiaras for popes ; he searches the world for the "gentilezze" craved by Lodovico ; tries to rifle Lorenzo's collection for him, succeeds better at Rome. On his great plaques and medals he scribes impetuous myths, especially those rapt incidents of horses and wings so captivating for Leonardo, locked Centaurs and Lapiths, rapes of Ganymede, beautiful youth caught on eagles' wings through heavenly air, or garlanded white Hippolytus gripping his frenzied chargers, or Bellerophon on the steed that was a god. The leonardesque note is not absent from the work of the goldsmiths and ironworkers. Leonardo himself somewhat disdained the goldsmith's art, though most painters possessed the craft, to supply impoverished times. The trade he chose as a standby was loftier—engineering and fortification. But he sometimes threw the craftsmen a design. He loved to amuse his mind with woven lines like magical spells, like enigmas of beauty. He makes pages of them. For whom did he draw that grille of trellis-work? Was it for Lodovico's Tesoro? All the ironwork was delicate as gold in Milan, whether it flowered the gates, or bound the coffers, or twisted the torchholders, or forged brasiers light and leafy with almost a Pompeian grace.

To the churches their due of pearls and amethysts, as of the flowered brocades. The reliquaries were a weight of pale and ardent jewels and pellucid enamels. The liturgy was told with changes of burning gems, the crosses were life-trees of jewels, such as blazed fabulous and imperishable in legendary golden temples of Heathenesse. The treasury of the Duomo kept its high processional cross of emerald and gold, with chalices and monstrances and holy things wrought over with great expense of spirit as well as of invaluable matter. The Sacred Cups were enamelled with angels, and rubied with martyrdoms; they were calyxes indeed where the blood of a god might glow in beautiful lines. Some of the crosses were at once crosses and lightbearers. Some were encrusted and spiked like holy maces, some were serene in silver and lucid enamel, some bore a little tempietto, some were sweet heathen things with lions' feet and sphinxes at the base, for in her heart Milan peculiarly knew that there are pagan roods on other hills than Calvary.

Leonardo would take pleasure in this "luxury for God." For though the gods come fluting like simple shepherds out of Asia, they are buried, after they have been torn and crucified, in palace-basilicas, like the Holy Wisdom, or the Holy Sepulchre, or the Dome of Saint Peter's, and all that mortal beauty can, is poured in vain passion over their dust. Indeed, Leonardo was friendly enough with goldsmiths and jewellers. His designs wandered to them as to the brocaders. It amused him to twine the Duchess a girdle, to link and interlink a chain for Galeazzo. No jewels, indeed, lie upon the grave soft raiment of his painted people, save some rare ornament of symbolic value. The brow-jewel, the cipher of the soul within, fascinated him sometimes. Goddesses in Egypt wore them. Once, we know, he confided to one elect chalcedony a little imperishable design to keep for ever. Imperishable, but lost! Lone and lovely chalcedony, opaque dead-green, was it with the head of a Medusa or the head of an Antinous Mondragone that he tried to seal you to Eternity?

Well! No wonder the chalcedony was lost in all the wrack and spoliation. Where is the great diamond Il Lupo, and where the rose-violet El Spigo, so famous for its dreamlike colour? Where is the pearled caduceus of Lodovico, imaginative sceptre of his desire? Lost with all the other glories, lost as the gold and ivory images of Greece. It is reckless of art to be snared within precious metal and rare stone. Better a little marble or mere canvas. Marble is ground and broken, canvas corrupts and spoils. Leonardo, who had considerable interest in the durabilities of the arts, would have been reluctant to admit that a few cadenced words, made out of " a mouthful of air," could outlive all visible beauty.

While Leonardo commits his device to the chalcedony, the " Sack of the French " looms like a livid cloud behind a stormy sunset splendid with the dissolution of beautiful, puissant, guileless and guilty things. Glittering vestigia sparkle along the dusty ways of mortality—only the mere diamond-dust of that dazzling place and period. The memorable, most covetable things have dissolved in smoke and flame, or been soiled and pierced and powdered and torn, and lost and thrown in ditches by the men of masterless armies.

Meanwhile, so jewelled is the whole picture that it seems to burn in clots of colour. The very sunset smoulders through the green trees in gouts of molten ruby; the very pebbles in the foregrounds of the pictures in Bona's *Book of Hours* seem to be broken from a reef of gems, and Stephen is stoned with lumps of sapphire and topaz. Even the swans go sailing like enchanted princes in collars of baroque pearls. It is as if a passion for preciousness wreaked itself on every visible thing, seizing upon surfaces intrinsically priceless to burden them with a ransomless excess of art. Beauty was clothed with gold-woven brocades, and these were dazzled down by gems, and the gems were caught in filigree meshes and charged with the dreams of art, till the lovely figure, burthened overmuch, went with a pale look of delicate fatigue.

xiii

These excessive people were not satiable. As in their play, they called " diviner air " to be their playmate in the fields when they tired of their palaces, and so, having imprisoned and concentrated the rarity and essence of materialism in their gems and brocades and miracles of handicraft, and all that seemed imperishable, they had another delicate inherited appetite for flowers, for things of an absolute beauty more adorable because it is fleeting and perishable. Famous for her lilies and deep roses Milan had always been. So they twined garlands for their hair, ladies and youths ; they held them more tenderly in their fingers than fan or profumatorio; they felt like flowers themselves, opening their corollas, yielding their honey, scattering their rare pollen to the winds in spendthrift joy—plucked flowers fading in their sheaths of gems. They laid the petals to their feverish hearts to cool them. Was it in some extravagant desire to prison the souls of flowers that they were so mad for perfume ? They scented their hair, scented their fine gloves (scented with poison sometimes), scented their birettas and their shoes. It seems sometimes as if Milan, like Lesbos and Cyprus, must have been known to wayfarers by the atmosphere of myrrh and amber created around it. The sumptuous essences were sold at their weight in gold, narcissus, amber, myrrh, iris, and violet, and aloeswood. " Cose oderifera," grains of musk and horns of civet, were among the gifts of princes.

Leonardo loved flowers even to tenderness, and perfumes pleased him too. He had always drawn corollas and leaves with sensitive sympathy. They now became more and more dreamlike, as if the seeds of earth had been drifted by western winds into immortal meads. Now they are reeds and lilies, water-flowers and alpine-flowers, children of secret marsh-meadows, cool and pure as if from the banks of Eurotas. Dearly, also, he loved the flowerlike swords of the Milanese. Perhaps the bright weapon of knighthood was losing the sacred symbolic prestige it had kept during the Middle Ages, when there was almost a myth of the sword, and Excalibur and Durandal and their kind were personalities in romance. But swords like Cesare Borgia's, papal swords of honour, and even the swords of simple Milanese gentlemen, sprang from the armoury of beauty. Graven handles and damascened blades, with beaten copper, gold or silver threads of broidered flower, blue-azure, clear-green or red spots of enamel, gravely insolent mottoes, beautiful sheaths, he loved them. He draws them with zest, for he is kin to them, aware that his personality is poignant and perfumed, as if he were born from some mortal bridal between a sword and a lily. He is unconsciously cruel, as is otherwise demonstrable ; this is the most romantic form his cruelty takes. Other weapons, ruthless symbols no longer used in warfare, he draws at this time to satisfy his spiritual sadism. Because Milan was the city of Sebastian, did he devise those immense bows as of ivory :

> " Pur comme la lune nouvelle
> Et criard comme l'hirondelle."

Lodovico and his Friends

Though the luxury of Milan is excessive, it is not omnivorous nor unselecting like Rome; it is more exquisite than that of Venice. "Nay, more! the insatiable humour of mortals hath added thereunto all the luxuries and refinements of the East, together with the marvels and rarities which our age hath with inexpressible toil and grievous perils sought out in the world unknown to past ages." Such is the comment of one chronicler.

They like the rare, they like things with associations that go echoing into the past like stricken bells. A dwarf is more precious if he come from Chios; a great diamond blazes more regally if it has moved through tales of great battle and splendid feasts afar, having been worn by the puissant lords of Burgundy. Lodovico wants the Medicean cameos, medals, books, "et simili gentilezza," because he knows them perfect of their kind. Caradosso cannot acquire them; but he does bring a lovely antique Leda and other things from Rome. The Duke should have had, one feels, sweet spoil from buried Naucratis, dredged from the deep delta-silt above her, some graven cusp of mother-of-pearl, its pale iridescence rippled with a tale of gods, some fragile gold-foil love-charm, some dedicated lotos-bowl to Bast or Aphrodite.

Leonardo's dream of bringing the snow from the mountain-peaks to cool the Milanese festivals of midsummer roses seems enchanting because so fantastic; it is indeed and literally a dream of Elagabalus. Leonardo himself is considered invaluable because he is unique, and is making a unique Cena and a unique Cavallo. True, at one time Lodovico loses his patience so badly that he thinks that a tame Perugino in the hand may do more than a phœnix-Leonardo on his sole Arabian tree. But there is reconciliation; and Leonardo begins the Cavallo again.

A taste for the rare usually means in its lower terms also a taste for the bizarre, even the grotesque. All the Renaissance people had a craving for the values of contrast and discord which was hardly Hellenic (though Thersites goes grotesque among the heaven-sprung kings), but which was, in its way, effective. So they placed at intervals among their great trellises of vines and roses, the dwarf, the Nubian, and the ape, as consciously as an Aubrey Beardsley might in his intensely plotted pages, though their decoration was life itself, and of a fiercer kind than his. All three motives of decoration were extremely evident in Milan, partly because its sub-Eastern mood found an intrinsic pleasure in these macabre images, partly because their rose-arabesque seemed so much the more sumptuous-fair thereby. When the ape escaped and ranged over the castle the thrill was keen. The outrageous figures of dwarfs and little monsters dressed in cloth-of-gold were set in the pattern with a fine brutality which put an edge on the pleasure of too-sophisticated nerves. Obscene little figures uttering obscene jests among the love-learned " fantastics " with their citterns and psalteries ! It was their frank way of recognizing a hidden horror, and smiting out an effect from it, a brazen gong among the viols. Modern music knows these devastating chords which leave us lacerated, to taste with agonizing sensibility the ecstasy of the succeeding passage of heavenly seducing sweetness. The Renaissance was brutal, of course ; and so are we. Appetites were delicate and monstrous : we hide them now and are all neurotics. Besides, wild appetites have sunk to ignoble itches : they have not the dignity of frenzies. I do not advocate a return to frenzy : I mean that we are only less vitalized.

Exotic beasts were also dear to that riotous frieze of life. Lodovico had his lordly menagerie, especially his beautiful African lions. All the Italian cities were at this time aware of the swift and fiery motions of animalism behind their superb spring towards power and splendour : they kept their totems ; they watched them increase with superstitious interest. But they took delight in them, too, for their wonderful shapes and ways, and old familiarities with the gods who often wore their visages. Cesare Borgia's slain bull invested him with a touch of the prestige of Osiris and Mithra, and was an admirable piece of imaginative policy. That Leonardo saw his totem sometimes in the lion, sometimes in the swan, sometimes in the dragon or serpent that fought him and yet was himself, is a matter I regretfully leave to the students of anthropology.

As for the Moors and Nubians, they were slaves ; and any loyal aristocratic household possessed one, if only to do honour to Lodovico's nickname, Il Moro, corrupted from his second name because of his dark complexion. The rose-white ladies of Milan were aware of the force of contrast ; servitors like these heightened the golden and crimson and pearly values. Isabella of Aragon may be a most unfortunate princess ; but she has her slave, and desires one blacker. Chiara Montpensier needs a " little Mauresque." The strangely white and vicious Circassians, in the opposite way, look equally exotic and decorative.

For the bizarre and the grotesque Leonardo's temperament had sympathy, and even appetite. The stern and immortal mood of his art exiled the bizarre from a beauty that did not need to jangle with any shock of surprise, secure and serene in the hush of its divine introit. But he loved the grotesque in Florence ; he loved it more in Milan. He draws those dreadful parodies of human countenances more frequently, and lets them play into the faces of beasts with more ingenuity and ferocity. The attack of the dwarfs and the Nubians and the exotic beasts on his attention is assisted by the obsession of the Lombard larvæ, and blindworms, and bats, resting in the churches of the Dies Iræ. It is strengthened too by his obscure reaction against the over-sweet wounded invasion of the beauty of the Milanese women, to which, intellectually, he has had to yield a little. So he introduces a ghastly coquetry into the painful feminine versions of disfigured and age-wracked heads. Doubtless he remained of a golden courtesy to women, doubt-less he was not subject to the sudden furies and mad illogic breaks with which others of his peculiar kind, less highly intellectualized, wreck their imaginative appreciation of ladies fair and noble and unexacting. Doubtless he relieved his ugly moods against both men and women in this play of draughtsmanship. It was a mode of artistic exercise? Yes! It was something more.

He was kinder to the beasts. With intense pleasure he draws the mighty feet of those noble lions; even when he caricatures a lion's head a certain nobility is left in it. When he caricatures a woman's head the eyes have often the pathos of a monkey's, of a distorted or dehumanized creature's. Apes, dwarfs, lions, and monkeys all paid some unconscious toll to his unwearied gaze. The Nubians, though engrossing in some ways, gave him a sick distaste. Even Leonardo was Florentine enough to write that death was better than the loss of liberty. Caged birds or caged folk, he did not like to see them.

xvi

" If music be the food of love, play on.
    Give me excess of it."

All the burning colours, all the lights, all the vines and roses, the beautiful, the haughty, the grotesque, the splendours and the shadows, were softly toned and harmonized by music. When Leonardo came to Milan he had a silver lyre in his hand, and he did not let it tarnish. Music had always been the angelic art of the city. " The workmanship of thy tabrets and pipes was prepared in thee on the day that thou wast created." The suspiria of her dooms and glories were woven in chorale. The story that Ambrose and Augustine had first sung in her old Duomo, the supreme antiphony of the *Te Deum*, was in its essence true. The great angel of the art moved now in quaint disguises, and might be an odalisque in a walled rose-garden, a wreathed lute-player for the dances, a grave pure acolyte in the court-chapel, a singing page in the Duchess' pavilion. There was music in the churches, rare music in the convents, where the nuns sang sweet, too sweet, like prisoned nightingales, music at the feasts, music at the chase, music at the water-revels, for Beatrice took her singers where she went, songsters like Narcisso lent from Mantua, and Angelo who sang like the sweet-throat white merle on the faëry branch, who charms a hundred years into an hour

The musicians were of many kinds. There were syrinxes of ebony wherewith a young faun in a pastoral play might pipe from a white thorn brake. The viol of Jacopo di San Secondo could soothe the Duke's fever. The singers of the warring Cardinal Ascanio could charm him into peace. The voice of Cristoforo Romano was a felicity. The Duchess herself had a most beautiful and perfect clavichord. Steadily the great liturgies went on in well-sung passional monotone, maintaining in delicate differences a Christian tradition more humane, more mystical, more of the Fourth Gospel, than that of Rome.

Every morning voices of cherubim sing the Messa Ducale in the chapel of the Castello. Musicians are stolen and lured from Flanders, and from San Giovanni in Florence, and from all sweet-sounding places. A company of Spanish musicians comes with very large viols. Ever and anon the proud and thrilling trumpets sound their silver sennets. The Trumpets of the Duke! The Trumpets even of the Duchess Isabella! The Trumpets even of the Commune of Milan, forlorn and ghostly sweet, undying!

Music was Lodovico's food of love. Music was Leonardo's atmosphere as he painted *The Virgin of the Rocks*. Music ran over the window-sills when Lorenzo da Pavia, grave and gracious friend of princes, tried his incomparable viols and organs, and when Atalante Migliarotti sang his great aria from *Orfeo*, and Leonardo drew him " lifting his eyes." In Milan, night and day, " were heard sounds of such sweet singing and such delicious harmonies of music that they seemed to descend from Heaven itself."

Music, with its reminiscence of some lost life, its reconciliation of all strange suffering and ultimate desire in beauty, its faëry substance of dreams, impossible dreams, the soft far-kindling surf of its overwhelming waves proceeding from some green abyss of Eternity, its fragrances, flavours and echoes beyond the sense, its sunken bells of undersea, its chiming stars beyond the verges, its visions of ultra-violet colour—what Leonardo called " the figuration of the invisible," the only art in which the spirit strives with angels, sins discarnate sins, and finds divine incomprehensible compassion, and that ecstasy of absolution which is at once bridal song and requiem, all within the holy pattern and rhythm of heavenly order, had not yet climbed to the Renaissance greatness of

Lodovico and his Friends

Palestrina.   For music soars in glory when great ages pass, the mystery of sound prevailing when the lust of the eyes is choked in ashes.   But there was " ravishing division to the lute," and a clear, appealing bird-song through all Italy.   When the regal sounds the note, and the viols, lutes and hautboys accord like innumerable larks or nightingales, all the too-brilliant Court etherealizes into a faint aurora.   The mind, surcharged with beauty as with tears, feels its mournful rare burthen dissolve into the imponderable dew of music.   How grave and sweet and chaste is the head now called that of Francesco Gaffurio, a precursor of Bach, master of the chapel, with fine worn face, hollowed by waves of sound. with listening eyes.   This presence of music in the loves of heaven or earth gave the dreamlike quality necessary to the excessive Court of Milan :

> " Doves it hath with music of moans,
>   Queens in throngs and damsels in throngs,
>   High tones and mysterious semitones."

xvii

Somewhere about 1490, the star of Lodovico, flashing its ruby fires, sings in its hour of azimuth, and the Duke and his Court in their fey and glamoured hour assume that insolence of felicity which offends the eyes of the gods.   The dark prince of Milan seems likely to be lord of Italy.   Il Pistoja dares to sing in the madness of the time that there is only God in heaven and Il Moro on earth.   It was the court-fool who said that Lodovico had the Emperor for his condottiere, Venice for his treasurer, the King of France for his courier, and the Pope for his chaplain. But rumour gave the saying to the Duke himself, and he was not the more beloved.

For a time comes when the Renaissance soul of Milan rises in a tidal wave, gathers its waters, smooth, silken, green, and irresistible, to its crest of wonder, delight, music, felicity.   The air of the Court is electric.   They ask feverish questions.   Will the Ducchetto live ?   Will the French come ?   Will the Emperor take his bride ?   Will Ambrogio da Rosato say the day is propitious to receive the last ambassadors ? The holy images have blazed with light.   The Christ in *The Last Supper*, now burning ethereal like a lunar rainbow in the refectory of Sta Marie delle Grazie, smiles remote and troubling as behind a veil, beauty rather than love, betrayed by folly rather than wrong, a mysterious prince lost rather than slain.   The great Rider looms like a Horseman of the Apocalypse, as if no earthly bowman could ever dare a sacri-legious arrow.   The golden apples fall softly in the green closes from the

Leonardo the Florentine

Hesperidean tree; and the Hesperids smile more dreamily at their golden dragon, for they do not know that the tossed spoil of their orchard has prepared intolerable war.

The picture of Milan thickens for some rich modern palette, nourished with jewels, like Moreau's. The air is shaken with love-songs, the west wind breathes perfumes. The faces are softly blurred; the eyes glitter or close among the music. The world is passionate with roses, the pleasure treads hard on pain, and dreamlike the sense of doom and disaster is tossed in Beatrice's defiant feather, glows dark in the heart of Lodovico's ruby, and veils the cupid-broidered alcove of Lucrezia. In painted halls lighted by innumerable gems, as by the great flambeaux and the gleaming mirrors, the ladies move hieratically through the dances in incredible bright robes, whereon the phylacteries of the religion of Venus are made broad and gilded. All the citharists are singing together, all the boyish pages with eyes of corrupted angels carry fruits and flowers. Beautiful young nobles, clothed in silver and puffs of delicate lawn, carry the rose-coloured rods of the revel-marshals with the gracious air of those who have great possessions in the duchies of Earth and Paradise. The fair women are hung with pluvials of pearls; their hearts are faint under pectorals of myth-graven sard or fabulous fair beast of cornelian. Their tissues of spun-gold thread are tired with the excess of their inwoven stones. It is a fatigue of pleasure. Milan is at its last moment, like a great rose-flower, when the leaves just hardly quiver to its fall; but the quiver seems to be only the fine trembling of delight. The Court has the soft, rich, ineffable bloom which is the mysticism of material things; it has the colour and depth of the heart of a black damask rose. Desire is a sob in the throat, and a shudder of gold. The reds are glowing rarely like the wings of the seraphim. The blues are deepening into grape-amethyst; the greens are gleaming like the eyes of Egypt's gods. Even the whites are rich as white enamel, or soft-glistering mistletoe, or moony pearl. The dark Duke goes on his regal way, magnificent dupe of the stars. Through the gold-dusted atmosphere and the rain of arpeggios he moves with his smooth-rippled hood of hair, his sweet smouldering eyes faintly importunate. Beatrice burns with a strange fever; the hyacinthine face of the young Bianca is seen dancing with Death like another argent lover. Cecilia moves pensive, white and golden, as if bearing her jar of spices very precious in a very precious manner—all in the soft-breathing flame of felicity.

Stately dances of heavily-clad ladies! Dreamily-passionate crying of the viols! Spirals of Eastern scent from the brasiers! Softly withdrawing feet of Leonardo the Florentine, his contemplative soul withdrawing also to its secret ivory chambers of quietness!

Lodovico and his Friends

But when the early dusk has the soft bloom of green and purple grapes he will linger by the moat, looking to find the snowy plumes of the resting swans, and thinking of Leda waiting among the reeds and lilies for the whir of great wings that will cover her close.

xviii

With a crash and a shock and a roll of the kettledrums, and the long wail of a torn viol, the music and the dancing cease. The Duchess has been weary and has wept for hours at the tomb of the dead Bianca. But they have wrapped her in crimson and wreathed her with jewels for the feast, and she has danced feverishly till the dreadful pain grasps and tears her out of "this so vain felicity." She lies in agony, and Lodovico suffers with her. Ambrogio da Rosate will never revive her, either with starry scrolls or powdered pearls. The walls of her own rose-garden have fallen down under the scarlet skies, and so in truth have the walls of Milan.

She lay in her most golden camorra in a darkness the hundred silver tapers could not temper. She had come to Milan in the bitter winter, and in the bitter winter she went, still clothed with her dear-bought golden vanities, but with an aching heart, to buy pity if she could among the dreadful masques of Eternity. With a kind of sympathetic magic her compassionate sculptor tried with carven brocades and gems to keep her on earth, which was her home, safe among the glades of emerald and the familiar cloth-of-gold.

For fifteen days Lodovico sate in a chamber hung with black, while some thin tapers fought against the darkened windows, while the mourning courtiers trembled in the altered air, and the rose-pale women grew grey, sensing the sieges of sorrow and fear. Prophecies of great disaster wheeled like ravens about the beautiful apses of Santa Maria, and sate on the supernal shoulder of the great cavalier on "that stupendous horse you know." Lent was near, and the darkness of the Cross fell across the carnival city. The Duke had the trivial investiture of the shadowy emperor; but he had lost his amulet-lady and the great collar of the red star Aldebaran, that was the investiture of the fatal stars in which alone his heart had faith. All faith is but some irradiated superstition; and, when Lodovico realized that his star could turn traitor to him, other treacheries followed inevitably. He did what he could; but, like other Italian tyrants suddenly disarmed by a supernatural conviction, he did it like a man in a weary dream, without conviction and without hope.

"But, when the Duchess Beatrice died everything fell into ruin.

That Court which had been a joyous Paradise became a dark and gloomy inferno, and poets and artists were forced to seek another road."

xix

In a little while friends and foes will have done their worst with Lodovico, and as he is borne into a dark captivity he asks, of all his spoiled and lovely dukedom, merely his copy of Dante from the library in Pavia. It is not well to think of Lodovico mouldering in his damp dungeon at Loches, and scribing piteous mottoes and devices on the wall, sad travesties of the gilded imprese and symbols of old. It is Francesca's deathless lament for the hopeless beauty of the past that creeps like flame about his dying nerves. Could his mind, feverish from the poet's flagrant circles, see white figures of the faithful rigid in burning tombs, while the towers of the City of Roses dissolved in some beautiful hell of the autumn-drift? No! For miracles of desperate loyalty went out of date with the Middle Ages. Only Beatrice is his, for she cannot be otherwise, and so is the little Bianca. Isabella is dancing with the King of France, all his golden courtiers are looking on; and Galeazzo his idol is still king of the jousts. Faintly he remembers the courteous, impassive ways and the enigmatic eyes of the great artist who painted and carved and builded and led the waters for his glory. The invaders have ruined the Great Horse; the Communion of Betrayal is fading already, and Leonardo the Florentine is also making friends with the French.

xx

The sad captive unchivalrously blotted out in Loches had given a mort of beauty to the world, and Leonardo had had his part. He had lived in contact with this Lydian Court of carnation colours and soft flutes, and had taken on something of its faint and delicate corruption, though his profile shows ascetic and ivory against the rosy tapestry. In this feast of Hesperidean fruits, the flavours of the peach edge upon wine; they have the mysterious richness of the moment before the rot has won. You must not keep the manna long. These flavours have a nuance and a value; they are dangerous and fine, and Leonardo could taste without peril. Some cannot know the charm and beauty of wine, some dare not drink the cup of love, the cup of Tristan and Isolde; some dare not taste any ecstasy whatever, lest the starry philtre become a wildfire in their veins, driving to madness and death of the soul. Those who must live by prohibitions are a hapless people, for whom is sympathy. But it is not right or possible for the strong to live at the

Lodovico and his Friends

level of the weakest brother ; since that effort would mean a general decline into intellectual and spiritual idiocy.

Certainly Milan fed all that Leonardo's varied nature contained of the feverish, the extravagant, the sensuous. Eyes of Naucratis, eyes of Lesbos, eyes of Cyprus, Lydian eyes, they dwelt upon him with their rare indwelling light, and disturbed him. His mind became surcharged with images of luxury. Circean magic crept like quicksilver through his veins. In his drawings the lids became more languorous, the spiral curls are heavier, the lips more like Erigone's. The pressure of imagery and music are almost intolerable at times, and he maintains his wonderful equilibrium by severe intellectual exercises that make him the more decidedly twy-natured. But there are new æsthetic effects in this great vision of luxury and luminism. The clear Florentine colours and lines do not disappear, but they soften and sigh when he buries Milanese hues in wet light, and blurs the shapes into dissolving sweetness with his enchanting sfumato. And, since these people are not lances and iris-flowers like the Florentines, but dreamy creatures fashioned by desire into affected and gracious attitudes, he finds a flowing contraposto for the tender conflict and soft surrender of their souls. For the rest, he melts all their dazzle of jewels in the merciless rare crucibles of the Sign of the Lion, and pours it out in the cool colours of the sea, liquid emerald, lapis, jasper and turkis, and a little dulled gold and a little carnation, while their subtle paradox of rarefied sensuality is transmuted in the merciless retorts of his intellect into the unimaginable sweetness of the gods.

xxi

In the world of luxury, for a time, Leonardo set a fashion. He was an arbiter of elegant things, of masques, robes, jewels, stuffs, fantastic shoes, embroideries, lutes, painted books, the lovely things of antiquity, splendid blades, perfumes, pretty fans, songs, disputations, imprese, flowers, decoration of duchesses' baths, for of all these matters, even the manuscripts, rough notes of another self, give careless evidence ; and the words of his contemporaries are collateral proof. The " leonardesque " patterns and images affected the flowering of the brocades, the chaining of the jewels, the heads upon the medals, the broidering of the swords, the angels in the painted books. His labyrinthine line of life coiled itself into the consciousness of Milan. In its innermost pavilion of luxury, in the drinking place of the contadini, in its churches and monastic places, in its hospitals and by its waters, you hear the soft fall of his feet.

He himself was temperate in all things. Of roasted peacocks and dishes that came to the sound of trumpets he was soon weary. He needed what every artist needs, the indispensable arles of beauty, which are, symbolically, a cup of wine, a red rose and a white, a silken shift and a great wax taper, and a golden ducat for a friend. To these necessities Leonardo would have added a supple fencing sword and a high-bred steed. But he liked the psychic atmosphere of luxury, and dreams of extravagant delight. He could be immoderate. To quarry the snows like Elagabalus and bring the pure drift among the roses was a delicious fantasy. There is some such imperial notion of luxury behind the decoration of the Sala delle Asse. He knew that his palace-people loved the notion of coolness in their fevered pleasures. So he said, "Let pleasure go with pleasure," and framed their courtly motions in masses of green leaves and spaces of blue sky, intriguingly bound into the sweet castle-chamber by the golden cords looped in "intremaccia." He will even paint the Leda every subtle sensualist in Italy desires, the sweet paramour of the gods who is the mysterious mother of immortal beauty, smiling strangely by great waters while the white plumes cover her. The Spirit of Milan goes with him at last as a dream of Leda.

His nerves were silk, his nerves were steel. With the servants of the Rose and the servants of the Sword he was equally at ease. "Such was I, Leonardo the Florentine, at the Court of the most illustrious Prince Signor Lodovico."

In Milan at times, even in the manuscripts, he touches from his hidden lyre some silver chords of pure romance, as if from some dreamy-looking lady, sad with loss, he had caught an intimation of exquisite disaster in the chronicles of the Princesses of Love who have become symbolic. Such the notion of the great crystal mirror proud as an epithalamy when it holds the Queen, widowed and dark at her passing. Such the stricken idea of the mortality of Helen that suddenly seems to awake the flutes of lamentation across the wine-dark sea. Silver flashing mirrors, silver waking of immemorial flutes that will outlast the earth !

> " Brightness falls from the air !
> Queens have died young and fair !
> Dust hath closed Helen's eye."

This most piercing refrain of all the ages finds even the heart of Leonardo in the Court of Milan.

xxii

But in the anatomy-chamber he shows a macabre scorn that is revealing. The pride of the mediæval ascetic becomes alive in the sunlike, sun-worshipping Leonardo, to accompany and encourage his icy-burning curiosity. His senses, imparadised in colour and perfume, he cynically forces into the noisome cell to endure the odours of corruption, the ghastly lights of putrefaction, the livid unholy hues of decay. It is the cilice and the scourge of the monk. Delicate nerves of silk can endure horrors better than coarser textures, when they are chilled by the anæsthetic of a desperate will, and strung by a mastering motive. Leonardo was seeking the secret of life in his anatomy-chamber; but unconsciously he had a dark irrelevant exultation because his way was horrible. It was a black antidote to luxury. When his emotional self is stirred so deeply by the deeply-lighted eyes of some fragrant and flowering creature that his consciousness is suddenly aware, it is easy for him to show that the lovely thing is but " a lane and a conduit of nourishment, a hostel of death, a sheath of corruption, sucking life from the death of others." " Un sac d'excréments," said Odéon de Cluny, the mediæval monk, of the human body. Leonardo was also anatomizing the horse. The mood of Baudelaire's *Charogne*, a poem carved in black obsidian, was not so alien from both monk and artist. Sometimes, when he comes out of that dread chamber he can discern nothing in the sunlight but the grim Dance of Death. He perceives even in the creative act the destructive, and knows that the sower must cast away the seed that he may reap. The squires are casting dice with the bones of the dead, the shepherds are bringing music from the tortured skins that still cry and lament in the cornamusa, the scholars are writing on vellum that has been torn from tender and sportive things, and the waxen lights on the High Altar are wicked with the death of the bees. The finches sing liquid pathos from their cages and hurt him, so that he says : " Death, rather than loss of liberty." (Probably he disdained Lodovico, who had not contrived to die.) Everything is bought by mortality and torture. The running waters, the falling mountains, the conflicts of swords, startling gouts of blood, a sense of human and unhuman catastrophe, affect him as in a bad dream. This is the ashen accidia of the intellectual who has dared too many things and with too much zest, of the emotional sated with music and colour and perfume. It is the hour when the grey cock crows, and there is no flicker in the exhausted heart, and no star speaks faintly in the dead silence. Then this is a ghastly material world of prey, to which there is cynical assent behind the veils.

He had a reaction keener and purer when he watched the swifts rising and falling in their farewell to the sun, or a charm of goldfinches glittering against the sky, or a triangle of migratory birds acute towards the ancient shores of Africa, or the crested larks singing antiphonies against the light, or even the great falcon motionless in pride of place. Then, with delight the birds begin to fly about the margins of his manuscripts, whatever his theme be ; and presently he goes to the room locked and triple-locked by Giulio, and gazes on the mighty shape of the great wing that shall yet raise him into the illimitable blue like a god indeed, prince of the powers of the air. Though he wandered far and wide through the duchy, he undoubtedly shows signs of claustrophobia. The city life of Milan was not like the city life of Florence ; both Court and University were cloistered, kept away from the commune, and, though Leonardo did not need the people, he needed the sense of wide spaces. He went to the dissecting-room as a defence against invading emotion : he threw himself breathlessly on light and air and the long far-travelling paths of perspective vanishing to horizon-point to escape from the sense of a splendid cage. These fantastical, jewelled, brocaded, and musical years were compelled, as they passed over the roses, to do hard penance of intellectual labour by night and day, to keep them fine and fit, passionate pilgrims to a passionless end. His eyes took pleasure in the fireflies, but his mind had put the stars on the rack of mathematics that he should know the terrors of their truth.

xxiii

There is something too flagrant and sinister in the Renaissance splendour of Milan. True, it was a guilty magnificence. The excesses of beauty's idolaters take a terrible toll, the excesses of beauty's iconoclasts take worse !

But all the tribute paid to the extravagant Renaissance of Milan was beautiful in itself. The armourers and the brocaders and the smiths and the other craftsmen did their work with zest and sincerity ; at least they were not vexed by wasting their monotonous hours in making matter meretricious in factories that spoil the soul and body. The craftsmen were haughty, the peasants fared well till the wars brought excessive taxation, the townsmen were prosperous, and they could always taste splendour in their churches and holidays. Plague and war came now and then, as plague and war still devastate the world, and that more thoroughly. And Lodovico at least, and his kind, were not cruel, not cruel as the race of Ferrara still was. For the craftsmen at least there was community with the nobles, that of a common enthusiasm for beautiful things. Think of that other period of lavish decoration in the eighteenth century, especially in France. The century of exquisite artificiality has its perverse charm, but how different is its luxury from the great way of luxury in the Renaissance. The very chairs and tables of the eighteenth century tell by their curves that they invite the amused regard of the listless libertine. What of the

Lodovico and his Friends

baubles of Crébillonesque amours, the pretty personalia of mere vanity, all the *mièvrerie* of the ornament that is but a mask for sensuality gone callous, and pride gone inhuman through the death of enthusiasm? I mean enthusiasm literally. For such nobles there was no God of any kind, and their luxury, for all its graces, was a monstrous offence against their kind, because it was perfectly cold and perfectly selfish. If Milan was a rare iniquity of splendour, the passion of her splendour redeems her. Besides, there is always that kind of holy innocence hidden within her, blending into a heathen sweetness kin to it, like the hues in a dove's neck.

Excess is dangerous. The Viper had become a dazzling emerald dragon in the Renaissance sky, too magnificent to be borne. The gemmed spines of its wings, and its Eastern spirals, and its ruby eyes, seemed to threaten. But if the great apparition of the city had burned in the holy halcyon blue of a kingfisher, or glowed mild as a bird-of-paradise, it would still have been considered too lustrous to live. The rival cities would have gone out to kill it. The human reasoning seems to be that, since nothing can become a splendour without having stolen strange prey, it is a duty to see that swift bright things come to confusion. So Milan perished because of its insufferable glory and the flamelike quality of its luxury. But when the great blazoned standard of the Sforza went down, the evil tale began which brought the masterless armies to the dreadful sacking of Rome and the worse violations of the sack of Florence, which meant the perishing of the Hellenistic dream and the end of the true Renaissance.

The Milan of the Sforzas was heathen rather than Hellenistic. At least she was not Athenian in her temper as Florence was. Yet in her own excessive way she confessed her dim apprehension of the Grecian story that, however mistaken and mistranslated, was a leaven of grace in every Renaissance city. And it was in this place of hybrid barbaric beauty that Leonardo created the work that proves him most the Greek, the picture where, with the might of maturity, he has drawn from the golden wells of his Athenian youth. What enchanted its idolaters was above all the great *sophrosyne* that dwelt in the unique *Cenacolo*, for, whoever the lord may be whose destined head is laid against that space of sky, his grace sends out the vital rhythm that controls all the agitation and brings it within that lucid, lovely peace of beauty for which there is only the great Greek name.

And the young men who came on Sundays to steep their souls silently in the rhythm of sophrosyne were citizens of " no unadventurous city." Were they also the lutanists and masquers of the luxurious Court? They were. They could be both. For they could reconcile their conflicts easily in Renaissance days.

Chapter vi

The Labour of Herakles

i

IT is evident that, if Leonardo had done nothing but attend to the works incidental to the courtly life and its habitations, he would have been busy enough. Fortifying the castle, decorating the rooms, finding devices and basilisks and wyverns for the jousting helmets, hanging a festival castello to the last cloth, squared in white and blue, ordering a masquing dress to the last peacock feather and a fair duchess' bathing-pavilion to the last eel-head, Leonardo was occupied, it seems. Yet such duties were but the gay fringes of his finely woven and densely rich activity. Sometimes a modern critic deplores the waste of Leonardo's miraculous energy in trivial matters. But the Renaissance thought that no gesture that expressed its superb vitality was a contemptible thing ; it loved the details of its glory. And Leonardo, himself of like mind, took pleasure in the knops and pomegranates so minutely expressive of the show. Great genius can include the minute and infinitesimal, the least being a symbol of the whole ; and great dreamers are always precise. Besides, this airy toil was restful, and it amused him. Neither pontiffs, nor princes, nor republics either, could induce Leonardo to do anything that bored him. These little tasks and toys were soothing to his mind when it was fevered from riding with immortal steeds, or strung with the bitter suspenses of *The Last Supper*.

He is a pervasive influence through all things, winding himself into the brocades, stamping his image on the chalcedonies, passing softly through the ways of magnificence till you hear his faint footfall vanish from the innermost pavilion, raising domes and ramparts, as if to the sound of his lyre, moving like a spirit on the waters.

That he was much in intercourse with courtly people, the implications or direct statements of Isabelle d'Este, Castiglione, the court-poets, Fra Luca Pacioli, Fra Sabba Castiglione, Vasari, Lomazzo, Cellini, Giuliano de' Medici, Bandello, the author of *Il Cortegiano*, Ippolito d'Este and Leonardo himself, the Anonimo, Paul Jovius, King Francis, all bear witness. But he is no court-chamberlain or master of the ceremonies like Goethe in his absurd little principality ; in that, as in other matters, there is no parallel. He likes the Renaissance princes because he is of their kind; his life is his own and he jealously guards that autonomy. And with the amorous, silken Duke, who was also a kind, regal, and imaginative person, Leonardo was well matched. It is difficult to think of another employer magnificent enough for a Leonardo, also sumptuous in his ways and kingly in his artistic demands. The mysterious prince that Italy watched with excitement, dark in his cloth-of-gold, the splendid creature too fortunate not to be dangerous, did not disappoint the arrogant prince of art that Italy hailed with wondering words, golden in his cloth-of-rose, till his star had fallen, burning disastrous through the frightened air. When Leonardo drafts the disturbed letters about his troubles it is as prince to prince. " I know the times—I do not wish to be troublesome—but what am I to do ? " Lodovico pauses from his sorrowful reckonings with insatiable Swiss mercenaries, and gives Dionysos-Apollo a vineyard. It is evidently a precious vineyard, for in the end the spoilt Andrea Salaino builds a house in it, and Leonardo's testament divides it between him and another. Admetus in his agonizing moment did very well.

ii

But though Lodovico did not claim the caduceus for a sceptre without some show of right, though, when Leonardo painted him, for a Madonna, a lovely lady to whose cypress-wood room he could slip from his oratory, she might be made a haunting image of faëry and a starry beacon of beauty, though the ephemeral beauty of the masques was so steeped in nobility and passion that they seemed to defile arrogantly into the pavilions of eternity, though Leonardo's strength went into his strong circumvallations, and his finely-calculating brain into locking the bright waters into loops about Vigevano and Milan, though, beyond all that, archetypal tasks, such as his soul desired, tormented and fascinated him, though he is happy in Milan, Leonardo stirs uneasily in the confines of the Court, in the confines of the city, in the confines of the duchy, and remembers Florence, with the little reckless airs of freedom wandering down from her intimate hills, the " liberties of Florence " that neither Lorenzo nor Savonarola could destroy. When he is most busily describing and analysing the ways of water, the " little mill at Florence " rises suddenly before him with the vivid pang of nostalgia. Leonardo obstinately remains the " Florentine," and the lilylike image of his city is his canon of perfection in the lax magnificence of Milan. He definitely behaved like an aristocrat, a member of a privileged class, made not by money, but by difficult and elaborate disciplines, initiations into the highest modes of life. In his more tolerant, less indignant way, Leonardo's attitude was not unlike Dante's, who could live neither with Florence nor without her, who regarded her as a cruel and wanton mistress, whose wild sweet eyes had nevertheless looked upon God, and kept His image tangled in the mesh of the retina.

He was the friend of princes ; but he was also their servant. In the Florentine streets he had laughed and talked and played his lute, and been no feudatory. Now he knows responsibilities and strictures ; the palace chambers and the studios shut him in. Is he so busy because of the pressure of claustrophobia, the sense of gilded bars ? He assuages the rebellion of his spirit by wreaking it upon the starry spaces. When Milan is a rainbow ecstasy, and the town a trembling felicity of masque and musique and dreaming faces, he knows the sudden trick of mind which turns the glory first into a drift of shed gold plumes, and then to a little gilt dust upon the Wheels of Time.

Be that as it may, he lives a thousand lives in Milan. Some live double lives ; Leonardo is a multiple personality. All qualities ripened fast in Lombardy ; and, moreover, he was at the midsummer of his life. When he came to Milan he was about thirty, when youth dazzles with almost a heart-breaking radiance before, with soft bright reluctances, it sighs away its irrecoverable sweetness. But Leonardo passed with grace into his maturity, and assumed the sovereignty of his powers. The furnaces of his mind were banked and glowing, ready to cast super-human shapes ; the deep wells and grottos of his soul, where the strange, rich cyclamen flowers grew, had drawn their fantastic rocks together into a hypæthral temple where searching light found in the shadow the smiling goddess and the angel, her acolyte and his dæmon. And in the outer chambers of his analytic self, the retorts were charged and the crucibles ready for all " experiment."

To even the casual observer his mind seems like one of those fertile plots in his native land that offer wheat, vines, and peaches all at once —sacrament and substance, and, in Leonardo's case, some secret garden-statue, whether of nymph or satyr.

He drew endlessly his studies for the great horse, and obtained a master-knowledge of the anatomy of steed and rider. He worked steadily at *The Last Supper*, and gathered the matter for treatises on light, perspective, the eye, and dynamics. He wrote a book on light and shade ; he founded a school ; he composed a treatise on painting. His art led him into all the ways of the universe, unheeding that before he could return with completed knowledge the day would be over, and his hand paralysed. He studied the flight of birds, and constructed his flying machines. He performed great engineering works and fortifications, and explored the " Why," implicit in all the phenomena he mastered. Whatever he touched he knew well, for in nothing was he superficial. Nothing escaped the passion of his interest.

One wonders when he slept. Even by night he was often shut up with flayed and noisome corpses. At other times we know he rested; and it is evident that he was one of the fortunate people to whom sleep comes and goes clearly and lightly. Yet he watched the shadows on the wall—it must have been when, too tired to sleep, he wrung from the dark hours more illumination for the kindly morrow. But the chill necromancer called insomnia must sometimes have defeated even those indomitable eyes with his veridical black magic. Then the chiaroscuro of leaping chivalry on the wall, shaped from shadow for the sake of the Cavallo, became sable hippogriffs, spurring no vanquished foe, but a fallen rider which was his own soul; and the soft, shifting mimicry of the faces round the great love-feast turned to the mop and mow of the Black Mass of some damnable god. In the apprehensive heart of midnight he would see his own drawings of the sorrowful or powerful oppositions of youth and experience change to a vision of the fiend Asomuel whispering low to his initiate while the horrified lilies dropt blood, till the cold half-swoon of dawn lay like a mort-cloth over his weary face and pulseless wrists. For Leonardo does occasionally speak as if he knew martyrdoms: " Dov' è più, più ne martiri, gran martiri."

iii

His intimate life lay in his happy house by the pleasance of the Castello, where he was surrounded with his servants and chosen pupils, and where his varied friends came in and out. He describes it, filled like other noble houses with costly trifles, concave mirrors, Venice books, Bohemian knives. As the years reluctantly left him, he softly resigned the rose-broidered mantle of youth, and assumed the air of a beautiful maturity, for he knew how to fit himself to his lustres, though at heart he resented, amazed and angry, the coming of old age. After all, if he does strike a chord of music in his manuscripts by the name of Helen, it is when he remembers her with sombre triumph at the moment of her humiliation, when even the golden queen, like himself, finds on her brow the communal seal of mortality. Only when the hounds of mortality are at her white throat does he evoke the child of Leda, and not like Faust. Instead of,

" Sweet Helen, make me immortal with a kiss,"

he writes : " Helen, when she looked in her mirror and saw the wrinkles which old age had made in her face, wept, and wondered why she had ever twice been carried away." The kind of threnody in which the passage occurs, however, is in singularly rhythmic and moving Italian.

But even when he leaves Milan he is a gracious person. His beard, now permitted to grow, is perfumed and curled, his hair smoothly combed into rippling waves, perhaps filleted with rose-colour, his hands soft and scented ; his beautiful lithe figure, still swift at sword-play and accustomed to horses, is wrapped in silk or furs as the season decrees. He must have resembled that lovely meditative Greek head sometimes called Plato and sometimes Dionysos.

It is of some size, Leonardo's house, as there is much to do in it when the artist needs studios for himself as a painter, a sculptor, and a scientist, and room for pupils and friends. Some of the rooms are locked with the Milanese ironwork by Giulio and Master Thomas, since profane and jealous eyes are not invited to experiments and statements that presuppose an earth not conformable to the canons of the Church. For the secrecy of his mind increases. That left hand writes its Eastern-looking script more and more fluently. Sometimes he traces odd foreign characters, as if practising some obscure Coptic of the soul, some language of twined hieroglyphics out of Egypt no stranger might read. And there are endless *entrelacs*, as if the twisted lines were some amulet to finger till he found the intelligible sesame word that made him free of the cave of magic. They seem woven of the silken thread that was the clue to the labyrinth.

iv

Those most caressed in his house are the young, some of them his pupils, chosen for their beauty, their charm, as often as possible for their birth, for Leonardo was not ill-disposed to make the education of his pupils a kind of Renaissance equivalent to that of the mediæval page. Besides, the perfect courtier of the time thought it well to be somewhat of a painter as well as much of a musician. The point is discussed in Castiglione's book. True, none of these charming amateurs, in both senses of the word, did great work ; but they certainly heightened their own critical faculty and helped to make the atmosphere in which great work is produced. Whatever else they did, they made music. " A boy made pleasant music on a clear-toned viol and sang thereto a sweet linos-song with delicate voice." On the shield of Achilles, in the studio of Leonardo, the linos-song goes rarely with the strings.

It is hard to know if Leonardo in his heart wished to found a school. Gently deprecating in manner, he was quietly intolerant of the second-rate. Like his friend the Borgia he told himself, " Aut Cæsar, aut nihil,"

The Labour of Herakles

and with a sweet cæsarian arrogance he smiled away the originality of his pupils, even while he taught them they must never imitate another painter, and must become the children, instead of the grandchildren, of art. He changed some of them from art students to charming people and friends. The gentle imagists of Milan (for " sculptors " is too hard a word), whose very names were sweet, Amadeo, Dolcebuone, made their lovely masks and wreaths for love's or death's festival, Leonardo's mighty and suave impress crushed such brethren of theirs as might have developed some analogy in painting, tender and rich and drowsy, for Lodovico's chambers and chapels. They never recovered from Leonardo, though some of their echoes are most attractive, and unjustly depreciated. Milan had yet formed no great painters. The cities of luxury require from their own population tapestry, gem-work, miniatures, the little arts rather than the great. Their citizens are too much part of their pageant to see it from without. And after Leonardo had carried his own personal art to its climax, nobody was left but his imitators, who had worshipped away their wits.

The arrival of a great genius, supreme in his kind, is a wrecking thing for any tradition of art, and agitating even for those outside the tradition. Since it is hardly possible to lift a hand without discomposing, wounding, sundering somewhere in the inextricable though impalpable web of life, or break a branch in the Dreadful Forest without finding blood on one's hands, what catastrophe and paralysis for ordinary mortals swept into novel swirls of emotion by the ghostly passage of the silver unicorn, the fiery spirals of the first descent of the gold-green paraclete.

The apparition of Leonardo's genius in the firmament of Milan was as disputeless ; and it did have the effect of an amazement. It abolished the past, and silently subjugated the future. Who were his predecessors in Milan ? The conscientious Vincenzo Foppa, unable to forget the rigidities of Squarcione, the dull Butinone, the amiable aged Zenale, who could paint brocades, and who was the gentle critic of the magnificent stranger when he hesitated over the face of his Christ. Ambrogio Borgognone, all silvery and soft rose in his painting, accepted the influence to some degree ; but mildly, firmly, remained his grave, pure self in his pictures. Bramantino, no Milanese, frescoed after the manner of Bramante, capably enough but without distinction, except in that little study of the child-duke, Gian Galeazzo, reading Cicero with an assiduity which departed from his later days.

The other painters were his own, sensitives whose wax was not rarefied enough to take the great seal of the Sphinx without blurring it, though softly willing to receive. They were delicate, lovely and even

Leonardo the Florentine

sparkling people, clairvoyant to his sensibilities rather than to his mind, effeminate, with sympathies too adoring. Boltraffio, a graceful young man of good birth, was the most imaginative of them. Ambrogio da Predis had been court-painter when Leonardo came, and submissively continued to paint under his direction, even with him occasionally. Cesare da Sesto, a talented but hesitant youth, frequented his studio ; Gianpietrino, Marco d'Oggione, and others, were of the group.

Yet others—some known to us only by a Christian name—came from afar, sometimes paying their way with " florins of the Rhine " ! The more famous of his imitators, Sodoma and Luini, were not yet evident. Francesco Melzo, with his admiring eyes, his young sensibility, his beautiful talent for devotion, was still a delicate child, though already destined to be the secret sweetness, the amethyst love-charm against bitterness Leonardo would never let fall.

Then there is Andrea Salaino, a youth beautiful and wanton and vain, possibly the son of a Hungarian armourer, dismissed by biographers sometimes as a servant. But a personal attendant in those days was often a well-bred and charming person. Great artists on embassy were sometimes paid for silken clothes for their servants. And Leonardo dressed Andrea in rose and green, with feathers, and fanciful shoes, and taught him painting, and helped him to be an expert in " gallant things," and to become an attractive ambassador in time to come, to people like Charles d'Amboise and Isabella d'Este. Sometimes Andrea is vain and petulant and extravagant, and Leonardo suddenly interrupts his scientific notes to write down a damning little account, and make a vague and bitter generalization about ingratitude. But Andrea Salaino had luxurious curls and heavy broad-lidded eyes and the kind of physical beauty that seems to attract a violet dream-butterfly to hover over it like a marrying moth. Vasari says Leonardo loved him because of his beautiful curls. He seems indeed to have had such masses of curled soft hair as the later Greek sculptors presented, undercut deeply to give an exotic pathos and mystery to the face. Leonardo did love it, twined and twisted it even for Leda's hair. So Andrea must dress in green and rose and have a cloak looped with silver, and rose edges to his shoes, and a feather to his cap, and hose of velvet, a sword and a knife like any other Milanese mignon. Leonardo sets down suddenly an account for Salaino's cape in April 1497. April—and the beautiful youth desires to look like a white daffodil, so there is silver-cloth, green velvet to slash it, and fluttering ribbons and little gilt meshes. " Salai stole the pence," comments Leonardo with cruel brevity. I would rather know why he rent the silver cloak with this secret stab than gain several pages of

The Labour of Herakles

perspective problems. In April mood and April raiment Salai had angered him, and forgotten the odd coins, to his damnation. The decoration of Salai is an æsthetic necessity, however ; and it naturally recurs in other Aprils. If Leonardo has a page like a Hyacinth he must set him in a beautiful sheath. He must also borrow golden ducats, and have his fortune told. Leonardo disapproved of soothsayers ; but he let the pretty spoilt page amuse himself with his future, just as he turned from his own great work to complete with some master-strokes the piece of mythology, the Pomona dream-white among the rich apples, the Flora in white veils crowned with Milanese roses, made by him or another like him. Many of the young faces which flower about the concentrated pages of the treatises, even among the intensely vivid dissections of the anatomy, must be of Andrea. There is one type almost Græco-Roman, with full dreamy eyes, a straight nose, a curled mouth, sullen or spoilt, a brief chin, all softened and clouded into beauty by the wonderful hair, which may be his.

The other young people who throng his studio, and play their lutes and mandolins, seem to be arranged around his room like flowers. They are not the flamelike creatures, the beautiful grail-children, their hair blown about by the great wind of the quest, that he drew for the Florentine *Adoration*. That ardent young man with the floating forelock, who quivers in the strung bow of his life, has gone. When he wants a face of clear dreams and innocent tenderness for Philip, he must gaze in his Florentine crystal of remembrance again, and recover Fioravante. These vibrating sweet folk were like darts and sword-lilies. Had he desired to create a reverie of Charmides moving like a great light, inviolate and proud, among his court of lovers, or Lysis, Critias, or Ion in the temple, he should have stayed in Florence. The Milanese children are not overapt in the palæstra. They are not proud Greek athletes, accepting ascesis, dreaming quiet and undefiled like the dawn. There is something of Rome, more of Bithynia in these too heavily bowed heads. The Milanese are rosy moths and mown narcissus. They are like the white flower moly. He cannot even draw them as Diadumenos, in that ineffable, lovely dream-gesture of perfection, inveterately Greek, for they have never thrown the disk. They are too slight for Antinous, for no vision of sacrificial Egypt such as bows that sullen entrancing head, heavily hyacinthine, can shadow their long limpid eyes. At their strongest they are like decadent young Roman emperors, at their weakest like frail angioletti. But now and then he throws a handful of these jonquils he loves to see about his way into the white-burning still of his imagination, and from the fragrant smoke arises some prince of faëry, some rare archangel lost from one of those unimaginable great compositions

223

of gods and men and heroes he did not paint. Is it only the strange mood of Milan, or is it the fine sadism in his strange heart, that makes him send an æsthetic arrow into these lovely figures of music-making youths, with dream-sorrow spilt among their lashes ? At least he is much occupied with imagining the Saint Sebastian. There are many images of that Eros and Adonis of Christendom ; Leonardo drew him eight times at least. At other moments he put delicate armour on his young figures, as if he drew them to a masque that would be a double-sexed Pyrrhic dance, greaved girls and helmeted boys.

Of one small wrongdoer in Leonardo's house he has left us a vivid little story in a scrap of diary among the scientific notes of his manuscripts. " Jacopo came to dwell with me on the Magdalene's Day in 1490, being ten years of age," writes Leonardo steadily. " On the second day I had made for him two shirts, a pair of hose, a doublet," he continues. Alas ! Jacopo stole some deniers, and never confessed, though Leonardo knew his guilt with a *vraie verité*. He then pilfered a silverpoint from Marco, who found it in his box. Next day Leonardo supped with his friend Jacopo Andrea. The boy ate enough for two, spilt, destroyed. In January Leonardo went to the house of Messer Galeazzo di Sanseverino to arrange his jousting festival. While some of the household squires were trying on the " wild men " raiment, the little boy thieved from a purse cast on the bed. A skin of fine Turkish leather was given Leonardo for boots. Jacopo stole it and confessed to buying aniseed sweets with the price of it. He then stole a silverpoint left lying on a drawing. At this point Leonardo meticulously adds up what he has paid for the year's clothing, mantle, shirts, pourpoints, furred vestments, girdles, lacings, and writes on the margin : " Robber, liar, obstinate, gluttonous."

Commentators make some quaint observations on Leonardo's merciless record of Jacopo, that ten-years-old villain. I think I see the child, that January day, curled and pretty in his furred cloak, creeping behind those gay young men at Galeazzo Sanseverino's, much amused at their savage attire, while Leonardo considers them attentively, and finding more coins to glut his unholy passion for aniseed. Leonardo is quite impersonal. It is a scientific tale of a non-moral child. Or else a comment of tired cynicism on the little culprit. He was an engaging imp in his furred mantle ; and doubtless Leonardo went on keeping him about the house as if he were a marmoset.

v

Famous and mature people came freely about the place. Bramante, so often Leonardo's colleague in court-commands, is blithe in the happy

The Labour of Herakles

Milanese air, indulging his fancy before the august service of Saint Peter's puts more airy graces to flight—Bramante, with strong, candid and springing face, furrowed and vital, a painter, also, of the stalwart and graceful legionaries of energy. He can be courtly too, and defend Petrarch's violets against Dante's roses of fire.

Leonardo was also friendly with the miniaturists, who were still nobly considered in Milan. Missal-painting is a strictly mediæval art, like carved ivory, and stained glass, and tapestry, and ballades, like all concentrated forms of angular archaic grace, attacking with a sweet violence ; but Milan clung harder to the mediæval crafts than other cities, loth to let any tradition of splendour die. The more insolent Renaissance curve of life, and the new " realism," smoothed out the old intensities and delicacies of missal-work. Yet Leonardo was so much attracted by the miniaturists, who still brought pages of great beauty to fastidious people like Federigo of Urbino, and who consented even to lend their decorations to their undoers, the printed books, that he himself thought of adding this detailed art to his other masteries. Attavante had been, and would be again, a friend of his. Fra Antonio da Monza was considered a precious person at the Court of Milan. He seemed to paint with smooth enamels, and copied courtly figures upon his leaves with that smiling and familiar confusion with beasts and birds which is so marked in the Milanese temper. Among all the Renaissance suppliance of harpies, angels, serpents, candelabra, censers, sphinxes, charming little shields and visors, and peacocks spilling their tails down a margin, you find a squirrel giving a paw to an amorino by a rivulet, on the bank of a flowery cape, or a snail moving as in a little skiff, or two rabbits holding up a shell, while leverets and hens and little dogs assist in the ceremonies. And things grow into each other, leaves into faces, volutes into harpies, in the Protean way that amused the great artist. He was drawn himself by Antonio, it is said, playing the lyre on a page of Cardinal Ascanio's great music-book.

With Caradosso, the great goldsmith, he had more equal talk, for he, with a great imagination, smote his consummate knots of mythology on his beaten plaques ; those two might converse of heroes and horses.

Of heroes and horses ! But these are beautiful phenomena, appearing and dissolving. What of the processes behind them ? What of the flux of the universe ? Comes Fazio Cardano, the father of the famous author of *De Subtilitate Rerum*, who told his son that Leonardo himself attempted an actual flight on his great wings. He is robed in scarlet, a grave jurist, and, like the Marliani family, and Leonardo himself, is locked deep in the cold rapture of mathematics. These mathematicians form a group, lending and borrowing precious volumes. It is in the capital of coloured

Leonardo the Florentine

images and excited senses that Leonardo finds so much serenity in this ultimate cold cloister of wisdom, this final lantern-chamber in the observatory of humanity, where the mind in a lucid frenzy of abstraction prepares its chart for exploring the void. But with beautiful equilibrium he specially notes among his mathematics that he must go often to the great baths to study the naked figures. Gazing at the lithe lines of the bathers, and drawing them in the Greek attitudes captured for beauty in the days of the gymnasia and the palæstra, he is not in danger of impaling his art on a triangle or vanishing with the vanishing points of his far-meeting lines. Music and mathematics, after all, were the chief elements of a Platonic education, and Leonardo was wise psychologically, perhaps, when lyre-playing and Euclid drew his attention from that trouble of Cybele which trembled behind all images in Milan. For even at the baths he will see young men too flower-soft, like her Atthis. They will not use the strigil after the disk-throwing. They may sit in the hot wet air, drowsily clasping a foot, or stand with down-dropped hand and one lifted arm behind a fair head, agaze in a pool. It is from Leonardo that Michelangelo derives his most beautiful " bound captives." But in what exquisite anguish would Leonardo's own dream-slaves, broken hyacinths of the gods, have stood round Trivulzio's divinely imagined tomb !

Fra Luca Pacioli, lively and eccentric friar, radiant over his mathematical lore, also consumes the hours with his great and gracious friend Leonardo, who will draw figures for his book, *De Divina Proportione*, with his *ineffabile sinistra mano*, or discuss with him his admired Piero della Francesca, who also mingled mathematics with the soft summons of his argent trumpets of clear light, or laugh at his buffoon-like ways. It is notable that Leonardo's taste for the bizarre is emphatic enough. He likes absurdity. He still has his own court-fool. Zoroastro da Pertola, much at home with the alchemists and diviners of Milan, devotedly attends his Florentine idol, and with a touching devotion grinds the colours for *The Last Supper*. Atalante Migliarotti, the old acquaintance of the lyre, is still a familiar, for a while at least, while he is young enough to be Music's beautiful bondager. Leonardo does a drawing of Atalante, lifting up his eyes, singing the songs of Orpheus. For Atalante is the " Orfeo " of the time, in Florence, in Milan, and in Mantua.

Jacopo Andrea da Ferrara, the architect, was a zealous experimenter of all things new. Leonardo was near to him " as a brother," it was said. And when Jacopo Andrea was quartered on the gates of Milan for loyalty to his lost Duke, Leonardo's heart may have sickened at the thought; Leonardo's brain was nevertheless surrendered to the French who slew him. He was even in hopes of raising a marvellous pyramid of statuary for the tomb of Trivulzio, whose decree had sentenced his

The Labour of Herakles

friend. Neither friend nor city was ponderable in the scale when Leonardo weighed his opportunities.

Lorenzo Gusnasco, of Pavia, is a dear and noble friend in music. Grave and sweet and cultured, the serene *bien-aimé* of princes, to whom he gives the courtesy of an equal, he lives happy in the devising of his perfect viols, lutes, clavichords and organs. One seems to see him plucking a chord of the clear, faint sound, the seed-pearl and dew-dust and grace-notes of melody coffered within his exquisite craft of ebony, ivory and mother-of-pearl, and living strings, with the rapt communing look of a Giorgione saint of sound. Another such, Francesco Gaffurio, master of the music, with sensitive mouth and twining hair, comes to be painted in the studio, though Leonardo seems too busy to do more than supervise. There are a number of portraits, long ascribed to the master, that seem much too good for Ambrogio da Predis, as we know that painter from his undoubted work, though hardly of the marvellous quality of the texture of paint supplied by Leonardo's own super-subtle fingers. If one had time and opportunity to be a Berenson, how gladly could one evoke in the softly curtained studio one or two sensitive and sympathetic spirits, rarer than Salaino, Ambrogio, Oggione, Cesare de Sesto, who could be the master's close understudies and interpreters of subtle looks. Amico di Leonardo and Alunno di Leonardo?—Amico rather. They shall do the little Princess and the Musicasta, and the head of Isabella of Aragon, and some of the central part of *The Virgin of the Rocks*, for instance. One might even—though the fancy seems heresy—have done the great Louvre picture called *La Ferronnière*. All these things are worthy of Leonardo in their charm and insight; they simply contain qualities of manner that hardly seem his own.

But Leonardo was kindly to all the musicians. The lutes sang always in his studio, an undersong like sweet spent waves, for so the faces of his people were altered by the rumours of immortal things. Cristoforo da Romano, the other artist who was so clear a singer, would sometimes meet Leonardo over music, and become animated enough to defend the sculptor against the painter in the endless debates concerning the priorities of the arts, though the diffident, delicate manner of Cristoforo was almost embarrassed with Leonardo. He had some grey-pearl and rose iridescence of interests himself, though he was no rival to the great Florentine, and he belonged to the Duchess with all his heart.

With another painter Leonardo surely met again at Pavia, when Perugino was painting the great altarpiece at the Certosa, all holy Umbrian sky, touched with feathery trees at the horizon, its three angels visible in the heart of its vast hollow of light, while the dreamy faces of the Madonna and her attendants consent to bliss and are sweetly satisfied, and the serene young Michael wears his very Peruginesque armour with grace. It is one of the painter's most engaging harmonies between great skies and tender pieties; and evidently the Duke liked it. So he might! That delicious movement between Tobias and his angel, that sudden confiding gesture of the boy, soft and quick as a shaft of sunlight, met by the faint simultaneous smile of the guide, all one rare flicker of perfect comprehension, is subtle enough for Leonardo.

In 1497 Lodovico tried to get Perugino to do some decoration for the Castello. At that point his relation with Leonardo was strained, and he begged Perugino from his natural lords, the tigerish and splendid Baglioni of Perugia, who loved the dulcitude of their artist much as the Borgia loved the innocent blue and gold of Pinturicchio. But he did not secure him, and Leonardo found time to do more castle decoration, as well as begin the Cavallo again. There was an understanding between these two artists, the ancient league of those who have been young together, and nursed in the self-same studio, or college, or whatever school of early experience betide them. Raphael's father had sung them as rising stars together—" Two youths alike in age and love."

Leonardo once made an intricate bandwork of his labyrinthine lines, and set in the middle the inscription: " Acha: Li: Vi: " Controversy rages round this device, which was engraved. Some say it wa the badge of his definite school of art, some that it was the seal of a occult band of scholars of which he was the centre. There is no definite evidence of an Academy, with rituals and symposia and festivals like the Platonic Academy of Florence, as a consequence, perhaps, of Lodovico's " duello." Certainly Leonardo was—and is—the kind of figure who tends to become the centre of a private cult, to form that *thiasus* of persons belonging to the aristocracy of beauty or wisdom or rare knowledge which becomes a kind of confraternity. He would have been Pythagoras in an antique era. He could have been Lucius Verus Apuleius. He could have been a nobler Apollonius of Tyana. Fra Luca Pacioli was a Pythagorean, and Leonardo must have remembered sometimes the ways of these haughty sectaries of antiquity. So Leonardo and his intimates probably did meet in symposia where they shared the hard-won reports of the disbibled heavens and earth, and new readings of Archimedean things, with starry stuff of another kind from Marsilio Ficino's book of mystical doctrine. For Leonardo read his Ficino as well as his Archimedes.

Perhaps he made the design for his younger enthusiasts, for youth delights to flaunt its blazons and favours. It is an ingenuity of interlacement, trefoil and quatrefoil, each twist completing and completed, a knot of symbol and comprehension in the esoteric Arabic manner,

The Labour of Herakles

whereby the beginning of a lesson or a treatise is illuminated only at the end, when the scholar's painful task flashes into a novel brilliance of wisdom as the last word is learned by heart. It may have been one of Leonardo's own imprese, shared with all his disciples. Imprese, personal badges and fancies, as distinct from civic or dynastic or conferred devices, were passionately used by people so proud of their personality; and these monomarks were both emphatic and exquisite.

Leonardo's conversation at this time was probably most savoured by his coteries in quiet hours. For mere epigrams and jest and set debates on the rival merits of paladins he had little fancy. For *contes drolatiques* he had no aptitude at all: but we find him practising in the manuscripts, sometimes, like an earnest archangel trying to comprehend the alien mysteries of human humour. He even learns the *Facetiæ* of Poggio, which seems droll even to pathos. His had been the Florentine monologue, like a sonata, hurrying, relenting, rising, appassionata, harmonizing sweetly to a close, a winding argument, moving with disarming grace to an end not soon recognized, eddying around the theme as if it were an iridescent accident, a phrase to be dissolved away in a melody, while the undertide of the great intention swept to remote and dangerous shores. And some in Milan were content with Leonardo's courteous manners and gracious comments. But there were many to listen to his lordlier speech, grave doctors, admiring artists, fair young nobles glad of that music of felicity and Leonardo's summer eyes.

VI

We do not know on what terms Leonardo gave himself to Milan, nor how much of his famous letter was definitely accepted. But we do know from his admissions and his attitudes that his chief task was the making of the great equestrian statue by which Lodovico intended to astonish Italy with the greatness of his race and his own kingly glory. Galeazzo Maria had begun the dream of a marvellous tomb covered by a magnificent Rider, the third Rider of the Renaissance, Francesco Sforza, as he passed into the holy Cathedral of Milan, raised in that hour of triumph to be more than the Conqueror-at-Arms. The sculptor was to lift him into the region of myth; he was to create a God, the Energy, the Triumphator, the Spirit of Italy *in excelsis*.

The gentle Milanese sculptors, accustomed to call, as easily as with a dewy tune on the pan-pipes, their amorini and fauns and ravishing vines from the rosy terra-cotta, shrank from the puissant vision to be dragged, with rough strife indeed, through the fiery gates into implacable terrible bronze. But all the sculptors in Italy had heard of that Cavallo. It was the horse, the marvel of pride and grace and strength, that engaged their minds. And it was a great tribute to Leonardo's shining prestige that he was accepted without protest as the carver of this Titan. No splendid sculpture yet lay to his charge, though he had been trained in a sculptor's bottega, and had enchanted people with those sweetly modulated heads of boys and smiling women so sadly perished. And sometimes he modelled in after years, for Lomazzo claims to possess a delicate head of a Christ-child. Perhaps it was the statue that drew him to Milan. In Florence it seemed impossible then that anybody should "ride brave in bronze." The Republic dreaded the conquering shadow of the Rider, the condottiere tyrant. When it raised great tombs it was for civic services, like those to the laurelled humanists in Sta Croce, who had done well by the City. Lorenzo and Giuliano were accomplished horsemen, but there were no images of them as riders outside the pictured cavalcades of the *Magi*. The image of the English condottiere who had been useful to the City had been painted in the Duomo; his horse was a concession to his trade. Nevertheless the Florentine artists longed to create an equestrian statue, the most trying and the most notable feat of sculpture. It was already in their tradition. Donatello's *Gattemelata* rode mightily in Padua. Verrocchio's *Colleone* was to be superb in Venice. The Pollaiuoli made two designs for the Sforza, but long before Leonardo went to Milan. There was no competition. Lodovico was jealous of all Venetian glories, and, excited doubtless by the infinite variety of poses sketched for him by Verrocchio's pupil, he was charmed to find one so gifted in other ways also adequate to the super-steed at last. Leonardo had been helping with Verrocchio's *Colleone* when he left Florence, and he had drawn many studies of superb and agitated steeds for the tilting motive of the *Adoration*. He was known as a brilliant rider and tamer of creatures like himself, strong, and delicate, and nervous. Besides, he could persuade with silver word and silver lyre. Evidently the steed was to carry the superlative king of a great monument, a little cathedral wherein the Rider should lie dead in state for ever, with captives round him like broken lilies. But that was a grandiose and impossible dream, that would have drained half the wealth of Milan. The steed was the great thing; the base, however splendid, could wait.

Whatever he built, whatever he did by aqueduct and canal, whatever ornament he added to the grace and colour of that decorated Court, Leonardo's life in Milan was dominated by two visionary figures: that of "the great horse," and that of the Prince of the bitter Love-Festival. It is unjust for his new scientific admirers to ignore the fact that all his painful researches into universal phenomena and universal law proceed

The Labour of Herakles

from his desire to be as an artist no less than absolute, and particularly to make these two works of his maturity sheer pieces of perfection, canonical chapters in the history of beauty.

During the whole of his first period in Milan he was absorbed in combining a Labour of Herakles with a Task of Psyche. He was grappling mentally and physically all the lines and masses that mean grace and strength into one amazing apparition of power that would seem to dominate the earth and take the sky. He was sifting all the expressions of humanity into twelve intense reactions against the most terrible accusation that Love can make. Whether he grasped the ineluctable steed in the masked passion of love with which the born rider tames the wild splendid creature to his vassalage, or delicately sifted like Psyche's helpers the innumerable shadows that alter the faces and the souls of men, he was using the whole of his being. The double toil did weary, I think, his superfine though perfectly trained fibre, and almost drained the fathomless reservoirs of his nervous energy. The famous comment on the fall of Duke Lodovico is neither resentful nor callous : " The Duke has lost his possessions, his state and his liberty ; and not one of his works has been completed." Here is simply the under-statement of flat exhaustion. Leonardo was not really in the habit of confiding his opinions or emotions to his papers. But what else remained to say ? Destiny had stricken the Duke and his splendid projects too early. They had cost the best years of Leonardo's life. Even he was tired. For a complete catastrophe there is no adequate comment. " The rest is silence " in a bitter sense.

Evidently he cast all his knowledge and skill as a sculptor into this mythic *tour-de-force* ; and after sixteen years of studying all the beautiful horses for which Milan was famous, after learning by heart the anatomy and features of man and beast, after perfectly realizing the horse as an artist, a scientist, a lord, and a brother, he saw the great model loom before the castle, colossal. The progress of the horse, from its initial stages, had been accompanied by the high-pitched epigrams of poets, and watched with an intensity of interest by craftsmen and princes that might well have unnerved a less serene confidence and troubled the processes of a less absorbed artist. He writes to the citizens of Piacenza who desire advice concerning the bronze gates they propose for their cathedral: " There is no one who is capable, except Leonardo the Florentine, who is making the bronze horse of the Duke Francesco, and you need take no count of him, for he has work that will last his whole lifetime, and I fear that it is so great an undertaking that he will never finish it." (Cold comfort for the citizens of Piacenza !)

Leonardo had even to begin his work again, after many years :

231

Leonardo the Florentine

" On 28th April 1496 [? 1490] I began this book and started the horse over again." There had been trouble with Lodovico, who, though an amiable tyrant, hardly expected to wait for sixteen years for the gradual distillation of genius. In 1489 Pietro Alamanni, the Florentine agent at Milan, wrote to Lorenzo, asking for one or two new masters to construct the statue. " For, though he has entrusted the commission to Leonardo da Vinci, he does not seem to me to have any great confidence in his capacity to carry it to completion." Possibly Lorenzo smiled, and possibly Lodovico was merely trying to pique his dilatory artist. At least they were pacified. But Leonardo was determined to make visible the Platonic idea of a horse, or rather of a horse and rider, for he saw these two as one—one will, one elemental energy. And evidently he did it. He had to surpass Donatello and Verrocchio. He was the challenger in this mighty effort, and he wrestled and threw them. So completely that nobody took the trouble to describe his masterpiece. There is no Pausanius for Renaissance Italy. Vasari is but desultory. All Italy had heard of the mighty monument ; all Italy had accepted it as an accomplished wonder. With a thunder of silver hooves it had galloped into the procession of supreme natural things, and people would sooner have thought of describing Bucephalus than the Cavallo of Leonardo. It was merely " the stupendous horse you know."

It surged into the astonished sight, when the town was shaken with the bells and colours of the imperial wedding, and this stranger from some true twilight of the gods, this phantom of a demiurge that mocked small ducal or imperial adventures, hueless and remote, gripped all the scattered standards of colour and sound and blazon into orderly cohorts of beauty, processions and rituals of the god of pride. For Leonardo had evoked his Lucifer, the Pendragon of his soul.

vii

But when he had finished, Lodovico had not money enough to cast it. Leonardo's peculiar fate came softly behind him and brushed away every certain footprint of the steed that had carried him into immortality. Not a statuette to tell even as much as the little images of the ivory and gold *Athena* of the Parthenon. Not a little wax model ! We gaze dubiously on some Caradosso plaque with a triumphing rider within a border of nereids, or search for some detail of a horseman whose steed rears over an enemy in the façade of the Certosa, or study figurines of triumphing horsemen in attitudes caught from the master's studio. We possess merely the conflict of those many amazing pages of beautiful horses, fierce or dreamy, rearing, pacing, galloping, fighting, filled with

The Labour of Herakles

rapture, disgust, mirth, fear—for Leonardo knew their psychology. The Gascon bowmen, on that first undisciplined and befouling entry into Milan, shot their arrows at the looming figure that seemed to crush their puny lives. Fra Sabba da Castiglione, that pleasing young Knight of Saint John, who had considerable sympathy with Leonardo, and who even wrote right to left as he did, has recorded the thing he saw. It lived on, wounded but inviolable shadow, mocking the darts with its immortal air. The Duke of Ferrara begged for the mighty remnant, and the French governor replied that King Louis had said he wished to keep it. Then it vanishes, as completely as if the divine energy in the shape of clay had trampled its own maltreated form into a little dust one dark hour, before it rose as on a winged destrier into the upper airs, and rode for Olympos.

So it was that, in the quieter way that was his, Leonardo, like his younger rival, had a " tragedy of the tomb." If anything exhausted him, the Cavallo did. Much as he loved horses, the gift of Poseidon, the lords of the waters, creatures with the rhythmic and gracious and inevitable motions of the waves, they seemed unlucky to his art. The *Adoration*, with its background of rearing riders, was never finished ; the Cavallo went to a dusty doom ; *The Battle of the Standard* was a frieze of beautiful fury, whose central knot perished from the wall and vanished mysteriously even in its cartoon, though fierily written on the eyes of the gazers. The tomb of Trivulzio was the fantastic project of a moment.

We do not know if the great steed paced or reared or galloped, and hardly even if it had its rider, though the drawings appear to say it had. Paulus Jovius seems to see a violently excited horse ; others saw it as a horse pacing. All men observe it in a dim wonder, and their words fumble in a maze, and give conflicting report, as happens when folk are aware of things new to their eyes, doubtfully, " as trees walking."

His atelier for the horse was in an ancient Visconti palace ; and there he drew, and wrought with clay, and suffered those wearinesses incidental to the sculptor's work. Also he himself endures much conflict about his horse. He would love the galloping or rearing thing, it appeals to him. It would be a taming of technique to suspend the untamable so that it hardly touched the base. But since he longs to cast it all of a piece ?— He murmurs that one must not desire the impossible, a maxim often on the lips of this born lover of the impossible—and then sets his rider " on a pacing steed and nothing else saw all day long." Till he wearies of that pacing steed, and turns to other tasks. But the leaping phantom of his steed pursues him, till deep in the rose-green glades of Vigevano he beholds the shapes of golden centaurs play, beating into silver dew with flying hooves the blue-violet ground-mist of the April dusk, or hears their thunder hush all the nightingales among the bride-white veils of the acacias of Pavia, till he sees in the midnight skies only the children of Leda riding, and feels the sun-god rise and set with the splendour of charioting horses.

Horses! Creatures tamed, untamed, tameless, of all beasts most equal with man in intelligence, beauty and pride, so splendid as a noble companion, so accusing as a drudge, so harrowing as a beaten slave, things of pride, courage and kindness, that imparted to man a virtue, that fair vanishing virtue of chivalry. (But it may be vanishing much to Leonardo's fancy, to the black-and-silver shapes that soar and dip in the sunset, on the taintless limitless ways of the wind and the sun, where even in battle, it is said, there lacks not the "magnanimous way of the falcon," and great salutation of equal foes, so that chivalry may be wrought like a thread of ancient gold into the new, hard, bright psychology now beaten out by the squadrons of the air.)

Horses of Babylon, apparelled for Semiramis; Carian horses with cheek-pieces of purple ivory; Thracian horses of Rhesus, white as snow and swift as fire, thieved by Diomed; immortal horses of Achilles; Xanthos, that spoke to him of death; wild horses of Hippolytus, gripped by swerveless fine hands; winged Steed of Perseus and rash Bellerophon; horses of Helios, that drink of the dawn and are stabled in the sunset; horses of the great Olympiads of time, driven by Greek riders serene in the quadriga; frieze of Athenian knights going gravely to festival on those little wide-necked Greek horses, stepping high and delicate with unshod feet (alas! that Leonardo should not have seen the Parthenon); charger of Alexander with a city for a grave; deified horses of Caligula with diamond frontlets; horses of charioting Nero; horses of Arabia, horses of Scythia, horses of Cathay, horses of Barbary, horses that bore the saints out of Egypt, "white chivalry of Christ"! Great white destriers that took mad fine lovers like Aucassin into battle, and stood still among the spears, while the young lord sat entranced; horses as brave as their knights and as wise as their masters, friends and companions of kings and condottiere! It was easy to frieze those stables with the great aisles in Milan.

Kingly, puissant, beautiful horses were among the great symbols of the Renaissance. One had borne Cesare Borgia blazing into France, with its mane twined with jewels and its proud feet shod with gold. The royal black steed Savoy defended King Charles of France at Fornovo and carried him into safety. The founder of the Sforza House had cared for his horses more than his men; and the Duke who was to be lifted into apotheosis had to the end of his life ridden them like a youth. Milan was a famous hostel for them. They were bred there, beautifully kept in houses planned by Leonardo himself. Galeazzo Sanseverino's horses were wonderful, kind as Cheiron, fiery as Diomed's immortal theft, proud as Pegasus. They were served like lords and clothed like fine ladies. Leonardo frequented their society when they were alive, and patiently dissected the tendons of their might when they were dead. He intended to make a treatise about them. Horses, as readers of Swift remember, sometimes attract those that love not their kind ; and they are ever dear to the lovers of great waters—images that rear themselves from the springs, the seas, and the clouds, sacrifices to the great rivers with whom they are kin, like the Trojan chargers thrown to deep-eddying Scamander. Galeazzo had a great Sicilian, with beautiful lifted leg, " Messer Mariolo's Morel the Florentin has a big horse with a fine neck," and a beautiful head. " The white stallion belonging to the falconer has beautiful hind-legs." " The big horse of Cennenino of Signor Giulio " seems to have been altogether noteworthy.

viii

In Leonardo's endless studies he varies between two kinds of steed. In one tense version the horse is rearing high, and the transcending rider is nearly upright on the fierce animal, swinging his exultant baton. But the position needed help from some support ; and Leonardo's subtle sense of measure was dubious if so instantaneous and violent a movement should be arrested. All the earlier studies are of a passionate vitality, however ; both Leonardo's and Lodovico's taste inclined to the astonishing, and especially to the unprecedented. The artist would hardly be content to follow in the track of the processional steeds of Donatello, and of Verrocchio, even then working in Venice ; and Lodovico's timidity abandoned him when he desired works of art and splendour. He did wish this figure of Renaissance energy, as personified in his race, to strike amazement in the beholder. However, Leonardo's contemplation of the statue at Pavia known as the *Regisole*, now vanished like so many of the antique riders, seemed to move him to more tranquil notions, as well as to a quickened admiration of classic models. " In that at Pavia [or Padua] the movement is more to be admired than anything else. The trot is almost the nature of the free horse." So he writes at this period.

Something of the horses at Monte Cavallo he must have known already, and of the four great horses from Nero's chariot that ramp so proudly before the front of Saint Mark's, as if they had risen from the sea to guard the temple of Poseidon. He must also have been aware of the quietude of Marcus Aurelius, riding a disciplined steed. At least he now presents a succession of serenely-moving horses, with and without riders, with noble and assured airs of sovereignty. Not merely conquering, but unconquerably lords of conquest, they pace remorseless and secure as Fate. Still, after these more restrained studies have confessed the calming hand of the antique, the dynamic energy rises to crescendo again ; the steeds gather force, though to a new and a rarer rhythm, and storm in great liberation across ethereal spaces. The naked young rider on the ramping steed would probably have been Leonardo's dream, though he might have rejected the fallen foe as obvious. And the mailed rider rising in his stirrups on the rearing horse, a Will incarnate, was probably Lodovico's. There are studies of moulds and furnaces for casting ; but they do not give away the secret. That horse and rider were to be separately cast, which was not altogether according to Leonardo's ambition, is all we learn for certain of that " stupendous horse you know." It was to be about seven metres high, and the monument demanded eighty tons of bronze.

ix

Meanwhile, there are the drawings, pages of horses, radiant and riderless, or rider-vassalled, but never rider-enslaved. If it be indeed the test of art that it should quicken the vitality of the gazer, it is hard to look at a stormy sheet of Leonardo's chargers without a leap of the heart and a sharply intaken breath, so certain the movement, so exultant the beautiful fiery line that sweeps splendid neck and quivering flank. Surely, dæmonic and delicate, they champed their silver grain from golden chargers like the horses of Caligula. They are disdainful, they are forbearing, they are ecstatic, they are cruel, they are patient and gentle, like one kind creature with a tied-up forelock. One enchanting rider goes off with a flying chlamys to gallop by Eurotas. Sometimes you see horse, rider and prostrate foe, mounted on an elaborate base. One nude youth, clinging to his horse, looks as if the fine silverpoint had chiselled him in metal. Another seems about to smite the foe. Again, the great triple group rises on an arch of triumph. Sometimes the passing horsemen are softened in a twilight distance as they just vanish out of sight towards some immortal river boundary. Some naked riders charge at dragons as if in a perilous frolic. In the drawings most of the horsemen are young—Leonardo's legions of youth, his chivalry of grace, his dangerous Greek cohorts of beauty. But, one thinks, can these be the equivocal angels he subtilized out of Milan ? These are insolent and alive, young Spartans who could curl their locks and smiling perish at Thermopylæ. Only they have been half-aware of a

YOUNG MAN IN MASQUER'S DRESS
(WINDSOR)

STUDIES OF HORSES
(WINDSOR)

The Labour of Herakles

barbaric dream, and their lithe figures seem to come riding from Greece under pointed Gothic arches. They are, indeed, the eager squires of the *Adoration,* grown finer, more disdainful, more imperious since he has mounted them on such horses that they must bear themselves as knights and cavaliers. Never does Leonardo's " ineffabile mano sinistro" move more lightly and more unswervingly over his paper than when he draws his horses. He must have been happy with them. They were happy together.

The great difficulty in imagining Leonardo is that it is almost impossible to think of all of his varying aspects at the same time. It is easy enough to imagine the cavalier and the sculptor turning to the low clear harmonies of colour and the vanishing landscape behind the head of the mysterious Lord in the refectory of Santa Maria delle Grazie, for an hour of quiet dreams. But it is not easy to think of him as also at work in the charnel-chamber at Pavia, and still less as writing bitter and rather petulant things against " abbreviators." Whatever he does, he does so completely that there seems no energy left for such byplays. I do not mean that he was not a great anatomist. He was proud of that, and of many other things ; but his primary interest at this time was " a me Leonardo fiorentino che fa il cavallo del Duca Francesco di Bronzo " ; and his labour on that Cavallo would have exhausted the attention of another.

Sometimes his horses ride off into the darkness that lies between his unconscious self and his imaginative reason, to fight with dragons, that everlasting contest all the more intense in the personality that approaches in power the godlike. The immortal bright steed that is himself, who rises from the great waters, from whose stamp springs Helicon and who often has wings, closes with the darkling dragon that also draws power from the air and the waters, and often has terrible wings, and is also himself. Much of the cruel and conscienceless energy that possessed him, that might have wrecked itself on a passive humanity in wild volitions, because of his intellectual passion escaped in splendid sublimation through his epic struggle with the great steed, the immoderate shape that, frayed with the arrows of France, vanished contemptuous among contending emperors and kings. I daresay he resigned himself. In his quest for perfection he had chased the wild centaur too long down the glades of Arcadia ; he gripped it too late to lead it to the subjugation of perdurable bronze ; he would not realize that some imperfection is the price every mortal must pay for a translation of his vision into the world of fact. Artists are easier now : they do not work from within outwards, they merely pull their material about till it suggests, however dimly, some kind of primitive half-baked form.

Leonardo the Florentine

At a rare moment we see him suddenly as if the door of his sculptor atelier opened suddenly in the sunlight. The amiable peasants are bringing him " a multitude of corals and shells from the mountains of Piacenza." They have seen him on those pensive wanderings ; and, like all simple people at all times, they take pleasure in lonely, incomprehensible and subtly sovran ways, for peasants, especially in Italy, are used to gods in the brake and on the hills, for whom they leave garlands, milk and honey, safe from the mass-priest. With some such homage, they bring this beautiful strange person shells, and so we see him turn from his models to take up a coral, his eyes gone suddenly dreamy with a thought of the elder waters. Doubtless he spoke sweetly to them—he did to everybody.

Leonardo the sculptor is a great legend. Perhaps it is a fine distinction ; but he was possibly all this time more intent on capturing an archetypal idea than on making a statue. He desired to impose a heavenly pattern on the world of matter, not, like Michelangelo, to release the lovely form lying implicit in that matter as if under enchantment. You do not see him attacking the frank marble with a chisel of impatient rapture, striking away the superfluous stuff from the Eros or the Pietà or the Victory he divined hidden in the lucid stone. You saw him endlessly drawing, dissecting, preparing, with an elaborate incantation of signs and symbols persuading his great image to take on the mortality of dimensional matter. Either artist achieved miracles ; but it did not seem inevitable that Leonardo's miracle should put on earthly form in sculpture ; it might have replied to another form of invocation. With Michelangelo it could not have been so. Both had the creative might of a god. But Michelangelo was demiurge ; Leonardo was like the spirit who moved on the face of the waters.

Well, he had brought his heavenly steed to the brink of the world of art ; but it was driven from its clay before he could tether it to bronze. Probably the fatigue of an effort into which he cast all his science, all his æsthetic, all his vision, and so much of his physical energy, did exhaust him ; and such anticlimax of that long-sustained effort as could allow a possible sneer on the lips of his enemies, and even suggest the insult which Michelangelo threw at him in later years in the streets of Florence, was bitter in his locked remembrance. He seems to turn hereafter, as the weary turn, from his burning chimera with its implacable demands ; and with " retreats " in the still cloisters of mathematics, with diligent brilliant labours at hydraulics and fortifications, that imply possible results for possible labours, he tries to evade the intolerable service of beauty.

Chapter vii

The Task of Psyche

i

PERHAPS he already had misgivings as to his Task of Psyche. Fortune had defeated him as Herakles; his own passion for experiment would undo him as Psychopompos. For it must never be forgotten that Leonardo firmly held that the figure is most to be praised which expresses by a gesture the pressure of the soul. His version of *The Last Supper* is painted on the wall of the refectory of the cloister of Sta Maria delle Grazie. Lodovico's beloved church, where he had enriched the sacristy with a great treasure of beaten gold and silver, and sacrosanct brocades, where Bramante had builded a fair chamber for the Renaissance within the courts of Lombard mediævalism, was to bear the seal of finality in a *Cenacolo* by Leonardo. He was to give supreme form to a traditional theme, and bring the mediæval mystery into the light of Renaissance day, to express by a reconciling harmony of moving gestures the panic of the soul accused by its God. Therefore, at times he forgot the Cavallo. From every face that passed he wrung with demanding look its possibility of fear, amazement, guilt; or persuaded from it with caressing eyes what faint sweetness it could surrender to the ineffable beauty of the one face he dared not paint altogether as he would. For this he would stretch souls upon a rack of steel as fine as silk till they yielded up their last residue in shame or beauty.

After Leonardo was dead, a boy who had seen him paint in the Refectory of the Graces, Matteo Bandello, wrote his novelle for the gracious ladies whose company he loved. When he was frequenting the " most delightsome gardens " of Camilla Scarampa, Lady Ippolita Sforza e Bentivoglio, and Cecilia Gallerani, all amicably happy, it would seem, in a mild Saint Martin's Summer, safe from sack and siege and plague, in the calm epilogue to their changeable lives, reasoning softly of the poet's office, and reading Cecilia's sonnets, he set down the one vivid impression of Leonardo we possess from an eyewitness. He is introducing his fiftieth story; and remembers the time when he stayed with his uncle, the General of the Dominican Order, in the Convent of the Graces. On Sunday, he says, certain gentlemen used to resort to the

Leonardo the Florentine

Delle Grazie monastery of the Friars of Saint Dominic, " and there abode quiet in the refectory to contemplate the marvellous and most famous Supper of Christ with His Disciples, which the excellent painter Leonardo da Vinci of Florence was then in act to paint, the latter being well pleased that everyone who saw his paintings should freely declare his opinion thereof." Bandello then describes with convincing accuracy the sequence of the artist's moods : " Now the said Leonardo was used oftenwhiles (and I myself have more than once seen and considered him) to go betimes of a morning and mount the scaffolding, for that The Last Supper is somewhat high above the ground, he was used, I say, from rise of sun to dusk of eve to lay not the brush from his hand, but, forgetting eating and drinking, to paint without intermission. On the other hand he would belike abide two, three, or four days thereafterward without setting hand thereto ; and whiles he abode one or two hours of the day, and only contemplated, examined and judged the figures, considering in himself that which he had wrought. Nay ! I have seen him, according as the humour or whim took him, at midday, whenas the sun was in Leo, depart the Corte Vecchia, whereas he was in act to mould in clay that stupendous horse which you know, and go straight to Le Grazie, and mounting the scaffolding, take his brush to give one or two touches to one of his figures, and then of a sudden come down, and betake himself elsewhither." Cardinal Gurk the elder, lodging in Santa Grazie, came with the others to see. While they were gazing, the painter descended from his scaffold, and the company fell to talking of the vanished paintings of antiquity, and lovely art, and the desire for great comparisons. The Cardinal, a gross person in the esoteric courtly company, asks Leonardo what is his salary, and is amazed to hear of two thousand ducats of regular pension, and manifold gifts. So Leonardo talks of the honour rightly done and due to painters, and, the unworthy prelate being gone, remarks : " My Lord Cardinal yonder marvelled amain at the liberality which our most excellent and magnificent lord Duke Lodovico useth with me ; but I myself marvel far more at him, and at his ignorance (be it said with all due reverence for his red hat), he showing himself little practised in the reading of good authors." He tells the story of Lippo Lippi, freed by the Moors for love of art, and fostered by Cosimo de' Medici, despite his amorous follies, because " rare and sublime spirits like himself are celestial, and not asses at hire " ; but not without elaborate reference to the famous tale of Apelles and Alexander.

This little piece of novelle writing is dipped deep in the personality of Leonardo, deeper than the blithe author suspects. It shows us Leonardo in that creative ecstasy which must have consumed so many

The Task of Psyche

of his days, and of which the manuscripts, mere scientific notes, give little trace, with which the *Treatise on Painting*, an inadequate series of hints taken down by some pupil more industrious than brilliant, is not concerned. He is revealed, though by an imperfect witness, in the splendid agony of that heightened and glittering state in which the mind is so buffeted by the besetting wings of ideas and images that it cries out in despair at the folly of seizing them with mere pen or brush or chisel, and almost tramples its mortality underfoot in vain desire to escape with the strong flight of beautiful shapes to some Platonic Heaven, rather than sadly to salve from that excessive illumination some broken lights and stifled colours and vanishing lines. Leonardo working in a fury of concentrated effort from dawn to dusk without food; Leonardo torn between the conflicting tyrants of the Renaissance, the conquering Energy that dominates the Kingdoms of the Earth, and the quiet Prince of immortal beauty for ever betrayed and adored; Leonardo sunk in trances of cogitation, whence he awakes to give the one touch or two that means so much to him, so little to the fretting prior, is here alive and lovable. The shaft about the red hat is also characteristic, for he loved not churchmen unless, like Ippolito d'Este, they touched his sense of greatness in some way. The implication that Florence knows best how to deal with artists colours the tale of Lippo Lippi, the moral of which—that artists live under a special dispensation of grace—is Leonardesque as well as Medicean. And it is easy to believe that Leonardo had Apelles much in his mind. He loved princes; but he did believe that artists were also princes. He was constantly called Apelles at Lodovico's Court, " this new Apelles whom he has brought from Florence," and certainly it pleased him. He was Greek in his way, but not purely Hellenic. Though he could have found friends in the House of Aspasia, the darker Leonardo would have waited for Macedon and Alexander to meet the kind of Greek most attractive to his temper. Alexander, born of magic Thracian Olympias and a serpent-god, as they said, bestial, divine, omnipotent, illuminated, he would have followed with Hephæstion and the great steed Bucephalus through Asia, and down through the fabulous passes into the carven white-jade cities of India, to stamp the indelible seal of Greece on the princely face of the Buddha, so that his images in the Kashmir region might wear an expression not altogether unfamiliar to the acquaintances of Madonna Lisa.

ii

The destiny of *The Last Supper* is written mournfully in the history of art. Leonardo could not endure the hasty fixation of the tried method of fresco-painting, which left no allowance for mood or afterthought, so he chose a modified and experimental tempera which permitted endless reverie and rectification to the passion for perfection. But the great picture, hardly finished, began to flake from the damp cloister wall, for the colours had not intertextured with its surface. Strange! Endless experiments and studies in perspective, colour, lighting, grouping, analysis of expression, harmonies of line, study of attitude! None, apparently, as to the durability of the paint that held these things together. For all his inquiry into the Laws of Matter, Leonardo was " Divine " enough to expect it to be faithful to him though irrationally used, as spirits are sometimes. This material wall, however, was too damp to be miraculous : and he did not persuade the sulky surface to become substantiate with his imagery. In Vasari's time the picture was blurred, in Lomazzo's it was a ghost.

The monks, who probably from the beginning viewed their treasure with more disquietude than the æsthetic nobles of Milan, let the smoke drift over it and drove a door through the middle of it. Napoleon's soldiers threw their missiles at it. The refectory became a stable and a hayloft. But the restorers were the deadliest foes. Some faint mirage might have persisted till modern wits had power to arrest that at least, if these tamperers, one being of singular iniquity, had not been so evilly zealous with the fresco, though in our own time a sympathetic skill has cleansed and fixed the perished remnant. You may admire the great composition, the rhythm of the grouping, the relations of the forms, the cunning adaptation to the room. Not here Leonardo's colour, nor Leonardo's faces, nor Leonardo's drapery, and little of Leonardo's hushed atmosphere of emotion! Nor are they in Marco d'Oggione's soft weak copy, and so not in Raphael Morghen's engraving. Only in Leonardo's studies for groups and single heads do you get some vivid notion of its spiritual quality.

Though the theme was a traditional one, it had not been overworked. Giotto's *Cena* was a series of dignified images, Ghirlandajo's was a competent arrangement brightened decoratively by peacocks and orange-trees. Perugino's did not lack pathos and tenderness. But the harsh Andrea del Castagno in Saint Apollonia in Florence with vigour and impatience had broken up the stiff row of figures and brought some rhythm into the emotion. Leonardo must have thought of a *Cenacolo* now and then, even in his first period. He had made so many studies for his early *Adoration* that the beautiful residue was a rich drift of motives. Groups on groups of people talking! Of people sitting earnestly at table, unified by the stress of some great argument! Knots of naked young men lost in some passionate disputation!

The Task of Psyche

Then the Duke wanted a *Cena* for his beloved Church. Leonardo knew that the Last Supper is difficult as a painter's subject. It is hard to give an enchanting visual impression to a number of companions sitting in a row, however sharply they be reacting to some given word. It is the given *word* which halts the painter. That is, the theme is purely literary ; and no painter could ever convey the heart-breaking beauty, the mortal simplicity of the different Gospel verses. No painter could knock so terribly at the soul's inmost doors with such ultimate tidings. Leonardo was given to argue that the painter's impression was always more puissant than the poet's. If *The Last Supper* survived now in all its original and ethereal beauty he could not convince us that, whatever the great seizure of his picture did for its gazers, it conveyed the poignancy of the silence that falls round love betrayed. The rhythm has conquered sorrow and shame. That suavity has dissolved any piercing quality. But the verses of the New Testament, for all their solemn silencing cadences, vibrate with pity and terror.

iii

Here is no occasion of a painter who holds that his subject is irrelevant to his picture. Leonardo expressly says that his subject does matter, and that any gesture, however skilfully and exquisitely presented, fails entirely unless it be convincing as a gesture of the soul. Christ was not unimportant to him and his gazers, as Whistler perversely held his subject to be. *The Last Supper* was not merely a symphony in rose and blue and green, nor a study in uprights and horizontals and ovals, nor even a triumph in linear and aerial perspective, nor a piece of rare illumination, nor an offering of tactile values, nor a realistic presentation of human types, though incidentally it was all of these. It was for Leonardo an imaginative vision translated into terms of human sight with all the science at his command. It is Pattern, supreme Pattern— the Pattern of a Passion.

That the serenely irradiated miracle of painting which opened the end of that refectory into a chamber of sorrowful mystery and a landscape of dreams did not fail of its æsthetic appeal we have impassioned testimony. The complete isolation of the supreme figure, its royal inclined head mystical within its own clear triumphal arch of sorrow, against the tender sky, the novel bowed movement of the beloved apostle who seems to swoon away from the beautiful breast where he has laid his head, the instinctive recoil of the others into the terza rima of Dantesque music—trinities of anguish and terror, yet subdued to that rhythm, subdued to the great pattern of art—the opposed isolation of darkness around the arch-traitor, the woven peace of the lines of the arches, tables, even the little rolls, the dreamy exalted landscape behind, attuned with the mood of its lord, the cool mysterious tones of Leonardo's colour, wrung from vanishing rainbows and stainless afterglows—all these altered the Last Supper of Christ into a symposium of beautiful things. It was in a way Leonardo's Renaissance tribute to that story of deathless symbolism which exasperated the Middle Ages into a fever of love and hate. He calmed it with some of the clear air, the olive groves and columns and the noble movement of Sophoclean tragedy, with his two intently opposed protagonists, and with the stricken chorus controlled by that overmastering rhythm as by a great sense of fate. The gestures of the apostles are those of people fending off a terror they dare not contemplate. With invisible divine hands the great rhythm steals over them, touching and composing the fingers of Panic.

iv

Yet the theme is bitter. Betrayal was for the Middle Ages the unpardonable sin. The amazing genius of those who shaped the story of Christ, carried betrayal with a kiss into the dark wild waste of unimaginable wickedness, and with Dante impaled the traitor in the apex of hell. This rage against the betrayal of love did not depart from the Renaissance, for all its military and political stratagems and treasons. True ! Their tyrants would dare damnation. They might poignard their friends in a fury, and hurry their enemies to the strangling-chair ; but deliberate betrayal was another matter. There was a black emphasis on personal treason. Cesare Borgia at Sinigaglia snapped the teeth of his trap on his captains as soon as he had smiled them within it. It was a *bellissimo inganno* ; he and his captains were playing life and death together, treason for treason. Grifonnetto Baglioni the beautiful suddenly murdered the sleep of his kindred after a love-feast, and Italy stood still with horror at " el gran tradimento," while the criminal went like a somnambulist, waiting only for his mother's lovely shrift and his purifying death. Lodovico the Duke broke his treaties, and undermined his allies, quite in a modern fashion ; and it was considered a wearisome habit. Still, that was impersonal diplomacy. Lodovico had no feeling for any of his political abettors except Lorenzo and Maximilian, to whom he behaved well, and Charles of France, whom he thoroughly despised. But when Bernardino di Conte, whom he had reared and spoiled in his extravagant way from childhood, whom he had embraced as the inviolable castellan of his impregnable keep, at once surrendered those mighty walls to the incredulous besiegers for a share in the spoil, all the cities as well as Lodovico, and the French themselves,

The Task of Psyche

said " Judas " till the traitor died of it.   Friendship at least, in the Renaissance, exacted the last fidelities.   So Leonardo would move them by his psychological skill in seizing the moment when the dreadful accusation of their Lord smote the ears of the disciples.   Not when He lifted the red loving-cup and broke the bread of sacrifice in consummating love did the soul of Leonardo respond, but when the sad air vibrated as with the wings of ravens with strange words auspicious of the Cross.

There was a strangeness in that picture and, for some, disturbance. For, though Leonardo used all his imaginative knowledge and his infinite science for the painting, his unconscious part stole in and changed the Christian theme.   " Tout est possible à Léonard, hormis de faire croire qu'il croit," says Suarés.   Well, he does not believe what the monks of the Grazie, what Lodovico, believed.   What he believes, however, is not so far from the Ephesian Gospel.

The murmured word has shaken the disciples into clusters of pain, like aspen leaves ; all of them stricken with horror, all of them cold with the secret sudden knowledge that, in some recoil from their burning enthusiasm, in the accidias of exhaustion, in the follies of surprise, in the grey moods of doubt, in the contagions of fear, in the extortions of anguish, in impulsive insanities, each of them might suddenly sell themselves to unimaginable guilt.   And their terror is not unjustified, for each will indeed deny his Lord ; even the Beloved clothed in the same sweet colours, whose head sinks away so wearily, will not cleave to the end.   Only Philip, too young, too dream-kindled, too innocent to realize, looks almost smilingly sweet and incredulous.   Love is wounded in the house of his friends.   In what other house has he ever been wounded ?

v

But is it Love's—this head of eucharistical grace that Leonardo said he could not finish, meaning that he dared not finish, exquisite heresiarch ! The story of Zenale's pretty reproach may be true : Leonardo would have listened and gently acquiesced.   He left incompletion like a veil over the heavenly face, for he would have moulded it in the image of his soul's desire, and the monks would not have borne it. It may be that the drawing in the Brera, all smirched over by alien fingers, was not even in the original his own.   But some such original existed.   And that heavy-lidded head, sexless, incomprehensible, with smooth curled hair, the " delicatissima figura," lost in a clear trance of dolour not known to the sons of men, held something of Leonardo's dream of God.   So might a great king's son look, surrendering to a fate that cannot mar him, dream-locked from the clamour, sweetly unsurprised, regarding with equanimity crucifixion or coronation as the last great act of courtesy on his way back to his throne in Eternity. He is the Alexandrian Logos, the Greek Christos, the one Light, he is essentially Beauty rather than Love, which, for Leonardo, is only beauty's divine accident. The gestures of the sufferers are almost shamed by this lucid and lovely sorrow, woven from supersubtle divinations. Can the immortal substance of the Logos feel the thorns, the scourge, the nails? Can this Beauty know the Agony of the Garden, this that seems even now to be away walking white in the seas of an emerald twilight? Ah, this is not the " Prince that in the sad orchard hung " between the thieves—this god of strange ecstasy, this leonardesque vine-god brought by sweet subterfuges and sub-ironic intentions to gaze wistfully at a treason he hardly comprehends. It is a beautiful Alexandrian mystery, and an æsthetic triumph ; but it is not the symbolic picture of the hushed and suffering Christian love-feast. Nor does the Catholic miracle of transubstantiation seem possible except to Philip the poet, to John the Beloved, and to Judas who is also divine, the principle of darkness, the antitype. The dazed and simple people suffer unillumined. Leonardo unconsciously has carried his aristocratic severance within even *The Last Supper*. His Christ is not saying, " Take, eat of my body, and drink of my blood," but " Verily one of you shall betray me. . . . What have I to do with thee ? "

One enthusiast compares the arrangement of the great *Cenacolo* with the grouping of the Parthenon pediment, because of the beautiful drapery, and the satisfying relation of the figures to each other and to the space they fill. I cannot feel that the remembrance of that supreme session of gazing gods, considering their dedicated processions of Athenian beauty, can be other than distracting to a mind desirous to be just to this intent and ultimate harmonizing of agitated souls round our Lord of beauty and sorrow, this burning-inward, not radiantly outward composition. Yet *The Last Supper* is probably of all Leonardo's works the most Greek in spirit, because of the sweetness, music and finality with which he subdues all the lines of quivering emotion into peace, the æsthetic mercy by which he resolves an intolerable situation into beauty.

But some might say there is a wounding kind of beauty whose thrilling arrows it is well to endure ; and that an imagery of the Betrayal should convey the bitter Gothic ecstasy.

vi

One seems to pass from the refectory within that Room with the coffered ceiling, all lighted wood and dark tapestry, where through the

The Task of Psyche

three arched openings at the end the heavenly light floods in. The wild emotion, leaping from heart to heart, sweeps the listeners into a series of waves, sweeps the protesting hands crying the same cry in different keys. The converging lines in the floor and walls vanish towards the vanishing prince. The illuminations and the penumbra of the chiaroscuro take up the battle of light and darkness. The slight hesitations and withdrawing starts cannot impede the dominant rhythm; they are like the delicate conflicts between verbal and musical accents in a great line of verse subdued by the mighty beat of its sovran scansion. The artist has drawn his wreathed work of beauty round them and laid the ends of the chain of emotion in the listless hand of the figure with the downcast eyes.

Nor is Judas outside the chain, though isolated so cunningly in his darkness of soul; from his hollowed and wasted face of pride and passion leaps the most direct response of all. The absurd stories about the drawing of this head, though probably encouraged by Leonardo's own enigmatic humour, while he silently had his own way with Judas, sound like popular fables. This is no " hardened sinner," no criminal. The great study at Windsor perhaps best gives Leonardo's conception: here is a powerful, heroic head, tortured, ravaged, exasperated. Leonardo knew well enough that there were worse traitors than the historic Judas, traitors to whom that kiss in the garden means no burning seal of remorse, and who live comfortably for ever after on the thirty pieces of silver at compound interest. But his divination went farther. This damned and defiant figure, clutching the bag in a nervous convulsion, is more than Judas. It is the Dark Angel confronting the god who is the Light; he is the apostle of the lost, predestinate to the eternal darkness by which the Light is known, without which it could do no miracles, the mysterious Antichrist whose pulses are akin to the beautiful god's. When even the brows of white Love, the beloved disciple, are heavy with the foreknowledge that even white Love may fail with delicate feet on the Via Dolorosa and flee naked into the darkness, the dark and dreadful Love acquiesces in his agonizing part. He, too, is necessary to the mystery of Redemption, to the deliverance of the god from his mortality, to the exaltation of mortality through the crucified crisis of his Passion; and in the kiss of betrayal he delivers to death, with one fierce throe of adoration and with all regret, with infinite reverberation of regret, the Lord of Light, for whom his darkness is forever the pavilion and the sepulchre. Manichæan Milan was urgent in Leonardo when he painted there; but he himself was naturally a dualist.

So shift on shift, if you feel the strong undercurrent of Leonardo's repressed unconsciousness, welling up through the faces of the protagonists, the great picture alters to a myth and a philosophy—shift on shift as Leonardo's masterpieces do. But it shifts back again, through phases of strange emotion, to a beautiful great pattern on a treacherous wall, made of some passionate people stricken to the heart by the quiet and lovely lord, and some exquisitely formed arches and perspectives and horizons of a clear landscape like a promise of peace. There was nothing casual or trivial on that accomplished surface that glimmered upon the wall. Every head was a marvel of strong humanity; and all the hands were expressive as the faces. The hands are always as eloquent in Leonardo as a Verlaine or any other French symbolist may describe them. And not only the hands. The whole body interprets, and the groups have their collective urgency besides. From head to foot these bodies are dyed from the pang of their peculiar surprise and pain. "Gesticulating Italians," says Mr Berenson, forgetting that Elizabethans or Galileans would also have so betrayed themselves in like manner, and refusing to recognize the powerful rhythm that charms the gestures into melody.

vii

When Lodovico was gone from his forgetful city, and King Louis had ridden down the way of white lilies and golden ladies to the Cathedral, he came to Santa Maria to gaze at the great *Cenacolo*. And with him there came Cesare Borgia and the Marquis of Mantua, and the lords of Ferrara, the princes of Montferrat and Savoy, and all the brilliant nobles who had taken great love and regal gifts from Lodovico! Ah! those of Ferrara, those of Mantua, splendid, who had helped to pull down the splendid, falcons who had preyed on a falcon, against nature, destroyers of evil omen! But gamesters have no emotion, and each of them feared for his own prestige. Leonardo the Florentine was amongst them, regretless and secretly ruthless as they: his genius needed another king to serve. What did they think, that glittering circle of treasonable princes, regarding the symphony of betrayal? They said it was "strangely beautiful;" and the king would fain have carried the wall to France. It was a mediæval knight who began his prayer: "Lord Jesus Christ, who hast commanded men to keep faith on earth"; and the day of such hectic loyalty was over. The artist stood apart, regarding them. He had wrought sixteen years for Lodovico; and was ready to serve his enemies, even if they quartered his bosom friend, Andrea of Ferrara, on the gates of Milan. The artist, Leonardo thought, must accept those who could give opportunities, and so was free to change as often as a condottiere. Besides—Lodovico

The Task of Psyche

had failed him. As for the father and brother of Beatrice, when they looked at her sweet effigy in the choir they must have had some fierce pang of shame, though the beautiful great picture commoved them not. Whatever the themes, the Renaissance princes were trained æsthetes, and a picture would not remind them that they had trafficked with Judas.

viii

The great composition of Leonardo's youth lies faint gold and wild like the early morning with lilies in her breast, and an unearthly wind sweeps all those true seekers out of the night into heavenly illumination. The airs are chill and fresh, the pure colours of the flowers are still unspoken, but their fragrance is in the air. The great composition of Leonardo's maturity lies like a departed sunset stained from the petals of much that flowered in vain. The rhythms of *The Last Supper* are of a harmonic undulation; the subtle linking of its chain of emotion is as involved and as complete as that of one of his Vincian knots. The rhythms of the *Adoration* are lyric and exultant; they have the leaping movement of the steeds of the morning. Still, *The Last Supper* has drawn much of its great quality from the *Adoration*. The beardless naked boys who once spoke ardently round a table, who sprang and gazed and quivered like Easter tongues of flame, young shepherds and magians and donzelle athirst for the Grail, knights of the Holy Ghost, or sun-children, who loosed the arrows of their souls like their lord of Delos, are all behind this stricken company, who find a serpent rising from the very Cup of Communion. From some Florentine reserve of clear types and noble lines he drew the energy to begin his picture of mature men in an ultimate hour, with grave draperies that conspire with the calm walls and the arches to control their passion. Only Philip with his dream face comes unchanged from the *Adoration*, and gazes still candid and ecstatic on his compeers so altered that they astound him. But opposed to his is the swooning Lombard beauty of Saint John the Beloved, with lovely fallen eyelids, soft hair and smoothly, tenderly modelled face. He is one of Leonardo's angels as he imagined them in Milan, with that air of mysterious sweetness, virginal and bridal. The delicate twine of pattern runs round the neck of his robe : the gem clasps it. He is lovely and beloved. And the Black Knight of the early picture ? He is divided now, and he is behind both Christ and Antichrist. It is, all the same, by the tense remembrance of the great Florentine rhythm of line that Leonardo's reply to a Gothic demand becomes the most Hellenic thing in Milan. The exegesis of its conflicting mood is too unrhetorical for Goethe ; the harmony is so complete as to silence all exegesis, except for such as are intent on discovering the soul of the master.

Henceforth he becomes reluctant even to plan great compositions. His organizing powers have expression enough in other labours. Of his art he will make a secret shrine wherein he will set the images of the mysterious beauty he loves, on whom his suppressed yearning concentrates, undisturbed by other emotional interests. The conflict of sex annoys his imagination. He loves a monotone of emotion, a brooding plainsong with all its delicate modulations changing and just aquiver like a shoaling sea. No music of the trumpets, drums, and clavichords of rapture, but a concert of viols rising and falling, a pure motet of blue and green colours, and one rare face with rare angelic echoes! This ark of music and light will bear the secret of his soul about the world, with a veil of blue and purple and emerald all wrought with cherubim.

He, the innovator, will keep to traditional themes. Into the traditional theme he will put sweet heresy like pagan incense in hallowed thuribles, and with all the new devices of his art heighten the strangeness of that exquisite trouble. Beyond all reproof he audaciously carries his mysterious soul into sanctuary. His initiates shall eat the white shewbread of art and be satisfied.

Madonna he paints " sitting behind her silver veils thinking delicate thoughts." But not a Madonna with saints and apostles about her. No ; the only woman type he can endure, serene in her own crystal world as he in his, shall be accompanied by sexless beautiful creatures, the child, the angel, or some strange sister. And, if he hides his unchristened emotion in the shapes of virgins and angels, he also brings his uncanonical knowledge upon the altar, beautifully astute. He must not tell the Inquisition that the Adriatic of molten sapphire once lay about the feet of Alps and Apennines, and that the great rivers running down to their inevitable end brought the rich deposits that made the Lombard Plain. But he can paint behind the Virgin a world in dreamy gradual parturition of land from water in silver rains and dawning light. With a divine camouflage, under the hood of lovely devotion the spirit that denies and the soul that desires softly captivate the altar place.

ix

If he did paint a *Nativity* for Matthew Corvinus or the Emperor Maximilian, one would give much to see it, for, if Leonardo detested the idea of physical love, he had a paradoxical reverence for the mystery of birth. As it is, the first revelation of his mature Milanese manner, and his considered type of beauty, is to be found in *The Virgin of the Rocks*. The whole drift of his subterranean emotionalism and strange baffled idealism, the mediæval asceticism so curiously involved with his Renaissance ruthlessness, gives an impression that he would willingly have accepted the theological doctrine of the Immaculate Conception, and dreamed wistfully about parthenogenesis, and identified himself with the child of mystical wonder. It is not improbable that he was unnerved by the strangeness and audacity of his imagination sometimes, and that he exercised himself so resolutely in the realms of the proven and provable because he feared that this divine dæmon of his imagination might become a winged victory and bear him too far into the worlds of fantasy.

It was really for the Brotherhood of the Conception in Milan that he first set this symbolic goddess in her hypæthral temple of strange rocks like menhirs—a Druid temple almost. They wanted an ancona for their chapel in San Francesco ; and, being mediævally minded, they made many stipulations as to carven wood and gilding. Leonardo, much engaged, had evidently named the da Predis brothers as his assistants. Perhaps the monks were startled by the new Madonna, not shut in some chamber of her ivory tower, nor in her garden close, nor even in a flowery mead, but throned as a marvel and a mystery in a faëry world " by perilous seas forlorn." This was not a picture of the Immaculate Conception yet, and it has been suggested that they even found something heretical in the angel's pointing hand. There is an old symbolism by which the presence of God is indicated by a hand, and the beautiful finger of the angel may be Leonardo's way of indicating that ancient significance, and recognizing that he was really painting the bride of the Holy Ghost. While, if the pointing hand gave the Saint John a sweet importance, well, Leonardo had a cult of Saint John, who was, moreover, the spiritual King of Lombardy from Theodolinda's day. But something alarmed the monks, for Leonardo did not suppress the lovely hand in the next version for any æsthetic reason. At all events there was a money quarrel ; and the painter appealed to the Duke against the monks' valuation. Leonardo, like Shakespeare, though generous and even extravagant, became exasperated when people tried to cheat. He was especially annoyed at being undervalued by some monks. It is a sorry business to deal in art, work for which no commercial value can be severely fixed, since its values vary, not only with the worker's mind, but with the soul and eyes of the receiver. What can one pay for the Protean thing ? It is worth a king's ransom for souls attuned and prepared. It is not worth a brass farthing to those initiate neither by grace nor duty. Leonardo must have been at least more at ease when work as engineer-in-chief paid for " things done that take the eye and have the price."

Therefore we know two Virgins of this kind, one in Paris and one in London. For Leonardo seems to have recovered his original painting of Our Lady, and sold it, so that in the end it was acquired by the French. Ambrogio da Predis, it is supposed, painted a duplicate in Leonardo's studio, with two single angels for the side wings; and this picture stayed with the monks till 1787, when Gavin Hamilton brought it to England. But Leonardo must have painted much of the second picture. Restored as it may be, it is hard to believe that the hand which worked the inanimate angels, and the dead surfaces of the wings, could have accomplished much of the beautiful replica, where the mere texture of the paint is still miraculously skilled in passages, where the points of the unfaltering fingers that tenderly handled the Child are discoverable in the glazes, while the hair of the angel and the Virgin twine into long softly thrilling spirals, such as only Leonardo could paint.

But the Louvre picture is unquestionably the original. It has a poignancy of emotion, a stabbing sweetness in its water-world colouring that fixes it within the earlier part of the Milanese period, before the Florentine edge had dissolved, rather than blunted, and the new beauty had still the charm of a challenge rather than of a seduction. Iris and cyclamen and pointed leaves, dove-delicate colombine leaning to its mirrored petals, enter more acutely into the unearthly mood; stranger rocks vanish into a more quivering light, the lovely hand of the angel is piercing in the pattern, the drapery of the Virgin has finer cadences, and gathers into a lapful of more sweetly broken gold, the blues lighten into the greens like the ascending cry of a violin, the faces are keyed high to the consummation of this mystical childermas. In the London version the participants are suaver, more dreamily sweet; in the angel the *sottigliezza* is almost morbid. The Louvre angel is divinely amused, as if he knew his pointing finger is heretical.

Still, both pictures are of surpassing beauty. For the first time Leonardo etherealizes the Lombard face to the type of his æsthetic desire, in both woman and angel, whose faces, rapt in dreamy contemplation, echo each other, androgynous, immortal. Already the Virgin gazes as Leda will gaze at the swan-children. For the first time he paints the mythic pyramid of the artist's triune soul, woman, child and faëry—faëry meaning god or angel. By gesture and expression the triangular group of forms and faces is woven together like a unison of viols. For the first time he reveals in its far-sought illumination the hollow land of spiritual adventures, where waters lapse to strange seas, amid dolomites of dreams, rocks like menhirs waiting sacrifice, an

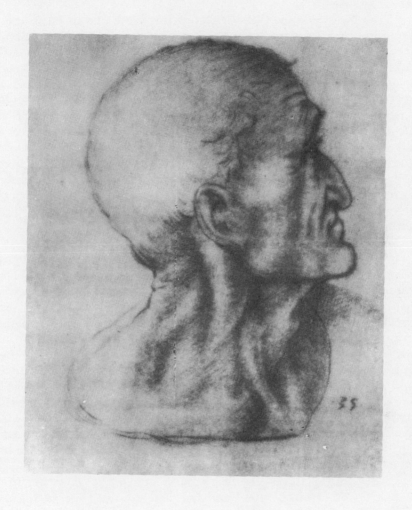

STUDY FOR THE HEAD OF JUDAS
(WINDSOR)

STUDY FOR THE HEAD OF PHILIP
(WINDSOR)

The Task of Psyche

uninhabited blue-green world dreaming of time to come. His unconscious self with a dark, soft flow of interpenetration supplies imaginative matter ; his shaping spirit persuades the pyramidal pattern to grow as easily as if it were a spiring hyacinth, wrings his chord of colour from vanishing hues of afterglow and undersea, and evokes strange light out of the darkness, for the immaterial soft embrace and conflict of chiaroscuro that most intrigues his artist's mind folds his whole vision in a changeable aerial tissue, shadow-bright.

The great beauty and sweetness of the children clarify and illuminate the mysterious spell of this picture without disturbing it. They are indeed the chief actors, and maintain their gestures with dignity unconscious and natural, for children not overtutored are always truly princely in manner—that is, original, courteous, and personal. The babies in both paintings are charming, and the drawings for them are even more tender. There is one where the delicious unaware nape of a child's neck brings one absurdly close to tears, so innocent and so vulnerable it seems. Leonardo indubitably must have been on good terms with children ; he probably met them on his own plane, a grave prince with princes. It is all part of the general Renaissance recognition of children ; but, before Leonardo, no artist so considered their beauty. His comprehension of the age of innocence is like the music of the shepherd's pipe in the pause of his suave harmonies.

x

There are rumours of other compositions, for instance a Rape of Persephone, surely a theme to please him, the beautiful myth of darkness and light, the dear brief victory of spring, filled with the plunging of the shadowy steeds of Hades and the rocky gates of the underworld. Surely he knew the flowers that " frighted she let fall from Dis's waggon " ; and the still gaze of the queen of the underworld :

" Pale beyond porch and portal
    Crowned with calm leaves she stands."

When he went up to Como and Bellaggio, and wandered on the slopes of Monte Generoso, clothed with wavering gold by laburnum branches, tender and tired with such burdens of beauty, and found deep meadow beds of valley-lily, sweet as Avalon, or hidden clefts of rare rose-asphodel and narcissus, or watched the fine-wrought colombine that pleased him stand tall and lone among the grasses—or on some other path caught sight of Lake Lugano like gleaming labradorite, like a dark angel's wing, the dream of it must have come to him. But horses and the dark lord ?

253

Leonardo the Florentine

Well! Persephone amid the flowers? Well! Yet he could not bring the two together. Some obscure anger blurred that composition. If, as the rumour went, there was a *Rape of Proserpine* burned by Francesco Melzi's confessor, a dark young Aidoneus may have seemed to bear thence a pale sister. Or did he transfigure them—Hyacinth and the sister of Hyacinth passing to Elysium?

No; but for the first time reflected on the hidden pools of his reverie is a white figure; and, from time to time, with a sense of rest he remembers one liquid name in the archives of beauty, and like a true Renaissance painter dreams of Leda. For while the Leda theme was a definite court-subject, and desirable for the Duke, it meant for Leonardo a harmony of all his dearest images, winding waters of a great Greek river, illumined emerald twilight, reeds and river-lilies, nonpareil white woman like a pure Attic vase, mysteriously spiralled hair, faint smiling of inconceivable bridal, and wings, great heavenly wings of snow. A dream of unearthly difficult colour, emerald and white, broken and ravishing in the mysteries of light! All the dukes wanted a Leda to tease their satiate senses; and all the artists wanted to do a Leda to solve a subtle problem of woven lines. Gazing at the swans in the castle moat, drawing strong wings in his locked chamber, considering the tranced Lombard faces that seem to wait in a dream for some amazing god, he thinks often of Leda. But not till he comes to Florence again, and the things of Milan become starry-soft and sweet in the richness of reminiscence, does he begin to design that picture, which he will finish only in his last years. And it will be lost, and coarsened copies will give no notion of the slim androgynous woman harmonized with the swan and the water, miraculous mother of swan-white beauty. Here is his symphony of æsthetic pleasure—the smiling of women beside the great waters, strange light, and the splendour of wings!

It seems matter for regret that Leonardo did no more great pages of myth, such myths as were familiar on the proud plaques of Caradosso, Phaethon lost with the horses of the sun, their fiery feet beating the ether into a faint golden smoke, Theseus and Hippolytus as he saw them masquing at Niccolo da Correggio's gay house. No; he paints his symbolic face, becoming more and more remote; deeply he isolates his stilled Herodiad, his Ecstasy at the heart of the eddying world. To the world of myth, his proper and congenial crypts of paganism might have given up their spellbound shapes altogether, and he himself might have been consumed at last by some wild passion, a beautiful monster like a flying dragon, strange to mortality, and all his disciplines and arguments and elaborated modes of living have vanished in some flagrant and insolent epiphany. He draws his mythology sometimes, he does

The Task of Psyche

not paint it; and satisfies his imaginative desires at the expense of the Church.

Some hold that the beautiful dancing angels at Venice, ecstatic figures in swirling rare raiment, were meant for an *Assumption of the Virgin* over the entrance to Santa Maria delle Grazie. Alas that the beautiful church should not have had its Lady like Astarte Syriaca with the new moon under her feet, and that "divers compositions of angels" did not find their place around her! That Leonardo also did some official portraiture of the ducal family in the sacristy we know, for the Duke, weary of the distillations and secretions of genius, issued orders to hurry the artist, rather as if he preferred not to do it directly. But the Duke and the Duchess, and the two children, are vanished, also, and it is doubtful if, with his own fastidious hands, he troubled greatly over a state family at its stiff public devotion. He seems to have had some purpose of an ancona or a sculptured screen, for he draws certain single figures of saints, notably Saint Louis of France, three lilies on his breast and his crown underfoot. And he decorated three rooms in the castle; but we know only the scheme of the Sala delle Asse, with its wood-lined walls, which he turned into a bower of green boughs, linked with his gilded cords. It was a courtly thicket of romance, set for living roses, rich-leaved laurels and oaks against a blue sky, all interlaced with gay devices. Another room seems to have been decorated with angels—or loves?—we cannot tell.

And he painted the great Court ladies, Cecilia, so long the Duchess-in-love of Milan; and if anyone was the Virgin of the Rocks I think it was Cecilia. He painted her as a Madonna of Roses, and he painted her with her cittern. And also he painted Lucrezia Crivelli, who may be *La Belle Ferronnière*. So that it is no wonder he did not paint the Duchess. They sat gleaming against the walls of his open-air studio under the linen awning, and gave him an hour of twilight and music. He changed them into acolytes of his own peculiar beauty, ironic, seducing, dream-holden.

xi

Again, as in the Florentine days, it is with pencil, pen, and silverpoint that he creates a world, a world of rare and lovely and terrible faces, of entranced and straining figures, of trees and fruits and flowers, of domical temples, of great bastions, of the cunning ferocities of war, the *curiosa felicitas* of peace. Of the pageant of horses evoked for the archetypal image of the Cavallo, something has been said. This great procession goes on from the days of the *Adoration* through the brief vision of Trivulzio's mighty tomb to the frenzied horsemen of

255

Leonardo the Florentine

The Battle of Anghiari. Round *The Last Supper*, again, cluster like vine-leaves many patient and vivid studies, conversing groups, or single magnificent heads, like those of Philip and Judas. Others by their poses indicate the theme of *The Washing of the Disciples' Feet* ; not a theme to hold him long—though some of the attitudes of antique grace arrest him a moment.

Strange machines and implements are drawn lightly over pensive figures. A gipsy captain, Scaramaccia, shows his enormous head with insolent, half-conscious power. The shadowy face of the Angel of the Rocks looks sideways : elsewhere is his mysterious lovely hand. There, a white daffodil, bows the dream-holden adoring head of Philip, veiled in diaphanëité, sweet as a maid's. There is raised the ravaged defiant head of Judas. And there an insolent young man with a Roman note in him, like Lucius Verus Commodus, is thinking of his gladiators. But Saint John Baptist returns to us, a grave Greek youth, earnest and pure, seated, with long, fine flanks and lifted finger. Saint Jerome also comes again, a young athlete now, fitter for his lordly lion. People plough and sow. An arsenal like a terrible hive is filled with straining attendants. Virgins sit under monstrous arum-trees with their doting unicorns. A woman moves in a car like Beatrice. Landscapes lie lost in cloud and water ; strange rock-worlds begin to dissolve into a drift of dreams, tidal waves are scrolling into great crests of immense corollas, a destructive fantasia. Great pieces of beautiful tissue are seen falling in cadence over noble limbs. Lovely fingers are lightly clasped. Glimpses are caught as through a white mist. Ecstatic dancers move like " a wave of the sea," their thin raiment curling about them at the edges like creaming foam. Naked riders grip with gryphons. A siren vanishing into acanthus clasps a volute—Leonardo must have been studying the Certosa. A youth gazes into a mirror while beasts devour each other. The head of the Duke appears and vanishes. Atalante lifts his eyes. Old men, young men with great curled hair, madonnas, children, girls, dragons, mermaids, horses, kittens, dancers, flying angels, flowers, gipsies, cuirassed ladies, virgins, courtesans, children, fluent veils, mailed girls or boys—strange epheboi for the rites of beauty— mingle together. Dionysos goes beautiful with wreathed brows. Leda's knotted hair, in spirals, bosses, knots, flames, and convolutions, on her bent and dreaming head is twined with her creative story. Napes of babies, the tenderest things to draw, throats of old women, the cruellest things to draw—his pencil is sweet as a mediæval carol for the one, more branding than Villon's ballade for the other.

Then there are the flowers, filling whole pages sometimes, or cast single and perfect among the geometrical figures, taking the eyes

The Task of Psyche

suddenly with gracility and fragrance. Fruits are delicately presented. Iris springs golden among his green leaves, his arrogant swords and standards. Lilies stand quivering among the reeds. The bramble flowers on its arc-shaped branch. Another bough bears its rose-fruit tenderly mothered by the leafy shoot. Colombines, sweetly isolate, hang their fragile bells over one page. Wood-anemones are laid down gently, as if dewy from secret glades, and violets strewn on the margins "live within the sense they quicken." And here is a clump of bulrushes which means that his mind is with Leda. With the flowers go the birds, suddenly flying about on many margins, flying solitary, flying in spirals, flying in triangles, poised in space. And wings of his own appear like portents, half bat, half bird, wings like a terrible Eastern cherubin's, fiery, spined, victorious.

But with these also go the cruel patterns of anger, delicate things become dangerous, as the law of life so often decrees. Rapiers and lances, ironical inimical things, implacable sword-lilies, rayed stars of cruelty, winged and spined explosives scattering vindictive asteroids and stinging seeds of slaughter, deadly dragonflies, scorpions of death. True, he offered engines of war to Lodovico and to Cesare ; and either of these may have used his scaling ladders, bombards, mortars and artillery-carriages, or tried his tanks and his poisoned smokes, though hardly his submarines. However, just as he draws flowers for some fantasy of tenderness, so he copies mortal weapons from ancient treatises, or from malicious fancy, merely to feed some æsthetic cruelty. It plainly delights him to imagine the ancient scythed chariot, rushing with plunging horses, reckless drivers with flying cloaks, and ruthless reaping wheels, like a malignant monster of the scorpion kind. His flamelike lines make the drawing a vitalizing thing ; but the motive remains diabolic. All Leonardo's pictures of destruction are of a peculiarly sharp-edged beauty ; they have a piercing, biting zest. As he says himself, one destroys to create. God and Nature and Fate have a dark rapture in destruction, and the men who have most of the creative energy are death-dealing as well as life-giving. Leonardo relieved his destroying moods by drawing and day-dreaming.

Characteristic of his dreamier states are the studies of the chain-work, the intrecciamente, sometimes as light and subtle as the impalpable garland that binds his figures in the unity of his pictures : sometimes heavily tressed, as in the panels of laced-work done perhaps for the Tesoro. Sometimes great pots of flowers are linked together by the knotted ropes : sometimes the twining loops of eternity seem a kind of thought-symbol. His pencil twines and intertwines the lines with the turns and returns and labyrinthine quests of his secret involuted argument concerning Eternity. The coils of that intricate symbolic ornament are so inveterate that if one of Celtic blood gaze at them long enough the knot will turn into a trance-making image, and he will pass into a sea-green twilight, and be aware of things like the amethyst-sewn hems on the cloak over the silver greaves of Maeve, and the ring of white birds round the golden head of Angus, and all the soft cruel music of the Riding of the Sidhe.

xii

There is also " la testa de nostra donna che va'n cielo," still bowing her head, one thinks, with faint and troubling smile, the new moon or the wings of life set in her luxurious hair, looking like Leda, looking like Ishtar, rising among a cloud of cherubim and seraphim. The record of " Una storia di Passione fatta in forma " shows that his fingers put aside the paper sometimes to draw in plaster, in gesso-work. And there were " eight Saint Sebastians " ! The image of the androgyne now begins to obsess him, the tender appeal of the girl softening the arrowy pride of a boy. Lovely, heavy-eyed, lips lifted at the corner, with spiral hair, garlanded as for a spring-sacrifice, with a point of suffering in their dream of delight, they are hardly aware that the first shaft has thrilled them. The old theme of the " conversation " between age and youth appears frequently, occasionally mixed with the manu-scripts, sometimes isolated. The theme is often half-sinister now, like the dark wrestling match on some Greek gems ; and the elders look sometimes like bitter satyrs at half-smiling insolent young men. Sun and darkness, heaven and hell, good and evil, beauty and ugliness, art and science, life and death, Leonardo desires to reconcile them all ; and even man and woman in one æsthetic image. Dionysos, Sebastian, Saint John, these will be the genii in his Temple of the Sun. It is not human sensuality that sends Leonardo to his ambiguous notion of sex. It is the excess of the intellectual, attempting an impossible synthesis.

xiii

But from the flame of the creative fury what ashes of accidia ! Even Leonardo knew such hours, void and dark of all but the sense of horror and of the slow decay which dragged him deathward, and deposed his sovran soul, and maimed his perfect body before it left him to the darkness. What he thought of death is contradictory. How he regarded the investiture of old age is clear. Sometimes, as in the *Old Man* at Windsor, with the sorrowful eyes and folded

The Task of Psyche

chin and neck, he allows it the dignity of resignation, at least. But with an exasperation of pain he more often drags it into the realm of the grotesque. Incessantly, indeed, his absorbed intelligence twists, and tries, and distorts, in the effort to find expressions for such heads as those of *The Last Supper*. Still, the pathological pages of *crétin* and criminal types are drawn partly to feed a genuine love of the macabre, partly as a savage reaction against that "ring of fair faces," the youths like the white flower moly, the ladies with Ovidian looks. And partly because he is sometimes in the mood of the wounded idealist, pressing fiercely on the aching nerve that informs him too acutely of human lapses from and grimaces aside the canons of beauty. Horrible mouths in elephantiasis, heads of frenzy, the mow of nightmare; the obscenæ and larvæ of human corruption! And here he will draw a tight plait of scanty hair, and there place a shamed vine-garland, or oak-wreath, and again a terrified gem, in ghastly coquetry. It is the cruelty of the indifferent god, of the outraged artist, and the revenge of a personality not woven into the kindly race of men. When in the worst moods of revulsion, in the most cynical image and caper of antic hay, Leonardo drew, and drew remorselessly well. Unlike Matisse, however, he did not put the mere disgraces of the human body on view while he had the bread of angels to give. His drawings were his matrix of horror and beauty, and his own personal affair. He has not marked them fit or unfit for art. Whatever his motive, he went no farther in pressing horror through his paint than the early head of Medusa, a tragical thing, but far from cynical.

xiv

As time went on, Leonardo became more and more the Duke's architect, fortifier, and engineer. Only scattered notes of these activities remain ; but we know they were varied enough to fill most of his days. With the Cathedral of Pavia he was much concerned, from the day when he rode with Francesco di Giorgio Martini, the Sienese, and a train of servitors, to consider the beginning. There he met geometers and anatomists who absorbed his attention, but from time to time he drew plans evidently in some way connected with the delayed Cathedral. The Duomo of Milan also kept him considerably preoccupied, he having done one model for the cupola, which he afterwards withdrew, though he was paid for yet another. Indeed he is much intrigued with domes, and meditates a treatise on cupolas. He draws them, some from existing models, some from his imagination. And he is thoroughly expert in the various constructions, and so original in his theories of stresses that he might be credited with sending, through Bramante, his imagination to

259

Leonardo the Florentine

hover over Saint Peter's at Rome. He copies San Sepolcro, he remembers the façade of Santa Maria Novella. His mind is indeed much occupied with architecture at this time, and it is characteristic that he is as much concerned with the resistances of walls, and stresses, and foundations, as with the raising of cupolas. He had a passion for detail.

His penetrating spirit passes into the vast masonries of the Castello defences. He plans a double-stair; he designs the two pavilions. Palaces with many loggie, houses with three terraces rise in his contemplation. He draws a strange fortressed cupola with turrets and bastions and flying pennons, raised on great columns. At times he seems to imagine " a palace like the basilica of an architecture at once Mussulman and Byzantine," like the building Huysmans ascribes to Moreau. Mighty steps, forests of pillars, vast architraves, are something chargeable to the oppression of claustrophobia that occasionally crushed him in courtly Milan. It is the double chord of immensity and loneliness that give Leonardo's fantasies in architecture their strange effect of Orientalism. For he does draw fantasies as well as actualities in his building moods. These monstrous domes and stairs, this sense of withdrawn and jealously-hidden life, affect one as if rigid tyrants sat somewhere on peacock thrones surrounded by motionless janissaries, while a waft of sandalwood betrays that, not so far away, jasmine-like sleepers lie in a carven seraglio guarded by Nubian mutes and scarlet-clad eunuchs. It is Turkish Orientalism, this, not Arabian nor Persian, that informs his daydream architecture, in which he has almost forgotten Alberti. After 1494 his deep study of Vitruvius calmed, not to say chilled, even Leonardo's more practicable plans. So potent was the effect of this immense prestige which, like a cold blight, froze the vitality out of Renaissance architecture.

In 1484-1485 the " divine displeasure " visited Milan in the form of plague. Lodovico, with a Greek or a modern desire for a " wide-wayed " Milan, and for the coming of light, had a sincere desire for town-planning. Leonardo made an extensive scheme for him of ten towns with limited populations, too vast a plan of course for even a Renaissance potentate. Many of his suggestions are admirable, and he has an advanced sense of hygiene. But, like his canals and churches, his cities become too much like ingenious problems in drawing, cold arrangements in mere convenience. Here his essential loneliness of soul destroys him, strangles his sense of beauty, bewilders his imagination. He cannot build a city, except as a diagram; he is not human enough to conspire with his kind to create it. He is not meek enough even to realize that Nature is the prime mover in the development of that vast organism. A dome is an ideal form, already risen from the seething dream of

The Task of Psyche

humanity; his mind can play with it as if it were a lonely cloud. He can make a duchess' pavilion because he has a languid notion of how to please a duchess, and he can devise great stables, being friends with horses. When he plans a new town, however, with a double system of high-level and low-level crossings, by the upper streets no carts nor similar objects should move; they are entirely for the use of gentlemen, the defile of the seigneurial life. The *canaille* may swarm in the lower storey, and the sea or the river can wash the town clean. He, the great flower of a civilization, has no sense of a community. The serene inhumanity of this immense proposal does not seem to have charmed the Duke, who, though nervous, was kindly. Leonardo's spiral cities hang in their concentric curves among spectra like isosceles triangles, unpeopled by lords or slaves. But one thing redeems Leonardo's toys from bodiless geometry, and turns them at least into carved crystal. In every piazza must be a fountain. The spirit of beauty could not utterly fail Leonardo at his coldest, and saves him here by a glitter, by a dream of flashing water. But she will never fill her Grecian urn at those fountains, never shall she walk on the walls of Leonardo's cities, nor shall any besiegers come in hollow ships to seize them. Great cities—Florence, Milan—have gone to his making as well as the stars and the gods of great spaces; but he is the anchorite of art, and the monk of knowledge, wilfully " idiotes " in human affairs; and, all alone, he cannot build for a people.

As the consulting engineer of the great irrigation works he was literally in his element. For with what were defensibly called the four elements Leonardo was indeed intimate. Fire, air, earth and water—these were powers he knew, the four great spirits of might who came together in the mystery of creation; and, because he learned patiently to spell over their true gramarye, because he knew something of the evocations to raise them, the incantations to bind them, their shifts and tricks and changes, the mere processes of their miracles and transmutations, he did not cease to wonder at them. One would imagine Leonardo had been born by the sea, or by great lakes, instead of merely by the Arno, which, like many famous rivers, is not mighty. He is like those who crave after the sea, for whom the mere presence of water quickens the hair and smooths the hands, eases the heart, loosens the strung nerves, drenches with rich tears the arid soul, and, when found only in dream-land, laves life's fever with tides of benison. Milan was at least in a moist plain, river-watered, with her broad lakes northward. He knew that where her birds flew now, strange fishes had once gone sailing with great flat eye and spinous fin. He works at the canals with joy, the free exercise of his mathematical instinct thrilling with the mysterious

261

pleasure of the water-diviner. He "knew water," he said. The despots in Milan had always realized the value of the rivers and the canals that united them. Duke Giangaleazzo had worked well in diverting and compelling them: so how much was already done in the riverain region we do not know. In this matter for once Leonardo is one of a dynasty, and his links of bright water are woven into a net whereat others laboured. Round Vigevano and Milan he patiently led his clearly running streams. The Naviglio Martesana was his chief concern ; and the completion of the navigable highway between the Adda and the Ticino. He gave exact instructions for draining the great marshland ; and projected a wonderful system of locks to overcome the difficulty of the levels.

XV

It is in Milan that the many theoretical sciences behind his art and life absorb more and more his reasoning intelligence, even as his art proves more and more a devouring and terrifying passion for perfection. He passes to them from that art in the first instance. How paint Nature without understanding all there is to know about Nature ? How paint man unless you know him to his last nerve and ligature ? How set figures in space without knowledge of every law of linear and aerial perspective, and the mysterious nature of light falling from moon and sun and star, and all the mysteries of dynamics, and the chemistries of earth and air and water and fire ? But behind all these are laws not to be apprehended without mathematics. He seems occasionally to be drunk with mathematics. Even Madonna begins to draw triangles in the ground, meditating some incomprehensible trinity, with Euclid out of Araby for a Gabriel.

Devotion to the sciences is at first, to some extent, his form of reaction from the great maturities and oppressions of beauty in Milan. From the palpable world he seeks relief in problems of weight, and reduces the sieges of sound, light, heat, colour, into a delicate tracery of lines not so ponderable as the faintest hue of lavender. He patiently sets down all his observations in his manuscript books, of which so many seem hopelessly lost. They reveal interests amazingly intense and varied, but for me they show primarily the modes of relief he found from the tension created by the intolerable strain of his two great tasks in Milan. In scientific result they carried him so far that we are surprised that he did not go farther. The lightning tore the dark air, but his keen senses did not shiver to the shock of electricity. The apples fell in the orchard of Milan, but he did not formulate the theory of their deposition. He watched the blood come and go at the soft vulnerable gates of the heart, and yet did not entirely grasp the cunning mode of its circulation. He was inhibited and he was secret. Science was a relief and an escape. From torturing art he turned to some experiment in which he could use his supple hands in an unusual restful way, and which would give him an exact and absolute result, so soothing after the eluding, fluctuating values of art, in which the sad fowler is never sure that the net he has woven so exultingly has not become a mere silly tangle under his hands, and that the flash of golden wings has escaped away so that all his craft seems madness and illusion. The experiments always had their positive value, and might also, at any moment of silky friction, flash a light on some great vision of law. Leonardo was working at a period of great excitement, when many enthusiastic contemporaries less secret than he were in quiet laboratories adding to that sum of knowledge presently to be fused by a Galileo. The skies were startling with new stars, the world was amazing with new continents ; and yet that earth, proud earth, elect of God and the Devil, sweet apple of their contention, cherished core of creation, keynote of the great harmonies of the bright-broidered spheres, fell through the diapason into a shivering, soundless solitude on a staggering orbit round an indifferent sun. Wrenched from the immense and unforgettable fabric of dream which was the Ptolemaic theory, she took her diminished, yet still romantic place in the solemn dance of the planets round the great fixed Star flagrant in unimaginable ether. But whether Leonardo beheld a Copernican universe we do not know. " The sun does not move," he wrote once on the border of a manuscript, as if suddenly astonished. Then, as if he were indeed sunstruck, he says no more of it.

But he glanced down scores of *aperçus*. The manuscripts reveal an insatiable mind. They are beautiful to look at, records of anatomy, physiology, geology, botany, astronomy, optics. The geometrical figures are like magical incantations, variations of pentagrams and circles most exquisitely drawn. The fiery swift stylus continually breaks into drawing, as if hieroglyphs of grace and distinction, unerring and consummate forms, could elucidate better than words. The organs of the body are like corollas and calyxes. " Those supreme fools, the necromancers and the enchanters " could not show books of gramarye more suggestive of sinister and unlawful beauty than the efforts of the " ineffabile mano sinistro " to write down those absorbing experiments towards revealing the laws of necessity. The machinery becomes *fleur-de-lisé* at any point of provocation, cannon are braceleted and graven, pistons break into stars, locks and clasps are broideries of steel ; defence and danger are pricked with beauty. The pantheism of his soul enters into waves, levers, machines, flowers, flames, shells as fine as colombines, till they become passionately, devastatingly alive.

Leonardo the Florentine

He has an instinct for secrecy, and there are some reasons. Anagrammatic words are mingled with the ingenious joints of his mechanics. From right to left runs his concentrated Arabic script easily locking away his conquered knowledge from idle eyes. Then Giulio the smith comes to double-lock the doors of his laboratories. In heretical Milan he is one more heretic, and the Inquisition is acute in the city whose religious temper resents dogma, and, from of old, especially the dogma of Rome. Unconsciously the last of the Manichæan heretics, Leonardo might, like many pioneers, be confounded with the necromancers he despises. But his precautions are not so thorough as to be more than symptoms of the jealous seclusion of his mind, the refusal of his soul to be candid in anything with a chance reader. He is at heart a stranger to humanity, and knows that it is natural to hunt the unicorn.

xvi

But the manuscripts are no record of his life and heart. Wonderful accidents happen when the artist breaks through the severity of science. Centaur-shapes, charging steeds and riders, bring Leonardo, tamer of horses, through the script : a fanciful page appears dreaming beside a record of mechanics : a lion's head looks out among the triangles and circles. In tales of trajectory fierily delicate figures are pierced by darts. In studies of motion, a vivid little climber ascends great stairs as if to all eternity. Among the notations of light, the raining and darting lines by which the centrifugal and centripetal forces are revealed, the faint glimpses of humanity take on the pathos of lost things, mere casualties rather piteous and fantastic. Swirls of smoke coil into shape, coil into a dragon, and the dragon into a helmet with a head on it. Flying folk are caught by snares. Water sleeps in great aqueducts, or lapses by terrible bastions, or pours into crafty locks. There are battles and sudden sieges, attacks by flying engines like bats and hawks of death. Lightning strikes a tower in Milan. Flowers grow so sensitively true that they seem indeed to love and suffer in this hurtling circling universe of his creation. Madonnas are caught among the wheels. Plans of great temples lie with wide-open round petals like geometrical flowers. Sometimes a sentence brings a sharp impression of the beautiful blue of distant hills. Sometimes, startlingly, another makes a carnival habit of black-and-white go giddily as through the hail of meteors, and the thrust and counter-thrust of the javelins of energy. The birds continually fly through the world of mathematics, mechanics, perspective. The migratory wings go, young and old, through the windy air, for they do bring their bright atmosphere with them. The tender

The Task of Psyche

younglings are beneath, the stronger keep the rarer altitude. And here one great wing is spread as if in victory, wing of a great flying basilisk rather than bird, wing of Eastern seraph, of Lucifer, prince of the air. The dream of Icarus is Leonardo's most passionate dream; it is the supreme fantasy where emotional desires and intellectual powers are at one; it is his unique image, his symbolic vision of himself as a god in that unprecedented ascendancy. When he does not see himself in the water, he sees himself in the air. But at some point, literally or figuratively, he fell—later, at Fiesole perhaps. There is only a confused rumour of sorrow around that period, and a sense that the creator of the manuscripts henceforth goes with a trailing wing.

But still the wings flash through a vision of sliding waters, flying arrows of the sun-god, a conceptual world built of aisles and pyramids, shifting lights, falling towers, and spring rainbows that are " not in the rain nor in the eye, though born of the sun and rain." Light falls splintering, dartling, dissolving, on the waters, the mirrors, the sea-pools, the fountains. There is eddy of spiral air, swirling of spiral water, spiral ascensions of birds, softly threatening spirals of smoke, softly dangerous spirals of smokelike curls, always the spiral line of life that dips to rise again! Even if you are no mathematician, if you consider Leonardo's books awhile, you will have a sense of cosmic preparation, of nebular triumphal travail gathering itself to some supernal throe for the unimaginable birth of universes. You feel as one walking in the Milky Way, with the star-dust covering you for glittering snow-crystals.

Softly dangerous spirals of smokelike hair! Some passages unconsciously betray obscure suffering in that controlled emotional life. A name is written, as if by accident, thrown sometimes like a gage of Eros in the midst of abstruse calculations. Then follow feverish, agitated pages. Riddling allegoric words conceal humiliation. Broken sentences begin generalizations about envy, ingratitude, false friends, the necessity of excising the worthless. The leaves are soiled, the calligraphy is large and slanted. Across attempted problems in stresses the words " amantissimo," " amicissimo," will write themselves imperiously, like heavenly hopeless tears. There is the shadow of crisis, and the sense of great ravages. Then he will observe " the magnanimous way of the falcon," or the like. And presently he resumes his fine and regular calligraphy with an intenter note on the circulation of water; and soon is happy with weights and counterweights again. But there has been distress, something like despair:

> " What my soul bore, my soul alone
> Within itself may tell."

Leonardo the Florentine

What hides behind these cloudy pages ? Some strange and fiery thing of an immortal's longing ? And did some of these dovelike Milanese youths seek an easier or a more caressing lord ? Leonardo's pain seems invariably to end in the assurance that the disturber is a transitory and inferior creature. It is likely that he was. And Leonardo is really saying : " Thy lyre will not avail thee, nor the gifts of Aphrodite, those thy locks and fair favour, when thou grovellest in the dust." But how sweet to fastidious senses are lyre, and locks, and fair favour, and the gifts of Aphrodite, and how much more conquering than nobility of soul, Leonardo knew as well as any. So the rose and cyclamen petals of Milan fall over even his scientific diaries and distract him.

xvii

The trivia of his daily life, the little coin of his great intercourse, slip heedlessly into the manuscripts, whether in Pavia he brood among the books and the skulls, or at Vigevano he foster the vine and persuade the waters, if in Milan he pass from the Cavallo in the old palace to *The Last Supper* in the refectory, or watch the Nail rise into position in the Cathedral, or meditate his treatises, or turn the dark hours to account. He has seen a nun at La Colomba in Cremona : she works straw-plait and her fingers fascinate. White-coifed nun, weaving fingers, and Leonardo ! Peaceful ! But with a strange pity and anger in his imperial heart, in heavy winter he regards " the beasts which in time of great snows come near to your houses, asking alms as from their masters." The gods had always a kindness for the beasts who were their true antitypes, and whose vizards they often wore. A physician has a steward without hands. Ears of corn of immense size come from Florence. A lady of the Crivelli family tells him that a drunken capon was persuaded to rear chickens and defend them from a goshawk. He is attracted by the unusual, the imperfect, the grotesque, like a child caught staring. He is hungry for books. Himself he has Ovid, Dante, Petrarch, Pulci, Filelfo, Marsilio Ficino, the Bible, the Psalms, a Lapidary, a Bestiary, the *Tesoro* of Brunetto Latini, a treatise on chiromancy. It is a characteristic commingling of Renaissance and mediæval interests ; and none is surprising. Even the treatise on chiromancy is the natural possession of a sceptic when he loves beautiful hands so much that he might even consider them, against reason, as apostolical of destiny. But Ottaviano Pallavacino must lend him a Vitruvius. He must ask the Marliani for their father's algebra. There's a Vitellius in the library of Pavia. Bartolommeo the Turk must tell him of the ebb and flow of the Black Sea ; and Portinari must explain how people go on the ice in Flanders. And Antonio knows how the fortified wall in Ferrara is contrived without loopholes.

Then will come a sudden waft of fresh odours. " Take good rose-water, and moisten the hands. Add lavender, and then rub your hands together. That is good."

One of his most lovable moments ! For Leonardo's hands are beautiful, and Milan is one wave of perfume. Lost in the astounding universe, stormily lit by the genii of Leonardo's mighty mind leaping from science to science, not without ferocity, one is steadied by the thought of a little silver ewer of rose-water, and a group of blue-grey lavender growing silken in the dusk to console the hands of Leonardo Rose-water and lavender ! These delicately betray why the great scientist and the great artist was yet found enchanting and beloved. Rose-water is a habit with beauty :

> " Oh ! whaur got ye tne rose-water
> That does mak' ye sae white ? "

xviii

Perhaps he had come from the dark work of dissection. Both during his first and his second Milanese period, Leonardo worked with intensity at anatomy, with more of a personal delight than he exhibits over any other tract of knowledge. It was of course the science nearest to him as an artist, and as a mortal. He accomplished much in his dissection studies, and is notably more outspoken in his opinions when he meddles intently with the sorrowful secrets of the body. Of the quality of his work more hereafter. What we realize now is that he adds to his scientific zest a note of savagery, which belongs to the sadist satisfaction with which he practises such a complete reaction against suave, splendid Milan. He maintains an imaginary dispute against the " Adversary " very disdainfully ; and is bitter against " abbreviators," who may be, as somebody has suggested, the students at Pavia who were so unruly a populace that Lodovico issued a remonstrance. In his anatomical science he is really conscious of doing something to " *épater les bourgeois* " and it pleases him. Moreover, he is proud of his courage and his nerve, secretly aware that in other matters they might be questioned. And indeed, even when contemplating his divining and perfect diagrams of the human body, one still feels inclined to say, with the lady in the play, that :

> " Thus to tyrannize upon the dead
> Is most inhuman."

267

Leonardo the Florentine

He throws his defiance in a pre-Rembrandtesque picture of eager and defiant words, breathlessly hurrying in their desire to tell what superhuman exactions this kind of study means for him. The dreadful patience, the fortitude, the terrible disdain—all climb up to that "Vale!" of supreme contempt. This is not the rose-water Leonardo, nor is it the crystalline scientist inattentive to mere mankind. It is a dark enthusiast who sits in the scorner's chair, and is justified. And all the time he delights in his macabre effect.

"And you who say that it is better to see the dissection than such drawings, you would speak well if it were possible to see all these things which are demonstrated in such drawings in a single specimen, in which you with all your genius will not see and will not obtain knowledge except of a few veins, for having the true and full knowledge of which I have dissected more than ten human bodies, destroying all other organs, consuming with very minutest particles all the flesh which surrounded these veins, without making them bloody except with insensible sanguinification of the capillary veins ; and one body did not suffice for so long a time, so that it was necessary to proceed by degrees with so many bodies that the complete knowledge might be fulfilled, which I twice repeated in order to see the differences.

"And if you do have love for such matters, you will perhaps be impeded by the stomach, and if that does not impede you, you will perhaps be impeded by the fear of living in the night hours in the company of such quartered and flayed corpses fearful to look at ; and if this does not impede you, you will perhaps lack the good draughtsmanship which belongs to such demonstration ; and if you have the draughtsmanship it will not be accompanied by the perspective ; and if it *is* accompanied, you will lack the order of the geometrical demonstrations, and the order of the calculation of the forces and power of the muscles ; and perhaps you will lack the patience, so that you will not be diligent.

"As to whether all these things have been in me or not, the hundred and twenty books composed by me will answer Yes or No, in which I have not been impeded by avarice or negligence, but only by time.

"Vale !"

It is a "Vale !" flung like a ringing gauntlet from the charnel-house where the curled and fastidious Leonardo, amid the stenches and evil phosphorescences of corruption, declares that the human body is a beautiful instrument for the soul he intends next to analyse, but does not. As he said, he was not easily disheartened. But if he had begun with the soul, he might have found more imperfections in the instrument.

268

The Task of Psyche

xix

This fierce valediction sounds as if anatomy devoured his nights and days. One gets a dazed impression sometimes that he occasionally came out in the fourth dimension, and juggled with his categories in parallel existences, or that he had forged a key to some crystal cistern of time whence he drew at dawn or dusk. For, with all his intensities of labour, he not only kept his air of leisure, but he did leisurely things. He stood by while the vines were gently buried at Vigevano for the winter. With the little book of prepared paper thrust in his girdle, he supped with the contadini, not without a certain Haroun al-Raschid effect. He had those trancelike hours without which the unrefreshed spirit must find its labour sheer slavery. He could loiter dreaming on the colour changes of the distant sky. He could maintain his early pact with the processes of silence and solitude. He drank the dew with growing things ; and watched the shadow enamoured of the light, and the blues and violets quiver at the edges of sun-white surfaces, and the leaves be born in the branches, and the waters mould and remould the face of the earth ; and he drew a tree in Pre-Raphaelite detail all one windless afternoon, or watched the hawk motionless in the blue air like golden Horus over Egypt, and tracked the pterodactyls in the ancient slime. He saw the caterpillars clinging to their leaves, the rose-buds change to rose-fruits, the ethereal shy ways of violets and colombines, the wanton ways of the great herodiad lilies. He found the flowers at strange moments of wedding or seeding. He heard the birds at matins and vespers and knew their language. His eyes were soft and sweet over the deathless lure of running water. His Ovid might be in his idle hand, but he needed no fable to make him part of the eternal meta-morphosis of nature : he could be beast or bird or flower, darkness or light, swan or eagle, river or laurel. He knew the old stories better than the humanists, all the phantom pursuits and changes, for his eyes beholding them made them part of himself. He went wandering in some strange place of rocks and found his Dionysos-John, with a cross of reeds and a garland of vine.

A French poet records a sympathetic impression of Leonardo's meditative hours :

> " Il aimait les cheveux annelés, la volute
> Que la boucle dessine au bord d'un front serein,
> Il aimait les vallons d'un pays uncertain
> Et les grottes qu'à l'ombre un jour voilé dispute.

Leonardo the Florentine

Il aimait la jeunesse ou la forme débute,
L'ambigu passager de l'épaule et du sein ;
Il aimait l'heure ou le poussière du lointain
Contre'un astre tombant s'élève, joue, et lutte.

Il aimait la fraîcheur, qu'exhalent les tombeaux,
Le dessin d'un serpent fuyant dans les roseaux,
Il aimait les détails découpés du feuillage :

Les traces que les pieds des dieux sur le rocher
Laissent, à l'aube, et que le jour vient effacer ;
Il aimait cette fleur, ces yeux, ce coquillage."

Yes ! He had leisure with it all. But it must be remembered that his was a miraculous quickness of mind, and that the manuscripts are mostly fitful and varied pages, with none of the concentrated and organized effort that means really exacting labour. The manuscripts themselves were at first only the notes of auxiliary knowledge for his art, and then a diversion from that consuming activity. And also, consider that, with deliberate grace, he refused all the mere adventure of life. No causes desperately fair lured him to disaster with gilded banners and silver sennets. No wasting romantic love of woman drew him down through the rings of rose-seraphim to drift impenitent in the fiery winds and rains. No holy wisdom trancedly withheld him in the clear sapphirine ecstasy of the cherubim. The powers and principalities never unloosed the lightnings of destruction stored up in his ruthless intelligence, so Leonardo, tamer of horses, did not gather the spears and take him cities. No great idolatry consumed his time and energy. Even Beauty he served like a prince consort, not in the slavish lover's way of Michelangelo. Therefore, since he did not love a lover to the stars or to perdition, nor lead an army, nor follow a flag nor die for a faith, nor save a city, no rich waste, no beautiful mania, exhausted his mind and soul. He lost no more energy over the changing affairs of humanity than did the Olympians over the fall of Troy ; indeed he gave them less attention.

Being psychically concerned wholly with his art and his sciences, he had a greater command of his time than most. Still, he used it miraculously : and most miraculously at Milan, because, after all, Lodovico was a forbearing and magnanimous prince, and Leonardo arranged his life to his liking, until the Duke's disaster began.

XX

Leonardo's Milan drawings include a series of allegories. Now allegory is not in Leonardo's temper ; he is, like all great artists, a

The Task of Psyche

symbolist. But his Duke wanted vivid ways of telling the story of his statecraft as he wished it to be told ; and Leonardo drew him some fantastical pieces of imagery on the themes of Envy and Ingratitude, Prudence and Justice and Fame. The strange shapes and symbols are quite passionately flung on the paper. Leonardo has a complex concerning jealousy and ingratitude himself ; some passages in Lodovico's vindicating story seem apt for his own, and he writes a bitter description of Envy beside one picture. Doubtless he was envied enough ; and his nerves could not endure detractors. The heavy details of the description become fire-fraught decorations in the drawing :

" This Envy is figured flouting at heaven because if she could she would use her strength against God. She is made with a mask of fair pretence upon her face. She is so made that she is wounded in the sight by palm and olive ; she is made with her ear wounded by laurel and myrtle to signify that honour and truth offend her. She is made with many lightnings issuing from her to signify her evil speech. She is made lean and dry as being in continual wasting desire ; she is made having her heart gnawed by a fiery serpent. She is given a quiver having tongues for arrows, a leopard hide because the leopard kills the lion by guile. A vase full of flowers is hiding toads and scorpions. She is made riding on Death because, dying never, she was given dominion over death."

Towards the end of Lodovico's rule, Leonardo's financial affairs became involved. It is chiefly the conflicts between notable personages, naturally, that get recorded in a way that gives them disproportionate importance. Lodovico had paid generously, but the wars had exhausted his exchequer, and for the time he had no attention for anything but his insatiable mercenaries. So Leonardo also had a financial crisis. It is a pity that the draft of his second letter of remonstrance is so torn, for it seems to show Leonardo at his best: sensitive, proud, unwilling to plead, aware of the " times," and the Duke's difficulties, also aware of his own responsibilities. There is a sigh over the Cavallo, still in the fragility of plaster, a surrender over the camerini, a proud apology for delay over some things—and, what is most important, an implied admission that his " art " was really the supreme star that controlled all the crossing tides of his being.

" It grieves me," he says, in one appeal, " that in order to procure the necessary subsistence I have been compelled to interrupt my work and occupy myself with trifles instead of carrying out the task entrusted to me by your highness. . . . I had to maintain six men for six months and received only fifty ducats." But, if he ever earns enough by other tasks, he hopes to concentrate on his art.

Leonardo the Florentine

The broken draft is more sombre :
" If other commissions are given me by . . .
" Remuneration for my services . . .
" I can do nothing . . .
" With assignments [of benefices ?] . . .
" It is not my art, I wish to leave it . . .
" I am aware that your Excellency is far too occupied for me to venture
to remind you of my small matters, and that the arts have been put
to silence . . . but my silence might occasion your Lordship's wrath . . .
" My life in your service . . .
" I hold myself prepared to obey . . .
" Of the horse I will say nothing, for I know the times are bad.
" To your Lordship that I still have to receive two years' salary . . .
" Two skilled workmen are in constant occupation at my expense . . .
" Important works by which I could prove myself to those who are
to come . . .
" Now I do not know what I can spend on my works . . .
" I have worked to gain my livelihood . . .
" Not having been informed what it is, I now find myself . . .
" Remind you of the commission to paint the camerini . . .
" Representing that of your Lordship I merely request . . ."

One may observe that the artist's letter is anything but servile.
It is a courteous, cold remonstrance. Breadwinning is a bitter game,
and poverty wears away the graces of life. It plunders grief of its
dignity, and stifles the heart of joy. It is a baleful fever that eats the
soul, a penance of nervous irritation that has no spiritual benefit.
Poverty has no leisure. Saint Francis' Lady Poverty was an Umbrian
princess-errant, a lilylike anchoress that toiled not neither did she spin.
Real Poverty is a poetic figure only when, exhausted, she draws the
violet hood of death over an arrogant defeated brow, or when, with
desperate eyes under the Phrygian cap, and a dagger in her hand, she
turns to slay King Jeshurun. But Leonardo was not really much
affected by this low fever and evil maceration. Poverty was an incident,
not a habit. No miserably irrelevant reason ever made him drag his
wings through the wind, or tore an idol from him, as bitterly befell
the great Mantegna. Even now Lodovico gives him a vineyard, and
he saves golden florins on it, with all his extravagant ways.

xxi

The years of 1499 and 1500 were evil years. The great Borgian
mystery-play, gilded and monstrous and hung with milky pearls, cast

The Task of Psyche

a red-gold shadow of mythical guilt over Italy; and became an amazement to distant nations. There were three suns shining during the night, spectres, strange cries, inundations. Gleaming swords and shields and ravens moved in the dim air. There were sanguine rains. The earth trembled, the mountains moved, and the valleys faded. In Greece the sun bled in the sky; in France there was plague: Germany, with Teutonic bad taste, did much in the way of abnormal births. There was thunder on the walls of Rome, and wrath in the swelling Tiber. The wind tore the papal shield from the Moles of Adrian. The Pope was struck down within the Vatican, yet lived.

Lodovico's star went out in these lurid years. In the end his jealous enemies closed round him. Why did he call the French? Why did he trifle with the obsolete legality of an Imperial Investiture? The investiture of his kingly quality, the investiture of the stars if he imagined so, was enough for an Italy where Naples had been won by the sword and held by bastards, where Venice lay gripped by an oligarchy, where in Ferrara legitimacy was no certain title to the dukedom, where Lorenzo had slipped by subtle wit into princedom at Florence, where Urbino, whose greatest duke had been a love-child, was adopting an heir, where the sons of popes and condottieri were grasping duchies and cities where they could. He was too scrupulous for a despot, and his possessions were too valuable not to allure.

He had summoned the French: he had made a League to drive them home again. But they had learned the way; and Louis of Orleans, become king, claimed Milan as well as Naples. This is not a history of Italy's dissolution, and there is no room to tell that Mantua and Ferrara fell away, that Florence refused, and Venice as usual betrayed, and Rome was inimical. Maximilian and his investiture had been dearly bought; but Maximilian was too busy with his own troubles to redeem his pledges to his great feudatory and the beautiful fief. The mercenaries were grasping and faithless, Galeazzo di Sanseverino was a bewildered general, and the alienated Trivulzio a strong one. Caiazzo soon played traitor. Alessandria inexplicably surrendered. Threatened on every side, Lodovico sent his children and his remaining treasure to Innsbruck, and, after confiding his Castello, with embraces and perfect faith, to Bernadino del Corte, and leaving his soul with Beatrice in that vigil of tears at her tomb, he rode away, clothed in black, to his one friend the Emperor. He would not now nor afterwards despoil his city to satisfy the Swiss; nor would he expose it to the dangers of a siege and sack.

Leonardo saw that departure. He was there when the castellan surrendered the invulnerable fortress to the French without an effort.

S

Leonardo the Florentine

merely for a share in the spoil, so that the invaders themselves marvelled and mocked him. He saw the great procession come in when Trivulzio and the King had done with their ceremonies at San Eustorgio ; he saw it pass down the way of white lilies and golden ladies, all hung with fleur-de-lis and the device of the ermine, all gold-and-white for King Louis, the victor in gold-and-white, and all gay with garlands. He saw the five hundred archers in green and red, with the device of the porcupine broidered on their vests. He saw King Louis under the baldacchino of golden brocade upheld by the learned doctors in purple and fur, great French lords and great Scots lords, friends of the French —the imperial De Ligny, the Duke of Bourbon, Stuart d'Aubigny, the Duke of Savoy, the Duke of Albany, fair, with piercing eyes and bitter speech, the " enfant de Fouez," Dunois of famous descent, Louis de la Tremouille—Vraye Corps Dieu, Jean de Foix, sieur de Lautrec, very young, with blond expressionless face, blue eyes and chestnut hair, and " tant d'autres comptes, barons, chevaliers, gens d'armes et souldatz que le noblesse et nombre d'iceulz toute admiracion d'excellent extime donnoit aux yeulz que le triumphe vinroyent regarder." Many were destined for Marignano and the stricken field of Pavia. Death like a gilded eagle hovered above them, choosing his prey.

Among the great Italian lords were Trivulzio, his long hatred satisfied, the Marquis of Mantua, the Marquis of Colonna, the lords of Ferrara, the Duke of Montferrat, the ambassadors of Venice, Genoa, Florence, Siena, Lucca and Pisa, all acquiescent with the ravishers of Italy. With the French cardinal, him of Amboise, rode Cardinal Gian Borgia, and Cardinal Giuliano delle Rovere, who was to be Pope Julius II., and cry "*Fuori gli barbari !* " And the fine courtiers of old were also decoratively about, like Niccolo de' Correggio.

And there, beautiful, serene, magnificent, figure most marked by all, fresh from his French bridal, wearing his French dukedom, rode Cesare Borgia. Did Leonardo first encounter him now ? They were alike in some ways, those two great Renaissance types. Both had risen above the conflict and stress of human emotion in pursuit of powerful ideas. Both took from life what they would, and considered not men nor cities in the fulfilment of their desires, though Leonardo's ruthlessness was naturally less obvious than Cesare's, for he was not the son of a Pope.

Still his way would be amongst them henceforth, the conquistadors and spoilers. Italy was ripe for plunderers. Her beautiful cities were to be forced like carven caskets by French, Spanish, Germans. And her own children would not be guiltless of her destruction. Popes and princes already were consenting to her death. Leonardo was not there

The Task of Psyche

when Lodovico came again with Swiss, Stradiot, German and Italian mercenaries. He was waiting on events at Venice, disinclined to commit himself while there was yet a doubt of the Duke's fate. There was drama enough, with Trivulzio's bitter pursuit, for the Duke regained his city, but not the insuperable Castello that he himself had so fortified. Drama enough when the princely Bayard over-rode into the enemy camp and came face to face with the princely Duke. Mediæval French chivalry and Renaissance Italian courtesy met ; and the more ancient civilization was here the victor. " He looked a lord whom little could astonish," said the released Bayard. So he seems unsurprised at sombre Novara, when the Swiss cynically refuse to fight Swiss, having made their own terms, and when they secretly sell even his promised personal freedom, he having covered his gold and crimson raiment in vain. Pale, composed, all his nervous panic stilled by the sense of complete catastrophe, he passed through his enemies. All the crowds mocked at the great courteous Duke, and the hating Venetians spoke of exposing him in a cage. But he asked for his own copy of Dante from his famous library at Pavia, and read of the Purgatorial Mount perhaps, till the mystic car of Beatrice approached him ; and then he thought of another Beatrice whose dancing feet and desirous eyes did not accord with transcendental philosophy, and who seemed to have led him somewhere nearer to hell than to heaven. Well ! She was dead, and Isabella her sister at last had her clavichord. He had long enough to think of it, scratching sombre imprese and dolorous devices on his prison wall in Loches. " Of the Duke there is no word spoken ; as if he had never been." Galeazzo remembered him for a while, till his cause became a hopeless matter. The Emperor Maximilian made friendly intercession. But the French feared him, so his over-subtle and too-magnificent mind became grey dust in a dungeon.

He passed, I hope, to some duchy in Paradise, where Leonardo could canalize the five rivers for him. No ! Since he was hardly Christine de Pisan's Duke of True Lovers, some fief under the Hollow Hill perhaps awaited him—where Leonardo could do the tunnelling, since he liked piercing mountains as well as controlling waters.

If it is an idle fancy, it is a gentle one, for I am not in accord with the stern historians who enjoy the notion that Lodovico languished in Loches, drawing those intolerably pathetic devices on the walls, as if fumbling after the imprese of his glory in the twilight of a dying brain, and scribing his low echo of Francesca's lament. He was undoubtedly a great lord ; and his enemies owed him a clean death.

Did he ruin Italy ? The French would have come without him. But undoubtedly Leonardo da Vinci would not have been so great a

figure without him. Lodovico had the best of both the Visconti and
the Sforza qualities, though he was inhibited by certain defects of the
elder line. He was an æsthete and he was humane, a rare combination
of qualities. With his opportunities and his liberalities Leonardo
satisfied his extraordinary range of interests, and created those greatest
works of his art which were doomed to destruction. And when it was
a matter of planning canals and streets, it was not the artist, intent on
his problems, but the despot, who informed the diagrams with some
sense of humanity. Lodovico gone, Leonardo might still be something
of a god at hire ; but he was much of a masterless man. He found no
other service in which he could have security and rest.

xxii

Those who depreciated the Lombards might have said that Leonardo,
"Tuscan and Greek," had preferred the service of a Milanese despot
as Master of Revels, Engineer, and Court Painter, to glorious labour in
his Florentine Republic. They might have said he sold his freedom.

Like other notable cities, Florence, so powerful in spirit, was a little
place, and reared more great artists than she could employ. Venice,
Rome, and Milan were the only three powers rich enough to employ
a Leonardo to his contentment. Lodovico was certainly much more
sympathetic as a tyrant than the Borgia Pope, for instance, who, like
all people learned in corruptions, wanted an art at once dazzling and
naïve, a taste admirably satisfied by Pinturricchio's ultramarines and
tender stories. Nor would the oligarchy of Venice have suited a temper
so individualistic. Milan gave him all that Florence could not, and
did not enslave him. He moved beautifully, and did great works, and
his fame went out amongst the cities. While his salary came smoothly
Leonardo was pleased with his state. "Such was I, Leonardo the
Florentine, at the court of the most illustrious prince, Signor Lodovico."

The dream of freedom is a spiritual condition that gives a value of
courage or of despair to whatever kind of bondage we must accept.
To Leonardo, with his besetting dream of wings beating the blue
air, the notion of freedom was a necessity. He could speak nobly
of the pride of liberty. But it was personal freedom he meant, the
joy of an uncaged mind. And with his rich and prevailing qualities
he could create his freedom around him anywhere. As for others—no
matter. He broke his contracts remorselessly as soon as he felt constraint. Even Lodovico had to wait long to have his wishes fulfilled—
another proof that Leonardo was never really without some wealth.
It is only the wage-slave who is bitterly bound to keep contracts.

The Task of Psyche

Honour, the most expensive flower of the virtues, is foisted on him ; and he most miraculously does try to carry the fragile red corolla in his clumsy hands.

xxiii

Leonardo took and gave great gifts to Milan. Yet some strange possession like a magical crystal made of air and morning-fire was surely lost on the road from Florence. He could never again paint the great light of that *Adoration*. He had quarried both *The Last Supper* and the Cavallo from the lordly excess and lovely extravagance of his preparation for that shining picture. But now even with the diffused illumination of *The Last Supper* he was done. He had come to love only the imprisoned gleaming of strange grottos now, twin to the shadow itself. It seemed as if the more he followed and analysed and pursued the ways of Light, the more he found it sister and daughter to the Dark, like Saint Anne and Mary. "May it please the Lord, Light of all things, to lighten me so that I speak worthily of the light." So he prays in the city of Julian, who also worshipped the sun—pantheist like the city, Manichæan like the city, worshipping the Light, but not offending the Dark, which will gather him softly in the end.

He had paid the rare petals of his youth for a heavy seed of glamour, for a rare fruit of honeyed and winelike and mandragora flavour, a beautiful hybrid fruit that shall itself be seedless. Or let us think that he had eaten the pomegranate seed in Manichæan Milan, and half of his soul was now the debt of Hades.

Of the paradoxical effect of Milan on the already paradoxical Leonardo already enough has been said. It softened him, hardened him, disintegrated him, enriched him, exhausted him. The emotionals, musicians, poets, lovers, æsthetes, women, prevailed at Lodovico's Court, children of magic, music, religion, human passion, with rituals of dance and luxury. Leonardo, for all his unparalleled intelligence, felt the passional self constantly implore great recognitions in his intellectual world. Instead of consenting to fair interplay he divided the twain with a dyke of squared circles. But the covered wells of life seeped through those walls and saturated his most abstract thinking.

xxiv

At the same time, if his vast consciousness seems ready to fall into segments in Milan, there were bright cleavages already when he arrived. I think he had a bitter shock in Florence, and that the dazzling globe of his personality was not intact. It was as if some stone had been

277

flung into a great crystal-golden bowl that revealed the impact by silently presenting in another atmosphere a many-pointed star, of which the rays glittered bravely till the noble thing was broken at death's strange fountain.

From nervous Florence to enervating Milan he came Citharædus. It was a serene Apollo who passed from Florence carrying the victorious lyre that harmonizes all the arts ; a midsummer god with other young gods. It was a serene Dionysos who returned from Milan, a midsummer god who had looked upon the Herodiad, the ritual dancer. He seemed like a sorcerer, and they called him one. It is dangerous to use scientific terms in a psychical sense ; but it does convey a certain necessary impression to say that Leonardo's early Florentine mood was unvexedly masculine, aware of women only in a purely æsthetic way, while the Milanese Leonardo has become in maturity bisexual in his imagination. I believe he was singularly chaste in temperament, and justifiable in his platonic loves. His lapses into cynicism would not give such a sense of shock if they were not out of keeping with his general mood. But if ever he was seduced and softened out of his engrossed narcissimus of soul, it was in Milan, wherein he gained and lost by the realization of the feminine principle. The colour of the emeralds in the processional cross of Maria-Aphrodite passed into his palette, and rose in mystical fumes behind his Circean Madonnas. Becoming more feminine, he is naturally less inviolable. Milan had a wounded kind of beauty, a dolorous sweetness. It is in the face of Saint John the Beloved, it is in the face of the Virgin of the Rocks, it is veiled in the face of the Christ.

This dreaming beauty took shape in his myth-making mind as a vision of that Leda, so like to Dionysos, he carried about with him henceforth as his intimate amulet of beauty—the " symbol," the lovely coin he broke as companion with the Spirit of Milan. Leda was Milan. He could not exorcise her till he had painted her. And with her perhaps he also laid the passionate Florentine dream of wings with which he bound her to his own city. On wings strong and pure as a swan's he was to take flight from the Mount of the Swan, and the world would be filled with his glory. So he prophesied ; but some disaster befell.

Yes ! if Leonardo had any passiontide it was in Milan. The Lombard Saint John is not the Florentine Saint John. He is a doubled lily and a hybrid flower. Henceforth Leonardo's effort is to combine the virile Florentine clarity with the obscure feminine love-wisdom of Milan. In his final picture he thought he had fixed the opposing principles, and made the impossible synthesis for which Greek artists tried in Hermaphroditus. After all, the psychical and æsthetic interest of the strange ideal were reinforced by Leonardo's vague but sincere biological notions. His flower-studies are numerous and tender during the Milan period. If a double-sexed flower be beautiful, why not a double-sexed flower in humanity, or at least, in art. His ambiguous people are dangerous henceforth, at least for the weak. But for the weaker brother Leonardo did not paint. His illuminati have crossed some perilous ford, they have stepped idly from the verge of some impossible abyss, and been borne up by angels of hell or of heaven. They are children of light who have made terms with the darkness ; but the darkness may be sweet.

It is certain that the long secret tradition of heresy in Milan strengthened Leonardo's contempt for authority. It was with blood and tears that the clergy of Milan yielded submission to the See of Rome ; the slight differences in ritual were jealously maintained as the symbols of their independence, and their minds were always inclined to feed on the more mystical Ephesian gospel. The Milanese had Orientalism enough of their own to dye their dream of God rare Tyrian ; from Provence, also, they accepted not only the sandal-scented romance of the " gai saber," but heretics as well as lovers. The Catharists, pure as desert anchorites of old, the fraticelli and apostolici who, like Athanasius, sought for the dissolving ordeals of sweet temptation, all the dreamy Antinomians who lived by grace, had modified the atmosphere for Leonardo, who by the grace of God felt a god. As a savant he was too intent on the laws of the universe to put much value in the little laws of man. He did not outrage them ; they did not get in his way, so they did not affect his profound indifferentism. As an artist he underwent the pressure of Manichæan, Antinomian heresy, and it stressed the natural dichotomy of his temper. The covert drew the hounds, of course ; and the Inquisition was more active in Milan than in most cities, which may partly explain his need of caution.

XXV

And, if the city was heretical to Rome she was, not willingly, being now a Renaissance city, heretical to Athens. Her history made her sensitive to the peculiar æsthetic charm of excess, so she was only as Greek as Antioch was. Leonardo's image of Saint Anne, half-Lesbian, half-Oriental in its effect, is a true image of Milan as a sacred city. He felt the Eastern angel in the legendary mother of Mary, the angel imputed to her by the Arabian sect ; and he drew her head often with strange Persian veils and Coptic coifs, as if she were a priestess in some ancient ziggurat. Yet her heroic pose and noble draperies are serene as Demeter's, for he did not lose the Greek eurythmy.

Leonardo the Florentine

Symbolic of these mingled moods, he took three æsthetic gifts from Milan, seductive and ambiguous too. These were chiaroscuro, contraposto, and sfumato, convenient names for æsthetic evolutions, closely associated with psychological states, as he would have been the first to declare. His early contest between light and dark grew stronger in the dark-bright city, where indeed the darkness begins to prevail, as something mightier, more ravishing, more absolute. Leonardo is the protagonist of the sun, and as a scientist he proclaims it the one thing adorable. But as an artist he unconsciously realizes that his light can only make patterns and irruptions on the darkness, create him grottos undersea for his immortal shapes. It is in the conflicts and surrenders of light that the swooning ecstasy quivers in tenderest semitones and penumbra of ethereal new colour. It is broken light that ravishes him now.

Thence the sfumato which enchanted his contemporaries, and which flowed partly from his love of these lighted shadows now so dulled by time, partly from the moist rich effect of the air in Milan. It was so much to his mood that he would smudge the paint with his thumb to get it, the wonderful frayed softness, as if the head became visible through the veils of some rich sorrow, some weeping cloud of sweetness.

As for the contraposto, it was his preferred way of showing the form flexible in its lithest lines. They were straight strict figures in Florence, figures of pride. The Milanese people, carrying grace to the point of affectation, swayed delicately in the soft west winds of feeling, turned sideways in appealing curves of lovely line, half-reluctant, half-desirous. The contraposto charmed Leonardo, both because it was more difficult to draw, and because it symbolized the sensuous conflict in his spirit. But let us never forget to recognize the tireless and versatile exercise of purely intellectual energy that covers these psychical conflicts, of which he is hardly aware. All his reasoning part was busy with those reactions to the close rarefied luxury of the city. From the claustrophobia of Court and studio, he fled to the spaces of air, and light, and water, and their irradiant laws. From the languor of the orchards, and the palace-chambers, and the cloisters, he passed to the contemplation of elemental forces, and endless problems in the wonder of dynamics. To the idle magic of soothsayers and alchemists he opposed the relentless laws inherent in matter. From the urgent sieges of physical loveliness he took cynical refuge in the dissecting-room. From the sight of splendid waste he turned to the conservation of energy. And all the city had of Superbia he threw into a challenge of the gods, with his unsurpassable image of the Triumphator and his mythos of Beauty betrayed.

The Task of Psyche

Nevertheless his great authority and princely manners at Milan unfitted him from his native city. He loved the pageants, he loved the atmosphere of luxury, he loved the perfume and the music, he loved the brilliant guests, he loved the delicate adolescents in their flared cloaks and jewelled bands. He loved the "natural disposition of the inhabitants to feasting and pleasure." The integrity of his æsthetic character is sapped as by a subterranean reverie of waters. It is richer, deeper, stranger. But it has lost the blithe Florentine singing note, though it is saved by the great Florentine line. Drenched by the emotionalism of Milan, he gains and he loses. The music-moulded faces of the Lombards perfect the type that once haunted his boyish imagination in Verrocchio's studio. But it is all an oppression of magic. His spirit, like his palette, shares in the corruption of the rose, for all his intellectual exercises ; there are blurred pages in his manuscripts where the blots and broken phrases are like sobs ; and his palette is nourished with precious degradations of colour, dying turquoise, deliquescent emerald, beautiful and dangerous. Dangerous at least for his imitators ! He achingly missed sometimes the Florentine penetrations of æsthetic delight, the pure poignard of beauty turning in the wound of bliss.

Still, if his work in Milan was haunted by the recollections of Florence, not till he had returned to Florence did he fully realize the emotional themes with which Milan had suborned his intellectual art. The first studies of Leda, with their note of heavenly wildness, the fair girl half-bent among the reeds and lilies, with faint subtle face and all that twisted hair, are something akin to the moods he took from both the cities ; but he first beheld her among the swans of the Castello. Distance is necessary to clarify an experience into images ; and it is only in the secret stills of reminiscence that the fragrances and essences of the past drip burningly sweet and strange. It is in the azure chamber of reverie that we see ourselves, as in a deep Venetian mirror, move clearly in lost places that have passed into the texture of soul and body. And, as the image of such a place is so inextricably caught in the supersensitive retina of the spiritual gaze, that we seem to have ravished some of its very colour and texture, as if in faint revenge for that so subtle theft, in any glorified scene that has served as a Station of the Cross, or a Bridal Chamber, or an altar of crowning, or a crypt of initiation, or even a charmed hostel of rest among the dews and sleeping daisies, we seem to leave some pale ghost of ourselves with the still bright air and the carven stones, a toll as slight as a summer gossamer, yet enough to bid the departed guest remember that he left a little of his spirit there upon his way to death. He does remember, merely hoping that the wraith is like a powder of roses. So Leonardo took a mystical spoil from Milan

Leonardo the Florentine

besides the golden florins ; yet left behind, with his tradition, much of his kingly security and sweetness of mind.

xxvii

After all, how could a soul that was formed by the rhythms of the Dorian lyre keep time with the heart of a city " that beat like the pulses of the priests of Cybele " ? Even a semi-divine spirit was troubled. The measures of the ancient city of Milan, where the seraphim of the four winds of the world had met, were too conflicting. Yet, in this capital of Renaissance beauty, freed from the criticism of frank intelligence, unbound from the authority of any tradition, with a Duke rich enough, until the armies exhausted him, to employ all his gifts and let him live serene and sovran among his kind, Leonardo flowered into artistic expression as never before or after. The strange fatality that, like a hound from Dis, dragged so much of his work into darkness, has left small relique of the marvel of his maturity. *The Last Supper* is a painted ghost ; the fard on the shadow is not Leonardo's. There is not a print of the pastern of the Cavallo on the roads of time, not one veridical little image of its incomparable pose. The portraits of enchanting women have vanished like themselves with the " neiges d'antan." What the domes of Milan and Pavia, the great canals of Lombardy, have taken from his genius is but obscurely suggested. But there the Virgin of the Rocks was revealed to him in her green-lit water-world ; and his twy-natured angels, who have looked into all that they desired, were finally formed to be the genii of his satisfied soul ; while, lord of them all, Saint John the Baptist, who is also Dionysos, becomes definitely the Choragus and the Psychopompos who invites the initiate soul to the caves and crypts of ecstasy.

Milan was not graved on his mind by the whirling disk of youth as Florence was. He has the traditional contempt of the Tuscan for the Lombard, the borderer, the son of mingled blood. It is the Florentine irony and the Florentine precision that save him from æsthetic and spiritual wreck in the "city of Venus." He bears himself a little haughtily, like a great apostle in a sweet barbarous place. He did not remember her like his own city, outlined in just and delicate contours of hills and towers and gates, with washes of pale pellucid colour. Milan was a soft sumptuous impression, a drift of crimson leaves. She was a great thicket of rose against the emerald-green, and he had kept her colour in the enchanting carnations that once so sweetly invited among his blues and greens and soft unburnished golds. His life had been rich and full there, where all images were richly blurred with a sfumato of their own

The Task of Psyche

immaterial bloom. When he sate in France at eventide, remembering youth and Florence, then, like a soft flight of rose flamingos upon a southern shore, he would be faintly aware of Milan. And, looking upon the beautiful devoted head of Francesco Melzi, he would realize that the strange city had given an inviolate love-gift that his own Florence had refused; and that the sweetness of Milan had followed him in those luminous, faithful eyes.

God thought of cities in many ways. For the cities of Asia were carven wells of white jade from which the West drew living water in urns of such pure and perfect shape as never Asia knew. And the marble cities of Greece were amazing lamps of beauty, made for the world's illumination. And the cities of Egypt lay, dead-gold shrines of antiquity older than time, keeping the immemorial wisdom of a magic that is the only possible converse with primeval night. And the cities of Spain were the castles of love and death whose foundations were pride. But the cities of Italy God made for sheer delight, and as a justification of the five senses that serve the imagination.

xxviii

Leonardo combined his cities very well. Only to Florence was he native, only in Florence was he young—in the clear city of violets and nightingales and bright air that seems as if some god redreamed it every night, the one city in Italy whose art and life witnessed to the thrilling sincerity of its imitation of Hellas. And only in Milan of the moist airs and falling roses could he have been drenched with the splendours of the later Empires, and the strange sacrificial gods that come out of Asia. Venice, Rome, gave nothing new. But it is something to regret that he did not wander southward to Naples, and thence to see, and see in its perfection of sun and headland, the golden eurythmy of the absolute pillars of Pæstum.

Part iii
The Wandering Years
(1500-1516)

Chapter i

The Way Back to Florence

i

LEONARDO was drawing the spiral smoke of the burning city when the French first captured Milan ; and he beheld the entrance of the King. But he soon withdrew to Venice, and of Lodovico's last mournful attempt to regain his duchy he witnessed nothing. It becomes evident later that he had already entered into some friendly relation with the French. King Louis had longed to carry away the refectory wall with the *Cenacolo* upon it. De Ligny, the magnificent captain, doomed to capture the Duke, had shown him friendliness. Florimond Robertet, the King's favoured secretary, an enthusiast for the exotic art of conquered Italy, had asked him for a Madonna. The serene and puissant son of the Pope, who had ridden post-haste to Milan to greet the King, coming with torches from a supper, and to squire him through his triumph, had discerned a temper not so unlike his own, and had realized that this genius could not only paint, but could strengthen walls like those of the Castello, and express advanced ideas about military warfare.

He had made his impression, but his mood was now set to return to Florence awhile. He had become a very famous prince among artists ; and we may easily believe that even Leonardo thought it would be sweet to breathe bright Tuscan air again, and hear some praise in the purer Italian of his own proud city. It was ill to linger in Milan at present, her Beautiful Way all trampled, her treasures roughly rent from her by aliens, smoke-soiled, broken, wounded, defiled by the barbarians. As for the seat of Lodovico's pride and strength : "In the Castello there is nothing but dirt and foulness such as Signor Lodovico would not have allowed for the whole world." When Leonardo sees Milan again she will be smoothed and graced once more for her conqueror ; the old Court life will exist in shards and drifts of peach-bloom colour in the villas along the waters without the town. But her Renaissance splendour will be over, though she keep some vivid suffering colour like a branch of a burning autumnal linden-tree, rich, tender and ghostly, a trembling illusion of vanishing crimson.

Leonardo the Florentine

" Flee from storms," said Leonardo, who now, like a white stormbird must hover long over so many storms with hardly a quiver of the wing. The time was begun for the destruction of Italy and her Renaissance, treachery on treachery, sack upon sack, invasion on invasion. If Leonardo be aware of the tragedies of the free cities, he does not reveal any sympathy. His indifferentism he wears like a secret silver mail of seamless mesh under his tunic of rose. It will turn aside all importunate attacks of battle upon his inviolable mind. His business is to find some peace where he can work out his soul in images of beauty, and engage his curious mind in the pursuit of truth. He holds himself exempt from the great quarrel of liberty, and immune from the strife of his fellows. For he is not of their kind. His duty is to his own genius, and he acknowledges no other duty. Besides, it is true that his mind has so accustomed itself to the vast processes and æons of time that go to the history of earth that he is almost disinterested in the contest of men about him. He cannot take sides in transitory affairs ; and if he sells his service to Cesare Borgia he is neither for nor against him.

But the departure from Milan meant a great displacement. He had formed his habits so that day and even night yielded all their opportunities for work and amusement : he had spun a web of superfine filaments connecting himself with numberless people who were friends and companions in grace, labour, knowledge. His house was happy and beautiful. He had grown into Milan, where he was an autocrat among the lovers of things unique and where his Protean variety of moods could find the versatility of tasks it desired. Henceforth he, the prince of artists, was to live very much as a genius-errant, his nerves restless because of the uncertainty of his future. When France gives him his hostel, and his recognition as a prince, it is too late for Leonardo the artist. The perilous habit of " living from day to day," which was soon imputed to him, wasted his hours like the locust, as they had never been wasted before. He is vexed by rivals, enemies and champions alike. He is undone by his qualities, for his fame had gone out with a flourish of silver trumpets from Milan ; and no State at the moment could afford a Leonardo. Even in the generous days of full Renaissance the problem of the artist's existence was at times embarrassing. Shall he traffic in his own blood and his dreams ? Can he be paid for his own progress towards perfection, his claims upon eternity ? No ! Yet he can make little valuable effort without some orderly and even comely way of life. Many of the Renaissance painters had the psychology of good craftsmen, and for an inventoried picture took their fixed price. Leonardo's chief effort at an inventoried picture had not been a success in the material way. In no respect did it fulfil the specification, and yet its value far exceeded the fixed price. It was during the Renaissance that the artist definitely separated from the craftsman and developed a distinct psychology. In Leonardo and Michelangelo, the lover of beauty and the creator of shapes that were " nurslings of immortality " found it a confusing and invidious matter to reconcile payment with their great qualities.

After leaving Milan, Leonardo behaved very much as a prince without a kingdom. He exhibited indifference towards his art, soothed his mind with abstract studies ; and, while he continued to charm his friends, showed no anxiety to compete eagerly for commissions, nor indeed to fulfil them when they were offered to him. He soon felt, not without bitterness, that he could not rebuild in Florence the fair house of music, security, and great friendliness, that was home to him in Milan. He had lived there too long ; and, when the excitement of his return to Florence had died down, he felt that, familiar as were the wild and witty ways of the Florentines, tonic as were their ironical scrutinies, he was no more the only prince of art in Florence ; he could not be in this Republican city, somewhat astringent after the expulsion of Piero de' Medici, the sweet and courteous autocrat with his lovely young court that he had been in Milan. He missed his house of friendship. Those who are isolated by the strangeness as well as the greatness of their qualities must feel at times that they move a dim and unreal flame by the habitations of men. Solitude is their tent of silver where angels come as guests ; but often they are consumed with craving to sit by a glowing hearth within kind walls and listen to common things, to make sure that all their lives are not a monstrous fantasy. So Leonardo invents a bathing-machine or a pump as a quaint clutch upon reality ; Michelangelo develops an organic passion for his family, though he justly finds its separate members detestable. Leonardo reassured himself by a ritualistic mode of existence : he needed his centre, his continuity of clear comely life, his ungrudged and undisputed opportunity. Ungrudged and undisputed it had to be. So he becomes a wandering star till King Francis gives him Cloux.

ii

When he left Milan he had Fra Luca Pacioli with him, that eccentric and cheerful mathematician, and also Andrea Salaino of the beautiful locks, as fond of fine clothes as ever. His store of florins he had lodged in the Treasury of Santa Maria Nuova ; but he did not go to Florence at once, for Lodovico might possibly regain his dukedom. He went to Venice by way of Mantua. Isabella, always good-humoured rather than sweet-hearted, was welcoming the exiles of Milan just then. She had arranged matters with the French, and was pleased to shelter such old friends as could not compromise her. Hospitality was a great pleasure to her, and she was nearly as charmed with people of rare quality as with a well-wrought intaglio or an antique statue. Nearly, but not quite! Her guests might find their lost idols in her palace, but would never recover them. She dearly loved Elisabetta of Urbino now, but she more dearly loved Elisabetta's sleeping Cupid, and in time to come she would beg prettily and effectively for that lovely piece of marble from Cesare Borgia, whom she tactfully made godfather to her son, and who seems to regard her with indulgent irony. Then, though she shelter her dearest friend and her husband most cordially, Elisabetta may recover her chair of estate again, but never her Eros.

She welcomed both Cecilia and Lucrezia for a time, while these fair martyrs, with many noble lords and ladies, considered when it would be safe to return to those revenues and villas which somehow cleave to people of high quality through the stormiest revolutions. At the worst they always escape with plenty of jewels, if they have not unfortunately been prevented from escape altogether. The bright migratory birds were well-advised, however, to settle on Mantua a while. The French did not wish the city of Milan to be deserted by its beauty and wit, though they could never reconstruct Lodovico's Court. Leonardo would yet see Cecilia and her friends back in their own villas, indifferent to plague and war, jewelled and brocaded, splendid as " the *Assumption* in Venice," says Bandello. Meanwhile Isabella shows them her studio, blue-and-gold, her astonishing little dwarfs' camerini, honeycombed in the palace (a spectacle that shocks us now), smiles her enchanting smile, and, her dark eyes sweet under her golden hair, plays an air on Beatrice's coveted clavichord, as if to say that perfect things naturally seek those who can use them best, or that beauty must have her way.

Therefore Leonardo and his friends came to Mantua, palaced Mantua, Virgilian Mantua, Sordello's, Vittorino's Mantua, a place of poetry with a rumour of old sweet sound haunting it, as it stood among its green lagoons, and the great swans drifted round it.

City of Pisanello and Mantegna, of things withdrawn, noble and yet tender in its tradition of art! Here had been Vittorino's House of Joy, of which the lucid lovely dream had been stamped by the famous medallist in a roundel great and pure. Cecilia Gonzaga sits by her calm unicorn under her crescent moon in her clear world, sweet witness to all eternity that the Renaissance had a holiness of beauty, and a religion as well as a fantasy in its love of Greek. It is of interest to compare this

The Way Back to Florence

lovely thing with Leonardo's best drawing of the theme of the girl with the unicorn. It is a lightly touched drawing, but enough to show his version of the mystery of virginity. The maiden sits under tall arum lilies, with the unicorn bowed on her knee : the rock-pillars of his sacred circle are in the distance. The sketch is sophisticate, strange, luxurious, for Leonardo's Unicorn, according to his own odd bestiary, is not the legendary guardian of chastity but an image of desire betrayed by the very delicacy of its greed. The virgin may indeed have some suggestion of the mediæval Madonna with the heavenly unicorn hunted by Gabriel to her breast ; the image would still be complicated, strange, luxurious.

He had brought Isabella lute-strings and viol-strings the year before, and so already knew the palaces, half-tragic even then, with peacocks and children in the ceilings of the bridal-chambers, and Mantegna's proud frescoes of the Gonzaga glory frank upon the walls. There was a great melancholy about the lake-city, that took even Isabella's bright imageries silently into its keeping, as if toning them instantly into a blazonry of the past. Yet she made a great stir of colour and music, and Leonardo carried her lute-strings. There is always a sense of music about Leonardo's movements ; as he says, it is an art of transitions.

Isabella's glancing mind flickered about the great painter with fine compliment and delicate advances. She had borrowed Cecilia's portrait not long before to compare it with a Bellini, and she was fain to see herself in Leonardo's eyes. She knows here is no artist to be imperiously used and threatened. He is not only a great painter ; he is intimate with her splendid and terrible brother. She must have his work in her palace of art. So, while he is in Mantua she is sweetly solicitous to Leonardo da Vinci, " who is our friend." When he is gone, she waylays him with unexpected ambassadors, implores him with something like humility. Isabella always wanted perfection, and wanted it in a hurry ; but, if she could get it from Leonardo, she would wait for it. She has waited for all eternity. She made a mistake, for Leonardo did allow her one piece of perfection when he left a copy of his drawing of her in Mantua. Her husband gave it away, and she thought she could replace it easily. But Leonardo paid no heed to the supplicating lady. One is glad almost that Isabella once met an artist and found he was Leonardo, the one man in Italy whom she could not persuade. It is hard to forgive her cruelty to Mantegna, and her perverse taste for allegory. At times it seems as if she needed G. F. Watts, at his worst. But perhaps her intellectual processes had become affected by the masques, which in the more highly conscious courts had a certain inclination to pass from myth to abstraction.

It is about this time that Isabella is dreaming of a statue of Virgil.

Leonardo the Florentine

An image of Virgil had been the palladium of Mantua, and the faithful city, with virgin choirs and sacrifices of flowers, had adored the poet who had become for them a kind of sweet magician and a gentle god, till an alarmed condottiere of puritan convictions (a Malatesta, too !) had thrown the profane thing in the river.   Vittorino da Feltre had renewed the rhythmic cult, desiring the Virgilian tenderness to leaven the souls of his pupils.   Now Isabella will have a new statue.   She writes to Mantegna for studies.   She wants an inscription to bind her name with Virgil's.   The diamond would write her bright name on the sweet Virgilian story.   But in the end she has no money.

The great Mantegna is still alive, in the street of the Unicorn, though the days of his pride are waning.   Austere and magnificent master, who with sincerity and pure faith evoked a splendid procession from a Rome like Rome's own dream of itself, an artist whose rhythmic movement is in the key of Lucretius, melancholy and mighty, whose saints and angels are golden and gracious and compassionate because they are strong, he succeeds through a belief in his pillared, arched, and ideal heaven as passionate as Fra Angelico's in his wild-rose, love-marvellous Paradise.   Wonderful his perspectives and the stately unsensuous beauty of his types, the swung garlands of great fruits that glow with solemn ecstasy ; but most wonderful the mere greatness of his manner.   The suffering indomitable mask of Mantegna still silently informs us that a sweet and haughty ethic may be a fine thing in a painter, and that sheer nobility is an æsthetic quality.

How did the weary and ailing Mantegna, one wonders, consider the silken courtly Florentine ?   A great Roman sword can sheer through webs of silk be they never so finely woven, and a simple sign disperse a subtle spell.   Did Leonardo see how splendid and yet how austere was the Pattern of Pride into which Mantegna had lifted the Pomp of Cæsar ?   Did he look at *The Madonna of Victory* which was the one lofty consequence of the ignoble battle of Fornovo, and feel that the solemn and pitying archangels, beautiful as early Miltonic verse is beautiful, unconsciously rebuked his gracile equivocal adolescents ? It is not a depreciation of Leonardo to say that Mantegna makes one realize where even his unparalleled genius falters.   Simplicity has a conquering power when it has a patrician grace ; and sincerity is doubly piercing when it proceeds from a mood so august.   Leonardo's mood was too " changeable " a tissue to be simple ; and, always a little strange to this planet, he hardly knew when he was sincere.

The Way Back to Florence

He drew Isabella, and said he would paint her. Leaving her one copy of his sketch, he took away the other, promising to make a completed portrait of it. It seems as if he had begun at some time to do so, for the prick of the transference pins remains on the Louvre designs. Vainly, however, will she say, " You promised," again and again. He thought the drawing a fine thing, for he clave to his copy ; but he was not disposed to linger over the painting. When he got to Florence, Mona Lisa was at hand, and Isabella was not. Mona Lisa's was a face that amused his æsthetic self ; and Isabella's was no enigma. So the princess for once gave way to the bourgeoise.

Probably he thought that he had done all that was necessary for Isabella's beauty. And, indeed, looking at that noble and delectable drawing, one has no wish to see it carried farther. Though a comparatively small matter, in this it is like the *Adoration*. He seems to have felt it complete, and so left it. In the pale-pastel softness of the sketch, Isabella's too-sparkling beauty, while it retains some vivid moment of her conversation, has sunk sweetly and just sufficiently into the withdrawn and dreamy twilight, the " smorzata " light which cleaves to all high beauty like a hinted halo or a Coan veil. The proud fair head turns in profile, swiftly intelligent to some occasion, some rare occasion. It rises fragile and princess-like from the spread of the great dim-striped sleeves, so that you get the moving effect of fragility flowering proudly from excessive regal pomp, an effect stolen and exaggerated by Raphael in his picture of *Joanna of Aragon*. Incidentally he thus finds, very naturally, the dignity of pyramidal composition in even a single figure. Isabella had let the divine painter dress her to his own taste. He seizes what is essentially good in her attire, and as usual sweeps away the accidentals. But here, as with Mona Lisa, he keeps a detail of fastidious sympathy natural to a painter who saw bodies unclothed, and saw them delicate. Softly he plaits the edge of lawn round the neck and bosom, under the thick sumptuous stuff of pale yellow. And the exceedingly tender and musical flow of the swept hair is caught within an impalpable net and just impressed with the faint coronal, while her patrician hands proclaim her Estensian and æsthete. It is far from the time when Titian will paint her in splendour, turbaned with jewels, all pearls and brilliants, sovereign and satisfied—but no longer gracile.

He has seized her at a moment that pleases him, with faint smile and attentive eyes ; he has given her the mystery of beauty's sibyl, as he gave it to Cecilia, Lucrezia, as he will give it to the others, notably to Mona Lisa. From this daughter of swords and saints and diamonds, herself too like a rapier and a diamond, hard, positive, the crystal formed in a house of plague and fiery war, set in her azure and or, *dardant per un désir*, he turns away courteously, arrested by no face that is not mutable, miroitant enough to promise the moment that fits his masque, the soft selenical moment remembering old initiations into lost lunar cults. Isabella's intelligence had some affinity with his in its glancing versatility ; but she had no gift to give him : for his strongly feminine side she was not gliding enough. So he leaves her in her paradise blue and gold, with her musical motives everywhere, to her pages and hounds and golden dwarfs, the falcons and the gerhawks, the poets and musicians, the Latin comedies and the shows. He respected her personality however ; he did not fuse it with his ideal. The drawing, we know from Lorenzo da Pavia, is very like her. And, since it closely resembles the portrait-medal done of her, with waving hair and pearl-clasped throat, by Cristoforo Romano, we know she was surely beautiful.

She was a tamer of beasts in her way. He is a hideous little person, Francesco Gonzaga, her husband, swart and savage warrior ; but he seems to look up at Isabella, not without pathos, as he does to *The Madonna of Victory* in Mantegna's great picture. He could flaunt his golden Teodora at the great Brescian pageant for the Queen of Cyprus ; but Isabella is first in splendour and in policy, and, when defeat breaks his nerve, he trusts to her abjectly. Leonardo does not dislike the ugly little Marquis ; for he has perhaps the best stable in Italy, with fifty superb war-steeds in it. He gazes with pleasure again, and with something of regret, at the noble destriers, the perfect horses of Spain and Thrace and Galicia. He is not done with horses yet : he draws these within the friezes of his memory. And over the Marquis of Mantua's famous menagerie of foreign beasts, bizarre or beautiful, kept as considered tokens of luxury, he lingers too.

But not long, for he was in Venice in 1500, having promised many things in departing. For the Marquis he did one favour, sending him, when he reached Florence, drawings of a Florentine villa he had admired, but warning him wisely that the house will not be really beautiful unless he can copy the site as well as the dwelling.

It is a pity that Leonardo was too early by a year or so in this region of Italy to see approach, with unprecedented pomps and masques, with marvellous web of golden hair and deep-gazing eyes, white as the innumerable pearls in her dowry, the beautiful, deadly Borgia bride. She came, they said, from loves more terrible than those of Egyptian gods or princes, from regal luxury and heathen festival and the flashing of poignards sheathed in beloved hearts by beloved hands ; and yet, it is also said, she came from these things like a simple child who accepts whatever is, as natural, to the high ceremonial and the reluctant haughty house of Ferrara, to accept that just as simply, and to rule over hearts because she had a love-breathing presence. An ivory lute, on her had great evil lutanists played unimaginable tunes that now merely haunted like a sadness her precious substance, immutably innocent. She who had gazed with her gay, gross father at the play of the stallions in the Vatican, now moved purely as a great duchess, and with a thick lock of golden hair scaled her pleasure in Bembo's platonic adorations, and knew that the perfect knight called Bayard wore her colours as the lady of his chivalrous love. Leonardo should have painted Lucrezia, and two Renaissance extremes would have met, the intellectual and psychical energy that overpassed the physical in mastering it, Florence at her highest, and the passive physical heathenism of Rome that took the stamp of a Cæsar in gold. Not for Leonardo, however, to paint Lucrezia, Herodiad as she was, most incomparable dancer among all the princesses, dancing her Spanish dances in green raiment and ringing her tambourines for the ladies of Mantua, Ferrara, and Urbino, as once for her father's delight. His business was to strengthen awhile the implacable and incarnate Will that was her brother.

iv

Leonardo passed to Venice, probably at that time and for long after the most beautiful city on earth, that could astonish and overwhelm the power of sight. The Adriatic Republic had been Lodovico's most cruel enemy ; but here the artist chose to tarry long enough to be sure that the Duke had lost Milan for ever.

He looked at Venice, and, one feels, instantly refused it. This great apparition, this insolent goddess, Anadyomene among cities, created by the marriage of sun and sea, dissolved all her artists into the mythos of her glory, and serenely obliterated the disobedient. She was more than the City Triumphant, she was the City Arrogant and Dominant, but her insolence was piled in amazing sea-sunsets and her tyrannies washed such Tyrian and Sidonian spoils within such dream-temples and dream-palaces that her cruel and ravishing ways seemed ethereal, her crafts, her greeds, the caprices of a loved woman. Beauty, beauty was her sole excuse, and men forgave her as they forgave Aphrodite. She was a city with a " genius " indeed that shaped and seized all her children, not subtle and delicate, ironic and wistful, like that of Florence, but exultant, reckless, Olympian—entirely conscienceless. She began heroically, she continued despotically. She had fought and trafficked so long with the Turk, that the Sultan's Byzantium was better known to her than her sister-cities in Italy ; and, while retaining a Western breadth of vision, she yet reinforced her diplomacies with the subtle intrigues of the Orient.

The sky and the sea had builded her, the East and the West met together to make her rich. Neither Emperor nor Pope could hold her : she lived to herself alone. She had sold a crusade to her gorgeous advantage. For her the golden raiment of Santa Sophia had been torn and stripped, the great Basilica in whose image Saint Mark's had risen. It was a kind of horrible incest and rape among cities. But she went on her path of superb spoliation, seizing on the Greek islands, crushing fair jealous Genoa. Padua, Verona, and Brescia cursed her. But her wicked adventures of plunder were hung with banners august and set with lyric trumpets, and in hours of desperate peril she was heroic as in her beginning.

Now she rested for a little, wondrous and serene, though wary, and took heed to her beauty and her great repute. Her golden integrity was assured by the finest chain-work ever woven by an oligarchy. The Doge had become her symbol, a creature invested with a sacred and solitary splendour, a pagan king-priest of old who wedded the sea in mystical marriage, and who, like the king-priest of old, was often a sacrificial victim. The dark and stately patricians whose names were written in the Golden Book were aware of all that happened in their city, in Italy, in Christendom, and Heathenesse. Her spies and agents and diplomatists were in every Court, and her bailo kissed the corner of the robe of the immobile indifferent Sultan in full cloth-of-gold. The " lords of the night " were jealously vigilant in her moonlit ways. The dagger flashed in lovers' gardens ; the precious bubble of her pure Murano glass, blown from tempered fiery air and a little rare sand, broke sometimes under an evil shock when the poison went astray from a hardier beaker. Dagger and poison were the State's. Her absolution still was her beauty. She was approaching her sheer apotheosis ; when as Antiope, Ariadne, considered of gods, and that not secretly, in her coronation glory of milky stars, she would daze the world with the sea-green, rose-red, sapphirine wonder of her Assumption.

v

Leonardo came into the full glory of light at Venice. Before him lay the world between land and water—the mysterious lagoons formed by the silt dropped by the tired rivers, the immense rose-lotos of a city spread out on the Adriatic. What Milan appeared to dream in her sunset languor was here more than realized. From the floors of aquamarine and peridot the golden-pale embroidered palaces rose in the rare

The Way Back to Florence

confusion of an original Gothic that ran into an Arabian reverie; Saint Mark's, with all its domes and radiant façades, with the four great horses before it, riding for their Lord Poseidon, and the three great standards of tumultuous romance, Cyprus, Morea, Candia, seemed like a wild mirage wrought by some sheer sea-magic. All things grew vivid as immense sea-anemones in the unsullied light that seemed one with the illumined ocean. No northern glazes of mist blurred their intensities. A green soft dusk dwelt through the temples; the daytime sky was burning azure. Tyre and Sidon and Cyprus had dissolved to feed this conflagration of ether. Sidonian emerald, Tyrian blue and Cyprus rose, they merely deepened the hues that were her own. The Bucentaur might pass in rose and green and gold. Rose and green and gold, the City was one with her. In the walled garden, the flame-colour climbed the cypress and the rose-carnation had all its passionate way. The city of adventurers and merchants was easily and always a city of lovers. Maybe it is the eternal passiontide of hearts surrendering to the flagrant seductions of sky and sea, and rushing together in rapture as in the House of Eros, that is the truly divine justification of Venice. In whatever mood her sea-paven lanes were laid, the feet of Love and Death drifted there on soft-winged sandals, and the desideria of longing youth rose up, conqueringly suppliant, to soften the arrogance of Venice into one vast world of compassion, one great lotos to receive two souls upon a sea of dreaming eternity.

Life passed processional. The masque was endless, for the ritual worship of the city was a long solemnity of colour and pomp of festival. All her occasions were hung with the spoils of the East and exalted into a High Mass of Assumption, even when, with ruthless pageantry, the city is merely despoiling a sole sad lady, her own acknowledged daughter, of the golden veils and diadem of Cyprus. But in the sweet fiery furnace of colour all her evil was purified away. Her oppressions, one repeats, were mysteriously altered to the exciting Cleopatra-tricks of a wonderful lover. Her excessive wealth was molten into an atmosphere of golden leisure and luxurious quiet, her insolence was altered by the lapping tides of blue and green into a rhythm of noble pride. Her cruelties were consumed away in the integral heroism of her isolation, that of the double star for East and West. The precious spoils of her piracy fitted themselves to her great sea-temple as if they had merely arrived at their destined places, from Rome, Byzantium, or Antioch. If they said she was become like a great courtesan, hers was the answerable defence of Phryne; like her, she was cast in the image of the goddess of the sea.

Through all the Orientalism of Venice, and the evocation of

sumptuous storming colour, flooding the soul that rises flushed and radiant, new-born from that baptism of splendour, there is a Greek note, something wilder and more wistful than that of other Renaissance cities, exquisite as a fugitive nymph. One doge brought a Grecian bride to the city, it was said, whose beauty was so rare that she could bathe it only in the morning dews; and her maidens rowed out to waking islets at dawn to gather it for her. So it is a faëry kind of Greece that wanders strange through Venice, like a privet-white Galatea from Cyclades lying in wine-dark seas empurpled from Asiatic shores. Or honey-white and golden, Greece of Sicily and Theocritus, the spirit steals within the sun-soaked idylls of Giorgione, and sings low in the pipe of his Shepherd Boy, incomparable and innocent Daphnis, and lies pure and Praxitelean in the divine sleep of his Venus. Less evident, but as potent, it dwells like a breath of hyacinth behind the quiet doors of Aldus Manutius' house of dedicated labour, through war and plague serenely persisting in rare and selfless humanism. It haunts the minds of those dreaming young nobles, many of whom have been Greek-speaking since the days of Guarino of Verona. Fragrance from Naxos came with the brown Levantine boatman bringing their little statuettes of winged and wistful things found in vineyard-soil. It finds the young Titian, who will yet paint one of the most sumptuous and least Hellenic pieces of paganism in the world.

Within this immoderate ecstasy of colour, a beautiful singing people drifted about their canals at tasks that seemed dipped in holiday, for the sensitive leisurely mood of their waters lapped round their unhasting lives. Golden the boatmen, formed like Greek athletes, that shifted their flame-coloured merchandise down by the Rialto. Courteous, grave, and Eastern, the merchants sat in the sweet-smelling Merceria, where the nightingales sang, where cloth-of-gold and rosed fabrics from the Orient hung every building till the air was dense with richness. As for the patricians, they almost justified their costly and jealous existence by the beautiful manners which clothed their pride as rarely as the great sleeves of brocade and the fine white lawn about their throats invested their beautiful persons. The princely young men went with music in their faces, for music rose up from the miraculously lyre-shaped city as if the strings vibrated with the pearly stir made by Thetis and Amphitrite. As seen in the Giorgionesque portraits, whether by that elusive artist or the early Titian, with dark fine hair, swept low and tenderly into silken nets, and earnest, meditative eyes, they seem the most truly aristocratic types that ever passed into painting, they are so sure, so delicate, so sifted of ignoble desire, so sweetly aware of poetry as an element of life, listening for the footfall of beauty, holding the token

The Way Back to Florence

of some great felicity lightly yet gently, like a rose, or a glove, or a book. Velasquez' Spaniards are more alien ; their pride is too near an insanity. Van Dyck's nobles, for all their lovely swagger, are too tenuous in their elegance ; their witless womanish ways, we see, will destroy them. Leonardo painted no perfected aristocrat; he drew Isabella. Not in the soil of Florence nor even Milan were such flowers grown as the Lords of the Golden Book. (But in the Florentine portraits you do not think if the subjects are patrician or plebeian, merely considering their humanity and their artist.)

vi

Leonardo, at first, one might think, would rest in the contemplation of all this miracle made out of sun-fire, sea-water, and a little silted earth, this Adriatica built of sunset and ocean. But he does not tarry long ; and he seems to move in the radiant city a little pale and weary. He could not fit into the scheme of Venice, that looked so aery and was so unyielding in its invisible golden strictures. He was the child of one great City that desired her children to be individualists, and had been the servant of another that had tolerated and respected his moods. Here was a place that carelessly claimed the artist as the mere acolyte of her glory, and gave him palaces and honours if he recognized her divinity, without in the least observing his.

Probably he was dazed by all that spilth of springtide light. By this time his pleasure was to concentrate it in a small space, and " smother " it sweetly with a suave and caressing brush. Personally he loved the twilight, and perhaps he found Venice best when the dusk came blue as a sublimation of Egyptian lapis, blue as that profound azure of the cherubim we see behind the wise Doge Loredano's head, blue as the chamber of King Ahasuerus. Maybe he deepened his blue in Venice— it seems to count almost as indigo in the Saint Anne.

But he was not in the Venetian sense a colourist. He loved the strange hues, the semitones that sound from the muted viols on the very verges of light. Green, blue, violet, mysteriously vanishing ! He liked the Eastern emeralds, the dying turquoise, the faint crimsons, the unburnished gold, the soft ivory of lilies, the morbidezza of the flesh. Best of all—green, blue, violet, mysteriously vanishing ! Symbolic colours, for he would convey a myth ! He had been drenched enough in richness at Milan. Now he hardly cared to look

"... where Colour, the Soul's Bridegroom, makes
The House of Heaven splendid for the Bride."

No ! The magnificent explosion almost hurt his tired and delicate nerves, and shook his wonderful line.

299

Leonardo the Florentine

But Venice had all the Leonardo she needed already. She had no use for a mystery. She was mystery enough in her own divine nature. It was peace time for her, and she was realizing the Renaissance in terms of pleasure, more and more aware that her artists could give her a sacred mirror, and yet more jewels for her play. She said she desired pictures to be pieces of great colour, dancing rhythm, treasurable and delightful pieces of paint, things for her to wear. The works of the Bellini, grave and pure, but aglow with light and Eastern hues, were honourable throughout Italy. Carpaccio had turned old legend into the procession of a Venetian romance. Crivelli had filled his Paduan rigidities with all the hushed golden splendours of Byzantine palaces and the lamps of sacerdotal gems, burning about a fantastic fine people from some sophisticated fairyland between Camelot and Cathay, recorded with a half-wild unearthly delight, as of a strange bird from Paradise. Titian was young and still uncertain. The day of Tintoret and Palma Vecchio and his kind was not yet.

The life of Giorgione slips away in its gilded shadows with some chords from a lute and some glints from a dagger, parallel with Leonardo's for a while, though it vanishes in the dark too soon. Delicate Giorgione, who sweetly kept the secret of his dream inviolate from his jealous city, and presented her with an emotional mystery of golden regret and visible music she did not comprehend ! Vasari says that Giorgione was much affected by the " extraordinary softness " of some works of Leonardo. It is more than possible that they met. Leonardo records no meeting with anybody—he did not keep a diary. But he had brought some of his Milanese work with him ; and he did not live solitary in Venice. Giorgione was twenty-four then, a love-child, lovely and a lutanist, as he himself had been in his youth. Dark and slender and glowing, with music in his eyes, he also had charmed his way with his lyre. Already he could paint his enchanted " poesie," those pictures of an imaginative substance akin to that of poetry, as lazulite is kin to Oriental turquoise, yet seeking shape in the medium of paint, not words. These golden idylls of the blessed, where life lapses amid music and murmuring water and sun-tranced trees, and far off sleep-charmed city gates, are the Venetian equivalent of the more intellectualized myths of Botticelli. How divinely beautiful is each, and how different ! The genius of Leonardo, which might have included both—the poignancy of the imaginative rhythm of Botticelli, the suavity of the sensuous rhythm of Giorgione—indifferently turned from the " poesia " form which seems to have been created for its pleasure. Already, for Giorgione, figures of Adonis and Paris stood fused in Elysian light, and the rare romantic figure of Adrastus for ever gazed at Hypsipyle. Already he was the painter of great patricians like the Knight of Malta, and those wonderful

The Way Back to Florence

young men with faces steeped in dreams, who, by processes of intense refinement, seemed to have reached a more rarefied state than most humankind. No need for him to remember the angels of the East when mortality can yield such flowers of grace. Now he is painting his great *Madonna* at Castelfranco, and the portrait of the richly-deposed Queen of Cyprus, who had great kindness for him.

Like Leonardo, Giorgione knew the sweetness of moulding chiaroscuro, the soothing glory of golden light, the satisfying effect of a triangular composition, even the expressive beauty of the hand. Like Leonardo's, his end is an impression of pure glamour, but different indeed is the spell. He receives us into the clear peace of an untroubled æsthetic experience. The æsthetic experience Leonardo gives is a sense of exquisite jeopardy ; there is intuition of a dividing sword somewhere, the sword between body and soul, the sword that forbids the way to Paradise, and whether you have passed it or not you cannot tell. Giorgione is Leonardo untroubled by any intellectual conflict, and steeped in a sea-soft, swordless, shadowless air, all rhythm and music and pure delight. His beautiful people have their mystery too ; they are grave young ambassadors carrying secret letters from some King of Kings, and none may violate their flawless chastity. But they are not equivocal, the high purport escapes from their deep-dwelling eyes and their pure hands. They have great assignations with felicity which may be fraught with peril, but with felicity they are fast-tokened.

Giorgione goes on his sweet-sounding way of muffled lutes and dream-hung festival, till he suddenly vanishes into darkness, stabbed or plague-stricken. He will yet paint more scenes from a hallowed yet heathen land, where the shrines are unstained from blood-offering, sweet with sacrifice of milk and honey and lutes and flowers. He will, with exultant heart and Praxitelean vision, sweep the pure lines of the loveliest nude figure of the Renaissance, and concentrate all the violin-like yearning love of beauty which did penetrate the too-deliberate paganism of the Renaissance with the sincerity of a bodiless desire, within its most expressive face: for the young monk-musician in *The Concert* is as Renaissance as Botticelli's head of Venus or Leonardo's Saint Anne. He is the painter of the purer Renaissance; he dissolves it all in golden light and a tremor of lovely music and the rich sadness of uncloyed pleasure. But like Leonardo's too is the after-tale of his works. Lost amazingly, repainted abominably, that golden-fine and flexibly sumptuous texture, at once so delicate and so rich that the sense of supersubtle touch craves for contact, wherewith the eyes dwell close as in bridal, the kind of texture such as, in the art of literature, one finds in *Lycidas,* or the *Ode on a Grecian Urn.*

Leonardo the Florentine

Leonardo's mind, however, may have rested in the sunset and the sea, though I fancy he was too weary for such an apocalypse of light and water, and considered without enthusiasm the magnificence of Venice, yet more opulent and dynamic than that of Milan, but less delicate. Even the halberd-iron on the prows of the gondola seemed to laugh a little too emptily into facile flowers. The pomp was too obvious, though the great spaces of sky and sea condoned it like fumes of coloured incense. The slim and gilded types of Carpaccio, Crivelli, the strange Veneziano, are disappearing in the Republic's glory. The Bellini still strew their music-making angels like flowers, Giorgione's young men are slender and reticent; his *Venus* is divinely chaste in outline; but his women seem inclined to heaviness. The fastidious Leonardo shrank from the sight of the famous Venetian courtesans, excessively golden and heavily white, set like great tuberoses on the balconies and public places, or led on the high *patens* inflicted on women by Orientally-minded lords. Privileged and flaunting, gorgeous, large-limbed, hierophants in the courts of the wanton goddess-city, their red-gold tresses twined in Eastern horns, they offended a mind inimical to gross display of the feminine principle in its crudity. The Venetian great ladies were sitting on the roofs, steeping their tresses in precious oils and spreading them in the sun to draw the sun's colour. Or they were locked in their seraglio-like rooms, or love-making dangerously in the immured gardens. Lately, Venice had absorbed Cyprus and the Cyprian together, with all their roses and all their poisons, as well as the immemorial sadist luxury from Crete; and sex was aflower both frankly and rankly. Up on the hills, Caterina, Queen of Jerusalem, Armenia and Cyprus, once mother of a Prince of Galilee, descendant of an Emperor of Trebizond, despoiled Daughter of a jealous Republic, kept her little court of lovers and idlers and philosophers of love, in a world of oak-groves and cypress-walks, set with apes and peacocks and dwarfs and hounds, with still a suitor to ride there on the fifteenth day, and the young graceful Bembo to melt " melodious words on lutes of amber " in honour of his fine fiction and variation of the Platonic theme, and a pageant with a car of white horses horned like unicorns to draw her when she made a state-visit. But Caterina also was now florid to see. The only women Leonardo could endure were fine and secret ; their lucid lids lay over their deep eyes, the petals of their arms and knees closed delicately over their sensitive beauty, and their heads, bowed heavily over their mysterious fatherless children, were oppressed by the brooding of wings. Not theirs the opulent inconscient clay that should submit to the images of the Aretine.

The Way Back to Florence

The Venetian architecture, so peculiar to the genius of the city, at least must have seized him, and coloured some of his " fantastic " projects, those in which the sense of the East surges against the cold barriers of Vitruvius. For, in this place of daring domes and exquisite pillars, all so arrogant and so inwrought, the Gothic arch wavered delicately into the curving horseshoe of the Arabic pavilion, and the mighty shape of Saint Sophia brooded beyond the golden cupola of Saint Mark. The most sumptuous façade in the world, gold, green, blue, rose, iris-changing like plumage, with the chargers from the bronze quadriga in Nero's Arch of Triumph come hither by way of Constantine and Byzantium to ride high in air on the balcony, that façade glorious with lily capitals, grouped pillars and columns of marble, pierced screens, and lamps burning for ever by Madonna, imperishable stains of ancient mosaic, all grown soft as a dream in the rare sea-weather, masked the gilded, coloured cupolas and the green-glimmering interiors of the temple that throve on the spoils of temples, absorbing them by sweet sea-change into her marvellous fabric, the sea-change that moulded her smooth and fluent as great waves. Ionia, Heliopolis, Damascus, Cyprus, Samarcand, Tyre, Candia, Lemnos, Naxos, Acre, Byzantium, the littorals of Thessaly, had fed her with beauty ; and the spirit of the East dwelt on the sea-jewelled pavements and golden aisles. The walls of gold and onyx and orient alabaster sent out a smoke of rainbow-colour ; the mosaics smouldered like burning embers on a golden cloth. Something of a hashisch dream ! But Leonardo took pleasure in a bubble of domes rising above a plan like a Greek cross, however intricate the complex of the cross. Saint Mark's at least seems in tone with his building fantasy, though the transfigured Gothic sweetness of the Doges' rosy house, with its rich angles, was more remote from his vaster conceptions.

The people in general pleased him. All their secular affairs were settled for them as absolutely by their Venetian secret councils as their spiritual affairs were settled by the patriarchs of the Venetian church. Their great sea-belfry, with soft strong tones, divided their days for them ; the gorgeous etiquette of their lives was arranged from birth to death by their puissant State. They were at liberty to be charming. The sweet-speaking children of the golden-strict Republic were humane, amicable, eloquent ; and pleasure was their art, even their duty, in this inverted sea-Sparta. They were even more versed in luxury than the other cities, for they had learned that sweet corruption long ago from Arabs and Byzantine Greeks. But they had not lost their gaiety in silken languors, and life went so dancingly that even the young betrothed, on first meeting her new parents, trod her ritual measure. Life went in pageant all day long. The music was the sweet melancholy of a pleasure that sighed into tears. " Our fiddlers here play so beautifully that they weep over their own music," says Albrecht Dürer, somewhat dazed by the radiance of life in Venice.

ix

Leonardo's senses being over-saturated in colour, sun, and sea, his scientific self protests. He is absorbed in studies of cosmography and geography, as is natural enough in a city whose Marco Polo had served the Great Khan in Pekin, and brought a princess of Cathay through many a journey to a strange throne in Persia, and whose ambassadors were her magnificent spies in countries old and new. Cathay had become a dense golden mist again, patterned with great peach-trees and bright dragons. Yet it was the dream of fabulous Cathay and rare Cipangu that had sent Columbus sailing through Saragossa seas, through the weather of an Andalusian April, to drop anchor in bright islets of feathery trees and glowing birds and gentle people, that were but the outposts of some grandiose continental shore, and had now brought John Cabot back to England with great reports of a mighty world of ice and snow and amazing rivers. In 1500 Columbus was enduring his bitterest year, returning in fetters to the sovereigns for whom he had already sullied the dominions of gold. Vasco da Gama, still in the daring tradition of Prince Henry, having rounded the Cape, and brought Portugal within the solemn gates of a novel India, was resting on his honours. And Leonardo's old acquaintance, Amerigo Vespucci, traveller and adventurer, returned from unauthenticated journeys, was already trying to set the piratical banner of his name flying over the vast New World. All these invaders of unploughed seas were inspiring the serene Republic with a jealous interest. The changing shape of the world had its fascination for Leonardo, who has a hunger for *mappemondes*, though not till after his death did Magellan's *Victory*, famous among heroic ships, come fainting, captainless, reeking of cloves, into Seville, having mysteriously lost a day out of time in her unprecedented voyage.

At times he may go to the Zecca, since he himself can advise his friend Antonio Segni, when he is mint-master at Rome ; and look at the beautiful coins of gold which are the sole proud issue of this tower. He will go to Murano, island of a strange air that is part of the ethereal fabric that bears its name, air aglow with a flame that never expires. The transmutations and liquefactions might attract him ; but the secret

The Way Back to Florence

Republic would not let him approach. How the fiery air and some precious silt changed into the violet-blue and the rare emerald of that ethereal crystal no stranger might know. He might wander instead to Manutius' gracious house, and look at the beautiful book of the *Dream of Poliphilus*, still young from the printing-press, and admire the rare devices, and smile at the intricate allegories of this monkish mind mad-about-Vitruvius. Or he might float out to the island of cypresses, where the jasper wave slept under rosy walls, and sense the languid rivers lapsing, relieved of burthens, through the mysterious lagoons. The mighty motions of the Adriatic tides repose his nerves, while his watching mind observes their hours and variations.

For the rest, there were disturbing things in Venice. Not in the proud Piazza, as the arrogant Condottiere dreamed, but set opposite the Hospital of San Marco, the great horse and man that made the image of Bartolommeo Colleone reminded Leonardo of his old master, of the days when he talked of horses in the bottega, and of his own crumbling insulted masterpiece in Milan. Already he felt that no steed of his would ever ride down the lists of bronze to prove its confident challenge to this. And perhaps he thought that some fatality did lie heavy on the sculptors of conquering shapes, for, if he had lost much vitality over his marvellous model, the once-loved Verrocchio had paid his patient and sincere life for this great piece of insolence. His happy, laborious existence in Florence had been tortured by the caprices of the Republic ; he had in one fierce fit of indignation broken his mould and fled homewards, to be recovered by persuasion and threats of assassination, and to die wasted by the fever of the lagoons, leaving his terrible captain to be cast, not by his dear disciple Lorenzo, as he pleaded, but by the crafty thief Leopardi, who wrote his own name on the bridle of the masterpiece. His disciple of old stood gazing long at it ; he drew it twice from memory thereafter. He had at least discussed and considered the studies for it when he was young and more Florentine than he could ever be again.

How nobly it had endured the searching revelations of the open air ! Leonardo again thought of the steeds galloping through his sketchbooks. A great patrician, Antonio Grimani, whose name was somewhat clouded at present by a defeat at Lepanto, but who had moved within the perilous magnificence of dogeship, was meditating an equestrian portrait, it was said.

x

He was glad enough to meet again Lorenzo da Pavia, who lived in Venice because in her great Eastern markets he found more easily the ebony, ivory, mother-of-pearl, sandalwood, and amber he needed for his beautiful craft, and because the city was as full of music as of spices and the sea. They talked together, and Leonardo showed him the portrait of the princess whose craving for Lorenzo's viols was as keen as her craving for Leonardo's own images of perfection. The lutanist writes to Isabella, telling her it is very like ; and for once that criticism of a portrait was probably heard with pleasure. " Leonardo da Vinci, who is at Venice, has shown me a portrait of your Highness which is of a striking resemblance. Truly it is as well done as is possible." So he wrote, and, taking up her newest lute, he delicately sank a star within the ivory and ebony, for such was her last caprice.

Leonardo departed in April, not even waiting for Ascension Day, when the Doge, with the standards of Saint Mark before him, and the six silver trumpets borne up by young pages, went dazzling down past the pierced balconies, aflower with ladies, to the mythic boat hung with marvel, the floating palace of the Bucentaur, when the gilded keel and the banks of serried oars were set for the Lido-point, followed by thousands of glowing shallops, and the marriage-ring of onyx, lapis, and malachite fell from his idolatrous hands into a bridal sea.

But Leonardo had enough of Venice. He had spoken with the geographers and adventurers ; he had taken more draughts of the East. Lodovico il Moro had been carried captive to France, so his mind was set steadily on his native city.

And, as a human detail, we observe that Leonardo's decorative attendant, Andrea Salaino of the beautiful love-locks, evidently found the gliding gilded ways of Venetian pleasure to his liking, for he borrowed from Leonardo, who makes a rather icy note of it, three golden ducats, because he desires to have made for him shoes of rose-colour with their ornaments. It is April, and the beautiful youth will have roses in his shoes for the spring. Leonardo will remember it with the curious cold exactitude he shows over money when he is offended. Nevertheless Andrea was a lovely popinjay in his rose-and-green raiment, with his faint suggestive smile, and floated like a bright humming-bird through carnival Venice.

Chapter ii

The Return of the Exile

i

LEONARDO had visited his native city at least once during his sojourn in Milan, for, as a Florentine of ever-increasing fame, he had been summoned in 1495 to a consultation concerning the great new Sala del Consiglio. But now he came invested with the authority of a singular perfection in painting and in sculpture, he, the desire of princes, seeking his own Republic, not without pleasure in becoming again a Florentine among the Florentines, home-born among the home-born, the texture of his personality as rich, as supple and as " changeable " as the unique penetrations, the novel evocations of his technique in art. Milan might seem to have dazzled down Florence for a while ; but the City of the Lilies had remained indomitably clear, like a pale acropolis washed out almost behind waves of sunset-colour that could but ebb away, leaving her all the more durably carved in inviolate pearl and ivory.

Possibly he returned with a true nostalgic wistfulness, for he does try for a while to fit himself to his city. Apples of gold on a platter of silver the rosy city of Milan had offered. But Florence held " a new-found agate urn as fresh as day. In the radiant repristination of her morning light, her classic moulded hills, her sharply-drawn vine-terraces and sparse fine decoration of silvering olive branches and pyramids of dark definite cypresses, her most personal dome and gates and towers, lay on purified spaces, lucent washes of colour, pale blue, rose-russet, jade-white and violet. Clear the sunlight, clear the moonlight. God dreamed her landscape over every night, so that, new-minted from sleep, she lay in her pale lustral gold, while her gilded flagstaves carried her rampant lions and her imperious lilies.

The blood-red flowers that had run startlingly under the olives in March were vanishing now, leaving some scarlet laggards here and there. Up in Vallombrosa the floodtide of crocus was hardly ebbing, and the great yellow primroses fell through the ivy into the brooks. The iris in golden companies had taken the reedy banks of the Arno. The temperate blithe air of the Tuscan spring, the nimble and delicate air, seized him again like a child's dream of Paradise. Up in mystic Fiesole, where the Etruscan and the Celt have made some riddling pact, he looked at Monte Ceceri, and already felt that tense bright air under his wings of power. He gazed at the hills of Carrara, amethyst in the sunset, aware of the pillars and shapes of beauty that slept spellbound within them. Weary from the fertile plains, and the glimpses of terrible Alpine heights that have no sense of man, he understood that some might say of the Florentines: " Their gods are gods of the hills, therefore are they stronger than we."

Dominant, splendid, the Palazzo della Signoria sprang, fierce witness to a pride not Milan's. More delicately haughty in its beauty was the loved romantic church of Santa Maria Novella than the loved romantic church of Santa Maria delle Grazie. Aerial in grace, serene in comprehending line, the dome of Brunelleschi put to shame the fretted cupola of Milan. And the fair campanili of that city were fantastic gladioli when you saw Giotto's rose-lily, fit for the bells of heaven, with its angelical sweetness delicately opposing the harshness of the Palazzo Vecchio tower. Nothing, after all, was so fierce and hard as Florence— not all the roses of Milan so sweet as one carved iris-flower.

For the ruddy vine of the Milanese terra-cotta, that clambered over Certosa and Castello alike, with cupids and shields hanging among its leaves and fruit, here were the sudden spaces as of white and blue hyacinths set in shadowy wood and shadowy stone, the Della Robbia roundels and panels and niches and cornices perdurably fresh and fragrant, sensitively giving themselves without riot or effusion, offering themselves graciously with a kind of high-bred courtesy. These were sweet again, with the Florentine sweetness that never loses its poignancy.

ii

The something hard in Florence, that made her

> Gardien pur,
> De la contour,

though it was necessary to her freedom and her intellectual life, the corslet of fine steel irony that covered her passionate heart, while it helped her to build and paint the things that became the criteria of their kinds, also made her difficult. Hers, like Leonardo her son's, was the love that was all crystalline with knowledge ; the blind ecstasy that sweeps away knowledge, dissolved into a mere colour of its obscure wisdom, was not Florentine. " Quia multa amavit " of Milan might sometimes be said, but hardly of Florence. She was as jealous of her

The Return of the Exile

sovereignty as Venice ; though she did love higher things. She loved her ideal of beauty, and she loved liberty. A great Winged Victory from Samothrace, with the immortal air caught in her pure raiment, was how this city beheld beauty. She had once accepted the Provençal doctrine of chivalric love, and lifted it to transcendental heights. Love in the air needs nothing but wreaths of lovely words. Now she had accepted the doctrine of platonic love, and that also was an affair of the intellect, requiring nothing but comely libations and more wreaths of lovely words. For love alone she would yield little ; but for her mingled dream of beauty and of liberty she would spend her treasure and her blood. Like Athens she was restless to set the imposition of her grace and power upon other cities, because she believed sincerely in the supremacy of her peculiar culture. And, like Athens, she looked a little askance at her children of genius, for she knew instinctively that, if her dream was mingled, theirs was single, and that indisputable beauty has her anarchists, on whom no laws are binding save by courtesy. She understood Socrates' policy towards poets who should be crowned with wool, and sent away from cities that feared for their integrity. Like Athens again, she was " the city of honey and hemlock." And when her famous son moved again in her streets, still soft and sumptuous, with his court of pupils and his throng of friends, perfumed and fancifully clad, with smooth, curled hair and beard, with a faint abstraction in his debonair bearing, and a certain satire in his green-hazel eyes, she was aware that his heart was also filled with honey and hemlock, and considered him critically. Moving with his quiet air of greatness, still clothed with that " certain fire and grace," fire not scorching, grace not oversweet, he seemed more or less like the son of a king.

But her honey was wild honey from aromatic hills, and the sweetness of Florence, Leonardo knew again, had a lyric, vibrating quality, a rarefied and piercing effect strange to trance-holden Milan, with all her witless, passive sweetness of crushed roses. It was the searching tenderness escaping from that great imaginative sympathy in which intellectual and emotional qualities are at one. It had a wild yet æsthetic note, like a cleft of rich rock-thyme, like the virginal veins of violet found in some of her fine white marble. The gracious story of the Merciful Knight, the rosy pillars of Samminiato, the ancient and lovely basilica in which he is remembered, such liquid lines of Dante as " In la sua volontade e nostra pace," the immature and touching girls carved by Desiderio and Mino, Verrocchio's primroses and the rare hands that hold them, the winglike pattern on Botticelli's sea, the flowery bambini on the hospital wall, Lorenzo's wistful songs, Poliziano's dreamy refrains, a sonnet of Michelangelo, a page of violets and colombines by Leonardo, are some of the things that betray in various degrees with what kisses Florence could heal when she wounded. He needed her kisses at this moment. For, when the May came singing through the City, he was glad the Lombard capital seemed already so unsubstantial, for if Andrea of Ferrara, with whom he had lived " as a brother," was quartered on its gates, even Leonardo could hardly be indifferent.

iii

Well ! he found Florence in her sweetest mood at first. He crushed the rare wild substance of her grape against his " palate fine," and found it more tonic than the peach-fruits of Milan. The press of eager, intelligent faces, witty with searching out all new things, was welcome. And the young Davids and Saint Georges of Florence, light-foot, vehement and smiling as Hermes, slim and tense like ivory bows, as in the old days of the *Adoration*, quickened his eyes with their airy motions, eyes drowsily surfeited with the dreamy narcissi of Milan.

Still, with that sharp sweetness came a sadness. The *Adoration* was the work of his youth, untired and prodigal of beauty. Since then his secret soul had been macerated with the perfumes of Milan, his imagination had learned to distil a secret spell, and all his intellectual energies had wrestled with every problem that can assail the craft of an artist, and the curiosity of a scientist. Down by the Arno went a ghost of himself, with more tumultuous golden hair, singing and idling when the air of sunset was " like lilies," golden lilies, closely surrounded by ghostly companions. No longer was he a kind of Alcibiades of the arts, humoured because he had beauty, genius, grace, and anything might be forgiven to such an irresistible combination. " My young lord's the lover of every perfect thing " they had said. Now his measure had been taken ; his worth, they thought, was proven. They held him among the highest, but they gazed at him no more in delighted expectation of sheer miracle.

Even he himself was not satisfied with himself. He had done great things, but he had painted too many fair women, and performed a courtier's tricks. " Nevertheless, I have something against thee, because thou hast left thy first love. Remember, therefore, whence thou art fallen," said the stones of Florence to him. So the ruthless, desirous spirit of youth, out of its heavenly place of wings and flames and crested waves, holding Earth between his hands like a mere crystal globe, for ever arraigns the wayfarer who dares to double on his failing track to meet him. It is decidedly the one wise thing for gifted youth to die early,

" And hold to the low lintel up
The unsurrendered challenge-cup."

The Return of the Exile

Now there were those who desired to pit his assured maturity against the fiery youth of Michelangelo. He was tired, for he had lived by consuming nerves and veins, using the very marrow of life in that impassioned Milanese existence; and the Cavallo had exhausted him considerably. When, at every stage, the portcullis falls on us we leave some shred of our soon-ailing mortality, and it is a maimed creature that, having just escaped too many harrowing grilles, at last falls upon the banks of the dark river where there are lilies and a boat.

Besides, the mood of the City had altered as well as his own. It is a trying experience to return to the city of one's youth after long sojourn in a strange capital. Other cities have been kinder, perhaps, like Milan, which gave him all the opportunities he could take, and recognized his autocracy in his arts. The native city keeps the liberty to chide, and old comrades the right to be jealous. Florence was critical; and Leonardo, though he speaks more than once of the value of criticism, did not accept it from all comers. Moreover, the criticism was not so tolerant as it had been.

The attitude towards the artist was almost consciously altered. It was no more the Florence of Cosimo and Lorenzo; and the times were troubled. Lorenzo was dead: the lesser Medici had vanished in exile. Lorenzo had proved once more that a dictator may rule for a lifetime, but will never found a continuous dynasty. The French had sullied the streets of Florence, almost like conquerors, and Capponi had threatened to ring the bells. Jesus Christ had been King in Florence; and two bonfires had troubled and irritated the City's conscience. One had been lit on that Shrove Tuesday when, instead of wreathing love-dances round the flame, the circles watched the hysteric folk cast their wealth of beauty to the fire—manuscripts, jewels, brocades, mirrors, fans, foreign hangings, chess-boards, ivory and alabaster things, perfume-balls and music-books, all lovely vanities and beautiful pictures of naked women. And another had been kindled round a gibbet before the Palazzo della Signoria, one of three. Ironical Florence regretted the first excess, but more she was ashamed by the tragic pyre in the Piazza, when she had forgotten all her Hellenism, and behaved like any barbarian city. Her rankling conscience made her volatile and feverish, readier than ever to divide over any person or matter. The crowds of Piagnoni, Arrabiati, Palleschi, became partisans over every affair; and the Republic was jealous of its dignity. However, Soderini was an earnest and simple gonfalonier. Machiavelli's pleading and power were reorganizing the militia, Pisa had been reconquered more or less, and there was a kind of peace.

Nevertheless, the jubilee year of 1500 was a year when all Italy was troubled with a sense of glory, guilt, and impending doom. It was the triumph of the Borgia. They saw him throned in Saint Peter's with Lucrezia, and Sanchia, and the marvellous young beauty Giulia Farnese, with excess of golden hair and golden brocades matching their glories at his feet, while Cesare, blond and beautiful, and most dangerous of the coil, laid down the Golden Rose to slay his totem bull before them. Yet the world crowded to Rome, afraid lest the indulgence of God, still shed even from such a sacrilegious vessel, might be lost. Expiatory figures in black and white, claiming the stigmata of Saint Catherine, move through that quivering air, conscious of mystical iniquity. It is an air that thickens with the gilded motes of Lucrezia's bridal pageants passing through conquered cities, and is mournful with many litanies.

Nevertheless, Copernicus lectured in Rome this year amid applause, and presently the ships of Spain and Portugal would confound Alexander's easy dividing line by meeting in amazement where East ran into West.

Florence was now a Republic, jealously watched, and sensitive with the apprehensions of danger. No longer did the artistic despot sympathetically recognize the despotic artist as a creature beyond law, subject only to the disciplines of his ideal, as Cosimo did, Lorenzo did. The artist was admirable, but there was no reason why he should not be a good citizen like another. This was now a city where puritans could stone Michelangelo's *David*, and begin to suspect Botticelli's sad beauty of a heresy. Whether Piagnoni or Palleschi cried, however, Florence was now in no mood to allow even her artists to be "idiots." The *Judith* of Donatello lent no more her sinister grace to the Medicean cortile; she was subdued to the service of the City. That fragile and triumphal heroine, with exquisite sadistic half-aversion, now stood sworded and memorial before the Palazzo della Signoria: "To all who should think to tyrannize over Florence." (As a statue she was a little wronged thereby, for the small luxurious figure was meant for an intimate setting.)

But Leonardo, while proud to call himself a Florentine, felt that he conferred a distinction and owed no duty farther. In the end Soderini complained that Leonardo had served the Republic badly; and no fair-minded person but will agree with him. Leonardo never fulfilled one Florentine commission. Milan had unfitted him for the asperity of a republic doubtful of luxury-loving artists. But is that the only reason? Is it not that ever in his consciousness wells the dark wound of a staunchless wrong? What was done to him "when young," he cannot forgive.

iv

With all that, he was rapturously greeted, and his house was besieged by students from the north, and by envoys of princes. Still, it was not

The Return of the Exile

the glad Renaissance morning of Verrocchio's bottega, when, exalted with high hopes, so many artists talked together of adventurous names and great discoveries. Not only had Piero de' Medici been driven out, but the Medicean palace, with all its power for creation as a school of art, had been sacked and scattered in 1494. Savonarola had broken the mood of the pure love of beauty. Verrocchio, the Pollaiuoli, Ghirlandajo were dead. Of the surviving artists all had been scarred by both the fires of the fierce Ferrarese, who with great images out of Ezekiel and the Apocalypse had lured their souls into the dangerous ecstasy of penitence. The artist, like a monk, is always a little given to self-torture ; and the idolater is more kin to a breaker of images than to a mere tolerator of them. Savonarola saw a dark satanic flame behind the figured things of beauty, and their makers, as if stricken by the fulminating compliment, rapturously threw them on the pyre. They caught the contagion of his terrible warning, they responded to the inverted sensuality of his denunciation, to the speech of darkness, splendidly embroidered with fierce lascivious images of great iniquitous queens who bruise the breasts of their virginity in Egypt and Assyria, of horsemen clothed in burning blue, "all of them desirable young men, even horsemen riding on horses," exceeding in dyed attire upon their heads, with monstrous visions, coloured like amber and fire and brass, of faces and wings, terrible apparitions of cherubim among their whirling wheels, and all baleful beauty doubly fair as, soft with doom, it falls to destruction. With nerves acute as his they listened for the armies of death and the galloping of the horsemen of the Apocalypse.

The mystic hill of Fiesole was now an image of Calvary. Lorenzo the Magnificent had been dead since 1498, taking the peace of Italy with him. Marsilio Ficino lay at rest in the comprehending Duomo. Poliziano also was dead in sorrow, wrapt in a Dominican shroud. The adorable Pico della Mirandola had burned his five books of love-verses, as he had burned his passion, his knowledge, his beauty, his wisdom of old religions, like some rare Arabian incense sweetening the bonfire to a jealous God. He had ceased his "climbing after knowledge infinite," put off his rare golden dream of the platonic and celestial love that alters its initiate from man to angel, and altered to a passionate flagellant, before he died in a vision of Our Lady, and was hid away in the cool cloisters of San Marco like a flower deflowered by a fiery tempest. His friend Benivieni, always devotional in mood, now went sombrely, a complete Piagnone, also trying to forget the ethereal climaxes of the "Symposium." These minds, sick of their subtleties, heard from Savonarola with an obscure flick of pleasure that "an old woman could have more saving faith than Plato." But that the Jesus Christ who had

Leonardo the Florentine

been King in Florence was not the sweet Galilean, the murder of that fair and noble young man, Lorenzo Tornabuoni, had too terribly proved.

As for the painters, Filippino was still working sweetly away in his fixed romantic manner. Fra Bartolommeo was now a melancholy monk, and a depressed copyist, though, like Filippino, he took some heart again from the return of Leonardo, and began to draw beautiful women like sad lilies, and essay larger ways with his drapery. That old studio friend, the impressionable Lorenzo di Credi, was trembling like a leaf in the wind of Apocalypse and refusing to touch a brush : he also steadied again under the old enchantment. Piero del Cosimo somewhat mechanically continued his work, with occasional gleams of fancy from his Greekish fairyland. A new painter naturally disposed to fuse some of Leonardo's suavity and soft light with his own gracious and resigned vision had arisen in Andrea del Sarto, soon to be at work where the lilies lay in the portals of the Annunziata. That other old friend, Perugino, was now equably at work in Florence in a bottega of his own, prosperous and reputed, turning out school-pieces with some cynicism, considerable avarice, and that steady recollection of the lighted arches of his Umbrian skies which atoned for much.

Botticelli he found in depressing case, his evocations of wistful en-glamoured paganism ended for ever. But his was still an example of the divided heart. He had cast his " many most beautiful naked women " into the flames, to satisfy that fierce prophet who, like all puritans, had shown his sense of the fearful fascination of beauty and the unchaste appetite of his heart by appeasing his desire with its destruction. Now he sate moodily in his bottega, still shaken by his recollection of that prophet, yet listening to the idlers like the prophet's enemy, Doffo Spini, who thronged his studio because he had that wilful taste for wanton jesting which is often merely a desperate counterpoise against the crushing weight of melancholia. He continued drawing the severe and exquisite arabesques to which he confined the shadow and fire of the cantos of Dante, and in that very jubilee year he painted his last great picture of the *Mystic Nativity*, with the memorial of the martyrs below, and that ineffable valediction of his early colour and unearthly emotion above, where the ring of angels with love-linked hands, and patterned palm branches, serenely keeps the pale-gold sky. The strange inscription upon it is the key of one mood in the Florence of 1500 : " This picture at the end of the year 1500 in the troubles of Italy, I, Alessandro, painted in the half-time after the time, at the time of the fulfilment of the 11th of S. John in the second war of the Apocalypse, in the loosing of the

The Return of the Exile

devil for $3\frac{1}{2}$ years, then he shall be chained according to the twelfth, and we shall see him trodden down as in the picture."

So the sense of unnatural doom and ascetic preparation, the brooding hysteria of the *dies iræ* over again, in a period struggling heroically and vainly to return to the Periclean days of Hellas, hung over lucid Florence. Conflicting and contemptuous, the reckless revelry of the gay companions, the dukes of pleasure, stormed down the narrow streets, but consciously defiant, without the old dancing radiance. Soderini, with simplicity, honesty, and some nobility, tried to keep his unnerved Republic true to a classic ideal ; and Machiavelli brilliantly and thanklessly tried with the wisdom of the serpent to reinforce the innocence of the dove.

Leonardo, who loathed a libertine and mocked at monks, who rejected the idea of dramatic supernatural vengeances with the triple rejection of the scientist aware of natural law, the artist convinced of God as an artist too, and the profound mystic refusing to see in the mere shadows of human terror the inconceivable heralds of divine purpose, resented the distractions in the Florentine air. The Hebraic note, which is distinctly present with all other notes in the full chord of the Renaissance, is hardly perceptible in Leonardo. (If there is any Bible in Leonardo's unconsciousness, it is a strange mingling of an etherealized Song of Songs and the Fourth Gospel.) His Jerome might be Job, who is not Hebraic at all. The poised and smiling, the Sophoclean, presence of Leonardo had its effect on the artists. Fra Bartolommeo and Lorenzo di Credi, at least, recovered equanimity, and took on discipleship again. The clear citadel of Leonardo's intelligence, adamant against hysteria, sent its diamond rays through the Florentine disquiet. His nerves might be irritated, but not his intelligence. And he could still prevail by his charm and his wonder-compelling art. That his city had not lost the power of æsthetic ecstasy he was speedily to prove, when the exhibition of the great cartoon of *Saint Anne and the Virgin*, with the liberating power of a beauty sovran and strange, subdued and reconciled the factions, for a little while at least, with the spell of mere delight. In this vibrating picture Leonardo struck with might that full chord of the Renaissance of which we speak ; and undid Savonarola by a beautiful subterfuge, including the Hebraic note indeed, but only as it dreams into the moaning of Syrian doves in the music of the Canticles.

v

But he was to become aware very soon of a new and definite challenge among the artists of Florence in the person of the young Michelangelo.

315

Leonardo the Florentine

On him, a boy of fifteen, Savonarola had also set the imprint of his burning personality. " The memory of his living voice still remaining on his mind," Michelangelo through strange confusions was haunted by the great Dominican till the end, though the remembrance seems chiefly the ache left by a kind of shock to the morbid neurasthenia that clings like the corroding shirt of fire to his mighty, artistic imagination, exciting it for ever to images of agony and doom. Yet Marsilio Ficino's Hellenistic gospel had been and remained dearer to Michelangelo than the monk's: he had wrought figures of Adonis and Bacchus and the platonic Eros in the year of the prophet's death ; and he behaved at the time as if unaffected by that historic pyre. Since Michelangelo had carved his mask of a faun in the gardens of Lorenzo he had been a Hellenist ; since at fifteen years of age he heard Savonarola preach he had been a Hebraist. The two cross-currents continued to vex his soul to the end ; yet the struggle between Greek god and Hebrew prophet resulted in the overwhelming and original images of the Sistine Chapel and the tomb of Julius.

From the beginning he hated Leonardo. At this time Michelangelo was still young, not yet marred by his pathological avarices and his furies of unconscionable labour, though already disfigured by the famous and infamous blow that Torrigiano dealt before Masaccio's frescoes. Probably he looked like one of those sullen and nobly modelled figures who stand round his Roman Virgin in the National Gallery, for, as Leonardo held, not only he but every artist is Narcissus. The young man, who loved to think himself a descendant of the great Matilda's, who had lived as a son in the lyre-playing house of Lorenzo, who had learned thoroughly the aristocratic arch-doctrine of platonic love, of which Leonardo was a more uncanonical scholar, who had already tricked the experts in antique statuary with the long, lapsing beauty of his sleeping *Love*, carved a proud low-relief of Lapiths and Centaurs, and invested his vision of the *Pietà*, a pure goddess mourning an Olympian fallen, with a crystal sorrow and a vestal fire, resented the court kept by the notary's love-child, resented the natural grace and courtesy of Leonardo, so much more princely than he. He detested the curled hair, the perfumed hands, the silk-sheathed figure, the assured beauty of Leonardo, and most of all his deprecating courtesy, as of a great sovereign. Already the conflicts of his irritable soul and body had made him avaricious, careless of himself as anything but an artist, and already his neurasthenic terrors and manias of suspicion drove him into loneliness. " The love of virtue, and the continual practice of the fine arts, made him solitary," says the biographer, inspired by himself. Though Leonardo also praised solitude, he certainly was no anchorite of art. His idolaters crowded round his

The Return of the Exile

doors, in the finely intolerant mood of those who would say to all tales of wonderful folk hereafter :

" I loved a Phœnix in my youth, so you may have your way."

An attitude despised by Michelangelo. But indeed everybody must have seemed dull after Leonardo, with his ironic smile and his lovely riddling way. The younger artist would then console his jealousy by mocking at the other's long periods of preparation, which seemed to him sterility. The two were just like enough to be wholly incompatible. For instance, Michelangelo had already studied anatomy to the point of illness in bodies provided for him out of San Spirito. What sickens the more muscular but less finely organized physique of Michelangelo, the subtler set of nerves and more delicately adjusted body will bear like chilled steel. In the grappling with statuary, however, the muscular grip will tell.

vi

When the first enthusiasm was over, Leonardo felt jarred by the critical and emulous atmosphere, and found it difficult to recover from the great discomposure that attends on all transitions. His art seemed more and more a cruel exaction in this air of conflict ; so, as usual, we find he is taking refuge in mathematics. When all the secret processes of the creative spirit have been disturbed by change of scene, rarely comes the fortunate moment when a thing of beauty may spring sudden and consummate from an electric imagination ; and a sense of frustration prevents him from drawing the flower of perfection through the slow leaves of patience, or nursing the sullen red to a bright flame of wonder. So Leonardo hides away from accidia in mathematics and geometry more than ever before. From the hyperæsthesia of his divine nerves, ruffled by the sense of Florentine, Italian, human disaster, he retires to the most remote and difficult cloister of abstract thought. His mind puts off the last vestige of troubling colour, sound, perfume, remembrance of friendly faces. For in the mathematical sciences there is indeed rest for such artists as can ascend the smooth vanishing stair of their spiral towers. To be a mathematician and a scientist, no need to delve in one's own aching and throbbing experience, to macerate the substance of one's love, hate, dread, mortal weariness and madness. In the calm immutable world of mathematics the soul walks cool and unvexed. It is not art that is an " escape from life," art that is the very concentration and passionate religious Imitation of life. In the world of art, ineffable fingers will find some ancient pain in the heart of the coldest æsthete. A colour, a chord, a marriage of words, a suggested fragrance will

317

suddenly break over again the astonied heart with the shock of some exquisite lost felicity. Safer the Tower of facetted Crystal than the Tower of Ivory.

vii

Glimpses of Leonardo at this time come through the correspondence of Isabella d'Este with her friends and agents in Florence. Her nets were fine, and they were cast wide. She drew them in with her greedy patrician hands, all glittering with beauty's plunder, and with arts and splendours cheated her diamond heart. Like Leonardo she cared chiefly for herself, and the courteous duel between the two proceeds admirably. But the lady has nothing to give in exchange for what she wants. She would willingly have stabled the unicorn himself among her rare beasts, but the unicorn must be more splendidly stalled than in Mantua. So she begins her long sweet siege of him in Florence. Fra Pietro da Novellaria, Vice-General of the Carmelites, who has been preaching at Santa Croce the penitential sermons from which the mobile Florentines wrung the true Lenten flavour of their hyssop after their vivid carnivals, is one of her friends. He must tell her what kind of life Leonardo is living, if he is working and at what, and how long he will be in Florence. Will he do a picture for her studio ? If so, she will leave all things, subject and time of performance, to the painter. If that be too much to ask, will he paint her a little picture of the Madonna, " devoto e dolce," as is his manner ? And, as " our illustrious lord " has given away her copy of the drawing he made of her, may she have another ? To which the churchman replied that Leonardo's manner of life is most changeable and uncertain, that he lives " from day to day." He has made only one sketch of the Virgin and Saint Anne. Here the preacher describes a cartoon in which the arrangement resembles that of the Louvre picture, and says that Saint Anne " may be a type of the Church who would not hinder the passion of Christ." So the orthodox cast their sweet apology over Leonardo's beautiful heretical picture, even as they had for long over the mysterious bridal figure of the Shulamite, seen through a silver smoke of spices among the silver lilies amid the passionate antiphonies of the Song of Songs.

The friar adds that otherwise Leonardo is absorbed in geometry and quite tired of painting. Two apprentices paint portraits in his studio, which, in passing, he sometimes touches with a caressing brush or the subtle thumb of the fine-fingered hand. The pupil, Salaino, is evidently the master of ceremonies. On Wednesday of Holy Week the fair young man with the enormous mass of curls, long and fleecy, like a brother of Rapunzel, introduces the diplomatic monk to Leonardo's studio. The

The Return of the Exile

painter is absorbed in mathematical experiments and can hardly bear the sight of a paint-brush, though he is at work on a little picture for Florimond Robertet, the powerful secretary of the King of France. He is very charming, however, and, if he can complete his engagement with King Louis by the end of the month, he would rather work for Isabella than for anybody else, which is obviously his debonair way of refusal, for the King of France is a competitor that can but crush the lady. In June, however, she writes to the Ferrarese envoy and ducal orator, Manfredo de' Manfredi, enclosing a letter written with her own hand for the painter. But neither the persuasive speech nor the sweet words " in mano propria sua " can prevail. He does not even answer it. When he is urged, he tells Manfredi at last that " I might say he had begun to do as you wished." (It is about this time that Isabella's father, Ercole d'Este, asks the Governor of Milan for the remnant of the Sforza steed ; and is told that King Louis has expressed a wish to keep it. We hear of it no more.)

In 1502 she asks her own agent, Francesco Malatesta, to inspect three precious vases from the Medicean collection for which she longs ; and, unvanquished, desires him to get the opinion of Leonardo, " who used to live in Milan, and who is our friend." Leonardo is nothing loth to do something in tune with the hours he spares from mathematics as an aristocratic flâneur and penetrative connoisseur. Wonderful toys ! Worthy the fine estimation of his eyes and the valuation of his long hands. Over one he is enthusiastic. It is a crystal vase all of one piece, with a very fine silver-gilt stand and cover. He " never saw a finer." You see a pure shape of silver fire and pale gold aglow between his palms. It is a Greeklike thing, you say, and he loves it. But next he lifts a cup of thin cloudy amethyst, rose and purple, studded with pearls and rubies, from its golden stand. That also he finds unique and most desirable. Ah ! Asia too, you say ! Nor does the tender hollow of agate, nor the curved shard of jasper on the silver stand go unpraised. Lorenzo's name in Roman letters is written on them all. Lorenzo's treasures, desired by Isabella, valued by Leonardo ! Well, she has spent too much lately ; she cannot have them. And she desists from Leonardo meantime, though not despairing yet. She busies herself awhile with Gian Bellini, who, more and more absorbed with grave Madonnas in a deepening sunset light, explains obstinately that he is not good at " fantasies." It is a " fantasy " she will have, so she loses her temper with Gian Bellini.

It seems as if, in his first reaction of pleasure towards the welcome and reviving air of his Florence, Leonardo had a fit of animated regression towards the time when he drew Madonnas more human, more intent on their children than on their own nymphæan reverie. It is admitted

319

that, for all his mathematics, he is making a little picture of a Madonna with a spindle for Florimond Robertet, a verse-making courtier who is a favourite of King Louis, and, as his secretary, powerful in Italy. There is a drawing for it in the Uffizi, the child grasping the cross-like winder with reverted tragic look, the Madonna gracious and sweetly ironic—not so tender as those whose children played with kittens long ago. But in another Louvre drawing of the same type the Madonna is faint and sweet, drawn and withdrawn like a dream, while the earnest baby, one hand in a dish of fruit, impulsively presses the other on his mother's face.

His actions seem to tell that already he has taken a decision, though it is hardly known to his waking mind. It is likely that, even when he pondered in Milan, he doubted if any state in Italy could employ him as he wished, and fatalistically foresaw himself assigned to the invader. With much of his inclination, with considerable good will indeed, he seems to have given his native city its opportunity. But he can never be whole-hearted about it, for he steadily maintains his relations with Milan.

viii

Yet he had a great triumph, and that in his art of painting. When he came to Florence he found that the Servite friars desired an altarpiece for their chapel in Santissima Annunziata. Filippino had been commissioned, but, hearing that the great Leonardo had a mind to supplant him, sweet-tempered as ever, and remembering other times when he had been the gentle inheritor of the master's arrogant negligences, he gladly yielded the task. The flattered monks received the lord of painters and his company within their own dwelling, while the mood lasted. Probably Leonardo had meditated his theme since the commission for the monks of the Conception in Milan turned his mind towards the great mediæval mystery of virgin-worship, half in sympathy, half in irony, for the point of derision in the real imaginative passion of Leonardo never altogether flickers out. The cult of Saint Anne, with its implications of more than one miraculous birth, had been growing in intensity even in high Renaissance—perhaps because the high Renaissance was pluralist in its attitude towards divinity. It must also be remembered that her festival was passionately dear to the Florentines as their day of liberation from a dreadful tyranny. In 1501 Leonardo exhibited his great cartoon, much like the picture, but more beautiful in some ways, for the draperies were probably as finished as in the detailed drawings. Then Florence gave herself up to holiday, oblivious of all faction and disquiet, renewed and exultant in a novel epiphany of pure beauty. Never had more " strangely beautiful " human forms been more wonderfully woven together against a more mysterious world. Never had picture disengaged a more poignant and startling emotional effect. Never had a mediæval half-heretical dream like this of the doubled virgin-lily been set so nobly and mightily to flower in Elysian space into something Greek and solemn and eternal. Lissom and august, regal and exquisite, the two goddesses interwove with the child, creating carelessly and perfectly their self-enclosed pyramid and climax of sweetness according to the serene laws of their own rare world. The people of Florence did not argue doctrinal validities. Holy Church had given and accepted the theme, and they were freed for mere pleasure when Leonardo the Florentine told them, in this mystery of the eyes, all that he had learned and felt in the sacred iniquitous City of Milan. They were " overpowered with joy." " The whole city was stirred, and you might have fancied that you saw a procession on some solemn feast-day." Girolamo Casio wrote a sonnet on the group, and people went about repeating it. As for the artist, he smiled at his Circean women so undesirous of mariners, and, sighing at the implacable extortions of art, sat down to plan new diversions of the Arno as a relief.

Of course the monks were left pictureless, and Filippino began to help them once more. He died, however, and Perugino had to spare them some Umbrian sky in the end. As the head of Saint Anne became more and more hieratical, coifed as with wings of a " covering cherub," more and more the image of all his soul contained and all that it desired, Leonardo felt more and more loth to let it go. The picture went to Milan with him, and there grew into a great " school " subject. He took it to France, and Francesco Melzi brought it home again ; but Cardinal Richelieu redeemed it for his country in the end.

ix

The theme of what might be called Leonardo's greatest personal picture seems at first surprisingly alien to his modern and unchristian psychology. Why did he deliberately choose a mediæval doctrine with a prescribed traditional attitude of mediæval naïveté touching absurdity ? He liked mediævalism ; the subtle mind which discerned the differences of light in the edge of a shadow could have balanced the angels on the point of a needle. He would have been at home with the schoolmen, and debated with the great Duns Scotus, who had indeed helped to raise Anne into her mystical state as the virgin mother of the Virgin. The ingenious recession of the mediæval conception pleased him ; the challenge of the traditional attitude to his powers of composition delighted him, for the more difficult a thing the more he cared to do it ;

and, finally, he was as much fascinated by the notion of virginity as any of the rapt makers of the litanies. It was a theme in which he could pour much of his own strange psychology, enriched and heavy from the emotional atmosphere of Milan ; he could steep it in all incense-like heresies of the soul and set it safely over the altar.

Saint Anna Metterza (herself the third)—that is, Saint Anne with the Virgin and Child as her attributes—had a cult that grew in importance during the great years of the Renaissance. The anxious doctors of divinity and the æsthetic enthusiasts of Virgin-worship had long considered her with mythopoeic, curiously-imagining eyes. Startling flowers of ecstasy had sprung in the deserts and cloisters, litanies like epithalamies, marvellous orchid-like lilies to lay at the feet of the mystical Virgin who saved their souls from the mire. The burning bush of her chastity was a wonder that consumed their earthly lusts. Pure, she must come from the pure, a mystery out of a mystery. Since it was impossible to push parthenogenesis too far back, some souls had been audacious enough to break as much as possible her line of human generation, and to emblazon her being by the introit of some divine creature, even as the women in the myths of old religions were deified.

At first content with providing a miraculous birth for the Virgin by giving her parents too old for physical desire, pure as white ashes are pure, they soon hated to think that the beauty pure as white altar-flame is pure, whose womb was the bridal chamber for a god, their garden enclosed, their fountain unsealed, their fruited branch, their tower of ivory, their lily beloved mystically with all the diverted passion of their souls and bodies too, should issue from such cold and unlovely copulation. So some said the Virgin was born of the light and delicate kiss given by Anne to Joachim when she went back to meet him at the Golden Gate, a herdsman among the white soft flocks. Popular tradition dwelt upon Anne, imagining sweet stories for the conception they would have as immaculate as the Virgin's own. The horrified churchmen intervened ; and, deeply learned in physiology, decided that Our Lady was stainless, not from the moment of physical generation, but from the moment of " animation," so that she was born in a state of original grace. Dreamy schismatics did more for Saint Anne. Ebionites and Nestorians and all fierce Arians tried to destroy her while they diminished her daughter, but Collyridians proclaimed her essential virginity, and a strange Manichæan sect of Araby declared her an angel incarnate. It was an æsthetic as well as a mystical desire that had worked at the legend of Saint Anne, intent upon creating things rich and pure, wafting strange pollen from heathen myths to double the lily, an æsthetic desire still inspiring a Leonardo.

From the Orient her feast had been carried to the sweet far-dreaming

The Return of the Exile

cathedrals of Winchester and Canterbury. Through the orchard ways of fantastical Provençal romance and the brooding mysticism of Spain it had come back to Italy, guarded and tended everywhere by the romantic Order of Saint Francis. She was, however carefully the Church might define her and differentiate her conception from Mary's, the virgin mother of the Virgin. She was the beautiful and angelical mother of beauty as Leda was, and some of her strange sweet apocrypha gave her a marvellous genesis. She was born of a fragrance, she had the tree for father, she was born of a prince, she was an angel herself. She was heathen, fragrant, prince-like, angelical. And at last Leonardo made her apotheosis, as if for the high-pointed pediment of some green sea-temple upon unimaginable Ephesian shores.

East and West conspired in the story, till Saint Anne became a mysterious figure, fit for the Renaissance and for Leonardo, seen under the " covering wings of cherubim." The theologians found mysterious verses in the prefiguring books of the prophets and most of all in the Canticles. " Under the apple-tree I raised thee up, there thy mother was corrupted, there she was defiled that bore thee." Such an inextricable song of strange passion, confounding a tenderness for birth, with a dim, sombre hatred for the physical cause of birth, and the immortal arrogance of a love transcending the conditions of life, gives the mystical text and unearthly rhythm for Leonardo's own mood as he paints the one type of woman he could have endured, a type not impossible to, but hardly compatible with, humanity, since he paints her in his own image, " his sister, his spouse."

x

So far as these goddesses are human they create a grave sweet unison of sex. He had made one undisturbed harmony in *The Last Supper*. He gives the other rare thiasos here. Woman, child, and hidden angel (for Manichean Milan had kept some echo of the Arabian story of Anne) he repeats the chord of *The Virgin of the Rocks;* but with what far echoes, what reverberations and repercussions of spiritual lutes and timbrels ! So transcendent of sex was the imagination of Leonardo that it could dare anything. The divine child looks back to his mother in love ; the mother leans to him tenderly from her mother's knee ; she who is the enigmatic First Cause of them both with smiling eyes charms them fast within the aerial pyramid of bliss, substantiate with her creative dream.

xi

He must have begun this great vibrating composition before he came to Florence, for there are many studies before he discovers exultingly

323

the solution of his triangular problem. Through hazes of vital spiral lines, cocoons of imaginative floss, the figures emerge, slowly visible, locking themselves gradually into their great pyramid of dreams. At first he is not aware that the poignant apex of his vision is the dangerous, beautiful head of Saint Anne, the face he has sought so long, discerning mere shadows of it in mortality. Through drawing on drawing he finds his way to her. Then he concentrates on that, dwelling luxuriously on the heavy eyes, the lovely mouth with lifted corners, and twines the woven hair with hieratic diadems, with the bizarre coifs and veils of an Eastern priestess. With all the intensity of a passion too perverse or too rare to wreak itself on anything but dream-stuff, he bids her put on divinity. The figure of the young Saint John disappears. Leonardo's saint has vanished into Anne herself. Type and antitype, solstice god and ritual dancer, begin to be as one. The Herodiad is stilled, she is at the centre of the spiral ; but from her dynamic beauty more throbbing beauty proceeds. The love-breathing woman who bows from her knee to the child, the beautiful child who is a god, are her marvellous attributes. Virgin mother of the Virgin, shrine within shrine, enchanted perspective and rich recession of mystery ! She whose angelic flesh created the pure womb of Mary, and began the mysterious canticle, gazes smiling and remote. God loves his mother and so does she. " Tota pulchra es, et macula non est in te."

xii

To the bending head of the Virgin, Leonardo also gives a solicitous consideration in his drawings. It is sweeter, less startling, more emotional. She is the tenderness of that strange figure so much more than tender. In the cartoon at Burlington House, Leonardo has drawn an alternative version, in which the women are more equal and more humanized. It is lovelier than the picture, as the picture is more beautiful than the cartoon. The juxtaposed heads are mystical in the soft chiaroscuro, soft as the Dove's breast ; but they are maiden-sweet. The Saint Anne of the picture is the sublimation of the virgin-harlot of many Eastern religions, she who stirs behind both Artemis and Aphrodite, she whose divine nature for ever repures and recastles itself from the embraces of her lovers. Here she is chaste as mortal women are, and only her pointing hand gives her an enigmatic and annunciant grace. As for the Virgin, she is sweet as Andromache. The two women are almost side by side, like dear sisters. They are Morning and Evening Star, they are Twilight and Sleep, they are the Music and the Song, they are like " the cloud-moon and the water-moon " and the children are jasmine flowers from their intimate double trance of grace, a psychical atmosphere that seems to become visible in the luminous moon-cloud of *smorzata* light. This delicate diffusion of the emotion steals dewy through the mind, though it cannot make the great attack of the pyramidal trinity, terrible as an army with banners.

It is in this cartoon, however, that the supple soothing raiment falls in such folds of beauty as have often recalled the robes of the three calm women in the Parthenon pediment. There is a drawing for the Virgin's raiment where the light and shadow lie as nobly as on a far hillside, and where the lines are inevitable and proud and sweet as cadenzas or cascades.

xiii

But in the great picture that went to France with Leonardo, and was for ever unfinished, the lithe and gracious limbs have fallen into their divine diagonals, and with the child and the lamb, drawn closer by seducing looks, have closed their monumental pyramid of grace ; their pulsating and ethereal incantation is complete, and beauty possesses them with a sound of violins, from the base of their perfect feet, set upon agate, among cyclamen, iris, and borage, to the apex, the paramount and paradisal face of Saint Anne. So they sit through all eternity in light and shadow and strange smiles, lost within their own enchanted world, that seems a birthplace of lapis and a sublimation of emerald, an un-chronicled realm of glaciers, rocks, and waters, bathed in its own green unearthly glow, while their rhythmic bodies interweave a mystic knot and pattern of immortal passion, communicating wonder.

It would be easy to dwell for long on the details of the beauty of this amazing page in the history of art. The tree that stands dark and brooding in its branches may be the tragic tree of life and death that grows first in the *Adoration* light, and is now like a sombre remembrance of the distant earth in these peripheries of sea-music. How gracious is the child ! The delicate surfaces are rubbed and spoiled, cruder hands than Leonardo's have touched the picture when his own began to lapse from their long and fine obedience to his will. But the fluent flesh is cool and sweet and inviolable as the waves : and the hands in the picture are of a sacrosanct perfection, like the hands that touch the holy things. The gaze is the remote far-gazing look of divinity in all the ages, Greek, Egyptian, Buddhistic, Byzantine, Giottesque. As the Praxitelean Hermes gazes with remote sweetness far beyond the child on his arm, so Saint Anne beyond the baby who seizes the symbolic lamb.

There are shifts and strangenesses in this vision, as in all Leonardo's visions. The archaic intensity of emotion, the Greek ease and greatness, the ambiguous gaze of Saint Anne combined with the strange attitude

Leonardo the Florentine

of Mary, which always surprises those unversed in the tradition, confuse the mind. Where can there be a great Greek line-pattern with intensity of emotion, but emotion Ionian and feminine? There is a dream of Lesbos. Could Sappho, with such divine irony, so have gazed at Anactoria on some Leucadian shore? No; the eyes of Anne might be Lesbian, but Anne is an angel. (No matter if Leonardo knew the old Manichean legend. She had become his angel, his dæmon, his own familiar angelic spirit, before he finished her, and no mere woman.) It was within the psychology of Leonardo to convey his own psychical mystery of Greek love to another sex; but his emotional web is more subtly woven. The women are not mortal, the chastity of such beauty forbids the notion of human and feverish desire. Only divine creatures can bear the weight of his nympholepsy. Are they Demeter and Persephone tending the child of Eleusis, and have the questing torches glimmered and died by the mysterious strand? Or is it Aphrodite fallen on Dione's lap? The tenderness is Olympian and mysterious; it is a revelation of an original mode of feeling, a passionate transcendence of sex, and its annunciants and acolytes are women because the eyes and hands of women have been hollowed and carved by immemorial religions to be the only things fine enough and sensitive enough for the lamps and lovers of new liturgies.

Except for scenes of state ritual, the Greeks, like Leonardo, separated the sexes when they desired a purely æsthetic effect. The consummate tenderness of the Ludovisi throne, where the covering grace of the acolytes yearns to the wistful, lifted hands of the goddess, while the isolated girls at the end intently burn the incense and sound the pure flute in another pale sea-world inviolate to man, has something of this exquisiteness, though it is more innocent and morning-wild. And in history, or rather in literature, there is a great instance of this triumphal interaction of psychical sympathy. When the dying Charmian binds the diadem of the dead Egypt, by whom Iras has already fallen on sleep, there is a unison and a league of all the passionate adorations and loyalties that women can bear each other. " Is this well done, Charmian?— Verie well, said she." It is a far cry from the last triumph of Cleopatra to the flawless unearthly sanctuary of Saint Anne; but there is the same transcending unison, and the same unassailable challenge. The presence of the child only deepens the note; the child is still one with his mother, and his mother is a virgin.

Leonardo had his notion of the only beauty of woman he could endure. The type he desires is an echo of himself: it is the face that rises through all the fair fountains to meet his own. He painted it most definitely in Saint Anne. And, since the only type of woman he could endure was nymph or angel, a creature irradiated with a quality not to be won from human experience, so strangely she smiles and looks, more than mortal. Yet she is credible as a feminine shape, and there have been women a little like her. Enough of Leonardo was feminine to make a convincing Renaissance dream of a woman—a woman in whom " a great prince in prison lies." And, having created her, he sets her jealously away from possible Joachims, as he exiles his Virgin Marys from the saints. Her attributes are another woman and a child, all interlinked in a rarity of unearthly sympathy. As an æsthete desiring a unison of beauty where the conflict of sex shall not be even as perceptible as the moth-wings of shadow on a luminous sea, as a mysterious soul desiring, for all his science, impossible genealogies where none may intervene but gods or angels with covering wings and searching fires, he recesses her in a double mystery of parthenogenesis, and cloisters her with essential companions in a cool green world outside space and time, like a crescent moon with a star within her lap and a spilt starlet at her feet. He abolishes physical sex in this amazing page of pure beauty ; he removes his virgin shapes from the embrace that for him is an unlovely duel of masked hatred. From their immunities they may provoke. None could violate. Though, from Leonardo's own account, they could move nympholepts like himself to bring a desperate ecstasy within the world of dreams, they themselves have ichor in their veins, and are as far removed from mortal desire and its satiety as if their strange rocks were the star-embroidered chair of Cassiopeia.

xiv

But all this picture is not meant to be definable in words. It is a marvellously woven gesture of Leonardo's soul. By this mighty arrangement of the Virgin, the Child, and the exquisite surrogate of the Angel, he intended first to surprise by a beautiful audacity, and then to soothe by the wordless wave of pure beauty that sweeps you to enchanted seas of eternity. He makes his fantastic knot of dream-experience, an emerald-burning cipher, haughty and sweet, not to be translated into human language, but to liberate and exalt and quicken mortality with a sense of deepening emotion, of communions and exaltations just beyond the senses. It is a kindling at the edges, a sounding of citharas among the asphodel just over the borders. Its literary parallel is the gold-and-sable poem of *The Phœnix and the Turtle*, which even so builds its cadences of exultant threnodic flutes into the soft climaxes of incredible epithalamia beyond space and time, a rapture for souls that have out-soared their ashes. These great creatures, born in original grace, lost in some island between Asia and Greece, maintain an ethereal and august existence according to their own unimaginable laws, keeping their own attitudes. echoing their own chords, sweetness in love with sweetness, a serenity of bliss. But that it is law, some mysterious law of love, that is revealed we know. There is nothing lax in the power that controls and keeps them in that pure pyramid ; and, in the strictest sense of the word, it is at a canonization of beauty that we assist. There are many tabernacles in the world of art where you say, " It is strange," and then, " It is beautiful." Whatever the fiery thicket encloses is indestructibly holy.

They sit still ; they are charged with divine energy ; they are dæmonic forces. They are the Renaissance, for they are mediæval, Greek and Syrian. Their artistic genealogy is that the Angel of the Renaissance looked on a queen on Rheims Cathedral, and found that she was fair.

xv

The Florentines gazed, and kept holiday for this new canonization in beauty's calendar. Not before had they seen figures so gracious, linked so rhythmically in such a noble monument of attitude. The combination of magnificence with exquisiteness captivated them immeasurably. To those who look long on those accomplished bodies, Michelangelo becomes crude and Botticelli almost pretty. Also, the morbidezza of style and of emotion, the something dense, rich, and mysterious in the texture of soul and body, with the pallor of the great heats and the relaxing moisture which Leonardo had known in Milan, was unusual and exciting to them. Michelangelo goes jealously to create the Doni Madonna, to show that he too can build a pyramid of gracefully twining shapes, and close it in a round. It is a noble composition too ; though the sculptor's Roman Virgin is no woman of strange magic, nor mirror of the artist's soul, nor has she the supple undulation Leonardo had captured from Lombard beauty. Yet the perverse and fretful Michelangelo has a franker mind. For mere beauty, in the deliberate Renaissance way, he preferred the youth ; and naked youths he challengingly set around his Madonnas, pure, serious, meditating their lord. Leonardo, indeed, also preferred that platonic beauty, and one may guess, not without reason, that it could even cause an agitation in his reverie, so that he preferred a supersubtle spiritual duplicity, and drowned his Narcissus, his Hylas, in the eyes of Saint Anne, whose face is interchangeable with that of a Saint John or a Dionysos.

As his pagan incense smouldered in a blessed crucible, so the high heresy of his love platonic passed like a shadow within the canonical beauty of woman. Indeed the irony of Saint Anne makes her look

The Return of the Exile

sometimes like Diotima, who, according to Socrates, understood all that.

When he had evolved the type of Saint Anne, it began to touch too close a nerve in his soul. He fell in love with that Dionysian Narcissan head, the image of his soul's desire. It went with him to Milan ; it was a far-journeying, never-finished affair ; and in the end his hand failed him, and others did some of the painting. His heart had failed him long before his hand did, however : " When setting to work in paint it was as if he were mastered by fear. So also he could finish nothing which he had begun, his soul being full of the sublimity of art, whereby he was enabled to see faults in pictures which others hailed as miraculous creations." So Lomazzo.

In Milan, as a centre of adoration, Leonardo's great school-picture was copied and recopied by imitators in deliquescences of colour and degradations of sentiment, its great Greek solemnity and harmony of lines broken up into refractions of prettiness, while the head of Saint Anne, enigmatic and angelical, submitted to all the indignities of age, fatuity, and sentimentalism. The spoilt Salaino had his way with it, the laborious da Cesto ; and they were not the worst.

xvi

There is another name for the head of Saint Anne, and that is the name of the mother of Helen. The Coan veils and fine coifs of Anne fit upon the bowed dreaming head of Leda—Leda less august, more feminine, more delicately voluptuous. The dreamy drift of Milanese reminiscence solidified into her image as an incense-smoke into thick spirals like her woven curls. Leda, first conceived among the swans and waters of Milan, is seen and seen again in the pauses of Leonardo's growing obsession of wings. She is the lady of mysterious birth, who, by the embrace of a god, became the mother of the golden beauty that walked on the walls of Troy, and the violet-dark beauty that spread the crimson-purple cloths for Agamemnon, and the inviolate beauty that rides as Castor and Pollux among the constellations—romantic, tragic, chivalric beauty. When, after the Borgian episode, Leonardo retired awhile to Fiesole, more and more preoccupied with the absorbing problem of wings, he paused at times to draw the Greek girl half kneeling among the reeds and lilies in the river-meadow ; and sometimes he braids her convoluted hair, as a more exciting substitution for the old abstract intrecciamente, and sometimes he draws her water-flowers. The hatching of the drawings becomes more and more spiral, as if the

329

whole vision of the bride of wings were passing into the wonder of flight. That theme was like the honeycomb of his later years, where he stored all the sweetness his mind had brought from roaming the amaranthine fields of the air, and assailing the dazzling pyramids of light. Wings, light, air, water, flowers, from these in immaterial, rarefied conspiracy he would create the perfect shape of the ideal, impossible woman embraced in the plumes of a god's desire.

xvii

The more mystical and ambiguous becomes the matter of Leonardo's painting, the more earnestly he works his practical intelligence, as if he had some instinctive motion towards a corrective. He has drawn models for Fra Pacioli's book on proportion (*De Divina Proportione*). His anatomical studies are begun again at the hospital of Santa Maria Nuova; and he is almost passionately interested in the engineering of a canal for the Arno. He broods a good deal over the Arno, its silts at Monte Albano, its coloured pebbles at Monte Lupo opposite. Once he sees the wind, like an angry god, hollow a sandbank in the river, till the gravel whirls up in the air " like a great bell-tower," a spiral fury of natural energy which must have enchanted his eyes.

Piero Soderini, about this time, offers him the great block of marble, somewhat spoiled by a previous sculptor, whose courage failed before the Mass from which Michelangelo's young Titan was afterwards to emerge. But Leonardo declines another Heraklean labour. If, for a little while, some more delicate and Lysippan shape, some young Dionysos, contended with the David within that gigantic piece of creative matter, it was elusive, and slipped easily away to use the strigil with a sigh in its palæstra of dreamland. For, psychically, Leonardo as a sculptor had been discouraged by the Cavallo; physically he was reluctant. His body was perfect and beautiful, and he was no prey to the maladies that ravaged and exasperated his young rival. But his strength and grace were more a matter of poise and equilibrium than of mere muscular energy—the nervous co-ordination and perfected rhythms of the dancer, the fencer, the horseman. If he could crush that shoe of iron it was probably in one of those superhuman spasms of power of which highly nervous physiques are capable even to miracle. But he had not Michelangelo's possessed and terrible physical energy. One does not see Leonardo fall on the living stone like him, and carve with passionate chisel the visionary shape into freedom. It was not only that his habit of long preparation refused such a sudden attack. By this time the illimitable expense of purely nervous energy in so many diverse forms

The Return of the Exile

had begun to tell a little. He was sixty-seven when he died, but he seemed much older, and had suffered awhile from nervous paralysis. It is as if age overtook him suddenly in those wandering years, and with some vindictiveness. Perhaps when the dream of flight slipped sadly away from him, so did his peculiar sense of divinity, passing in mournful music through the gates of Fiesole, as the spirit of Antony's god forsook him to the sound of lamenting lutes when he became mere mortal, doomed to defeat. Leonardo, however, the passing of Herakles left still indomitable.

Meanwhile, he is restless still. Too many friends importune, too many enemies annoy, too many commissions offer. Florence is a distracting city. Then comes a request from one who seems riding invincibly from point to point of the road of conquest towards the dominion of Italy. Cesare Borgia, beginning his new campaign of the Romagna, has need of all the daring inventions, crafty maps, and sieging skill that Leonardo can supply. It is true that Cesare is bound to find Florence an obstacle in his way if he rides far enough, and that the City already regards his dominant figure with more than distrust, and that his most notable captains have definite designs in Tuscany. But Leonardo merely thinks it will be attractive to serve a prince again whose iron will keeps undistracted days. So, in 1502, he is Cesare's engineer. He, who said " Flee from storms," departs to the sieges, sacks, and stratagems of one whom his world acclaimed the prince of magnificent treasons.

Chapter iii

The Camp of Cæsar

i

WHEN Leonardo and Cesare Borgia stood together, this singular chance of the Renaissance brought all that it had of unflinching intelligence to squire an indomitable will. It seems a disproportionate consequence that the contact should serve only to strengthen a campaign of conquest that was made futile by the death of the Pope. But Renaissance energies often seem too limited in their scope. At a period when humanity was as if recharged with dynamic power, it found only a tired and parcelled earth to work upon. True, on far western horizons arose new continents ; but, if a man would be king, he preferred to be king in a country with a great history—he would be king in Italy. There was too much energy in the desirable land, hurtling and confined between sea and sea, while still more furious forces poured over the Alps and through the valves of Naples.

Cesare, in his twenty-fifth year, had already a long story of splendour, cruelty, and crime behind him. He was at that moment the most fascinating figure in Italy, the masked lithe personage round whom eddied fear and wonder and strange enthusiasms. With delicate craft, cool murder, great alliance, politic mercies, and ready genius for action, he went among his captains, his poets, and his bombardiers, from town to town of Northern Italy, impassible, his golden profumatorio-ball between his hands, his poignard in his girdle, carving himself a great kingdom as other men wrought their different works of art.

The excess of vitality that boiled in the veins of Rodrigo Borgia, so that satyriasis broke out in lampsacene festival in the halls of the papal palace, and orgiastic rites in golden swirling lines of unholy patterns recalled the days of late Roman emperors, was tempered in his dangerous son to clear-burning purpose and undeviating will. " Virtú " had Cesare, the power to behave like a god, to remove offenders from his path, and to conciliate the rest. His father, organically excited by all emotions, loved the children of his flesh as if they were his flesh—loved them with " carnalità," as if their beauty and splendour were seductive food. Of such a father Cesare was certainly the child best qualified to make amazing uses of his unique position as the son of the Vatican.

Now he had perfected his personality till it was like the great symbolic sword made for him when he was still a cardinal, the sword that was the queen of swords, with hard pure silhouette confining its broidery of Cæsarian mottoes, and of heathen sacrifices with naked dancers and music-makers entoiled with garlands to the religion of the Bull, all stamped in fine niello on a ground of sequin-gold. Hard and pure to its purpose was Cesare's spirit now, and the dancers and music-makers and victims that it required were only a graceful niello pattern to make the blade at once more fair and more ominous. Leonardo loved swords. What he had of swordlike willingly responded to the Borgia. Even the humane and sensitive Castiglione could not withhold admiration from that superb figure riding so ingratiate by the King of France towards some dimly-suspected golden blur shaped, it seemed, like a throne of his own. He had courage, genius, daring ; even his enemies regarded him with a superstition of fear. He had a " fortune," they said. His passion-less mode of passionate concentration unnerved them—the implacable soul that smiled away injury, and kissed an enemy honey-sweet till he found himself all in a horrible surprise in a strangling-chair. " Aut Cæsar, aut nihil," he said, and went his dread dazzling way to what seemed shaped like a throne, the golden blur that dispelled as naked nothing.

At seventeen Cesare had lived like a prince of the blood, keeping his court within a court, a beautiful young cardinal very attractive when he pleased, moody, however, because that dissolute lovely brother, the Duke of Gandia, was secular prince and gonfalonier, and in his feminine sweetness more delightful to the doting father than even he, more of a rhythmic dancer with their drowsy gold-lily Lucrezia than even he. Though he would understudy his father on occasion, with waving fans, sedia gestatoria, and globe and sword before him, he had worn his cardinalate even more airily than most, dissembling it with golden raiment, with pearls on his very shoes. He had gone dressed as a Turk with the Sultan's precious and melancholy brother Djem through the basilicas ; he had ridden as a soldier ; he had taken the women he wanted, like his young brother's wife Sancia, the light Neapolitan prin-cess, since to women, whom he regarded as mere casual pleasures, he was irresistible, as his father had been. But the Duke of Gandia had been dragged with pierced body from Tiber mud, and the agony of a father crying like an outraged god of Egypt had suddenly passed into a stupor of silence and fear. Soon Cesare had sword and gonfalon and Golden Rose. Loosed from his cardinalate, he had gone with a great company into France, burning like a Roman dream of the young Tiberius, crimson and gold, wearing a diadem with rings and rings of rubies, riding a steed all rosed and houselled and shod with gold and gems. Red and yellow and golden his troops, slim and glittering his pages as dragonflies, with players of rebecs, clarions and trumpets clad in haughty silver, sounding haughty silver at the gates of Chinon. And there he had won the heart of the doubtful Louis, and wedded a fair French princess, and left her derelict and desolate, so that he returned Cesare Borgia of France, the Duke of Valentinois, and quartered the lilies with the Papal keys and the familiar Bull. He had thrust his dagger in his father's minion Perotto, even while he covered himself with the cope ; he had ended the life of Lucrezia's husband, Alfonso de Bisceglie, with a certain impatience, because he too had become a hindrance and seemed unconscionably hard to kill. Father and sister had been angry, wept, and reconciled themselves with their tyrant. He had not killed because there came on him the desire to kill. He had no dark blood-lust like some of the Malatesti or Visconti or Baglioni, as he had none of their incomprehensible ecstasies of beauty, and astonishments of mercy.

ii

Now, while the Pope weakened and plundered the great dynastic families of Rome, not without poison and torture, Cesare was making himself a kingdom in the Romagna ; encouraged by France, reluctantly allowed by Venice, anxiously watched by Florence. Rimini, Pesaro, Imola, Forli, Camerino, Faenza, Urbino, had been declared forfeit to the Papal Power.

Cesare, with cool insolence declaring that his aim was not to create tyrants but to remove them, was even welcome to some of these little city-states, exhausted by their own despots. He was gentle to his inferiors, and, when war left him leisure, had administrative power. He regularized justice, and ruled inflexibly. In the first campaign Imola was easily his, and Cesena. Pesaro cried "Duca, Duca !" readily enough. But Faenza, Urbino, Camerino were to show that some cities could love such despots as by grace and sympathy had pledged themselves their blood-brothers. The city of Forli surrendered easily, but the Rocca, superbly held by Caterina Sforza, a woman to match him, caused him a bitter siege. She fought him tower by tower, before she rode out with the honours of war between him and the French captain Yves d'Allègre. He had shown military genius in his first campaign ; and on his return to Rome, at the great formal reception, his pride-rapt father caught him to his breast that would kneel. "Biondo e bello" he sat in the final car of his triumph, clothed in cuirass and chlamys, and the Pope must see twice over that sumptuous chimerical pageant. Yet the French resented that triumph, and never considered Cesare as " galant uomo " afterwards, for he could not resist leading the Lady of Forli captive in his procession, chained in gold like Zenobia, the rumour ran.

iii

He was now the most potent and the most fascinating figure in Italy. Giangaleazzo of Milan had gone as far towards the throne of Italy before him ; but that cold basilisk, gazing quietly from his secret chamber with fatidical eyes, did not proceed with meteoric swiftness, nor dazzle with the dramatic quality so dear to the heart of the Italian Renaissance. Cesare was the most self-possessed person in the land ; he could deploy his personality as well as his armies ; he knew how to capture the imagination of prince or peasant as well as a castled city. The stark anomalies of his past he translated into sinister but imaginative values. This golden Spaniard with his icy flame of pride, they said, was a cardinal who had deliberately abjured his vows. This suave Italian, with scented sensuous ways as sweet as clove-carnations, was a French prince wedded in the inimical dangerous country. This sacred gonfalonier had overloved his bright sister and murdered her husband. Crowned and hung with the white pearls like her, he could pass you death closed in the black pearls with a smile. He could accept the Golden Rose in cloth-of-gold and ermine, with the Dove of Pearls and its gilded nimbus upon his head. But more he seized the eyes when he went blond and beautiful in black velvet, with merely the collar of Saint Michael lying brilliant on his tunic, conspicuous by simplicity among his retainers in red and yellow.

For his peers he chose to be an enigma that fretted the mind. He had none of the wraths and the penitences, the sensual fits of emotion, the large mirths of his father. He made himself rare, a myth, a mystery ; he was not accessible even to great envoys. At dead of night he would receive them lying on his couch, though he had spent the day masked at Carnival. He made himself an aureole that quivered with the hues of Paradise and Hell ; he fascinated like " un grand diabolique," and charged with the cold fascination of a satanist the purely intellectual policies of his one great lust for power. He could be enchanting, diffident, debonair, in his speech and manners, when he definitely wished to beguile, but for the majority he chose to be a significant silence, which might speak, not in threats, but in daggers that sprang deadly true, cords that twisted like serpents, irons that branded, headsmen that struck at dawn. Don Michelotto, his *âme damnée*, was the dreadful translator of Cesare's silences when others opposed him, or merely got in his way.

But he had his court, his court of scholars and poets, who praised the "libertas Cæsarea," and restored the House of the Bull to mythology. He had those who clave to him with adoration even to his end, like Agapito, his pale, devoted secretary. Though, unlike his father, he wasted little time on women, plucking them hastily in his gauntleted hands when the mood took him, they seem to have found some enchantment in him. One tall, mute girl followed him everywhere ; and a Florentine Fiammetta burned sweetly enough for Cesare. His subjects were often willing subjects. It suited his policy to be kind and just to the lowly. His Spanish captains and troops had a cruelty he could not always restrain ; but he had a gift for government and a friendliness for the peasants and citizens who trusted him. He did not hold his dominions long enough to prove his regal qualities, but certainly there have been worse kings than Cesare. The gentle idealizing spirit that dwells wistfully in the souls of simple people, even when they are trodden into a mire of blood and tears, like a dove among the pots, making them so long-suffering to the splendid, so terrible when they realize that the splendid are indifferent, was better understood by Cesare than by that aloof Leonardo. He could use it. The shepherds in the Romagna, which Leonardo despised as "the realm of all stupidity," thought of Cesare riding as a deliverer, golden and rare, an apparition who would wrestle with them in their sports, and slay the Bull like Mithra who was lord of the shepherds as well as of legionaries, and promise them peace and abundance. So they made songs to their pipes of the bright new Sovran. If he killed another tyrant here and there, they were not much interested. The people of the towns he favoured came cheerfully to his banners. The great governor he had established, Don Ramiro de Lorca, was an oppressor like all the Spaniards, but his power had been diminished, and presently it would dramatically end.

iv

What was he to Leonardo ? A power—a power that seemed one with the velocities and lightnings of the gorgeous and indifferent universe in which his own mind was at home. Like these, Cesare did not strike for striking's sake ; it was merely that the things that spoilt the track of the lightning were blighted. The power was closed in a personality swordlike, secret, and "squisita." He was "l'unico Cesare," and the unique Leonardo was willing to serve him. The arts of war interested

The Camp of Cæsar

his mind ; and, if Cesare were to become a great king, his magnificence could not require of art less than Lodovico's. Meanwhile Leonardo, in a state of revulsion from the dim emotional agitations whence he has evoked the sea-coloured vision of Saint Anne, is in a mood when the spectacle of devastation is not disagreeable to him. To the Necessity that puts the Universe in motion he would say of Cesare, as of other velocities : " How admirable is thy justice, O thou First Cause, who hast not willed that any created thing should fail in this power of the order and quality of its necessary effects, since if a puissance must drive a vanquished thing one hundred braccie, and if that in its obedience it is arrested by some obstacle, thou hast decreed that the violent clash will cause a new movement which by different leaps will cover the entire journey it was predestined to make." So he looked at Cesare as a force driving conquered things in the paths of necessity, and revealing new potencies in their collisions.

Cesare's chief centre was the dignified town of Cesena, which had accustomed itself to carnival masks, to the come and go of great captains, and the march of Cesare's personal guards, all red and yellow, with his invincible name in silver on their breasts. Cesare, at twenty-five " the most beautiful man in Italy," was still golden, though slightly marred in his aspect because he was suffering from that evil the French called Italian and the Italians French. East and West had embraced too furiously, blind exultation grasping at stars had plunged through satyric excesses, the furious armies had poisoned the cities, and syphilis corroded popes, princes, and poets. Torella the doctor was in attendance ; but Cesare forbore from neither siege nor carnival. He was surrounded by brilliant young captains, French, Italian, Spanish. The Scots d'Aubigny and the French Yves d'Allègre were effective though fitful auxiliaries. Cesare's campaigns were still audacious enough to seem like *romans d'aventure*, so the young dukes came to learn conquest. Ercole Bentivoglio was there, and Cesare Spadari of Modena, Gian Paolo Baglioni, head of the remnant of the magnificent house that held Perugia, a tigerish, heathenish lord openly his sister's lover, but a famous condottiere like his kin. "El gran tradimento " of Perugia had been among the portents of the Jubilee year, when so many magnificent, beautiful, and dangerous creatures were slain by that one of themselves most like " an angel of heaven," a story of violence ending as sadly and sweetly as a Greek tragedy. "The High and Mighty Giovan Paolo " still seemed scathed as by fire from the unnatural stratagem in which perished the aged and kingly Guido, the sumptuous Astorre, the great captain on the golden-houselled steed, Semonotto, the cruel, fair young warrior of dreadful daring, Gismondo slight and lovable, all slain among their lovers, brides or pages, their gold and silver brocades hardly put off, slain in their extreme moment of gaiety by Grifonetto, " who for beauty was a second Ganymede," and who perished fate-stricken in his turn without a motion of defence. Giovan Paolo was the Captain of Siena's forces, bought for the time by the Pope, while his brother Morgante led the armies of Florence. He had a horse, " el Savallo," taken in battle, not big, but " made of steel and fire." So rode Giovan Paolo, unconscious that he would escape the suspicion of two terrible popes only to be lured into that castle of the dreadful dead, San Angelo, by the indolent Leo. The Count of Caiazzo, Galeazzo Sanseverino's brother, was sometimes seen in the councils. The most experienced warrior was Vitellozzo Vitelli, the lord of Citta di Castello, a pale man lame from Cesare's malady, from time to time hatefully regarding Florence, which had executed his brother Paolo for suspected treason ; though from this city the King of France had debarred the companies of Cesare. Slim and effeminate, with vicious eyes, went Paolo Orsini, member of a great Roman family ill-regarded by Pope Alexander. " Madonna Paolo," his own men called the languid youth. The " wolf Oliverotto," young, yet stained deep with the blood of his kind, moved stealthily and powerfully beside him.

Vitellozzo was the most distinguished of them. Leonardo borrows books from him, a volume of Roberto Valturio, and one by Fra Pacioli, so that we know the condottiere captains did not go to war without their treatises of theory. Others may capture towns ; Leonardo is also anxious for loot in the shape of a Codex of Archimedes. Vitellozzo promises to get him one from the Bishop of Borgo san Sepolcro. Cesare promises to get him another from Padua. You may imagine a group by the camp-fire, or in some vanquished library, Cesare smiling and rolling his golden perfume-ball, Vitellozzo like a sick and anxious eagle, Leonardo with sweet voice, persuasive gesture, and waving hair, kempt and comely despite his hasty travel—all talking about Archimedes, while the captain is meditating Cesare's end, and Cesare is perfectly aware of it, and Don Michelotto, his dark familiar, is even now preparing the trap of Sinigaglia.

In war Cesare " était gentil compagnon et hardi homme." He carried with him more than his captains—secretaries and writers eminent in their day. Agapito da Amelia was an amanuensis with whom he could indeed write as with his own hand. Francesco Sperulo was a poet and a fellow knight-at-arms. The Divine Aquilino, Justolo, Orfino, were eulogists with some style. Vincenzo Calmeta, a Knight of St John of Jerusalem, sang to the lute while improvising. Bramante advised Cesare sometimes. Antonio di San Gallo was frequently a consultant, but he belonged rather to the Pope, eagerly following the war from

The Camp of Cæsar

Rome. Leonardo was Cesare's personal engineer. Once again he encountered Francesco di Giorgio Martini of Siena, with whom he had ridden to Pavia long ago—ailing now and near his end. In the ranks of the army went that turbulent sculptor Torrigiano, whose artistic qualities are so little remembered because he broke Michelangelo's nose and was proud of it.

One other figure, present as a spectator, half-forgetting the vexations of poverty and the caprices of his city in a detached absorption in Cesare's chess-playing on the board of the Romagna, taking his queen, his kings, his bishops, and his knaves with masterly moves, was that tormented figure with the itching senses, the crystal brain, and the melancholy thirst for nobility—Niccolò Machiavelli, Secretary for the Republic of Florence, acutely and uneasily aware that its overthrow might become part of Cesare's policy. A slender person, dark, aquiline, with bright eyes and close lips, he gazes at Cesare the inscrutable with a certain imaginative terror, fascinated by his unflinching advance, while, for sweet balm to his unreasonable craving for human nobility, he hides the *Heroes* of Plutarch in the sleeve of his gown. That Leonardo was friendly with Machiavelli there is some evidence. It is even surmised that he may have written thereafter in the notebooks a page concerning *The Battle of Anghiari*. Though with what cool compassion Leonardo must have regarded both Machiavelli's suppressed idealism, burning him like a secret malady, and the cynical sensuality with which he tried to relieve it ! Probably he appreciated the great lucidity of his mind, while lightly considering that it was turned on transient affairs. " Italia di dolore ostello " was terribly inhabited ? Yes, for she could not find him his decorated rooftree. Well, he could leave her.

As for the armies, they were most various. Spanish cavalry and infantry and Gascon mercenaries were useful in attack, but so ruthless that they menaced Cesare's personal popularity. He controlled his own armies with a stern discipline ; these raveners were not responsible to him. The excesses of the siege at Capua were laid to his charge ; but in that case he was probably inattentive. He was taking the city for the French king, not for himself.

There was variety enough in Cesare's army to interest Leonardo, who had an acute curiosity in arms both antique and novel. The light cavalry was composed chiefly of Stradiots, with their broadswords and lances twelve feet long ; the Spanish infantry marched in light armour with short swords. The Romagna militia, wearing head and breast pieces, carried pike and broadsword. Dressed in white and scarlet and yellow, flying the Borgia flag, and sounding the maddening throbbing music of the kettledrums, they were distinguished by their swift

339

movements and their staying power, for Cesare seems to have aimed at speed and fire in his armies. Leonardo draws musketeers, archers, Swiss pikemen, among his studies of assault and defence, as well as little flying figures wearing nothing but hats, as if to relieve his mind with a little fantasy.

v

Cesena, with its important Rocca, once defended by emperors, was meanwhile the Duke's capital. It was a dignified place, and had been made beautiful by that Novello Malatesta who was Sigismondo's lovelier brother, whose head, indeed, struck on Pisanello's medal, is worthy of a Renaissance Eros. The palace was fair and embroidered, there was a great library, and a tradition of a court of scholars and poets. But Cesare also loved it for its name, and because the Rubicon ran clear not far away. His mind, set on an arrogant parallel, cherished Cesena, and plotted for its welfare. With wrestling matches like that in *As You Like It* he amused the contadini, and with the bullfights, where he shone perilous and imperilled. It was to have a university, a new Hall of Justice, a canal to Porto Cesenatico, and an important harbour there, all of these being matters for his new architect and engineer.

Imola was another city flattered by him, and Fano had submitted to liberal terms. Pesaro and its strong Rocca had received him, calling him " Duca ! " while its lord, that Giovanni Sforza who was once Cesare's brother-in-law, rode hurriedly away.

In May 1501 he had taken Piombino, a windy proud stronghold high on its promontory spur of the Apennines, gazing across at Elba, and in the spring of the next year had received his father there, who had much pleasure in a great golden Mass as rhythmic as a ballet, and a great golden ballet as punctilious as a Mass, otherwise seeming forgetful of Lent.

But Faenza had a beloved lord, and had for six months made an epic defence, with desperate and defiant banners inviolate through the bitter winter. The very women, under Diamante Jovelli, laboured steadily at the defences; and Astorre Manfredi, their signor, young, beautiful, chivalrous, interlocked his soul with the city's that loved him. Even Isabella d'Este spent some admiration on Faenza, though she was Cesare's ally, and though, through all the conquered cities of the Romagna, wound glittering the bridal procession of Lucrezia, passing through clouds of music and colour and epithalamy, with the Cardinal Ippolito for escort, to be the Duchess of Ferrara and her sister-in-law. Faenza did surrender, but on noble conditions, and at the persuasion of Astorre, agonizing for his city. He also had been promised freedom and safety,

The Camp of Cæsar

and with young enthusiasm had been so enchanted by the victor's magical manners that he had joined his group of captains. But he was too young, too sweet, too much a dream and a bright incentive to his romantic city. With his still younger half-brother he was soon hidden in the sinister crypts of San Angelo; and, when Cesare next visited Rome, the two bodies were found in the Tiber, terribly wronged by lust and death. Vain Astorre's candid eyes and his golden curls and his delicate rose-colour and his sweet " aria di malincolia," vain his innocence and chivalry! While he lived he was in Cesare's way. This happened in June 1502, just when we first find Leonardo deep in the Borgia's service.

What the inscrutable Duke wanted with Leonardo is clear enough from the remarkable patent issued by him at Pavia when he was visiting the French king. With one haughty and unqualified gesture he opens all the gates before Leonardo and his servants. He may go where he will, do what he will. It is quite evident that Cesare had confidence in Leonardo's powers to be useful in war—more, evidently, than Lodovico had. It was an absolute freedom that was rendered him by Cesare Borgia of France, Duke of Romagna.

" To all our lieutenants, castellans, captains, condottiere, officials, soldiers and subjects hereafter cognisant of this decree, we constrain and command, that to the bearer, our most excellent and well-beloved servant, Architect and Engineer-in-Chief, Leonardo Vinci [prestantissimo et dilectissimo familiare architetto et ingegnare generale]—whom we have appointed to inspect strongholds and fortresses in our dominions to the end that according to their need and to his counsel we may be enabled to provide for their necessities, we afford a passage absolutely free from any toll or tax, a friendly welcome both for himself and his company, freedom to see, examine and take measurements precisely as he may wish, and for this purpose assistance in men as many as he may desire, and all possible aid, assistance and favour, it being our will that in the carrying out of any works, in our dominions, every engineer will be bound to confer with him and to follow his advice."

He needed Leonardo in both his aspects: for destructive and constructive purposes. Leonardo's many devices could enter into sieges and attacks; Leonardo's genius was equal also to problems of defence, and valuable for the consolidation of vanquished cities by new building and care for the waterways. Cesare's bombardiers were notably among his strongest troops. Machiavelli observes their fine order and state. Heavy cannone, slender serpentino, he essayed them all. The artillery at this time was specially cherished by Vitellozzo, with whom conversed Leonardo as a specialist in arms. He had new ideas about firearms.

Leonardo the Florentine

He drew them with care, and tenderly set a bracelet of fair pattern about them. It is probable that he did a good deal of siege-work with Vitellozzo, and helped to order new guns of French pattern from Brescia.

Invaluable and original Cesare should have found Leonardo's six large-scale maps of Central Italy, revealing the direction of the waters, the structure of the soil, the distances between the fortresses, the towns, rivers, mountains. These maps cover the country as far north as the Val d'Ema, as far south as the Lake of Bolsena, as far east as Perugia and Cortona, as far west as Siena. They present all Central Italy from the Adriatic to the Tyrrhenian Sea. Another shows the town of Imola. His intelligence must have realized that these maps were dangerous to Florentine security, one thinks. That Leonardo was busy the broken notes of his itinerary show. Bertinoro, Imola, Faenza, Forli, Rimini, Urbino, Pesaro, Ravenna, Buonconvente, Casanova, Chiusi, Perugia, Foligno, Cesena, Porto Cesenatico, to Siena, Sinigaglia, Urbino—he appears suddenly in all these cities, written in red on the conquering progress of Cesare.

vi

Leonardo himself does not record his professional deeds, though we have accidental glimpses. The names of these cities flash vivid and dreamlike in connexion with dreamlike accidents. "Where is Valentino?" he writes in a memorandum full of the distraction of a hurried departure. Nobody indeed could be certain of Valentino's swift and deadly movements. On 13th July 1503, however, Leonardo is in Urbino, peacefully drawing a dovecote. Urbino, that truly gentle and exquisite hill-centre of Renaissance civilization, had been taken by Cesare forty days before by one of his most conscienceless sleights. For he had borrowed Duke Guidobaldo's artillery and soldiers, and then seized the defenceless city. Lofty Urbino was of great strategical importance, and necessary to his kingdom. Life had been at its delicate flower there, in the fine white limestone palace that Laurana had built, a city of a palace high on the hill, with hanging-gardens on rocky pillars, and balconies gazing on the sunset, and sweet extravagant stairs, and rooms decorated with angels carrying pots of lilies and carnations, and studios in cunning intarsiatura work, and the tale of Troy emerald and rosy in the tapestries, and the famous library of precious painted books and famous codices, all one hush of peace and felicity. With a Court as finished as that of Ferrara, with none of the tigerish quality that spotted with red the poetic lilies of Ferrara, a Court that carried out more faithfully than any in Italy the sweet tradition of Vittorino da Feltre, the gentle invalid Guidobaldo, who maintained, as well as he could, the

The Camp of Cæsar

wise and generous attitude of the great Duke Federigo da Montefeltro, and his wife Elisabetta, a wistful and lovely lady, were intimately and sweetly attuned. It dissolved like a breath before the onset of Cesare, and the fair castle was his to pillage. But the loyal rosy city would not forget the dukes with whom it had lived in amity ; it would not acquiesce in the new cold tyrant whose red and yellow seemed so crude in the pale rose and grape-purple spaces of high Urbino, which antique courtesy had mellowed for the lovers and poets. The Court returned in the end, and the lords and ladies sat talking of many things in the lifted chambers, with Castiglione to keep their words in rue and lavender for sweet and sad remembrance. They would talk even of Leonardo himself, careless that he had been in Urbino with the enemy, consenting to their flight. And indeed among those who talked would be Giuliano de' Medici, an exile, in time to come a protector to the artist, and unwillingly a danger to the city that sheltered him.

But meanwhile Leonardo listens to the doves as he draws their cote, and sketches a part of the great stair (for stairs gave him pleasure), as if Cesare and his armies were a mere hallucination.

In August he is found at Pesaro, drawing machines indeed, but more attracted by the library. A peaceful place it looked beneath its woody hills beside a smiling sea ; and the people had got used to Cesare's gaudy guards with the serpents' heads at their belts. But in a week he is at high Rimini, easily surrendered by a captain unworthy his valorous name. Stark and splendid rose the terrible Rocca, the Gate of the Marches, towering over its desolate coast and its violent little river. Yet a splendour had burned by these pale sea-edges ; and the symbols of the elephant and the rose spoke everywhere of the great lost soul of Sigismondo Malatesta, a beast and a god, a tyrant who was a poet, whose flame would have consumed Cesare, though he never could have matched him in policy. There was much in Rimini for Leonardo's eyes, for Valturio had been engineer of the Rocca, Alberti the architect of the Temple, Piero della Francesca had painted Sigismondo in devotion, and Vittore Pisano had been his medallist. The Arch of Augustus proclaimed the Roman dignity ; repeated in the famous " Temple " by Alberti it masked the Gothic church of Saint Francis, so strangely transformed to a heathen shrine of love. Leonardo must have looked at Sigismondo kneeling before his saint against that sky of solemn sacred blue, and at Isotta carved in the likeness of Saint Michael in the decorated chapel of the archangel, a baffling triumphal image that should have pleased him, and all the mythic brede of lovely shapes wherewith Agostino and others had made enchanting the unfinished undomed church with its bizarre, broken look. Within, signs of the zodiac, charioting goddesses, fluting, twining draperies like the Mænads' on antique reliefs, all out of Sigismondo's verse ! Leonardo should have found favour for a plumed Mercury holding a caduceus and a viol, and wearing an Eastern headdress. And if he had sympathy with Botticelli he must also have known some affinity with Agostino, great though exotic sculptor, with his feminine lyrical genius, speaking in floating veils of gauze, languid lids, and winding hair, and shapes of singing fantasy.

So far as we know, he listened in Rimini, listened to a sweet falling fountain whose waters chimed in a pure prismatic harmony. As if they were the falling tears of Francesca and Isotta ! He thought not of them. But the fountain-loving Leonardo especially loved this fountain in the hot August, and longed for a fugue of fountains. He tarried but for a day or so. Soon he is back at Cesena, drawing the fortress and planning the glory of the Duke of Romagna's favourite city, considering also the canal to Porto Cesenatico, where he goes one day and draws a gate. But round Cesena he observes how the vines grow garlanded round the trees, and notes the rude cars of the country. Images of antique peace—vine-dressers and peasants walking by their slow white oxen !

October finds him at Imola, working at its defences, for Cesare is shut in that city. The captains of the Duke, fearing to be devoured one by one " as by a dragon," have been conferring secretly at La Magione, with Orsini cavaliers and cardinals, with the representative of the Duke of Urbino and the confidant of Pandolfo Petrucci of Siena, the brain of the conspiracy, and the Bentivoglio lord.

Panic stirs stealthily among Cesare's company, afraid that the conspiring condottiere have contrived to checkmate him. Leonardo has a note somewhere about the mysterious contagion of fear, swift and secret leprosy of the spirit. French troops, however, move swiftly to succour. Ancient Imola, on the great Roman Road, had belonged to the Sforza, had belonged to the evil Riario family. It had its sweetness, for by a strange miracle of tenderness the Madonna of the Pear-Tree had touched the heart of even Girolamo Riario, and now in rose-time all the people went out to give roses to the new-builded shrine. Yet Imola was also tainted, and Guidarello Guidarelli, that knight whom we know as sculptured most lovely in death, one of the sweet sleepers of the Renaissance, was obscurely murdered here in the dark Borgian war.

The conspirators of La Magione, by lack of mutual faith, and in superstitious fear of Cesare, have drifted back to uneasy allegiance, and have been effusively reconciled. Gian Paolo Baglioni does not like the atmosphere, and rides for Perugia. On Christmas Day the peasants, coming in at dawn to Cesena, are stricken to see, on the piazza under the Rocca, a headless body in rich raiment lying by the block, and a head on

The Camp of Cæsar

a pike. These bleeding fragments were yesterday Don Ramiro del Lorqua, the Spanish Governor of the Romagna, inferior only to the Duke. He has been an extortioner. This is Cesarian justice, sudden, remorseless, irrespective of persons. But some say that Lucrezia's brooding eyes, as she passed midst her bridal procession, drove the Spaniard to some fiery madness, not to be pardoned by the terrible brother.

Leonardo goes with the Duke to Sinigaglia, which Oliverotto has captured for him this month. Machiavelli is in Sinigaglia too, for, in that square town on the high almost-islanded cape, its brick wall set with four bastions, Michelotto had made ready, and the air was quivering with apprehension. But Cesare, dulcet and " squisita," meets his uneasy captains, Oliverotto, Paolo Orsini, the Duke of Gravina, and Vitellozzo—the last reluctant, and drearily fatalistic, drawn forward with a kiss. How deftly they were tricked across the fatal threshold, how soon the strangling cord silenced the frantic Oliverotto and the resigned Vitellozzo, was matter of admiration to all. The two prisoners were also soon strangled " in the Spanish manner," while Pope Alexander attended to the " biberat calicem " policy for the other Orsini in Rome. Cesare had disembarrassed himself by the " bellissimo inganno." Machiavelli remained enraptured by the perfect finish of the affair. If Leonardo thought anything, he did not say it : he probably regretted that one hope of an Archimedean Codex was lost with Vitellozzo.

He was at Acquapendente when Isabella d'Este sent to Cesare her quaint felicitating gift of a hundred masks, very beautiful, made in Ferrara. True, Cesare did use masks a great deal, but Isabella seems nervous for once. She overdoes it. She expresses " joy and pleasure " at his success. " We think you should take some rest and recreation." " We burn to have news of you." " Very illustrious and excellent Madonna," begins Cesare, " honoured Commère, very dear sister," and proceeds to say that he has justly punished the perfidy of his enemies, and that these masks are precious as a new proof of the singular affection she bears him. He sounds a little ironical : Leonardo, too, may have smiled faintly over the masks.

The architect and engineer flits in other cities. Proud and lovely Perugia sees him, and Chiusi. To sweet and cordial Faenza, with its fair Florentine basilica, still moody, weary from the siege, mourning for the death of its young lord, to Castel Bolognese, where he dismantles fortifications, to sea-girt Piombone, swept by the wind and rain, to restore them, where he stands long by the shore, his eyes on the silver line of the breaking wave, to Camerino, two thousand feet above the sea-level, a noble city brooding over the evening earth, also gloomy because the oldest and the youngest of its feudal family have been wiped out by cool murder. (" A truce having been made with the lord of Camerino by the Duke Valentino, the latter rushed into the city when he was least expected.") He saw Fano ; he went to little Ceri, with the balisters and catapults, and the new scaling-ladder made of a series of platforms. He went as far south as Orvieto, where the illuminated, three-pointed front of the cathedral, with roses, inset pilasters, points, mosaics, fluted, spiralled, crusted, sown and carved with a mediæval passion surexcited and enthralled by Renaissance images, stood in exquisite astonishment in the lonely air. And at some time he was in Siena, that soft fierce place couched on her beautiful hills like a gleaming dragon at the feet of the Virgin. Did he pause by the striped and arrogant cathedral, or wander round the soft-slid edges of the white conchlike piazza that lies under the most challenging town-tower in Italy, those dream-soft slopes of the piazza round which the coloured riders still rush fiercely for the *palio* ? Yes, he stood there, gazing at La Mangia. Whatever he did in high Siena, he ended by saying simply, like Galahad : " Also I heard a bell." For it is the motion of the great bell that fascinates him, swinging him away from Cesare's affairs.

In the end Cesare went to Rome to see his father, and that fatal supper-party in the vineyard by poison or by fever concluded horribly the life of Pope Alexander, and destroyed the fortune of Cesare. As Machiavelli observed, he had arranged for every contingency save that he should be dragged to the doors of death in the wake of the Pope. Leonardo the Florentine may have gone to Rome with him. When we discover him again he is back in Florence, painting Madonna Lisa to the sound of lutes. Discomposing as it was, he probably had to live by a rhythm of revulsions. What he did not like was the lack of a fixed centre. He preferred to stabilize one point of himself, like Donne's compass.

vii

The direct effect of his campaigning experience will appear presently in his studies for *The Battle of Anghiari*, and in his merciless close descriptions of unidealized battle, that " brutalissima pazzia," in which descriptions, nevertheless, there lies some obscure zest of a savage idiosyncrasy. Savage and delicate was he, like his god who tore the young kid on the hills of Thrace. It is evident that he had observed battle closely, and analysed its horrible incidents. When he is writing vividly about cardiac matters, and says he has seen one flying in terror whose heart literally burst, so that life passed from him in streams of blood and tears, he does not remember the heart of Christ pierced over again in that

insufferable trepidation.   He has not even the Achillean tenderness for
the young victim of the spear.   In the Borgian war he must have seen
this suffering of a panic too intolerable, and marked it for his notebook.
In a way, Leonardo, who thought it mere mortal stupidity to destroy
the body of man, because it was so admirable a piece of mechanism,
was crueller than Cesare.   Indeed at this time the more merciless
exultation of the universe seems to possess him ; and images of deluge,
destruction and eclipse sweep through his brain in mighty waves of
dissolution and vanishing spirals of smoke ; of which more presently.

The world of Northern Italy was torn and scorched by little wars
and great invasions.   Round Perugia there had been a massacre of the
trees, even the fruit-trees, and even the olive-trees, as the chronicler
tells with the horror due to sacrilege.   The happy fields were burned.
About the cities wolves multiplied, for they found Christian flesh to eat.
Sometimes in extremity of rage frenzied folk tore arch-enemies to pieces
and ate scraps of their flesh in dreadful revulsions to primitive sacrament.
The Spaniards left everywhere a trail of innocent blood and hateful
dirt.   The forces of Vitellozzo were reputed not even to leave the nails
on the walls.   Yet the condottiere captain, bred only for armies, had
peculiar virtues for his comrades-in-arms.   Fierce foemen, also, are suddenly stricken with chivalrous courtesies.   The Baglioni girls, escaping in
boys' dress, a dangerous disguise, from their unsafe city, are given honourable refuge by an enemy governor.   The whole battle is stayed when the
young Carlo degli Oddi falls pierced so mortally, and his " fair limbs lie
on the green sod," and men weep for his perished beauty.   Miracle
blazes up in the fevered atmosphere.   Perugia and Siena hate each other
because of Our Lady's ring ; Suor Colomba, translucent, feeds only on
the Bread of the Angels.   Priests, in an excess of compassion and fear,
begin to say masses for all the dead and dying.   Madonnas speak out of
thorns and pear-blossom.   But there is also a rain of scarlet blood that
stains the leaves (rain dyed by the driven sands of Africa).   And from
the branches like evil fruits hang satanic ravens, surfeited with the blood
of doves.   Such mediæval things of dread and pity were still happening
when Leonardo, the high lord of the Renaissance, went to war with the
crossbowmen and the bombardiers.   But through all the bloodshed and
contention the Tree of Art quietly put forth its amazing corollas of
beauty, as if it throve on the rich compost of blood and filth.

viii

But the red and yellow phantasmagoria of Cesare's armies, the noise
of the kettledrums, the bloodied earth and the dust-clouded skies, tired

the æsthete in Leonardo. He took his harvest from this as from all experiences. And for his intimate secret spirit he separated away the few crystalline and exquisite things he considered as symbolic values for eternity. He reveals himself through the red mists in tense and concentrated attitudes of listening, as if the eye, that proud organ, had been blinded and dazed from its serenity by collapsing walls of cities, and clamorous colours, and groups of frenzy round the standards of the Bull and the argent Gryphon, and had, plucking merely some sprigs of silver euphrasy, some white and crystal and selenical things like white doves, white vanishing stairs, white line of breaking wave, white spray of singing fountain, resigned for once its primacy among the senses to the ear, the vibrant and mysterious cell that receives, from beyond all the shouts and shrieks and drums in the foreground, the ethereal echoes of eternity. For the sense of hearing is swift and fine to restore the edge and temper of a disaffected æsthetic perception. Even Cesare, though given to "stratagems and spoils," had a symphony of lutes for his hours of quiet.

So Leonardo hears the doves draw softly out the far-burning perspectives of summer : he hears the fountain chime supersensual rainbow chords : he hears the waves break on the edges of the world : he hears the great bell toll in its remote suspension like the passing-bell of time. From the rage and the perfidy, the scarlets and the kettledrums of the investiture of Borgian war, he creates like a cool silvery mirage an unearthly pastoral, of vines garlanded about the trees, of a dovecote and vanishing palace steps, of a fountain, of a tolling bell. These are the eternal and essential things, the symbolic souls of the cities, not marred with smoke and blood and tears. Their names come like magical faint echoes out of the battle ; their images rise as fair as fountains, ineffably fair, to the sound of solemn bells and the washing of waves, when we see the random records on Leonardo's page.

Another idyllic note tells us that the shepherds of the Romagna bury their pipes in the hollows of their hills to sweeten the music. But the rationalist in Leonardo binds the eyes of his imaginative soul—or is it his curious fear of the earth-mother that prevents him from sympathy with this antique chthonic rite that besought melody for the cornamusa by laying it between the breasts of Cybele ? Somewhere, we remember, he remarks that the Romagna is "the realm of all stupidity." For the superstitious earth-wisdom of the shepherds he had no respect. There are moments when Leonardo's great genius is embarrassed by mere intelligence, as Socrates' often was, as Shakespeare's never was.

Still, it is evident that Leonardo's unconscious, more divining self is at work transmuting this experience, like all other experiences, into a

The Camp of Cæsar

transient crystal wave of Time that will be subsumed by another and another, before it break pure and colourless and soundless upon the impalpable shores of eternity, " chon grave e superbo andante," in his own phrase, and again repeated, with a musical difference, "chon superbo e grave andante."

ix

But this resolution he could not wholly achieve till, by the studies of frenzied men and horses, the turbaned heads, with faces convulsed by the rictus of agony and rage and panic or by the madness of shouting, by the sublimation of that dark flame of battle in the group that interlocks round the standard of Anghiari, he had purged his mind of the terror of the Borgian play, though pity was there none to purge. He describes a night-scene in red and black, with figures silhouetted against the camp-fire—Rembrandtesque in its vision. So, cloaked, he must have mingled with the soldiers, his little book still in his girdle. " Vigil strange I kept in the field one night," he also could have said ; and, if he saw no image of transcending pathos like the face of an ivory Christ, he found some sword-lilies. One young warrior, kneeling behind a high pointed shield, with steel cap, figured coat, and great sword, is a lovely figure plucked from the armies. Indeed, when Leonardo drew men and horses in any business, fierce or tender, the result was beauty. War might be a bestial fury, and the battle-painter must remember that " there must not be a level spot that is not trampled with gore." For all his realism of speech, in his great cartoon he liberated the " fire and grace," the flashing bitter beauty inherent in combat, and, having done that, desired to do no more, for he had finished with this experience.

The spirit that had animated him awhile dissolves itself in the universal, in the wild swirls of sea and sky, where the world seems molten as one omnipotent, crested, suspended wave such as a Japanese might imagine. Great winds from outer space, born beyond earth's atmosphere, sweep trees and men from the globe, terribly diminishing it away into spirals of sand and water and cloud. His imagination in its cruel fit loses itself in the vision of a Deluge in which his reason definitely does not believe. In the conflict of wind and water and earth and fire that eddies away into darkness, once more " chon grave et superbo andante," the infinitesimal foray of the Borgia has vanished like one drop of blood. And presently this curve of experience endures in Leonardo only in the fiery zest with which he turns the volutes of his drawings, and in the half-sensual irony with which he imposes his narcissan dream on the equivocal smooth face of the Neapolitan lady.

349

Chapter iv

Mona Lisa & The Battle of Anghiari

i

IN 1503 Leonardo was back in Florence at the time of the iris. There may have been some faint cloud of remorse in his clear mind. He must have realized that Cesare's policies would ultimately have been inimical to Florence, and his fine senses must have sickened at so much violence and agonizing death. His eyes took their harvest undeterred, perhaps : it was not a fragrant nor a musical experience. There was a corrosive residue, after every transmutation. Besides, these flights and suddenly-shifting scenes were too kaleidoscopic. After all, he wished to strike a root somewhere, so that the organic processes of his genius might resume their patient and exquisite works of concentration. Once more he desired to be truly a Florentine, at home in his city. He failed ; but it is not entirely the fault of the City.

It was long-suffering in some ways : and did not openly reproach him with being the friend of the dangerous Borgia, and the companion of its arch-enemy Vitellozzo ; though these things may have been remembered against him. Artists and men of genius generally, it was known, were condottieri in their fashion.

Significant of his intention to refranchise himself in his native town, his name is firmly restored to the record of Florentine painters. Soderini is now gonfalonier for life—a kind of doge ; and, though the Pisan war drags wearily on, and Florence is tired of paying her mercenaries, there is a renewed excitement in matters of art. Leonardo, surrounded by idolaters, is creating new types of human beauty and precipitating new æsthetic emotions in his veiled and beautiful studio where the lutanists sit at ease, their fingers in their thrilling strings. Michelangelo is furiously quarrying his sombre gauche adolescent from that huge mishandled block of stone. Perugino's bottega is assailed by violent people desirous of dreamy Madonnas and skies of absolution and benediction. Raphael, a beautiful girlish youth with dark curls and madonna eyes of his own, has come from Siena to absorb what congenial matter he may find.

But Leonardo's mood is still coloured by the sights and sounds of the Borgian war, and perhaps by dark uncoiling of the dragon stirring in his own soul. The catharsis was not complete ; the sublimation was not achieved. But the dangerous yeast of the sadist mood worked off its violence, not only in the dæmonic energy of the spiralled drawings, but in a double effort of great painting, directly in *The Battle of Anghiari*, indirectly, and as if by contrast, in the portraiture of women, especially of Madonna Lisa.

This kind of parallelism in imaginative expression appears to suit his mind. Sometimes, of course, there is " contamination," in the artistic sense. Strange cruelty slips into Mona Lisa's gaze ; soft sfumato, from whatever choking cloud of horror obtained, sweetly enwraps the group of warriors as if a goddess would fain snatch away some Paris of the mellay in a lighted cloud.

Leonardo amused himself with these portraits of women, some of which he merely touched here and there with his brush, some of which he drew, and left to his assistants to paint. But he finished the picture of Ginevra Benci, the sister of his friend ; and he spent a long time over La Gioconda because she brought him an intriguing new problem in æsthetics. Only at the end did he paint the kind of beauty that he preferred : but he could always find it drowned like Hylas in the nymphæan pools of a woman's eyes. He was not frank, like Michelangelo ; the transitions by which even Mona Lisa, so feminine in her aspect, is made to approximate to the Dionysiac type, are so strategic as to be almost furtive. It is as if he were afraid to see his Narcissus except in a disguise. However, while he worked at the extreme masculine in *The Battle of Anghiari*, he was more inclined to balance it with the extreme feminine in *Mona Lisa*. But I think the Borgian war a little turned the edge of Leonardo's sensibilities at a time when he was beginning to tire— to need some rest, at least. There is a kind of cold imaginative sensuality suspended in his vision while he paints this lady ; and he did paint her over too long a period. She affected his type. There is Saint Anne and the Dionysos in the final John the Baptist, but there is also Mona Lisa. This is something of a pity, for it spoils the virginal contour of the ephebus, and brings too much of Salmacis into the Renaissance Hermaphroditus.

It is often said that Leonardo devoted four years to *Mona Lisa* ; but this is a misleading statement. He had spent a year with Cesare since he began the picture, and, while he remained in Florence, he continued as usual to keep dozens of different interests at play, like a juggler effortlessly maintaining his coloured balls in suspension. The battle picture ran parellel with this, so that he had, with the study of frenzied bodies and horses, the study of a hidden soul. It is, on a smaller scale, the parallelism of the two great Milanese efforts over again.

Leonardo the Florentine

Madonna Lisa, daughter of Antonio Maria de Noldo Gherardini, was a Neapolitan, wedded in 1495 to a wealthy Florentine merchant, Nanobi del Giocondo, whose third wife she was. She had had one daughter dead in infancy, buried in Santa Maria Novella. Nothing else is known of her. She did not even " lift a pearl-pale hand, and bind up her long hair, and sigh." She simply sat still, and listened to Leonardo and the music, and looked at the jugglers ; and by so doing she entered into the procession of immortal women for whom every generation raises up a tribe of lovers. She is as famous as Helen of Troy ; she is as disputed as Sappho. She has become Our Lady of the Renaissance, with her legend and her litanies. She unites lovers and she creates feuds. Through the half-mocking incantation of a great painter the bourgeoise lady is much more potent to-day than Isabella d'Este, or Vittoria Colonna, or Elisabetta of Urbino, La Bella Imperia, or Lucrezia Borgia, with whom she probably had much in common. But in this case Leonardo has achieved an effect usually peculiar to those workers in words whom he despises. He has created a mythic personality which continues to be discussed as if it were that of a live woman, though it is from his own psychology that Leonardo has scooped so much dense, rich, dreamlike matter to knead into the drowsy Neapolitan spirit, even while he intimately modelled her strange face, persuading it to be made over again in his own image.

The portrait of Mona Lisa is the most written-about picture in the world. There must be something almost miraculous about a canvas that provokes so much love and hate. It has become a wonder-working eikon rather than a picture ; and suffers the adventures of priceless reliquaries. It is as well known as the Parthenon, or Chartres Cathedral, or the Praxitelean Hermes. I have always had a doubt in my mind since hearing that some preposterous thief had stolen her. When I saw her afterwards, her colours seemed brighter and her expression duller—but then, La Gioconda is not sceptral over every mood.

Of all her eulogists Walter Pater remains the most distinguished. At present, indeed, he seems to have done her magnificent disservice, for he has antagonized not only those who dislike beauty in painting, but those who dislike beauty in prose, or beauty in any art whatever— that is to say, the noisier sect of twentieth-century painters, writers, and their appreciators. Pater's beautiful and beautifully placed words are really evocative of what was in Leonardo's consciousness when he painted this woman. It is a psychological appreciation ; but it is just and fine. When a picture has satisfied the æsthetic criteria, it may be allowed its psychical value. Indeed, Leonardo himself would have insisted on that. It is more descriptive of Leonardo's soul than Mona Lisa's, but she has become only a gesture of that soul, after all. The sentence that enumerates the forces behind her closes with the " crimes of the Borgias." That is no mere rhetorical phrase. Leonardo's mind was fresh from a campaign begun with the heathen sacrifice of that beautiful youth Astorre Manfredi, continued through the blood-libations of Cesena, Imola, Camerino, Sinagaglia. *Mona Lisa* was a post-war picture, and some of the dark ferment of strife is troublous in that as well as in *The Battle of Anghiari*.

iii

Yes! Leonardo's senses had been flayed appreciably. For once, instead of the hard and rare conception, he wanted the rich and soft. He wanted also to be amused, to be diverted by a problem. Mona Lisa was soft and rich in her texture and contour ; and she presented a new problem—how to fit his nymphæan and immortal type to a face mortal enough, though inclined to smile and look in the way that he approved. Naples was the city of ancient pleasure ; the sirens lay in its waters, and the satyrs played in the sun. Its women had as a heritage tricks of desirousness, pagan arts learned in the days of Tiberius. The Renaissance busts of unknown Neapolitan ladies, heads by Laurana and his followers, have much fascination. Ladies smooth and still, with delicate hoods of hair, ivory-lidded long eyes and secret lips with a little smile lifting the corners! Ambiguous like fine lamias they look, and their preoccupation is ironically voluptuous. They seem princesses of sunken cities, and high-abbesses in Paphos.

The war had frothed Leonardo's mind. It had made him more aware of sensuality than usual, the sensuality of hate, which is much the same as that of desire. It is hard to understand the sentimentalists who imagine that this was the mistress of Leonardo's love. No tradition even breathes such an incredible notion. He understood women, and analysed them with the subtlety of that part of himself which was woman. He was indifferently friendly with them—so long as they did not trespass ; and sometimes he amused himself—that part of himself which was panther—rather wickedly with their images. And sometimes he shaped the impossible, inviolable face of his dream.

He painted Madonna Lisa with the comprehension, not of love, but of secret cruelty. It amused him to knead his dream into her beautiful flesh, to call out her enchanting faint smile with lutanists and tumblers, with the jesting talk he thought fit for her, and to set her loggia in a blue-green world of barren rock and wandering waters, with only the little bridge to show that one may hardly escape from her. Not hers the

z

predestined face, the face that might have lured Leonardo to mysterious love and supersubtle embrace. But, moulding her soft sensuous shape, and her siren look, not only with his brush, but with his dream-charged soul, he created something novel and wonderful from the conflict, not from the harmony, between them. From her smooth bodily beauty he wrung the Circean shape he desired to see. And as the veiled head detached itself, more and more actual in the unreal atmosphere, he was fascinated with the solution of his own problem.

He could not let it go. He had done something unprecedented in the art of portraiture. He had used all his technical skill in compelling that figure to live in three-dimensional reality in her own atmosphere. So he kept it. The French critic who suggests that he was allowed to do so because he had given the lady an expression that no husband could long endure is sensible, though over-solemn. And, indeed, there is something dubious about Madonna Lisa. The pictures in which she appears naked to the waist against a wall of flowers are by Leonardo's pupils ; but it is supposed that he made some study of the kind himself, which merged afterwards into the Saint John and the Dionysos. If he did, she must sometimes have looked a little like a Lesbian hetæra ; and the transition would be natural enough. One feels he did consider her with some cynical intellectual whim of sensualism, for it is only in *Mona Lisa*, for some reason, that one remembers that Leonardo was the Anatomist of Love.

But time and restoration have brought tricking shadows over her beauty. When those gazers who reported to Vasari saw the drowning lustre of her eyes, the soft carnations, rose and white, of her texture, the silken eyelashes and fine eyebrows, the tender nostrils, the pit of the throat where the quick pulse seemed to beat like a sweet pathos, they thought of nothing but that she was fair. Evidently such was also the effect on King Francis, who bought her for a great price in the end.

She had her own secret, however. Some say she was stupid, because she liked the tumblers. Our Lady gazed at the juggler doing his best somersaults before her altar in the cathedral, and was pleased, so that Mona Lisa had a heavenly precedent for her taste. But what she really did was to forget her mask in some pale amusement, and Leonardo caught her in the unguarded hour. There is a fusion of two enigmas in her. One is his ; but she has her own mystery. For once the twy-natured angel does not subdue the woman altogether.

> " What potions have I drunk of syren tears
> Distilled from limbecks foul as hell within ? "

say some who are most discomforted by Leonardo's famous portrait. But " Strange queen, why art thou desirous now to beguile me ? " is more often the apostrophe of those who find her challenging.   Such is Gautier's love declaration : " Ne dirait-on que la Joconde est l'Isis d'une religion cryptique qui, se croyant seule, entr'ouvre les plis de son voile, dût l'imprudent qui la surprendrait devenir fou et mourir ? "   Men like the portrait because they feel there should be something *aiguisée* in all her sweetness, a finesse and a point in her surrender that would keep it for ever a surprise and a climax.   Women, as a rule, regard her a little uneasily, for they are dimly aware of her simple riddle—that she is enchanting but disenchanted, with the disenchantment of every woman who has found love's consummation destroy the rare pattern of her illusion.   All women who are mature in Madonna Lisa's way suffer from profound disillusionment.   If she so desires still to beguile, it is for her mere amusement, for the days are long and flameless that give the lie to the Annunciation.

She is not a high type !   No !   Some special pollen-bread of illusion is really necessary to keep the high type in the heavenly airs.   But from her ironies and her reveries she has distilled a wordless wisdom.   Such was Mona Lisa when Leonardo caught her off her guard in his soft-lit studio at close of day, when at some chord of music, that unmasking art, she half-smiled, and so did he, understanding her, for love's earthly consummations he too despised.   It was therefore a more subtle smile than usual, and needed all his cold lore, gained from the anatomist's table, to bring the thirty-six muscles or so into super-exquisite play.   He knew that ring of nerves and minute fascicles round the mouth, more sensitive than any musical strings, that would set square in terror and become three-pointed in despair, while pleasure began about the eyes to fade sweetly at the corners of the mouth, lifting and shortening the upper lip.   It was a nervous phenomenon, slight as the trembling of an eyelid, an alteration as fine as the cunning shift of an accent in a line of verse.

iv

" Always make the figure so that the bosom is not turned in the same direction as the head ; for Nature gave us for our convenience the neck, which can easily be moved in different directions according as ye seek out different directions."

This is Leonardo's apparently naïve explanation of those easy and noble attitudes which give his portraits their gracious rhythms, the quiet music of his contraposto more composed than rectitude itself.   So La Gioconda detaches herself, turning slightly in her chair in her dark loggia overlooking the green water-world, with soft hands so lightly clasped before her.   " There are no tactile values more convincing than

Leonardo the Florentine

those of *Mona Lisa*," says the great authority on tactile values—at least he said so once. The famous portrait illustrates what Leonardo intends by " imitation of nature," and study of images in mirrors, and maxims that sound as if he were a literal realist. He merely means that your painted image must seem actual to you, graspable by your senses, something that your eyes recognize as having validity for other senses. But so you perceive images as in a dream, and Madonna Lisa sits in a dreamland. Strange rocks, winding water, green-blue light! No earthly scene was ever assembled quite like that. Leonardo's fantasy assembled it, drenching the beautiful lady in a rarer mystery : her strange head appears native to her green dusk of dreams. He is kind to her, after all. Like a god, he has rapt her away from the soiling touch of a much-wedded bourgeois (not unresembling Ser Piero) to the inviolate shores of lapis and emerald where only sacred virgins and angels and holy children breathe the rare ether of the suprasensual world. And indeed her quiet attitude and the arrangement of her beautiful calm raiment gives her the timeless and universal look of a fate and a goddess. She is Leonardo's subtle Melancholia, so exquisitely at home with despair that she can smile.

With great pleasure he dwells on the suavity of the details. He almost seems to insist for once, like Agathon, that the soft feet of Love seek soft ways. The soft green velvet is fluted on the beautiful satin-soft breast, the faëry-fine golden broidery, the soft suggestion of lawn, the soft hair, the faint veil, the hands much softer than he usually paints them, the soft-wreathed drapery over the arm, the softly ruffled sleeves where the light makes a pattern of its own, like the river pattern behind, all the soft noble raiment whose folds harmonize with the landscape, the soft and sensuous fibre of the lady herself—over all these soothing contacts his eyes and his brush linger with deceptive painter's solicitude, stroking his own nerves, on edge from the kettledrums and the dust and the crude colours. There is immense æsthetic tenderness in the picture, in this painting of details. For the rest, it is an aery collision of ironies, hers detached and unconscious, his attentive and a little cruel, a difficult delicate duel to set his jaded wits glittering again. Yet she pleased him somewhat : she was at least a version of the Circean type—coming from the city of the sirens.

v

Whatever else the picture did, it marked an era in portraiture. This penetrating and impassioned pulsation of personality had not been realized in paint or stone before. We, who are staled by reproductions of Mona Lisa's image, must try to realize the amazed delight with which this new way of presenting a subject was received.

Mona Lisa & The Battle of Anghiari

Nothing in classic art, nothing in mediæval art, nothing so far in Renaissance art, had prepared Tuscany for this imaginative mode of interpreting a real person. In Florence, portraiture had so far been most successful in sculpture. Desiderio and Mino da Fiesole had moulded with a chaste sympathy the virginal young Florentines with their straight long necks and intelligent looks, their back-brushed hair and candid spirited bearing, the small shadow under the full lower lip softening like a sigh their provoking little smiles. Verrocchio's lady with the lovely hands had achieved nobility as well as a cool sweetness like her primroses. It is sad that we have not Leonardo's picture of Ginevra dei Benci, done at this time also, a " cosa bellissima " that was considered very like the lady ; for one would gladly see how Leonardo interpreted a true Florentine. But it was *Mona Lisa* that made the sensation, *Mona Lisa* who attracted the imitators. Evidently Leonardo got his best effects when he had an exotic type to work upon—Lombard or Neapolitan. There is a kind of lovely animalism so dreamy in its texture that it seems mysterious ; it is as if every cell of the *mate* moist flesh secreted reverie from the atmosphere. And perhaps it is mysterious, sacred stuff woven again and again by the gods of life in places like the islands of Parthenope for their peculiar priestesses. The Neapolitans had it ; the Lombards had it, and it was more mystical wear with them. Dwellers in wet, mild places have it most often, as if they grew like the water-lilies.

What the treatment of *Mona Lisa* looked like when applied to the wrong person you may perceive in Raphael's *Maddalena Doni*, which looks like a well-painted caricature. This heavy, over-domesticated woman, like a boiled gooseberry, was surely the last person to be done " after " La Gioconda. The painter, in his extreme interest in Leonardo's stylistic achievement, must have forgotten his model.

vi

There are many famous portraits of women—or of their attitudes. Not to speak of the sculptured women, though many of these are among the rarest, there had been fair high ladies by Piero della Francesca, and Botticelli had turned Simonetta Vespucci's wistful and bizarre face to a dreamy wonder both as Mary and as Venus. Through succeeding generations the mind, reminiscent, strays at random. There is Raphael's *Joanna of Aragon* ; and the great lady with the white veil, whom, they say, he loved. There is Titian's *Laura Dianti*, soft, rich, and luxurious as peonies. There are the sharp fine outlines of Jean Clouet's ladies. There is that unknown woman, painted by Velasquez, with mantilla and fan, whose eyes attack you, and whose expression says she has a history

Leonardo the Florentine

—an admirable picture of course, and a human document as well. Rubens' Hélène and Rembrandt's Saskia live within the canvas. There is Holbein's Duchess of Milan. There is El Greco's startling and lovely daughter. There is Goya's Duchess. Rose and blue and white you have the powder-soft images of the Pompadour. There are Reynolds' Kitty Fisher, and Romney's Emma, and Gainsborough's Graces, and Raeburn's deep-glowing, love-textured women. There is Albert Stevens' Mrs Collman. There are Whistler's diaphanous ladies. Think of to-day, and Augustus John's *Laughing Woman* seems to be invested with the strange quality of air, vibrating around her tragic strident head and sleeping in the great folds of her red gown, that dwells within a timeless picture. But, whether you like *Mona Lisa* or not, even if your fancy has been staled by thousands of bad photographs of the portrait—these all seem common clay beside her whose fluent flesh was moulded by the puissant and delicate waves of Leonardo's contemplation, waves like that he saw at stormy Piombono, which was "all foam-water." In spite of the *fadaises* of too-sentimental idolaters (the worst being the French, who, though admirable Leonardo scholars, cannot quite get over their national longing to have a "mistress" in the case) this presentation of the *femme de trente ans* of the Renaissance remains the supreme portrait of a woman. Others may be more obviously beautiful ; she remains inexhaustible in surmise. True that for many she has an inimical air, and seems to offer not peace but the thrust of a hidden dagger. So does Nature. Mr Berenson bitterly calls her a foreigner ; but she is not therefore an undesirable alien. For this once Leonardo had the whim to try his aery mask of mystery on a human face with a Neapolitan secret of its own. He was in an excited mood after the turmoil of his Borgian year ; and, with something of a cruel sympathy, he did idly try to tamper, with an amused mind, at a lock whereof he knew the wards, though he did not desire to force them. Once he did this—evidently only once, for even by his contemporaries *Mona Lisa* was considered unique among his portraits. I prefer Saint Anne. But La Gioconda is woman, she is natural woman, seen and seen through by Leonardo.

vii

It is likely that Leonardo allured his patient sitter to come at the end of the day, to sit among the music in the merciful light he loved. It would soothe him, this detachment of the quiet lady in her still pose, this painting of silences and consoling surfaces and hazes of green light, after the day spent in working at the convulsed figures of the first live battle-picture ever painted. Leonardo created many precedents. It is as if Destiny destroyed his nonpareil exemplars so that others might not be discouraged from attempting the new path—not entirely a happy notion of Destiny's.   Piero Soderini, a determined rather than a discerning patron of art, was now gonfalonier.   War with Pisa was still troublesome ; but, aware that Florence had her greatest geniuses within her gates at the time, he thought that the city should take tithe of their labour, and the citizens feel like Athenians at some great game and contest of straining wits, with Leonardo and Michelangelo together painting the walls of the council-chamber of the Palazzo Vecchio.   The Florentines had always loved to use the spur of competition.   Michelangelo's eager and angry mood welcomed the duel.   Leonardo must have hated it ; he who kept his unique way shuddered from the vulgarity. Yet his mood was still charged with great fiery images of violence that could be precipitated only in large spaces.   A battle ? He knew how to paint a battle, not an amusing game of hobby-horses like Uccello's, nor the calm pageant of Piero della Francesca, but the very orgasm of brutality, the stupid " bestialissima pazzia " of men.   So he accepted the commission, somewhat stringently expressed, for the great artist was by this time considered as hard to hold and bind as Proteus.   Whether the battle of Anghiari, in which the Florentines defeated the Milanese, was a theme maliciously inflicted on the friend of Milan we are uncertain. Certain it is that Leonardo would have turned any battle into a battle of horses ; and that Michelangelo would have used his as an opportunity for his vision of naked and splendid athletes, whoever the combatants.

At first Leonardo seems quite concentrated on covering his wall with deathless forms of strife.   On the 24th day of October 1503 he took from the Signoria the keys of the Sala del Papa in Santa Maria Novella, the studio allotted to him for the great work, and in February 1504 he had finished his cartoon and begun the great group of *The Battle of the Standard* in the Sala del Consiglio itself.   But now his delicate and deadly nemesis, as with insouciant grace, came lightly once more across his path.   It is hardly likely that Leonardo's mind acquiesced completely in its task even from the beginning ; but he was carried along by the æsthetic, and even the ethic, desire to rid himself of the feverish Borgian experience by expressing it.   When he had designed the cartoon, its central ecstasy of wrath around the Standard communicating its furious beat, by riderless chargers and agonized fugitives, to subsidiary knots of rage and torment ; when he had drawn the heads of frantic men and frantic steeds, and projected all this passionate realism into the airs of beauty by the rhythm and the dæmonic energy and the grace of the lithe, finely-armoured figures and the divine horses, he had relieved his mind— and was tired of the battle.   Then little irritations vexed him unduly ; he seemed like one unnerved. It is almost as if, half dreaming, half awake, he brought about his own defeat. He already knew that one long-studied painting on a cloister wall was insecure : he felt foredoomed in fresco, or its equivalent. The conviction that he had once jeopardized his work made him jeopardize it again, almost consentingly, at least unresistingly, like a somnambulist carrying out a suggestion of failure. He seems to be overcome by one of those strange fits of Renaissance fatalism that paralyse even the men of action sometimes in moments of great consequence. Else why trust the burden of this tremendous cartoon to the chance of an ill-understood recipe out of Pliny ? " He took from Plinius the stucco in which he painted." He wanted to paint in oil, and trusted to this antique stucco as a binder. It needed heat to make sure of fixation, and when Leonardo lit a great brasier of fire in the Sala del Papa, all went well. But when he lit another in the enormous Sala del Consiglio the heat would not reach beyond the feet of his combatants, and the colours of the group of *The Battle of the Standard*, which he had already painted, began to run. Dolour must have wrung him hard, especially as the historic taunt of Michelangelo still jarred his ear and flushed his cheek. So far as we know, at least, he said nothing.

But, if his unconscious part had been passionately attached to that wall in the immense room, all blighted now by Vasari's industry, would not the vision of that tide of war have found its encaustic permanent ? Could not Leonardo, who measured the waves and calculated the effects of light and heat, have taken account of the height of the chamber for which he had built a special bridge of scaffolding, and considered to what level a manageable flame would affect an atmosphere with which he was familiar ? In art and in science Leonardo, who knows so much and is so elaborate in preparation, often fails by some initial error into which no ordinary man would have slipped. The mistakes of the brilliant are always mistakes that no fool would make. But they are mistakes which, by their very obviousness, betray a condition of nervous embarrassment, peculiar to Leonardo at work. He was " overcome by fear," says Lomazzo, before all his pictures, seeing always the perfect pattern he could not complete on earth.

Nor were his conditions as fortunate as usual. His princely bearing had its infatuates ; but a critical bourgeoisie considered that it savoured of Medicean sympathies. Evidently he felt stifled and stung by the petty authorities of the town officials, who probably were not sorry to ruffle the artist with the kingly manners. The story of the *maussade* cashier who tried to pay him in quattrini betrays an unhappy state of affairs. " I do not paint for coppers," said Leonardo. And he was but ill-paid after all, Florence not being affluent, with all her mercenaries to keep.

Mona Lisa & The Battle of Anghiari

He would have resumed, perhaps, had he not been called to Milan. Michelangelo also got no farther than his cartoon. The great Pontiff whose will blows through the sculptor's life like a great wind, while he never stirs an eddy in Leonardo's, was imagining his mythic tomb, and demanded him. Both artists departed because of a tomb, for the proud Trivulzio was dreaming in Milan of his. These visionaries of Renaissance tombs had great artists for the " bound captives " of their arrogant mortuary desires. In the end, the Signory had at least both cartoons. While these were to be seen, one in the Medicean palace, one in the Hall of the Pope, Cellini says, Florence was " The School of the World." All the artists thronged to see them, and Leonardo's vanishing knot of frenzied horsemen painted on the wall, and carefully preserved for some time. But, under the pressure of admiration evidently, the drawings fell to pieces and disappeared. They vanished. Rubens drew a free study of *The Battle of the Standard*, and Edelinck engraved it ; but Leonardo translated by Rubens is a light gone out in smoke. Rubens' thicker sight cast in lead the leaping figures, loaded the fiery lines with flesh, hooded the strange heads with stupidity. Raphael's drawing of the horsemen is too softened and unstrung. Different studies of Leonardo's own are more potent in conjuring back that group of agonists.

viii

Leonardo prepared thoroughly for his painting. Somebody wrote out a description of the battle of Anghiari for him—perhaps Machiavelli. He even visited the scene, though it really was a mean skirmish enough, Leonardo's battle of the tribes of the dragon, although Niccolo Piccinino commanded the Florentines. He wrote a study of war in a note of fierce disdain which cannot disedge the mysterious secret zest with which he regards his fantasia of carnage. His words create the suffocating atmophere, the trampled men leaving dreadful traces of their glissades in the bloody mud, the writhing and digging teeth and nails of the dying clamping themselves on vital matter of any kind in the ultimate spasm.

With what intensity his cool eyes recorded the details of agony ! Eyes that had looked unshrinking at wretches led to execution easily devoured the torments of those who at least died in hot blood. He sees how the wings of the nostrils are cut by wrinkles, recurving back from the nose to the eyes, dilating and lifting them in a grin of ghastly finality. Faces he draws, faces in extremity of rage, faces yelling senselessly in the lust of struggle, but working into some pattern of ferocity not without beauty, some enduring mask of an eternal mood, a mood of the frenzy that is not merely in man but in Nature, whose grimaces of fury are cyclone, and earthquake, and deluge, and volcanic flame. Such faces might be frozen under the gilt antennæ and strange vizor of a Samurai armoured in tiers of gold and scarlet lacquer. They appeared under the crested helmets of Leonardo's warriors, graceful and lithe of limb, with armour flexibly moulded and finished on breast and navel with calyxed ornament as fine as the tender little broidery round the neck of Mona Lisa's robe. Casques, scimitars, and ornaments like those of his great drawing of the condottiere knight, he lavished on his battle.

He idealized after all. That he has seen a battle in its brutality he convinces us by words. In picture he merely conveyed its splendid rage, nor could he do otherwise, for his lines never lost their inherent " fire and grace." If Leonardo drew horses he drew beauty, even if the horses bit each other like their riders. With the cold art of the anatomist, the sympathetic art of a cavalier, he brought them springing from the sod. " One is not able to describe the invention which Leonardo showed in the habits of the soldiers, all varied in different ways by him, or in the weapons and other ornaments ; much less the incredible mastery which he showed in the forms and lineaments of the horses, the fiery spirit, the muscles and shapely beauty of which Leonardo drew better than any other master." Their riders were graceful too. He had seen the sullen beautiful features of the Baglioni house, and the Orsini's girlish face, and Cesare's serene profile among the battle smoke, and many another young and reckless mask. This is a personal conflict, and even a madness of rage has its splendour when that conflict is locked round the great symbol of a Standard. Intensity is always a silencing quality : it burns magnificent whatever feeds it. And that atmosphere of dust and smoke so intolerably confusing, Leonardo's brush would alter into a troubled, dreamy glory of sfumato, and strange grace would play heedlessly like lightning over the warriors. " And there must not be a level spot that is not trampled with gore." He would have kept some green sod, where beautiful youth might die. He harrows in words : he will not harrow in his art. He has a great æsthetic mercy : as a painter he will not trade even on your pathos, much less on your sense of anguish.

Still, the whole thing was an apotheosis of terrible movement ; the riders were seen in one instant of that great flux of violence, not entranced or paralysed in it. Not again should Paolo Uccello make of a battle a decoration of orange-trees and lances and attractive hobby-horses with a lyrical figure in the midst, like the victorious boy with the bared gold head. Simone Martini, in his fresco in the Sienese town hall, had carried the incident of war still farther into the concluding peace of romantic decoration. There, against the dense apprehensive blue, towards the locked and castled hill-city on the west, rides the erect, the bright lone captain, while only a prick of gilded flags and spears suggests his advancing host appearing on the farther edge of the east. No ! And not even Piero della Francesca's statuesque grouping in a clear light would again suffice the theme. More's the pity, one thinks, for, though Leonardo's vanished masterpiece has been the great first cause of miles of dreary battle-painting, there is nothing caught from his mood even till we come to Delacroix, who has something of his spirit, though not the fiery volatilization of his line. The great Velasquez applied his complete style only to a moment of noble melancholy ; and made the old tradition novel and original by the tall lances that stand so superbly against the skies of *The Surrender of Breda,* communicating I know not what of destiny accomplished and chivalrous honour unbroken in defeat. Goya and Callot did the horrible details of war. At the vast neatly parcelled reviews of toy soldiers in the eighteenth century one yawns ; at the empty confusions of Vernet and his followers one says, " sound and fury, signifying nothing." Of the official battle-painting of to-day, think what you will. It seems as if war were certainly good material for poetry ; but fit for painting only through symbolism.

The artistic wrong done by Leonardo's cartoon has come about through its vanishing. If it had survived, the rhythm and the beauty of line would have carried it into harmony like his other pictures, and discouraged imitation—perhaps. Love of realism, jarring with the sense of sophrosyne, created one of Leonardo's major conflicts. His soul inclined to a Greek army, an army of lovers like the Thebans, or Spartans, marching to terrible things enough, but marching to the sound of flutes, and ready at desperate moments to sit down and comb their hyacinthine hair. In his final cartoon the flute-music, so to speak, the beautiful curls, the fiery horses, and the bridal passion for the great Standard, would have woven some pure reconciliation of war with beauty. It is when the best things, not the worst things, are withdrawn from what is considered a social evil that it perishes. When the love of comrades, and the sound of a peculiar music, and the blind rare rapture for a flag, are utterly wrung out of war, then war will end in ashes. And that will be when war becomes entirely a conflict of gases, I suppose. The League of Nations may become effective when it includes somebody who really understands how to exterminate the dreadful beauty entangled with war. Nearly extinct now, but not altogether, since it flies like a great golden eagle in the air.

ix

Leonardo's own life, as usual, is consumed by many interests besides painting. Hardly had he returned from his Borgian episode when his

363

own Florence sent him to the walls of that weary indomitable enemy, Pisa, to consider the diversion of the course of the River Arno from the proud ancient city. But rivers do sometimes cleave to the towns that are theirs, and in this case the Arno seems to have refused to be " conducted from place to place " even by Leonardo. " Rivers should be coaxed and not treated roughly or with violence," he says in one place. This theft and rape of the Arno comes under the heading of violence.

Evidently trying to be a good citizen at this period, he renews an old dream, and proposes to raise the sunken floor of the Baptistery and lift the pile on a basement of steps, as originally intended. This was not so extravagant a notion as it seemed to the Florentines, whose ancient Baptistery, on a site hallowed to the gods long before Saint John came with a christened solstice, seemed to have taken an organic grip and sent its roots ramifying through the soil of the city. Yet Leonardo's eloquence half enchanted their wits. " Among these designs and models, there was one by which he often demonstrated to many ingenious citizens who then governed Florence that he was ready to raise the temple of San Giovanni in Florence, and place steps under it, without damage to the building ; and with such weighty reasons he counselled it, that it appeared possible ; although each one of them, after he had departed, would recognize, when alone by himself, the impossibility of such an undertaking." He was too eloquent for city fathers ; even in Florence they distrusted those that charmed their ears.

In 1504 Leonardo is one of a council assembled to decide the placing of Michelangelo's giant *David*, now quarried from the stone he had rejected. With Andrea della Robbia, Cosimo Rosselli, Botticelli, Filippino Lippi, Perugino, Lorenzo di Credi and Giuliano di San Gallo, and others, he discusses the matter. Finally he approves the opinion of San Gallo, that the statue should stand before the Loggia di' Signori : " Io confermo che stia nelle Loggia dove ha detto Giuliano di San Gallo, in su'l murricciuolo dove s'appiccano le spalle allato al muro, con ornamanto decente, et in modo guasti le cerimonie degli Uffici." So he states his opinion, without enthusiasm, with reasons faintly depreciatory. One feels that he did not like the *David*. Michelangelo had his own way, and the statue was erected in the Piazza ; and the gay Florentines began to sing amusing songs about it, as they do to this day. But a watch had to be set on it for some time, because the puritans stoned it, for the dark spirit of Savonarola arose from the scar of the pyre that had been built too close.

In 1504, also, the comfortable Ser Piero da Vinci makes his exit from the world. Leonardo twice writes down the fact with a grim precision : " On Wednesday, at seven o'clock, died Ser Piero da Vinci, on the 9th of

Mona Lisa & The Battle of Anghiari

July 1504 " (C.A.). And again, " On the 9th of July 1504, Wednesday, died Ser Piero da Vinci, notary at the Palazzo del Podesta, my father, at seven o'clock, being 80 years old, leaving behind ten male and two female children."

Piero da Vinci had become a notary so active that no attestation was complete without his signature. Leonardo seems to have maintained some civility with the gross prosperous bourgeois who was once a romantic young man ; but all his decided comments about the method of reproducing the species imply a singular distaste for an old gentleman whose youngest child was a mere infant when he died. In the inheritance he had no part. His illegitimate birth was hardly a reason why he should not have been remembered in some way by his father, who, however, probably died intestate. The other children refused to recognize him in the matter ; and he did not protest. At the time he had money enough. " With his liberality he used to gather together and support any friend, rich and poor, if only he had wit and quality." It is also evident that he had his servants and horses still, and some unusual animals, for it was one of Leonardo's princelike ways to affect a menagerie, as his imitator Sodoma did after him, more extravagantly. The member of the family with whom Leonardo does renew alliance is Alessandre Amadori, the brother of his first stepmother. " Le prete Alessandre Amadori e vivo a non ? " he writes in a memorandum. Amadori was " vivo," and Canon of Fiesole, and amicably proud of the connexion. When Leonardo is thoroughly weary he seeks the bright heights of Fiesole. Early things have their deep claim on him. He reserves some shelter at Vinci, where he first knew the thrill of both panic and nympholepsy, flights and terrors among the woods—fierce, fine appetites, nevertheless, the only sensations unforgettable that still can bite his disciplined soul with ecstasy.

X

In his graceful way Leonardo, like other painters, it must be remembered, received students in his house—Italians, Flemings, Germans. The fame of his beautiful manners and his predilection for charming and dandified young people probably made his house as much an aviary of humming-birds as a busy bottega. Some came to him, no doubt, to get an æsthetic equivalent of the mediæval education of page and squire, some to learn that gracious intimacy with painting which the rare Urbinate courtiers held to be necessary, on the whole, to the perfect education of a gentleman. He attracted sensitive spirits of delicate oblation. He set them preciously about him like flowers among the musicians, young things with fragrant mignonette qualities, wistful qualities too elusive to have names as ethical virtues, too sweet to need other than flowery names as graces, swift suppliances to conciliate a troubled mind, and to stroke tingling nerves into smoothness. Names, and florin-fees, hastily scribbled on fly-leaves or boards of notebooks, cause many young transient figures to flit faintly in the distance. Some painted steadily enough, sedulously imitating the master's ways. Andrea Salaino, renewing the roses in his shoes every April, and burnishing carefully the mass of luxurious hair which, it was said, sometimes served to show that the coils of Leda's were possible, moved about, very attractive and serviceable, good at painting " gallant things," and at getting into mischief. He had a pretty if a malicious trick of presenting Leonardo's ladies naked against the flowers, like romantic courtesans. Leonardo smiled, completely indifferent. Andrea was annoying at moments, but he had piquancy. The little accounts for housekeeping that wander into the notebooks are frequently quoted as a proof of Leonardo's great simplicity of life. They merely prove that he was temperate in food. Andrea of the bright raiment buys the food usually, but such a duty was no disgrace in Renaissance Florence. Indeed, the picture of Andrea of the great curls in his silver cloak and his rosy shoes carrying back bread and grapes and wine, sacramental food for his lord in the tapestried house, and looking like a fantastic Pompeian Eros, is sufficiently agreeable.

In 1505, Botticelli was sixty-one, Perugino, fifty-nine, Leonardo, fifty-three, Michelangelo, thirty, Raphael, twenty-two. Lorenzo di Credi was now drawing sweet epicene heads and mignon angels. Fra Bartolommeo was trying to grasp, with the success of Ixion, some of the largeness of composition he admired in the Saint Anne. Perugino was painting placidly, with a studio so decorated with pretty girl-models that visitors were loth to depart, though the beautiful girl with the sumptuous hair whom he had married was kept close enough. Botticelli was become so weary and so uncertain of humour that commissions had ceased to visit him. It was full Cinquecento, and he yearned back to the chill sweet seas and the virginal goddess of the morning. But in the cell of melancholy he found a theme, and, more modern than any, he painted despair in *The Outcast*. Andrea del Sarto, still very young, was feeding his dark eyes on Leonardo's images. A small, unruly, and impudent child was growing into an age at which he would see salamanders in the fire and be plagued into learning to play the flute. One day, as Benvenuto Cellini, he would demand of the King of France that he should pay him as Leonardo had been paid.

Raphael, come gently from Siena to learn what he could in Florence, found favour in Leonardo's studio. He was modest and girlish, with eloquent shadowy eyes and flowing hair, a pretty youth, though a trifle sentimental. He was meditating a *Pietà* for Atalanta, the fair, unfortunate mother of Grifonetto Baglioni, the mother " that was herself so young," for, like Perugino, he too had been used to bring these violent people into the dreamy quietude of his pictures. Leonardo's sketchbooks were open to him ; and he drew motives from the old drawings and the new, and copied, copied assiduously. It is a strange effect when Raphael imposes the Early Victorian type of which he had such a clear prevision on attitudes borrowed from Leonardo. There is the picture, for instance, of the Madonna who always is to me the portrait of Laura Pendennis—her so popularly known as *La Belle Jardinière*. You generally have Raphael at his worst when he imitates Leonardo. The theft is too obvious, and, what is worse, too unjustified. Raphael was temperamentally rather than mentally disqualified from understanding the greater painter. He copies the pyramidal forms, the attitudes, the dulcitude, but not the ironic dulcitude. For all his fluid paint, his gracious lines, his happy gift of decorating spaces, his benignities of motherhood, when he imitates Leonardo he becomes dull. He could exalt Perugino, he could assimilate the terribilità of Michelangelo to some quality that went with his soft genius. But Leonardo dwelt beyond his sphere.

xi

It was Michelangelo who really embittered Leonardo's Florentine life. Perhaps it cannot be expected that great geniuses of diametrically differing temperaments should love each other. But Leonardo was courteous to everybody. He had worked very harmoniously with Bramante ; and seems always on good terms with his fellow-painters. Michelangelo, however, with his stormy melancholy, and his corroding neurasthenia of suspicion and fear, could not endure another brilliant artist near him. Leonardo's aspect, Leonardo's dress, Leonardo's gracious ways exasperated him. They were working in rivalry at the council hall —and Leonardo looked like that ! " He was of a fine person, well-proportioned, full of grace and of a beautiful aspect." He still wore a rose-coloured tunic, short to the knee, though long garments were in use. " He had, reaching down to the middle of his breast, a fine beard, curled and well-kept." Rose-colour was the colour for aristocrats in Florence, it should be remembered.

He looks like that, and he seems as great a gentleman as it is possible for a concealed angel to be. Also, he can *flâner* in the streets talking, always talking, when he should be working to death, trying to hold his own with his younger rival. He, Michelangelo, is overwhelmed with

labour, he has to wear an old felt hat and can hardly take his boots off ;
though he is a young man he is ravaged with unpoetic internal pains.
Moreover, where does Leonardo get so much money that he can lend
freely to other artists, and keep horses and servants like a noble ? Nobody
knows where that money comes from. He, Michelangelo, can afford
nothing. (So he thinks.) But then he is solitary and poor because he is
virtuous. Besides, he has a family to help. Bastards are lucky : they
have no responsibilities. Also Leonardo pretends to be a Platonist,
like him ; but he has not the true high doctrine. He is only a notary's
son, while he, Michelangelo, is a descendant of the great Matilda. (Art
should be confided only to well-born persons.) How dare Leonardo be
always the Beloved while he laments for ever as the hungry Lover ?
And Dante, whom he also learned to adore in the house of Lorenzo,
so that he had the true canon of Dante-worship always—Leonardo
pretends to understand Dante ! So runs Michelangelo's reverie in his
irritable mood, provoked by Leonardo's unconscious serenity. But it
is not fair to condemn him. There was divinity also in Michelangelo ;
suffering and darkly dreaming of things to come. When he said that,

" I was born for Art : from childhood given
A prey for burning beauty to devour,"

he was right. Devoured he was. Not only his body, but his personality
was wrecked by it. He was a Titan ; and the feud with the Olympian
was predetermined.

As for Leonardo, like all people accustomed to use their personalities
with magical effect, to persuade easily with a trick of the eyes and a
curve of the mouth and a slight motion of the beautiful hands, so that the
farther favour of musical speech seems an intoxication and excess of
giving, he found it disconcerting to see somebody so notoriously outside
the spell. Sensitively he disliked dislike. He would make advances to
Michelangelo. Perhaps he had not been enthusiastic about that gawky
huge *David*. Neither had he cared for that young drunken *Bacchus* of
his, smooth and sleepy, not like his Dionysos god. But Michelangelo is
destroying his native air for him : after all, perhaps the distrust is due
to the fact that they share some psychical resemblance. He has heard
Michelangelo's defence of the incorruptible nature of Our Lady's beauty,
and it pleases him. It remains young and perfect because it is never
wasted by a single sensual motion, even of thought. So he himself likes
to think of virginity : they knew psychology, those monks. Perhaps
Michelangelo and he are anchorites of the same order. And Michelangelo himself has his own obscure undertow of attraction. " When I
see a man who knows how to do or say something better than the rest

of the world I am constrained to fall in love with him, and then I give myself so completely to him that I no longer belong to myself. . . . Even the dancer, the luteplayer, if they were skilled in art could do what they liked with me." So his heart said, but the genius in him could not endure a subjection which meant its own dissolution in love. When, in his later phase, he became a childlike beggar for tenderness, it was from Vittoria Colonna, who had a calm pure soul, still more from Tommaso Cavalieri, beautiful, honourable, but limited, it was from stupid young men with lovely faces, that he implored it. The wisdom of his genius saved itself from suffering through his prostrations by preventing him from adoring anybody who was likely to dominate him. For all his jealousy, his just sense of beauty divined the greatness of Leonardo, and the danger of his magic. There is a strange twist of hatred, there is love gone wrong, there is a resentment mad with morbid attraction in his impossibly boorish attack. This historic insult, in which Leonardo's tentative civility ends, is perhaps so brutal and so childishly gross because he feels his hatred imperilled. The true neurasthenic cannot accept an advance : it amazes him, and the immediate surprise expresses itself by a crazy rudeness which is his own undoing.

Leonardo is walking in the Piazza Santa Trinità, near the river. An eager group of acquaintances is discussing a point in Dante. They see Leonardo, and gather him quickly to them, urging him to give an opinion. He observes Michelangelo coming moodily along " like an executioner," as Raphael will say in Rome, his hat over his tortured angry brows ; and remembers he is a disciple of Dante. So, in his persuasive way : " Michelangelo here will explain the verses of which you speak." " Explain them yourself," comes the vehement irrelevant cry of abuse. " You who made the model of a bronze horse, and who, incapable of casting it, left it unfinished, to your shame be it said ! " Then, as if fury chokes him : " And these ' capponi' of Milanese thought you could do it ! " Leonardo, it is recorded, flushed deeply—and was silent. You feel the blank embarrassment of the group, as Michelangelo goes off raging.

The deep flush that dyed Leonardo's cheek is perhaps the most emotional thing recorded of him. True ! It was Lodovico's wars that had prevented the great Cavallo from passing through the fires of the foundry. But, if he had not wrestled with the Centaur for sixteen years, it might have reared itself in gilded bronze before the Duke's star had set. It was not without great pain that he remembered the terrific effort with which he had striven to marry grace and strength in a Rider that would be the Energy of Italy. The mere shock of the crude insult jarred him to the centre. He did not reply. Why should he ? In the lucid

2 A

369

courts of his intelligence swords might be crossed, but there was no mud-throwing. Michelangelo might as well have thrown a handful of filth at his candid rose raiment. Leonardo's flush faded and he made no sign. "As if the Emerald said to itself: 'Whatever happens I must be Emerald.'" Leonardo remained smaragdine. Michelangelo went on his way, hating Leonardo a little more, having wronged him.

Still, his detractor found him strangely stimulating. If Leonardo built his pyramid of mysterious emotion in Saint Anne, Michelangelo set his Holy Family piled within a round—powerful forms, masculine sibylline woman of austere beauty, vigorous child, beautiful nude youths also severe and pure. Did Leonardo dissolve his shifting shimmering moods into fine rich paints and glazes, fumes of soft light and colour? In stern distemper and cold clear hues Michelangelo arrogantly set out his soul. Does somebody say that Leonardo's chargers are more beautiful than anybody's horses? Michelangelo also draws horses of his own. Was Leonardo preoccupied with the theme of Leda? Michelangelo did a great Leda, sister to Dusk and Dawn, with his usual candour; though the prudish shrank from the mighty embraces of his calm chaste gods. With jealous eyes he had looked at Leonardo's drawings. The loveliest creatures Michelangelo ever compelled from marble, the dreamy agonists called the *Bound Captives*, are like great supernal lilies laid by Michelangelo's genius at the feet of Leonardo's in some true Platonic world of beauty's patterns, where nothing survives of the mortality that hindered one and marred the other. Michelangelo, like lesser men, copied from Leonardo, who copied nobody.

xii

While Leonardo has been considering his battle-picture, Isabella of Mantua has renewed her courteous petitions. She has become somewhat ruffled by Giovanni Bellini, steadily protesting that he is of no use at "fantasie," especially hers; but she approaches Leonardo as delicately as ever. This time it is by the Ferrarese agent Angelo del Tovaglia, whose villa in Florence Leonardo had drawn for the Marquis. She desires exceedingly that the artist would paint a boy-Christ for her, not hurrying in the matter, as a diversion "from his heavy labour "—not knowing or not heeding that *Mona Lisa* was diversion enough. To Leonardo himself she pleads for this little piece of charm and sweetness. "If you will grant our desire," she writes, "apart from the payment, which shall be fixed by yourself, we shall remain so deeply obliged to you that we shall never be able to acquit our debt." And, "Our sole desire shall be to do what you wish, and from this time forth we are ready to do your service and pleasure." She could not say more; and perhaps she sealed her letter with her precious turquoise so absolutely graven with a *Victory*. But it was vain. She repeats mournfully her great desire, sighs that the orders he receives " make me fear that you have forgotten mine." " We beg you, when you are weary of Florentine history, to seek relaxation in this little figure." But Leonardo, giving vague sweet words, promising " without fail " to Angelo del Tovaglia, does not seem to reply to her. Angelo evidently suspects the artist's absent-mindedness. He has also gone to quicken Perugino on Isabella's behalf, and sceptically observes that in the struggle to be last he thinks Leonardo will win. When Isabella herself comes to Florence to give thanks for recovery from an illness among the festival lilies of the Annunziata Church, Leonardo is in retreat, watching birds at Fiesole. She sees both the cartoons, and gets the gentle and gracious Alessandro Amadori to intercede for her, with the usual consequence of fair fruitless words. So she desists. Again he " really promised "; but he left for Milan in May. Meanwhile it is suggested that Andrea Salaino shall paint her " cosa galanta " (some gallant thing). This did not sound to Isabella's Renaissance mind so startling a substitute for " a little Christ " as might appear. Life was very much of one piece with her, a gold-changeable tissue with jest and devotion in the interplay. She was the tender intimate of the Beata Osanna, the special mascot of Mantua ; but she could write a shocking story to her very young son in Rome. She did not, however, use the curled Salaino as suggested; but some time after she invited his opinion on Perugino's work, for the *Triumph of Chastity* had not satisfied her. He praised the fantasia and altered some defects, which, one thinks, must have considerably annoyed the distinguished and elderly and popular Perugino. But Isabella must have thought this was a subtle way of pleasing Leonardo ; and her manners with Perugino were distinctly imperious. Her tact does not avail. The Grotta will have no trace of Leonardo. No heavenly head with mysterious eyes and soft bright curls will gaze with faint smile upon that place of gilded intarsiatura, paven with rich majolica. Perugino will deliver his canvas in time ; Venice will send her rare stuffs, and furs, and rosaries of roses, enamelled roses. Mantegna has served her to the end. Cristoforo da Romano, that fine connoisseur, would frame for her a door in Greek vases, gryphons and doves. She has another viol of ebony and sandalwood from Lorenzo da Pavia. Manutius will give her copies of Catullus and Propertius and Persius, fresh from his press, printed on special parchment. Fra Sabba, from exile in Rhodes, will send her heads of Amazons and morsels of lucid shapes from Chios, Delos, Naxos— enchanting names—and sweet calamus for a new lyre, and cherish a daring stupendous dream of transporting Artemisia's great tomb from

Halicarnassus to Mantua. So she must be content. The world is her glittering fair.

xiii

As usual Leonardo is much occupied with many things not obviously relevant to painting. While Fra Pacioli lingers in Florence, he can spend tranquil hours in the multiplication of roots. With a "maestro d'Abbaco" he exquisitely squares the circle. Bartolommeo Vespucci, the nephew of the explorer, lends a book on geometry. Pandolfini lends another. Sirigatti has priceless information to convey concerning astronomy. With Giovanni di Amerigo Benci, that studious boy, he keeps up a lively interchange of books and *mappemondes* and "jaspers": for at times he is all for cosmography. Antonio Segni, described as "very much his friend" in earlier times, is rich now and a patron of painters, and glad to renew the ancient pact of friendship. Still, I prefer to think that the decorative cartoon of the *Triumph of Poseidon* was given him in the early generosity of youth. The surging sea-chariot of the god at Windsor is drawn at the period of exultant spirals and volutes, certainly ; but it may have been done in a fit of reminiscence. With the miniaturists Leonardo has pleasant intercourse. Gherardo at San Marco he knows ; and to the distinguished Attavante he lends four golden ducats, though not without making a note of it. (He frequently puts a casual account in his scientific notebooks. At this period, indeed, such little memoranda become rather frequent. He seems occasionally, with an irritated wonder, to explain to himself what has happened to some small sum, as the times become more straitened.) Wherever he goes, he is friendly with the miniaturists and illuminators, casting a wistful eye on their entrancing art. He who could be so captivating in detail was not averse from the idea of practising even this form of mediæval intensity. He had the patience, too. If Michelangelo could contract himself into a sonnet, Leonardo thought sometimes of binding his flowers into a tender page of unique illumination, strange violet, and verderame, with touches of rose-blood and unburnished gold. A siren-broidered, vine-trailed page ! Or one so convoluted with mysterious dragon-beasts and labyrinthine lines of eternity as to look like a leaf from an Italian *Book of Kells*. But, so far as one knows, he did not. He must have realized that the cloistral art would run like a little soft flame through his heavily chartered hours, consuming them with a small absorbing felicity of toil.

And he had so much else to do.   Geology snared him along the banks of the Arno, and round his old home.   Near Monte Lupo he sees piled up the coloured gravels conglomerate.   By Castel Fiorentino he perceives the tufa. There are mixtures of shells of all ages and kinds (shells he loves also for their own sake, gathering them like flowers). The contours of Monte Albano tell of liquid erosions. Milan was once in a sea ; Florence was once in a lake. But anatomy is better. That needs as much exactitude and concentration as illumination. He had begun it for painting's sake. Now it was one of his intellectual habits. If it was less fragrant than the blazoning of flowery pages, it was more exciting. He was the illuminator of the dark red centres where the last secrets of existence flickered and throbbed ; he was the first miniaturist of the Life-tree sunk palpitating and vulnerable in every human form, protected by an armour of bone. And might not his scalpel, that pried more curiously and with more poignant tact than any other probing steel, slide through some recondite valve, press on some occult secreting gland, and discover what is more marvellous to him than an America or a ringed Jupiter—that final retreat yet a-shudder with the amazement of a just-departed soul ? He is working in the hospital of Santa Maria Novella, and passionately interested in blood-vessels. " Draw the arm of Francesco the miniaturist," he notes, " it shows so many veins." The patient arm of the miniaturist does him a kindly turn. Here is a still interlude between Leonardo and a very old man, sitting motionless as a Buddha on his bed in the hospital, while his faint pulses fade out in the after-noon sun. " This old man, a very few hours before his death, told me that he was a hundred years old and more, and that he felt no discomfort in himself but weakness ; and so, seated on his bed in the hospital of Santa Maria Novella in Florence, with no other move-ment or sign of any accident, he passed from this life. And I made an autopsy of him to see the cause of so gentle a death." He found the veins quite desiccated. Soon after he dissected a two-year-old child ; and stated an admirable comparison. Those children he drew and painted, so infantile yet so royal, with whom he must have conversed as prince with prince—he certainly knew them through and through. No sigh of wondering pity for the imperceptible cessation of that apolo-getic old man, whose disclaiming and obscure existence is part and parcel of a grey and passive subsoil of humanity whence great orchids like Leonardo draw their flamelike substance ! It is a strange human parable that for a moment opposes the most vivid of Renaissance personalities to the most obscure. Oh, of course, of course, Leonardo was a true scientist ; and his interest for the moment was " this tunic of veins," which, he said, men wear as oranges do.

Michelangelo was an anatomist too. They were very kind at San Spirito in allowing him bodies. In later days his surgeon-friend, Colombo, gave him the corpse of a singularly beautiful and graceful Moor as a valuable favour ; and the artist made a demonstration on it for Condivi. But the docile Condivi is made to say : " I speak of that part of the science which is necessary to the art of painting and sculpture, not of the other particulars which the anatomists study." There is possibly a bitter side-glance in retrospect at Leonardo's researches into " the other particulars." For his part, Leonardo, when he comes to Rome, writes down his impression that painters should not draw their figures as if they were only anatomists. Probably he has been contemplating the vast thews and mighty sinews of the prophets and sibyls in the Sistine. He, the best anatomist of his day, never made that mistake. Indeed his physiological drawings are so beautiful because the æsthete in him never dies, so that the figures are nobly proportioned, and the weft of the muscle is never coarse. Yet it was Michelangelo who became ill over his anatomy ; not the sensitive æsthete. An æsthete is more ruthless than anybody except an impassioned scientist, and Leonardo was both. Nevertheless, he had that glamour for which infatuated mortals gladly forgo compassion : " There was an endless grace in all his actions."

xiv

Even anatomy, which was probably to some degree auxiliary to his battle-painting, failed to steady his quivering equilibrium. Life was too agitating in Florence, with its intrigues and its cliques, its whispers and denigrations, and, most wearing of all, the excessive expectations of his partisans. His spirit is fretful ; his great wings are taken in a net. Wings ! The swifts are circling to the eaves in the sunset, and the hawk hangs poised on a clear March morning over the way to Fiesole. He will go to the heights, and work at flight awhile, till his mind too rises serene and pure, motionless and golden as the god Horus over Egypt, having " outsoared the shadow of their might." Even as a bird out of the fowler's snare he escapes away to the holy hill of Fiesole to do a new thing of divinity. Sweet air, and the affectionate priest Amadori for company ! Perhaps he will work at hydraulics too, as he looks down on the winding waters. Perhaps he will think of Leda also, to keep together the divinity of wings and waters with her mystical smiling.

So he begins to write and draw with passion, to concentrate on flight. In this recoil from human society and its intolerable demands he seems more determined than ever to bring his long studies in matters aerial to a stupendous climax. Over there, naked and challenging, rises Monte Ceceri, by its very name tempting him to spread the wings of Michael, of Lucifer. If he did fly, how satisfied for ever would be the aching sense of baffled power that has always fretted faintly his great composure, how silenced for ever the tiresome voices that, with good or ill intent, insist that the winged victory of his genius has closed her pinions. He writes and he draws with patient marvellous precision. His astonishing eyes and his unerring stylus record the instantaneous movements of wings with camera-like swiftness. You seem to see them sweep out from the page, to catch them a moment in the rapture of their ascent, with no effect of arrest or sudden catalepsy. He argues intensely that, though one might state that birds are more powerfully organized for flight than man, since the breast is woven, bone, muscle, and cartilage, of a piece with the wing, skin, muscle, and ligament, all very powerful, yet this flexible energy is used also for such purposes as holding the prey, so that the bird needs little force, really, to move in the air. Men have far more power, he is assured, than they need merely for walking. So he toils at the great wing as of an immense bat-bird, more of the Dark Angel's than the Bright, indeed—and so, predestined.

Meanwhile in viscid wells in alien wealds of Asia seethes the power he needs. The instinct of the diviner, perhaps, turned his fancy sometimes to Caucasian realms.

But he is hopeful, and for once, in the recesses of his manuscripts, utters one of the few personal cries that irresistibly rend the obstinate silence of his soul, the soul that stands by, watching the " ineffabile mano sinistro " write its secret Arabic way. The name of the neighbouring hill, the vision of the æsthetic beauty he bears within his mind as Leda and Leda's lover, the exultation of attainment, bring him one of those moments, filled with plumes of snow and flame, when Leonardo for an instant reveals how much of a god he sometimes felt : " From the mountain which bears the name of the great bird will take flight that glorious bird which will fill the whole world with its infinite splendour."

XV

The studies of Leda which belong to this period are among the most beautiful of Florentine drawings. Half-kneeling among the sweet sedges around the water-lilies, whose hearts are steeped in divinity like hers, her delight yearning back to the great bird, and forward to the children, the glad naked Leda seems aglow with a soft light of dreamy consummation ; and the wings of the swan are bridal. The spiral shadowing has a triumphal zest, as if the whole rich fable were rising into a lyric ecstasy of flight. But indeed these drawings of the kneeling Leda seem to reveal a true Leonardo that is almost a lost Leonardo—the painter of the meads of cool water and lilies, and white naked shapes dreaming in rare golden air, of a sinless paganism, part Elysian, part

Arcadian. It is only one part of the Hellenic dream, but it is the Greek paradise—something idyllic, and something wildly sweet. And in this ethereal, purely enchanted peace, where no beautiful shape is monstrous, Leonardo should have moved paranymphus. But the Middle Ages lay between, and from their lovely wasting fever he could not but inherit some sense of the forbidden, some subtle doctrine of Manichæan conflict between light and darkness, some Syrian ecstasy. When he painted the *Leda*, in the end, it was considered a " dangerous " picture, a Leda chaste and conscious, looking like the Dionysos, and more aware of the strange nuptial knot than of the covering wings. Somewhere in his soul lay the amber light and the lucid dells of Elysium, and the singing of the Hesperides, Hyacinth and the sister of Hyacinth growing side by side, and Achilles racing in his beauty on sands where breaks that crested wave of time which is Hellenism. But the dread out of Asia clouded it, and he never painted even a Sicilian idyll, as Giorgione did. Among the silver shifts and soft substitutions that slip and vanish in the fluctuations of Leonardo's fancy, the Leda myth may but suavely supplant that of Ganymede. Michelangelo it was who drew the *Ganymede*, and Raphael *The Death of Adonis*. Leonardo was truly the paranymph of a Narcissan dream-type ; and he desired not only the wings but that miracle of birth which he could never reconcile with his sense of beauty unless it were supernatural.

Who knows what climax and crisis of life was upon him as he wrote those pages of the ways of birds, and drew his *Leda* ? Somewhere in Leonardo's prime there seems a fall of Icarus, and a great soul, whose folded wings may be broken, henceforth keeps his eyes for the dust of the earth that besets him, waiting for his mortality.

xvi

That he had been vexed during the period of *The Battle of Anghiari* is fairly apparent. It is at this time that the Duchess' circle at Urbino, people with large intelligent eyes and subtle mouths (destined some of them to sorrowful ends, though now so sweetly discoursing and gliding into fine bassets), while talking of the painter's art, chance to consider those who excel in one thing, yet make it their business to do another. Of which perversity Leonardo is cited by Federigo as a chief exemplar. " Another man, one of the first painters in the world, despises the art in which he is most rare and has set himself to study philosophy, in which he has such strange conceptions and new chimeras that he could not with all his painter's art depict them." If Federigo means natural philosophy, he is ill-informed. But of this note of admiring remonstrance, from those who " cannot dispraise but in a kind of praise," as well as of more insolent reproach, Leonardo was hearing far too much for his sensitive mood. If another wall-painting had betrayed him, he was weary of an art in which he could never see his dream and desire glassed in true perfection. All artists have their æsthetic " nights obscure," when they blaspheme against their art. In the black horror of their extinguished torches their accomplishments seem but the broken toys and baubles of an idiot, the spilt glass of a shivered kaleidoscope. Leonardo consistently did consider his art of painting as his supreme business ; but he was, like all many-sided people, perverse enough to resent depreciation of his other and more unusual masteries. After all, he knew those who could employ them, and be glad of them, who could employ all of him, too vast for this little Florence. And say what they might, who matched him in painting even if he did not cover walls to please town councillors or popes, or repeat himself endlessly for any prosperous bidder like Perugino ? He never staled his theme. He was the unique Leonardo, and unique was his every image. As for fertility, he had but to leave his sketch-books open, and the pollen-dust drifted about, and Raphael's Madonnas assumed an air of quality, Michelangelo's youths put on a Bithynian grace. But of him some new thing was always expected.

It was true. His own disdain of trodden ways had begun that fatal expectation which afterwards the artist disappoints at his peril, and which has no mercy on his human weariness. Leonardo, just declining from the zenith of his great maturity of power, was beginning to realize that, by being an athlete both in mind and in body, he had drained too deeply even his profound crystal reservoirs of vitality. He had not slackened yet. But the error over the stucco in the battle-piece was an initial stupidity which was part of the phenomena of exhaustion. The chimera of perfection wherewith he wrestled had sprung unawares and staggered him, so that, wearied with long preparation, he blundered like an amateur at the first step of the practical phase of his creation.

xvii

The more casual drawings of these days show some restlessness. The convolutions of Leda's hair become queer soothing symbols. But the excitement of the Borgian period dies sullenly away in a drift and disturbance and fantasy of deluge and destruction. Scattered clouds, torn sky, bent trees, overthrown men, knots of drowning cavaliers ! Why does he draw a Deluge in which he does not believe ? Why does he even write a purple passage about it ? All the brooding resentment of his mind, all the drift and disturbance of his emotional existence, find relief in this vast and careless purgation of the earth from humanity by the Flood. Conflict of wind and water and fire, cloud-bursts, frenzied groups, then eddying water and rarer rain ! He broods over it, elaborates it, even while the æsthete in him refuses the theme for a picture. It is his secret way of saying : " Après moi, le déluge." After him indeed, the Sack of Rome, the Sack of Florence, and the subjection of Italy.

All this time there was some suppressed emotional trouble in Leonardo's life, to be guessed at and felt like muted strings behind the shifting scene, a shadow of leaping flame upon the painted wall, a disquiet too delicate and fugitive for history, a flicker and a scintillation, an ethereal rose that vanishes and comes again among the blues and greens of the great opaline soul of Leonardo. We only know the manuscript is troubled sometimes, and that among the relaxed pages fair figures intrude, like that of a beautiful young man with exotic mitre and grave eager visage. Among pages of fortifications come arabesques of interlinear pattern, so irrelevant that they seem to record Leonardo's way of pursuing some strange labyrinth of memory, to be the hieroglyphic chronicle of Leonardo's way of loving, untrodden before save by epheboi and angels.

The problem of *The Battle of Anghiari* tortures him. The lively cabals in the studios ; the disputes over Machiavelli's new militia ; the rumours concerning himself, are all wearisome. The might of his lifted wings fades from him, and the vision of golden Leda pales on the heavier air. Where shall he go ? " Anywhere, anywhere, so it be out of your whispering," he might say, like the desperate lady in the play. " Dove mi poserò ? Dove de qui a poco tempo tu'l saprai," he writes on a distracted page in the Codex Atlanticus. But Leonardo was beloved. Someone came behind, with long fragrant curls that touched the page, and profound sweet eyes, writing underneath :

> " Leonardo mio, non avete,
> O Leonardo, perchè tanto penate ? "

So the under-music wells out in Leonardo's life ; as through a suddenly opened door the sound of flutes afar, and a high and tender sympathy as of the lovers imagined in the House of Agathon.

Nevertheless Leonardo and Florence had failed each other, he in patience and the City in kindness. The nervous crisis ended suddenly. An urgent demand came from the French in Milan : some high personage had need of Leonardo to fulfil " certain plans." So he was permitted to depart in May, for three months, under pain of a fine if he did not return within that period. That witty foreigner Erasmus was in Florence in October ; but, as he seemed blind in that city, and merely went on complaining that he was not in Rome, he did not miss Leonardo, who had not returned. Michelangelo, Raphael, Bartolommeo, Andrea del Sarto, had no attraction for him. Even Machiavelli he ignored. He lost his time and his temper ; and translated Lucian for his comfort. For he had no sense of art, and Italy was for him merely the land of the Latinists. But he saw a surpassing thunderstorm, with a sky of dead silver and clouds like ashen cliffs, and lightning darting wildly about the walls. Leonardo may have regretted not having seen such spectacular firedrakes around the horizon.

Leonardo had gone, and would return only as a transient guest. Yet he went with that half-sad, half-smiling remonstrance written in his heart as well as in his book. In his bright bitter City, all angry wits and jangled nerves, he had his orris-sweet friends whose penetrating grace was of a rarer quality than the unquestioning, adoring Milanese could give. Let it be said again. Leonardo da Vinci remained the name of the conqueror in the car ; Leonardo the Florentine sounded for ever like the fluted phrase of a lover.

Chapter v

With the French in Milan

i

LEONARDO was immeasurably relieved when he was called to Milan by a voice of such authority that the nervous Republic, now fast-soldered to the French alliance, dared not refuse. He was weary and bitter over his spoiled fresco, jarred by the hostility of Michelangelo, unnerved by the uncertainty of his revenues. Even the bright beauty of the City—the happy harmonies of its towers and domes, the frescoes glowing without and within, the pure spaces of della Robbia work, waking here like grave *Ave Marias* and there like the sennets of great heralds, the arrogant fair images of bronze and marble gathering beneath the Palazzo della Signoria, all the bright genius of Florence that, through faction and error, proved itself indomitable by reason of these rare idols—was not unrebuking for Leonardo, glad to be torn from the duress of its demand, languidly relenting from the proof of his nativity. Even the quick and nimble air, which quivered in the summer heat, was become too tense for him, whose spirit craved for moisture softening through the sense, and a dream of great waters and great water-flowers.

True, the French now held a scattered and spoiled Milan. But Leonardo really liked the French. He liked their gay, quick wits, their flattering ways towards Italian art, especially his own. He had made friends with some already, and found them keen and amusing, and impressed by his brilliant versatility, especially curious concerning the wonder-working keys he carried as gate-ward of the "paradise of the sciences—mechanics." They were ironic like the Florentines, but not so critical. And surely, he thought, the Florentines had lost their edge just then, for ever running to the Piazza to look at the gaily-dressed companies of Machiavelli's absurd new militia. They seemed disoriented with apprehension over the Venetians, this battlesome Pope, and the Medicean exiles, to whom he, at least, had no great objection. To the fussy simple-minded Soderini, indeed, he would prefer Giuliano il Magnifico, whom he had met, and found most intelligent about both portraits and experiments. Would his indifferentism have been stirred even

HEAD OF YOUNG MAN IN AGITATION, WITH
DESIGNS FOR MILANESE ARCHITECTURE
(BRITISH MUSEUM)

KNEELING LEDA
(CHATSWORTH)

if he had realized that this period of unrest was the beginning of the long war-game which would pass through such bloody episodes as Agnadello, Ravenna, Marignano, Pavia, to the intolerable crises of the Sack of Rome and the Agony of Florence? For that long tragedy Michelangelo, despite his craven nerves and physical frenzies of terror, would be the looming Æschylean Choragus, with brush and chisel writing out his great rhythms of lamentation, with all the sacred arrogance of an immortal imagining death and judgment in the chosen chapel of the warring Pope from whom his fearful body fled, with the inviolable might of beauty suborning by a sublime stratagem the very tombs of the disastrous corrupted princes who had wrecked his city, and raising them into an indestructible mythos of stricken gods, the mourners for the pierced heart of Florence and the immolation of Italy. (Far off, there seems a sweetness, as of harpers with unearthly harps, sounding soft muted things of how fair was the Past.) In the Medicean Chapel Leonardo seems a remote and perverse shadow. Yet even that isolated soul might have grieved if he had lived to be aware of the sack of his city. He departed now, to call himself " fiorentino " again in Milan. But as he drew his great studies of cloudy wrack and eddying storm and stupendous waves stirred as by great wings of silver behind the drift, he may have thought these skies were fit for dissolving Italy.

ii

Yet Leonardo had his case. If he was not conscious of civic demands, or of active patriotic duties, he was aware of personal obligations, as the true æsthete, who hates a deformation in his spiritual attitude as much as a defect in his body or a flaw in his work, invariably is. Beautiful manners are the æsthete's morals ; and Leonardo was beloved. He considered it necessary that an artist should move through the world with contacts that were as rarely as possible collisions. His contacts indeed are usually of velvet ; and, if he seems to avoid a quarrel by elusiveness, it is because he detests argument and uproar and even emphasis of any kind. Nevertheless, though he possesses the Renaissance virtue of " cortigiania," a lovely blend of courtesy and courtliness, deep, fine and perfumed like a great wine offered by a noble host, he surrenders less actual independence to princes and pontiffs than Michelangelo does, although he goes noisily in a wind of sighs and tears and complaints. Leonardo was no Goethe : there was nothing of the court-chamberlain about him. If he served princes it was as a prince, who gave inestimable service for a mere comely livelihood. And not for Prince any more than for Republic would he force the perverse difficult dæmon of his art. He suffered some blame for caprice sometimes, because he had early set his own criterion. Those who begin by practising the impossible adopt a self-destroying policy, for they create an implacable expectation which human weariness cannot invariably satisfy. So Leonardo occasionally abandoned a piece of perfection in apparently inexplicable fear, for some nervous failure arrested him again and again. The chimera of art preyed on him more fiercely than on most, for it was a marvellous and terrible chimera ; but his ethos did not go to pieces under the strain. He remained fastidious in his habits, courteous and considerate in his attitudes. He steadied his imaginative malady (for, since all pure imagination is accompanied by a certain degree of wasting fear and strange pulsation, it is, I daresay, a malady) with the discipline of science, and so moved with dignity through a period which promised tranquillity and broke into confusion. Michelangelo is a weak human being ; this prophet of doom and cloudy splendour had a central spirit capable of mystical and rare emotions, but it was bound up in a mesh of irritable personality that made him peevish, jealous, and terrified as a neurasthenic child. Michelangelo angrily set the artist among the prophets ; but Leonardo graciously set him among the aristocrats of humanity.

iii

The French were still holding Milan for Louis XII. Charles d'Amboise, lord of Chaumont, lived in some state in the Castello, a military keep now, no longer a faëry palace within. Gian Giacomo Trivulzio, whose military genius and wounded pride had won for France the city in which Lodovico had derided him, was the general of the forces, mighty in splendour, a little vexed that he could not shape his magnificence into forms of enchanting grace like his fallen enemy. Without the walls, the orchards and the fields were patiently, pardoningly healing their own ravaged souls and greening the burned ways of the invaders, who, for their part, recognized that who held Milan must take up the bright trust of her waters, and unsully those pure streams.

But Lodovico had been an artist ; and his Court and assembly of beauty had been his intimate dream, even as the lifting of his whole city into light and air had been his social vision. The French had done violence to Italy ; yet they desired the soul as well as the body, the white Hesperid as well as the golden orchard. They wanted the luxurious imaginations of the brain that darkened in Loches, as well as his rich-bearing lands and his strongholds. They were inexpert as yet in Italian matters. Proud knights as they had been in their narrow mediæval castles, and punctilious as was their intercourse in tournament

With the French in Milan

and carven gallery and garden-close, they had not the great golden way of the new Paganism, and the subtlety of the woven magnificence, the passion of sheer beauty, and the ever-escaping vision of something radiant and Greek, the ritual dance and large rhythm of existence in which you forgot the poison, the dagger, the kiss of betrayal till all three were mortal in your heart. The French who came and went in Italy were the last haughty princes of mediæval knighthood ; but they felt somewhat barbarian, except perhaps Bayard, passing unchanging through his "very joyous history." As for Louis XII., he was a kindly, conscientious sovereign, but not munificent in largess of art—not a true Renaissance king.

Charles d'Amboise, though he owed his pride of place to his kinship with the famous cardinal, and though he proved somewhat indolent and jealous towards his colleagues in difficult passes ahead, was intelligent, and ambitious to recompose the glory of Milan. The roseal reliques of the old pleasure-city still lay like the shards of a great peach-blow jar, like petals from a shaken peach-branch, along the waters, where in cool loggia and clear garden the Milanese nobles and ladies, who had easily reconciled themselves with the French, sat with princely visitors telling stories, and plucking ravishing divisions from Bembo's pretty Platonism, like a silver dolcimelo tied with love-knots, as if plague and famine and fire did not from time to time terribly dismay, and wolves come prowling through the city. For them indeed the light slipped softly through the apple-boughs, and sleep stole through the quivering leaves. Through all the story of Italian war and plague, there is always the bower of musicians hid from the Triumph of Death, the secret Decameronian garden of fountains immune from the pest. Cecilia, still fair and tender, received her diverse guests, with a pensive thought for her growing son, Lodovico's child. Her friend, Isabella d'Este, had interceded for her with the French, explaining what a desirable ornament Cecilia was. So she kept her little court of ladies, "dressed like the *Assumption* in Venice," and Isabella, brightly oblivious of ancient beauty-blinding festivals in the Castello, came to exchange fantasies with her, and talk of lutes and vanities and victories—always of victories for Isabella.

Sometimes Trivulzio gave a great feast, and wondered why it lacked the fine romantic fever of the Duke's day. Colours enough, gems enough, viols enough, princes and ladies ! He was generalissimo of the forces. He had a long tale of glory, though some part of his triumph had been escheated to the French. Well, he had an idea. That Florentine who had been so useful to Lodovico, and had shaped the great steed that had faded on the air—what if he deified him instead of Francesco Sforza? He, not the upstart, would ride against mortality on a yet braver pedestal.

Leonardo the Florentine

He would be " pyramidally extant." Also, that artist could do many things. Chaumont more than agreed with him.

Whether Trivulzio or Chaumont was responsible for Leonardo's advent, or both acted together, we are not sure. As soon as he arrived, it seemed everybody's interest to keep him there. For Trivulzio's tomb he later made a thorough estimate, so there was some reality in that proud business. Dreams of Greek islands where harpies or sirens bear away the soul, of Roman triumphators, sweet genii failing under the excess of Renaissance pride, were summoned for the execution of the sepulchre ; and again Leonardo looked at the great destriers rearing or pacing, for its crown and consummation would have been the equestrian statue. But probably Trivulzio did not become decisive about this tomb till he was sharing the military dictatorship with Gaston de Foix ; and then Fortune sulked towards him in his turn.

Charles d'Amboise, lord of Chaumont-sur-Loire, was young, only twenty years old, when he became governor of the duchy of Milan. He wanted to bring back the glory of Milan as a centre of the arts, of vast architectural and hydraulic enterprises, to restore its days of genius, in brief, so he desired Leonardo ; and he got him, not without some struggle with Florence, and the intervention of King Louis himself. Leonardo first came to Milan for three months, bound to return under penalty of a fine of one hundred and thirty large florins of gold. The governor asked for an extension of leave once, and was allowed it ; but another request was countered by a bitter protest from Soderini, who said that Leonardo was a "dilatore" to the Signoria, had acted unfairly, and owed the State money. He states the case brutally ; but quite truthfully. Leonardo responds by gathering the debt from his friends, and sending it to Soderini, who will have none of it. After all, it was the unfinished and soon-perishing group of horsemen abandoned on the wall of the council-chamber that seemed to the gonfalonier, tense with anxiety for his fair Republic, an insult to Florence. Leonardo could have said that the governor had detained him ; but, even when Chaumont has written a tactful and conciliatory epistle to make easy his return, with merely a delicate inflection of surprise that Florence does not seem to realize the versatility of this Leonardo, he does not go. The fact is, he never faces an abandoned masterpiece ; and he dreads hostility in the atmosphere.

But in January of 1507 a letter to the Signoria from the Florentine ambassador, Pandolfini, at Blois, reveals that King Louis is determined to possess Leonardo, and specially desires that he should not leave Milan till his own arrival there. The most Christian King admits that he would like Leonardo to paint him " some little picture of Our Lady and

384

other things according as the fancy likes me. Perhaps I shall also ask him to paint my portrait." Pandolfini replies for the Signoria in the only way possible to that body, and finds that he becomes more interesting to the King because Leonardo is a personal acquaintance. He also is bidden write to Leonardo urging him to stay where he is. " All this," comments Pandolfini, with the slightly cynical note of the true Florentine, " is because of a little picture from the hand of Leonardo which has been recently brought here, and which has been considered an excellent work." This is probably *The Madonna of the Spindle*, painted for the King's secretary Robertet, the intimate theme, with its tender but simple symbolism, being tactfully chosen for the eyes of King Louis, a tenacious, obstinate monarch, conscientious in his way, whose somewhat bourgeois Court was dominated by the virtuous, devout, and slightly disingenuous Anne of Brittany. Since Louis himself proceeds to require Leonardo from his " tres chiers et grands amys," Florence resigns herself to do without her painter. As for Leonardo, having a pension and a fixed place again, he breathes easily, absorbed in his old tasks of irrigation. In May 1509 the canal in San Cristoforo is finished, and soon after he is granted a concession of twelve inches of water upon it. His ancient vineyard having been restored to him in April, the Naiades and the Mænads appropriately minister unto him still.

iv

Serenity settled through his soul again like dew. The passionate languor of Lombardy, the moist airs, the great velarium of the skies, soft and deep in a blue between amethyst and lapis, relaxed his overstrung spirit. The patient slow processes of reparation for ever at work in rich earth and living water, absorbing and kneading away the traces of harrying armies, the patient slow processes of human toil, hardly interrupted by war, in the continuities of the great canals, the growing Certosa, were soothing to his mind, seeking to recover the organic rhythm of its peculiar activities. Even the incense-breathing mysterious ways of a city that could not forget that it was a sacred capital, insensibly sweetened the diviner obscurer part of him, and filled his mind again with images of some beautiful unearthly apparitor, Dionysos—Saint John.

In the year 1507, Milan is momentarily flushed with a shadow of her former pageantries, when King Louis, as victor at Agnadello, enters in triumph through weather all crystal and golden. Streets hung with tapestry, towers of verdure builded high and peopled with gleaming figures from fable and myth, children carrying lilies, three hundred silver armourers, and soaring arches of triumph devised by Leonardo, are among

2 B   385

the gorgeous devices. Trivulzio gives a pompous banquet, and they dance in the castle hall. Isabella of Mantua is there, for she is ever among the garlanded. She is dancing incomparably as usual, and King Louis, unused to dancing, must tread a measure with so lovely a lady. Great cardinals are there, d'Amboise, Sanseverino, Ippolito d'Este; great captains like Jean Crissot; and Galeazzo Sanseverino, now Grand Ecuyer de France, beloved by all Frenchmen, his chief care still being to train beautiful horses and chivalrous young men. He is their unique exotic prince of cortigiania won from Italy. There is also Leonardo the Florentine. Next day, in the giostra in the Piazza, Galeazzo is as notable as ever; but, it may be, a little like a somnambulist. No water-festival as of old with sweet lamenting lutes presses the passion of the past on these hearts like carven jewels. As things were, for these three at least, missing the dreamy fever, the rapture of excess that ravished a moment's immortality, the delight and the wonder that swept all the colours into ethereal flame and sound, the music must have had its own Italian undersong, its Renaissance variant of : " Nous n'irons plus aux bois ; les lauriers sont coupés."

v

This radiant Easter weather became a famous drought. Soft and perilous like a spell, the summer passed into the rere-summer called Saint Martin's, and so brooded over the land, and put its insidious charm upon the fields and orchards. The reapers reaped a second harvest, and the amazed red roses flowered and fell till Christmas. Perhaps, while the apples burdened the branches, Leonardo, who had been reading his Ovid, had a first vision of that Pomona picture which we can guess at only as revealing a princess of fruited boughs rose-white through faint triple veils of Cos.

He was not left in peace, looking at the miraculous harvest-fields and the drowsy winter roses, and, unfortunately, at his vanishing canals, for he was not put immediately in " possession of this water," the " twelve inches " given him by Louis, because of the drought. He was dividing his time very happily, living sometimes in the Castello with Chaumont the governor, whose conversation was evidently sympathetic to him, sometimes at cool Vaprio among the woods and waters, in the Melzi villa, where he found the child Francesco grown into an adorable and adoring youth, beautiful, gentle in the finest sense, ready to throw his young heart like a white anemone before the feet of greatness, to spend his early grace like rare spices for the favour of weary greatness. Leonardo seems to have answered with a special and more poignant kindness to a spirit so unspoiled and generous. He cast his glamour over

With the French in Milan

Francesco, and shut him delicately in the crystalline felicity he could still bestow. Enchanted, Francesco stayed enchanted, and even as a " beautiful and serene old man " went dreaming of that supreme discipleship which ended when he was still but twenty. For imaginative people did not weary of Leonardo ; and Francesco seems a gracious creature, a lovely Phædo to hang his flowery head by Leonardo's death-bed. He was the rainbow in his evening sky, the sweet serenade at dewy shut of day, he was the image of Italian grace memorial under the silver-lit skies of Amboise. His was the perfect sacrifice, consummate not in tears but in joy. " Entreat me not to leave thee or to return from following after thee," said Francesco, and he rode with his lord Leonardo over the unfriendly Alps to Cloux. Therefore we know that Leonardo could love in the end, that malady and exile wrought softly with his soul, that he was glad to find roses in the snow, to see the almond-tree flowering through the white thick drift of sleepy flakes, and that, for once at least, tender with the tender, he cherished a squire of beauty, gracious Beloved with sweet lover, in the great platonic way—that at least Francesco, pure enthusiast, was consanguine with his heart.

From Vaprio, the Castello, the new studio where all the artists of Lombardy were flocking to idolize the images of Saint Anne and Mona Lisa and the visions of Leda, from his vast schemes of hydraulic works and fortifications, he was rent by his own just anger, which had carried him into the exasperating trap of a lawsuit in Florence. It was with great reluctance that Charles d'Amboise let him go ; but Leonardo, bitterly stung, was determined to have his right, though it meant return to a city where he was still a little under a cloud.

That uncle, Francesco, who had lived in the quiet house at Vinci with him when he was a child, and who probably much preferred the bright amusing prodigy to the dull children, the legitimate infants who came so much later, remembered him kindly in his testament. Living quietly, with no definite profession, he had little to leave ; but for good will and remembrance he gave Leonardo a small piece of land near Fiesole. The stepbrothers and sisters, instigated, it is said, by Giuliano, one more active in greed or spite than the rest, disputed even this trifling and affectionate inheritance, as if refusing the great intruder any part or lot in their father's family. Leonardo did not love money as Michelangelo did, nor had he an organic passion for his family folk, such as some lone spirits, also like Michelangelo, do have, a kind of melancholy mania proceeding from the strange temperament that denies them the children of their blood. Leonardo thought of money only when he was at a temporary loss for it, or when somebody who had been expensive seemed ungrateful. But, like Shakespeare, he does not like to be cheated : it enrages him

387

to be considered a fool because he is an artist. Besides, in this case he probably desired the bit of land, both because he valued Francesco's recognition after his too deliberate outlawry from his father's inheritance, and because he liked Fiesole. How little he cherished rancour after he had gained his rights is obvious from the fact that his own will assigned the Fiesole ground to those who had disputed it. At this moment, however, he probably required fulfilment of his father's promise as well as his uncle's ; and he moved viceroys, kings, and prince-cardinals, that Florence might do him justice, and that suddenly.

But Florence, despite these august appeals, does not hurry. Chaumont urges speed in real anxiety, underlining the fact that Leonardo's lawsuit has become a regal affair : " Loys," by the grace of God, King of France, Duke of Milan and lord of Genoa, presses for the return of " Nostre chier et bien-aimé Leonardo di Vincy, nostre painctre et ingenieur ordinaire " ; the mighty Cardinal Ippolito d'Este pauses in his leopard's wars to intercede with a member of the Signoria for Leonardo. All they ask is that the lawsuit be hurried. But Leonardo has made Florence wait, and wait in vain. So he perforce lingers in the City in that state of mental prickly-heat familiar to the victim of delay. From the extreme condition in which the spirit is really stung to death by flies he was delivered in time.

He consoles those days as well as possible, living quietly behind strong barriers of devotion in the kind warm chambers of intimate friends, painting, studying. He dwells six months in the house of Piero de' Braccio Martelli, close by Giovan Francesco Rusticci, both students to his liking. As for Piero de' Braccio Martelli, he is a mathematician. In his house, some pensive twilight hour, while working at his natural philosophy, Leonardo has a sharp realization that it is really time to remould and arrange all those fragmentary and conglomerate treatises of his into one vast encyclopædia, a novum organum of knowledge. He begins a small treatise with determined exactitude : " Cominciato in Firenze, in casa di Piero de Braccio Martelli addi 22 di Marzo 1508." So he writes, and begins notes on natural problems, and mathematics. Rusticci is a young nobleman, once a pupil of Verrocchio's, one of those amateurs in art for whom Leonardo had a preference, their more general intelligence, as well as their fair manners, recommending their tentative art more highly than should be, perhaps. This Rusticci seems to have had tastes in science of a more bizarre kind than Leonardo's, for he wasted time and money in trying to freeze mercury, a whim Leonardo would surely have condemned along with the search for perpetual motion and such pointless freaks of minds unlessoned in " experience." But Leonardo is slightly disingenuous in his professed scorn for the alchemists and their kind, for he consorts with them quite amicably, as if dimly suspicious

With the French in Milan

that they may find at the end, by their transmutations and sublimations, if not gold in their crucibles, yet some precious accidental precipitate, some by-product of odd-coloured truth. Or perhaps even he is not certain in his heart that the glorious intelligible and law-locked universe has not left unbound some lost loophole or silly postern whence the reasonless raids and impulsive spells of the magician may not drag through an incredible, irrational plunder.

Rusticci at present is very busy as a sculptor, working at a group of Saint John the Baptist, between the Levite and the Pharisee, for the Baptistery. Vasari says Leonardo gave much help to the artist, especially in the casting. He could hardly have refrained entirely from an image of his peculiar saint ; and the figures do look as if they had seen Leonardo, and faintly reflected his grace.

So he passes the time till Easter approaches and the end of the law-suit is in sight. Then he is assailed by a nervous longing for certitude about the position to which he shall soon return. Has it been injured by the long delay? Salaino, his curled Mercury, " mio discipelo," hastens to Milan with three letters : one for Chaumont, one for the President of the Waters, one for Francesco Melzi. The governor he earnestly entreats to inform him where he is supposed to live, whether his pension is in force, whether his congenial benefice of the waters may not begin to yield him toll. He will bring " two Madonnas " for the King, or for Chaumont, or for any friend of theirs. The President is also entreated to put the affair of the canal in order. These two letters are written with a certain diffidence of haughtiness, but with every form of courtesy. The last, to Francesco, is in the imperious mock-angry voice of intense tenderness which pushes away sweet words as ineffective and stale, and finds relief in the sharp device of using the language of anger to edge love's exquisite temper : " Buo di, Messer Francesco, why in God's name of all the letters I have written to you have you never answered one? Now wait till I come, by God, and I shall make you write so much that perhaps you will become sick of it." Leonardo

> " Must needs express
> His love with unmeant bitterness."

Underneath it, Leonardo is something of a suppliant. But " caro mio Francesco " goes to Cusago, and to see the President on his account.

The " two Madonnas " which Leonardo brought back to Milan at Easter are among the many sweet shadows that wander doubtfully in Leonardo's name in the ways of chance. Some think the original of the *Madonna Litta* was one. It seems of an earlier conception ; but Leonardo evidently considered the simpler Florentine Madonnas to be of a type more appealing to the simple Louis than his later mistresses of vision. And, while the theme of a *Virgin of the Balances* harmonizes with the taste of an artist so preoccupied with weights and measures, Leonardo's own pondering Madonna would not have been accompanied by any Joseph, such as the copy has introduced.

vi

At Easter, however, Leonardo is back in Milan. The lively French lords that come and go about the Castello are his friends and admirers. His pension is assured him, and that double life of scientific activity and artistic vitality reassumes its mysterious rhythm of high and low. The young Milanese painters, and disciples from distant places, throng his studio, and carry abroad his smiling ladies and his blue-green hazes as never before, when he was more strictly in Court service and less accessible to the general. When he is tired there is always the leafy villa at Vaprio and the plashing of water from the great mill-wheel ; and there is always Francesco with a jewel on his brow and great waves in his hair, like the other Milanese youths, but with the delicate ways of an aristocratic dreamer, and the fragrant solicitudes of a born disciple. All now seems reassurance for Leonardo again ; but it is in a world of red shifts and scenes of bitter battle, with changing sides and violent mutabilities, that he tries to pursue his luminous way. Italy has become the dolorous stage for the deploy and the clash of Europe's greeds and ambitions. France, which had crossed the Alps, partly as an invader with a flourish of old claims in Milan and Naples, a little as a deliverer, mindful of the trust of Charlemagne, had become by the league with Florence almost a champion for the spirit of Italy, though a champion with a guerdon. Naples in her fall had brought the sombre Spaniard, with his ruthless, devastating armies. Venice in her isolation took help from any Power, and kept faith with none. The Switzers poured down from their Alps, selling their efficiency to the highest bidder, sounding the insolent indifferent horns of Uri through the trumpets and kettledrums of the contending hosts. Florence, alone faithful to the French alliance, was more and more uneasily aware of the sons of Lorenzo—Cardinal Giovanni mellifluously making friends with Julius, Giuliano friendly and gentle, beloved in many courts. And the terrible Pope goes thundering, first with the French against Venice, then, Venice taken, with all the rest against the French, demanding from the god of battles a temporal dominion for the Holy See. The armies of the indecisive Maximilian, his black velvet a little frayed, his knightly gesture a little derided, his intention always a trifle too needy, mingle with the cross-currents of destruction. But the issue will not be clear in Italy till the great duel is set between Francis the First and Maximilian's pale grandchild, lord of the Spains, the Sicilies, the Germanies, the Low Countries, and, at last, the Italies, the fatal, anxious Emperor Charles the Fifth, who would finally steal away from his intolerable dominions to a cloister-cell.

Milan, that hapless city, is ever in the way of the armies, ever a coveted spoil of the victors. Through the smoke of the Italian confusion fierce figures loom in menace and in triumph! Mediæval gallantries of single and desperate sally, knights with splendid plumes and lances and glitter of angry gems, on proud heraldic chargers, are breaking through the ignoble new masses of infantry, and the base cannon-fire unfit for chivalric warfare. Nevertheless this despised infantry is being shaped into a swift and mighty force, though the great cavaliers are so contemptuous, and the beautiful destriers are so at one with their riders that they impart more wisdom and grace than they take, like the steed Savoy, which could ennoble even Charles the Eighth. French knights-at-arms seem still to ride out from the pages of Froissart; but, imitating the subtle Italian lords, crested cardinals and crested princes, and free-lance captains carving out their crests, with swift military instinct they soon adapt themselves to changed military conditions.

vii

The war-psychology of the time is as full of contrasts, horrors, grotesques, illogical transitions, treacheries, mad metamorphoses and wild lightnings of beauty as a feverish dream. Will you hear the great Pope crying aloud: " Ferrara, Ferrara, I will have thee by the body of Christ! " Or see his beloved, insinuating Cardinal Alidosi, effeminate, subtle, thieving the pride of victory, till the furious nephew strikes him down, and is like to go for ever unpardoned? Or Gian Paolo Baglioni, again, gazing at Julius, willing and able to destroy him, yet not daring because of the invincible prestige of that fierce figure that holds himself the Vicar of the Prince of Galilee? The shifty Marquis of Pescara, with Vittoria Colonna's pure love-letters like silver doves' feathers laid in his breast, since in some sphere, abstract from these camps and easy women in spoiled cities, he did love her; dark Alfonso of Ferrara, holding his cannon as his kin, and with gross mirth turning Michelangelo's statue of his Papal enemy into a bombard; Gasparo Sanseverino, called el Capitano Fracasso, because of his amazing strength; Yves d'Allègre, the candid, honourable leader; the wise Stuart d'Aubigny, leading the Scots archers in red and white; the terrible Cardinal Ippolito d'Este, driving through Venetian war " like Darius in his chariot "; the aged unbroken Gian Giacomo Trivulzio; the proud Colonnas, Gonsalvo del Cordoba, " the

Leonardo the Florentine

great Captain," later the young Constable of Bourbon, very magnificent and pale, his foreboding eyes burning between masses of dark hair—all are seen in glimpses through the smoke. The French have the most glittering soldiers. Though Louis XII. was bonhomme and bourgeois, with too much conscience about taxation to please his feudal princes, and no fanfaronade of gold and flourish of silver about his Court, the lords made up for it, waiting in gleaming armour for the day of young Monsieur d'Angoulême. Among these had been the superb and much-adored Comte de Ligny, who went to fight dazzling in cloth-of-gold and white and violet, white plumes flying from his golden hat, looking like the gold and azure lion of his blazonry. Indeed the generals still led their armies into battles like bridegrooms going to their bridal chambers, as the old books desired, all conspicuous with dazzling armour and great collars and chains of jewels, sumptuous marks for death and capture.

Of all the bright eagles of war who swooped most often across Leonardo's vision were two most famous. Unsullied rode the incomparable Bayard through his " very joyous history," last and perfect flower of the mediæval ethic, a sworded archangel in the baffling Italian world, beautiful, honourable, generous, so innocent in his antique faith to God and King and Lady, that before these limpid and simple eyes, disconcerting as Ithuriel's, lovely as a child's, astute and cruel and sophisticated people hurriedly put on strange virtues—eyes before which Alfonso of Ferrara remembered his honour, and his golden Borgia her virginity ! For single combat and daring sally none could equal "the good knight, his heart pure as a pearl." Yet his great courage went with intelligence : his schemes of reconnaissance were surprisingly adequate—surprisingly, for Bayard always had his scruples.

Scruples hardly mixed with the meditation of the young Gaston de Foix, Prince of the Blood, Duke of Nemours, Viceroy of Milan, "foudre d'Italie," a moodier lord of princelier and more violent blood, descendant of a race long renowned for heresy and song and beauty like the sungod's, and an arrogance equal to that of the kings of France. He won five victories before he died in his last, twenty years old, with a dream of a crown in his heart. Merciless like all who are betrothed to Victory, he was a great general and a dauntless one, with regal courtesies both for friends and enemies. Though a perfect cavalier, he could leap from his horse, and, kicking aside his steel shoes, show his men how easy it was to climb through a slippery breach. But Gaston's figure remains in history as last seen in his surcoat, heavily charged with the heraldries of Foix and Navarre, lifting against the red, red sunrise of the day of Ravenna his bared forearm, fantastically fighting so, " pour l'amour de ma vie." It is the true mediæval gesture, the vow irrationally sweet.

With the French in Milan

And Gaston's figure lies enclosed in art, divinely at peace on that pure monument in Milan, simply clad and virginal, the Collar of Saint Michael on his breast, youth undefeated, his lilied banners untaken, his early-laurelled head more content with sleep than ever it would have been with the crown of Navarre.

viii

Him Leonardo must have encountered sometimes when he walked slim and pale in the twilight through the streets of Milan, for Gaston de Foix had his melancholy fits, when he went solitary, followed by a single page. But despite all these strong clashing vassals of popes and emperors and kings and republics, and the havoc of their hosts—indeed to some degree because of these paradoxical beauty-loving leaders of armies—the sacred commune of art and wisdom maintained unbroken its triumphal standards, and inviolable its immaterial walls, as if it floated more glorious above the blood and tears, as if its apostles merely wrested the oriflammes of a more puissant beauty from the vehement conflicts of human wrath. All this time Copernicus was slipping quietly about Bologna, Padua, Ferrara, working at canon law and medicine, talking gently to the " Pythagoreans " of the day, meditating the heliocentric writ by which he would one day summon the planets and their moons to reveal themselves in solemn chapter and ritual procession around the sun. Ariosto was unwinding the rich and dreamy music of his coloured cantos. Aldus Manutius was wandering patiently through Lombardy collecting Virgilian script for his great edition of the Mantuan poet. Leonardo, with all his mind, spirit, and imagination, was now endeavouring to bring his parallels together, to light the myriad wedding-torches for the union of two transcendent species, himself the Hymen of the incredible nuptials of Art and Science, Power and Beauty, Leda and the Swan. Michelangelo was evoking Hebraic, Hellenic, Roman witnesses, fates and oracles of the unity of God—prophets, sibyls, demigods, choirs of epheboi, vestal virgins, thrones, dominations, principalities and powers. Raphael, with happy fluency, was painting the synthesis of theology and philosophy over the great walls of the Vatican. Bramante was working at the vast cathedral which was to bring Plato and Peter, flamens and priests, together under the supreme and reconciling dome of Christendom. The Renaissance made its last superb attempt to create a universal harmony of beauty and wisdom, in which all the lands and all the ages and all the categories should find their chords and colours in diapason. For these warring folk had immortal dreams. Perhaps the immortal dreams distracted their excited flesh the more with fierce appetites, dangerous desires, since heavenly fire plays havoc sometimes with mere mortality. The antagonisms of the earth were to shatter the cloud-gold domes of heavenly beauty dear to the hearts even of the sensualists, the fierce captains and cynic cardinals. The revolt of the average man in the Teuton country was to destroy Renaissance Italy as surely as the leaderless armies of Charles the Fifth ; but rainbow-ends of great purpose and fragments of the imagined symphony haunted its sorrowful conclusions. To this day the spirits that reply to the stainless music of Palestrina are different in kind from those that join in the shouted hymns of Luther. They are the true heirs of the spiritualized Renaissance that rose like a fair phantom from suffering and vanished, lost to Time, between Reformation and counter-Reformation.

ix

Leonardo was probably weary by this time of military operations. He could have offered the combatants many mortal devices, from the antique Greek fire to a screen of poison-gas, and moving masses of death from scythed chariots to tanks, and submarines for those who fought by sea, and a new kind of breech-loading cannon. Leonardo himself had scruples of conscience only about the submarines ; but Renaissance condottieri would probably have shrunk from war by chemistry. Though he might be fantastic in his arrangements of war-machinery, he mixed his chimerical chariots, as of Scythia, with terribly practical notions. On one page he sets a scythed car with ramping steeds, and naked driver with flying chlamys in the middle, a racing shearing scorpion before, a fleur-de-lis spear projected from the sickled wheels behind—an ingenious piece of devilry for obsolete combats. And he will bring great bowmen among his drawings of firearms. But he realized very well how the deadly mine could annihilate strong defences ; he drew his ingenious cannon ; he thought of his deadly gas. Sometimes his super-bombards send out great waves of smokelike flowers. So might the red horror of the burst shell change suddenly into a white cloud of narcissus and nepenthe and lotos. Perhaps he thought it might. It seems as if for Leonardo all things, dissolving in smoke, or cloud, or flood, broke at the ultimate edges into that foam of narcissus and nepenthe and lotos.

But his great spirit was now anxious for days of labour to its liking, and inclined to some closer husbandry of the hours at last. Time for the linking of rivers and canals, for the smooth clear pour of water over his new locks, satisfying to his mind and soothing to his nerves ! Time for the studio where the lutes and the cithers yet spoke softly and the idolatrous pupils listened to his simplest words ! Time for the anatomy-chamber, especially now that Marc della Torre, that brilliant witty

With the French in Milan

youth, son of a noble house, was willing to be a disciple in this lonely science, and admire those faithful beautiful drawings without precedent. It is indeed a pity that he does not yet find " port after stormie seas."

The story of Leonardo's personal art at this time is fuller of vanishing suggested shapes than usual. Most of the final work that still survives to us, or does not survive to us, belongs to this second broken period in Milan. Psychologically it shows some changes. His great pictures make so strongly imaginative and intellectual an attack that Müther's cheerful statement that Leonardo brought sensuality into Italian art seems at first amazing. Nevertheless, his imitators, unable to capture the great enigma of Leonardo's imaginative way, did concentrate on some easier mannerisms which do convey a cunning appeal to the senses. Leonardo himself, puissant human being as he was, knew something of the proud sensuality of the " ascetic erotic," and caught great ardours from suppressed desire to charge with flame the mystery of symbolic shapes and numbers on the planetary plane of his imagination. The first period in Milan had assailed him with the mysticism of the senses, drawn him within the dance of the Herodiad, but drawn him to the centre where intense vitality is silence and the soul is crystal. It had given him a type whereby he could make visible his dream-type. During the violent contrasts of the first years of his return to Florence, the vision of Cesare Borgia mingling with that of Mona Lisa, he imposed it, half curious, half amused, on a Neapolitan whose reverie kept obscurely some of the secrets of Capri. Now he was back in disordered Milan, with patrons, both among the French and later among the Medici, the better pleased if art should serve their senses as well as their souls. The city itself lay shattered in its passive sweetness. Deprived of Lodovico's sincere sense of romance, and his love of emotional setting, bewildered and listless, it becomes the Milan of Bandello, where all is glister, spilt perfume, green leaves, cool deep chambers, and soft adulteries, with sudden horrors unfit for tragedy. That Leonardo's studio was complaisant at least to the gay soulless life carried on between the entrances of new conquerors appears from the novelist's description of a room in which a lover lays a snare for a lady that would have been considered shocking in Lodovico's time, though not in that of his brother. The red and golden room, perfumed with aloeswood and " Cyprus birdlets " contains seducing pictures by "Messer Leonardo." Not by Leonardo, certainly, but, it may be, by some of the young men who painted pretty women like puppets made after his great model. There was a rather child-like voluptuousness in one or two of those disciples which turned to rich new flower in the fertile soil of Sodoma's more powerful temperament.

Leonardo's imagination never consented to the mere art of the senses, which, even as an anatomist, he steadily considers the acolytes of the soul. There is more trouble and vibration of the spirit in any design or picture of his than in any work of the great Venetians, apart from the golden shadows of Giorgione. But he is weary, and the unquiet, softly desperate atmosphere weakens him a little.

x

Something too sweet to be a degradation, something too fascinating to be a corruption, passes into those pictures which he now rarely finishes himself. The great *Saint Anne* picture stands in his studio, remote and magnificent, a reproach to the pupils who try to complete the colouring. Madonna Lisa hangs there too, destroying Gianpietrino's pretty mincing ladies with a flicker of her lashes. And there glows a sketch of a changed Leda, lovely still, but no more the wild naiad of the Greek river, innocently rapt by beautiful wings, half caught by them, half by the wonder of the children-trove, with something inconceivable and uncapturable escaping between them to carol above her. This new Leda is a Cnidian Venus; her body is a white amphora of sweet spices; her oval face and her dreaming eyes are surcharged with the reverie of desire. She is more clothed with camellia-white flesh; the beautiful knees alone remind you of the nymphlike figure among the reeds, while the ruffled plumes of the swan are drowsier, no longer symbolic of the chastity and flight of supreme beauty. This is too much the smooth melting sweetness of Ovid. Lost the wilding note of the hyacinthine hollow land of hill and river! Only in the ever-coiling conchs and whorls of Leda's hair does Leonardo still write his more mystical signature.

As the *Saint Anne*, the dove that hid in the cleft of the hard, pure rocks, was the type adored by the hard pure angel in him, so the *Leda* was at first the type desired by the questing heathen god in him, god that fain would take the shape of swan or eagle. The fetishistic passion for lovely hair, which reveals a symbolic appetite, spends itself in real rapture over Leda's. For Greek sculptors, shaping rippled heads like the Lemnian Athena's or undercutting the locks heavily for shadowy pathos; for most dissimilar Flemish painters, drawing long veils of smooth-waving tresses over the moon-calm faces of their Madonnas, and for many other enthusiasts in art and life besides Leonardo, the efflorescent hair of women and youths was adored, not only because of its beauty, but because of the intense vitality it symbolized. For Leonardo, long curls, like swirling waters, obey the spiral law of life. The winding river of Leda, the winding hair of Leda, meant mysterious natural life and the birth of beauty. Among the many studies for this dedicated head are

TYPES OF DESTRUCTIVE MACHINES
(BRITISH MUSEUM)

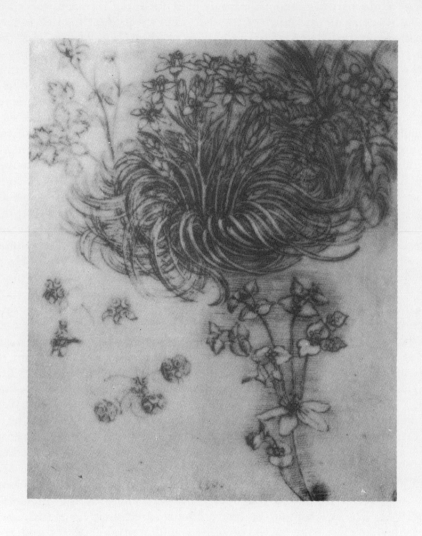

FLOWER-STUDIES
(WINDSOR)

With the French in Milan

coils and soft twists vanishing off in faint rings—"inanellata" is the delicate Italian word—smooth strands of it breaking into a lily-foam of corollas, even as do his waves of the sea. The river and the curls indeed mix strangely together. Here and there are little ringlets, as if shorn for love's sake, to be " a bracelet of bright hair about the bone." Sometimes a smooth strong curve of water pours from some square hydraulic arrangement, and simply boils into a great foam of curls, as of a hundred naiades. Or the descent from mighty weirs plaits itself into intricate braids. Or the lightly indicated face appears ethereal under that heavy coronal of woven fancies, with a fine and fugitive look, the flying air of the virgin undespoiled in the mystical bride. In these studies, the scientist, the æsthete, and the strange cold delicate amorist that slipped white and secret in the green twilight among the reedy pools of Leonardo's soul, are as interchangeable as light and shadow, and that which is neither light nor shadow. It was Salaino's hair, the story went, but I think Leonardo used the curls of this ornamental youth merely as a soft interwoven spell to enter the rockbound dreamland where, as a swan, he found the spirit of the waters, like a young moon white and androgyne. He is at home among the reeds. In some odd childish way in Vinci, the place of the osiers, he had found a wild surprise with something of love, something of dread. Leda was the nymph who caught him into aversion from mortal woman ; now he is the swan-god, by the strength and splendour of flight supreme over every dread, covering his mystical love at last in the pure birth-chamber of reeds and waters. He did ill to change Leda into a beauty fit for a king's paramour ! He began her as if she were his own. But, as if in a fit of obscure anger, he sold her, like a slave who had vexed him, to Giuliano, to Francis, or another, having humanized and degraded her.

As for the finished *Leda*, that existed, and vanished from Fontainebleau. Some think that it was painted in the end for Giuliano de' Medici, some for Francis the First. The beautiful figure must have had a Praxitelean grace ; probably it would now have raised a sweet contention as to whether, as a perfect nude, it conquered the sleeping *Venus* of Giorgione. The crude copies can hardly murmur in their hoarse whisper of solicitation what were the possible lines and attitude. Leda and the Swan was the supreme Renaissance theme for a picture. Greek beauty embraced by a winged energy that is half-beast, half-god is the symbolic knot for the centre of the Renaissance mystery. And, if Leonardo built his sensuous pyramid of pagan beauty thus, beside the mystical pyramid of *Saint Anne*, with the Swan for the Dove, he was expressing the immoderate fantasy of a soul that would include every vision, not only for himself but for his time.

Leonardo the Florentine

And if his naked Leda, crowned with her mysteriously knotted hair, did " solicit the hands to feel, the lips to kiss," we must take it that he meant it so. He was praised for the chastity of her attitude, the pressed knees, the lowered lids, the bent head, the closing of her white petals. " In women and young boys," he says serenely, " a lightly closed position is necessary." Well, she was beautiful and dangerous, and looked like Phryne, whose image drew the ships to Cnidos. But the girl among the lilies and rushes makes you homesick for Elysium.

xi

He had an Ovidian mood in this brief luxurious reverie before his peace was again shattered. A Pomona, it is said, he painted, her beauty half hid in triple veils of gauze. " Under an apple-tree I raised thee up," once more, but not like Saint Anne ! Francesco Melzi painted a *Pomona and Vertumnus*; but Leonardo's Pomona seems to have dreamed smiling against the apple boughs, smiling alone among the waters, of golden consummations and fruitions. " Di Leonardo e la ridente Pomona da una parte coperta da tre veli che è cosa difficilissima in quest' arte."[1] His mind seems to be dreamy and drowsy with insidious felicity. His themes are frankly pagan now. So far as he is on any side at this time, he is with the French against the Papacy, with Milan who was always against the Papacy, with his own Florence undone by the Papacy. He draws a Flora, for Francesco to paint, Amoretti says, some sweet androgynous figure among groups of his sensitive colombines, jasmines, his double-sexed flowers. He draws a beautiful Dionysos, with his thyrsus, with crossed knees, and lifted finger, delicate as a woman, wreathed and mysterious, among the anemones and the hellebore, smiling like his own soul—his own god visible at last, though he is too busy and too tired himself to paint the blue-green landscape and the rest. His own god nearly, but not altogether ! His own god has had another name since his earliest days. He is more dæmonic, more ambiguous, more the precursor of impossible miracles of experience. He begins to draw the strange antinomian head again, calling it Saint John—the incommunicable love-god of his youth.

It is perhaps possible that Leonardo, just before he became the conquest of time, felt even his adamantine will and his ascetic spirit subdued to some degree by the subtle alteration with which advancing age ironically commutes an original intention and a sustained attitude that deliberately defies the human limitation. The bitter Michelangelo grown old was a childish bedesman for love, glad of alms not only from Vittoria Colonna

[1] Lomazzo : *Idea del tempio delle pittura.*

With the French in Milan

and Tommaso Cavalieri, but from any beautiful fool. Leonardo grew old at an earlier age than the ailing Michelangelo ; and in this penultimate phase, painting his Ledas and Pomonas, he seems to consider in a reverie whether he was altogether wise to pass by any crystal pool of pleasure—an anchorite of art, to refuse the human lot. For a brief period it is almost as if, like Pygmalion, he would fain surrender to the type he has created, and to desire with his senses as well as his soul, to ravish with his eyes at least. The delicate and monstrous dynasty of Pygmalion was such as might indeed have proceeded from the chill sweet life of a creature whose parents were marble and the desire of the sculptor who craved her in a kind of imaginative incest, so it is as well that the subtly-smiling Cyprian refrained from sending a veridical Leda to disorder the arrogant mind of the painter who gave not a dove nor a rose to her altar. Yet his exquisite equilibrium is unsteadied a little, as if his disciplined senses had been on the brink of disloyalty to his soul, and, though he returns by way of Dionysos to his own spiritual mystery, it is with a poppied spirit and a failing hand.

"Formerly," said Leonardo himself, "it happened to me to make a thing divine which, when bought by the lover of it, he wished to take away the attributes of divinity to kiss it without reproach. But at last conscience vanquished his sorrowing sighs and his passion, and he was forced to tear the picture from his house." It is conjectured that this victim of art may have been the gentle sentimentalist Giuliano de' Medici, the champion of ladies in *The Courtier*, and that the picture was the *Leda*. I doubt if the " divine attributes " of the *Leda* would deter the conscience of a Renaissance pagan, and I think the image must have been of some lost Madonna. What seems strange is that Leonardo considers this passional deception of his picture a legitimate and logical effect of the delight of the eyes in any picture, and that he regards with sympathy and approval this bizarre penitent from that inordinate and fantastical sect, bridegrooms of statues and infatuates of images, that so confound the categories of experience as to overleap the barriers of matter, and commit an immediate rape in the world of dreams. The solemn ecstasies of Saint Anne have their dangers in reaction ; and Leonardo, the painter of the soul, becomes philosophically libertine in his contemplation of the senses of others.

It was at this time that he saw Giovannina. " Giovannina has a fantastic face : she lives in St Catherine's Hospital." Evidently she was young. Hers was the only face of living woman of which Leonardo wrote one word. Did he dissolve her winged eyes and her lifted lips into an angel as he did sometimes with the drawing of a girl ? He could deflower with a look, and draw the heart from out the breast with a smile. Giovannina had a fantastic face ; and she grew faint when Leonardo passed by. That was all.

But if there be any trouble and confusion at this time in a great spirit that with all reluctance submits to the bitter abdicating processes of time, there are always white violets set about his ways. Michelangelo writes his sonnets in the passion of his age :

> " Bring back the time when blind desire ran free
> Too strong for bit or rein to curb its flight ;
> Bring back the buried face once angel-bright
> That hides in earth all comely things from me."

Leonardo composed no sonnet. But on one idle page is written :

> " Maestro Leonardo fiorentino in Milano
> Francesco . . ."

This is one of the cryptic and symbolic simplicities that come from an automatic pencil. There the wild violets have been shed with the dew on them, youth's offering. Elsewhere broken lines and vivid phrases like " Amantissimo in Cristo," soft faces drawn through the diagrams, lightly embracing naked figures, scattered flowers, these only show the faint rose-crystal colour of Leonardo's hidden emotional life. One head comes through often, with massed hair, very short and pouting upper lip, with no more intelligence than is implicit in soft locks and large eyes. It looks like Andrea Salaino. But it reappears with clear iris, swept lashes, seriously closed lips, grave and tender, modulated into beauty. And then it might be Francesco Melzi. Other faces appear—one a fierce square mask, dominant and suffering.

xii

Well, in the studio where the young painters came, he was king and autocrat ; and his great pictures were considered by idolatrous eyes. It was at this time that Leonardo paralysed the originality of Milanese painting, it is said. But Milanese painting had not shown any great originality before his advent. Being a kind of capital, Milan naturally fed on foreign influence. With all his words Leonardo deprecated imitators, but the seduction of his manner and the sheer enchantment of his art withdrew all the sting from his talk about the sons and " grandsons " of nature, when it came sweetly, as if half-seriously, from the master's smiling lips. Besides, he was not unkind when they did copy. He created an atmosphere around him drenched with a pantheistic reverie. His studio was like an hypnotic æsthetic clinique where, under the fascination of his personality, his scholars passed into a drowsy enchantment wherein they unconsciously repeated some part of Leonardo's own vision, altered and lowered according to their temperaments. The gentle and charming young people who filled his house were fragile vessels that broke under his potent spell, keeping but some faint perfume of it. Some could do no more than remember Leonardo, and in love rather than hope repeat the magic formula of which they had not caught the essential syllable. Others, of a cruder type, copied and vulgarized mere mannerisms. But the greatest artists are always paralysing for their followers ; and the imitators of Michelangelo and Raphael are more wearisome than Leonardo's because they are so much more blatant. True, all the effort and patience and severe intellectual process of Leonardo his followers softly decline ; they accept only what they think facile. It is ironic that the school of Leonardo should end in the pretty ; but the school of Michelangelo ended in the pompous, which was worse. The weakness of their disciples is hardly to be imputed as a fault to either of these supreme masters. The passion had died out of the Renaissance and out of Italy, and *vanitas vanitatum* inflated the swelling sails of the baroque. Leonardo's greatest contemporary effect is that which he had on his rivals. His drawings and theories might have founded a dozen new schools of illuminists and formalists, and restored Renaissance painting in its decay. But the rhythm of history could prevail against even Leonardo.

Yet, though Leonardo's Milanese disciples lived but in the peristyles of his genius, and some of them were only like anemones set about his studio to brighten it, others were assiduous and earnest enough to refract some beam of his light with a broken soft colour of their own. The singularity of his type could be carried no farther ; they left out the intellectual beauty, and made engaging masks of it. Giovan Antonio Boltraffio, one of these well-bred and beautiful amateurs living gracefully a fashionable enough life, whom Leonardo specially affected, enriched the school with work of a peculiar romantic refinement, carried, as in the portraits of his poet-friend Girolamo Casio, to a dainty endearing excess. He sometimes signed his name as Leonardo's pupil, so devoted was he ; though he could bring his frank, soft vision through to paint with a sincere conviction and the warmth of an original colourist. He worked so sensitively with one motive of the master's that his pictures of the sweet Narcissus, his wreathed head bowed over the pool, against the branches and a blue-green sky, reveal how strong was the " love of the fountain " conveyed by Leonardo's own imagination. Indeed, all his disciples, dwelling deeply on subtly sadist or narcissan themes, bid us realize how powerful was the mere sensuous fabric of Leonardo's great intelligence, which comprehended so much more of sublimer matter that in him we are hardly aware of sense at all. But he was responsible for the love of his school for Herodiads, and Dionysos figures, and Judiths, and androgynous naked women among flowers, and Saint Sebastians. Deprived alike of their symbolic values and their proud lines of power, they sometimes look charming, but always equivocal. The steadfast young disciple Francesco Melzi could design with some sweet imaginative sympathy a *Vertumnus and Pomona*, and a Colombina like a great startling flower among little flowers painted with the brilliance of a miniaturist. Andrea Salaino, we know, worked considerably under Leonardo's supervision, though it is difficult to distinguish his works. One powerful, voluptuous, and richly-coloured personality did touch Leonardo, either now or later in Rome : Sodoma translates the enigmatic and chaste content of Leonardo's art into terms of frank bisexual appeal. He himself is like a gay Oriental prince, living expensively, flaunting his sobriquet, keeping his racehorses, his menagerie, his double harem. As a mere painter he has greatness ; and the swooning beauty of his figures, as well as the vivacity of their movements and attitudes, has its own seduction. His animalism is fiery, and the Leonardesque leaven makes it radiant. He had the lordship of the senses five, and could do a beautiful Leonardesque Madonna, so velvet-soft with pollened bloom, so made for human love, that the sweet hypocrite seems more flowery-innocent than the master's goddesses.

The Church of Saint Maurizio was rising slowly between 1503 and 1519, and there the noiseless shade, Luini, went softly painting, painting. It is Luini, the gentle and devotional, who, by some paradox, shows the Leonardesque sweetness in its corruption. He merely is not strong enough to handle the master's subtleties, nor to realize that a white intensity of intellectual life vibrated in the " things divine " of Leonardo, reserving them from any effective imitation. The famous " sottigliezza " distracts all who would thieve some of that truly incommunicable beauty. They are confused. So Luini's Herodiads and Madonnas smile like lilies on the verge of rankness, engaging and unconscious harlots unaware of sin, because they cannot realize anything. Saints modelled on the Countess of Cellant did so gaze. But Luini's figures have their interest, creatures of dream-guilt and trance, with ripe chestnut hair and heavy lids and moist passive lips, contagious with the Lombard fever of pleasure which was Milan's way of expressing despair. They are not vital. Yet Luini can do charming things, and the pure lines of the Saint Catherine, laid by angels in her pagan sarcophagus under a cloudy sky, excuse many a lifeless pretty picture. Solario could do a portrait sometimes against a deep background of woods and waters ; and Gaudenzio of

With the French in Milan

Ferrara would keep a thought of Leonardo in his yellow-haired crimson-clad figures. He had more originality and air-stirring movement than the closer disciples. Gianpietrino is very sentimental, with brilliant shallow effects ; but he is a " little master " of *mièvrerie* in his portraits of pretty ladies. Marco d'Oggione is cruder and harder. Cesare da Sesto is not over-faithful, and seems to lose himself between Raphael and Leonardo. Yet he too has some sincerity of his own. Altogether, Boltraffio, Ambrogio da Predis, with his courtly folk, Gianpietrino, Bernardino de Conti, good at pensive musicians, and Marco d'Oggione, create a pageant of young lovers from that part of Leonardo's formula they have been able to take. Some determinate minds will have it that Leonardo maintained his secret " Academy," and that Boltraffio had carried it on during his absence. They give a literal significance to the peculiar knot with the inscription " Acha : Li : V." Leonardo drew six models of it, all different ; and one was certainly engraved, and one was stamped on a palace in Milan. " Academy " meant " School," in the widest sense of the word, a place of reunion for sympathetic spirits. Or not even a place : it might mean merely a loose group of friends thinking harmoniously. The suggestion of Léon Dorez that Leonardo used the device because it recalled the woven reeds of his birthplace (Vinci, from *vinco* = osiers) is arresting. It became a kind of armorial bearing for him who had none save this play on the fluctuating double-entendre of his name, reminiscent of both slaves and conquerors. It would serve also as the mark of his atelier. And since all friends and pupils were his idolaters, and the linear devices were often called love-knots, the labyrinthine cipher was the dearer since it could seem at times dipped deep in fine emotion.

Flemish pupils also were carrying away their impressions to their lands of still waters and leaning poplars and flat quietudes, to bring the blue-green lights into calm paradise-pictures, to melt the mysterious smile in the serene quietism of the saints.

xiii

That all Leonardo's followers are uninterested in any part of the figure but the head is an odd comment on the teaching of one who so steadily held that emotion was expressed by every fibre of the body and that every muscle should be known to the last ligature. The training was arduous, and the Milanese youths were dreamy, and it was not Leonardo's way to insist or even to chide. He had no time to force these kind lax pupils into ways of crushing patience. They had his example. But he himself drew enchanting heads, and they could make copies like sweet death-masks from them. The greatest draughtsman in European art had no pupil that could draw really well. It needs a virile mind to send the line leaping true and fair. Besides, they had not his immediate sense of natural law. His pen or pencil so constantly describing a cupola, or casting a great mole, lightly indicating mountains and rivers, pouring widths of water over mighty weirs, did bring

> ". . . a world in a grain of sand
> And a heaven in a wild flower."

Since he drew from the very centre of the universe, " the Tower of Zeus," as the Pythagoreans call it, he could send the spirit of that universe into a curl, and bring the vision of Life within a dreaming face. Nothing was small or large to Leonardo ; every delicate thing he drew was invested with greatness, for he was drawing the Scheme of Things, and the water-lily was as marvellous as the great flood. But, if he told his pupils useful things about attitudes, he did not communicate his secret wisdom concerning the laws behind attitudes, so they drew their little vanities, with uncertain outlines. Probably he preferred to see them like children playing with toys.

None of Leonardo's pupils was a sculptor. If they could not draw, they could hardly struggle with matter so much more rebellious than paint. And Leonardo's own preferences, loftily disdainful of the manual toil of a sculptor, affected the inclination of his pupils. Sometimes he modelled a little head like that of the young Christ possessed by Lomazzo, or some such exquisite thing, to assure himself that his fingers could still communicate life to the clay. And that he was not unwilling to confront an immense opportunity again is shown by the fact that his brain was suddenly once more crowded with horses when Trivulzio meditated his monument. Among linear knots and faint faces, lions' and sudden horses' heads, we find a careful estimate for the carven and cast pile of marble and metal, the pillared and arched ædicula, wherein the proud sarcophagus was to lie. On the summit " uno corsiere grande al naturalle coll' omo sopra vuole per la spesa del metallo." Candelabra, and harpies that carry away the soul as they did long before in Lycia, entablature and frieze, captives like broken lilies, rearing horse and dominating rider, all costing twice as much as the Colleone statue ! The pedestal showed eight fluted Corinthian columns, placed on a high base and carrying a richly elaborated entablature, with a frieze adorned with reliefs round the projecting roof, with a figure in front of every column and open arches between, through which the sarcophagus and the resting statue of the dead were visible. But when he came back to Milan from Florence, military affairs were engaging Trivulzio, who was undermined in the end by his rivals, and died in bitterness at Chartres.

With the French in Milan

So Leonardo's horses once more fled indignant and disdainful from frustration.

It was a grandiose death-palace he had imagined for Trivulzio, kin to one of his colossal architectural dreams of a great Oriental mausoleum shaped like an immense terraced cone, its top crowned by a temple, a pyramid pierced by labyrinthine sepulchral chambers where might lie some golden and mystical dynasty of Sassanids, Seleucids, Ptolemies, balms within their breasts and masks upon their faces. Leonardo's patrons were singularly unfortunate. But the drawings and statuettes prepared for this dazzling epiphany of Renaissance sculpture influenced stronger brains than those of his Milanese pupils. I do not think the fair and beautiful images were ever more than dreamlike to Leonardo himself. I think he played with the figures of the estimate to feed his fantasy, as Balzac works with such fortunes as César Birotteau's. If he had not been the unique Leonardo he might have carved some single reaped lily of youth, like Ilaria, Medea, Gaston, Guidarello, Beatrice, and made the loveliest of the lovely sleepers over whom the Renaissance spends a sacred tenderness. But whatever Leonardo did had to be without precedent.

xiv

If Leonardo suffered trouble, not so much of the senses as of the emotions, he calmed it as he did before, by his passionate concentration on anatomical studies. These gave him more delight than any other of his scientific inquiries, for many reasons : they were most difficult, they were theoretically forbidden, they were lonely, and they brought him to the limit of the provable. They might even build a palpitating bridge to what was yet unprovable. Evidently it was his intent to essay that dangerous transition.

So he works earnestly, and not so much alone, this time. The distinguished young professor of anatomy at Pavia, Marcantonio della Torre, was a radiant spirit seeking the secrets of true healing through the ordeals of the dissecting-room. He was young, of a great Milanese family, attractive, and gay. In *The Courtier* he is merrily reported as buying off a sinful but amusing friar with wild wit. But his levity was the relief from ardent and valuable toil, and a heroic humanity of compassion which brought his young face to the grey death-dust before he was thirty, for he perished in his efforts to help the fever-stricken on the shores of Lake Garda.

Leonardo worked well with such a pupil, for his pupil della Torre undoubtedly was. The contact seems to have been exciting ; and he was more absorbed than ever, forgetting his Leda and all her kind in the exploration of the human body, in whatever macabre conditions. Della Torre had the alleviation of human suffering in view. The conviction that every muscle and nerve should be known to a painter of bodies certainly drove Leonardo ; but pure desire for knowledge, intense curiosity concerning this strange instrument of being, steeled him more invulnerably to his task. These bodies moved him not by their ghastly tales of corruption and suffering. Though his subjects must have come from prisons and hospitals, distorted from their original intention, repulsive with horrible maladies of the skin, he rarely alludes to defects. He is enthusiastic ; he finds the human body a wonderful expression. He draws its organs like opening flowers, its dorsal bones fanning out as beautiful ivory-work. And indeed Leonardo's anatomical works are of singular perfection. Any layman, confronted with the usual medical diagrams, has a sense of shock and incredulity at the crudity of the sight ; but Leonardo's drawings are so exquisite as well as so accurate that they frequently convey sheer pleasure in their pattern. His intense pencil, which softly leaves their perfume to the flowers, here deodorizes and prepares the section. For all illustrations of movement and proportion he draws beautiful figures in attitudes that are strong and fine as those of a Greek athlete. His own perfectly proportioned body often served him as a model for those straight figures of finely-woven muscle, tendons, and nerves. Leonardo's eyes seem to have an X-ray power. The flesh-less arms with long-fingered hands delicately turn in attitudes of pronation and supination. If he wants to draw a slim arm with a sensitive trick of the fingers, beside its articulated skeleton mimicking the motion, some lithe youth is at his service. Beautiful bodies and parts of bodies, straight and tense and thrilling with vigour like glimpses of bathers in a silver mist of dawn, communicate freshness and vigour, as if he turned suddenly to the living from the chamber of the mortified dead.

The curvatures of the spine and pelvis, the inclinations of the thorax, he transfers to his paper as none has done or seen before. The perfections of the cranium give him pleasure. He routs the mysterious " Adversary," the Spirit who rises in the solitude to mock at his work. " O that it may please God to let me also expound the psychology of the habits of man in such fashion as I am describing his body ! " And with triumphal accents, gazing at his own superb drawings, he discomfits that shadowy rival who always annoys his mind slightly—the dealer in descriptive words : " And you who claim by words to show the body of man with all the aspects of the arrangement of his members, cast away this notion, for the more you minutely describe, the more you confound the mind of the reader and the farther you separate him from the true idea of the thing described : it is therefore necessary to draw in demonstrating."

With the French in Milan

Over anatomy, he will even tell you what some of his opinions are, so excited is he. It is in this impassioned curiosity concerning the body and its mechanism that he makes most emphatically the great postulate and assumption of a soul and a God that seems necessary to every artist and every true philosopher. The five senses are but "the officers of the soul." He is concerned with the body now. Still, he is not afraid to think of so analysing the soul—in another world, possibly. For mortal time failed him, was failing him now. When he describes, with concentrated cold words that yet dissemble some recoil, those tragic movements of the cold, the fearful, the paralytic, that happen without the soul's permission, futile and imbecile gestures, did he already divine that such failure and disobedience of his own perfectly co-ordinated muscles would slowly drag him to the earth that craved the son of light and air ? Hardly, while he could still draw like that.

XV

Small things distract him. Sometimes he is designing choir-stalls for the cathedral in Pavia, the inimitable quality of his design in minutiæ, as if an immortal could be elegant, being still sought after. The Certosa goes on rising in its colours of milk and wine ; but a heaviness has befallen the chisels. The library at Pavia has been desolated since the old days, for the French kings have looted the learning as well as the wealth of Milan, and the armies have trailed home, loosely grasping their spoils of beauty, precious manuscripts as well as jewels and brocades. Most of the books he will meet again in Blois. In 1511 he is taking an interest in the discovery of marble quarries as white as snow ; the pure dense richness of the stuff delights him, this packed and trapped lily-matter of earth, like the solidified foam of the great dissolving waves he draws in fantasy. What was "Antonio" doing on the 26th of September 1510, when he broke his leg and was not able to move for forty days ? Antonio's fall disquiets a peaceful period of scientific study. He may have been rashly attempting Leonardo's wing-models.

His renown is spreading greatly among the French. Jean Lemaire, mourning Louis de Luxembourg, Comte de Ligny, in the *Plainte du Désir*, refers to Leonardo with admiration, and the versatile Jean Perréal speaks of :

"Léonard qui as des grâces suprêmes."

Jean Perréal was of that lively and eccentric kind that appealed to Leonardo, who liked a touch of grotesque in character as well as in faces. He was a clever tumbler among the arts, immensely popular. Leonardo makes a note that he must study tempera with Jean de Paris. The

407

French admired without comprehending ; but already they use the one sweet vague word for his indestructible quality—grace.

xvi

But all is smoke and change. Leonardo has created his charmed atmosphere even in hapless and disturbed Milan. These terrific metamorphoses of cities, slipping bloodily from one fierce rape to another, flick away his house of crystal like a castle of cards as soon as his patience has restored it. "Cosa bella mortale passa e non d'arte," he says pensively at some such time of upheaval ; but even art, though the air of immortality be imprisoned within it, can vanish from human eyes. The dubitant sentence, so very often quoted, is but a poor platitude in English. It is significant in Italian, because of its mere music. Leonardo had the song-improviser's sense of the sound-value of words and the undertone of emotion carried by mere accent and syllabling. He breathes the soft sighing syllables of lamentation like a lovely phrase caught from a Requiem Mass.

In 1511 Charles de Chaumont died before Correggio, and Gaston de Foix, with Trivulzio, governed Milan and the armies. Julius, having no more use for the French after the subjugation of Venice, now brought Venetians, Spaniards, and Switzers against them. "Fuori i barbari !" cried he, superbly forgetful of the day when he rode gladly into Milan with Cesare Borgia in the wake of the conquering Louis. The League of Cambrai was snapped, and within his new Holy League the Pope had drawn Frederick of Aragon, Henry VIII. of England, and the Emperor Maximilian, as well as Venice. But Gaston de Foix had military genius as well as contagious courage, and when his cousin the King signalled to him that a victory was necessary he threw it to him like a " sanguine flower inscribed with woe," for he cast it in dying. On the Easter Sunday of 11th April 1512 the two armies met in an ominous red dawn under the walls of Ravenna, and under that crimson sky the Most Christian King and His Holiness the Pope dyed the earth to the same tragical colour in blood of France and Italy. Spanish and French and Italian nobles were there in glittering panoply. The fifty scythed cars of Pedro Navarro galloped with guns upon them : the bowmen and the bombardiers were mingled in the half-mediæval, half-modern battle. The Cross of Pisa was the standard against the Cross of Rome. Gigantic Cardinal Sanseverino rode mailed like a captain on his huge destrier. Obese and purblind, making a virtue of necessity, Cardinal Giovanni de' Medici heavily paced on his white Arab stallion in his pontifical scarlet, blessing the men-at-arms, and wishing himself elsewhere.

With the French in Milan

The victory was to France, but the death of the victor left it barren. Gaston, with fifteen wounds between brow and breast, would no more toss his armies lightly about from town to town, like feathers. While the indecisive French still held Milan, Cardinal Giovanni lived there as a very honourable prisoner, with his inseparable nephew Giulio, afterwards Clement V., stealing espionage from captivity, and contriving to slip away as his easy captors retreated. Leonardo must have seen him at this time, as he suavely dealt out the plenary indulgences allowed him from Rome, to the annoyance of the defecting Archbishop of Pisa. For the painter remained where he was even after, by Julius' decree, the 20,000 Switzers brought Maximilian Sforza into Milan in the month of December. He seems, indeed, to have been very calm, as was his way when some irrational earthquake of outward circumstances suddenly defaulted the fabric of his existence. The Swiss, rude and destructive invaders, lit a great conflagration ; he sat still by the angry glare and made his spiral studies of smoke and flame, of destructive energy, vast wraiths of vanishing beauty with softly foliated edges like immense flowers as usual. "The Swiss lit these fires," he writes pleasantly, as if they had made a bonfire to please him.

xvii

He did not fear the young Maximilian at all. Doubtless he would have served him like his father. But it was soon apparent that Maximilian Sforza, though he had entered in state, with Cecilia's son for his banner-bearer, would have no time or money to spare from his distracted position as a prince maintained by mercenaries over whom he had no power. Meanwhile the Congress of Mantua, urged by the violent will of the Pope and corrupted by the promise of great bribes from the Medici, whom the simple Soderini dared not in his honesty and nervousness outbid, had decided to reinstate the sons of Lorenzo in Florence. There followed the outrageous Sack of Prato, sweet city of flowery gardens and lovely women, infamous even in that time of violent sieges, where neither age nor sex won mercy and no sacred thing was left inviolate, a crime of which the smooth Leo X. can never be held guiltless, and which made moody his gentle, irresolute brother Giuliano. "O Dio, O Dio, O Dio, che crudeltà ! " wrote one spectator. Soderini disappeared from Florence, after his last speech of pure patriotism, and died in exile, whereupon Machiavelli with bitter wit committed his too guileless soul, not to hell or purgatory, but to the limbo of unchristened babies. Giuliano de' Medici came quietly to the city of his birth as a private citizen, and by gracious and liberal ways made himself easily beloved.

So he would have remained, but Giovanni the cardinal had planned no deprecating existence in Florence. He delighted the Palleschi by entering in state, smilingly changing the councils, and with costly masquerades and societies of the Diamond and the Ring, and one unprecedented carnival, creating a passable imitation of the bright city of the great Lorenzo. In February 1513, however, died Julius, the Pope whose vices were as many as the Borgia's, whose destructive powers were more widespread, but whose dynamic energy, whose terribilità, formed a spectacle so unique and amazing that vices seemed trivial and venial things, cast off with centripetal velocity from his whirling career. He had wearied out the Sacred College ; the young cardinals were hungry for peace and pleasure, Giovanni de' Medici was young enough, extravagant enough, humanist enough to be sympathetic. Moreover, he had a revolting malady, which probably meant another early election. He was ill enough to be respectable ; and yet he would enjoy a libertine Rome. Also he was a humanist. In all things he was "papabile" ; so Medicean Florence hailed Leo X. with frenzied delight.

xviii

The cold and cynical heart of Giovanni de' Medici was capable of little affection, though he had loved the young cardinal nephew of Julius with such tenderness that he remembered him invariably with tears. Now his old-young spirit had real cordiality only for his delicate and charming brother Giuliano. For his nephew Lorenzo, child of his elder brother Piero, he merely had the family instinct. His half-brother Giulio was a habit. When his patient worming ambition began to raise its head, it proved close kin to the rampant dragon let loose by a Riario, a della Rovere, or a Borgia. While Leo ruled the Church, some member of his family should acquire a principality in dear Italy, and become a king of Tuscany. This was the lot he had cast for Giuliano, who was temperamentally averse to it. But for living like a prince he had every inclination and some of his father's grace. He had spent his exile in noble courts—Milan, Mantua, most of all Urbino. Leonardo and he were friends already ; and when Giuliano went to Rome so did Leonardo, to whom he had willingly assigned a generous pension.

It was bitter for Leonardo, who had just succeeded in charming for himself a new resting-place, and in creating the peculiar atmosphere in which he could maintain his many industries, to find himself uprooted and unprovided for at sixty. What he did in the pause between the departure of the French and his reception by Giuliano de' Medici is not clear. When he left Milan, however, he did not go alone ; he was beset

With the French in Milan

by fair friends, Francesco Melzi, Giovan Maria Boltraffio, and Andrea Salaino, besides other pupils. He carried an atelier with him. "On the 4th September 1513 I set out for Rome with Giovanni, Francesco Melzi, Salai, Lorenzo, and le Fanfoia." He did not suffer actual loss, nor did the breath of the fires of the Swiss pass upon him ; but for some time he must have considered the future with dubiety. He had served Lorenzo, Lodovico, Cesare Borgia, the Florentine Republic, the French ; and the variation of his patrons, which meant nothing to him, and little to them, whose alliances were so mutable, yet perplexed him, for he had become suddenly old, and all the power of Italy seemed drifting towards Rome, which had never attracted him.

xix

At some point during this Milanese period Leonardo was suddenly overtaken by the enemy he dreaded, and without one defensive parry surrendered his mortality to age, or so it seems to us, who find it so natural to think of Leonardo young, garlanded like Sophocles, or Leonardo old, invested with an avalanche of white locks like Homer. The drawn-out period of his summer prime, when artists painted him like Plato, is not sufficiently realized. Leonardo made the most of all his ages. But apparently this honey-breathing maturity, which had long repelled the leaguers of age, now submitted, as if all at once weary of the "wrackful siege of battering days." The famous portrait in Turin, supposed to be a self-study, has probably over-impressed its mask of tragic winter on our eyes, and suggested the minds of his critics into their damnable iteration of the word "sage." Leonardo, though his physical self began to fail him, did not feel by that failure instantly qualified to sit still, and formulate a cool philosophy for ardent youth in gnomic speeches. No! He continued to draw, to invent, to speak sweetly, to play tricks with flying lizards, to arrange masques, to entertain his visitors till the end. He had a Greek contempt for the mere body of age, and an unchanging pleasure in contemplating "the happy flower" of youth. He continued, like Socrates, to refresh his eyes and his soul by converse with beautiful youth. He warmed his hands in the very end at the spirit of a very gay young king whose fires then gave out a lively light and heat, though they were to prove but a blaze of crackling thorns.

The famous self-portrait was done in one of his bitter moods, when he had the Narcissus-fit in its extreme reversion. Gazing in the mirror, with fierce hatred of the "deep trenches in his beauty's field," he drove the furrows deeper into disaster with ruthless pencil, locked heavily the weary mouth, and with savage exaggeration dishevelled the white hair and beard. The bitter-burning eyes, such eyes as could indeed with hurt soul challenge the hurt soul of their double only from the sincerity of a mirror, gaze authentic from that self-macerating hour.

The " most beautiful face in the world " had been ravaged by endless toil. The passion for perfection had drawn a merciless claw across its composed features, and lack of sleep had dragged and wasted the eyes. Not " Venus entière a sa proie attachée " is so devastating as that passion for perfection. The grotesques of age he draws at this time are peculiarly cruel. They also are often exercises in self-torture ; there is a suicidal lust in them. He is like a fading woman, who in the glass twists and exaggerates her mobile face and neck to the finalities of shame in a morbid fit of horror : indeed his hatred of age belongs to his feminine side. All the disgraces of sagging or dried-up flesh are known to him, the hooked nose, the locked toothless mouth, the debasing and brutal folds that ruin the contour and division of neck and chin. Some of these old men are shrewd, some libertine ; some have become grossly animal, as though, unleavened by soul, they putrefy ; some rage with thrust lip ; some seem to wear a lovely oak-chaplet like an obscene ornament. In his heart, however, Leonardo knew he was not as these, and he recovered his serenity.

The head at Windsor with the silver-rippled hair is probably much nearer to the reality. Charming kings and cardinals, he finished his life in furred robes with comely aspect, the golden ashes of youth by time's alchemy buried within a fine aquiline image of ivory and silver, where still the eyes burned green at times, and beautiful enough to keep the young Francesco happy at his side. Whatever age might do to him, he was of those whose sympathies are always with youth, who, for all their maturities of power and conquests of experience, seem changelessly contemporary with the thrilling hearts and eyes blinded by morning glory that are beginning the foredoomed Adventure which for them must have, they think, some true consummation. Leonardo's life was like one long prelude to an epic story continued in eternity. " When I thought I was learning to live I was but learning how to die," he said in some stricken moment, suddenly realizing that all the lore so sharply tested by his disciplined proud senses would abandon his mind when, those five fine senses stopped with dust, his naked spirit sought a realm impenetrable to the laws of matter, where only his strange-flaming knots of imaginative vision, perhaps, might serve, rekindled heavenlier, to be the lampads for his ethereal way.

Chapter vi

In the Vatican

i

THE great Lorenzo had imparted some of his personality to his children ; but, whether because his peculiar imaginative wisdom was intransmissible, or because the arrogant and stupid blood of the Roman Orsini was powerful to counteract and to spoil, no descendant of his was destined to prove that the Medicean quality could last out even a brief dynasty. His own " desire to live," which exhausted him to death so early, did at least vibrate through all his descendants ; but, more ignoble in its range, it was in them much more disastrous in its consequence.

His eldest son, Piero, handsome, foolhardy, a brilliant cavalier, translated his father's half-wistful and poetic gaiety into an incurable folly that lightly carried him into that outrageously frivolous betrayal of his own city's strongholds which resulted in the furious expulsion of the Medicean family and the sacking of the beautiful house in the Via Larga with its exquisitely harmonized collections of art. He had been drowned by accident, and was not mourned. Giovanni, afterwards Pope Leo, had his father's gift for diplomacy reduced to a patient guile and a serviceable tact which was always somewhat suspect. Giuliano, who was, according to Lorenzo, the good child, remains the most attractive of the younger Medici. The passionate and tender part of Lorenzo became a dreamy sentimentalism and an art of eroticism in the gentlest of his sons. Giuliano has been called a Renaissance Hamlet, a phrase which endows him with a tragic intensity alien to that sympathetic and pensive figure, with sumptuous ways, with eyes too hectic and desires too questing from the consumptive malady that wasted him. He has a pathos and a grace : he desires to live out his life luxuriously indeed, but tolerantly, liberally, amicably, in company with sciences, arts, and lovely shows. Reluctantly he is swept into great dignities in the oily but implacable current of Leo's smooth ambition, setting towards the goal of a Medicean kingdom.

He was considered an accomplished courtier, at Urbino especially, where he lived for some time in a wing of the high white castle. Castiglione

wrote him down Giuliano the feminist. Still you may hear him in
The Courtier, with eloquent climaxes and storied instances defending the
honour, beauty, and intelligence of ladies against Gasparo Pallavicino
the misogynist, while Emilia Pia's quick tongue dances in and out the
dialogue like a silver adder. He was an idealist, though he had his
neurotic fevers, and the restless bright child Ippolito was the consequence
of one hidden love-story. Therefore, to his brother's annoyance, his
heart and will refused to plunder power from the charming duchy that had
cherished him in exile. He had been made gonfalonier of the Church ;
and, with interminable stupefying ceremonial of cavalcades, high masses,
orations, intermezzos, plays, performances of every kind, with a colossal
banquet, exploding guns, beating drums and blowing trumpets, with
three days' fulminating festival, a patrician of Rome. Bembo, the
Platonist, and the serious Sadoleto had been his friends in exile ; and
from his sympathy they passed into Leo's favour as his chief latinists.

His slightly fantastic mood, his taste for splendour, his curiosity
concerning sciences as well as arts, his frank generosity, his half-sensuous,
half-mystical sweetness, made him harmonious with Leonardo, who
seems to have mingled happily with Giuliano's personal group, even with
his nephew, the dissolute, arrogant Lorenzo, son of Piero. Leonardo,
it is said, painted for Giuliano a Florentine lady who was dear to him ;
and in his letter-drafts he expresses some cordial solicitude concerning
an illness of his. One of the Magnificent's friends who has wandered
to India, Andrea Corsali, writing to both Lorenzo and Giuliano,
refers to " il nostro Leonardo " and his vegetarian theories, comparing
them with the beliefs he finds in the mild-mannered tribes of his
travels.

Giuliano was understood to have a speculative mind, and he was
drawn to mathematics and mechanics ; " tenendo intorno a se uomini
ingegnosi, ed ogni nuova cosa voleva provare." His odd device was
the triangle. Like all Leonardo's patrons he had a passion for alchemy,
which the artist did nothing to disturb. Apart from one exasperated
passage, his attitude to alchemy and its allied arts is equivocal. Some
of his own discoveries seemed magical enough to such as were not, like
him, the sons of " experience " ; and those who imputed to him the
fillets and charming-rods of Hermes Trismegistus, strange traditional
creature commingled of the Greek god and the Egyptian Thoth, did not
altogether displease him. Else why did he love to draw at times fuming
tripods with the star of earth sunk in them, and brasiers and serpentine
bandelettes, and other attributes of the magician ? For many reasons,
Giuliano, amorous, dreamy, extravagant, seems to have valued Leonardo,
even when Leo shrugged. But the Magnifico, though death-struck, was

In the Vatican

still young and earnest enough for Leonardo: the old-young Pope was too incurably frivolous. Moreover, Giuliano was feminine of mood; Leo seemed emasculate.

ii

Giovanni de' Medici had been fed with sees and abbeys from the age of seven. At fourteen the pale and heavy boy with blemished eyes was a cardinal, with Rodrigo Borgia and Ascanio Sforza for his sponsors. He was educated at Pisa with the witty Bibbiena as the guide of his household, and when he passed to Rome, that " sink of iniquity," his father wrote him the famous letter of death-bed wisdom in which he advised all those politic virtues that Leo conspicuously did not acquire. Some politic virtues, however, he did have. He had perilled his red robe when Piero fled from Florence, but he escaped in a brown Franciscan habit. While the Borgia ruled, he went travelling in France, Bavaria, the Low Countries, with Giulio, his inseparable half-brother; but without acquiring any sense of the Teutonic psychology which might have helped him to realize that Luther, who in 1510 had already made the pilgrimage of the Roman basilicas on his hands and knees, had a serious bearing on the fortunes of the Church. His suave smiling ways and great personal tact had made him popular with the College of Cardinals; and he had courted the distrustful Julius till he won him. He seemed unambitious, devoting himself to maintaining a princely house in Rome where artists, musicians, jewellers, latinists, might find that patronage inadequately bestowed by a military and wandering Pope. Always enjoying life, he had yet been early afflicted with a loathsome and incurable malady. But, when the young cardinals made him Pope, they expected a coloured and exciting Rome from him, and they were not disappointed, though they were surprised sometimes when the mask of complaisance became a little set as he regarded a safe-conduct as one of his practical jokes, and strangled one of them, as Michelet says, " en riant."

Leo, though only thirty-seven, was not pleasing to Leonardo's senses. He was tall and stout, with a thick-fleshed neck and an immense double chin: his broad figure was supported by spindly legs. The smooth, blind face of a eunuch, empurpled by this time, presented a vague but effective defence to the world. A spy-glass helped the protruding eyes that could not see. Evil effluvia from his corrupted body infected the air. But his Medicean hands, the hands that his grand-niece Catherine would carry into France, smooth, white, plump, were laid beautifully before him like idols, glorious with triumphal rings. His soft low voice and his divining tact, however, were supposed to render his friends oblivious of his physical defects. Leonardo, weary but fastidious, was

415

probably not oblivious. If he failed to charm Leo, it is likely that the soft rotten Pope antagonized him.

The Pope's passion for pleasure included humanism, comedy, music, never-ending spectacle, tapestry, goldsmith-work of every kind, hunting, and buffoonery. That he had a real though limited zest for scholarship of the Ciceronian kind is true : humanists like Erasmus found Rome a spiritual city indeed, though the love of the classical tongues was cooling now from a wild adventure to a noble superstition. His enthusiasm for splendour was of a lordly enough kind to run into monumental expression in the Vatican and Saint Peter's. His palace ran over with the sound of lutes and viols and sweet voices. He dropped largess of gold and silver at table, at processions, in the hunting-parks. True also that he considerably cleared up and purified the fetid jungle of Rome outside the palaces, though he did less than Sixtus and Nicholas. But a trivial Latin couplet by an ill-conditioned pedant could obtain great bounty, while Ariosto, old friend as well as great poet, was put off with a malodorous kiss. Any kind of art that did not magnify his name could go stinted. And if the music was sweet in the little rooms and the chapel, it was often a brazen dissonance at the *outré*, jazz-coloured, jazz-sounding banquets. If he cleared the ways of the city, it was to make room for his extravagant personal pageants. Nevertheless, for all his secret blood-lust slaked in massacre of driven birds and beasts, his hypocrisy of mercy that cowled violation of safe-conduct and secret murder, the crude humour satisfied only by ferocious practical joking, the implacable stealths and ruins of his quiet hatred, Leo is often grandiose in his effect. It is hard for the central figure in Rome not to be grandiose, and Leo was cæsarian enough. There was little of the Florentine in him : he had repaired too early to his mother's city. But with his beautiful pampered hands, his cold corrupt heart in his cold corrupt perfume-drenhed body, his fine latinity, his pagan thirsts, as he sits with his toys and his cardinals in Raphael's faithful portrait there is a heavy greatness in his air. The shadow of the imagined Dome of Saint Peter's is behind him, and some dim dream of a Christianity that shall cover his classical world seems to visit his half-waking hours. Poliziano, Marsilio, and Pico had stood round his infancy, and the wistful reverie of Fiesole has become a hard and pompous vision in the airs of Rome. Still, a vision !

And though there was nothing Greek in him he respected Greek, and did something for the encouragement of its scholars. A " golden age " which had Bembo and Sadoleto as papal secretaries, communicating the opinions of Rome in Ciceronian Latin, was irresistible to Erasmus, though uninteresting to Leonardo, who had learned Latin merely that he might read scientific treatises.

In the Vatican

When the centre of the Renaissance shifted from Florence to Rome, that passionate climax of many centuries was already frigid with approaching death. Rome was always committed to her own conquering past. On what she had once taken from Greece she had heavily sunk her proper seal. Upon the genius she now drew from the Hellenizing cities of Italy she impressed her own clangorous rhetoric. Michelangelo had been early subdued to her temper, had been at once wasted and fulfilled, and charactered, by the exactions of Julius, Imperator and Pontifex Maximus combined. Raphael, the eloquent, decorative, conceding, was born to be the minion of her softer moods. Leonardo, son of the proud Early Renaissance, is never so Florentine, never so Hellenic, in his attitude as when he is steadily, distastefully refusing to become a part of the sublime, insolent, and uncomprehending capital of the Seven Hills. This great Hostel of the World to which, more than ever, all the pilgrims of the earth came in, was too indiscriminate for him, and the colours that hung her gloriously builded or gloriously broken walls were too garish.

No other city in Italy presented such startling contiguities of splendour and squalor, rising and falling architecture, such a disconcerting vision of mighty things preying on each other, and on themselves. Within the ring of mouldering walls the capital itself covered but a small space. Without, among the vineyards, the groves, and the thickets of myrtle, the deer and the wild boar went freely. The Capitoline Hill was Monte Caprino, where every spring the goats browsed among the Pentelic fragments of frieze and pillar. The mausoleums were shells stripped of their marble. Round the Pillar of Trajan clustered a mean huddle of buildings. Within the Forum, the Thermæ, the amphitheatres, were squalid nests of houses and shops. The Colosseum and the Theatre of Marcellus were quarries for the builders of the Pope, his cardinals and his bankers. Churches like classic temples were rising from Romanesque basilicas that themselves had been composed of the fluted columns and entablatures of a more antique consecration. Round the confused but splendidly-growing Vatican, and the new Saint Peter's developing behind the old façade, palaces and churches were rising in a half-built medley of plundered prone pillars and quarried stones. While the latinists sang of Leo as the second Augustus, the Rome of the first was passing in the consuming limekilns, and Fra Giocondo, the Sangalli, Peruzzi, Bramante, and Michelangelo were consenting to the iniquity. Brunellesco, with visionary eyes, had read the noble vestiges of antique Rome till she stood before him perfect in her imperial shape ; and had gone home to build as enduringly in his own strong way, not to destroy the very patterns of

endurance and strength. Renaissance Rome had its own rage for building ; its architects would create their own Golden House and their own
Pantheon, and, almost unthinking, hard-pressed for material, took the
stones that were nearest. It is to the praise of Leo that he gave Raphael
leave to stay the destroyers, though neither Pope nor artist might be
among the guiltless themselves.

Bramante, with his crowd of helpers, was busy, though soon to die.
He had changed in mood since the blithe Milanese days. Now he lived in
a palace of his own, dug out like others from the antiquity he reverenced;
and quarrelled with Michelangelo. Leonardo, again talking with him of
domes, may have sent another impulse into the building of Saint Peter's.
At present Bramante was busy by the Belvedere, where Giuliano had
provided studios for his own artist. He was laying out the gardens with
parterres and fountains, with laurel and cypress and mulberry and rose,
with here a great aviary and there a park for wild beasts. The Vatican
stood a conflicting assembly of the conflicting elements of Rome. Magnificent stretched its great chambers with the coloured crowds below
repeated brilliantly above in Raphael's flattering review of the splendour
and wisdom of Renaissance Rome. But a bridge bound it to the Castle
of San Angelo. This sepulchre of a humane and various Emperor, over
which the wistful Gregory had seen the reassuring Angel, should have
been a Citadel of Mercy ; it was the Dark Tower of the Vatican, where
the popes dealt death to their victims, yet found a final security for
themselves.

Round the Vatican the palaces of the cardinals mingled with trumpery
wooden houses, and the turreted keeps of the feudal Roman families.
Churches, chapels, monasteries, palaces, libraries, residences, jumbled together. The lines of the new palaces were cold and formal and Vitruvian,
and sometimes disgracious with the folly of empty pediments. But
they were gaily painted within and without, so that they were not unlike
their elegant owners with their vitrified tastes and their ostentatious
desires. And the villas that were rising among their great gardens by
the river, on the hills and in the Campagna, were more fanciful and
romantic.

Between the Capitol and the Tiber crowded a fetid and fever-
stricken district. Different nationalities huddled here and there sordidly
enough, though Agostino Chigi, the banker, in his great palace strove to
rival Elagabalus.

iv

But all the strain and struggle was arched by the dark-blue Roman
sky, and bathed in its radiant light. The Tiber ran dead-golden over its

In the Vatican

tragic dead and its buried statues : the people drank of it, yet lived. The rhythm of the Seven Hills quieted the dissonances ; and the great surviving lines of Roman building, horizontal, vertical, semicircular, contemptuous of depredation, indestructible almost as the hills, continued their cæsarian meditation, with as great an assurance and dignity. The Flavian amphitheatre, the Forum, and the Capitol still prevailed against the Vatican, and imposed their mood upon Saint Peter's.

The sense of ruin, however, amid all the feverish pomp of Leo and the cardinals, still created a shiver of desolation in an artistic mind. In vain did Leonardo gaze at the great steps guarded by the Dioscuri, at Marcus Aurelius, riding in gilded bronze, the figure that had enchanted Verrocchio. He had seen them before ; and he would draw no more horses. He saw as in a dream the ghosts of the Cæsars and the Antonines. The legend of Rome was too trampling and obvious a glory to kindle the tired soul of the subtle Leonardo. And indeed its puissant ruins as the setting for the turbulent Roman life of shows and carnivals made existence too like a harlequinade. The conclusion of the Renaissance seemed a startling *danse macabre* of cardinals with their courtesans and pages, while musicians fiddled and humanists went humanizing in gross comedies.

No ! But the true genius of ancient Rome ran out from the city across the Campagna in the great aqueducts, still almost complete. There the spirit of Leonardo found peace in Rome and touched her soul, magnificently bearing the bounty of water as with the eagles and the trophies of the legions. Out in the Campagna he wandered, considering the storied soil with a new geomancy, the great ways of the sun, the sacred long-worshipped trees and groves asleep in the pulverized sunlight. He found the secret primrose-beds, and with softening eyes saw the violets he loved fragrant in the broken closes of Hadrian's Villa. By the foot of a silvery pine grew the blue and purple anemones. From the depth of some thicket amused wild eyes of invitation, long since hidden under the holy hood of Saint Silvanus or Saint Silvester, glittered and were lost. Leonardo took his notes of the geology of the Campagna, drew some tender flowers, thought a little more intently of the faunlike angel of Annunciation he had begun to evoke from the darkness, and was more serene.

v

Since the Renaissance in Rome was an affair of popes and cardinals and ambassadors it was naturally a matter of latinity, architecture, and shows, but most of all, latinity. Leo was early perfect in his Latin, and at least a student and appreciator of Greek. Bembo and Sadoleto, his secretaries of state, to their knowledge of Latin added some true

419

Renaissance idealism. Bembo was a pagan who told Sadoleto not to spoil his style by reading Saint Paul ; but the one was capable of a beautiful " rapture " over his reading of platonic love, and the other had an essentially grave and devotional mind that would take him presently to the Oratory of Divine Love, the little group of saintly souls that, down by the Tiber, would try to pray back the Dove of Ecstasy over the High Altar, as sweetly and as effectively as moonlight endeavouring amid the loud shocks of political confusion to reform the Church by grace within. Meanwhile, as to Bembo, Bibbiena, Inghirami, and Leo himself, they savoured their Latin epigrams and debated Ciceronian philosophies under the trees at Agostino Chigi's villa.

All this latinity had caused a riot of conventional mythology which seriously confused thought, while it stifled vision, by conventionalizing the images of those gods who had returned in wonder. Rome was never good at gods. There they became always rather abstract and heavy deities, who left mere charm to the genii that haunted the oaks and the vines. But even during the lurid reign of the Borgia the atmosphere of Rome had been more mysterious, more quick with a sense of dread divinity, than it was now. That temperamental Alexander, who had a kind of sinful greatness, seemed to have brought heathen gods alive into the House of the Bull, and locked the forces of Christ again with the dæmon host of Eastern powers. The shadow of the wrath of God lay across the city, and Alexander, shaking his cardinals in full consistory with his terrible repentances, seemed more of a believer than Leo. But the mysticism of sin, idolatry, expiation, heathen and Christian conflict, was over. The cool Medicean Pope " enjoyed the papacy " with perfect good faith, and played at mythology without conviction. It was commendable for " The Thirteenth Apostle " to be also the Pontifex Maximus, or even the " Jupiter of Earth." Christ is a Hero, or he is Apollo, a priest is a flamen, the Virgin is Diana. The great latinist Inghirami, preaching on Good Friday, compared Christ with Cæsar, Cecrops, Aristides, Epaminondas, and even Iphigenia. He was held to have surpassed himself. The artists kept more lightly and graciously the mythological way, and Bibbiena's bathroom, painted with the history of Cupid and Psyche, created a fashion and an appetite for that sweet history.

vi

Leo's imperfect eyesight abetted his personal inclination in diverting his mind from subtle painting. He did not love it for its own sake. He allowed its presence when it glorified himself and his race, and was easily visible in large compositions like Raphael's. He tolerated it when it impressed itself with undeniable brio like Michelangelo's, though he admitted he was afraid of that artist and preferred him away in the quarries of Carrara. He liked violent colours, quick transitions, spiced attacks upon his filmed vision and his chilled nerves. He liked shows and spectacles and triumphs—sudden and momentary things unclosing gorgeous petals of a day for one who was deliberately getting as much pleasure as possible out of that day. Things had to be flagrant to get through Leo's thickened senses. Hence the jumbled and excessive pageants, without poetic sweetness or cohesion, not like the lovely masques of old in far Milan. Music was the art he loved most finely, it seems, that ethereal art so often found, like an angel in a brothel, in folk of an otherwise gross and sensual habit. Hearing is perhaps the last remote sense to be stopped by self-indulgence. Music, at least, could throw Leo into a beatific ecstasy as he sat with half-closed lids, listening to the blind musician Raffaello Brandolini perhaps, and beating time with one soft hand.

His chapel was filled from Milan, Mantua, Germany, France, and the Low Countries. Leonardo was no longer friendly with his lyre. But he encountered some old friends in music. Atalante Migliarotti, no longer fair as Orpheus, was now a pontifical architect's clerk. But Jacopo di Sansecondo, once Lodovico's violinist, was painted by Raphael in apotheosis as Apollo on Parnassus.

Better still, however, did Leo love his wearisome improvisatori and intolerable buffoons. Such is the baffling frivolity of Leo's mind that any admirable preference of his is immediately discounted by some other preference more acute but infinitely absurd. He loved classic statuary, for instance ; and held his *Apollo*, his *Laocöon*, his *Ariadne*, exceedingly dear. But one feels that the anxious collector of unicorns' horns, knives, lapis-lazuli, and liquid amber, might have been best pleased with the black obsidian elephants from the Temple of Concord or the tusks of the wild boar of Calydon brought by Augustus from Tegea. His taste for the bizarre and intrinsically precious in small things gave great employment to the goldsmiths and their kind. The carven and graven minutiæ of the lives of the Pope and his cardinals, whether sacred or secular, were of intense and delicate beauty, the only intense and delicate kind of beauty in the overflown magnificence of the city. Caradosso, who did wonders for Lodovico in Milan, is still doing wonders for Leo in Rome.

vii

Still, the statuary of the classic past was worshipped and copied. Within the Baths of Caracalla yet lay hid a great treasure of gods, demigods, friezes, reliefs, hermaphrodites, busts, bronzes, cameos, medals, lamps ; and deep in the kind soil of orchards and vineyards slept many a naked Venus and lotos-like Antinous. In the court of the Belvedere, close to Leonardo's dwelling, Bramante was laying brick-paved walks between rows of orange-trees. In the niches had been idolatrously placed the papal treasures won back from antique earth. There the Apollo Musagetes haughtily lifted his arrowless hand. There Ariadne turned marble to soft sensuous sleep. There Father Tiber lay mighty ; and Herakles was puissant, and noble sarcophagi stood broidered with myth. Most worshipped of all, there Laocöon and his sons writhed involved in their eternal agony. No wonder Michelangelo had stood breathless while this image of an art that had come to a point so like his own was laboriously resurrected from its vineyard near the Baths of Titus; and had refused the sacrilege of a restoring chisel. Leonardo was no Pergamene, and probably felt as we do, that this arrested torment, with the boy so harrowingly near escape, was not controlled by the law of rhythm. As for Ariadne, his lonely and complete Dionysos had ravished no bride in Naxos. And the Apollo was not subtle. Lovelier revenants yet to come—the Praxitelean Hermes, the Lodovisi *Throne*, the seated Demeter, the Youth from Subiaco, the Leconfield Aphrodite, the Lemnian Athena, the Riders of the Parthenon, some fine athlete diadumenos, some sweet archaic figure faintly smiling and stiffly held in fluted raiment even, might have charmed his sense with their purer fire and startled away the excess of Syrian sweetness that sometimes weakens the heavy heads of his youths.

viii

Renaissance life in Rome was the life of the young cardinals. And the young cardinals were a delicate and brutal people, with tastes at once literate, cynical, and gross, wearing the sacred scarlet like a masquer's habit, with a spoilt privileged air not always unattractive. The younger princes of violent dynasties, Riario, d'Este, Colonna, Petrucci, restless at the undesired immunities of the porporati, were given to insolent effects. Their existence had its æsthetic qualities ; but it was bizarre, confusing, plangent, a matter of strong flavours, crude colours, syncopated sounds. It was *faisandé*—it was like the world of Trimalcio's banquet qualified by the world of Petronius Arbiter's own villa ; and the " suavo " Leo had some of Nero's attributes other than the spy-glass.

Those young cardinals, the Cardinal of Aragon, Cardinal Petrucci, the " Cupid " of the Sacred College, all unaware that his beauty will be tragically smothered by an Oriental hangman in a noisome cell, Alessandro Farnese, Giulio de' Medici, handsome, with shifty eyes, Cybo, Ridolfi,

In the Vatican

Salviati, Ippolito d'Este, towering among them with a certain dangerous Ferrarese grace, a startling and poetic figure among his retinues of beautiful pages and exotic athletes, live as proudly as princes and as softly as women. So, for that matter, do the older cardinals, Bibbiena, with his large witty eyes and amused mouth, Inghirami the eloquent, grown fat since the days when he won his nickname of " Phædra." the pale effete Raffaelle Riario, most luxurious of all, whom Leonardo had seen go livid from the Pazzi plot, now dwelling in a great palace of polychrome marble by Bramante, built from the ruins of a Roman arch. They lie in great beds of rose and violet in tapestried chambers, where the last picture of Madonna or of Ganymede stands waiting their eyes. They are clothed in fine *étamine*, stuff woven only for women and children and cardinals ; they glow in scarlet and darken to amethyst ; they are wrapped warm in priceless ermine and silk ; their sapphire rings are chiselled by Caradosso ; their aglets are great Eastern rubies. Their cups are of vermeil, chalcedony, and decorated jasper. Their hunting horns are light and gilded and damascened. They eat rare foods from gold and silver plate, and after the pheasants and peacocks, gleaming in their proud feathers, have been borne in and out, noble young gentlemen serve them with rose-water from graven silver ewers as the fantastic pastries enter to the sound of fifes and trumpets. Sometimes their banquets are served by dwarfs, and occasionally by naked girls. Sometimes children in shepherd guise will dance for them ; sometimes a Moorish maiden all alone. Sometimes a rigid figure (fit for a Russian ballet) adorns the feast : a Spanish buffoon all clothed in gold is striking double strokes on a silver-garnished drum.

The cardinals emulate Agostino Chigi the banker, a king of high finance—evil portent !—whose august dining-hall proves at the end of his collation to be merely his stable, and who has his dishes of gold and silver thrown from his windows to prove he does not use them twice in the same revel. The Pope's own table is the coarsest in its manners, for Leo, who has a wicked pleasure in human inferiority, must have a butt when he sits at meat ; the dwarfs, the buffoons, the miserable arch-poet, even Fra Mariano himself, the beloved jester, must feed this rude humour.

Their gardens enclose menageries of rare and furious and beautiful creatures. The roots of their vineyards twine round an Antinous-Dionysos. From blague, or for rococo ornament, they keep Chaldæan diviners. Their mules are caparisoned in red ; the stirrups are gilded. In the wild carnivals, clothed like superb Turks, they go riding on Turkish horses. They are great hunters : their gerfalcons from Pisa are black as night ; their dogs from Mantua are swift and sure. When Leo goes hunting to slake his stifled blood-lust with battues of helpless beasts and birds fenced within great enclosures, he leaves for La Magliana "without his stole, and what is worse without his rochet, and what is worst of all, he wore great hunting boots." He has hounds from France and falcons from Iceland. In one hand he carries his eyeglass, with the other he will take a dagger, when he descends from his white steed and his calm as a spectator to slay the driven quarry at his feet to the sound of flutes, fifes, and lutes. The tall Cardinal Sanseverino, wearing his Heraklean lionskin, is at grips with the boar. On the homeward way courageous peregrines attempting great eagles fall bloodied to earth, earning stylistic epitaphs. Leonardo, friend to noble beasts, must have loathed these unfair slaughters. He had known fair hunting in his day, when Beatrice the Duchess rode reckless after the boar at Vigevano.

Shows go on all the time. The Sacro Processo of Leo at Eastertide began an unflagging continuity of masque, ballet, triumph, moresque, interlude, drama. They were flagrant rather than exquisite ; but a certain hard bright zest and hilarity of colour swept them joyously through the green arches, past the brocaded houses bowered in box and ilex. In 1514 the Portuguese ambassadors came bringing gifts. An Indian herald led a panther. There were leopards and parroquets and Indian fowls, and Persian horses, and priceless impearled cloths. But best of all, there was an elephant bearing a castle of wrought silver and led by a Saracen. He could weep like a woman, and he understood two languages. Leo loved his elephant nearly as well as his *Laocöon*. Like Leonardo, it was housed in the Belvedere. The artist, who had a high opinion of elephants, preferred it to the Pope.

Bullfights, races, Jew-baiting, arranged fights among the populace, enliven the cruel carnivals of the Holy City. The spirit of the amphitheatre is active still ; and harlequin hangmen execute chosen victims, for Rome keeps the dark craving for human sacrifice at Easter. Cruelty can take a merry form ; and the practical jests of Leo and his cardinals are colossal. Baraballo rides grotesquely past, wreathed and fatuous, upon the elephant, amid the sound of trumpets and inextinguishable laughter proceeding to his mock coronation in the Capitol. In gentler mood you can always go to see Pasquin. Pasquin is dressed like Apollo : Pasquin has complete licence to say anything, and Leo is more amused than anybody. If you are serious, you can go to talk with the fifty elect young Greek nobles who are studying under Lascaris so that true Hellenism may steal within the cruder veins of Rome. If you want a pretty sight, there is the new Procession of Venus, the bastard girls of the Convent San Spirito walking behind a slim gilt girl-Hymen, with her little torchbearers. Some, nuns elect, are in wedding raiment for their

In the Vatican

bridal with God : some are decked with gold and pearls, bespoken for earthly marriage : some await their destiny. Lovers choose : the desirous steal. It is a great festival with trumpets. All the great ladies look on, dazzling in changeable sbernias and wide cinctures of gems ; but their faces are hard, the colours are crude, and they are parroquets rather than peacocks. You may go out to the church of Saint Sebastian in the Appian Way, whither repair—a habit peculiar to Rome—the more daring of the light women, riding in doublet and hose and gallant hats, coming like youths to pray to the youthful saint. At Pentecost you might look at the cardinals loosing the doves from the altar at Saint Peter's, while *Veni Sancte Spiritus* rises from the flawless choir. The golden knights of Saint Peter are always magnificent. The audiences rush the gates of the Vatican to hear l'Unico Aretino improvise. Some great event is always loosening the bells and the trumpets. Giuliano receives one of those delicate pontifical swords sheathed in beauty, blessed for destruction. The dubious Maximilian is given the Golden Rose, grown to an exquisite bright branch with musk hidden in the capsules.

"Cypria semper ero," wrote the wise goldsmith under his marble Aphrodite in reply to Chigi's pompous Arch of Triumph for Leo's Sacro Processo, which proclaimed that, Venus and Ares having been satisfied by preceding pontiffs, it was now the turn of Pallas. For refined conversation, lute-music, and a little serious business in diplomacy sometimes, the dignitaries passed to the great houses of the " cortigiane honeste," a strange, sumptuous, and pathetic race created by the humanists in Rome in steadfast imitation of the Greek hetæræ. From Milan, Naples, Venice, Genoa, Spain, France, all the regions famed for enchantresses, they came. Only in Rome, in that soil of powdered brutalities and learned sensibilities, could they richly put forth their gold and saffron calyxes. With modest eyes and dulcet voices they refined the crude atmosphere into an illusive silver light in those salons of theirs which were also chancelleries for Europe. La Bella Imperia was lately dead, Imperia who, sandalled with gold, fair and slight between her great velvet sleeves, quivered, like a white butterfly in the leaves of an immense flower, in the depths of her blue and golden palace, filled with lutes and books. Beauty was her virtue ; and there were others like her, and like Tullia d'Aragona who used her Greek and Latin like perfumes and powders of enchantment. Both Vittoria Colonna and Michelangelo agree in considering beauty as a virtue in itself, and the " Roman courtesan " as a radiant apostle of the quality. Yet, behind all the brave curtains of purple and gold, behind all the grandiose wefts of music and poetry and colour, albeit their sophisticated caresses were kin to

425

those of the Cynthia of Propertius, were they not sold like others in the city of the Floralia, though the price was high? "Are we not worthy of pity?" wrote Beatrice of Ferrara suddenly to the young Lorenzo de' Medici—a strange confidant for a Renaissance Marguerite Gauthier.

Then there were the comedies, comedies of Plautus, finely acted and well embroidered with interlude and moresque, and set with novel, wonderfully deceptive perspectives by Peruzzi, and comedies like those of Plautus, by Bibbiena, Ariosto, Machiavelli, who, with the hard sob in his throat turned to an evil chuckle, made the wittiest and wickedest of Italian comedies for the thieves of his Republic, and, in a kind of satiric despair, a manual of princecraft for the iron autocrat who now seemed the one bitter hope of salvation for troubled Italy.

But the comedies rose to their glory when Rome had a visitor, and of all gay visitors, none was so pampered and delighted as Isabella d'Este, coming there in 1514-1515, to the Court where her young son Federigo had been educated as a hostage. That restless brilliant lady has her famine for original sights and experiences royally satisfied. Giuliano de' Medici and Bibbiena bring her to the Vatican, where Leo seats her beside him like a queen. Thereafter Isabella among the cardinals is distinctly a pretty sight, as, faintly flushed with glittering eyes, delighting and delighted, she dances through golden Rome surrounded by her extravagant pontifical courtiers. She saw the hard bright paganism of Renaissance Rome at its height, just as she would see it in the very agony of its fall, for occasion waited upon Isabella. Her brother Ippolito's festival in the Baths of Diocletian, whereafter they hunted the stag and danced till dawn; the visitation of the Seven Churches with an escort of young cardinals; the concerto of violins, lutes and harpsichords; the banquets of peacocks' flesh, with children coming out of pasties to say naughty verses; the battles of oranges among the mob; the interludes, the racy comedies; the allegorical scenes; Bibbiena's *Calandra*, perfectly produced, seasoned to bite through jaded palates; Raphael to show her heathen and Christian temples—everything charmed her. Amid coloured balloons of carnival she goes laughing through the ruins and the palaces. The infinite variety of dances pleases her; but she sends to Milan for Lombard dancers to show the cardinals what grace can do. She has forgotten Leonardo by this time: in Rome he is not the fashion.

ix

I have described that side of Renaissance Rome and its papal prince which exasperated the weary nerves of Leonardo, and made him the

In the Vatican

glad guest of Francis. There is another side to it. The combination of music, humanism, tolerance, and great elegance of manner, made the young cardinals enchanting in many of their moods; and Leo could be witty and had moments of fine enthusiasm for classical studies. There were great houses of beauty and simplicity, like that of Grimani, through whose open doors and empty sunny halls Erasmus went wandering till he found the cardinal in the loggia in pleasant conversation with friends, cordial in welcome. Erasmus said that only the floods of Lethe could drown for him the memory of Rome. The vast libraries, the sight of the ancient arches and pillars, the absorbing conversation of scholars, and the " sweet liberty," the great intellectual toleration, so delighted him. The young cardinals at play round Isabella d'Este are most attractive; they are blithe and graceful like kitten-leopards. If they go to see witty comedies that jest with the cold priapism of the intellectual sensualist, you feel that these are ritual phallic sacrifices to ancient gods, and that they really like dancing better. Among the ambassadors one discovers the calm blue eyes and dark hair of Castiglione, with perfect courtesy watching the interests of his jeopardized Duke, yet not disliking Rome.

But Leonardo, versed in Florentine art, and not so forgetful as Isabella of the masques of Milan, found the shows ponderous. The humanists seemed pedantic; and, worst of all, the " sweet liberty," the great intellectual toleration, which made conversation scintillating and comedy audacious, failed inexplicably in his own case when he was attacked by a German mechanic. Throngs of parasites, copyists, secretaries, lackeys, every kind of pander, courtesans, mimes, and noisy buffoons, offended his sense of gracious existence. What to him was the Roman Academy? What to him the purity of the Greek Press, and the care for the beautiful cursive type of Manutius' books? The lucid Latin of Bembo and Sadoleto carried no delight for him. Vida might write hexameters on chess; Jovius might emulate Livy; five books of Tacitus might be restored to the world with a kind of rapture almost rekindled from the earlier enthusiasm. Leonardo, who could make Archimedes participate in wars between Spain and England, had no sense of human history; and had as much regard for the written word as one of the Olympians whom he resembled. Jovius, however, was intently aware of Leonardo.

x

Raphael was the painter for Leo and for Rome. He resumed in his radiant and easy art all the notable Renaissance qualities, and carried them easily home to minds disinclined to spare much attention from the brilliant business of life. His gift for covering great spaces with animated

427

Leonardo the Florentine

and arresting compositions that mirrored with flattery the people of his day under great disguises of names they reverenced, his reconciliations of the traditions to which they were accustomed, provided exactly the kind of state-painting desired by the Halls of the Vatican. He himself was made for Leo's Rome, easily the darling of pontiffs and women. Poetically beautiful in a Madonna-like way, charming, spendthrift, conceding, he made the cardinals feel that he was one of them ; and they did their best to adopt him into their brotherhood. Leo loved him because he was full of *gentilezza*, because he would do anything, from painting the Stanze to inventing a humorous drop-scene, or amorously illustrating a cardinal's bathroom with delicate little loves and dolphins and swans. In all pleasures, as in all devotions, he was readily accomplice, which was most convenient. Did Leo's conscience begin to ache over the ruining of Rome's ruins ? Raphael will be Inspector-General of Antiquities, besides all other things. Is Leo tired of the endless quarrels over Saint Peter's building ? When Bramante dies, in 1514, Raphael will be Superintendent of Saint Peter's. From that princely studio proceed sweet nursing Madonnas with no Seven Swords in their hearts, clasping pretty children doomed to no Cross, while designs for decorating villas, portraits like Castiglione's or Leo's own, or of noble ladies like La Donna Velata, or provocative women like La Fornarina, and sweeping designs for magnificent tapestries are poured easily out. And with his very adequate pupils he would readily fresco a summer villa. He improvised as brilliantly as l'Unico Aretino, and all in a happy glow and rush of festival laughter and love-making.

Leonardo, contemplating this overfluent version of his own early facility, felt blunted and weakened. Before this ardent talent his difficult genius became the more chilly. They were courteous enough : Raphael painted him as Plato, it is said. And he copied and domesticated the *Leda*, still enthusiastic in imitation. Sodoma, overshadowed by Raphael but protected by Chigi, understood Leonardo better, though clogged and cloyed by his own rich animalism.

From the Raphael party nevertheless Leonardo receives indifference or a certain irrational dislike, for who that was an enthusiast of Raphael would not recoil from the evasive and ironical air that hardly left even the *Leda*, though now she might stand seducing within the tender cover of the great wing, and throw round the bird's neck a languid lovely hand? From the Michelangelo party, since there was one still, he had active hostility. The Sistine Chapel was Michelangelo's terrific apologia for his bitter humours. That terrible thundercloud of brooding and hurtling forms hung like a portent of judgment over the carnival cardinals ; but they knew it was a great work, and the confusion of prophets and genii and sibyls pleased their minds with a sense of brio, and flattered their great relish of a synthetic knot of Hebraic, Hellenic, and Christian figures. Michelangelo had been the special Medicean artist; and Leo, who was discomforted both by his personality and his work, felt bound to employ him, though he sent him afar. The sullen sculptor is a Timon-like figure in Rome. Cardinal Farnese meets him on a winter day wandering in the Colosseum. Where is he going? "To school to learn something," is the reply. He is agonizing over Julius' neglected tomb. But the cries and persecution, manias and protests of Michelangelo at the period of transition make us glad that Leonardo moved with such composure in equal trial. Without naming him, he notes Michelangelo's weakness of over-emphasis in his nude athletes: "O anatomical Painter! beware lest the too-strong indication of the bones, sinews, and muscles be the cause of your becoming wooden in your painting by your wish to make your nude figures display all their feeling."

In the ceremonial rhetoric of Renaissance Rome there was no desire for Leonardo's lonely and personal and lyrical art. Lyrical it was, for all the long preparation, lyrical as the builded odes of Milton and Keats are lyrical, since the motive pulsing through the harmonies is a single indescribable cry of wonder and pure rapture. As an artist Leonardo was not contemporary with Raphael and Michelangelo. He belonged to a more radiant period and knew a diviner air. He was a son of the morning, whose true contemporaries were Piero della Francesca, and Botticelli and Mantegna. Greater and more many-sided than these, he did not lose that first felicity, that winging imaginative delight, with which the Florentine painters rediscovered the beauty of the body and the strangeness of the soul, and caught up the blithe imitation, not of the Greeks, but of the Greek attitude to Nature. He became alien to his time when his time passed to overbearing Rome—to Rome that could overbear any painter, but not Leonardo. His lovely and preoccupied art refused her service. Listless as it had become, the personality of Leonardo was still more powerful than the personality of Rome.

xi

Giuliano de' Medici had installed his friend the artist in the studios of the Belvedere, with the Pope's assent. There he worked, a little at painting, much at mechanics. Leonardo has his own friends, his own disciples about him. And Giuliano's set, more insinuating than Leo's, come about the place.

But he is vexed and weary. The dust of Rome is gritty on his palate, the texture of Rome runs coarse under his finger, the cymbals of Rome

Leonardo the Florentine

are harsh in his ears. It is august, but it is not fine. There comes a time when those most steadily victorious in charm enter some alien territory and know defeat. With an evil astonishment and a complete inhibition they find the flame of their spirit gutter low in that thick atmosphere. Their very voices cannot carry, and their eyes are despoiled of all sweet authority. The axioms of their being are not accepted. Much more easily might Orpheus - Leonardo enchant the beasts than the Romans. Their hard, bright materialism was self-sufficient ; and they had no interest in processes of perfection. The indifference of their misconception was a kind of brutality for him. It is only at this penultimate stage that Leonardo presents a harrowing pathos, for it always seems shameful to the onlooker to realize a great soul in wrong, incongruous plight.

When weariness is so increased by this kind of dismay that the spirit closes its eyes awhile in its desperate fatigue of defeat, only some nervous spectre walks abroad, betraying the sick true lord by its fierce resentments of little things. Mere sensibility is so raw that a slight bruise draws blood ; and any trivial human spite seems to drive a stiletto charged with an assassin's malice. Hence Leonardo's Roman visit seems to be chiefly composed of the tragedy of an ungrateful German. Three times does he draft a letter concerning the iniquities of the " ingannato Tedesco " for Giuliano, who has been ill. That Leonardo is also ill, is evident enough. He is obsessed by the wickedness of this mechanic and his accomplice. Perhaps he never sent this so elaborately drafted letter ; perhaps his indignation ran away in the expression of it, and left him Olympian again. The consequence of the incident was serious enough psychologically, and more than anything sickened him of Rome.

Within the Belvedere are many ateliers, one of them being occupied by a German mechanic, Giorgio, working for Giuliano under Leonardo's orders. This workman is idle, dissolute, dishonest, and disrespectful to Leonardo, and shows every kind of ingratitude. He is influenced by another German intruder, John of the Mirrors, tries to steal Leonardo's models, and spies upon his anatomy. Finally he demands excessive pay ; and, being refused, sells everything in his atelier and abandons it to the glass-maker, who coolly sets up a factory and makes mirrors to send to the fairs. He fills the whole Belvedere with workshops for mirrors. You seem to see this Court of the Vatican glittering with Teutonic impudence. Dwelling on Giorgio's ingratitude, Leonardo explains that he has even given him the opportunity of dining with him, so that he might improve his Italian. The " inganno Tedesco," however, flouts both Leonardo's salads and his pure Tuscan : he eats with the Swiss guards, and spends all day hunting with them in the ruins. This last detail gives a lightning glimpse of a genre scene in Renaissance Rome. "Afterwards he went to dine with the Swiss of the guard where there are idle fellows, in which he beat them all ; and most times they went two or three together with guns, to shoot birds among the ruins, and this went on till evening."

The vagaries of the "Tedesco" would seem rather humorous. But both the insolent workmen evidently curried favour with some of Leonardo's more powerful detractors. For he, who has been working at his anatomy in the most favoured hospital, finds the Director suddenly refusing him admission, and the Pope condemning him for heretical practices in his studies. The men, Leonardo says, have sown "the usual scandals."

> "That thou art blamed shall not be thy defect,
> For scandal's mark was ever yet the fair."

All his life he must have been thus scandalled, and thus consoled. Still, that he is grieved and angry is natural. In Leo's Rome, famous for toleration, where Pasquin might be as insolent as he pleased and the comedies made mock of the clergy, where cardinals rode like Turks, and all the churchmen debated subtly the immortality of the soul, where Michelangelo anatomized with encouragement, why was the hospital shut on Leonardo at the instance of such informers, and he protected by the beloved brother Giuliano ? Leo's famous toleration was certainly the toleration of Gallio, and Gallio is much safer on the seat of authority than Paul. Still, the easy-going Pope banned Leonardo's anatomy. The persistent calumnies were full of implications ; probably Leonardo was embittered. In his age as in his youth, he, so admired and super-excellent, had been challenged where lesser men went free. It was the penalty of his singular powers ; but it stung him. He wished to leave Rome. "In fine I come to the conclusion that it is bad if they [men] are hostile and worse if they are friendly."

xii

He was not altogether unhappy. We find him indulging in play. Perhaps inspired by the sight of the cardinals playing with coloured balloons in the court of the Belvedere, he has been studying the problem of flight on the balloon principle. He does it with *espièglerie*, and the more vivacious princes, such as Ippolito d'Este, with keen faces and amused and dangerous eyes, those of Giuliano's following, find mirth in Leonardo's studio, where odd-shaped creatures of inflated skin, toys of wax and quicksilver, go sailing through the air ; and an astonishing little monster, made from a grotesque lizard given to him by the vine-dresser of the Belvedere, glides about like a familiar dragonlet in a queer dream. He has given it quivering wings made from the skins of other lizards, and horns and a beard. His other notion of blowing up a handful of prepared ox-gut till it drove everybody out of the room, shows that he did not leave all the practical jokes to the Romans. Vasari's state-ment that he did this, " comparing it with virtue," sounds incredible. He is amusing himself with startling mystifications, even as he did when he was a young man in Verrocchio's bottega, composing dragons. The point of malice just gleams in his amusement, as he compels his sciences to be diverting. He is a changeling still ; and has not lost the mockery of the god in exile.

He is flashing mirrors in experiment, and intently composing varnishes and oils. He is at work also on that system of treatises which, arranged and completed, would have been an encyclopædia of Renaissance knowledge in arts and sciences. He writes in the Belvedere *De Ludo geometrico*, an abstruse work on the quadrature of curved surfaces. And, his shaping mind, at least, fiery and tireless, he wakes the languid Giuliano to a great scheme for draining the Pontine Marshes. Or within the fosses of the sinister round bulk of San Angelo he makes absorbing experiments in sound. Also, as we have seen, there was always the great Campagna, where among stones and flowers one could forget irritating Germans.

He even does some painting. His pupil Boltraffio has to content the San Onofrio convent when it desires an altarpiece, and does it in a leonardesque way. But, if he never painted that picture for the Pope for which, said his enemies, he first made the glaze, he found a more sympathetic friend in the Pope's datary, Baldassare Turini, for whom he did a Madonna and a little picture of a beautiful boy, something of the kind once desired by Isabella. We do not know the Madonna, and the sweet adolescent has been lost.

But beyond the Alps the striving forces are not quiet because Leo is enjoying his Rome. It is a world of gathering conflicts. In the year 1515, Leonardo records with his significant brevity that the Magnifico has departed to Savoy to marry a wife, and that news has come that the King of France is dead. Giuliano has indeed gone to bring as a bride Philiberta of Savoy, young half-sister to that Louise whose heart throbbed so wildly at the other piece of intelligence. King Louis the Twelfth, anxious kindly sovereign, considerate of his people, who loved him, had died in a wild fit of belated romance, sweetly offering his death as a New Year's gift to his lovely English bride ; and the disquieting heir, " ce gros garçon " who, he said, would spoil all, leapt upon the coveted throne as Francis the First. He was young, he was fed on romances, he had seen himself from infancy as a Cæsar in the idolatrous eyes of the other two members of what Cardinal Bibbiena had called " the Trinity." He meant to dazzle out the memory of Gaston de Foix, his early companion, and to create a new epic of Charlemagne. He was of Orleans, and his eyes were on Valentino's Milan. His mother's little Court at Cognac had been very Italianate. A brilliant Spanish engineer, Pedro Navarro, was at his service ; so, while Italy was looking elsewhere, his armies slipped miraculously over the Alps by an unsuspected bypath, and he was amazing Lombardy. Leo, uncertain, dispatches the ailing Giuliano as gonfalonier of the Church, with the Papal army, to watch and to intervene if necessary. Leonardo accompanies him, probably as engineer. Weary as he is, he does not shrink from camps again. They are better than Rome without his friend and protector. But Giuliano becomes very ill in Florence ; and his nephew Lorenzo takes his place as captain. Leonardo leaves this later Medicean Florence, already invested with the languid affectations and melancholy grace of decay, where, in his beloved Santa Maria Novella, that keeps a climate, they say, like a perpetual spring, the masked gallants at vespers are whispering what they will. He goes with Lorenzo to Piacenza, it seems, helping with fortifications this incapable and arrogant young man, whose chief distinction was to appear clothed in gold and cramoisie at carnival battles of oranges and lemons. The sudden and dramatic victory of Marignano, where Francis, accompanied by Trivulzio, Bourbon, Bayard, broke the Spanish forces under Cardona and the Cardinal of Sion, and destroyed the reputation of the Swiss, put an end to Leo's shifty inactivity. On that September day, Francis, vanquishing like a real king of paladins, recklessly blazing through the two-days " battle of giants," with the rose of carbuncles in his casque and the blue surcoat powdered with lilies over his proud armour, romantically taking knighthood from the sword of Bayard, had the climax of his heart's desire, and shone a chivalrous hero in the eyes of Europe, the peer of Roland and Oliver, Godfrey and Baldwin. It was too early. He did not himself suspect that he had no staying power.

The Pope, aware that he had been dealing doubly with the French, agreed to meet Francis at Bologna. Leonardo was already there. According to Vasari, Leonardo left Italy because a dispute threatened concerning the façade of San Lorenzo, at which Michelangelo was working. It is not very clear. But probably the likelihood of continued friction with Michelangelo, if he continued to work for the Medici, made Leonardo feel that there was no room for him in Italy. He had left Piacenza, and journeyed quickly by Fiorenzuola, Borgo San Domino, Parma, Reggio, Modena, comparatively tranquil places friendly to

Leonardo the Florentine

Giuliano's sway. We do not know if he had been more or less in touch with the French since he left Milan ; we do not know if he was introduced to Francis by some of his courtiers, or if Philiberta of Savoy had communicated to her nephew the impressions of Giuliano. We do know that he met the King, and that the ancient spell of mysterious sweetness, which had sunk low in the gross and heedless atmosphere of Rome, flamed up again in the glow of new interest and approval, and swiftly enkindled Francis. That disappointing young man was at his best moment of pride and enthusiasm. His mind was loosely woven, his ambitions were showy, his vigorous senses were overblown. That excessive indulgence from idolatrous women, which would have turned a more delicate being into something fine though perverse, had merely made the " gros garçon " ill-conditioned in his appetites and disappointments. But he was generous in his easy way, and that he had some instinct for beauty and subtly-textured personality his frank recognition of Leonardo's quality completely proves. His very decorative device of a crowned salamander in the midst of the flame betrays at least a flamelike intention. There is no reason to doubt that he took pleasure in Leonardo's conversation, which was not likely to be entirely woven of philosophy and information. Leonardo's grace could not but wear its learning easily, like an ornament ; and his talk was of a dancing kind, lighted with wit and irony. The spell had worked ; and Leonardo, reassured by his last victory, felt his powers renewed.

Bologna, the grave arcaded city of learning, leaning towers, and brooding churches, with grave piled apses, looked on sullenly at the meeting of Leo and Francis. It had its pride and its violences. Within its cloisters lay the beautiful Enzo, son of the great heretic emperor, whom no gold could ransom because the city had such pride in its captive, and who died at last in his prison-chambers of love and music. Within its cloisters also lay Saint Dominic in an angel-guarded tomb. It had fought Julius II. hard, had turned his statue into a cannon, and still sullenly regarded the Papacy, crying, "Sega!" at intervals for its Bentivoglio tyrant. When Leo came, having passed, throwing silver, through Florence amid the demonstrative excess of a decoration more in the Roman than the Florentine manner, with trophies and obelisks innumerable, Bologna spared him not an arch or a wreath. But when King Francis came, quietly, with no procession, this parsimony of show disappointed them. He was graceful and handsome enough at this hour of his youth, however, very red and white, brown-haired and slant-eyed, his long nose not so evident ; and his figure seemed magnificent, in a great cloak of gold with zibelline furs. There were anxious intrigues for the threatened Duke of Urbino, whose duchy Leo still meant to acquire. Castiglione was there, fervent for his master. Felice delle Rovere, and ten ladies romantic in peacock velvet and white ermine, visited the King, and enchanted his susceptible heart. Leo and Francis met with great courtesies, and exchanged concessions, neither being really satisfied. The dying Giuliano was made Duke of Nemours, among other things. They renewed the ancient conversation concerning a crusade, which, as a faëry Eastern exploit, had glamour for Francis ; and then Leo said Mass at the High Altar in San Petronio, with the King for server, pensively reflecting as he held the basin that he had failed to secure the investiture of Naples or to save his friend the Duke of Urbino.

Then the Pope gave Francis, for a *baiser-de-paix*, a piece of the True Cross in a reliquary of diamond and gold. This jewelled Cross had once been Lodovico's. With other treasures he had committed it to the keeping of Ascanio Sforza, his cardinal brother, at whose death the Pope had taken it. But King Francis considered this a mediæval gift for a sovereign who tried to combine the New Ideas with feudal chivalry. He said he would prefer *The Laocöon*. The astonished Leo hurriedly assented, was overwhelmed with thanks, and, safe in Rome, sent a bad copy.

Raphael came to Bologna in Leo's train : he and Leonardo were together for the last time. They looked like morning and evening star ; but for both their setting was soon to be. Leonardo, watching the interplay of King and Pope, was talking with the King's Household and quietly arranging his journey. In 1515 he has followed Francis, and sees the sweet city of Milan for the last time. The gentle and wearied Maximilian, son of Lodovico, has thankfully accepted a pension and an asylum from the King, being exhausted by a Swiss-guarded state. Inexhaustible in pageants, the city wakes to revels again at the approach of the new lord. And probably it is now that Leonardo's famous mechanical lion makes a wondrous appearance. The glittering beast walks to the feet of the King, a handsome young satyr with long nose and equivocal eyes, clothed in wide-sleeved magnificence ; and its breast opens in a river of lilies. Leonardo, having found a prince with the radiant masquing mood upon him, gladly recovers his own. With a Renaissance pageant he ends his life in Italy.

There must have been some mournful leave-takings in Milan. Andrea Salaino has no heart to go beyond the Alps, so he is left, to build a house on Leonardo's vineyard. But Francesco Melzi will ride with him across the mountains and to the last ferry. A successor to Salaino as a personal attendant, a young man called Battista da Villanis, goes with them.

On the sixth day of a rigid January the group of Italians rode away in the suite of Francis. There is something heroic in the spectacle of

Leonardo the Florentine

Leonardo, old and nerve-shaken, his right hand already quivering on his rein, riding across the Alps to an alien land, serenely confident in his power to please a young, changeable, and fantastic king. And there is something symbolic in that little group. It is the Renaissance passing from Italy to France. Swallows and harbingers of that exotic beauty had already rested in music and floriation under the eaves of the French castles. But Leonardo was the Italian Renaissance, keeping all the lucidity of its morning with the paradoxical perfection of its prime, refusing the chilly languors of its decay. He rides adventuring now as he did when he went with a silver lyre in his hand to try romantic impossible gestes in Milan. Over the dreadful defiles and up through the solemn silver-stricken ridges of Savoy he rides ; and, if death be following him close, yet love, Italian love, is his squire. It was the romantic, the unappeasable knight-errant in Leonardo, prevailing over the savant and even the artist, that endeared him to Francis. Never forget the interplay that makes a changeable tissue of Leonardo's ages, calming the young insouciant cavalier with the serious preoccupations of an incomparable mind, mantling the tired old man with something seigneurial and fleur-de-lisé. The iridescence of youth plays over the rider who sets his horses across the Alpine passes violet in the end of day.

Part iv

The Hostel of Francis

(1516-1519)

Chapter i

The Hostel of Francis

i

WHEN Leonardo rode into the strangers' land, Europe seemed to be requickening under a constellation of Youth, as the three stars of Francis, Charles, the grandson of Maximilian, and Henry VIII. of England, strove for the ascendant ; and a false excitement of hope for great deeds ran through the nations. France particularly, or rather the Court of France, which was all that seemed to matter then, was aglow with triumphal pleasure. Italy was a garden of pillage, and the spirit of the Renaissance seemed to have passed to the land of the Loire.

Leonardo came to France at a time of bewildering transition. It was a conscious affair in France, the Renaissance : it did not awake with a sense of wild wings and Greek asphodel as it did in the Italian cities, whose hearts had never been transpierced by the great spears of the Gothic. France had expressed the soul of mediævalism more passionately, terribly, and sweetly than any other country—in ecstatic building like that of Amiens, Rheims, Chartres, Rouen, Paris ; in a sculpture of exquisite and noble shapes with raiment fluted as purely as that of the archaic figures of Greece ; in ivories, missals, and stained-glass of heart-moving intensity ; in Arthurian romance in the North, and Provençal song and cantefable in the South ; in crusades of knights and courts of love ; in all of best and worst that was implied by the word chivalry.

Now, restored to some vigour and lucidity by the simplifying of its dynastic troubles in the accession of the House of Orleans, personified by Francis the First, this Latin country, that dissolves the North and South within its gay ironic intelligence and its covered wells of emotion, was ready for new impulses in art and learning. But the soul of France was delicate, violent, and wearied from its long trances and fevers. It could only take the Italian contagion daintily, coquettishly, a little perversely, since, to its persistent mediæval mood, Italy still seemed something forbidden. And so it remained. The Gothic points are woven within the fretted patterns of the new pavilions, if only like

439

thorns with the roses. Slim saints and queens from the cathedrals enter into the fluent nymphs of Jean Goujon and Germain Pilon. The French Renaissance had not the great and impassioned ways of the Italian Revival. But it was a poignant and exquisite intrigue, for it was a much more feminine affair.

ii

Louis XII. had felt the enchantment of the wine-red, rose-red city of Milan, and had brought home some of the foreign beauty that had crazed his hapless predecessor. He, however, was a king with a conscience about his revenues ; wherefore his people loved him. But the young Francis, formed by idolatrous women, hearing from infancy a mother murmur " mon roi, mon seigneur, mon César, mon fils," bred on the romances of Roland and Amadis, encouraged in luxurious appetites, disciplined only by personal encounters with romantic young nobles all eager for glory in Italian wars, considered his kingdom as a mere stage for his own magnificence, and Italy partly as a rose-garden of sophisticate delight and partly as the gilded lists in which he would ride for the crown of the Holy Roman Empire. He and his young companions deliberately desired of life nothing but a gorgeous court for gallantry and a glittering field for war.

His mother's sensuous and flowery little Court at Cognac, the " second paradise," had been " italianisant." His games with " le jeune Adventureux " were " games of Italy." As if bound by some new vine, the keep of Amboise was putting forth sweet ornament. The brilliant Gaston de Foix, a prince whom he envied and Marguerite loved, had won in his brief life more laurels than he could bear. The old Italian title of Milan was doubly his by his marriage with Claude. So, after a dazzling coronation, in which he shone like Monseigneur Saint Michael in a great light of silver, he achieved the surprising Alpine crossing, and was made and marred at Marignano.

Leonardo's experience of Francis fell in the best years of that showy sovereign's life. His great victory had lifted him into a glowing enthusiasm that became him well ; and he was determined that his Court should be as artistic an expression of the new paganism as any Court in Italy. There is indeed something crude and " voulu " in the early years of Francis' reign. The mediæval refinement has passed, and the italianate refinement has not quite been caught. There is too much mere gold and silver, too much animal vigour, too casual an air in the love-making. The King loved women, art, poetry, but with a certain grossness. Even in youth the weft of Francis' character is slackly wrought, and his mind is too insensitive through vanity to let him be subtly touched ; the fine though perverse issues of the French Renaissance appear in its art only when the sweet poison of Italy is indeed dissolved by Catherine in the blood of the Valois.

But Francis' gay good-humour, his easy generosity, the natural quickness of his spoiled mind, his vivid appreciation of rare quality, his gift for gesture, his sense of drama, made him for the moment seem the most important figure in Europe. He was still handsome. Not yet had the vitiated blood suffused his face, turning it to a heavy mask of carnal satiety. He was tall : he had masses of brown hair ; he was red and white. With his daring equivocal eyes, his quietly-laughing mouth, and his amusing long nose, he looked like a young satyr who had found his way to a throne. Rather drunk with beauty and opportunity, his frank and sensual air poetized by youth and some real imaginative delight into something mobile, faunish, and engaging, Francis was found lovable by many. And that he could be regal in the wide-sleeved magnificence of his white brocades even the stately Venetian ambassadors admitted in their secret reports.

There is enough testimony to prove that he was capable of appreciating Leonardo not only as an artist, architect, and engineer, but as a personality. Cellini's report long afterwards of King Francis' cordial recollection of Leonardo's witty and philosophic discourse is probably correct enough : that lively artist did not often record the praises of another, dead or alive. Leonardo, old and ill, was nobly used and honoured by Francis : it is perhaps a proof of what waste there was indeed in the scattered spirit of the " roi chevalier."

iii

As long before, in Lodovico's great day, Leonardo found himself entirely committed to a Court. It was indeed perplexingly like and unlike the Court of that imaginative tyrant. There was an extravagant lord, there was a court of women, there was a life of masquerade, falconry, hunting, and sometimes mere charivari. But there was no breadth of imaginative design, for Francis had not the mental sweep and the artistic passion that dwelt behind Lodovico's wide-winged eyebrows. The women were of a different type from the sweet love-dreaming Lombards. Greeds and ambitions often chilled their hearts ; and plot and counter-plot constricted their amourettes into wilful intrigues, spiced by mere desire.

Above all, there was no city. As time passed, Francis showed an inclination to shift his centre from Tours to Paris ; but he never had much interest in the scene without his gates. Leonardo reveals an apprehension of this volatile spirit when he begins to plan cities for

Leonardo the Florentine

Francis. "Let the men of the country partly inhabit the new houses when the Court is absent," he says. The restlessness which grew upon the King after his return from exile made him feverish from the beginning. Ever longing to try the effect of his own figure in a new setting, he carried his extravagant Court from place to place, dancing, hunting, masquing, singing, unaware of "le paouvre peuple," save when some momentary twinge takes him or some other great duke. A grim warrior like Anne de Montmorency, whose character has its depths, is rueful over the wars that he loves, "par pitié du paouvre peuple qui ne peut mais de leurs querelles." Even Francis takes some thought at first "pour le soullagement du paouvre peuple," and pays the mercenaries. There was some stir of conscience, even in France, during the high Renaissance. But pity died, speared by both sides, in the implacable wars of the religions.

There is a complaint in *The Courtier* that the French nobles are too unceremonious in their bearing to their king. And indeed Leonardo found himself now serving a group of feudal aristocrats more insolent in their assumption than any Italian tyrant, who held his difficult princedom so long as he placated his subjects with some kind of *virtù*, were it only a show of splendour. The great families of France still considered themselves the peers of an overlord whose sceptre had but recently been accepted in Burgundy and Brittany. They form a group sacrosanct and unassailable ; their flesh is so kneaded with the sense of some divine privilege that they feel themselves not of ordinary clay. Outside their personal code, outside the haughty whim of their largess, they are insensible to sympathy. Bayard is the last noble flower of mediæval education, disinterested, candid, courageous, though perhaps a little stupid in his undisturbed simplicity of motive ; but he sees the peasants hanged at random on the castle walls with the indifference of any knight in Froissart. They are not of his kind. The mottoes of the great families have an insane pride :

> " Roy ne suis !
> Duc ne prince aussy ;
> Je suis le sire de Coucy."

and

> " Roy ne puis !
> Prince ne daigne !
> Rohan suis."

So they will continue, superb and conscienceless through the centuries, as if reliquaries of some sacred blood, more and more sterile in their magnificence, till the only virtue of their order is that of passing under the guillotine with such a great air that we forget for a moment what centuries of oppression paid the price for that fine and final gesture.

They were warriors that stood round Francis—like Anne de Montmorency, fierce and steadfast in will, famous from Ravenna, Philippe de Chabot that shall be Admiral of France, the blond Sieur de Fleuranges, with cold blue eyes, the " jeune Adventureux," experienced in Italian war, Odet de Foix, Sieur de Lautrec, arrogant, with sleepy lids, scarred also from Gaston's great battle, La Tremouille, La Palice, the good soldier with the astonished look, Trivulzio, the great Italian condottiere. And there was Galeazzo di Sanseverino still pursuing his delicate way, beloved of kings, destined for Pavia ; and Bonnivet with disarmingly ingenuous brows, the professional lover, always waylaying Marguerite with stealthy glances, because she ever gave a "doux Nenny, avec un doux sourire." Prouder than any the Constable of Bourbon, consanguine with Italy by his Gonzaga mother, mighty prince of the blood, kinglier to see than Francis, his tragic eyes burning in the white wedge of his face dividing his black bell of hair. But still he moved indifferently loyal ; and Francis felt like Charlemagne among his paladins.

iv

It was with women that Francis, whom they had formed and adored, took his greatest pleasure. His ideal was to go glorious to war, and return victor to Venus and her garlanders. His Master of the Household, Artus de Boisy, a courtier whose personal charm and noble presence kept him steadily the favourite of kings, was heir to a tradition that linked him with Agnes Sorel, and the cult of the tender "dame de beauté" sentimentalized the Court. Not a word of Jeanne d'Arc ! Her poignant gift of martyrdom was too intolerable a debt : besides, her faëry blood had only the red blazonries of a saint. Not for these pleasure-hot eyes to see the greatest lady in history :

> " Dans un encadrement de cierge et de flamberge,
> Et le casque remis aux mains du petit page.
> La fille la plus sainte après la sainte Vierge."

They look a little too much of the transition, those ladies of King Francis' Court, during the first years of his reign. Most of the challenging Renaissance figures are still in the wings. Those that are on the stage halt somewhat doubtfully in their parts, not yet practised in the new attitude, or they dash gaily about, madcap as Nomerfide. In their rigid bodices, wide stiff skirts, great sleeves and hard little coifs, looped with jewels, they seem a trifle vigorous and robust, having lost the mediæval

Leonardo the Florentine

fineness and not yet acquired the Renaissance finesse. They are Poitevin ladies, understood by Rabelais. They have the something fantastical of the *Roman de la Rose*, the something gross of the fabliaux. They remember the lady who educated Petit Jehan de Saintré, and they promise the Abbey of Thelema. With frankly inviting eyes they continue the tradition of chivalric love, only dyed a new purple in Platonism after the manner of Bembo. But the men are finer and more complex than the women, being much more italianate : even their fashions are more attractive—black velvet berets, hanging hair, jewelled collars, and wide sleeves. While Francis never fails to appreciate his Frenchwomen, it is for love as well as for war that he goes to Italy : the morbid lovely faces of Milan haunt his imagination, and siren voices sing him sweetly to the disaster of Pavia.

But soon the new spirit will work the Frenchwomen fluette and Spring-like as the gracile pavilions and the poesies of Ronsard, like the white Diane, like the rose-white Queen of Scots. If, at present, between the mediæval garden enclosed and the Renaissance spiral stair, they are gauche and coltish, and their looks are too brightly urgent, they will become more " devins et delicats " when the Demoiselle de Heilly, that blonde girl, slides into the facile throne of the King's heart. It is held as yet by Françoise de Foix, Madame de Chateaubriand, passionate, sombre, opulent, and milky-white, with great dark eyes. A richly surrendered Danaë, a romantic jealous lady, loving the King with verses ! Unconsidered, the patient Queen Claude keeps her quiet state, making a silence about her with her pure devices of swans, lilies, ermines, and moons. Tyrannical over her and all others, Louise de Savoy, the King's mother, chestnut-haired, with eyes of cold blue-grey, and slender shape, conceals behind her equivocal nunlike air fierce passions of desire and avarice which will yet undo her glorified son. With this terrible neo-pagan " Madame " Leonardo doubtless exchanged courtesies, especially at Romorantin, for she loved flowers and music. Round her hovered a band of ladies gay and desirous, the maids-of-honour that will become the flying squadron of Catherine de' Medici.

But the famous and attractive Thelemite of the Court was the most devoted sister in history, the Marguerite of Marguerites, the Pearl of the Valois. She moves among the " dévisantes " who will one day enter *The Heptameron*, deprecating and distinguished, her whole soul dissolved in the art of pleasing. Her thick fair hair, her violet half-closed eyes, her wistfully smiling mouth, make all the Court forget whether she is a beauty or not ; and men go mad for the ravishing unravished air of one who has a wild and witty head and a calm cold heart that kindles only with a mystical imaginative idolatry for her brother and her King. She is more passionately "italianisante" than any, for Boccaccio's book has become part of her. Yet those who think Marguerite's Decameronian tolerance anything but an intellectual frolic find themselves transpierced in the duel of wits she never refuses, sure of her final defence in the invincible distaste of her senses. With the chastity of a chilled or repressed or poetized mood, she finds a purely mental mirth in matters of which she never quite realizes the actuality. A *subtilité* in the way of adultery is a comedy in the air ; and though she loves a lover's love she loathes his appetite. She is coquette as well as mystic, materialist, epicurean, and reformer. She is rather uncertain, in fact, among all the pleasing Renaissance attitudes. Now she leads the madcap ladies during the first rapture of King Francis' reign, capping verses and playing on her viol, learning *les langues hérétiques*, laughing the *petit ris folâtre*, not foreseeing the time when, in her litter of weariness and pain, she shall write her shameful piteous book, vibrating and cordial, exotic and vulgar, to wring a smile from the marred dishonoured shape of the "roi chevalier" that remained preposterously godlike for her.

Leonardo, it is said, devised masques for her when her brother came to visit her in state at Argentan. Doubtless she spoke to him with that penetrating voice of hers, and wrapped the great Italian in silken scarves of sympathy ; but Marguerite was, like Isabella d'Este, too deliberately intelligent for Leonardo, even though she was "born smiling." The Court of which she was the chief sunflower must have bewildered him, if he could be bewildered, with its ancient dynastic prides, and its crudities in the new culture, its libertine, amiable, headlong way of romping into the Renaissance culture in a fit of high spirits between Ravenna and Pavia. Along the Loire the landscape was breaking into the iris flags of its turreted chateaux, some just putting forth a lily-border at the top, some unfolding a sudden swan-wing ruffled with pointed pattern at the edge, some springing exultant like a group of purfled white hollyhocks. Soon the ladies would be singing the psalms of Clement Marot to their pretty love-tunes, even if they did still visit a magician now and then to waste the waxen effigy of a rival. Stiff in their splendours, they dance pavanes among the lighted torches on the lawns, and fly among the statues with little shrieks. There is much duelling, and the tourneys are cordially approved. The stables are filled with horses from Turkey, England, and Spain. The dogs are of pedigree. The falconries are noisy with falcons, gerfalcons, tiercelets, emerillons, éperviers, herons : some of them are from Candia, Syria, Venice. Lute-players mix with the soothsayers and astrologers. The banquets are served with elaborate etiquette ; the golden pheasant and the wine in great carven ewers come in while the musicians play in the gallery. After Marignano, it is a climax of joy and pride. The King and his friends are masquing, hunting, singing, laughing, building, in a charivari of gay extravagance. They are childishly inventive in their luxuries, and enthusiastic in their pleasures. King Louis and Queen Anne had lived soberly, and tasted the dangerous soul of Italy but sparingly. Now there is some yeasty ferment as of new wine in old bottles, but presently the bouquet and the flavour will be sure, subtle, and novel.

V

It was in the pleasant land of Touraine, in the dreamy valley of the Loire, that King Francis' gay processions of silken litters and gleaming cavaliers passed from castle to castle. Tours, the city of the fine French knight St Martin, was still his capital in Leonardo's day, and Amboise was one of the great residences. The electric quality of the moods that seethed around the thickset of towers and spires that was Paris had not yet magnetized him to the centre of France. It was in Amboise, keep and palace and town of Charles VIII. and Louis XII., where Francis himself had spent his youth, that Leonardo was installed, for the King, like all superb spendthrifts, intended to alter the architecture and the landscape to his pleasure ; and Leonardo, whose hands were failing him, was for the French as distinguished in building and engineering as in painting, so that his head was still invaluable to his hosts.

Touraine was always dreaming south to Italy, and at times Leonardo might think some faint mirage of Tuscany hung within the faint sweet landscape, undulating in gracious rhythms, rich in woodland, cornland, orchard, and vineyard, with castles fairer in the winding waters, all the colours gone bodiless under the pearly sky, as if it were seen in soft suspension in his camera obscura. There were the wide rivers, the rocky cliffs, the deep glades and woods he loved, all so strangely dim and different, with silver lady birches for his fine olive-trees. Round Loches and Amboise great forests slept ; ridges of copsewood edged the tranquil lie of the land beyond them ; slender oak-woods stood faëry in the soft light, while the arrayed poplars pricked the air with the authentic clarion of France. In March you found the hidden violets under the drifted leaves of yesteryear. And when the spring came it was indeed a delicate world, all trembling white and green and ethereal rose, for then the myriad orchards woke, and in all the glades and covert places the lily-of-the-valley ran wild and wondrous, fragrant sanctuary for the driven white deer. Manors and priories lay lazy and charming in their gardens. But the coils of enchanting water consoled Leonardo most, reaches of shining river lapsing under castle walls Those rivers run fluent and fresh through all French Renaissance sculpture, laving into delicious mannerism such as the sinuous nymphs of Jean Goujon.

vi

The spirit of Italy had already touched the scene. Even the mediæval strength of Amboise was putting forth strange flowers. The masters of Tours and Poitiers had gone to Rome : Fra Giocondo had been here twenty years before, brought by Louis XII. From great spoils of books and paintings and tapestries had grown trails of arabesque vine, exotic and pagan, round the mediæval gargoyles. Tours had its "beautiful galleries." Not often did any repair to Loches, though Agnes Sorel lay there in a royal tomb. Those terrible towers arose in the distance—Loches where Lodovico had mouldered, drawing his desolate childish patterns on the wall. Not far from Amboise was Blois, famed for lilac-laden air and women coloured like red-and-white carnations. There Fra Giocondo had already devised a labyrinth and a terrace : now the ancient château was kindling into a new Renaissance wing, and, wonderfully fleur-de-lisé, a most ethereal and lovely lyric of a spiral staircase which some would assign to Leonardo himself. Langeais was still a fortress, but its battlement was changed to a cornice, and its inner court was decorated. Enchanting Chenonceaux was rising, a true pavilion open for love and lovers. At Bury, Florimond Robertet, that lover of things Southern, the great noble who was favoured by a line of kings from Charles VIII. to Henri III., had made himself an italianate dwelling. At Romorantin, Louise de Savoy decorated her château among the vines, strawberry-fields, and poppies. At the Château de Gaillon the famous Cardinal d'Amboise had made a frank lodge of delight among bright parterres and led waters, a delicate dentelled place, painted within by Andrea Solario. Wild Chambord, St Germain, Madrid, Azay le Rideau, Fontainebleau, Anet, and the rest, were all to come. But the architecture of pleasure and intrigue, of a Court amorous and delighted, of labyrinth, spiral stair, peaked roof, open gallery, thrown bridge, wide rooms, many windows, daring effects, was candidly and radiantly beginning.

The great pile of Amboise castle stood up above the town, beautifully placed high over the shining Loire where the Amasse ran to meet it. Its two massive round towers had slanted brickways for staircases. A Roman camp the fortified city had been once, and the queer rockholes called the Granaries of Cæsar might intrigue Leonardo's geological

447

curiosity. Merovingian story haunted its ancient walls, and the seigneurial race of Anjou, fierce red Foulques and Geoffreys, had held it long. Charles VII. had made royal this powerful castle ; Louis XI. had built it the chapel of Saint Blaise ; Charles VIII., ever amorous of the Italy that had been so dangerous a conquest, had softened its menace with flowery gardens before he found such a sudden squalid end in its neglected corner ; Louis XII. had given it a great clock-tower, and planted a quincunx of limes, and thrown a light gallery to overhang the river, where now the gallants made love as they gazed at the running water, still innocent of noyades. Yet Amboise was a mediæval setting for Leonardo, with the Gothic throbbing in the Collegiate Church of Saint Florentin, a little dark place yet lit with golden tapestries and burning glass, and projecting from the castle wall in the little chapel of Saint Hubert, a quickset of tender and thorny fancies. It was also a great centre of moralities and passion-plays, with a tradition of authors and actors. *The Mystery of the Passion of Our Lord* was presented in the open air with great pomp. And in near-by towns and villages you might behold *The Mystery of the Sibyls*, that of *King Solomon and the Queen Saba*, and *The Mystery of Madame Saint Anne.*

But Leonardo need not pass through the narrow Gothic ways of the town. His little manor of Cloux, afterwards called Clos-Lucé, a pleasant square house of brick and white stone, with a winding stair, sheltered from the North by a hill, lay courting the sun among its own gardens and little woods by the brook of l'Amasse. Louis of Luxembourg and Louise of Savoy had owned the place as pleasure-hostel and hunting-lodge, so it was devised for comfort. The revenue of seven hundred crowns was noble ; and Leonardo might wrap himself in his furred mantles, and work at peace.

vii

It is but dimly that we perceive the exile in the excited, ostentatious first years of King Francis' reign. He was much in contact with the King, and evidently liked him. Francis had a quick mind and an intense curiosity ; in his youth he was evidently an engaging young satyr. His very flush and glow of mere vitality were cordial to the chilled artist, and revived his flickering soul. " He affirmed that never any man had come into the world who knew so much as Leonardo ; and that not only in matters of sculpture, painting, and architecture, but in addition he was a great philosopher." So Cellini, reporting Francis in after years. The King probably meant that Leonardo was apt in the criticism of life, when he sighed this variant of

" His ghost be with the old philosophers ! "

The Hostel of Francis

It is unlikely that, as d'Ollanda narrates, he appointed noblemen clothed in silk and brocade to wait on the great painter; but every reference to their relation indicates that he used him like a scholar and a gentleman. Leonardo, even Leonardo grown old, was a stately guest for France, not like those industrious painters of the King, Jean Perréal, the Modenese Belin, Guyot, and Champion, and the notable Janet, who first began to take the insolent self-willed faces of that Court in the fine meshes of the pure, cold, and simple art of the Clouets. These were all *valets-de-chambre*, honourable enough, good for any task of standard-painting or blazonry. Leonardo was the King of Italian art.

But his mind still kept step with the masque and the *pas d'armes*. With easy courtesy he lent his long-versed Italian taste to mass the colours and rearrange the groups more rhythmically, at Argentan, at Amboise, at Blois; at state visitation or nuptial feast he could heighten the spectacle with some gleam of passing exotic beauty. Pageantry was a complex art when it was well done, rekindling all his talents of architect, engineer, decorator, mechanist, and musician; and he still liked to see the whole sumptuous vision glow and fade on the dark amid the light of torches.

He did most willing and valuable service to his land of refuge, however, in renewing his old power of linking the rivers. He was still an engineer and a hydraulic specialist. At Blois he could see the canal-works done by Fra Giocondo twenty years before. Now he was setting the canal near Romorantin with his own impounding locks, and deciding to link the Loire and the Saône. He was near La Sologne, a country of marsh and fever, yet wooded and pictorial, where the King would build a new palace. He patiently studied the country and the river-system, seeking from the Saône to establish direct communion with Touraine and Lyons, repairing often to Romorantin, to the domain of Madame. " The Eve of Saint Antony I returned from Romorantin to Amboise, and the King went away two days before from Romorantin." He works pensively " as I did before at Friuli." According to Ravaisson Mollien : " The indications of Leonardo allow us to guess that the canal, beginning either near Tours or near Blois and passing by Romorantin, with an embarking place at Villefranche, should, beyond Bourges, cross the Allier under the tributaries of the Dore and the Sioule, to go by Moulins to Digoin, and at last upon the other bank of the Loire, to cross the hills of the Charolais and rejoin the Saône near Mâcon." It must have been with relief that he found himself at his old work of canalization : in some ways he was certain of being no profitless guest.

It may be that his influence on France expressed itself definitely in the new kind of building, for he was the King's architect, among other things, having been so entitled even in Milan. It is true that the new châteaux are definitely French, and that they seem to take from Italy little beyond their open galleries, their floriation, and their gardens. But Leonardo would not have resented the fretted line of their turrets and high-pitched roofs, the piercing note of the Gothic modulated to romantic jubilation. The effects desired were Italian—room, light, air, decoration.

Francis thinks vaguely of a great new palace at Amboise. Leonardo makes a design for it, lying vast, clear, serene, in spacious courts, gardens, and lakes. It is rectangular, with massive round towers ; and it is surrounded by a wide moat, like the Castello that kept Milan of old. Did he design the lovely spiral stair at Blois, so embroidered with beautiful devices, the line of which trills up as sweetly and as surely as a boy's carol ? It is an enchanting thing ; it is a sinistral spiral ; it is indeed like the spiral of one of Leonardo's beloved shells ; we know also that he was interested in stairs. But no definite record clinches his or any other name to that, so it is as you will. Much more definite is the case which M. Marcel Reymond makes out for Leonardo as the initial architect of Chambord. That strange Oriental pavilion of cupolas and turrets, the rich fantasy of which has been marred in several ways, especially by the filling up of its terraces and great bright moats, does indeed in its original rapture show a startling affinity with some of Leonardo's secular-looking domed churches, and imaginary projections. The French architects, it is suggested, may have seen these. The immensity of the place, the cupolas, the surprising intrigue of the double stair, the faëry repetition, as of a sunken Eastern city, among the lilies of the moat, the mighty carved lantern in the middle of the château, suspended like that on the dome of Florence Cathedral, are all in Leonardo's mood. Hidden in the deep forests of La Sologne, this château must have had an incredible and Arabian air dear to the heart of Francis, who took delight in the East, like Leonardo, and was friendly with the Sultan. It looks indeed like the pleasure-house of a green-turbaned Emir rather than the Very Christian King. The towers at the corners are French ; but the campanile and the lantern, the arcades and the polychrome marble effects, seem to remember Florence, while the luxurious wild air of the whole is of a dream-Orient. This eclectic charm not impossibly belongs to the artist who was capable of drawing a castle like a mosque. Though the palace at Chambord is not so exquisite as some of the other pavilions of the Loire, it has a certain greatness of handling : as in the Renaissance parts of Blois there is a mastery and magnificence which refuse the *mièvrerie* that is at once a quality and a defect of entrancing Chenonceaux and dream-girdled Azay-le-Rideau. It is easy to believe that Leonardo had something to do with Blois; and that the architects of Chambord had at least seen his sketches.

viii

As a painter, Leonardo could serve King Francis little with new work. By 1517, we know, his right hand was paralysed, and, though he drew with the left, he needed both for painting. In any case he could not have affected French painting greatly at this time, for French painting was not ready for him. Jean Fouquet's precise and delicate work had been the art of the miniaturist, and miniaturists still were the King's painters, though ready to do anything, from painting a standard to town-planning, like the versatile Jean Perréal, so famous in his lifetime, so soon and so completely forgotten. The great art of Dijon and Tours, of mediæval France, had been sculpture; and Michel Colombe, the gracious ymagier, and Jean Juste, the sculptor of noble tombs, had hardly ceased from their devout pure work of beauty, though Leonardo probably considered their figures stiff and archaic. In the extravagant Church of Brou and its sculptured tombs mediæval art was flaring up in the changing air before it died. The newer artists, like Janet and Bourdichon, were busily drawing the crayons *d'après le vif*, which the Court collected like other whimsical toys. Leonardo's art was too far beyond the eager adaptable draughtsmen for them to emulate it. The phœnix was lone and marvellous indeed in France. At that superb technique, that wonderful sleight of light and shadow which, like magic, compelled from dark or emerald atmospheres dream-figures actual as mirror-images, but much more lovely, they could merely exclaim, thinking not of imitating a miracle. But Leonardo's great pictures were little seen by any but Francis and his friends. Gazing at the profound and disquieting faces of Mona Lisa, Dionysos, Saint John, Saint Anne, Leda, Pomona, the chattering courtiers, silenced by that divine company risen from the green twilights and caves of eternity, perhaps felt something of the superb rhythm and the intense imaginative passion of the Renaissance prime. It is likelier that these novices, like other followers of Leonardo, caught too much of the refinement and none of the greatness. The French Renaissance became more perverse as it became more delicate; and if " Valois " has acquired a connotation of poignards and perfumes, nymph-broidered stone, rose-golden verses, springtide grace and springtide languor, too febrile to come to fruitage, sterile and morbid beauty spoiled by odours of blood, the misunderstood eyes of Leonardo's Dionysos may not be altogether irresponsible.

Francis, at least, presently acquired *Mona Lisa* for a great price. And, looking at the vigorous strong-nosed ladies drawn by Janet, one

451

does not wonder that he desired the mysterious and smooth Neapolitan for his cabinet. But French art was not now strong enough to bear this alien greatness, the spiritual disturbance of unquestionable might. Rosso would come ; Primaticcio would come ; Andrea del Sarto would reveal his easier, more readily charming art. That dangerous *naïf* demon, Benvenuto Cellini, would bring his cups and jewels. Meanwhile François Clouet, affining his lucid pencils, would set down, with ironic fidelity and exquisite touch, a truly French tradition. Leonardo's great pictures obscurely maintained their power in palace chambers till the day when, hung on the walls of the Louvre for all to see, they should convey for ever, even though spoiled and darkening, the contagion of Renaissance Italy to the art of the world, and make and mar personality again. Despite the evil chemistries of time, the wrongs of rash restorers, the excesses of magicians, and the revolts of new schools, they continue to alter the psychology of nations, for no dreamer can be immune to them.

ix

Perhaps to flatter Francis' longing for the lovely Lombard dream-type, he continued to paint the *Pomona*, smiling visionary in her triple veil. For some time at least he was at work on one picture to please himself. When his hand failed, no pupil tried to finish this, so, without the last refinements of Leonardo's suave modelling, the figure does look more startling than it might otherwise have done. Possibly it is more frankly revealing. For undoubtedly Leonardo painted with all his intimate nerves when he evoked the figure he called Saint John the Baptist.

His conscious life had been complicated and distracted for long by superficial troubles. Now, as his failing hands strove to paint a last picture, his unconscious part had its way at last. Dreamily, half-aware, he painted his angel, his dæmon, his peculiar love-god, he painted Narcissus and his own soul. He painted a face in which the virginal nymph dear to his imagination ran like pure water into the lineaments of the dionysiac god his æsthetic senses desired. He brought together two natures in beauty and confounded many oppositions, the Herodiad and the Baptist, the nymph and the god, Christianity and Paganism, soul and body, masculine and feminine. And he made something that shocks at first, partly because the picture, not being finished, is the more acute, partly because no shape could but recast itself as a strangeness under the imaginative philtre that Leonardo poured, partly because the candour of genius must always be startling. Every spirit that rises above the safe level of the talents must contain some of the mocking, anarchistical and violent elements that leap about the universe, however triumphally it may control them. Its fires are fed with far-fetched fuel though the flame burn white and steady ; and any unsindoned image of its secrecy is discomposing to the laity. Leonardo looked the veil-wrapt dreamer within his breast in the haunting eyes, and painted it, not as Saint Anne, or the Virgin of the Rocks, or Leda, or Pomona, or Persephone, or Dionysos, but as Saint John the Baptist, since some unforgettable climax of nerves and emotions still quivered with the burning air upon his midsummer day. With the last refinements of his momentary contraposto, morbid sfumato, and a dramatic chiaroscuro that would have no parallel until the days of Rembrandt, he evoked his occulted soul, the beautiful dæmon he never exorcised, the magian creature, the heathen lord behind the solstice. But he did not finish it : his hand fell paralysed as if in fear.

Out of the darkened air the strange prince of midsummer appears half-turned to the right, his head bowed a little to the left. A thin cross is held in one hand, that also presses the slipt panther-skin to the shoulder. The right forearm is lifted over the breast and the upthrown hand points mysteriously to some wonder. It is contraposto exultant in one swift movement, so hard to hold that the figure seems indeed like a momentary apparition vanishing in the darkness. The shadows invade the serried fine curls and mask the great deep-seated eyes. The cheeks are soft, the mouth is more lifted in the dionysiac smile than ever. The image seems revealed by some reflected illumination : as the artist seeks for darker darks and more highly keyed lights, so he stresses the plangent violin-like vibration of the face and attitude. " Shadow," he said, " is derived from two sources—one substantial, the other spiritual." Lost indeed in mystic shadow the promise of this enigmatic Renaissance love-god. The vision is incredible ; this precursor promises unprecedented things. But it was the characteristic of Renaissance psychology to desire impossible things, and Leonardo's Saint John will at least quicken your sense of the imaginative range of emotion if you can equably confront the delicate detonation of that face. He is the saint of the impossible ; but there is no satiety on his track of white fire.

Perhaps it was the purely technical problem, the fascinating play of light and dark, that discovered the strange apparition. Artists whose style is of one texture with their metaphysic do sometimes find their desired image while they finger rich perplexities of expression : the breded door gives way beneath their touch. But it is likelier that here the haunting image came through some duskling reverie bringing its own mysterious chiaroscuro. Still, that same haunting image hardly in itself conveys all that Leonardo intended. It was charged with emotional fantasy too rarefied, with intellectual concept too subtle to be

Leonardo the Florentine

made lucid and lovely through the eyes. He overstrained his medium. Visual symbols cannot fluctuate and echo as words and music can. Androgyne beauty dimly suggested, nymph, genius, angel, girl, and boy, and created as if by wasting sighs and the pure hands of dreams desiring inviolable translunar things, might be revealed by words, caught icy and remote like a silver seraph, or folded in fluted veils of sorrow, or sexless and flamelike like the bright shape that steered the boat of the Witch of Atlas. The attack on the eyes is too disturbing because it is too direct and simple. Leonardo's intention is always manifold, and it is not impossible that he meant to disturb the senses as well as the soul. Still, it was to the soul he ultimately spoke ; he consistently maintains that. This figure has an intense intimacy, as if it were a projection from an image at the inward end of the optic nerves, and so not lawfully ours to see. It is a personal lyric at the conclusion of Leonardo's painting ; and a cipher for those who refuse him sympathy. It was the last preoccupation of his great genius, and the frankest expression of his psychology.

It was quite in the Florentine tradition to let the imagination play with Saint John, who was often confounded with an angel, even by the theologians, and identified with the burning love of friends. You might, like Donatello, represent him through the stages of his visionary and ascetic life. But his midsummer festival, falling at the time when the hosts of faërie and heathenesse had power even in Christendom, the story of Herodias and the dancing Salome, the dramatic opposition of desert and court, the loneliness of the sand and river spaces in which he appears amazing and remote, made him seem to fantastic minds an angelic prince of Syria, a bright shape like the sun-god with whom he was confused. He appears in many guises in Florence, especially in Florentine sculpture. There is a bust of him in the manner of Verrocchio, in which he seems a curled young Florentine, smiling a secret and somewhat affected smile. When Michelangelo does a Giovannino, it is evidently as he does a young Eros or Apollo, a slim supple heathen child, beautiful but slightly sullen. Saint John the Baptist, like David or Saint George, often serves the Florentines as a mere image of inviolate youth. Decidedly Leonardo does more with him : he charges him with sensuous beauty. That is, after he has felt the Herodiad in Milan. Other Florentines, Donatello, Agostino, Verrocchio, had tried for the delicate androgyne effect since Ghiberti adored the Greek Hermaphroditus with thrilled and reverent fingers. Leonardo carried it to its peculiar perfection. For him Saint John was interchangeable with Dionysos, the lord of nature-magic and of ritual rapture. This is only a more intense version of the god, the solemn giver of ecstasy, entranced in divine solitude at the centre of the dance of creation. Of Dionysos are those imperious, luminous eyes, the dreamy smile, the soft and feminine breast that tells the delight of his double nature wrought of Greece and Asia, Hades and Heaven.

Vasari calls the figure an angel, and some discern the shadow of a wing. As a messenger from the divine, a lone annunciant, the Baptist was frequently considered as angel. Here he is essentially an angel, kin to the serene seraph that dwells with the Virgin among the hard pure rocks. Angels were dear to the Renaissance artist, who, like the Greek, preferred to work out his more intimate type of beauty in the form of a beautiful youth. Angels were peculiarly dear to Leonardo, who liked their shifting incalculable essence. Saint John was an angel for him—an angel, a dæmon, a haunting Idea, his Love-god, his Narcissus, his emotional self. To impose an angel on a Greek god was the kind of intricate paradox that delighted him, who loved the fluctuating shadow-play of the emotions as well as the chiaroscuro of paint.

Restless Greek artists in the more languid periods, restless Leonardo seeking a new beauty unstained and incorrupt, create the hermaphrodite type. The trouble is—it is too much the effort of an intellectual.

> " Cum dubitat natura marem faceret ne puellam
> Factus es, O pulcher, pene puella, puer."

That frank paganism of the sense, delighting in an exciting frustration, falls blunted before Leonardo's figure. It is inviolable, except by those whom Milton abolished with the great saying : " We cannot make them chaste that come not hither so." It is charged with a puissant imaginative energy : it is over-intellectualized. Only an arrogant brain can so interfere with the dreadful divisions of sex, in its conflicting effort to keep a sensuous beauty while placing it beyond sensual desire. But the picture is serious and lovely ; there is a whole philosophy behind it. And there is irony still in the deep-challenging eyes. Is the breast delicate as that of Mnasidica's girl-friend ? The eyes, with a deep immortal mirth, mock the cloyed and cloying sensualist. The artist is playing with a dangerous matter ? Yes, but with the cold hands of an implacable idealist.

x

It was half-heartedly and mechanically, in the chilled Northern air, under the cloudier skies, among the gorgeous coarser people, with their frank amours and their unripened taste, that Leonardo did his part for their entertainment and their needs. That put no strain on his attention. He had become absent-minded, lost in reverie in the long blue Northern dusks ; and he sat wondering that life seemed nearly over, and that it was all so frustrate, and that he ended in this shadowy poignant place, where even the saints, Florentin, Denis, Blaise, Hubert, seemed slim Gothic knights, serious sweet chevaliers of the Cross, with pointed faces like Aucassin, sad seigneurs who had never worn a girdle of gold like Sebastian, duke of archers, who had never seen Italy. This came out of the darkness, sinister, smiling, beautiful, wringing from Leda and Dionysos and all the grape-vine of trance-holden images their ultimate sweetness, looking with equal eyes on man and woman, offering the gift of ecstasy. Down in turreted close-penned Amboise they are playing *The Mystery of the Passion of Our Lord*. This canvas stands on the easel in Leonardo's studio, as if in divine and delicate derision and sympathy.

But for all the indissoluble rare irony of the air, for all the smile too Pagan, the extreme sweetness and baffling kindness behind the challenge of the eyes, the canonized gesture that seems a heavenly travesty, the womanish beauty of the form, the figure is an expression of Leonardo's hidden mysticism. It is mysticism deep, dark, speechless, exultant as that of any Christian saint. The gaze is neither good nor evil; it is neither Greek nor Christian. It is dionysiac, however, it is that of the god of Greece and Asia, the god of ecstasy, of sheer beauty, the state beyond good and evil where the soul is purified and recharged. Or you think of Orphic and Eleusinian mysteries, Greek faiths that woke like spices from a sleeping root borne from Egypt. After the dark fast of the night the anactoron suddenly opens ablaze, and you see the hierophant clothed in ritual jewels revealing the last holy things, the white flower and the reaped ear of corn which is the sacrificial god. The ritual jewels are that faëry cross, but the hierophant still represents Persephone and Dionysos. The gaze is that of Dionysos, it is that of the Holy Ghost, who also came on wings out of Asia. It is mere ecstasy that Leonardo's art offers ; and he tries to paint its annunciation angel here. Saints and artists seek the same thing ; and if some of the images of the saints were translated into paint, they would startle more than this. There is indeed some sub-flaming affinity here with the most ecstatic thing in mystical literature. It is not Saint Teresa who has used the extreme Sapphic intensity to describe the love of the soul for its mysterious lord. Nay ! But some such angel as this, with deep-set luminous eyes and smiling lips, might dawn through the " Night Obscure " to promise the garden of lilies to Saint John of the Cross. In its desperate haste to find a heavenly language great and holy passion wreaks itself on what images and parallels it can ravish from earthly experience. Leonardo in his dying mood makes his effort at a mystic reconciliation. It is the Renaissance figure of a Renaissance synthesis, all beauty in one cup. And the figure is set within Leonardo's own æsthetic synthesis, the conflict of light and

The Hostel of Francis

dark resolved by the knowledge of Love into a nuptial embrace from which Ecstasy is born.

Darkness is the great mother of the light, as of all things. In this eternal conflict her bright offspring cannot prevail entirely over her, for he is her child, as well as her prince and her lord, conditioned by her. With soft fall of obliterating veils she softens the transient brilliance. In Leonardo's last picture, the earth that he never completely accepted, for all his interest in her drifted sands, has disappeared. This is but a scintillation of light in a world of dark ether—the prince of the powers of the air visible at last, Michael and Lucifer, the ambiguous angel of all the antinomies. Whatever he is, earth is dissolving for Leonardo in one of the great waves of his scientific vision, a wave of darkening water, a wave of darkening cloud ; and the figure of Saint John is one of those last corollas of ethereal foam, kin to his own soul, melancholy, and exultant, and unimaginable. Time and skill are failing him in the dusk : he cannot quite convey how melancholy and exultant it is on the edges of the breaking wave, nor how unimaginable the visions that assail him. For the Saint John, like Leonardo's other symbols, is washed over by all the cross-currents of his conflicting mind. Whatever he dreams in the wild faint corollas, the twy-principled flowers, of all his waves of cloud and smoke and water, however, they do mean ecstasy. There is a certain nihilism in the troubling twy-natured apostle upon the darkness ; but he does mean ecstasy.

Will you call it a strange hieroglyph ? It is the cipher of Leonardo's mind and soul. It is more Leonardo than the *Treatise on Weights and Measures*, or even the *Treatise on Light*. Michelangelo also left a hieroglyphic knot of personality in his locked *Victory*—puissant and repellent. Michelangelo, old, was love-tortured. Leonardo's love was closed in his brain. This remains a disquieting image ; there was no adequate shape to express Leonardo's final encounter with beauty, and you may say he pushed symbolism into the monstrous, in the Egyptian manner. Yet for some it is as subtle, as strange, as daringly pure as *The Phœnix and the Turtle*, for those deep-dwelling eyes keep their divinity.

He would possibly have smiled at all those who have been exasperated by his hermaphrodite, and, gazing at the gracious form in which he had played the part of creator, and perhaps merely attempted to mingle the charm of both sexes in the supreme and sterile beauty which his perverse or fastidious mind preferred, have murmured, like a poet whose vision of nature something resembled his own :

> " My last delight ! tell them that they are dull,
> And bid them own that thou art beautiful."

This final picture is at least a proof of his indomitable mind, original

457

and impassioned in its quality to the end. Leonardo is not an extinct and venerable old man muttering platitudes through his beard : he is not even a wise Shakespearian elder. He is an untamed and adventurous soul, still seeking his unique experiences, facing the lovely dæmon of his secret existence, and following the exciting rarely-promising eyes of that strange prince across the border. This ultimate thing he does makes no inadequate generalization concerning life, recognizes no defeat of imaginative passion by the years. There is a fierce poignancy in Leonardo's last picture, as if he had taken the hidden dagger from his heart at last, and looked at it. For piercing-soft as a dagger-lily is the god. Leonardo, still challenging, daring, curious of mysterious emotion in his last years, is consoling to the many spirits who with dignity and pathos cover the burning love of romance with the ashes of Time, and at seventy secretly desire the trumpets of beauty's tournament as ardently as at seventeen, however sweetly they that were knights resign themselves to be her bedesmen.

xi

Only one priceless document survives by which we part the curtain of the dark, and gaze on an authentic scene in the sunlit studio at Cloux. Antonio da Beatis is the secretary of Louis, Cardinal of Aragon, the natural son of Ferdinand the First of Naples. He writes his careful account of his master's visit to the great painter. You see Leonardo, shrunken and white, reviving again in the crowd of glowing Italian faces, in the freedom of the liquid Italian speech. The consciousness of something *criard* and coarse in this French Court vanishes mellow into the October light, as he talks in the old way, of painting, of anatomy, of science.

" On the 18th October 1517, from Tours we went to Amboise. In one of the suburbs, we went with the cardinal to visit Messer Leonardo Vinci, the Florentine, more than seventy years old, the most excellent painter of the time. He showed his Excellency three pictures : one, drawn from the model, is of a certain Florentine lady, executed at the request of the late Giuliano de' Medici the Magnificent ; the other of Saint John Baptist young, and the third of the Madonna and the Son who rest in the lap of Saint Anne, all the three very perfect, although from him, since he has been stricken with a certain paralysis of the right hand, no more masterpieces can be expected. He has been the benefactor of a Milanese disciple who works very well. Although the said Messer Leonardo cannot paint longer with the ' dolcezza ' which was natural to him, he can still make drawings and teach others. This gentleman has written on anatomy in its relations to painting in an

The Hostel of Francis

admirable fashion, describing the bones, members, muscles, nerves, veins, joints, intestines and all that one can study in the body of man or woman as none has done before him. We have seen it with our eyes ; and he told us that he had dissected more than thirty bodies of men and women of all ages. He has also written on the nature of water. With various machines and other things he has filled an infinity of volumes, all written in the vulgar language, which, published, would be of the greatest utility and the greatest charm." [1]

Who was the Florentine lady ? Did Leonardo take the picture back from Giuliano when he rode away to Savoy to wed Philiberta, who was twisted and plain ? Was the portrait that of the dark arresting woman afterwards called *La Belle Feronnière* ? No ! She is Milanese. We do not know this canvas ; but with sadness we realize how age had gripped him, and in what weak, weary way he must die, through the slowly growing disobedience of that well-tempered instrument, the body in which he had gloried. Even the cardinal must have looked with regret at the mournful hand, deficient from its unparalleled intentions.

They took their leave of him like a stately embassy of farewell from his Italy, the great cardinal moody a little because the strange prestige of dionysiac eyes, dwelling upon him from the divine faces of Leda, Pomona, Saint John the Baptist, the Thyrsus-bearer himself, Madonna Lisa and Madame Saint Anne, had become a trouble in his blood ; and, as he rode away from the manor-house through the October weather, rare and golden, it seemed as if he could think of no destination that was not for the moment rather pointless, and no kind of love that did not seem stricken with some banality. As for the young secretary, his mind was confused between the rose-white amphora of Leda's pure body and the frightening great books of images for which at least thirty hapless dead had been rifled. And he remembered the burning eyes and the wasted, useless hand of the old man wrapped in his furred robes, and wondered at the fine young Milanese noble, in his flowering devotion.

Leonardo sat on, looking at the images of his soul's desire, while Francesco Melzi, using his hands as if they touched the Holy Things, put away the manuscripts so jealously kept from unfriendly eyes. His dear lord had bought with this great concession some longer period of the press of kindled Italian faces, the melodious rumour of Italian tongues, the sudden waft of Italy, sweet as clove-spices. Leonardo was lonely. They were all kind and admiring in this Northern place, but they were gauche and uncertain, not assured of the high Renaissance manner like his own people.

[1] Itinerario di Monsignor il Cardinal da Aragona . . . descritto per me Dom Antonio de Beatis clerico melfictano. (Uzielli—Ricerche.)

Leonardo the Florentine

When Leonardo took his pen to write significantly in his manuscript book for the last time, he inscribed no platitude about a well-spent life, no impersonal scientific observation on the creeping grip of paralysis, no philosophic irony on the " animula blandula," no resignation to the laws of necessity. " A 24 di guigno, il di di San Giovanni 1518 in Ambosa nel palazzo del Cloux." So he writes, and ceases, turning to gaze at his unfinished god, saint, angel—the lord of light, life, the solstice, dividing the darkness with his smile, the lovely darkness which is the condition of his existence and the cave of his repose. There are leaping flames about Amboise ; the girls were out gathering fairy herbs in the late evening the day before. But he is back in Lorenzo's Florence, and he is beautiful, beloved, unique, youth's legendary own. The ease and grace of divinity are in his heart : he is shadowed only by a faint misgiving about these mortal ways. He is aware of ranked lights on the altar, fantastic processions with beautiful boys dressed like sibyls, and gilded moving castles, decorated streets and the proud kingly horses, glittering folds of the *palio* borne home at dusk of day, great bonfires blazing through the summer night, crying and complaining of the tender lutes. Then, like a dissonance and a crash of sinister drums, the memory of an evil fair face and an ancient sense of wrong ! Well ! The lord of the solstice, darkness and light, beauty and dread, the duality of the universe, had maintained his power ; and the last face he painted was that of Saint John, the last intimate words he wrote made the name of his day. Saint John is the funeral genius : but his torch is not inverted.

Something of Florence came to Amboise before Leonardo died. In the April of 1518, Lorenzo de' Medici, nephew of Leo and Giuliano, now known as the usurping Duke of Urbino, arrived at Amboise to be god-parent to the little Dauphin, and also to be wedded in France. When Leonardo had last seen Lorenzo he had been hovering with the papal army in Piacenza, hoping for the French defeat. He was a dissolute duke of carnival ; but Leonardo had been on friendly terms with him in Italy.

Excessive carnival had mocked its lord, and the young man came painfully that long way, consumed, says the frank chronicler, by " la grosse vérolle." Nevertheless he was pompously welcomed, he and his retinue in crimson velvet and his thirty-six horses, and Leonardo did not stand aside from the month-long marvel of pageant and tourney. He even remembered the mechanism of his great *Paradiso* for the grim bridal. The Duke of Urbino held the Dauphin at the font, lords of Lorraine and Bourbon on either side. The fountains of Amboise ran wine and ypocras. Banquets, ballets, and dances declared the triumph of this christening; and seventy fair ladies in bright disguises shook the clashing silver rain of their tambourines through the music. Three days after, the beautiful girl, Madeline de la Tour d'Auvergne, daughter of the Count d'Auvergne, was wedded to Lorenzo. They smiled, and did not pity her. Yet Fleuranges, that hard blond young chevalier, with his insolent half-smile, writes: " Quant Elle épousa le ducque d'Urbin, elle espousa la grosse vérolle avecque, quant et quant." He perhaps had a half-regret. From the great festival spread in the castle court, canopied and hung with splendid cloths so that it seemed a vast tent, lighted so richly with torches and flambeaux that all was bright as day, with trumpets and hautboys they brought the fair flushed bride to the cruel marriage-bed, a beautiful thing given by Pope Leo, of tortoise-shell inlaid with pearl and studded with gems—" la mariée qui estoit trop plus belle que le mariez "—to her sinister and sardonic doom. They all knew it; but the sacrificial games were superb. It is the most dreadful wedding in Renaissance history, and it is the last where Leonardo is a spectator. Well! All weddings are sardonic and sinister to him. Next day the jousts begin, the most elaborate jousts that ever had been in France, lasting eight days; and Lorenzo is magnificently victor "pour l'amour de sa Mye." The gross, gorgeous story, rigid with jewelled ceremony, is more coldly savage than a Maupassant *conte*. Through the summer weather they feasted and masqued and fought. What delighted Francis most was the siege of a mimic town of wood, surrounded by moats. This was a brilliant and breathless pastime; but, Fleuranges says mildly, it did not please everybody, for many were killed and hurt. Then the bridal pair passed away. They were both dead within the year, leaving an infant, Medican Catherine.

xiv

Silence closes round on Leonardo dying, slowly weakening, lost in reverie, his mind presenting him with broken pictures from the Renaissance scroll of his life. Cities and solitudes—stained-ivory Florence, girdled by the Arno green at evening when the air was like golden lilies, and the pure heights of Fiesole, windy Pistoja with friendly eyes, rose-dreaming Milan with ancient Pavia and leafy Vigevano, orchards with heavy apple-boughs and murmuring water, Como by the siren lake, Chiavenna among the foaming falls, Mantua on her green lagoons, Venice like shed rainbows on the sea, Florence again, bitter-sweet, Milan again, shattered and kind, little high cities of the Romagna glimpsed in between, through a cloud of angry smoke (Urbino on a moon-hung height, Ravenna by a desolate shore, Piombono on its wave-washed promontory), Rome impenetrable, imposing, desolating, an impression of coloured balloons of carnival among imperial ruins, Bologna grave and indifferent, little Tours, aprickle with spiny turrets like a French thistle, massive Amboise, strange hostel where he should lie for ever ! But his fleur-de-lis is all " florençée " : he has kept the perfume of the iris, sweet from root to flower. So in the end it is Florence again, where he was young and a god, and life seemed long enough for a god's intent. Upon that golden self, so nimble and delicate in every gesture, it is as if only some devilish trick had suddenly imposed this detestable vizard of age and weakness. He had only begun his infinite business. " While I thought I was learning to live, I was but learning how to die."

For, though he did not piously lament a misspent life, as Vasari imagines, his last months must have been dipped in that great Renaissance melancholy that waits on all extremes of passion and delight, and which wells up occasionally through the interstices of his life at its most intensified periods. " The search for the impossible has for punishment melancholy and despair." He had such moments.

His divinity shrank and shuddered from the gates of death. He had found the body a supple instrument, a noble organ, as he said, for the breath of the soul, and, though some of its stops were broken now, he was reluctant to leave it. He loved its dear familiar ways, especially the pride of the eyes. The soul did not die ; but what fortunes it might have in a universe of unguessed imperceptible categories, unfed, uncherished by the senses it cannot even remember, he did not profess to imagine. " The soul can never be corrupted with the corruption of the body," he says definitely, but almost with a sigh. There is no light on the destiny of that incorruptible soul after it has suffered "the supreme evil " that is death. There are no travellers' tales and ghostly reports of Eternity. " With sighs and tears the soul laments in taking leave of the body, and not without reason." Ah ! What more excruciating destiny did this diviner suspect for the tortured soul, what more unimaginable agony of love and loss and betrayal, what more intolerable doom ? By this we know that, whatever Leonardo's experience held of transcendent power, he did not transcend in suffering.

xv

Yet his great power of equilibrium and his perfect courtesy would subdue the natural regret of an insatiate mind. He is left alone with

The Hostel of Francis

Francesco. It is a last and living version of the " conversation " he has so often drawn, between the opposed heads of age and youth. Disciple and master, neophyte and magician, squire and lord! Leonardo has designed some of these conversations in the satiric key, a little terribly. But Francesco is the lovely idyll, the shepherd's flute in the dews. He is altogether gracious and beautiful for him, and his remembrance will keep the boy gracious and beautiful too when he is old. As the paralysis creeps about the tired heart, you almost expect to hear again the immortal words, "To-morrow, O Phaedo, thou wilt shear off those beautiful locks," and to see the fair young Greek, reborn in Renaissance attire, again bowing down where he sits, and weeping over himself because he loses such a friend. You feel, as Francesco himself thinks, that love and loss will always keep him stilled and withdrawn a little, as if he could but go softly after the singular solemn experience of this valediction. He will go back to Italy and live quietly in Milan. When Vasari sees him in his age he will yet seem to be existing pensively. He had exquisite sensibilities and a delicate diffidence, and a genius for devotion. But as he religiously cares for those relics of his saint, the manuscripts, he will often sigh to think he can never dig the crystal treatises from that rich matrix.

"•Si come una giornata bene spesa, dà lieto dormire ; cosi una vita, bene usata, dà lieto morire." Leonardo wrote that once, in a tired mood, not for what it meant, but for the grieving sweetness of the sound. It is nothing in English. It ripples like running water at evensong in the sweet Italian. It is rare as the simple satisfying toll of the cadence in Fidele's dirge :

> " Thou thy worldly task hast done,
> Home art gone, and ta'en thy wages."

But Leonardo is always many things at once. His wage and his loveday and peace were the mysterious dreams promised by the eyes of Saint John, and the unsated curiosity which he brought to the last adventure.

xvi

One feels that, as he sank deeper in weakness, sweet sensations came to him like the breath of night-flowering plants, that for a moment he escaped from the coloured coils of mortality. It might be that he had swung like a god in one gold-green iridescent Renaissance ring of the unimaginable Spiral of Life, which dipped down pale and cold into death before it lifted him with unearthly flutes into another whorl of being. For a penultimate moment he must have been loosed from that burning obedience, to lie merely listening in the quiet while all the merles were fluting clear on the pale pure edges of the refraining light, and the world went softly violet before the nightingale began. With a sigh Leonardo slowly put on the soft silk robe of absolute sleep, and forgetfulness as a chaplet. The windows were open on the April ; and in the deep glades the fragrant wild lilies were faulting the trail of the white wild deer. He had not lived canonical hours ; but there are stations on the way to Eleusis as well as on the way to the Cross. And if his heart were not pierced at vespers, nevertheless calm compline came with its dews and myrrhs. The senses he had nobly used might be blessed with the eucharistical oils, and between his lips that praised the wonder of life the body of the god that died and rose again was not desecrated.

It was the morrow of the May Day when he died.[1] Away in Florence the red flowers that were the blood of Dionysos were waking on the pomegranate-trees, the young Thessalian moon swang silver over the height of Fiesole, and the nightingale lamented among the cypresses. The may-songs had been hushed and chidden because the young duke and his year-old bride lay dying in their palace, not because one who had in his youth been a Prince of the May was passing from life in Cloux. He had indeed looked like a King of the May once, privileged, garlanded, with hearts to walk upon. But he had evaded the mortal moment, and lost the final initiate whisper of wisdom the earth gives her sacrifice. The May Day waited for him none the less.

King Francis did not lift his dying head, as Vasari imagined. He was celebrating the birth of his second son at Saint Germain en Laye. The ebullient king would have been too much an intruder at the mysterious passing of Leonardo's soul into the May morning. Doubtless he sincerely mourned for his artist ; but he was very busy practising picturesque gestures and glittering effects for the Field of the Cloth of Gold.

xvii

On Easter Eve Leonardo had sent for the notary, feeling that life was hourly uncertain, and made a simple and decorous will, dividing the goods he left among his friends and servitors, giving his relatives the property they had tried to take from him. It is chiefly remarkable for the elaborate provision made for his funeral. He commits his soul to " Nostro Signore Messer Domine Dio, alle gloriosa Virgine Maria, a monsignore Sancte Michele, e a tutti li beati Angeli sancti e Sancte del Paradiso." With Michael and all the angels at least he always had understanding. But some have marvelled that the ironic mind that

[1] 2nd May 1519.

464

mocked so much at monks and friars should so surround his death with the ceremonials of the Church. " Item, the said testator desires to be buried in the church of Saint Florentin of Amboise and that his body may be borne there by the chaplains of the church. Before his body be carried into the said church the testator desires that there may be celebrated in the said church of Saint Florentin three high masses with deacon and sub-deacon, and that the day on which are said the three high masses, there be said thirty low masses of Saint Gregory ; Item, that in the church of Saint Denis, the same service as above be celebrated ; Item, also in the Church of the brothers and minor religious, the same service." Seventy poor people also were to receive alms, and carry torches in the funeral procession : and a lavish donation of thick wax candles was to illuminate the celebrating churches.

It is entirely in Leonardo's attitude, however, to pass from the scene with music and flambeaux, with a sombre pageant plumed with light. He was ritualistic in his mode of life, and for him a processional effect had a great symbolic value. Besides, he was a personage in France, with something seigneurial in his position. So all day long Amboise was murmurous with sacred Latin and Gregorian chant, and soft from swinging censers for the soul of Leonardo.

No more than heathen pope or prince did he think of dissevering himself from the Church at whose priests and monks he laughed according to the Renaissance fashion. Like an ironic abbé of later days, he smiled. Like a gentleman he suited his gesture of farewell to the custom of his time and place, for it would have been foreign to Leonardo's great courtesy not to observe a princely etiquette in dying. Like an artist, also, he knew that Catholicism had more in it than Christianity, and that its ritual of death might prepare the passing of any sincere and suffering soul, and commit to peace any forsaken body.

Moreover, Leonardo would consign that body which he had so loved not without some sad ostentation to its obsolete destiny. What ceremonial beauty he could command should give mournful sweetness to its exequies, and solemn masses should provide that not all at once should the implacable gates of remembrance be closed upon its reluctant departure. Was he not right so sincerely to regret the death of the body ? The most passionate mystic, the spirit most enamoured of dreams of immortality, wounded at times by a memory of how the lost beloved could break the heart with tenderness by some trick of smiling or some liquid look, suddenly and wildly refuses like a chilly fantasy any existence without the pathos and mirth inextricable from mere dust-doomed humanity. And if Leonardo thought that tangled with his tired physical fibre was something of himself that was enchanting, and yet

Leonardo the Florentine

had not been caught in any web of paint or draughtsmanship or any page of curious inquiry he left behind, he was justified. With speech and expression he could work a magic greater than art or science could convey.

Yet the implacable satire of fate that went behind him, trying to obliterate all he wrought, undid the care with which his mortal part was put to rest. You cannot stand by Leonardo's tomb. The cloister kept no memorial of its illustrious dead ; and the bones of this aristocrat among artists seem to have been thrown at some time into a common grave.

xviii

Francesco Melzi wrote to Leonardo's brothers, simply and exquisitely and nobly, with a quiet and heavy sense of irreparable loss. " I believe that you are informed of the death of Messer Leonardo, your brother, and for me the best of fathers. It would be impossible for me to express the anguish that I have suffered from this death, and while my body holds together I shall live in perpetual unhappiness, and for good reason. The loss of such a man is wept by all, for it is not in the power of nature to create another ! May almighty God rest his soul for ever ! "

Part v
Leonardo da Vinci

Chapter i
The Personality of Leonardo

i

SUCH is the history of Leonardo as he passed through his Renaissance world, artist and savant, courtier and engineer, sceptic and mystic, beautiful and beloved, reconciling all its contraries, harmonizing all its conflicts, expressing all its violent aspiration in his intricate fugues of fulfilment. He seems the supreme lily of this passionate order, pollened by rich winds from Samothrace and Syria, complicated, double-sexed, sterile, amethyst and ivory, too cryptically perfect to reproduce itself, merely forming its marvellous starry pattern as a sign of what humanity can do.

For not the darkened and mishandled canvases that once were triumphs of his art, not the surprising fragments of the records of his curiosity, not even the tireless beauty and energy of his drawing, that plays like lightning, and leaps like fountains, and sings like birds, and breathes like asphodel, not all his godlike gestures in leading the waters and attempting the air, altogether explain the silenced impression that attends the spoken name of Leonardo. Think of other astonishing minds in European history—Plato, Aristotle, Dante, Galileo, Shakespeare. Their effect is explicable. The leonardesque quality that disconcerts while it fascinates is peculiar to the greatest of the Florentines. It is something original and intransmissible, something angelical, dæmonic if you like, a faëry strand of alien life caught glittering through the fine stuff of his human personality. By what exquisite equipoise of nervous organization, what unique harmony of soul and body, this nameless charm was generated or ensnared we shall never discover by any critical analysis.

ii

If you would feel—not comprehend, but by supersubtle tacts and etherealized sensations dimly surmise—the mighty backward and abysm of Leonardo's mind, you should look long at some collection of his great studies of atmospheric effects. These things give the impression of being seen, not from earth, but from some unimaginable point beyond.

as if the soul of Leonardo hovered, unhooded eagle of the empyrean, beyond all the shifting airs of his world. Astonishing cloud-cauldrons swirl and boil into transcendental foliations. The fuming matter of the mortal atmosphere is twisting into spirals, always spirals, softly, dreadfully, coiling and fanning into mysterious shapes, curled, couchant dragons, monstrous capitals of incomprehensible pillars foaming over with impalpable lotos-flowers, dim palm-oases at once delicate and monstrous, as of ruinous arbours of lost Assyrian gods, widespread wings, radiating, dawning terrible and fair like the wings of the symbol of Egypt. Sometimes this world of upper air, where the creative spirit whorls and unleashes and unfurls and flowers, the place beyond symbols whence symbols are born and fall like milky stars, approaches the little earth-planet in flood and tempest. The dim silver sky-dragons descend to mingle with a world turned to foaming waters that cataract into eternity, while only the wronged fallen trees, mournful and sweet as petals in this elemental catastrophe, are the ultimate relics of the mortal scene, torn along in the vehemence of the flood, the last lost notes of a far-away non-human tenderness, so helplessly yielding and curving to the pitiless force that rends them. A sudden shift in the artist's mind—and the visions become fantasy and symbol of creation ! Sometimes it is a transit of earth's magnificence, seen merely as falling and shattering Cyclopean blocks, vanishing once more into wild spirals of dissolution. This is " simplification " of vision long before the term was imagined ; and it is beautiful as well as tremendous. Again there is a dream of high white peaks soft and mysterious, an ethereal Alp broken into clustered snow pillars. It is passed and half-shattered by some storm-gust from Eternity, that breaks beyond it like a colossal bouquet of blown white azaleas. Snow-peaks, blown storm, white azalea flowers ! It has a perfection of immaterial beauty, beauty ransomed to sight by delicate destruction from a void and chasm where only non-human eyes can see, a wreathen rare paradox of the infinite in a drift of soft snow-powder, a sublime phantom of a storm sweet as the white wings of some wild Psyche of the Outer Isles of eternity.

Winds that sweep the interstellar spaces, cyclonic currents from those Outer Isles of the universe, marvellous tempests of a blotted world, dim-lit atmospheres with here and there the shape and shadow of monstrous Egyptian spread wings ! Earth and earth's time dissolve in a great wave, whose ghost becomes a pale flower-shape shedding petals and pollen into infinitude. Dark currents flowing into foam of immense corollas, shaken tresses of the stars, cascades lightening into trails of unimaginable bell-flowers, a mystery of dark and light growing into dimly perceived pattern, things overflowing the apprehension of language, an

The Personality of Leonardo

ineffable stir by which the mind is mingled with the dawn-dream of creation.

The patterns of these supernal storms are too impalpable to be called Chinese, though there are allied effects in the work of the great dynasties of Chinese draughtsmen. They are like original symbolic figures shaping themselves out of the creative duel of light and dark in the shaken wind, out of the great waters that destroy matter to whirl it again into ascending spirals of life. All things dissolve, blown by the great winds of time and space, fluctuant from form to form ; they dissolve and pass in great waves eddying into more great waves that rise to their crest and break ; but break in the corollas and pollens of a new order and creation of beauty, a new foam of gods and horses and arts and mortals. Creation out of devastation, eternal flux of beauty and might ! So far as Leonardo has any philosophy, it lies in some such vision of the universe in waves that break eternally, but break in beauty ; and it often seems as if such philosophy were only an infinitely remote reminiscence from the very heart of primal energy. His vision of the world beyond life is a kind of recollection of storming cloud, vast vans of silver, conflicts of light and dark whence creative stars are born, and the raining javelins and coiling spirals of the forces of necessity. And if sometimes he considers it with exultation, occasionally it is with unmistakable dread.

This is the background of beauty and terror, destructive and creative, which Leonardo carries in his mind, whence he with such exorcism of grace compels its fine and fiery elements into shape. He seems to descend like air and flame and water from some such primordial and nebular womb of darkness. It is as if one of the blown lily-corollas that are the foam of those cosmic waves had been tossed through the stars from a flowery breaker to fall among the vines of earth and exult with the embrace that made a Renaissance love-child. Behind all Leonardo's sophisticated manners, behind all his gestures of science, art, courtesy, behind his impassioned patience, is the swift and surprising motion of an elemental. His mind is kneaded with some original matter flung from the unpolluted urns of creation. It has never before been patterned, never subdued to any degree of passivity by the fatigued generations. And it is matter incredibly rich, charged with all the potencies that make a world, with a tranquil puissance of sex that knows not dichotomy, with a wisdom not yet drained away into ethics and philosophies, with an imagination not committed to any one art, with an unsated energy sufficient for every exercise of mind, soul, and body, an original grace not conscious of original sin. It is for Leonardo to create his own categories. He seems to be almost a species in himself, thrown off by Nature from a period when humanity, wrought into a high crest of flower

471

and foam and fire, provided more passionate opportunity than usual. Leonardo is pure Renaissance ; but he is rarefied Renaissance, made of that flower and foam and pure white flame. The impression of his contemporaries strives to convey this notion of him as a marvellous accident, an unprecedented and unpropagating meteor. His power over all the liberal arts, says Lomazzo, was " received from the sun." The Anonimo insists that he was " brought forth by a miracle of nature." The gentle Francesco, bewailing him, says that Nature cannot make his peer. Benvenuto Cellini simply observes that he was an " angel incarnate."

This sense of nonpareil and august authority from the very fountain of life invests Leonardo with the greatness of his brothers, the wind and the light, and fire and water. Wind and light pass over all things good and evil with indifferent pure feet. Fire feeds on any fuel, impersonally bright. To this power familiar with the genesis of stars what are fair faces more than flowers, domes, demilunes ? If its very embraces are strange, it is that its radiant energy cannot realize the traditions of a race striving to perpetuate itself. Self-perpetuation seems a little pointless to a dæmonic force from without that creates in destroying. To destroy and to create, the profound dynamic paradox of Nature, was the burning duplicity that invested all Leonardo's paradoxes, conflicts, harmonies.

For Nature, who by some whimsical plot created Leonardo as a kind of microcosm, disqualified him to a certain degree for mere mortality by her very excess. Its ways were too strait, its opportunities inadequate, its nights and days too brief, its physical flower too fading. Moreover, some qualities cannot be coefficients ; and part of his rich conflict was resolved not by harmonies but by cancellations. He was too critical for such a creator, too fastidious for his energies. So, however deeply his immediate task involve him, he is always shadowed by some *arrière-pensée* ; some other curiosity or some other vision is importuning his attention like fretting flame or rising incense.

To some degree his inhibitions were due simply to that tyranny of the reason. Early he began to dread the flaming unhesitating power of his emotional and imaginative self. He said :

> " Bright reason shall mock thee
> Like the star from a wintry sky."

He suppressed and denied it, and used it like a slave, till it almost split away from his thinking part in its resentment. His bright, remorseless intellect preyed on its hidden twin, trying to devour and assimilate not only the obscure grapes of violet, the white wheat of its darkness, but the very dæmonic substance itself. The suffering soul separated itself and moated itself against the sworded tyrant, and sank into silence, only appearing like a ghost again and again, till, a wild and laughing phantom, it triumphed in the end. During the long rich period of his first residence in Milan, fed with the rose-perfumes and rose-colours and lute-music of sumptuous and feminine images, his unconsciousness became strong in itself as an entire personality, and softly prevailed against the iron intellectual disciplines. But the shifts and changes of his later life deprived him of that deep reverie in which the profound pantheistic part dreams as in a siren sea, and is enriched. When the priceless sense of leisure again possessed him, and reverie settled through his soul like rare dews, it was too late. Only one lotos came through the twilight waters, like the lotos that sleeps on the Nile by far Antinoë, and he called it Saint John the Baptist.

iii

Yet this nameless incandescent quality, as if aboriginal from the Sun he hailed as lord of the universe, was cast within a soul and body that had all their inheritance of race and time. In his air and aspect there is nothing wild or amorphous. The " shaping spirit of imagination " is mighty as the puissant stuff she handles. He may disconcert ; but he is sophisticate in all the ways of grace. " Fire and grace " indeed are the two qualities that are always instantly allowed him, ethereal qualities so exquisite and so rare in unison. If his spirit seemed to have leapt fresh from the fiery fount, his mind appeared to have instantly caught from Earth whatever she had flowered of wise and fair. It is hardly that he speaks as if much concerned with human history, for his serene anachronisms concerning the recent triviality of mortal chronology are as amazing as his accurate and unique sense of geological time, and his divination of dynasties mighty before man put out a fumbling hand, strange fishes, monstrous birds, terrible pterodactyls. These bland confusions but heighten that odd impression of him as a bright spy and curious intruder from another realm. It is with mythic story that he seems to have mingled, with the changeable tradition of gods and symbols that cloudily and fierily accompanies the winding progress of humanity, stuff compact of its dreams and desires. There are clear-flying notes and scattered lights in Leonardo's personality that suggest a fanciful past. You seem to see the rocky isle of Delos, the river Eurotas among its sweet sedges, the crags of Parnassus where the many torches betray the mystic rites of Dionysos—wherever there is water, hard, cold rock, and a flowering fable of sumptuous white beauty, and preferably a sense of wings. Leonardo, the scientist, ignored the pseudo-mysteries ; Leonardo, the artist, continually reveals " the wants of those who have need of gods and mysteries," and the smiling of his women is like the music of ritual flutes.

Leonardo the Florentine

It is Hellenic myth that haunts the image of Leonardo in Hellenizing Florence ; and indeed all these flamelike young men he draws, and draws, for his great *Adoration*, are creatures beautiful and chaste, fit for the palæstra, though they are excited by some quest as never were Charmides and Lysis, who in the grave composure of their beauty accepted, not sought, the gifts of wisdom ; and their bright hair is blown by some wind of the Holy Ghost into cloven tongues upon their brows. When he has passed to sweet sensuous Milan, so mingled in her mood, at best Aspasian in her Hellenism, the orientation of his spirit becomes, unconsciously, more decided. Then you feel that Dionysos who came out of Asia, the lord of all natural magic, is indeed his god, and that he has watched Alexander and his friend run races in the Troad for Achilles' funeral games, and later gone with Hadrian into Egypt, and seen a strange love's head sink among the lotos to be deified in the image of the vine-god. Yet, every now and then, in some pure and severe head that seems to await the white fillet of Hippolytus, some group of lilies too gracile for any but Hellenic soil, he seems to have a faint nostalgia for low golden shores, deep vales of asphodel, and some Elysian air that would breathe away the dim-violet dust of decadent ages that has settled upon his reverie.

iv

It is this original energy blent with harmonizing power that gives Leonardo his great air of being godlike and Greek. He is the " divine " Leonardo because of the detached and equal vision he turns on creation : he is Greek in his effect, for all his Asiatic softness, because, with eyes unhooded, accepting from his predecessors merely the skill of craft he will carry yet farther, he builds his great images of ecstasy with solemnity, harmony, restraint, so that Saint Anne and the Virgin in their cadenced raiment strangely remind you of the figured Parthenon. He considers the Greeks alone " worthy of imitation," because they worked straight from Nature and used their own eyes. Working like them, he often arrives at their effects. But the Eastern seething trouble of mysterious life, which they subdued to lucid pattern, he will not altogether subdue. There is mediævalism in him, and the thirst for the impossible. There is Italy in him, the dark spirit of the Etruscan's secret race, and the patience wherewith they granulated their marvellous gold. Indeed, in the infinite iridescence and scintillation of Leonardo's mind, and in the drawings that most reveal it, you catch gleams and flashes of all places and periods. He will snatch you as far east as the soft ineffable flowering and the flying dragons of far Cathay, and set you down in the ultimate west among faëry islands and labyrinthine knots of broidered stone by sea-green eternity. He will hood himself like a Persian Magian ;

The Personality of Leonardo

and, coifed with the ibis-wings of Thoth, lose you amid a sinister forest of pillars in the sun-temples of Egypt. But behind it all he is ever aware of the metamorphoses and spirals of merely natural life, sometimes sweeping man upward, sometimes looping him into a dark agony. He knows the change and the shift in mortal mood, beasts into men, men into beasts— the shadowy drop on all-fours, the obscure lycanthropies of the soul. And with all his Greek, Roman, Eastern distances, he has mediæval values of intensity and concentration, as if he had discussed Saint Anne with the Angelical Doctor, wrapped in a brown cowl, or listened to Abelard in close-pressed Paris, or considered theories of static law with Albertus Magnus.

But he was the Renaissance love-child of a beautiful love-broken mother who may indeed, in a dim imagination, have passed like a compassion into his lonely Virgin-mothers, safe within their pure desolate rocks ; and he could develop all singular qualities of beauty and power with an ease and applause unlikely to attend him at any other period. We are used to call Leonardo " modern," whatever we mean by it. All the Renaissance people are " modern " in their outlook, thinking and feeling for themselves, developing their personalities to a degree which would now be absolutely denied them. Leonardo is lonely during the Renaissance because he is the Renaissance superman. He would have been lonely at any time because of that amazing creative quality. He would be miserable to-day, for with our little supermen he would indeed be arrogant in silence. Look what we have made of Leonardo, who by all reliable tradition was " fit for verse," even for mythology. A blameless moralizing old man, respectfully studying " nature " ; and all because he shed a few platitudes among his scientific notes ! (He also shed some caressing words : they are ignored.) This of a spirit, for all its glamour of sweetness essentially hazardous, haughty, and heathen from the sun, burning his own track through mysterious thickets of emotion as well as spreading the wings of Lucifer on the inviolate realms of air. From the tangle of the manuscripts you may guess many things : but from those pictures left to us, the stations in the progress of his soul, we learn more of the princely and dangerous mood behind the most psychological art in all the world.

The Renaissance age fitted Leonardo. It gave him employers and companions, also with insatiable curiosities, ruthless passion in conquest, large and liberal notions of the artist. If he remained a little solitary it was merely because of his unparalleled endowment, comparatively ineffective in production, because of the conflict among those excessive qualities ; and he was slightly inhibited, because he would be indifferent to the ethos and the polity of any time, although, courtesy being of his essence, he would never violate them if possible.

Leonardo the Florentine

The lordship of his shaping power masters and bridles the wild steeds of Leonardo's original energies, even as his sensitive strong hands dominated the untamed horses that he loved. Never did the charioteer of the soul drive fierier things more consentingly to beauty's goal. Yet Leonardo could have been extravagant as any condottiere prince. He could have outdone a d'Este or a Baglione in violence, or astounded Cesare by his ruthless will and his Machiavellian mathematics of conquest. Perhaps it was as well for Italy that his appetite lay in the psychical world, and that in him the lust even for fame was only fitful. His natural inclination to the fantasy of power is distinct, though repressed. It is in some lonely and immense architectural projects that the wild and monstrous note is audible like an echo of drums. Not that they are irrational in design or less than superbly and logically created on his page. But these vastitudes of domes and pillars and stairs sometimes have a little the effect of a haschisch dream ; and the colossal temples strike out something of the terrifying power of Heliopolis or Baalbec, where a great wind seems to have swept all puny worshippers like dust into the desert-spaces. This passion for puissance in itself awakes also in the strange little cries of delirious exultation that escape Leonardo when he thinks he really will conquer the air.

With this unequalled endowment of natural force, however, his dominating reason turned a thousand wheels of intellectual effort. Body and soul, he was disciplined, trained perfect. Any rumour of dissipated time in his youth appears only to mean that he rode and fenced and danced and made music and loitered in the sun with his peers, as a beautiful young man in Lorenzo's Florence was bound to do. He gathered his flowers in the maytide, and wrung out their perfume for his later years. That supreme sense of form, having first elaborated his own personality to a degree that dazzled his contemporaries, was directed without, to reduce the imaginative trouble of the world to the rhythm and pattern of pure beauty, to reduce the phenomena of the universe to an orderly vision by an inquisition and a survey as complete as the duration of his life allowed. The inspiration of Leonardo, both in art and in science, is dionysiac, dæmonic, ecstatic, carrying him easily among the untrodden dews and the unpathed waters and caves occult, and inviolate moon-floors lit by pale earthshine. But it is controlled by the ruthless demand for measure, the exactitude of the god who flayed Marsyas. Lorenzo's famous antique seal, which held that cruel myth sunken in cornelian, set by Ghiberti between the wings of a golden dragon smothered in ivy-leaves, seems to leave its impress on Florentine art, and most of all on

The Personality of Leonardo

Leonardo, whose white passion for perfection consumed the rose from all other passions. But he had power enough. For to control the waters and to explore the air has been for time immemorial the tasks of gods who descend to be kings awhile.

vi

The formal reason was sceptical in Leonardo and critical, though all the tides of his æsthetic being set towards the morning star of mysticism that hangs low between earth and heaven. This fundamental antithesis of spiritual attitude underlies all the antinomies and paradoxes which he wrought into a suave music of double expression. His cool and ironic intellect, fencing, dancing, riding fast, like his physical self, saved him from the sentimentality and sensuality that lie stealthily in wait for the complete mystic in his ashen hours of nonchaloir and accidia, slyly offering their drugs to relieve that horrible exhaustion. But it also withheld him from using quite candidly the instinctive or intuitive power, the imaginative logic of throbbing pulsations, though he does seem to recognize it as a legitimate organon for the discovery of the cloudy dead-golden region of experience on whose borders the reason becomes blind and mute. Like all people of lucid intelligence, he was reluctant to use his divining heart, and to say : " This is the voice that I seem to hear murmuring in my ears like the sound of the flute in the ears of the mystic," because the credulous had tarnished its great validities. So, though it was his deliberate intention to write of the soul and her august and mysterious ways, he left that to the very end ; and, among all the many treatises he meditated, this consuming essay, which must have hovered cloudy-bright as he wrote of the body, has dropped but one sombre feather or so. He lit great lamps of myth and symbol in his pictures, but he veiled them with emerald veils of tradition. The conflict between the sceptical mood, which is the delicate justifying flower of the destructive principle, and the fiery intuitive mood, which adumbrates the creative force, is often too equally balanced : there is a kind of nihilism in this controlled and exquisite artist, and he comes lonely and disguised to the house of Ecstasy.

vii

Leonardo was profoundly aware of the flashing singularity of his own mind, a mind ready to leap on any problem and grip it hard through all its changes till it confessed its reality, ranging at ease through the universe from the infinitely great to the infinitely little. Confidence dwells deep in his speech and actions. He knew he was a many-faceted diamond whose mere lustre princes might be glad to possess. Yet, with all his justifiable assurance, Leonardo seems not altogether at home in the world of mortal affairs. He knows that his intellectual difference from other men is a cleavage that goes to the very roots of life. He is a brilliant efflorescent graft from some strange Tree of Paradise : he is a dazzling departure from the beaten track like a rainbow bridge that ends in mid-air. He is parentless, childless, as if to make him a god had found a peasant-girl in the guise of a Hawk, not a Dove. Of the ways of the world he is never quite certain. His spirit is all masked in a beautiful courtesy ; but he is often perplexed. And he is not really fortunate. Life, for Leonardo, should have been one smooth, rich experiment, a succession of crystallizing and sublimating stages taking place in a polarized state of impassioned contemplation. But after the fall of Lodovico, existence is all disturbed by catastrophes and irritating contacts. He is destroyed because he can find no centre of rest.

" Fly from storms," said Leonardo, who was so often lifted and borne from his quietude by the fierce mutabilities of the tempest of Renaissance war. But why should he counsel evasions who was formed competent to pass through fiery crises ? The strangest note in the great orchestration of Leonardo's character is the low sighing wood-wind moan of fear. This audacious mind, this fiery and bizarre spirit, this personality that was a civilization in itself, knew the paralysis and defeat of that sudden, sterilizing, and prehistoric emotion. One does not mean that Leonardo was not more courageous than most : the besetting weakness is usually but the defect of the king-quality in a character, and it is the strongest gate that is most carelessly guarded. And fear is the vertigo of the lonely. Leonardo knew the spiritual solitudes where the head reels and all things become phantasmal, since he was by the very richness and complexity of his pattern incompatible with his kind.

Panic affected him at times like a low fever, an illness of the nerves that shook him suddenly at all conclusions, arresting his hands at the face of the Christ, his scalpel at the mystery of the heart, and his mind at the notion of an immovable sun. He dared not paint the face of his desire in *The Last Supper*, he dared not find that the septum of the heart is impenetrable, he dared not step into a heliocentric universe. His pictures and his treatises were alike unfinished. It is true that the vast variety of his coincident activities implied a kind of multiple thinking that would have been almost destructive of the brain-tissue of most people, and must have been exhausting even to Leonardo's. But it really was his desire to complete things ; he would put an exquisite finish on some trivial toy of design like a duchess' bath or a masquer's dress, as if to find the mere pleasure of perfection in small indifferent matters, since the great monuments of his art and his science refused

The Personality of Leonardo

him the joy of their consummation. Down so many ways of truth and beauty he goes, the prime adventurer. Always at some bend it is as if he met with his Medusa. He is a god, but a god in conflict ; a Michael, but with his dragon.

This is a psychical fear, tangled hard with the passion for perfection and the uncertainty of spiritual loneliness. It has a physical reflection in Leonardo's dread of death. He was not on such intimate terms with this world, one thinks, that he should have shuddered from a release that was like a return to his native dells of light. Evidently his contemplation of the outer universe left him in much the same mood as the warm young sensualist, Claudio, who had no scientific vision at all.

> " Ay ! but to die, and go we know not where ;
> To lie in cold obstruction, and to rot ;
> This sensible warm motion to become
> A kneaded clod ; and the delighted spirit
> To bathe in fiery floods, or to reside
> In thrilling regions of the thick-ribbed ice ;
> To be imprisoned in the viewless winds,
> And blown with restless violence round about
> The pendent world."

So he avoided death as he avoided love, with which death is so strangely plighted. He would ride wild horses, and wear a sword that he knew how to use with beautiful dexterity, and he would peril himself in Borgian camps and flaming cities, when he was intent on the demands of his own personality. But it is in vain that we seek in the annals of Leonardo for any rashness for the sake of friendship, gratitude, love of city, or even the love of truth. He was tactful over his science. The notes were as inaccessible as he could make them, written in his sinistral secret script and double-locked in his studios, divulged only to the discreet. With a camouflage of platitudes he sometimes pleased to cover his indifference to the ethical ; while the drawings that better told his heart betrayed his personal code. His unchristened imagination stole into ambiguous security over the altars of the monks at whom he jested. Whatever he might say, he did not covet martyrdom. Science was an excitement and a relief to him, but not a religion, and if the Inquisition had threatened him with such agonies as he curiously watched in others he would hardly have offered as much resistance as Galileo. He would merely have said with a debonair gesture : " Of course the crowned writings are infallible, and the Church is their interpreter. I have been amusing myself." Possibly he would have been right. A Copernican universe is not worth dying for to us, creatures of night and day, for whom the sun for ever rises in the mysterious chambers of the east, and sets in the rose and emerald pavilions of the dreaming west. A scientific truth does not convey the anæsthesia of the vision of all things in divinity, and men seldom die for the ultimate Necessity as they do for the glory of God. Leonardo, one feels, would never even have said with Socrates' ironic flame of pride : " I would rather die having spoken in my manner than speak in your manner and live." But then Leonardo was never particularly anxious to convey his wisdom to anybody. He worked and contemplated to satisfy his own craving. In his anatomical notes he tells us that he has seen the heart of one who was burned alive whole and perfect among the ashes. The side-remark is a little startling : he seems to think it a casual matter. It is the physical fact that interests him : what brought the too audacious or merely unfortunate heart to the gates of fire is of no account. Sorcerer, freethinker, conspirator against ethic or doctrine, that victim perished obscurely, and his heart lay vivid among the ashes like Shelley's, to intrigue with the calm eyes of Leonardo, whose locked crystal-box of a heart kept safe the keys of all his heretical knowledge. None can deny that Christianity has given the world some mystical paradoxes that are worth all the wisdom of Socrates in their vibrating emotional truth. " He that loveth his life shall lose it," is one that Leonardo refused.

viii

Leonardo himself, in his pictorial parable of the cave, hints at a mystery of fear and desire cloying and turning the edge of his spirit. The caves of the earth-mother he did not dare. Though he goes farther than most men he yet stops short in all his ventures as he stopped short at the entrance to the cavern. He knew the sublimated nymphlike spirit of Nature, the imaginative soul behind all creation.

" He felt that wondrous lady all alone :
And she felt him upon her emerald throne."

Perhaps in the last instance it is his dream of Nature herself that he paints dangerous, enigmatic, alluring among the hard pure rocks and green pure waters. But there is another aspect of Nature, a blind and furious force of life that demands a sacrifice or a placation he could not give. He knows that in some ways he is a renegade to life. There is a sense of dream-guilt in his painting : he refused to be of the *kouretes* of Cybele.

He had not really quite the courage of his qualities, though he had their arrogance. The touch of insistence in the brave words that escape from him sometimes, in the manuscripts and in certain letter-drafts, betrays a lurking doubt. What began the inhibition and the mystic

The Personality of Leonardo

fear ? In the woods of Westermain did he, a child, sicken over some loathly fungoid sight or shudder from a coil of snakes or a half-eaten bird ? Or did he chance on some too-faunish thing among the vine-dressers ? Was he shocked and shaken by some blunt cruelty or heedless mockery as an over-sensitive miraculous child, and did the impression, lost awhile in the radiant assurance of his Florentine youth, all music and light and praise, revive with septic throbbing intensity under the sudden buffet and indignity of the public arraignment of his soul ? Or was it only that nature, having created a meteor among mortals, muffled it in a milky cloud lest its burning track be intolerable for human kind ?

Leonardo's exquisite nerve-system must have been unusual in its quality ; but he overtaxed it. Not even he could exact from his body the deeds of an athlete, an artist, an engineer, and a manifold savant, by day and by night, without paying in terms of exhaustion. Age fell on him early for a Renaissance man, and fell heavily, though he ignored it as much as possible. But he is not free all his life from the hyper-æsthesia of the *névrose*. Those eyes of his devour with a fierce intensity : images are printed like fire on his retina. Sometimes the world is distorted into caricature, and he sees men as beasts walking. Hearing and smell and touch, the alarmist, fugitive, prehistoric senses that send the swiftest shocks to the heart, are also supersubtle in him : the acuteness of all his sense-impressions must have been a torture as well as a delight. And it is noticeable that, sun-worshipper, he keeps to the shadow. Like most nerve-wrought people he loves cool, dusky, and soothing impressions, the twilight and the rain-washed silver airs that are kind to flowers and faces and bring out their aroma ; the movement of great waters that float into beauty the fevers of the soul. And, like all faintly morbid spirits whose desirous moods are of the faëry and psychical kind, so that the rarefied sense turns to mysticism, the colour he loves is green. A strange unchristened colour from Saracen or Babylonian worlds, for the Greeks had no word for it ! It belongs to the strange paradise of dreams between heaven and hell, Christendom and Heathenesse, where gods and angels meet, and where the soul that would feed among the lilies finds them in fields of emerald.

He has touches of claustrophobia in the painted chambers and feverish studios of Milan. He has spasms of furious sensibility when his young pupils behave lightly : he has indeed a definite complex about ingratitude and envy. His pictures become an agony to him ; the passion for perfection consumes him. In Rome he is aware of the devouring burning exasperation over trifles that betrays great weariness. Though his heart be invulnerable, he is clothed sometimes by his nerves like a cilice of fire.

Leonardo the Florentine

The nerves and the emotions are inextricably interwoven ; and the enigma of Leonardo's emotional life is left unsolved. He was a beautiful person whose actions were all instinct with grace. He looked like the Ionian Apollo Citharœdus, like the dreaming Dionysos. He had lovely, riddling ways ; with the strings beneath his delicate fingers he loved to charm away a soul. By some unfair endowment, his intellectual and imaginative qualities were attended by the inexplicable glamour, enchantment, love-spell, which is in itself sufficient to supersede all intellectual qualities. If he could not love, he took pleasure in being beloved, an attitude for which poor humanity is often pathetically grateful.

That Leonardo's emotional existence does not affect his achievement, and is of no interest, is a thesis held by many of his biographers. Certainly matters of the heart distract Leonardo's life less than that of most great artists. His purely intellectual activity was incessant to an unparalleled degree ; his senses, rarefied, and swift as an immortal's, fed him with visual images so richly that he did not need the passional tremors and illuminations of beauty. Yet, even if the love-attitude be shut away as in an agate casket of the soul, it will escape like a colour or a scent and diffuse itself through thought and expression. To-day, its denials and dissipations are causes of Mr Wells' angry exasperation and Mr Shaw's crackling and arid philosophy ; and its rebellions preoccupy all the little novelists who write against romance, as much as its devotions preoccupied Plato and Shakespeare, and Dante, whose implication is that love is the key to the universe. Leonardo's lack of continuity in his researches has its obscure relation with his deliberate refusal of the continuities of life. His supreme indifference to the feminine principle as anything but an æsthetic idea had something to do with his dread of the complete Lucretian vision of Nature. He dare not say, with superb and careless acquiescence : "Et Venus in silvis jungebat corpora amantium." Again, his sexless preference for pure enchantment as the psychical effect of his art explains why it needs an initiation, and is not invariably potent in its spell, why it sometimes seems, beside the art of Velazquez or Rembrandt, even beside the art of Giorgione or Botticelli, who are more kin to him, a kind of exquisite ducdame, even though it be indeed a great " Greek invocation." It is not that it excites disparagement or blame ; but sometimes it is disquieting and unsympathetic to a mortality that loves and dies and suffers. Sometimes he seems merely to bring faëry contraband into a world of tears, and any old woman of Rembrandt's, or any arrogant and pathetic Infanta of Velazquez, is alike more beautiful than Mona Lisa. Within a divine tenderness he does cloister the miraculous mother and the child ; but even the sole mysterious perfection of their unity has something ambiguous and supernatural in it, except perhaps in the early Florentine madonnas that we know only in drawings.

x

The everlasting dualities of human intercourse could not enrich Leonardo.   As he seemed to reconcile good and evil, trance and activity, emotion and intellect, mystery and illumination, so he appeared to unite in himself lover and beloved, male and female, master and slave.   The great give-and-take of complementary lovers and the poignant unsating delight of their union is not within his experience.   A lord of life, he is isolated from life by his perfection.   It is difficult to describe his attitude without scientific words that do not unjustly convey a pathological implication and a reproach.   Leonardo sits with Socrates and his friends in the House of Agathon, a psychical lover of beautiful youth, indifferent to the wasting feverish love of woman.   Michelangelo, his familiar enemy, is with him there, though Michelangelo found a restful feminine type in Vittoria Colonna, even while his adoration of Tommaso Cavalieri was still more rapturous.   Neither of them could be called perverts or inverts, the unsatisfactory names given to the sad and suffering children of distraction to whom Marcel Proust has offered a courageous service.   The sheer intellectual power of Leonardo gripped like a despot the insurrections of desire, and soothed and spirited them away into a haunting smile.

We cannot apply our standards to Renaissance psychology.   There was a kind of great confusion in these bridegrooms of the antique Venus whom they sometimes preferred to see as Adonis.   The new liberating paganism seemed to unchain their senses as well as their minds ; and through their uncritical Hellenizing delight Greek love sometimes ran a little like Greek fire.   But it was an ideal love in its essence, dreamed after the platonic pattern, succeeding the mediæval woman-worship, of whose wasting sweetness and moon-soft delicacy of texture they were a little cloyed, though in their reluctance to lose any lovely tradition they did not yet abandon that fine fashion.   It was beauty, beauty of the holy human form broken from its mediæval sheaths, that enchanted them, the beauty of Greek or Roman statuary.   They found this bodily beauty only in courtesan, Madonna, and boy. Perhaps a little confusedly, they thought the boy was the most Hellenic image.   In the figure of a woman was something too much of insolence, something too much of pathos, the over-insistent challenge, the overwounded soft suffering of the body that Nature has crucified. Giorgione and Leonardo himself were the only two Renaissance artists that deified the naked figure of a woman ;

and they did so only by steeping it in the airs of Elysium. They regarded with sculptor's eyes the beautiful austere unwounded forms of youth, perfect as lekythi or lilies. The women provocatively followed their lead themselves, dressed in armour sometimes, wilfully teasing figures like Isabella d'Este and her women, wearing caps of boys with jewelled feathers, yet revealing the beauty of the breast, shocking and delighting France. They consented to the exaltation of masculine youth, and aped it prettily : it was all part of the vague aching nostalgia for Greece.

They were overstrung with the neo-Platonic effort towards a great religion and metaphysic of love. They saw Phaedrus under the plane-tree listening to Socrates in his ecstasy, and Charmides, modest and exquisite among his lovers, and the crowned Lysis like a fair vision, and Autolycus like a bright torch at the festival, and Ion pure in the temple, and Phaedo with bowed curls under the hand of the dying philosopher, and Alcibiades with his thick crown of ivy and violets, exalting the continence of his friend. They heard of the lovers of Achilles, who won his way to the Blessed Isles through love, and the Spartans who died at Thermopylæ, and the Sacred Band of Theban Lovers all dead upon the ground. Michelangelo would echo Plato in his exaltation of this love too impassioned for friendship, too noble for appetite, this masculine and intellectual Eros born of the Uranian Aphrodite, who in his aspect of Himeros delights the soul only through the aery pleasure of the eyes.

xi

Yet this Athenian dream, that had never belonged save to some high aristocrats, had been softened in Alexandria and coarsened in Rome, and damned by Christianity (though it had a wistful baptism in stories like those of Amis and Amile, or Roland and Oliver), so that even in Florence, where it was most passionately revived, there was something equivocal and shadowy about it. Nevertheless, this glorification of male friendship, and this tender delight in the beauty of the boy, was one of the chief characteristics of the Renaissance, and sent its spirit into France and England. It was an attitude that persisted long. The attitude, at least, dyes deep the Shakespearian *Sonnets*; and the ascetic Milton, in celebrating pure and lovely youth, not only in his Latin verses, but in the great stanzas of *Lycidas*, is chaster as well as more tender than when with cold animal sensuality he expresses his notions of nuptial bliss. In modern times it is an attitude that blazes into strange beauty in the music of *Calamus*, where Whitman is most a poet. Fashions have altered, and seem inclined to alter again, in literature at least. The Renaissance worship of the youth was its effort to realize a Greek ideal,

The Personality of Leonardo

and to escape from sex. Greek love at best was a great sunlight of sweet feeling undisturbed by craving; at worst it was a lust like another. The Renaissance, however, unable to rid its mind of the troubling romantic effect which women had achieved during the Middle Ages, and, indeed, reluctant to surrender it, especially as the women were hellenizing and platonizing with them, desired, as usual, to combine contraries; romantic love and Greek love showed "contamination"; and most of the great Renaissance figures were bisexual in mood—sometimes, admittedly, in more than mood. They were too highly charged with too many conflicting currents.

Leonardo did not write sonnets like Michelangelo, so we cannot tell how much he was affected by the platonizing habit of the philosophers of Fiesole and Careggi, Marsilio, Poliziano, Pico, and the rest. It was the Alexandrian and Plotinian version of the platonic philosophies that obtained in Florence, and a Christian emotionalism charged this hybrid faith with something yet more fantastical, rose-coloured, and tender. It created that vibrating atmosphere of an aristocratic religion and a secret cult in which the feet are sometimes caught suddenly by snares because the eyes are blinded by the stars of enthusiasm; but Marsilio was a sincere hierophant, Pico della Mirandola a beautiful celebrant, and the ironic Lorenzo a wistful adherent. It is almost impossible to know what Leonardo thought or felt in platonizing, adonizing Florence. The æsthetic notions at least of the esoteric philosophy of Lorenzo's Court floated through the City, copied and sometimes travestied by artists devoted to Medicean patronage, like Verrocchio. With exaggerated praise and classic analogies they spoiled the slim conscious boys who posed for the Davids, the Saint Georges, the Baptists. That it was Leonardo who found himself suddenly called to account is still distinctly inexplicable. But that the notary's love-child was the most gracious and brilliant figure in Florence is probably explanation enough. He was too "strangely beautiful."

Be that as it may, it is true that Leonardo did not set his conduct to the rhythm of any very definite metaphysic, though he is more Platonic in his implications than might seem. After all, if he had written that treatise on the soul he might have told his philosophy of love. But the Platonic theories of earthly and heavenly beauty did not subdue him as they did Michelangelo, who, in his stricken age, loved Tommaso Cavalieri with a mystical adoration, and could write to any beautiful person with the idolatry of a Juliet. He had many ways of loving, the furious Michelangelo with the craving heart. If he had his Andrea too, he could write of his high Platonic rapture that "he who would understand it must first of all die," a despairing sweet simplicity of a cry that holds true of all ethereal and poetic passion. And he was fortunate, for, if he found his feminine type in Vittoria Colonna, she was remote and starry enough to keep him content in his worship ; and did not endanger her peace by an intimate kindness. The strange drawing he made of his dead lady, with pensive face and wasted breasts, showed what acrid flavour lingered from the secret sadistic anger with which any true Platonist loved a woman. Michelangelo could carve the platonic Eros, not at all unlike the terrible Lord of Dante—severe, fair, implacable ; and one of his Bound Captives is as divinely lovely in its so different conception as the Praxitelean Hermes. Probably he stole the latter idea from Leonardo : but that great artist, one reluctantly feels, could not have created such a proud image of youth dreamily striving against his bonds, princely, virginal, heart-moving, yet pure as Dorian flutes. Leonardo's fair young friends dreamed with a hyacinthine difference.

xii

But Leonardo was the beloved, not the wistful mournful lover like Michelangelo, who was marred and harsh. He read his Marsilio, and was aware of the atmosphere. In his youth perhaps he was nearer Alcibiades than Socrates, though, being Leonardo, he knew when to develop into the sage. His friends were many and varied ; for beautiful young men he seems to have had an æsthetic tenderness removed both from the Platonic idealism and from its sensual delation and defect. Leonardo did not theorize much over his inclinations, one feels. Like most children of grace, he had a conviction that what he did must be gracious, a heresy strengthened in the dreamy air of Milan, heavy and mild with ancient antinomian doctrines out of Africa and Asia, all in that suggestive key. He loved them like the flowers, and liked to have them about him in the same way. He loved them because they had beautiful curls, and large eyes, fine straight noses and dreaming lips lifted at the corners, and an androgyne charm of manner and bearing. He was with Agathon rather than Socrates, and would have agreed that " love never settles in a body that is not flowerlike, or in any soul or place where the bloom has died." Wisdom, even virtue, he did not require of them. With smiling sophistry he would have held that, since the body was the first work of the soul, then the soul that spun such fine floss of curls, and swept the lashes on the cheek like a sweet sorrow, must have a mystic beauty. And perhaps he was right. There are those who offer a mystery by the mere dwelling of their strangely-irised eyes, an initiation by the shadowy smile hovering on the curvature of their lips, or the very wave carved within the hair above their lucid temples, or the meditation of their long hands,

The Personality of Leonardo

or even the matt and sacred texture of their veil of flesh.   Sometimes a gesture or an expression of youth is so charged with physical grace that it takes the heart with intolerable tenderness, like the last fine ghost of a wave vanishing on silver sand, or the young moon shy in a jasper eventide.

Leonardo never reached that final stage of Platonic enthusiasm when the lover may " regard bodily beauty as a little thing."   Being honest, even Leonardo admits that sometimes lovely shapes are bestowed on the creatures of mere appetite ; and this waste annoys him to petulance. He says that the unthinking and the swinish should have nothing like the wonder of a human body spent on their low existences : a rude fleshly sack with two orifices would do.   They are " mere canals for food," and fit only to be sewer-cleaners or charcoal-burners.

xiii

From the early biographers we gather only that Leonardo was singularly beloved.   The colour and quality of his emotional life can be but guessed from his pictures, drawings and manuscripts.   It seems prismatic, fluctuating, a matter of dreams and nerves rather than shaken pulses and fiery moments.   Love is but an accident in the pursuit of beauty.   He loves beauty, he loves truth.   He has a tenderness for some sweet people.   Sweet and gracile people !   There is no strength and persistence, no rhythmic high pulsation of an equal friendship.

No !   There is little definite information as to Leonardo's emotional hours.   The manuscripts are not in the least intended as a diary or a personal expression of any kind.   They are laboratory notebooks, ciphers and formulæ set down to assist the memory, with elaborate beginnings of treatises now and then.   Any comment or intimate note is accidental ; and its significance is dubious without its context.   It is easy to infer too much even from the hasty memoranda that slip in by mistake.   He has a complex against written language, perhaps because he is so mailed in secrecy, and words, after all, do not really hide the soul that spins them.

But from a long contemplation of Leonardo's imagery, from the blanks and blurs and pauses, from the sudden growth of lilies by the margin of the page, the dip of the birds, the bubbling of the domes, the challenge of soft young faces with cæsarian eyes, the spirals and eddies of flames and smoke and clouds and water, the patterns of laby-rinthine line, we get an impression of desire and dreams behind all this astonishing activity of mind, a faint rose-crystal flame of desire and dreams—chimerical, paradoxical emotion that softly wearied him as he wrought, till he often dropped silverpoint or pencil just when he should have gone farther. Again and again the hand is seized by his unconscious self as he sits musing, and a group of anemones, a spire of lilies, a cloudy-fair head with bistred eyes, a fantastic dome, an involved intrecciamenta, betrays the wistful, profound, and convoluted reverie. Sometimes among the careful studies of motion swings a naked figure with a great sword. Ever and anon the doors of his cold chamber of experiment seem to open, and the cry of the singing strings comes through. He takes off his mask, sweetens his hands with rose and lavender, and goes. Sometimes he sits in the dusk, gazing at a blank page, hurt and uncomprehending. " Amantissimo," he writes, and " carissimo " across the page serried with lines and figures. Nothing more ! A drop of blood, a drop of ichor, has fallen there. Sometimes he writes a name, sometimes the handwriting becomes large and irregular. On the 10th of July 1492 somebody wounded him. " The wood feeds the flame that burns it," he writes, and murmurs of " the hand of ingratitude," and laces his twisted knots in agitation.

But all through his painting, all through his marvellous drawings, what dark rays of defiance, what diaphaneities of emotion, flash and flicker, as if the burning-glasses of his hidden soul projected their sudden shifting light upon the paper. Invisibly through his scientific notes he writes his reverie in symbols. As the great philosopher says : " The soul divines what it seeks, and traces obscurely the footsteps of its obscure desire." Flowers he regards with infinite attention for their own sakes ; and also with a drowsy mysticism, for all the waves of being seem to break in a rich foam of flowers, phantom shapes of the bridal-lily kind. The spiral line he finds in magical shells, in the whirlwinds, in the climbing plants, in eddying pools, in the waterspouts, in rising smoke, in luring hair, betrays his vital ecstasy. The waters themselves are the great creative birth-waters, spiritual as well as physical, the milky fantasia where the dreamer may drown or bring his black pearl to land. Sometimes he writes a word in some lost Coptic ; sometimes he twines his patient knots, his amulets, things of sesame to finger till they let him through to his vision. When the fastidious mood deepens to cruelty, he draws swords—pure and romantic and beautiful, the sword that slept between chaste lovers in forests of mediæval romance, the sword that divides soul from body always. He also draws his clefts of the hard pure rock in which to see his dream of virginal ecstasy. When he sketches the body it is but a symbol of the soul's intentions. He concentrates his interest on great deeply-set eyes, on softly-twisting hair, on rhythmical long hands, till the symbolist takes on almost the passion of the fetichist. The fastidious symbolic soul sits like fierce little flames in these.

The Personality of Leonardo

" Great love springs from great knowledge of the beloved object, and if you little know it you will be able to love it only little or not at all." This axiom of Leonardo's is generally quoted with great approval ; but it is not very illuminating, since he has not defined knowledge. " Il n'y a rien de plus suspect que l'amour, même envers Dieu," said more acutely the wise monk, imagining Love, the black hood falling from his wasted face, and his ivory hands grasping the crucifix, while the inextinguishable rose of his heart still secretes some heretical dew of sweetness from the mere passion of his penance. Yet flame can consecrate anything : and, if love can turn a renunciation to a sin, it can change the sin into a star. But there is little track of the flamelike Eros in Leonardo's existence. Here and there is the moisture of crystal tears, but never the fiery footprints. Here and there shed rose and violet ; but never the bruisèd myrrh. Sometimes there is a name suddenly written among the speculations, the calligraphy goes wrong, the pages are blurred and blotted, broken sentences about ingratitude and ill company appear. Then the diagrams steady, and the writer is presently absorbed in some new theory. You apprehend that merely his pride has been wounded and his nerves have been unsettled. If you have been contemplating Leonardo too long, you almost wish that if no woman could hold a heart even more subtle than her own, he could have broken it over a Fioravante, say. But it was the love of himself that he loved in others : the eyes of Fioravante and the rest were the mirror of Narcissus. What matter if he wrote " Amantissimo " masculine or feminine, if only he came through the fiery door and grasped the key of life. He did not : he holds only the key of dreams.

Leonardo himself has commented on the narcissimus of the artist and his unconscious repetition of his own peculiarities in the figures he paints. His own narcissimus went deeper ; and his own marvellous soul with its dæmon was what he most cared for. He looked like Love himself, " a philosopher, mighty in magic and philtres and a sophist." Even in the early *Adoration* he paints the different aspects of his own soul, in the timeless seekers who have watched the stars from Babylonian ziggurats, in the dazzled youth shaken between joy and fear, in the adoring face that is of his heart's desire, in the dim cavaliers who tilt in the distance, most of all in the Black Knight of melancholy who refusingly looks away from it all. During his Florentine youth, he is naturally more awake to the things without him ; and it amused him to draw incessantly at a charming genre theme that intrigued the virtuoso in him, like *The Madonna with the Cat*. But after he went to Milan, and the two parts of his consciousness separated more definitely under the strain and the spell, whatever he painted, the theme was only his own soul preoccupied with its own angel of strange beauty.

Again he gives the vague impression of a species that Nature has elaborated and lost, as too sensitively complicated for the harsh simplicities of environment. Late in the biological day, that is the kind of fate that befalls him. So he does not enter into the blood of humanity so much as into its mind, as a dazzling but uncongenial enigma. Leonardo himself seems to seek restlessly for some consummation of peace impossible to his peculiar mood. His amazing intellect blazes path after path for him : he abandons them all, and none comes after to carry them to the end which suddenly ceased to interest him.

xv

But Narcissus loved a nymph, and her name was Echo. Leonardo, like others not born to the love of woman, loved a feminine dream-type. It was a nymphlike type, with a soul of natural magic, and it echoed his unearthly desire : and it mirrored his own eyes also. In humanity he never found it, for its essential quality was angelic, naiad-like, immortal. And as time went on, it became confused with the beauty of the youth, and more and more androgyne, like Dionysos and the Saint John.

xvi

The world revealed in the scientific manuscripts is an entirely masculine world. That the Duchess must have her bath and her pavilion, and an old servant called Catarina her priests for burial, that, most surprisingly, " Giovannina has a fantastic face," is all we hear of woman. If the great name of Helen once rings from the page it is only to record that even her swan-born beauty became the weeping prey of Time. But in the world of his art he draws women, he paints them with intense æsthetic interest and comprehension. There was a strong feminine part in Leonardo for all his virilitá—the hyacinthine sister of his Hyacinth spirit. He did not need woman ; with a terribly disinterested air he understood her. His hands were plunged in the hapless secrets of her tragic body ; he drew and drew the child she carried in her womb, regarding her then with some sympathy, like a skilled physician. For this mournful and imploring creature he had neither distaste nor desire. He dipped her in immortality as if to deodorize her before he cared to paint her. With one famous exception, perhaps—but

The Personality of Leonardo

even to Mona Lisa he gave the throne of Circe. He charmed away their importunate hearts, and closed them in hard pure rock from any lovers that were not winged.

Wherever women congregate there is a cult and a mystery because only in their dark pagan souls is the authentic incense hidden ; and even Leonardo had to find a priestess to convey his dream of beauty. When the day's work was for the Church, he called her Saint Anne or the Virgin ; when it was for his own pleasure and a secular patron's, she was Leda ; when it was only for his own pleasure she faded into Dionysos, the mænad into her lord.

He knew there was one impossible type that could trick his strange spirit into love and peace because it was contained in himself, an imaginative, dream-holden, yet divinely ironic type. It was not that of Madonna Lisa, though he laid the mask of his æsthetic ideal lightly on that mobile and provoking visage. If it had materialized in life, it is doubtful if Leonardo would have been moved to conquest or surrender. His fastidious spirit desired no violent gesture to bring disenchantment, despair, and the silence of the flutes. He could not in the bed of Cleopatra have conjured up the ghost of a rose ; but he might have had some original rapture for the faëry Queen of Sheba, for one who came wisdom to wisdom, prince to prince, brother to brother almost. " Now there was no spice like the spice which the Queen of Sheba gave to Solomon." If Saint Anne had come clothed in Oriental veils through the ways of Milan, so he might have met her, star with star, in some sophistication of delight.

xvii

He brought strange stuff from the borders of the world to charge these dreaming faces. He had drawn the straight young girls of Florence, arrowy and virginal like their brothers, so little distinguishable. But to the haughty and equal Florentine ladies, who were hailed " signore " and " amico " by their love-poets, his art did not respond. The lovely Lombard faces gave him the pure oval, the deep eyes, the tranced lips, the rich hair, that seemed fit as a chalice for his philtre. But he fetched the wildness of the nymph from the oaks and reeds of Vinci, the secret mystery of the Annunciation angels from the mediæval story, ethereal foam from the strange wine-dark seas where the head of Sappho lies among branches of rose-coral ; and sea-magic from the caves of Calypso and the isles of Circe, and the violet Western waters where walks the white witch Morgan le Fay ; and with this potent hydromel he intoxicated the Lombard beauty into the woman of faëry enchantment that dwells in all the legends, ambiguous and irresistible, a creature of doom and delight,

491

his ecstatic sister and spouse, whom he "raised up under the apple-tree" in the orchards of Milan.

He wedded in her face the sweetness of the virgin and the mother, the woman and the nymph, the Narcissus and the Echo, the East and the West. Jealous as a monk of this creature made out of his own substance, he isolated her among virgin rocks by virgin waters, and left her lone with children and angels, elfin fiery spirits, his "still unravished bride of quietness." Strange sumptuous love from heaven might find her on wings, wings of the Dove, wings of the Swan, wings of his own pure and sumptuous dream-desire. Or the heavenly white unicorn would do for an image, seeking her under a great group of towering lilies, for that is also lone and splendid.

xviii

For all his amazing energy and the haughty freedom of his spirit, there really was something monkish in Leonardo which kept his pagan imagination on terms of friendly interest with the mediæval tradition. He was beauty's monk—that is, he was, even more than Socrates, an "ascetic erotic." Perhaps it is in the very pathos of the dissonances of human character, in the wild crevices between soul and body, that the passion of life throws its fierce and urgent seeds and roots its yearning tendrils. The fine equilibrium of Leonardo rejected such ungovernable intercessions; his senses, trained to subjection, the "officers of the soul," became too fastidious to work as for common clay. He refused the great democracy of love as he would fain have refused the great democracy of death. He loved himself and his own image as if he were a god, partly because to love another might seem surrender to a merely physical force he despised. It is by his implications that one realizes how much Leonardo was an idealist, refusing the Nature he professed to adore. He carried all imaginative qualities to their climax; and, like all the great Greek and the romantic lovers too, would not admit that a spasm of nerves and muscles he definitely considered hideous might be anything but an advantage taken of an emotional rhapsody by insurrecting desires. The soul was like a delicate prince castled in gold and ivory. He could not bear that its vassals might shatter the ivory, deface the gold, and drive the lord, like a white flame leaping from dyke to dyke, to the obscure finality found by any fool or sot. He knew that the soul could become so much more complicated than the sense that it might pour a wine at once so fierce and penetrating that the narrow vessel of clay might dissolve as if it were poison, that it might sink so mysterious an image of Eros on the crude world of fact that the dull matter might blur it into something between angel and satyr. His violet-burning imagination fled to art as it were a cloister of dreams.

But he had a great tenderness for the mystery of birth. As a Renaissance pagan he is nympholept, ravished by a vision of immortal beauty; like any mediæval monk and schoolman he is charmed by the mystical vision of virginity. He hates the act of procreation, but he loves the child. As an artist he solved his problem by a dream of parthenogenesis, or by bridal with a god, which, while remote and miraculous, yet casually admitted to the imagination the haunting sensuousness that could not be entirely laid, in a subtle and etherealized and perhaps perverted way that pleased him.

xix

Leonardo's refined materialism and the paradoxical mysticism that hovers over it form an antinomy he might have attempted to resolve in his lost treatise of the soul. The body is an instrument so complicated that few spirits are mighty enough to use it well; yet the act of transmitting life is a brutality. Death is a disaster for the soul that separates itself from its marvellous senses, and vanishes into the terrible universe forgetful even of its dear experiences, vanishes wailing as it came. " And I certainly think that its tears and lamentation are not without reason." He could not have understood those that find the flesh a trammel, a fetter, and a cross. Yet he has those morbid moods of an almost Baudelairean kind when men seem nothing but sheaths of corruption, feeding on and generating death. Sometimes he draws the "man of bone," strong as the human will in clean and beautiful framework of ivory, with intense relief, as if all else were a softness of desire and a corruption.

None the less that part of his anatomical study which deals with the development of the unborn child is as reverent as it is curious in mood. He is absorbed in this creative wonder. The child in the womb is himself, whose whole life is a myth and a mystery. He too considers birth " the immortal act in a mortal body." His original and astonishingly correct drawings of the child in the womb are not only of great scientific value : they are things of beauty. The small curved figure of the unborn seems bowed like a minor prophet in an ecstasy of lamentation, foreboding through the veils of its birth-chamber all the woe to come. Only here does he make any concession to woman, whose soul is the artist fashioning the piteous child in the " crystal cabinet," and whose impressions of pain and delight communicate themselves to that unsevered heart. He is so emphatic on the power of prenatal impressions that some red thread of personal feeling seems to glisten here.

Leonardo the Florentine

Yet when he refers to the very article of love in which the child began it is with superb contempt, as a low contraction and spasm of nerves and muscles most like the spasm of death and nearly as destructive of the soul. For him love in its frenzy is " a thing so hideous that humanity would cease if the victims could see themselves." With drawings of horrible anatomical unions, once at least heightened by a cynical trick, he analyses the erotic emotion. " L'atto del coito e le membra a quello adoprata," wrote he. " Son di tanta bruttura, che, se non fusse la bellezza de' volti e li ornamenti delli opranti e la sfrenata dispoziene la natura perderebbe la spezia umane." Against voluptuousness, his attitude is uncompromising. " He who does not discipline the desire for pleasure lowers himself to the level of the beasts ! " When his stepbrother has a son, Leonardo tells him he has raised up a new enemy. Indeed, his obscure anger against the life of sense defeats even his artistic fantasy sometimes. He begins to describe an imagined Temple of Venus in the island of Cyprus. You see great steps mounting a rock to a meadow on the plateau, carven pilasters, water falling from vases of porphyry and serpentine, glimpses of lake and woodland. But you divine something weird, monstrous, solitary, soundless. There are no moaning doves, no chanting choirs, no shed roses, no chryselephantine images with deep eyes smiling under the low-tressed brows. The unconsenting soul of Leonardo suddenly withdraws from the scene : there is an imaginative collapse into the grotesque effect of nightmare, and you are left on a ghastly beach strewn with bones, relics of mariners victimized by that treacherous shore.

He wrought out his arrogant ethic for himself, not for the crowd. If it amused him to draw a brothel he drew it. If his patrons desired portraits of their mistresses he painted them, and made them lovelier, by veiling them in the sweet sfumato of his own peculiar dream. He imposed his attitude on nobody. Those intolerable virtues so unwavering in flame that they consume all who cannot live at their highest level and so subtly interpenetrate the texture of life that they search out mercilessly all the little weak places of mere indulgence, the implications of illogical assent, he left to saints and reformers more passionate for their humanity. But his own imagined women he set in their lonely circles among peaks and strange airs of accomplished sacrifice. He closed them round with phallic rocks and strange birth-waters, jealously recessed in legend, Anne rather than Mary, Leda rather than Helen, the virgin-mother at the heart of things, watched by angels, in direct contact only with God, the pure giver of life. Yet even then there is a certain *arrière-pensée* in the vision, as if the bones of mariners might lie here also, somewhere beyond the enchanted circle, bones of mariners who had

The Personality of Leonardo

not the wisdom of Ulysses or Leonardo, and so could not with impunity share the cup of Circe. But the initiate spirit, by communion with that arrested look, that stilled gesture, that Eleusinian smile, partakes the intangible substance of ecstatic life.

It is his instinct to minimize the sex-appeal, however, that tends always to make the feminine beauty disappear in the youth's. This is most evident in his drawing, especially in his later drawing. We know from his definite statement that he thought the will of the painter should try to defeat his narcissism, so he is much more spontaneous in his drawing. There the figures of women and girls, jealously closed on themselves, leaf on unfolded leaf, become confused with the virginal youths. Is Narcissus girl or boy ? Is that heavy head, oppressed with the covering wings of a strange vision, the head of the Virgin or of Saint John the Beloved ? Does this straight-gazing look belong to Hippolytus or Artemis ? As the years pass in Milan, the figures become more mignon-like, more spoilt in their air, more lustrous in their splendid curls and dilating eyes, more like the gold-fleeced Gilderoy of the Scots ballad. The rarely-armoured creatures drawn from the Milanese pageants look like young Amazons. Says Taine : " Pareil aux androgynes de l'époque imperiale . . . confondant et multipliant, par singulier mélange, la beauté des deux sexes, il se perd dans les réveries et dans les recherches des âges de décadence et d'immoralité." Which is perhaps too emphatic, though one or two of the heads that suddenly come through the anatomical notes at Windsor do have a kind of sensual and a nearly soulless insolence that makes them almost Græco-Roman. One of them looks like a Commodus scenting the arena. And his final arrogant determination to make the best of both sexes in the *Saint John* is probably an æsthetic failure. He is expressing that interplay of the masculine and feminine principles which modern psychology recognizes in every character of any perplexity ; but he does not quite succeed in his mystical intention. The disciple of Nature should hardly have tried to bridge what she has for ever sundered for the ends of her " fruitful feud."

XX

It is in the eyes, clear in iris, dark in pupil, deeply set under heavy lids, that Leonardo refuges the desire of the soul. The broad, smooth lids he touches with his own far-gathered euphrasy. His own eyes, bitterly burning, still beautiful, gaze indomitable from the ravaged mask of his age. Even in his most horrible grotesques, the eyes alone remain uncaricatured, they look out from their cruelly swollen or twisted features with the wrath of lions or the hurtful pathos of monkeys. He never tires of exalting the lordship of the eyes.

Leonardo the Florentine

His own, one feels, took from the beautiful all the consummation he desired.

> " And pictures in our eyes to get
> Was all our propagation."

As an artist he begot fair images on his cool æsthetic love, an ethereal and sinless propagation, as the soft-flaming delight in beauty set fire to the consenting air.

The type of ideal beauty for which Leonardo tried was less the god than the angel. For all their passion for Greece, the people of the Renaissance had known a Syrian religion, and their Greek manuscripts came by way of Constantinople. In picture and sculpture they wrought the genius of their reverie in these ambiguous winged figures that meant both synthesis of East and West and some heavenly reconciliation of sex. Angels out of Chaldæa, angels out of Babylon, with terrible spined wings and fiery hearts, cherubim guarding the mercy-seat, watching through all changing patterns the eternal Tree of Life ! They had looked on the daughters of Hellas and found them fair ; and in the form of soft-pinioned Thanatos had led them tenderly by the hand round the great pillar-drums of Ephesus. They had altered into genii of Love and Death, thrysus-bearers and torchbearers. The lukewarm Council of Laodicæa feared those fiery eyes and terrible wings before they came with the roses to the tombs of the martyrs, and the Christian virgins covered their bright hair " because of the angels " ; but the tender Council of Nicæa accepted them, and wafted them (on " those Nicæan barks of yore," perhaps), about the time that the saints came riding on white horses out of Egypt. During the Middle Ages they settled like a flight of doves on the tombs and cathedrals, intent and exquisite in ivory or stone, bearing large lilies of annunciation or dancing over the Epiphany. Then they remembered they were sons of the morning, kin to dæmon and beast and the gods of Greece all together. The Renaissance was beset by angels, messengers of burning beauty. All Leonardo's people are of angelic strain ; and, it must be admitted, some of them look as if they have been entreated in Sodom though they did escape. He drew them : he loved their great wings, the flowery conspiracies of their reverie, their unearthly substance.

But Leonardo's attitude to any phase of life is so iridescent that it is impossible to catch even its colour. The famous smile which illuminates all his mysterious faces was the perfect image of his mood when he considered the strangeness of love. Shadows of it had been seen before, on the down-dropt heads of Greek genii, Eros, Narcissus, Adonis, sweetly, unconsciously, enchanted with delight at their own beauty ; on mediæval

The Personality of Leonardo

angels and precious virgins committed to a divine mystery, refined, sarrasine, ravishing, a little rigid and archaic from the cloisters of Byzantine ivory in which they were first carven ; and on the rather insolent and mocking youths of Donatello and Verrocchio. Leonardo added to it the profound irony with which he contemplated all things, human and divine. If the smiling of the East, like that of Kwannon, seems sisterly, it is merely that, East or West, all the gods seem to smile like that.

xxi

When the presence of genius does not create anarchy in the personality that finds the dread burden insupportable, it complicates and rarefies the power of love even as it sublimates all other powers. The strangeness of Leonardo's emotional life is as an aurora through his brain. He kept his beautiful basilian way, with an absent tenderness in his eyes for all the flowerlike ; and, if his great example was dangerous for the weaker brother, then, emphatically, Leonardo did not care what happened to the weaker brother. The ban they had put on him in his youth possibly turned to a provocation and an imaginative danger in his veins. "This law is not for thee but for another," he seems to say. One is certain that he felt, like the Valentinians of old, that " it is impossible for the spiritual to become corrupted whatever their actions." So believing, living as one concentrated on his spiritual and intellectual affairs, did he ever—like other magnificent sleepwalkers whose hearts are engrossed with dreams that none can share while their indifferent and abstracted bodies move through the coloured crowds, mechanically making their courteous gestures—wake suddenly to find mud or blood upon his hands? There is no record. As he says, people spread " the usual scandals." There are knots and anomalies of spiritual trouble in Leonardo's art and even in his science. He has some kind of imaginative desire too mysterious to express itself in the material world, and its searching parables have a touch of the wild and the monstrous, loves of Zeus and Hades, shadows of wings and horses, the coming of fire and wave in the ecstatic rapes of gods. He seems to keep intact the physical chastity of beauty : we are disquieted by the vanishing enigmas he writes in the world of souls. And at times we feel that one so impassioned in experience as Leonardo probably tried his dangerous experiments in living moments before he resigned his mystic dream of consummation to the plane of heavenly patterns.

Still — why should his great genius not have its anomalies like another ? In maturity, at least, he refrained from greatly disquieting lesser existences with them, as few Renaissance folk refrained. His heart might have its sadisms ; but there is no record of cruel acts in his life—he seems careful to avoid enmities. His twofold desire might constellate strange emerald stars upon the darkness ; it never sank to simple earthly lust. He became an ascetic who avoided passion as a dethronement of reason. His fantasy of virgins and angels and birds sufficed a mind disposed to fastidious chastity and a body inured to temperance by feats of grace and strength and by exacting labours. Genius of the highest kind controls even its earthly life to a pattern of beauty : it is not disorderly. It is the secondary group of artists, those of weak and supersensitive bodies and purely lyric temper, whose characters split under the dæmonic force, and who, conscripts of the fiery principle, go, crazed and wandering lights, through their black morasses with trails of broken song or quivering colour. These are the Villons, the Marlowes, the Verlaines. Plato, Sophocles, Leonardo, Shakespeare, as persons and as artists, preserve a suave and regal attitude.

xxii

It is written that Santa Teresa wept once a week for somebody " because he could not love." If we shrink sometimes from the great Leonardo it is not because he loved too much, but because he loved too little. It is not merely that his divine mind is untouched by what is, after all, essential to the understanding of human experience. If, as beauty's monk, he loved virginity, it was with a certain cold distrust of the imaginative senses that often deflowers in some disdainful way the beautiful creatures he draws. After the first Florentine period, at least, his pencil hardly creates such girls as wove in clear cloisters the holy veil of Athena, and went up in fluted raiment to her proud festival. It becomes, in the final years, hardly austere enough even for their riding brethren. Perfect Greek forms of youth, unravished and unconsummated, pure and regretful as a bridal-vessel of Callirrhoë over a maiden grave, you rarely find in all Leonardo's later pageant. His types become too languorous. Even these he did not love sufficiently : his ruthless intellect tampers with their integrity, betraying them to dubiety by its hesitations as to what it will wring from them, of sweet or soft, of cruel or tender.

It is not merely that he did not, like the great Dante, know the love that makes earth and heaven and hell over again in the insuperable soft-breathing flame of its great catastrophe, and turns the senses to roses and wounds of ecstasy, the heart to a crying violin and the brain to a silver star, though such experience, however brief may seem its duration in time, is an initiation in the mystery of life necessary to those who seek to interpret it completely. He does not enter into the love of humanity

The Personality of Leonardo

at all : he is not one with his kind, despite his gracious ways as of a condescending sovereign. It is true that it is a terrible thing to build a castle on the quicksands of human affection, and that there is no lonelier creature than a lover lost in the dark forest of another's heart. But these tragic subversions and intimate solitudes are part of the marvellous mortal lot. The isolation of Leonardo cuts him out of the continuity of human existence. And this injures even the pride of his intellect. There are confusions and irrelevances and " faults " and sudden cessations in his continuity of thought which betray something abnormal in the thinker. Sometimes in this consummate mind there is an inexplicable infantilism, as if it had not arrived at maturity by all the necessary experiences.

xxiii

Still, the norm is but a figment of man's reason, a law set up as he desperately and blindly chooses among his fantastic motives those that may best comfort and preserve him, a law to which no individual really conforms. There are those whose service to humanity consists in refusing the norms of its safety and disconcerting its fundamental attitudes. They are born athirst for pure truth or pure beauty ; and Leonardo has the double ruthlessness of both these abstract desires.

As an artist he is, in a great sense, a sheer æsthete. There are those who are doomed to hunger and thirst after pure beauty. It is not love they desire, for the sense of beauty may become an angel-damascened sword to pierce love's heart to death. They are discontented with the warm hearths of their friends, and have no appetite for the daily bread of human affection. Their caresses are distrait, and they do not hear the silver flute of Hesper that brings all lovers home. Through processes of magic and enchantment they find the moment of æsthetic ecstasy which is for them the sole justification and absolution of life. Leonardo knows what song the sirens sang. His art is incantation and evocation, pure sorcery and sea-magic of emerald and amethyst. He takes us beyond good and evil, love and hate. Leonardo is a Platonist in his art, a believer in absolutes. This is his dream of absolute beauty, beauty of the double principle, in which, by the lovely unconscious Manichæan heresy of his later life, good and evil, light and dark, find their only reconciliation. In the æsthetic ecstasy of white flame lovers forget their stigmata, traitors their shame, warriors their rage, gods their cross, and human souls their mortality.

For absolute Beauty, religions, philosophies, and loves may be great accomplices, but they are not necessary to her. There is ultimate irony under her dreaming eyes, and when her long hands uplift the chalice the wine may be the blood of Dionysos or Christ. The religions of the Far East deny her with enmity ; but she alters their renunciations into sweet litanies and builds dreamlike temples over the naked and mortified bodies of their saints and prophets.

Leonardo, with his double-flowered heart and double-starred brain, reveals her dangerous and divine. She sits by the mysterious unfurrowed seas, she who set tall Troy alight. In her dream she builds great cities, and, when she is tired of their ways, she throws Greek fire on them and destroys them. She is for the strong, who can safely drink her circean cup because they have driven the animal from their souls. Let others admire and fear, and put off their shoes and tread delicately, for the ground though heathen is holy. He exalts the divine nostalgia for faëry isles that ravishes away the spirit now and then from all its human securities, that makes a man tire of the sight of prudent Penelope, and a woman dream of a rarer lover in the arms of the best-loved husband.

Did that last treatise on the soul and its ways contain the great Arabian word of finality that illuminated all that was written before with a gnostic brilliance ? Possibly it would have revealed not only his philosophy, but himself, for none can write of the soul without betraying some personal secret of bliss or bane.

xxiv

It is true that Leonardo had his effect wherever he went. This iridescent mind shed its blues and greens on the people who loved him, his noble gestures created a fashion, his manners set a criterion, and his imaginative reverie was a contagion. Yet he is not so closely correlated with his time and place as lesser men. The singularity in his mood isolated him ; and at heart he was anti-social. Individualist and aristocrat to the last degree, he refines and heightens his personality, even while he limits it, by a secret estrangement from his kind.

" So that prosperity of body may not ruin prosperity of mind," wrote Leonardo, " the painter must live solitary. Alone you are all yourself ; with a companion you are half yourself. And so you squander yourself according to the indiscretion of your company."

Leonardo did not " live solitary." But he never partook his soul. Of all withheld people the loneliest are those who walk through crowds scattering a largess of courtesy, and who conceal by dazzling. Secrecy is a habit of his mind. His unusual Eastern handwriting from right to left shows at least the instinct to conceal his studies from the vulgar. If he thought at times of arranging more of his notes for publication he made no real effort towards lucidity ; and did not train even Francesco

The Personality of Leonardo

to use them otherwise than as relics.   He is of those who think wisdom
and knowledge should be guarded as privileged doctrines by the elect ;
and in this attitude as in others is kin to the mysterious Pythagoras.
" The truth of things is a supreme food for fine intelligences, but not for
vagabond humours," he declares.   In this way, perhaps, he kept flawless
the crystal of his intellectual sincerity : but so there crept into his vision
the touch of the sinister and the chimerical that quivers like burning air
in the self-doubting mind of the solitary who, by refusing to touch the
existence of another, begins to disbelieve his own.   When Leonardo is
most at the service of his bright peers, when he is young in Florence, he
devises the crowded canvas of the *Adoration* containing sixty figures of
men and seventeen of beasts, in which he shares his great personality
among many types, and conveys with easy magnificence of design a rare
community of emotion—though even there the Black Knight enters a
sceptical and regal refusal.   But he breaks away from the eager press
of young Florentine faces.   It is hardly, it is with vigils of effort and
conquests of reluctance, that he brings the twelve passion-distracted
figures into unison and pattern with the god undistracted in *The Last
Supper*, for his deep inclination is to set one lonely figure in its inviolate
world of rock and water, an inclination hardly satisfied till his softening
finger-tips drew the strange Saint John through the wet paint with the
eyes and lips of the Herodiad.   *The Battle of Anghiari* wearies him, once
he has relieved his mind of its pent violence.   Neither in its beauty nor
in its rage does he love a communal ecstasy.   He deliberately forfeits
the largeness of his imaginative design, except in the great *Saint Anne*,
where the lonely figure has her sisterly, angelical, and childlike attributes
and echoes.   In the end it is as if part of Leonardo's art had broken free
of the pattern of humanity and formed an isolated rose-whorl of emerald
and azure fire in the darkness, still so " strangely beautiful " that we
almost try to alter the pattern to contain it, which excitement of ours is
its homage.

XXV

This loneliness of mind gives a strange impression even to the manuscript pages most vivid with sketches and plans of buildings, machines,
canals, and other matters meaningless if they are not for human needs.
Leonardo seems always intent on the mere problem to be solved by his
intent isolated mind.   Nobody, one feels, will worship in those many-
domed churches made for an intellectual's whim and not for a god's
desire.   People and nobles alike would refuse his cities like hygienic
Thebaïds.   Nobody sins in his lupanars.   They are spirits that sit on his
fiery chariots of war : the naked creatures in his arsenals and elsewhere

on his mighty levers are not the masters but the slaves of his machine. His arrogant spined wings are spread for some lone Icarus.

But it is in Leonardo's science that his isolation tells most. Both in Florence and Milan he was in lively contact with groups of students, insatiably stripping their minds and borrowing books. But the work of his laboratory seems lonely work ; and he does not appear to have communicated any of his researches. Only with della Torre did he have some definite kind of collaboration for a brief period, meditating with him a work on anatomy. Circumstantial reasons helped to conceal his manuscripts no doubt ; but his natural inclination readily accepted them. Sometimes words are interpolated by unknown hands. Evidently the spoilt bright children with the curled heads might take a liberty with the papers they were safe not to understand. But he was an Archimedes who never said " Eureka ! " and did not want to say it, whatever he may have discovered. Accomplished flight, even, was to be presented like a sudden miracle to a stricken world. Therefore, although in the dazzle of his manifold activity he seems to rule the elements, at times he is but a Sisyphus with his rock of earth, an Ixion with his great cogged wheels, a Phaethon with his flaming sun, and with his wings that aforesaid lone Icarus. Conclusions triumphal evade him. He gazes down far untrodden vistas with a ringing of reins, then turns aside and gallops away. He is always " going elsewhither," as he is described.

When the Renaissance passion dies out of its art, the Renaissance curiosity remains and carries its pride far into the world of scientific discovery. But Vesalius, Galileo, Kepler, and in their different ways Bruno and Campanella, Bacon, Descartes and Newton, seem to be unaffected by Leonardo, and would have come to their diverse ends if he had never lived. For all the painful investigation of Monsieur Duhem, he does not seem to enter inextricably into the tradition of scientific truth. Because of his isolation he remains the most brilliant and versatile of all amateurs, lost in fascinating experiments, making wonderful guesses, handling all problems with originality and dexterity, stopping short of great conclusions, inventing many things that have been reinvented since. It is all an amazing spectacle, an unparalleled play of mind, a triumph of the subtle and sceptical part of his supreme intelligence, an incitement and a delight. Without the manuscripts we would hardly have suspected the radiating colourless energy that maintained this life of laborious research parallel with the mystical and absorbed existence of the great artist, so different is the psychology revealed. Yet it is complementary with the pictures, not contradictory ; and it is wrong to ignore the testimony of Leonardo's art and to prefer the notebooks, for art strikes deeper roots than scientific research in the human personality.

The Personality of Leonardo

If it be admitted that the sadhu, tranced motionless under his holy tree, or the nun, lost in vicarious agony before her lamp of perpetual adoration, may affect by supersubtle vibrations the lives beyond their solitudes, if beating hearts and burning brains can communicate to others their intense images without the intervention of language, if no gesture is spilt on waste air but enters into and alters the charged waves of the atmosphere that ripple against mortal nerves, then the concentrated mind of Leonardo, by its patient electric contemplation and impassioned search helped to predispose the minds of Vesalius, Galileo, Kepler, Descartes, Watts. This is a spiritual theory that seems to materialize daily. Still, when every admission is made, Leonardo's value as a scientist was sterilized by his isolation.

No disciple quickened him with questions at doubtful moments, or with blind enthusiasm urged his reluctant vision into the final danger of a complete hypothesis, eager to plant an exultant flag on the peak of an astonishing discovery. So also in art he had no peer and companion in the world of wonder to send the strong pulsations of humanity through that imaginative twilight of emotion.

xxvi

The isolation of Leonardo was but the condition of his pride. Pride has been the keynote of Italian genius, of Lucretius, Dante, Lorenzo de' Medici, Leonardo, Michelangelo, Leopardi, Alfieri, Carducci, d'Annunzio. Pride was the great virtue of the Italian Renaissance :

" Let the devil
Be sometimes honoured for his burning throne "—

and pride ride out on his rearing destrier from the low company of the Seven Deadly Sins. For it is this kingly pagan virtue, not blessed, I know, in Galilee, that alone defeats overwhelming odds, and carries you into impossible achievement. The saints have it : they find some christened name for it.

For pride in its essence means fastidious refusal of what stains and hampers and degrades the essential spirit. It always serves a flamelike ideal, and consistently governs the soul by some fair and fruitless quixotry. Recovered pride in the beauty and power of humanity gave the Renaissance its great way, and stamped with magnificence the very tyrants who wreaked their violent wills evilly in their amazement, and bought a golden shrift with an enamelled *baiser-de-paix* that delights the eyes of the hungry generations. But the artists for once were proudest of all, for never were artists so convinced that they wrought for immortality. It is a conviction absolutely necessary to supreme style.

503

Leonardo the Florentine

Conscious of his sovereign powers, Leonardo moves the haughtiest of them all—haughtier than the superb Mantegna, than the indignant Michelangelo, than the knightly luting Giorgione, than the princely Raphael of Rome. He has the insolence of the gods, disguised in courtesy ; he has also the scorn of the heresiarch, who denies the gods. What does he find in Dante, the great mediævalist, besides the ingenuity of scholasticism, which quite appealed to his subtle mind ? The indomitable pride that insensibly passes over to greet Farinata in his burning tomb, and sympathizes with the unbroken spirit that makes the fig at God.

But there is no evil greed in Leonardo : he has no desire to destroy by possessing : his æsthetic scruples keep him cleaner than all the Tables of the Law. He has always in his mind that image of the white ermine who will die of a stain : indeed, his liking for this fair fabulous thing betrays the quivering sensibility which flickers behind all his disdains. The quiet narcissism of his soul fed upon a pure and noble figure. He speaks once with envy and approval of the Eastern kings that showed themselves only when hidden by masks and veils—Leonardo at his haughtiest, refusing to reveal, much less exploit, his personality. He is scornful of gold, " that monstrous element." In any general declaration of his might, he reveals the startling composure of a divinity, as in the famous letter to the Duke ; but requests concerning his just needs are veiled with extreme hesitation and shyness, the nervous reluctance to " teach a tongue unused to plead " even to state his case. He cannot cry out like a humanist, or even like an outraged artist, like Michelangelo. He uses courtly phrases : he writes as one sovereign to another. There is something beautifully withheld in his attitude. From fiery pontiffs withdrawing, to great princes neither suppliant nor reproachful, he keeps his eagle way.

And he is too proud to quarrel. If one insults you, your patience must be redoubled. Leonardo's haughty forbearance moves him to express a certain fine stoicism at times, the nearest he gets to any ethical doctrine.

But his pride is not shadowless, and the shadow of pride is cruelty. You feel that here is a personality anti-social in its instincts, yet making imperious assumptions, and kinglike exactions from humanity, silently compelling tribute by its very graces. He exercised a kind of suave tyranny, against which Michelangelo once broke in blind and savage resentment, and knew not why he did it.

All the despots are asleep in Leonardo—their sweetness, their cruelty, their magnificence, their impossible desires. Like Alexander or Caligula he would invest his birth with miracle and myth, and hawks descend

The Personality of Leonardo

from the sky to hood his head with their wings. He conquers his realms of the spirit like a condottiere, like Orion the heavenly hunter. He shatters the spheres and establishes bright tyrannies in the kingdom of knowledge. Worse than the despots, he invites no man to his lonely and secret banquet—or only some long-curled dreamy children, to look like amaranths and sound like flutes, with no thirst for his forbidden cup.

A natural aristocrat, he is also an aristocrat by conviction, and his contempt for humanity as a whole, though he disciplines and represses it, betrays itself strangely. It is by an extension of aristocratic pride, perhaps, that we find him amusing himself with the peasants, disdainfully intoxicating them with wine and wild mirth that he may draw their features caricatured out of probability by a gross hysteria. He is the grand seigneur coldly carving poor humanity into " L'homme qui rit " for his curiosity and entertainment. For he has the added mercilessness of all those who live in the first instance by their eyes. The glances of the draughtsman and painter have a ruthless despoiling power. They strip, they search, they accuse and violate, they indifferently tear out the heart from all appearances. And, in Leonardo's case, with the facile grace of a lovely relenting look, they compel their own absolution. All his fierce and delicate senses, trained by his imagination into fiery points of apprehension, could deflower with a flash, and like a priest give consummation with a touch.

This is the indifferent lightning-play of the intellectual and the æsthete, the mood also of the superman whose great desire is for wings to make him a god, the implied cruelty of disdain. But in the manuscripts we glimpse occasionally a darker sadism, a cold pleasure in cruelty, something organically sinister. It is twisted with the Orientalism that veils with purple the Greek within him, and with the macabre love of the horrible because it is horrible. But in all comprehensive, puissant, and complicated natures there are odd atavisms that have their power in shaping and colouring the whole curiously convoluted mind. The richer the character the more it covers the history of the race, and remembers even from the days before morality. There must be anomalies, imperfect resolutions, in such a gorgeous clot of psychic matter. But Leonardo is supercivilized : he is the master of his atavisms. In a manner now regarded as psychologically sound he releases them by expression ; though he never lets them through to his finished work, except when they can be allies to art, as in his battle-piece.

There are moments when one feels that the marvellous Leonardo, with his enchanter's renown, reminds one of the legendary Merlin who was the son of a virgin and a devil—he seems so passionless, cold, and sinister. Why did he watch executions and tortures, why did he in his radiant youth so precisely draw that hanged man ? Even an artist in his passion to record human expression will stop short this side the horror that only hangmen can bear, unless his name be Leonardo. This is spiritual vivisection, and, for all Leonardo's love of animals, I do not think that he who could put scientific poison in the young peach-tree would have shrunk from the material form, if it had been permitted. Many pages of the manuscripts reveal him in the state of fantasy. His dreams, he says, are of falling flames, bright colours in the darkness, talking beasts, falling from heights, rushing torrents. The waking dreams he puts on record are all of human terror and destruction. Disdaining words, he rarely troubles to be eloquent. But when he describes battle, deluge, annihilation, he passed easily into a sombre yet exultant music. When he gives an account of the " pazzia bestialissima " he does it with zest. When he loses himself in a reverie of that flood he has lucidly argued out of the history of the earth, he is one with the wind and water that sweeps into nothingness the groups of fierce or tender, heroic or wretched—all desperate—people. He imagines an entire book on inundation and earthquake and abysmal catastrophe ; and he would have written it well, with the defunctive music of eclipse. But in this he is at one with Nature : like her he thinks " destructive thoughts." The volutes of sea-storms, sand-storms, and wind-storms are the spirals of the great Dragon he delighted to draw in mighty conflicts—the dragon of darkness, of rushing water, of fury, that everywhere patterns the veil of things. After all, it is his version of the Dance of Siva. It is idle to pretend that Nature is benevolent, or to take comfort from a " pathetic fallacy." Blake says the angels, contemplating that sacred mystery of destruction let loose in the gleaming tiger, flung

> " down their burning spears
> And watered heaven with their tears."

So did not Leonardo. Blake also held that a tear was " an intellectual thing." Whereas Leonardo said, " Tears come from the heart, not the brain," intending, I think, to condemn.

xxvii

Though Leonardo may deprecate war in theory, he was very ready to serve it. And if he drew weapons of death, there mingled with his many motives the fact that he really liked to draw destructive objects. His poignant pencil is relishing over flying darts and serpentine slings, halberds like implacable fleur-de-lis, slim driving lances, devilish blades and hungry sickles, balls of flaming horror. With what an evil vivacity

The Personality of Leonardo

the slings and great catapults writhe and rush to their work. With what zest rush the light diabolic scorpionlike chariots to their deadly reaping. He troubles even to choose incisive piercing things from the battlefields of antiquity. In the Codex Atlanticus there are some amazingly beautiful studies of pierced balls, filled with poisonous vapours, rising from their mortars with goblin delight, radiating and seeding their malice in decorative designs like Aubrey Beardsley's strange sporing flowers. In his parterre of sword-lilies, his wood of blossoming lances, the spirit of Leonardo walks delicately in its fiercer moments, and even there gathers a springlike beauty from that agonizing blackthorn. Great bombards he makes, womanishly ornamented ; and thinks of new ways of destruction—tanks, poison-gas, breech-loading guns. Oddly enough, he has a scruple of conscience over the idea of a submarine, and somewhat piously observes that he will not explain all this notion in case men would fain do murder in the depths of the sea. He will be their auxiliary in slaughter on earth, or air, but not in the water. It is as if Leonardo were under a sacred pact with this pure element which, in his dreams, his art, and his daily labour, meant at once soothing notions, cooling lullaby, glimmering beauty, and work that was good, puissant, and achievable.

That miraculous draughtsmanship of his can ransom most things to the kingdom of beauty. Almost it redeems the grotesques. The theory that these are all due to Leonardo's strenuous exercises in human expression does not seem adequate. True, he won to his subtlety of lips and eyes by steadily practising and memorizing all the tricks of human features. True, all the grotesques that are ascribed to him are not genuine ; yet there are too many undoubtedly his. Also it is possible that he sometimes deliberately corrected by these drastic exercises a certain personal taste for almost pretty types that weakened him in Milan. After all, the distortions are too fiendish. The fineness of the drawing heightens the savagery of this notation of ugliness : there are ghastly little tricks of adornment in some that look like wicked and ribald jokes. This is no horrified comment on a state of things that reduces humanity to *cagots*, like the grotesques of Callot or Goya. It is no witty satire on human absurdity or a wildly humorous mode of teasing, like the work of those caricaturists who appeal to the intelligence of the race which they satirize and whose weaknesses they share. No ! It is the cynical attack of an anti-social spirit upon a despicable alien kind. What there is of emotional in these pages is a mere exasperation of the nerves over the horrors which mortality is capable of weaving. Leonardo must endure this veil himself : there is some agony in his rage of cruelty, something of self-maceration, the rending of a wound, but more of hatred.

507

Leonardo the Florentine

He steeps his lion's paw in ink, and mauls the visage of man and woman. Leonardo, who glorifies the human body, here secretly blasphemes it. He reveals all that it is capable of in the way of grace and beauty, and then deforms it. Sometimes his cold fury is obscene, like Swift's. He makes man in the image of a god, and sets on him the mark of the beast.

There is a hateful plausibility about these terrible heads, marked with that loathsome stigmata. The monstrous warts and unholy pouches of that accursed flesh are exaggerations of the sad scars and dragged muscles of time's distortions. Malice, envy, idiocy are behind those eaten noses, those thrust lips, those sunken brows, those bulbs of flesh, these awful degradations of the mouth and chin, worse than the dim brute features of lemuroid and gibbon that have never yet known a soul. He draws senates of monstrosities, councils of crétins. Some are but slightly stamped with malice, like one group which looks like a company of shrewd old Florentines, just withering into base candours of avarice and folly. But generally he does bring out the animal in the human face. You seem to see the herd of Circe sometimes, in the penultimate moment of transformation. He is worst when he crowns some hideous head with a sardonic chaplet, or twists the hair of some hydrocephalic woman with a piggish underface in a little braid, and sets a flower at her deformed neck.

The world of Leonardo's drawings is in some ways comparable only with Shakespeare's world of drama. There might be some parallel between Leonardo's grotesques and the caricaturing scenes in Shakespeare, if anywhere they were lightened by the spirit of humour. But they are not. The dramatist who relates the soliloquy of the porter going to the gate, in *Macbeth*, is interested in his soul as well as in his hero's at the flaming climax of his fate. It is not only by human pity that great minds betray their sympathy with their kind. It is also by their humour, which is nothing if not another form of communion.

The Leonardo of the " facezie " and the " profezie " is painful. He writes down seriously jokes he has heard, and they are unspeakably bad. He is awkward over it. Like most Latins he is ironic and often witty. He is too stately, too detached for humour. He even learns up Poggio's *Facetiæ*. With baffled and embarrassed ways he caricatures the speech of the average man, though here his travesty is unintentional. No ! Few of his monstrous heads are redeemed by humour.

Still, the grotesques are probably a wise and deliberate release of his unconscious enmity towards a humanity with which he was not on wholly equal terms. He is only making a wry mouth at some of the detestable flavours in the cup of life. The cruelty of Leonardo is subjective. He would not willingly have made his grotesques public

508

The Personality of Leonardo

property, and doubtless relegated them among the notes of his workshop. How far the cruelty translated itself into his life remains unknown. Only in one drawing of another kind does he give such an odd shock of cynicism that for the moment one believes he was capable of anything, and, even after the notion of his harmonious personality is restored, the memory of it recurs uneasily, as if one feared to find a heinous crack in a beautiful vessel of Venice crystal. People possessed of his indefinable charm—spell, enchantment, wordless allure of personality—more than all others have this disconcerting trick of turning even on their lovers, at sudden terrifying moments, the mask of a smiling fiend, of revealing behind the webs of faëry glamour a heart in texture no softer than a heart-shaped faëry flint, impenetrable to tears or desperate hands. The touch of the unearthly which fascinates makes them also capable of the caprice of a bored or disgusted immortal.

Once, then, at least, he made a drawing which seems a kind of inhuman insult. In one of the cross-sections of his *Anatomy of Love* he gives, by a completely cynical trick which recalls nothing but the chill eroticism displayed by the dark Etruscans couched with odd smiles on their enigmatic tombs, a shock and a confusion. To come upon this drawing in Leonardo's great world of lovely shapes where, after all, the grotesques move in the shadows and the general impression is live and lovely as lightning, is like finding an obscene gold image, the horrible fantasy of some aged Tiberius, in the gardens of a lucid and smiling Temple. The touch that, by an indication of waving hair and sidelong eye, turns a scientific statement to a piece of wickedness is amazing and abnormal. There are chasms of derision held in the smooth suave lines : the thing grins and is cold. Gripped by Leonardo's matchless drawing, the theme offers a detached and nonchalant diabolism like a Felicien Rops.

You can stumble on strange obscenæ in every great genius : it seems part of its vastness. So you find phallic rites and symbols tolerated in the clear rituals of civilized religions. Why should one outraging trick of drawing so disproportionately shock in Leonardo that it seems suddenly to cancel the charter of his felicity ? It is so incongruous, of course, to find the great artist, the scrupulous savant, the ascetic of beauty wrapped in his silk and fur who refuses common appetites, play a prank like the Aretine's. But it is this very fastidiousness, pushed almost to mania, that explains it all the same. He draws his cross-section with a glee of disgust, and finishes it off with a chilly devilry to convey his inhuman loathing. And we seem to see an archangel make an indecent gesture with his dedicated hands.

You say he was tender to the beasts. He had that almost excessive comprehension and consideration for them which you find in the misanthropic who, like him, consider with a pleasurable zest hecatombs of the human race, but shiver at the death of a rabbit. All the outlaws and denunciants of their kind extol the pathos and devotion of the inarticulate creation. And the gods understand beasts better than men, for they wear their shapes, and have been hunted as well as hunter. Leonardo regards them with a touch of this pagan divinity ; he sits alone among their images sometimes, like Orpheus among his charmed audience. There is a shadow of totemism in his brain : he sees himself in the lion, the phœnix, the steed, the unicorn, the swan, the eagle, the hawk—anything that is splendid, anything especially that has wings. He draws near to the beasts in fables, and hears them talk : he pursues them into fantasy in old bestiaries ; and finds affinities with the salamander, the basilisk, the dragon. His pencil is exceedingly amused by the twining surprises of the cat : he is deeply moved by the suppliant beasts in bitter winter : he breaks open the cages and sets the captives free : the lithe and lovely motions of animals invade his house : he cannot bear that life should feed upon their death. When he caricatures lions and horses, he does not destroy in them a nobility of which he leaves his human distortions no vestige. And sometimes he is so playful that these become as amusing as the kindlier mediæval grotesques. His elephant-headed rider playing on his trunk is cousinly with the ass who uses the vielle on Chartres Cathedral ; and his crumple-faced lobster is like a teasing smile.

xxviii

But it is impossible to put any case against Leonardo without repentance and misgiving. In the final effect all things turn to grace, and one is silenced. All things turn to grace, even as his destructive powers of wind and wave and battle break in foam of flowers. After all, these lonely spirits, these apostles in the wilderness like his own Saint, are not to be considered in their attitude towards other mortals. Their relation to humanity seems accidental : it is their direct relation to the forces of art and nature that matters. Their great preoccupation is merely to set a lamp and blaze a track. They increase the sense of the splendour and spaciousness of life by their mere existence, and their hands throw open wide casements on Eternity. Theirs is the vindication of the spiritual aristocrat. If they suffer from loss of the warm human contagion, since they take not their new fire from the communal spring-altar, with inspiriting defiance they strike from a virgin flint and ethereal tinder a flame of some colour never known before.

And Leonardo's great sense of fitness, his desire for harmony in his life as well as in art and science, gave him kind and courteous ways.

The Personality of Leonardo

There is no bloodstain or sensual violence, no degradation of avarice or sloth or greed, to drag down and rend the fine texture of his existence.

If he was like a planetary stranger hung low in the stainless, strange ether that echoed but coldly and clearly the troubles of the heavier air, the musing sweetness of his eyes and the penetrating cadence of his voice came like solace to the heavy-hearted, for beauty, even when distrait, can heal when love halts too mute with sympathy. He had that hypnotic power which is an effluence and by-product of some permutation of personal qualities not yet defined ; it soothes and enchants and heals by dissolving away the poison of pain in the trance and truce of its charm. It affects the sensitive mood like music. He wove a web of beguiling words and cadences and hieratic gestures ; and in all fair sensitive places his listeners consented to the spell. And of his great tenderness for lovely remote creatures, like children and flowers and delicate young people, there is no possible doubt. When he was sweet, one feels, looking at his happier drawings, it was with a rare and piercing sweetness, like a woodland spring set with roundels, with crowns, and with bouquets of great primroses, sweet as jasmine in winter, or a bird on a flowering apple-tree, or a branch of double-cherry against a dead-gold sky, or an almond-tree among April snowflakes, or a fountain playing alone in a rose-red cup in a sunken secret garden, or a white, sacred, and sumptuous falcon on a decorated perch in a silken Sung painting.

xxix

There is a certain unconscious pathos in Leonardo, nevertheless, as he moves in his great, rather vague amiability through the scenes of his life, or as he stirs restively and bitterly sometimes in his manuscripts. He appears as if somewhat lost and puzzled in earthly affairs, and ever so courteously at odds. "What is your will ? " he seems to say. " I do not wish to offend your customs." But he is much aware of envy and ingratitude. The intricate allegories he draws for Lodovico's justification are done with such an amazing beauty of lightly burning line that they look like mysterious scenes from a necromantic story of conjurers, fabulous beasts, dæmons, benignant spirits, tripods, flashing mirrors, shining waters and blazing lights, and shambling deaths. He has made the theme of calumny his own, and writes "Intollerabile " upon it. Like scenes of wicked magic, the malignant mystery of human motive affects him. Sometimes this wonder deepens into a lucid sorrow, the melancholy of a divine being taken in a snare of mortal treachery he cannot condemn since he does not comprehend it, the sad reverie of the lord of his *Last Supper*.

Leonardo the Florentine

When dealing directly with human life as a whole, he is never at ease. As we have seen, when he tries to be humorous, he writes down the jokes of the average man, and looks at them pensively, wondering why they seem no longer funny. The " facezie " and conundrums are tiresome, though sometimes there is a flash of wit ; and the " profezie " are full of *bêtises*. The finest silken swathel of sensibility has a flaw, and some rude threads are interwoven in Leonardo's written humour : it is all part of his bewilderment. Sometimes, however, a flash as of a stinging knife hints what Leonardo could do when he dared to be himself in conversation, and did not need to consider his audience. His generalizations are frequently platitudes. They seem part of his camouflage and rarely express his true temper. But written words are always suspect by Leonardo. He speaks most sincerely and most sympathetically when he is analysing the pitiful mortal tabernacle that the human soul wears and breaks and spoils before leaving it to the worms, whose cells have been so much used by the smouldering flames of suffering or delight that it has secreted a perishable pathos and tragedy of its own which the reluctant spirit must relinquish as alms for oblivion.

Chapter ii

The Expression of Leonardo

i

LEONARDO tried to live between his Ivory and his faceted Crystal Towers : he was aware of hurtling in the dim air and the strange salt smell of blood. The sombre and passionate pride of melancholy which dwells through all the greatest art, and sounds mightily in Italian imagination, through Lucretius, Virgil, Catullus, Dante, Michelangelo, Leopardi, Alfieri, turned in Leonardo's veins to a great indifferentism. Mortal affairs were small to him who lived beyond historic time ; to him who in his Protean vision saw men change into beasts and beasts into men, it mattered little who reigned in Florence or Milan. What did matter was the shattering of these fair cities as forms and arks of beauty whereby his spirit was content to rest and labour.

" The painter requires such knowledge of mathematics as belongs to painting, and severance from companions who are not in sympathy with his studies, and his brain should have the power of adapting itself to the tenor of the objects which present themselves before it, and *he should be freed from all other cares*." So Leonardo remarked with a sigh. In his land of warring Italians, Spanish, French, and Germans, in his personal fortune attendant on luckless Sforza, shifting Medici, destined Borgia, violent d'Este, fluctuant Francis, it was not easy for the artist to be freed from cares. Still, he probably fared better than if he were living now. He did not force his genius in any way for his princely patrons. His manners and amusing conversation were at their service : his art obeyed their pleasure when it was also his own. Through the dissolving scenes of his life he remains unalterably himself. " He who is fixed to a star does not change his mind," observes Leonardo ; and we assent, murmuring, " As though the emerald should say, ' Whatever happens I must be emerald.' " Starry and implacable, he kept his patient way.

ii

Of Leonardo's great double expression in art and science, I cannot here begin much farther analysis. For the suggestions of his art are endless and a true examination would require a volume in itself. I have

Leonardo the Florentine

tried to confine myself to the study of his personality in his environment, and of his arts and sciences only as the illuminants of his elusive character.

As an artist, Leonardo desires by flattering the senses with an illusion of reality to achieve a psychical effect. He " paints the soul," by his own admission, but in images so actual that they seem apprehensible by the cheated eyes and longing hands. Both in art and science, Leonardo first states firmly his attitude towards the soul, and then talks like the most convinced realist. He sounds like a materialist till you remember that matter, for him, is an expression of spirit. He is intricately and almost trivially concerned with processes ; but even miracles must have processes of some kind, however instantaneous. The end of his pictures, with all their mastery of design and great composition, was to create a state of emotion, and that emotion was the mere æsthetic ecstasy, the lyrical response by which the gazer enters into beauty by communion, and quivers with new life.

They convey the great perturbation of beauty's attack. For while there is a beauty that takes you softly like sleep, Leonardo's sweeps you like a wave to the Enchanted Isles, where you find the eidolon of his soul's lonely and nonpareil cult, the faëry Magic that sings you from your mortality, the siren spirit at the edge of the world that lures the mad and star-stricken dreamers whose beautiful disaster makes undesirable all earthly fulfilments. It is the central quality of his personality that enters into his art of painting. It is glamour, it is divinity, it is the pure æsthetic principle which is not ethical nor representative nor decorative nor emotional nor intellectual, though it may be confused with elements so described. It is the timeless intangible call that imposes a spell, and does so loosen the coils of mortality that some astonished souls, a moment anchorless in eternity, naked to sheer enchantment, lost in the innumerable foam-asphodel, are afraid, and call it dangerous.

Yet, with this rare fantasy in his mind, with what amazing patience Leonardo could attend on processes his notebooks do reveal. When genius takes the laborious method it is more concentrated than industrious talent ; its patience is mastered passion, and eats its way through studious labour like a creeping flame that shall rise towering, purified, unquestionable at the fortunate moment. The concentrated attention scintillates in its steady advance till it fuses. Always he professes his disdain for " impatient geniuses." People are disappointed in the *Trattato della Pittura*. That is only a collection of hints to inexperienced students. Sometimes he reveals himself. Sometimes he seems to trifle, as in his rather petulant and quibbling comparisons of the arts, which suggest the verbal encounters of a Court debate. Perhaps these paragraphs are notes for one of these half-serious discussions of really

The Expression of Leonardo

unarguable things in which Renaissance people tried their wits. " More time is wasted in talking about the problem," said Michelangelo of the comparison between painting and sculpture, "than would go to the making of figures in both species." But the *Trattato* is Leonardo reported by a mind more anxious than intelligent, not one of the elect. You hear him talk of how he laid his snares of perspective, and plotted the light, and posed the figures, and mixed the rare impasto that was the lime to hold the feet of his gods and angels, with an odd mixture of childishness and wisdom, and occasional beautiful instances of nuances captured by his surpassing eyes. He did not babble of the beauty he meant to glass darkly. For that he fixed his eyes on the darkness and wrought his evocation with light and shadow.

Leonardo's is the only mind of great quality that is also a painter's mind. Painters do not think much as a rule ; they seem not even to feel much, except in simple and absent-minded ways. Of all artists they are most absorbed in their craft. Their matter may be the stuff of human life ; but it need not be. They exist in terms of light and colour and line ; and if these things are a symbolic language, it is not their concern. Light and colour and line are mystery enough in themselves.

It is said that Leonardo, like the other great Florentines, was over-intellectualized, and that he was limited and inhibited by his meditations. Doubtless, as a painter, he thought overmuch, and his intellectual passion for perfection destroyed to some degree the instinctive rapture of his hands. Yet a great painter possesses an imaginative substance peculiar to his light and colour and design, interpenetrating it as the grape lies aromatic in the wine. And, for the Renaissance men, an art that did not occupy itself with the shapes of humanity was not yet conceivable. They were extraordinarily proud of themselves as a race ; and to set the human body in a world of light and colour with a three-dimensional effect, giving out strange values of imaginative Greek reminiscence and living emotion, was their end and aim. Perhaps art does not work out paysagistes and impressionists till we are a disillusioned folk, so ashamed of our humanity that no brilliant study in contemporary modes of existence but seems to hint at satire. We do not feel like gods any longer, and it is only rarely that a Rodin learns from Donatello how to charge even desperate and wasted shapes with the tragic intensity of beauty, and to slide subtle planes to obtain an atmospheric sweetness. The greatest painters, after all, work so well that they affect the soul and the imagination, and we should be able to forget at sacramental moments how they convey their effect of beauty, as we forget craft always in the æsthetic ecstasy, with whatever pleasure in more critical moods we caress and try with our eyes the mere texture.

Leonardo the Florentine

Leonardo could have been a paysagiste also. Not only his dream-landscapes, composed of unprecedented rock and water, vibrating richly from the mysterious pulses of the figures throned within them, reveal that power ; but in his drawings little groups of trees in the pulverized sunlight show that he might have drawn hayricks and poplars with Monet—and certainly nenuphars—while his notes record that, like any Impressionist, he watched the white light break blue and violet at the edges. Indeed there were in Leonardo the hints and beginnings of all the modern schools that are. He can get his high lights like any pointillist. He can uplift or deject a figure in lit atmosphere with the delicate inflexions of a Dégas. Even to-day he who drew those trees vanishing in mad storms could sympathize with the alarmed and furious flowers, the forests spiralling into hallucinations of colour in the sun-struck world of Van Gogh ; and his Pantheistic spirit would not refuse the sense of organic nature that broods in the ponderous luminous fruits of Cézanne. He can apply his exquisite draughtsmanship to human deformity like Matisse, though he is too civilized to carry that into paint. There is at least an æsthetic mercy about Leonardo. It is possible that even Picasso's cubes might convey their import to him who could make all mathematical figures look brilliantly portentous as magic pentagrams. To his tolerant and flexible power and his original vision many ways of painting were open. His time and his temperament together decided that his brush should build a cave of sea-colour, and lure the light within it to reveal and model the shapes he preferred. Definite demand could extort from his patient wisdom the elaborate eurythmy and the catholicity of type in *The Last Supper*. Otherwise his repressed psychic desire compelled his various genius to become almost the bigot of one fatidical face.

iii

It seems as if he, who considered the sun as the supreme adorable thing in the universe, and who would have agreed with Manet that the light is the important person in a picture, who planned treatises concerning the eye and luminism, should have left canvases filled with graded tones like Manet, canvases dazzling as Renoir, glowing as Seurat. Yet it seems almost as if completely brilliant pictures could be painted only by people with little imagination, for the definite refusal of imaginative values by the Impressionists was chiefly due to the fact that they had none. It is impossible to suppress an imagination : it will out, if only in distortion. Leonardo, Rembrandt, Velasquez even, great interpreters as well as painters, loving the light are lost in shadows. Leonardo comes to his *Saint John* ; Rembrandt to his *Nativity*.

The Expression of Leonardo

For, whatever his theory, Leonardo's temperament loved the shadow, the lit darkness, where strange emotion breaks. He is a " plein-airist " in theory ; but his secret Basilidean soul is ravished to see the light at play with his sister the dark.

> " Follow thy fair sun, unhappy shadow.
> Though he be all of light
> And thou be dark as night,
> Yet follow thy fair sun, unhappy shadow ! "

Leonardo practically confesses that he often dreaded the hounds of light, and loved the soft fall of the obliterating veils of dusk and mild rains. Green caves of twilight and undersea, with veiled light moving and cherishing the dreamy faces like another angel! "The bright shadow, the dark light " is his " delicate Ariel." In the end, however, the darkness seems to prevail, and light becomes but her swordlike offspring, conditioned by her. Time and the restorers were on the side of the dark, alas, and Leonardo's subtle semitones and softnesses of penumbra, the innermost phrases of his enchantment, have been lost in the obscurity.

> " Oh ! La nuance seule fiance
> Le rêve au rêve et la flûte au cor."

It was what his unconscious self desired, the light of Dionysos half-way to Hades, not the great luminism of Apollo, whom his lips praised.

But it is hard for our minds to realize Leonardo's great originality in art. The soft miracles of his chiaroscuro were an amazement in their time, more astonishing and more delectable than cubist patterns are now. These bodies caught in lithe motions, sometimes momentary motions, were marvellous to folk accustomed to see figures in stilled and pensive attitudes that had not quite forgotten their golden or ivory Byzantine niches. The soft modelling touches of the light, caressing and persuading sweet images out of the darkness, and the tender mysticism of the green-lit shadow, seemed mere magic to those who had not yet tried to paint the impalpable.

iv

Sometimes it is urged against Leonardo that he is not a colourist, but colour is a matter of taste. The clamant and triumphal tones of the great Venetians are not for him whose art sought to serve no clamant and communal mood. He finds among the greens and blues the ultra-violet, violin-like notes of his reverie, the faëry colours treacherous to mortals. He does not give " les tons d'or et puissants, quelque chose qui soit royale

517

et qui reste," for it is not his will to rest you. He will fetch those greens and blues, and faint carnation and pale gold, to be conditioned by his learnèd luminism, the colours of dreams and mysticism, colours of great peacocks, sacred doves, June twilights, Western seas, Egyptian glass, Oriental lapis, and Persian smaragdes, colours of the cherubim and of Astarte. But alas! these sacred evasive colours that hover in lighted landscapes and vanish on rainy horizons are imperishable only when fixed by fire in enamel or gems or glass. Leonardo's blues and greens were cunningly composed, but they were eaten up by nitre; as his dark shadows grew darker, invading his light. Still the green passing within the blue was a fit tonality for one symbol dissolving into another, bizarre, delicate, even monstrous. All the luminous painters, regarding colours only as the dreams of light, prefer the ethereal and evasive hues. Piero della Francesca was silver-grey and black, lavender, pale blue, pale rose. Velasquez was mother-of-pearl and rose. Rembrandt had ambers and topazes. Monet is dim dust of gold. Manet is black and grey to relieve the light. Dégas is ivory, dusk, and soft sable. Leonardo was viridian and sapphirine, with lights of gold and rose. Perhaps too earnestly he worked at the cunning chemistries of his palette, and precipitated treachery as a bi-product when he used a device for a greener green. It is hard to judge justly of his colour-intentions now. Time is on the side of the simplicities in this matter.

v

The story of Leonardo's adventures in chiaroscuro is like a lyric cantefable to him, wherein he pursues the flying feet of light through cave and wood and wild cascade, through camp and court and charnel and great campagna and lifted alp; but in the rhythmic pattern and architectonic quality of his designs he remains hard, noble, and Greek. Not one of his followers realized the Greek element that strengthened and purified the interplay of Leonardo's imagination, investing all his images with an air of greatness, something august, rhythmical, and pure, blending strangely with the sense of romantic magic. He had learned his mythology from the antique gems in Lorenzo's house, where he had seen Meleager ride naked on his prancing horse, and Phaethon hurled from the sun-chariot, and his soul had drunk the milk of an ivy-wreathed Bacchante. From the reminiscent plaquettes and medals he became familiar with Apollo implacable, Dionysos unveiling Ariadne, Love riding in a chariot, Diomed daring his puissant theft, Centaurs and Dancing Fauns. He had heard Ghiberti talk, with sweet intonations breathing the words of a lover over the smooth rare beauty of an antique divinity ; and, though he was not so excited over sculptured fragments as most, he could not altogether remain insensible to the sweet heathen madness that escaped from the opened graves of beautiful buried statues, as if, during their long wedding night with darkness, they had acquired a soul, and undergone a wistful alteration. His one reservation, when he condemns the iniquity of copying, concerns the antique. You may imitate the antique, he says, for the classic sculptors discovered the immutable law of right proportion. But like a Greek he wove his own design, he made his own selection, observing the rules of harmony. For Renaissance enthusiasts did not copy ; they merely caught fire from newly-discovered beauty ; and they got more divining joy from their Græco-Roman fragments than later listless days from all the broken bredes of the Parthenon.

Florence made Leonardo a Hellene, and all the softer airs of Milan did not dissolve away his Greek love of rhythm and architectonic effect, or allow him to forget the dream-country whose very flowers bear the cry of a god's lamentation. The Florentine austerity saved him from the soft corruptions of the Milanese mood. In the *Saint Anne* you are cast strangely on a faëry shore, but you know it is a mighty and superbly curved wave that brings you there.

vi

It was with an intense delighted agony that Leonardo prepared his pictures, drawing design on design in which the final intention grows as the flower from the bud, emerges as the Psyche from the cocoon. He builds it greatly within the pyramidal lines he accepts as the best framework for his imaginative play, like all great artists, like God himself, powerful to charm infinity into a strict symbol, desiring a certain straitness of bondage that the dream of light, colour, music, may come not forth shapeless and vague. He practises the details with pencil and silverpoint ; he prepares his cunning degradations of light. But he never could please himself, for he was cursed by the passion for perfection. It was the triumph of the design that moved him, and sometimes he left it at that. He could see all the difficulties overcome ; and lost interest in mere fulfilment. Even his wonderful patience sometimes broke its continuities ; and he would say, anticipating *Axel*, that execution was work for servants. Leonardo desired the impossible, a consuming habit which he himself deprecated. Every picture was to be an inexhaustible well of beauty, a microcosm of human knowledge. So he wearied before the precious substance was complete, as if suddenly arrested by the reflection that time and perfidious fingers would undo and coarsen the supersubtle layers of his too sophisticated palette, that the technical triumph of *Mona Lisa*, for instance, might have sad sequels of altering hues and darkening lights. Anxiously he thinks of the durabilities in media, remembers sighingly the Della Robbia enamel, meditates novel processes of fixation. In listless mood, vainly hoping for the bright moment that carries the vision into perfection, and fires it imperishable there, he left his masterpieces abandoned by the way, or carried them about with him like a cross. If he knew any Via Dolorosa it was this life of art ; and his great pictures were exquisite stations on the way to a crucifixion of pearl.

Very few of these exquisite stations remain on his iridescent track ; and these have been wronged, not merely by Time but by the unholy fingers of the restorers, who wished to say that they had tampered with the work of a legendary artist. And so much has been lost.

It would be quite possible to make a Ballade of the Vanished Things of Leonardo, for few great artists have been so plundered by some mysterious chance, obscurely dissolving these stealths from perfection with the " neiges d'antan." Lost things and things unfinished ! Where are the waxen heads of smiling women and of boys, that he fashioned so engagingly in his Florentine youth ? Where is the dread fair head of his *Medusa*, a frozen image with a faint smile and the snakes wound in bandelettes, much liker the ivorine Rondanini masque than the travesty that found some nerve in Shelley ? Where is the cartoon for the King of Portugal's tapestry, of Adam and Eve among the flowers of Paradise, just awake to the passion of desire ? Where are the two Madonnas with fruits or dewy flowers, and where the amused Madonna whose child plays with a cat ? Where is the *Adoration of the Shepherds* with their flutes and their lambs, a dewy folk with young pagan faces ? Where is the exultant drawing of the *Triumph of Poseidon*, foaming hippocamps on foaming water ? Where is the *Nativity* that was a bribe for Maximilian ? Where is the Madonna Cecilia with her lute in an odour of roses, looking so " giovanetta " ? Is it Lucrezia Crivelli that passes in the dark Louvre canvas with that arrested and arresting look ? Where is the perfect model made for the proud Duke's statue whereof we shall never know if the steed paced or reared, if the rider sat steady or stood eager in his stirrups ? Where is the head of the Duke, and the little bust of the Christ ? It is hardly possible that Ginevra dei Benci can be that white dense woman among the junipers. Where is the original of those " school " versions of the naked Mona Lisa, smiling frankly like a Bassarid, set about with pentecostal twy-natured colombines ? Vanished all but the design of *The Last Supper*. Vanished the great knot of maddened men and horses which was all men ever saw of *The Battle of*

The Expression of Leonardo

Anghiari. Who was the Florentine lady he painted for the splendid and gentle Duke Giuliano before that Magnifico rode into Savoy for Philiberta ? What did he devise for the Pope's Datary that he would not for the Pope ? What rash hand dared to destroy the dangerous great *Leda* that could seduce the souls of men ? There are ravishing figures in the half-light. Did he ever bring any of those drawings into pictures, since they are named by name—Saint Sebastian, an Eros pierced by his own arrows, the head of Our Lady in *The Assumption,* Our Lady or Ashtaroth, the "compositions of angels," delectable companies of heavenly narcissi. And there are some entrancing rumours. What sad and sumptuous Herodiad, perhaps, what Pomona under the heavy apple-boughs, smiling drowsily, rose-white under her three veils, what lovelier Leda kneeling among the reeds and lilies, what Ganymede on wings invincible ?

It is a drift of images dread and tender, as perished as the music and songs of his youth or as unachieved as the dream of that desirable book on the soul and its great subtle ways. As irrecoverable as the beautiful masques wherein, in true Renaissance fashion, he confounded the kinds like a capricious imperial tyrant, setting muted citharas in the hands of the burning colours, and globes of rosy light over the silver singers.

What is left to us ? There is probably the early Louvre *Annunciation.* In a way all the motives and figures of Leonardo's work are gathered in that early *Adoration* of amber touched with green, and in the numberless studies he made for it. He left it unfinished ; yet it was his quarry all the while—the seekers, the light, the trees, the mystic woman and the child, the virgin rocks, the vast fragments of architecture. The conversations are there, and the riders, that will become *The Last Supper* and *The Battle of Anghiari.* But there will be a change. These young men, dreamy indeed, but exultant and ravished by a hope, whose bodies are blown flames, will become drowsy and languid in Milan. They will learn strange ardours, strange ironies, strange satieties. Their lips will shorten, their eyes and curls grow ever larger ; Saint John will see his Herodiad ; and the Madonna will become a siren of souls, the Mistress of Vision at the heart of the ecstasy, in the land of Luthany, the beauty beyond the verges of life, sunken undersea. Painted or imagined in Milan are *The Virgin of the Rocks* and the great *Saint Anne.* We have a shadow left of *The Last Supper,* and a rumour of the Horse. Probably he drew *La Belle Ferronnière,* and left another to complete her. Indubitably he painted *Mona Lisa.* Probably also he drew the *Dionysos* in the Louvre ; and he painted the *Saint John* till he had to desist.

Leonardo the Florentine

To realize most the range and power of Leonardo's art, it is necessary to enter into the world of his drawings, for he is distinctly the greatest of European draughtsmen. Botticelli's is a delighting line, it sings like music; but Leonardo's is fire-music. The line of Dégas in our day can swoop and soar like a bird, but Leonardo's is like a fire-bird. As others speak or write, so Leonardo draws, mocking at those who must use words. Indeed perhaps the ethereal and winglike intention of Leonardo never quite got through to his elaborate paint: it became clogged, sometimes faintly caricatured, by the density and emphasis of the medium. Pen, pencil, silverpoint could more delicately delay the volatile image, sometimes with lucid insistence, sometimes as softly, as faintly as a sigh. All things are rarefied in the glass of his vision, as if reflected in the water he loved. Something glittering and fine in Leonardo's point seems to consume the paper it touches, and all other drawings seem dulled with torpidity if you have been looking at his. This is his language, this absolutely sure, sudden, and fiery line. His drawings are his natural kingly gestures and they give an organic satisfaction. His flame-plumed spirit has a swiftness that does not come flying through his over-meditated paint.

There are elaborately drawn heads like that of the condottiere with the fanciful armour and the elaborate spined helmet with the lily earpieces, or the head of the enigmatic girl who passed into the angel of *The Virgin of the Rocks*, or the great sumptuous pastel of Isabella d'Este, or the yelling head of a warrior, or of a sad square elderly man with folded mouth, or handsome sullen busts like that of a young Roman emperor, or those of dreamy long-eyed adolescents farouche and tender, with ambered lids and luxurious curls, or Scaramuccia's enormous gipsy mask of unconscious brutal power, the chaste brows of Philip dawning out of a reverie of love, and bowed heads, mysterious, of women whose veils fall like twilight about them, oppressed by doom and delight, mingled of Cassandra and Helen. Dreamy Madonna heads with folded hair: seducing Leda heads with fabulous tresses! There are faces corrugated with suffering and will, mignonette faces sweet and smooth as a tuberose. His people have that intimate air that claims all gazers as confederates and auxiliaries in their psychical secret, requiring not only the sweetest extenuation but sympathy, as with their cult of some spring-god.

There are figures of serene Florentine girls and ardent Florentine boys, flower-like decadent pages of Milan, virgins sitting with their unicorns in wastes of dreamland, wild dancers with foaming raiment.

The Expression of Leonardo

Disciples unsandal among the sections of machines; and Virgin and child commune with Saint Elizabeth and John in faint white evocation, suggested by a hardly touching silverpoint. The hylozoism of his mind feeds the vitality of his pencil, and even the triangles come alive. Naked figures work at great levers. Beautiful riders grip their equal chargers. An old man sits pensive under a tree. Remote from life rise pointing pinnacles of rock, such as may be seen in tormented corners of the world, or on the broken edges of the wild Atlantic he never knew. Or it is a great clanging arsenal, and little toiling figures in feverish bondage to the gigantic pulleys make it look like a Piranesi torture-chamber. A lancer seems to fly in the air with the impetus of his attack, on a horse that carries lances too, a transpiercing cavalier. Royal unconscious children interpose like violets the pathos of their weakness. There are armed boys in fantastic Penthesilean armour for such jousts as Galeazzo di Sanseverino's. Arrogant young heads suddenly give the lie to diagrams of skulls and vulnerable blood-vessels. You find the charming sleeve of the *Annunciation* angel in pen and bistre : and the studies for the noble draperies in the *Saint Anne* picture, where the light sleeps and slips in the sweetly broken folds as it does cold and bright on a far hillside. There are allegories like fiery fantastic hallucinations. There are sessions of distorted faces, and one old woman, majestic in her ugliness, is throned with her pathetic eyes, a monstrous princess in the world of the grotesque. There are dramatic confrontations of youth and age, the adoring young eyes asking for a wonder or sullenly refusing it, the steadfast eyes of experience that have seen the Medusa declaring it miraculous merely to survive. There is intrecciamente work like pale-coloured honeycomb, or woven hair, or implicated desires. The water pours from mighty locks, or swirls in spiral pools.

> " Siren there
> Winds her dizzy hair and sings."

There are studies and studies of lovely hair. Some of the heads wear it like ring-feathers or sorrel-leaves : sometimes Andrea Salai seems to shake his long locks. There is a prehistoric fight with a dragon. Nothing can be more dæmonic than Leonardo's combats of lions and dragons. Nothing can be more delicate than his flowers.

Leonardo's flowers live their own life; they are dipped in their peculiar ecstasy ; they seem to create their own Elysian air about them as they grow on his page. They are exact, and yet they are heavenly. Certainly he had an intimate feeling for them, for a mystic floralism seems part of his implied philosophy. Rarefied flowers, especially of the gracious prodigal lily kind, do mean for him that ethereal intensity of bliss to which all the tides of being yearn. So he draws them lost in their own reverie of love and desire, for he seems to have realized the sex of plants, divined their ravished hearts pulsating with some clear ichor ; and they look like the flowers in the garden of the Sensitive Plant, for all their exquisite fidelity to earthly pattern.

The water-worts and iris-leaves and sedge-plants are often apparent, for he naturally loves the mysterious water-flowers whose roots are lost in darkness, nenuphar and iris, the sacred kin of the lotos. For wrought fragile things he had a divining tenderness, especially for the fine colombine with its fragile session of doves, dear to the Holy Ghost, and the cloistral violet. The rich romantic effect of the bramble arc appeals to him : he draws it often in leaf, flower and fruit, sometimes altogether, for with characteristic Renaissance greed he likes the double effect of flower and fruit. He draws a sceptral spire of tiger-lily, and repeats the pattern on the hairy chest of a fierce warlike person. There is a dedicated arrangement of anemones and lily-flowers drawn as for Easter-tide. He gathers rare boughs of rosaceous plants, and spendthrift blossom of apple and cherry, and precious rods of jasmine, and other poignant deliciæ of spring. There are wild roses and fragile cyclamen. Also there are the dark roses of Milan and the guelder roses from its campagna. Sometimes tall grasses feather into flower. The fruit of the oak becomes sacred and regal under his gaze. You can see the bloom on those sumptuous grapes. He finds his growing things at shy moments of flowering, fruiting, seeding. Sometimes he draws a whole grove of trees, their stems and boskage a dreamy reality. To all growing things he gives so rare an innocence of the eyes that his absolutely true report of their beauty comes almost with a delicate shock. He sees the leaves turn to receive the dew and the light, and tenderly mother the dawning flower. He sees them as faëry Ledas and Madonnas, with mystical winds and wings achieving the mystery of a beautiful and stainless propagation ; and his waves of cloud and water, all his waves of being, begin to break in those dim great corollas.

viii

Leonardo was an artist in more ways than one ; but pre-eminently he was a painter. " O superexcellence of all things created by God, how praise thee, how express thy nobility ? " This art seemed most to satisfy the Renaissance craving for power that fierily wrought in him, urging him also to tame the air and lead the waters, for he explained that the painter could in his art possess all that delighted him, regard with impunity what horrified him, and avenge himself on what seemed

The Expression of Leonardo

hateful. "He is Lord and God of them." So he "armed himself with his sensuality" like the so different Catherine of Siena, or, in the modern jargon, sublimated his imperial Renaissance mania for power into an artistic fantasy.

He could have been a great sculptor; and the magnificent series of drawings concerned with the famous Cavallo sufficiently reveals into what a shape of kindled energy and might he transformed the condottiere Duke. But his temperament was averse from sculpture; and there is something quite sincere in his dislike of the mechanical toil involved in it. The sculptor's is too like a workman's job: he thinks it degrading to perspire over a work—degrading to art and artist. Sometimes the divine Leonardo sounds a trifle of a snob: but this may be simply an effort to find a cover for the fact that the great Cavallo had physically wearied him out. The little heads and reliefs we hear of must have been handled very sweetly; we seek them in vain. The Cavallo would have been a superb *tour de force*, but the imager might have equalled a Praxitelean sculptor on a more tranquil theme, with a statue of the Renaissance genius, dreaming heavenly in a soft atmosphere, plane gliding into plane of tenderness, or surpassed Scopas with a figure of Himeros, lord of the love that is the passion of the eyes.

Leonardo was also an architect, and a most practical one, who understood all about stresses, and strains, and the composition of walls, except when he painted on them. He could be intensely utilitarian in suggestions concerning civil and military architecture; indeed, with his engineering, these works made his steadiest form of livelihood, even as goldsmithery served the earlier painters. He could make an ingenious and singular plan for a *eatro*, where all the listeners should hear. And in his city plans he does plead that the streets should be wide as the houses are high, and that great squares and market-places be flooded with light and air.

He was an earnest student of the theory of domical construction, especially of the type of some that Strzykowski calls Iranic; and he meditated a treatise on cupolas. He studies the domes of Brunelleschi and the domes of Milan; and thinks out a skilful and surprisingly sympathetic cupola for the bizarre cathedral. His fanciful domes rise from octagonal bases, richly clustered round by chapels of various combinations, sometimes fantastically rising into shapes of tall candelabra. The serenity and majesty of the Dome suited his synthetic Renaissance mind; and it seems to become one of his symbols. He exhausts the plan-forms, sometimes circular, sometimes octagonal: the dome has always the central seizure of the building. Indeed he may have glided with Bramante into the long tradition of the dome of Saint Peter's. But his semilunes look

Leonardo the Florentine

strangely unchristian. Not like these is such a dome as overarches the Christian mystery of the Grail, and the sacrament of *Parsifal*.

"Et, ô ces voix d'enfants chantant dans la coupole!"

For all his poring over Vitruvius with Gian Andrea of Ferrara he could never have been severe enough or pedantic enough to devise a neo-Roman building, as he could not have been limpid enough for a pillared eurythmy like the Parthenon's, or religious enough to accept the singing and volatile Gothic vibrating with its passion of prayer. Yet he might have with more opportunity begun a Byzantine-Iranic revival, and brought some church of the Holy Wisdom foaming up in domes and semilunes from one of his exquisite and magnificent plans of the Greek-cross variety.

One of his distractions when he is weary—and perhaps suffering from some claustrophobia—is to build an immense temple with an audacious breaker of domelets round a central dome with a plan like a geometrical flower. Sometimes he imagines a kind of herodium, an artificial mountain crowned by a temple, wound about with terraces and pierced with sepulchral halls that seem to glow dark red as Halls of Eblis. Sometimes he is of one mood with the Pyramid builders. Sometimes his fabrics are excessive enough to wear that touch of Heliopolis or Ecbatana which invests them with a sombre Oriental might of sensuality and splendour. Sometimes they are a Sultan's pavilions, airy and Arabian.

"In Xanadu did Kubla Khan
A stately pleasure-dome decree
Where Alph the sacred river ran
Through caverns measureless to man
Down to a sunless sea."

And so on. Here are Leonardo's cave-broken landscapes, his subterranean rivers, his Eastern domes, his loneliness of effect, his atmosphere of magic.

But for all his expert skill and ingenuity in changing patterns of plan, one cannot feel that Leonardo was happiest in architecture. No man can build to himself alone; and the isolation of his soul separated him from the civic or patriotic mood that is the most exciting auxiliary of the architect. Even when he is most reasonable, when he insists on setting free great churches from the clustered human dwellings round them, or wishes to separate campanile and dome because each should keep intact its own perfection, you feel that the æsthetic reason grows from his instinct to set high things as well as high people away from their kind. Thinking of different kinds of beauty in building, of the great Grecian urn of a temple at Pæstum, that golden house of the sea-god, solitary now, not always; of the silencing sight of Chartres, built by the seigneur and the serf equally yoked, of the wild wings of Troyes

The Expression of Leonardo

and its kind risen from the mad rapture of love and hate in the soul of
the Middle Ages, of San Marco, more to his mind, the gratified altar of
Venice, of the gracious Santa Maria della Grazie even, sweetly adorned
by Bramante understanding the spirit of Milan, you feel that Leonardo
was limited by his lack of love, in the widest sense of the word, and that
the exquisite lily-like plans are sterile exercises of an ingenuity that casts
no pollen.   But it may be he did affect the châteaux of France like Blois
and Chambord, the jealous pleasure-houses of a separated class.

ix

Leonardo was a musician by habit, and thought it was the figuration
of the invisible, but regretted its impermanence, or said so for a quibble.
To the most synthetic art, the art of words, he was not friendly.   The
poetasters of the day evidently annoyed him at the Court of Milan ; but
in his laboured comparison between the pictorial effects produced by a
poet and a painter (as if a poet's end were to describe), he may have
suffered from an early jealousy of Poliziano, who rendered embroidered
landscape, dreamy figures and dancing motion with charming effect,
and who certainly inspired Botticelli.   Leonardo himself in his notes
frequently suffers from some incompatibility with the written word.
But he was a rhetorician and a conversationalist ; and people much
given to the art of speech, dependent on the echoes and glances of their
listeners, are depressed by the inhibition of the pen.   Leonardo could
always draw instead.   Sometimes, however, when he is really moved,
his skill as a musician comes to his aid.   This is Leonardo's loveliest
æsthetic effect as a writer, the famous passage in which the name of
Helen strikes through the mournful music :
"O tempo consumatore della cose, e o invidiosa antichità, tu
distruggi tutte le cose, e consumato tutte le cosa dai duri denti della
vecchiezza, a poco a poco, con lenta morte ! Elena quando si specchiava
vedendo le vizze grinze del suo viso, fatte per la vecchiezza, piange, e
pensa seco, perchè fu rapita dice volte.   O tempo consumatore delle
cose, e o invidiosa antichità, per la quale tutte le cose son consumato."
Observe the art of the refrain, caught over from the extemporized
flower-songs of his youth, and all the echoing effects of his beautiful
andante movement.
It would have annoyed him to foresee that he would be so much
appreciated by the literary.   Yet it is easier to get sheer glamour into
words (or into violins) than into anything so material as paint must be.
For a medium vanishing at the edges, a symbol opening out leaves upon
leaves, ringing faint undersea bells upon bells of wonder, dropping a

527

sudden bizarre chord on the dulcimer, words are apt and echoing as he did not realize. The fugitive things that he loved, that often escaped even his subtle nets, the melting of the light, the vanishing of the smoke, the breaking of the wave, the wind in the trees, the flight of throbbing swifts upon a sunset sky, the fading of a smile, can be taken in the gossamer entanglement of a few sighing words. But the Italian Renaissance lived in its eyes : if you take pageant away from its poets, from Poliziano to Ariosto and Tasso, the beauty is sadly diminished away. Dante was now canonized, and being canonized, was no longer a living inspiration to them.

Gazing at *The Virgin of the Rocks*, one remembers the " perilous seas forlorn," even as Leonardo's visionary domes recall Kubla Khan ; and again and again in the wilderness of the manuscripts one suddenly remembers Shelley, when, music-blind and music-true, he sings like a fountain or a flame or a cascade, Shelley, who felt the cosmic ecstasy more than any other English poet, who was a little like Leonardo himself in seeming sometimes like a non-human natural force, when he forgot the anguish and injustice of man, and, with twisted mouth and flying hair seemed to flash and burn like lightning about the peaks of the earth. Shelley also loved domes, flowers, lutes, deep caves and Caucasian mountains and changing clouds. It is possible that Leonardo might have approved the cosmic vision of *Prometheus Unbound*, with its pale dances of stars, its lunar rainbows, its masque of shifting mountains. It is the nearest literary parallel to the effect of some of those passages in Leonardo's manuscripts in which you most feel the radiation of energy, the rush of waters, the shattering of light. It is much nearer than the Prologue to *Faust*, which is a Hebraic antiphony. Leonardo was not really in the least like Goethe.

Still, he lived in the Italian Renaissance, and despised poets. But, as he is the only painter who does make sheer glamour a visible affair, the traffickers in words have avenged themselves by an appreciation which seems unfairly to do him wrong as a craftsman among the painters. After all, even a painter is all the better of a little imagination. And Leonardo's imaginative substance is really inseparable from the body of his art. It is not completely translatable into words. But, while he does not tell a story, or convey a moral, or appeal to a traditional senti-ment, or commit any other painter's iniquity, he does, by the weaving of his lines and the plotting of his shadows, predispose to an illuminating reverie, and communicate a spiritual adventure.

x

When we lament the frailty of Leonardo's direct disciples we forget his effect on his contemporaries. Leonardo was a contagion, and it is hard to estimate his unwordy influence. Of all the painters of the time, the nearest him was Botticelli, also ethereal and sensuous in his temper, also a great master of line, and a mystic with floralism in his mood. He too loves symbolic tones and forms of nature. But Botticelli is feminine through and through ; and the sweet fever of his great designs is like the music of Chopin. Botticelli was an emotionalist, and his rare fragile people are all taken in the rhythms of his captivating line as if snared in a sad mystery of love.

" And what of Beauty ? saith my sufferings then."

And Giorgione also was surely of Leonardo's kin, another love-child, dealing also in poetic landscape and mysterious type. But Giorgione seems to "remember Sicily," and love also of a gracious pagan kind. The lovers lie clothed in their music, and their extreme felicity trembles like the golden air that charms their idyll. He too can give a more unqualified and sympathetic delight, for his imaginative temper, great and golden as it is, is not strange to the human experience. There is a candour of tenderness in his soul. *The Shepherd Boy* at Hampton Court, with sweet mouth, sensitive nostrils, soft hair and glowing eyes, is a child of some golden age, an Elysian Daphnis, a creature inno-cent and appealing as the melody in his flute, moulded from a simpler dream-kindness than either Leonardo's eager young Florentines or his languorous Milanese.

And yet Leonardo's mighty shaping intellect and greatness of design seem to relegate these two enchanting painters, nearest to him in temper, to a more limited, more lyrical order.

Of all Leonardo's direct descendants the greatest was Sodoma, who strengthened with leonardesque quality the melting beauty of his types, and turned the famous smile to a flower of fine sensuality. In the end of the Renaissance day one side of his genius was brought to over-sweet perfection in Correggio, the luxurious Ovidian painter, pagelike and woman-trained, who with all the art of sfumato and chiaroscuro heightened the luscious sun-steeped limbs of his latinized gods and goddesses, while he carried the audacious art of perspective into the realm of acrobatics.

Michelangelo and Raphael were touched by Leonardo, as we have seen, as well as smaller people. Albrecht Dürer came upon his traces and made himself into a Teutonic Leonardo, fine curled hair, fine raiment and all the rest. A great artist without magic ! The Flemings bore away his colours and his suavity to their flat dreamy country, and Matsys and Mabuse were touched by his lyricism and dolcezza, while Rubens caught from his fading *Battle of the Standard* some dynamic radiance that purified his energy somewhat. Not till modern days did France realize her great visitor. Then some of her Romantics stole splinters from his dense matrix of emerald. So Delacroix took fire like Rubens ; and the strange Moreau remembered him as he created his world of jewelled seas and rocks and wild fauna round hieratic Herodiads and their kind. So did at times the exotic Chasseriau, when he was most divided between Greece and India. Yet those who really most resembled him, the experimentalists, were ignorant of all his tentatives, and broke their way into new fields of vision for themselves, which, after all, is liker Leonardo's way than any imitation.

But France has been most affected by Leonardo in her literature. She has eloquently recognized him as a great painter ; but some kinds of imaginative stuff are fitted for more arts than one, and his morbidezza, his subtlety, his suggested ways of strange experience, have affected the writers. Taine glorified him ; and Stendhal felt his power when he shaped the sweet ironic forms of Gina and Fabrizio. And, probably because of those pictures in the Louvre, Seraphita moves poignant on icy peaks with the trembling auroras behind, and the golden eyes of Paquita, lit from paradise and hell, darken upon the terrible *dénouement*, the wild surprise of the rival sensualists. And still to some degree because of him, Gautier, eloquent among Leonardo's interpreters, sent that audacious cavalier, Mademoiselle de Maupin, riding with radiant pagan eyes through the golden forests of his wilful delighting romance. There is many another moved by Leonardo. To-day, Rémy de Gourmont has some of the leonardesque quality, not only in the smiling seductive texture of his style, but in the dexterity of his intellectual play and the catholicity of his interest. *Une Nuit dans le Luxembourg*, for instance, has an evasive quality quite leonardesque. You have Leonardo's effect of liberation obtained by slight shocks, though the dream-soft shapes of duskling women among the flowers are reminiscent more of Luini than Leonardo. You might find an effect of Leonardo also in the work of d'Annunzio, who is certainly something of a Renaissance figure in an Italy that has revived its Renaissance despot. But none of Leonardo's remembrancers, either in paint or letters, has any shadow of that masculine and all-embracing intellect in which the strange beauty he preferred became so instinct with power and grace that it entered into real divinity. Leonardo is nearly all intellect : the rest is glamour. " And all the rest is but enchantment," as Malory says. Yes ! But all enchantment is a miracle, and this a lasting miracle.

Chapter iii

Leonardo the Savant

i

IT is not possible here to consider Leonardo as a savant, for that is an intricate subject that needs another world of exposition. I have been concerned with him as a dreamer and an artist, steadily remembering his scientific work, but only as a condition that qualified his psychology, and seemed, though only seemed, to be contradictory. As an artist Leonardo was a mystic; as a scientist he frequently expresses himself like a complete rationalist. The contradiction is merely superficial. He has made his mystical assumptions; and as a savant he is concerned only with processes.

Since it is not so very long ago that Leonardo's manuscripts became realized by critical opinion, the enthusiasm they have excited is still perhaps a little overpitched. For an artist to have a scientific mind is even yet considered as amazing as it was once for a woman to be intelligent, and he is encouraged with the fond pride given to bright children. Leonardo's guesses are sometimes credited with a reach which he would have disavowed. Now that the young schools of painters have disowned all their predecessors, there is even a certain desire to make him over entirely to science. It will not do. Any mortal who can be an artist at all is an artist first, and everything else a long way after. Leonardo himself is so clear about this that he spends few words in declaring it. He tells proudly the unexpected things he can do. But " as to painting, I am the equal to any master, be he whom he may," he says in a casual royal way. It was painting that led him to science, to inquiries into light and perspective, so to optics and physics, to the anatomy of the body, to problems of tensions, levers, forces.

But, once involved in the quest for knowledge of the natural universe, the analysing and curious intellect of Leonardo began to sift and prove and acquire for the love of it. For him art was an implacable and wasting chimera, preying for ever on a fever of the nerves. There are times when the best is the enemy of the good; and the cruel desire for perfection thrusts a bright sword into every innocent infant effort. Scientific research was laborious, peaceful, restful. It needed no determined initiations of effort, no desperate struggle with a dream. It was all a matter of law and order : you inevitably pressed on from point to point. And how divinely lucid, cool, perfect, was heavenly mathematics. Leonardo escaped into the sciences as into the cloisters, away from the images that tortured and importuned his mind for a place in the immortal Pattern. They stole in after him, and brought him back. The flowers grew by the geometrical pages ; the domes rose visionary among the graphs ; the sweet sullen profiles looked their challenge through the strange script. He was an artist, and all the sciences were but loops on the winding way by which he went to his procrastinated duel of agony ; loop on loop he lingered, for the creative effort cost him too much life.

The artist must pay for his art, and no man of woman born can spend his mortality in both creation and analysis. But Leonardo maintained his psychical double life with a concentration and a catholicity of interest that present a really unparalleled phenomenon in the records of intellectual activity. Nobody else was ever interested in quite so many problems at once. It is this simultaneousness of interest that takes the breath away : together with the unflagging exultation of the worker. If the calligraphy wearies, and the page blurs, it is but for a moment. Presently, with racing pulses he is writing hard over some problem of dynamics or hydrostatics. And probably he found that the conquest of the laws of matter gave him, more easily than his art, the sense of power so necessary to his Renaissance psychology. He was at home with air and light and earth and water, a truer magician than any, for he had learned the laws that did control those mighty spirits.

ii

Leonardo himself speaks of a hundred and twenty books of manuscript. Since there are so many lost pages, it is difficult to estimate the value of his scientific investigation. But on the whole his qualities and defects are those of the greatest of amateurs—who is also a pioneer : isolation drags him, lack of technical vocabularies makes him obscure. The everlasting discussion concerning the inductive method I leave aside. It is so often solemnly debated ; and it seems as if any intelligent person had to proceed by a mingling of both induction and deduction. Leonardo certainly is an apostle of experience and experiment. He is naturally a rebel, impatient of authority ; there is an intellectual anarchist in him. He does not refuse tradition ; but he interrogates Greeks and Arabs, Aristotle, Euclid, Pliny, Vitruvius, Avicenna, Archimedes, as if they were contemporary witnesses. Indeed, he is so

Leonardo the Savant

enchanted by the new attitude of universal scepticism, laboriously qualified by testing experiment, that he is like a child with a new toy, and sometimes proves what is axiomatic. Still, as he says : " Experience has been the mistress of all who write well. And so as mistress I will cite her in all cases." " Experience never deceives." Yes ! The eye may deceive, the touch betray, the ear make a false report, all the senses be tricked and ensorcelled by the sore need of the spirit. However, he did also say : " Before making a general rule of this case repeat it two or three times." He proceeded from a notation of fact to a deduction of law, and left out theology. The anarchist in him placated, he began to rebuild the new Idea.

Concerning the fundamental science of mathematics he was an enthusiast. " Let no man who is not a mathematician read my book," he writes proudly, copying in this Plato's inscription over the Academe. Yet mathematicians say that his mathematics can often be faulty, though he has a brilliant notion of their trend, and a keen sense of their unlocking value in the worlds of the other sciences. He had a geometrical imagination and made ingenious constructions of pure form. The cone, the sphere, the cylinder he loved for themselves. But the truth was that Leonardo's science leaped most vividly into radiance when it was quickened by his artistic quality ; and his patient experiments are sometimes suddenly discarded in flashes of brilliant intuition. And it must not be supposed that this flexible magnificent mind was without its follies and prejudices. There is a childishness in Leonardo's maturity which argues some defect of experience, and in quaint analogies and quibbles and abrupt transitions of thought he sometimes exhibits not only mediævalism, but infantilism. Yet this *naïveté* of vision had its value. Like a child he saw the shells on the mountain-tops, and like a child, not like a savant, he instantly began to think of the sea that must have brought them thither. Like a child he reasons naturally about the Flood. He keeps his freshness of outlook : he sees things as for the first time and goes on saying ' Why ? ' As an artist he divines the spirals in all things, and finds some analogies that are not mistakes. The child and the artist led him even farther than the mathematician.

It is in the humaner sciences, those nearest his art, that he seems most brilliant. The soul, he thinks, is the artificer ; and the body is its intricate expression. He is considered the greatest living anatomist of his time ; and his lovely drawings, strong, delicate, calm, show that diagrams can be beautiful, like the fine silverpoints of the throat, or the studies of pronation and supination ; and that the truthful observation of the organs of life can conciliate rather than shock. He knew Galen, Avicenna, Mondino, and Benedetti, though he speaks of " authors "

533

much as Blake speaks of " angels." Other artists had worked at superficial anatomy ; but Leonardo explored the human body. He described
the physical life of man from his generation to his slow decay. He nearly
discovered the circulation of the blood ; he gives an accurate account of
the uterus. Blood-vessels, muscles, nerves, he traces and describes with
surprising accuracy, and all the processes of movement, and the story
of gestation. Correctly he articulated the skeleton, noted the curves of
the spinal column, and worked out a canon of proportion with strong
straight figures copied from his own form, it is said. With original
daring, he contrived to take casts of the brain. With the eye he is not
so fortunate ; but he worked out the resemblance to the camera obscura,
and the pinhole theory. Sometimes his artist self seems to revolt
against this preoccupation with what is hidden. A fair curled Salai-like
head, confident in young beauty, suddenly looks out from a description
of the vessels of the abdomen, mocking at mere mechanism.

Leonardo was also absorbed in the anatomy of the horse, and founded
the hippic canon. He began comparative anatomy, making comparative
studies of locomotion ; and intended " a special treatise " for the description of four-footed animals, among them man—" who in infancy walks on
four feet." He had glimpses and hints of the idea of evolution, to which
both his love of metamorphosis and his deep pantheistic reverie pre-
disposed him. At times he seems to feel man like a bird scale the air,
like a fish descend into the sea, like a snake coil in the woods, like a
lemuroid cling to the branches, not unconscious of some loss in the
development of a creature who in finding his feet loses his wings.

iii

From man he passed to the earth, the structure of which, by one of
his closest and oddest analogies, he compared with the human body,
with the living water in its veins for blood. There are times when his
pantheistic mind seems to endow the planet with a kind of vegetative
soul maintaining a life of its own. In the contemplation of nature,
indeed, his mind is continually awake to " correspondences."

> " L'homme y passe à travers des forêts de symboles,
>   Qui l'observent avec des regards familiers."

As is well known, he was a good geologist, disproving the notion of
a general flood, and calculating with fair accuracy the time of earth's
development. He imagines a map of Italy immemorial ages ago. It
was in curiously pondering shells and fossils as a palæontologist that
he came to this conclusion, more deadly to the Church than a Lutheran

Leonardo the Savant

heresy, at a period when it tolerated anything but such a subversion of doctrine as was implied in Leonardo's apostrophe :

" O time, rapid destroyer of created things, how many people and kings hast thou annihilated. What a sequence of revolutions and catastrophes since this amazingly formed fish died here in these deeply twisted caverns ! Now, destroyed by patient time, it lies in this completely enclosed space, and with fleshless and naked bones it has made an armour and a support against the mountain which weighs upon it."

But as he imagined the enduring mountains change and pass, and the valleys lifted up, it was chiefly on the movements of water that he fixed his concentrated attention. For he had an organic kinship with water—in seas, and under seas, and landlocked pools and rivers. He knows how to walk on water, but will not tell the secret because of the wickedness of man, a singular and unexpected scruple, for he is ready enough to use rivers as his auxiliaries in the art of fortification, and to tell " how to throw poison in the form of powder on ships." He sees it nymphlike, Thetis-like, eternally changeable in form, as vapour, rain, ice, dew, white hail. He sees it bridal in wild cascades, spiral in whirlpools, sombre in undersea rivers, serenely captive in his canals. He knows its speeds, currents, tides and moods : he meant to write a treatise on water. He is happy and tranquil in this great work of canalization, mastering with dykes and ramparts and barrages the crystal element he loves, even as he tamed the horses that are kin to its springs and waves. He draws the Hermes-staff in various disguises, flying off into bandelettes, quivering like the rod of the water-diviner. With singular pleasure he maps the mounded country of the intersecting rivers and canals, marking the towns and villages with towers, lifting the very landscape into the shape of his waves.

The fascination of those waves carried him into more sensitive inquiries ; and he seems to see like any modern the universe vibrating and mysterious with correspondences of waves in sea and light and sound. His acute artist's apprehension finds the image of the light in the mirror like the echo of the sound. Watching the wave on the wheat, he explains the nature of that wonderful motion.

Now and then the flame begins to creep among the little straws of recorded facts and experiments, and all observed things rush together in a law so transcendent that it seems to lighten the world like a great flame. It does indeed when he suddenly writes : " Il sole non se muove." But in what mood he wrote that sentence we are uncertain. As a dazzling hypothesis, not permanently adopted ? He has illuminated moments when he sees the Earth as a star among other stars. He challenged

Leonardo the Florentine

the Aristotelean notion of the incorruptibility of the planets and affirmed "la nobelta del nostro mondo," its kinship with the planets. The music of the spheres he stayed. The contact would be wasting, he said; the music would cease, and the dancers stop. Yet at times, for all his sun-worship, he thinks in terms of the Ptolemaic conception. The notion of a heliocentric universe made even the mind of Leonardo a little shelterless sometimes. Meanwhile the diffident Copernicus was finding his way to that bright centre by the red light of Mars.

But Leonardo said that the moon had her continents and valleys flooded by pale earthshine : he had become a lunographer, gazing at her silver disk from Fiesole height with his special magnifying-glasses.

iv

It is useless to attempt except in some special volume any survey of those notebooks with their used covers. Leonardo's sciences were continually interacting : they were so much alive that they ran together, refusing to stay in compartments. They are confused chapters in human thought ; and if Leonardo had written all his treatises he would have composed an encyclopædia of Renaissance knowledge. Evidently he thought he would do that, among other things.

There is hardly a modern science of which he does not consider the first steps. Nothing escaped him : he questioned even the meteors and rainbows. But Mechanics, he said, was the paradise of the sciences, for there one gathered all the fruits. It is like Leonardo to see mechanics as a fruited garden. Here he certainly had more definite predecessors. Archimedes is his idol, whose codices he wistfully tracks through the Borgian war. Leo Battista Alberti, whom he had seen in his youth as a tranquil old man who had something anticipated his own universality, had made his inquiries, and Leonardo was aware of them. That he was acquainted with mediæval precursors in science like Albertus Magnus, Nicholas of Cusa, and Roger Bacon, the learned book of M. Duhem proves to some degree. That he was " deeply read in the nominalists of Paris " I doubt a little, though he was evidently acquainted with some of the more mystical doctrines of the schoolmen.

In mechanics he came to what was nearest his mind, the fundamental problems of force and energy. His draughtsmanship darts and radiates over these matters. The natural force in himself is kin to these great forces. He thinks lucidly of them and mocks at the fanatics of perpetual motion : he plans a treatise of weights and measures, and has some sense of the law of the parallelogram of forces and velocities.

His hydrostatics and hydraulics are mostly empirical, relating to his canal-work. Duhem thinks his ideas of statics and dynamics are unoriginal, and he certainly proves that in this Leonardo owed much to forgotten mediæval thinkers. But he draws great pulley systems so that they look like a fierce merciless drama, and delights in levers with their magical power of displacement. He forefeels the idea of gravitation : though he does not quite elucidate a law. Temperamentally, none the less, he would incline more readily to the theories of Einstein.

v

His knowledge of the forces of nature he applied to inventions, with great skill and daring, and with the reckless joy of the creator. Such is his incessant activity that he will invent anything from a flying-machine to a roasting spit. His equal interest in all things heightens his effect as of a planetary stranger, to whom the smaller needs of man are as odd and interesting as his greater. He invents light bridges, moving walls, bastions and ravelins, ladders, catapults, mines, and steam-cannon for the art of war. Turbines, mills, and barrage systems are devised for his rivers and canals. He can measure the winds, and count the speed of ships. Swimming-belts are drawn " to save life on sea." But he does not care much if his inventions are never translated into terms of fact. Just as he explores the cosmos merely to satisfy his great Greek curiosity, so he applies knowledge to things to amuse the restlessness of his fancy. When he draws levers and pulleys Leonardo is very happy. Sometimes little figures drag and strain, the slaves of the machine, melancholy precursors of a crushed humanity to come. Sometimes the devotees, in more radiant mood, seem incarnate spirits of the tensions and forces —spirits of air lightly impulsive on wheels or ropes, flying or flitting as on the riggings of a ship, running clothed only in swift beauty and a petasus.

But the passionate desire of his soul was to be the first mortal to scale the air. For this he gathered together all his lore of dartling energies and opposing strains, for this with marvellous eyes he noted those instantaneous movements of the flight of birds. For the conquest of the air he wove his great mechanical plots with the concentration and ambition of a Cesare Borgia ; it was probably his heart's desire. For this notion of flight the mystic in him, the terrible æsthete in him, the unfamiliar god in him, met the intent observer, the tireless recorder ; inordinate pride waited on exquisite patience—but Leonardo did not fly. As the first person of the Renaissance he merely desired the kingdom of the air, the virginal inaccessible realm where he should be sole and sovran ; but Leonardo did not fly.

Cardan observes that he tried it, and came to grief. But though

Leonardo the Florentine

Cardan's father was a friend of Leonardo, surely so conspicuous a failure would have written its drama on more minds. Perhaps he did make some secluded attempt from the Corte Vecchia, hard by the fanciful campanile of San Gottardo. Perhaps he did indeed attempt it from the Hill of Swans at Fiesole.[1] There is a time after which he moves with the effect of a trailing wing.

He studied his birds with maintained intensity, drawing all the fluctuations of their beating wings and their steady poise in the blue, all the gentle habits of their pathetic and lovely migrations. He knew the principle of flight; and the great wing he evolved at last, more a bat's than a bird's, would have flown if he could have found the motive-power. As it was, he had to depend on the inadequate human impulsion. His waxen toys show that he meditated the balloon-principle; but his imagination was held by a vision of wings above a sunset hill.

"And the cherubim shall spread out their wings on high, covering the mercy-seat with their wings, with their faces one to another; toward the mercy-seat shall the faces of the cherubim be." A Syrian image for this Greek spirit of curiosity, an image full of wings and mystery—but it makes one of the symbolic knots that express Leonardo! It is concerned with that fierce centre of original life from which Leonardo seems to come.

One sad comment the meditative mind makes on Leonardo's love of mechanics and inventions. The fruits he gathered in this peculiar paradise were of the Dead Sea, for, all unconscious, this lover of beauty helped to prepare the Mechanical Age. He who would star and fleur-de-lis and coil and pattern machinery into the likeness of great ships and wings and living majesties, and set lithe spirits in the riggings, might now gaze in horror at the monstrous cage of iron and steel fitted over the green and shuddering earth, mortified with black wounds, as if enduring some enormous travesty of an ancient martyrdom of windlass and pulley, in a great suffocation of smoke.

vi

"He arrived at thought so heretical that he submitted to no religion, thinking it much more adventurous to be a philosopher than a Christian." So Vasari in his first edition of Leonardo's life. There is quite enough ironic Voltairean comment in the manuscripts to justify the somewhat shocked statement. A Cyrenaic philosopher he seems here, with satire

---

[1] "The great bird will take its first flight on the back of its great swan, and filling the universe with stupor, will fill all writings with its renown, and glory eternal to the nest where it was born."

Leonardo the Savant

of established doctrine concealing his own more dangerous mystical heresies. Still, Leonardo is never simple in his attitude. He mocks steadily at all churchmen, but monks are his friends, his hosts, his patrons. So also he mocks at the astrologers and necromancers, yet some quaint experimenter in the occult is usually among his intimates. Once, by one of his odd transitions, he compares his fate with theirs before instantly abusing them, as if he secretly feared he really was one of their brotherhood, perhaps because he found his researches so exciting that they seemed magical. " It was more *adventurous* to be a philosopher than a Christian "—a characteristically Renaissance reason. To these highly charged minds, insatiable for new knowledge, true reports from the outer universe were as amazing as any magical story. It was a marvel to find mountains in the moon. It was a kind of mysterious terror to feel the stars lapsing from their spheres indifferent to man, who thought himself their nursling whom they damned or desired ; and the kind Earth falling from her place, not only as the centre of the universe, but also, it seemed, destroyed as the core of God's desire, naked of her futile dream of Redemption. The ways of science in Renaissance days were indeed as full of wild wonder as any. The reports of the lonely and audacious pioneers were grave and fair and terrible tidings that shook an authentic heaven and shattered a credible hell. There was a dreadful excitement in the tale of a planet ; and a fossil shell was a token from astounding antiquity. We have lost that sense of wonder : so vulgar and trivial is our ennui that a signal from Mars would be staled in a week.

vii

There were other minds of universal interest before the Renaissance passed away. Bruno and Campanella in Italy had caught fire from science for the service of humanity : they are noble types, but not astonishing. Beside Leonardo, Montaigne, for instance, that tolerant attractive philosopher, is an intellectual Autolycus, with the tastes of a magpie. Erasmus, on a higher philosophic grade, is fearful, anæmic, controversial. Some hold that, through Cardan, Leonardo affected Palissy and Pascal. There are certainly temperamental affinities between the suave Italian and Pascal, that dark lord of melancholia.

In these days it is a habit to mention Leonardo with Goethe ; but it is not a comprehending habit. The German, indeed, combined his art with some scientific work. But his science was not nearly so wide in its range nor so courageous in intellectual attack ; and as an artist his sense of style is most unequal. As to life, he was a Court Chamberlain and a Grand Turk. Leonardo's impassible eyes would have annihilated a Faust who leagues himself with the powers of Hell to seduce a silly village girl. Infinitely higher Leonardo's austerity and psychical subtlety than Goethe's long record of sentimental undignified amours. Of course Goethe had his great moments, especially his lyrical moments. But *Wilhelm Meister* and *Faust* are absolutely devoid of Leonardo's powerful sense of æsthetic order. He is not woven of the same fibre as Leonardo, this calm Teuton posing as an "augustan" Roman. I am not considering Goethe as a phenomenon in himself—merely Goethe as compared with Leonardo.

viii

It was matter in its eternal dance that fascinated Leonardo—flux and reflux, existence like a blown candle-flame, or a falling wave. For all his passionate care for detail, it was the dim shape of the larger vision that held him ; and, as his waves of cloud or water might break in foam of lilies, so all his wisdom, he thought, might rise crescent in a great wave to break in his art. "This cannot be taught like mathematics or copied like letters. . . . This alone remains noble, this alone does honour to its author," he says of his painting.

For the savant is not the essential Leonardo. The essential Leonardo is in his art. You feel that here he went by borders so strange that not only his passion for perfection but the dim sense of danger in his dreamland was a motive that made him steady himself by the sciences. The manuscripts reveal Leonardo's efforts to tether himself to actuality. He knew too well what many know a little, that strange click of the brain, that sudden shift of meditation by which the whole universe becomes unreal, while with unsensuous wits we apprehend an unearthly sphere, when even the painful heartbeats, the nervous senses that like nails clamp us to the cross of life, alter into pale dead roses. Some obscure instinct warns us that it is dangerous to let the soul escape, a kind of treason not to exhaust the Via Dolorosa. If Leonardo did not wear the stigmata, he walked all the more unreal by the strange edges of his psychic life. Mystics are practical : genius loves detail. Leonardo proves to himself the laws of reality, admitting tersely and definitely that spirits are, but are in another sphere, not communicable with this ; trying to forget psychical affairs awhile, for the sake of his sanity, perhaps. Yet every now and then he sees that blown flame, that breaking wave, and the universe passes in a cloud of mystical dust.

Besides fulfilling the actual cravings of his mind, then, these scientific researches saved Leonardo from accidia and tristitia, the disease and wastage of all monks, whether intellectual or emotional. The scientific stoicism which formed the ethical code of the cold religion of stupendous

Leonardo the Savant

Necessity was a fortifying power for one whose imagination sought after a rare sensuous mysticism. Castled in impregnable adamant, sure of its safe retreat, his soul made its subtle sallies across the marches of reality. The artist was supreme in him, but the scientist was necessary to the fine equilibrium of his mind which balanced him beyond all possible psychical disaster. The only trouble seems to be that the scheme of Leonardo's intellect was not on a scale fitted for mortal time.

The Epilogue

i

STILL he walks in rose-colour, Leonardo the Florentine, young by the green bow of Arno in the golden sunset, his lute in his hands, all his notebooks unwritten, all his pictures unpainted, all his riddles unguessed, the most enchanting prince of the Renaissance—for thirty years inclined to leave it at that. Of all the beauty he created, the bright legend of his youth is the best. He continues to challenge, to excite, to annoy, more perhaps than any other man in modern history, more like a great queen of romance than anything else. They try to hide him in the grey habit of the scientific worker, and put some uncandid tags in his mouth; but his noble "divinity" burns white through the disguise.

It makes the English so happy to say Leonardo was mostly an engineer. They are afraid of him and afraid of Italy; and they think that an understanding of mechanics robs him of the last mote of his magic. He who saw the "paradise of mechanics" as a rare garden hung with fruits would have been surprised at their artless conviction.

But all the Northern minds that have been liberated by the golden largess of the Southern sea are still half afraid of the shores locked by God to be the hollow of His wisdom and His delight. There the East has tossed its dark mystery of life in a foam of rose and lotos. There the gilded coffer of Osiris has rested beneath the germinating branches. There the ships of Greece have sailed for golden Helen, and Sappho has sunk her head in the waves by Lesbos. There the sacred Snake has been worshipped in Carthage; the mariners have heard across the waves that Pan is dead. Barques laden with mysterious colour have come from Tyre, and peacocks, apes, and ivory from Sidon. The Celtic folk have found it in the azure twilight, and left their deposit of dusking dreams. All the races of the ancient world have mingled in Sicily, and Provence has sung across the wave to Tripoli. But the Sirens chant on the shores of Italy. God made the cities of the East as chalices for His dark wisdom, and the cities of Greece as lamps for His illumination, but the cities of Italy He dreamed for mere delight.

Delight is the richest contagion, and again and again the nations for whose vanity the "Nordic" myth was recently invented, having become

The Epilogue

i

STILL he walks in rose-colour, Leonardo the Florentine, young by the green bow of Arno in the golden sunset, his lute in his hands, all his notebooks unwritten, all his pictures unpainted, all his riddles unguessed, the most enchanting prince of the Renaissance—for thirty years inclined to leave it at that. Of all the beauty he created, the bright legend of his youth is the best. He continues to challenge, to excite, to annoy, more perhaps than any other man in modern history, more like a great queen of romance than anything else. They try to hide him in the grey habit of the scientific worker, and put some uncandid tags in his mouth; but his ironic " divinity " burns white through the disguise.

It makes the English so happy to say Leonardo was mostly an engineer. They are afraid of him and afraid of Italy; and they think that an understanding of mechanics robs him of the last mote of his magic. He who saw the " paradise of mechanics " as a rare garden hung with fruits would have been surprised at their artless conviction.

But all the Northern minds that have been liberated by the golden largess of the Southern sea are still half afraid of the shores locked by God to be the hollow of His wisdom and His delight. There the East has tossed its dark mystery of life in a foam of rose and lotos. There the gilded coffer of Osiris has rested beneath the germinating branches There the ships of Greece have sailed for golden Helen, and Sappho has sunk her head in the waves by Lesbos. There the sacred Snake has been worshipped in Carthage; the mariners have heard across the waves that Pan is dead. Barques laden with mysterious colour have come from Tyre, and peacocks, apes, and ivory from Sidon. The Celtic folk have found it in the azure twilight, and left their deposit of duskling dreams. All the races of the ancient world have mingled in Sicily, and Provence has sung across the wave to Tripoli. But the Sirens chant on the shores of Italy. God made the cities of the East as chalices for His dark wisdom, and the cities of Greece as lamps for His illumination, but the cities of Italy He dreamed for mere delight.

Delight is the richest contagion, and again and again the nations for whose vanity the " Nordic " myth was recently invented, having become

The Epilogue

pale and cold, wring out some of that vintage so sweet that they think it forbidden. They drank deepest during the Renaissance years. Leonardo is the flower of the Mediterranean culture in all its ages, spiring splendid in the fertilizing air, with the passion rarefied away into an imaginative reverie. He communicates with us still across the years by the mysterious power of a personality strong enough to enter into the human imagination. Sappho, if no fiery fragment of hers had ever been found, would have remained a cry among the nightingales and a wave of violet in the waters. Alcibiades is for ever a sound of flutes among the philosophers. Hell is deeplier sunk because Dante hated. Saint Francis is a tenderness in the temper of humanity. Leonardo is an alluring gesture, and an enchanting smile. All the notebooks fall away, all the pictures draw together in one dream-face on an immortal shore discontenting us with this world.

ii

He is clouded sometimes by perverse people who call themselves his initiates, trying to wrap their fevers in the purple of a quiet king. And he remains enigmatic. Did his name mean captive or conqueror indeed ? If he wore a chain, he forged it with the flowerlike delicacy of a fantasia dei Vinci. True, he is not bound to us by love : he regards us with the irony of a god : he offers his liberation of the æsthetic ecstasy in accents divinely sweet but strange, even incomprehensible. When as an artist he has vanished too far through the blue and the green to seek his strange beauty, and the lovely exciting heads bend too ironically from their dark air, one murmurs : " While the earth remaineth, seedtime and harvest and cold and heat and summer and winter and day and night shall not cease." It is steadying. Then one remembers that he has said this also himself ; in the marvellous catholicity of his drawings. He is the apologist of the lonely reverie ; but his great intellect could endure that dissolving mood which for some is a poison. He is like a music, entering sweetly into the blood, kindling the heart with a wistful desire for love beyond the boundaries of sense, dying away in dewy vanishing notes, echoes angelical, beyond good and evil.

iii

The burning passion of the Renaissance temper is not obvious in its great exponent. Not his such wild rapture for Hellenism and beauty as bound the tortured brows of Sigismondo with a divine dæmonic laurel, or helmed with silver the sensual clay of Lorenzo de' Medici. But if he, to whom all things seem possible, acquiesced in the calm

The Epilogue

synthesis and equilibrium of his spirit, he may have obeyed some imperious warning in his blood. If he had given himself to any frenzy, a being of such amazing energy would have paled the despots. He was the god with the dragon : he kept it underfoot. Perhaps he suppressed the emotional life too much ; and it shaped his dream the more strangely. It is at the end, not the beginning, of his æsthetic career that he paints the triumphal *Saint John.*

But it is not really for us to know if a unique personality felt triumph or defeat, for he lived on a plane remote from the ordinary judgment, far from lovers' vows and safe hearth-fires, where a more angelic or dæmonic force charges the spirit.

> " Thus, for a saint's apostasy,
> The unimagined woes
> And sorrows of the hierarchy
> None but an angel knows."

Leonardo had something of Lucifer and something of Michael. The dark and the light strove in him towards creation ; and gods, beasts, angels, and mortals passed in his vision. Who has his passion for perfection now ? Who can create a new and lasting Pattern of beauty as he did ? Who can alter the dreams of men ? Who can pass easily from point to point of wisdom like him ? Who can enrich the human psychology with a new mood and a new curiosity ? What spirit is fine and fiery enough to be Leonardo's apparitor ?

iv

Leonardo was born perfect in mind and body ; but the ways of the world have been worn by the desperate defiances and the heroic weaknesses of the imperfect. He had to carve his original paths with his too precious diamond tools, and to charm his jealous kind with music and courtesy. There are hapless " faults " and chasms in his earthly world, which a lesser and more human intelligence would have overleaped. But he kept his course like a star ; and kings and warriors could not deflect this bright vassal of the sun from his fixed orbit, and his remorseless duty to his own soul. He could not love much ; but he enchanted so that his lovers were satisfied ; and his grace of liberal indulgence had all the effect of tenderness. He was of those idealists whose passion is only for absolutes, and who are invaluable to the development of the race, for they keep burning those white torches of truth and beauty that Pity and Faith are always willing for Love's sake to reverse. And, if it be true that the humblest, risking his heart in a mortal passion, may gather a

2 M   545

The Epilogue

keen rose-laurel where Leonardo failed, it is even truer that the haughtiest will never equal the renown of the figure, shod with splendour, that walks through time and place, a taunt, a challenge, and a mystery.

V

Let it be always remembered also that in one way Leonardo did enter irretrievably into the earth, and serve Italy with his genius. The plain of Lombardy became so rich that it could not be ruined, and Leonardo's spirit there married the shining waters and came smiling to obscure and lovely immortality in the foison of its fruits and flowers. But indeed he was more of Italy that he could know—perhaps till he dreamed in the castle of Cloux. Whatever strange type of sibyl and siren he painted by the waters, she would serve better than any other image for the Italy of the Renaissance as the Northern nations saw her, sitting by her shining lakes and rivers with magian eyes, inviting their souls to all delight and probable disaster, yet certainly to an adventure so unique as to be irresistible.

There are places it is good to be born in, for they shape the soul as a Greek amphora contained the wine. Such was Athens, such was Florence in Lorenzo's time. Leonardo had seen men and cities and things, and had dissolved them away to a colour in his personality; but the Florentine mould received all the rich libations of Lombardy, and kept the lucid outline through all the soft wet light of dreams. Florence shaped him, Milan charged him with reverie, and gave him noble opportunity, Rome rejected him; it was Florence that haunted his exile, though his tired eyes rested on the bright head of Francesco of Milan.

vi

But there is something dreamlike in the eddying people, the gold and crimson patterns drift into vanishing spirals of coloured smoke; the voices and the gestures grow faint as the light of dead and dying stars. Like a waft of hautboys and lutes, Florence, Milan, Venice, Rome, and Amboise, go fading down the spaces of eternity; and Leonardo is left contemplative.

And to others it is he that seems visionary. All the folk who try to speak of him describe him dimly in terms of nonpareil and ineluctable brightness, gestures of greatness and grace, a preoccupied sweetness faintly apprehended, as somebody they had dreamed rather than known; and his conversation is indeed like music, not to be reported save in its effects. He appears really like Prospero sometimes, a dream-duke of

The Epilogue

Milan, serenely disguised, literally a lord of winds and waters and yellow sands, amused at the bright children, served by Ariel and the " slaves of music," ready for a masque, ready to scatter it in a vision of fading and dissolving earth, lost in the clear melancholy of a wisdom that has resigned and forgotten the dear crimsons of life. But, unlike Prospero, he never broke his staff ; he offered to the end his cup of troubling beauty, to save the soul from sloth and contentment, and ravish it awhile with ethereal desire from the gross habit and dulled senses of its mortality.

He widened the borders of life, and he diffused through the psychology of Western nations a new kind of delight and a passionate expectation of wonder, such a mysterious hope as invades you if you see the dawn begin unearthly over the ultimate islands, or the hills vanish into paler hills that again are but the foothills of heavenlier ranges, or the birds on the golden horizons climbing their castled air.

Appendix A

Note on Leonardo's Family and Early Life

IT will be best, perhaps, to record briefly here the dated facts of Leonardo's first thirty years. He was born near the little hamlet of Vinci, five miles north of Empoli, on the right bank of the Arno, on the way to Monte Albano, not far from the strategical point of Anchiano. He was the natural son of a peasant girl, called Caterina, and Ser Piero da Vinci, the notary son of a long line of notaries of some repute both in Vinci and in Florence. His birth-year is known to be 1452 from a taxation return made in 1457 by Leonardo's grandfather, Ser Antonio, in which he numbers the residents in his casa at Vinci. Besides himself, it contained his wife, Monna Lucia, aged sixty-four; Ser Piero, now thirty; Francesco, another son; Albiera, the young wife of Piero; and Leonardo, aged five, the illegitimate son of Ser Piero, his mother being Caterina, " now married to Chartabriga di Piero del Vaccha da Vinci." An aunt, Alessandra, also seems to have been of the household.

The Anonimo Fiorentino says Leonardo's mother was " of gentle blood "; other accounts refer to her as a peasant. But in the year of Leonardo's birth, Ser Piero married Albiera di Giovanni Amadori, of a nobler house than his own, while Caterina was wedded to her allotted cattleherd.

The boy grew up in his father's house, mostly at Vinci, sometimes in Florence, where the family rented a half-house. When Leonardo was nine, his first step-mother, for whose family he ever had a kindness, probably because they were of gentle manners, died, and in 1465 Ser Piero married a Florentine girl two years older than his son, Francesca di Ser Giovanni Lanfredini. About this time Leonardo was probably taught simple things at home. He surpassed in arithmetic, learned with great facility, and from the beginning was exceedingly versatile. Music, mathematics, singing and literature formed part of his education. Latin he probably acquired later. But very early he drew and modelled.

Ser Piero, being of a fifth generation of notaries, prospered greatly in his craft. In 1469, Ser Antonio being dead by this time, the family moved into Florence entirely. Ser Piero lived in a house behind the Signoria in the Piazza di Firenza on the site of the Palazzo Gondi. There was also a house at Fiesole. The notary was greatly in demand for contracts and public documents. In 1471 he was procurator to the Cloister of Santa Annunziata; he also became financial adviser to the monks of S. Donato, legal assistant to the Medici and other public families, and Notary to the Signoria. He probably used his professional influence on behalf of his brilliant son, which may explain to some degree why Leonardo was so perversely cavalier towards his early Florentine commissions. At the age of forty-five he married a third wife, with a dowry of three hundred and sixty-five florins, who presented him with five legitimate children. With the advent of the first, Leonardo, beautiful Ishmael of the family, at last knew the disadvantages of a stepmother, and finally quitted his father's house to live in Verrocchio's. After the death of this dutiful lady, Ser Piero nobly denied himself a wife for some years; but at the age of sixty he indomitably wedded a certain Lucrezia di Cortegiani and had six more undistinguished children.

Leonardo seems to have maintained some kind of acquaintanceship with his relatives, though his stepbrothers in later years ungenerously disputed his part in the inheritance, trying even to withhold from him some roods of land left him by his uncle Francesco. Leonardo, having gained his point by the intervention of cardinals and French captains, resumed his aloof but tolerant attitude sufficiently to receive an admiring message from an intelligent sister-in-law, and to acknowledge his brothers in his will by a legacy of the disputed property. Probably in the loneliness of age, unknit to his race by any organic bond, he felt even a stepbrother a kind of witness to his humanity. The one friendly quasi-relative was Alessandro Amadori, Canon of Fiesole, who called himself his uncle, and interceded for Isabella d'Este.

As for Ser Piero, in the second phase of his Florentine years Leonardo briefly chronicles his end, in a chill entry which, to say the least, is without emotion. Some biographers admiringly remark that the father's physical energy helps to explain the psychical fervour of the son. Perhaps! Others are a little horrified at the development of Caterina's romantic lover into " this Bluebeard of a notary," as Gabriel Séailles calls him, though " Bluebeard " is slightly harsh, for his wives all died naturally. His fastidious son would regard his commercial activities with contempt and his senescent uxoriousness with disgust. Some acid sentences about money-getters, and others more than worthy of the *Kreutzer Sonata*, we probably owe to his cold contemplation of Ser Piero, who may have caused still more profound reactions. As it is, the notary seems somehow a subject for a Florentine Arnold Bennett. In 1869, a peasant descendant called Tommaso Vinci, whose forefather was Domenico, Leonardo's stepbrother, was alive.

At least the notary was intelligent enough to give his son a magnificent name, and to take his early drawings to his friend, Verrocchio, who, astonished by their quality, received the boy of fourteen or so in his bottega, where he found Lorenzo di Credi an earnest pupil, Perugino as a kind of post-graduate research worker, and many others. At seventeen he was living independently among various companions, and earning a great reputation for versatility, grace, and power.

He drew, and he modelled waxen heads of boys and of women smiling. His originality in inventions, his chamber of horrors where he gathered terrifying reptiles from which to compose the Platonic idea of a dragon, his interest in engineering, and his skill on the lute, all attracted popular curiosity. The story of his painting an angel in Verrocchio's *Baptism* with such beauty that the discomfited master renounced painting for ever, since " a child " could vanquish him, is well known ; but Leonardo and Verrocchio, as well as the angel in question, are mute witnesses against its veracity. The tale of the " rondache " or shield, on the other hand, is likely to be true. The *naïf* peasant who brings Ser Piero the curious round of wood with a desire that it should be painted with some device, and who receives in the end, with overwhelming gratitude, another shield painted with an arrow-pierced heart, a symbol for ever dear to simple souls ; Leonardo, who shuts himself up with noisome lizards and spiders and bats till he has created on the true circle a monster so veridical that his father is at first terrified to death ; Ser Piero, who, recovering from his fright, rejoices and stealthily sells the work at a great price, so filling his pocket, delighting the peasant, and amusing the fantasy of his disdainful son all at once, in his adequate bourgeois manner, make a pretty comedy. The anecdote has its value because it illustrates Leonardo's way of preparing a ground of realism for his romantic fantasy. In the same mood he painted a Medusa head, which no longer exists, and a cartoon of Adam and Eve in the Earthly Paradise, for a tapestry of the King of Portugal, that never found its way to the looms. An uncle of Leonardo's, it is said, possessed it for some time and gave it to Ottaviano de' Medici.

In 1472 Leonardo's name is entered in the Red Book of the Company of Painters in Florence as being admitted to membership. The painters of Florence were enrolled among the Guild of Physicians and Apothecaries. The Company of Saint Luke had its residenza in the great hospital of Sta Maria Nuova, which Leonardo used as a bank for money and a school of anatomy. Entries show that he was guilty of forgetting the candles due to Saint Luke, of forgetting to pay his sub-scription, and of working on holy festival days. To 1473 belongs his first dated drawing, bearing an inscription written from left to right.

In 1476 an anonymous accusation, in the " drum " of the wall of the Signoria, levelled against him and others a charge of unnatural vice in connexion with a certain model called Jacopo Saltarelli. The charge, which has been already trans-

Appendix A

scribed from Solmi's biography, was repeated, but finally rejected as not proven. The early study of St John belongs to this year. Leonardo was still living with Verrocchio : it is supposed that he left him about 1477. According to some accounts, it was at this point that he accepted an atelier in San Marco from Lorenzo, and more or less was in his service.

On the 1st of January 1478 the Signoria of Florence offered him a commission for an altarpiece in the Chapel of S. Bernard in the Palazzo Vecchio. Eight days before, the work had been given to Piero Pollaiuolo ; some influence, probably Lorenzo's, diverted it. But, though the Signoria waited five years, and the artist was paid twenty-five florins on account, the picture was never painted. When, in despair, the Council turned to the busy Ghirlandajo, he also failed them, and Filippino Lippi at last sufficed their need, in 1485. It is possible that Leonardo considered an Adoration of the Shepherds as a theme for this picture.

Leonardo is known from a fragmentary note on a drawing to have been "working at the two Madonnas " in October, 1478. He seems to have been staying at Pistoja for a time. In 1479 he certainly was in Florence, for he drew the hanged conspirator, Bandino Bandini.

The monks of the rich convent of San Donato, outside Scopeto, by the Porta Romana, now asked Leonardo, in March 1480, for a picture to set over their High Altar. The contract was complicated. The artist was allowed twenty-four or thirty months for his period of labour ; the monks reserved power to terminate the contract without compensation if the work was not done. The price was to be one-third of some monastic property in the Val d'Elsa, or three hundred florins, if the owners desired to resume the land. A girl's dowry came out of the estate, a condition fixed by the testator. But, for all the intricate arrangements, no Leonardo masterpiece ever came in wonder to the altar of the monks. In 1480 and 1481 he appears to have stayed at times in a monastery outside Florence. His employers paid him sums on account ; they sent him barrels of red wine and measures of wheat. In 1481, probably when he was in residence, they allowed him a load of wood and one lira, six soldi, for painting the clock, which he did partly as a caprice, partly because his purse for the moment was empty. The time and care spent during this period over elaborate studies and designs for an Adoration of the Magi suggest very strongly that the great picture in monochrome now in the Uffizi was intended for the patient monks. The somewhat pathetic counter-plea that, though the contract bound Leonardo to provide his own colours, his anxious employers nevertheless allowed him some expensive blue and yellow, that these have not been used in the *Adoration*, and that Leonardo could not possibly have diverted them to another purpose, is negligible. With great insouciance he could have diverted them to any chance purpose whatever. Ultramarine and gold he did not esteem greatly ; the monks, who, as a rule, loved bright colours, were trying to make sure of them.

Leonardo was " in casa propria " in 1481. Thereafter, from 1481 till 1501, his name disappears from Florentine records. But, from evidence deduced from Sabba Castiglione's description of his sixteen years' work in the great studio, he must have been in Milan in 1483. In 1487, Bellincioni mentions him as settled in Milan and definitely part of its Court—" Da Fiorenza un Apelle la qui condotto."

Because of this lapse in dated record, some students of Leonardo look favourably on the hypothesis of Dr J. P. Richter—based on some scraps of fanciful letters to the Devatdar of Syria—that for some years Leonardo was absent in the Orient, that he was appointed acting-engineer to the Sultan of Syria, and accepted the religion of Mahomet. This theory looks plausible, for Leonardo's odd letters to the Devatdar describe vividly an earthquake that did happen at Aleppo and Syria ; his architecture has an Oriental air, and some of his moods, burning-cold, inflexible, and gorgeous, are not out of tone with the temper of the fatalists of Allah. But those letters do not contain anything that Leonardo, curious inquirer, might not have heard from far travellers in Florence or Milan or Venice, for explorers did go to Cathay, Constantinople, Russia, Timbuctoo. Great Italian cities were visited by embassies from Asian and African coasts ; Armenian headgear is drawn in other sketch-books besides Leonardo's, in that Ferrarese book attributed to Mantegna for instance ; also, there were slaves in all the cities, Nubians, Russians, Circassians.

Appendix A

The letters, divagating into an extravagant key, are merely some of Leonardo's realistic day-dreaming, incidentally making him the originator of epistolary romance. As for the architecture, there were Oriental effects in Italian building long before Leonardo. And there is no trace of the fanatical, sensual side of Mohammedanism in Leonardo's tolerant, agnostical attitude towards the universe. Besides, it is impossible to believe that Leonardo could have gone to serve a Sultan, and wandered in the Orient, without some Eastern episode appearing in his legend. One artist went to Moscow, another to Constantinople, and so it was written. Vasari would have heard of Leonardo, in Phrygian cap and Asian robes, seducing barbaric princes, bridging the awful chasms of Afreet-haunted mountains, watching the immemorial motion of those great waters, the Tigris and the Euphrates, pondering mosques and churches in Cilicia, pausing divinely over fabulous buried cities, wandering lost amid the tremendous pillars of ancient sun-temples, received as an enchanter by Mazdæan priests, becoming a kind of solar myth in the savage heights and lost waters of the ranges of Taurus. No! Some mithraic rumour would have rippled to Italy from Leonardo's Eastern progress.

Descriptions of Etna and Stromboli in eruption, an odd account of Cyprus might witness some Mediterranean travel. But Leonardo's habit is to set down matters of hearsay as vividly as things seen. No artist has to see a place in order to have a vision of it.

In all probability he left Florence about 1482, or early in 1483, and proceeded to the Court of Lodovico Sforza at Milan, in company with Atalante Migliarotti and Zoroastro da Pertola. He himself was carrying a silver lute of his own invention, shaped like the head of a horse; and he was either directly sent by Lorenzo, or went with his commendation. Whether the famous letter in which he describes his own powers was addressed to Lodovico before his arrival or after it remains uncertain. It had been a matter of general knowledge for some years that the new Duke, anxious to dazzle, desired to erect the superlative equestrian monument dreamed of by his brother to their condottiere father. Antonio Pollaiuolo had been making designs for it, but there is no evidence of an open competition. Leonardo had been working with the sculptor of the Colleone statue; his renown was great, his confidence was superb, his personality captivating, his music seducing. A person who could not only create the super-steed, but could also be courtier enough to handle the masques and paint the mistresses, Apelles enough to glorify the Duke's name in cloister and castle, architect and engineer enough to carry out his schemes of irrigation and building both in Milan and Pavia, was exactly the kind of genius that Lodovico would accept at his own valuation. What that valuation was we learn from Leonardo himself. Before he enters on the second and more mature phase of his existence, it should here be printed once again. The calm and rather terrible arrogance of its terms is due not only to Leonardo's unshaken confidence in his powers, but also to that secret snake of pathological doubt and fear which lay in his breast, just faintly constricting its coils from time to time. There is nothing like an unrecognized terror for turning pride to vanity. Leonardo's letter is marvellous; but it leaves a strange impression. If the writer is indeed not more than mortal, we think, here are the characters of megalomania:

" Most illustrious Lord,—Having now sufficiently considered the specimens of all those who proclaim themselves skilled contrivers of instruments of war, and that the invention and operation of the said instruments are nothing different to those in common use: I shall endeavour, without prejudice to anyone else, to explain myself to your Excellency, showing your Lordship my secrets and then offering them to your best pleasure and approbation to work with effect at opportune moments as well as all those things which, in part, shall be briefly noted below.

(1) I have a sort of extremely light and strong bridges adapted to be most easily carried, and with them you may pursue and at any time flee from the enemy; and others, secure and indestructible by fire and battle, easy and convenient to lift and place. Also methods of burning and destroying those of the enemy.

(2) I know how, when a place is besieged, to take water out of the trenches

552

and make endless variety of bridges, and covered ways and ladders, and other machines pertaining to such expeditions.

(3) Item. If, by reason of the height of the banks, or the strength of the place and its position, it is impossible, when besieging a place, to avail oneself of the plan of bombardment, I have methods for destroying every rock or other fortress even if it were founded on a rock, etc.

(4) Again, I have kinds of mortars; most convenient and easy to carry; and with these can fling small stones almost resembling a storm; and with the smoke of these causing great terror to the enemy, to his great detriment and confusion.

(9) [8] And when the fight should be at sea I have kinds of many machines most efficient for offence and defence; and vessels which will resist the attack of the largest guns and powder and fumes.

(5) I have means by secret and tortuous mines and ways, made without noise to reach a designated [spot]. Even if it were needed to pass under a trench or a river.

(6) Item. I will make covered chariots, safe and unattackable, which, entering among the enemy with their artillery there is no body of men so great but they would break them. And behind these, infantry could follow quite unhurt and without any hindrance.

(7) Item. In case of need I will make big guns, mortars and light ordnance of fine and useful forms out of the common type.

(8) Where the operation of bombardment should fail, I would contrive catapults, mangonels, trabocchi and other machines of marvellous efficacy and not in common use. And in short, according to the variety of cases, I can contrive various and endless means of offence and defence.

(10) In time of peace I believe I can give perfect satisfaction and to the equal of any other in architecture and the composition of buildings public and private; and in guiding water from one place to another.

Item. I can carry out sculpture in marble, bronze, or clay, and also in painting whatever may be done, and as well as any other, be he whom he may.

[32] Again, the bronze horse may be taken in hand which is to be the immortal glory and eternal honour of the prince your father of happy memory, and of the illustrious house of Sforza.

And if any one of the above-named things seem to anyone to be impossible or not feasible, I am most ready to make the experiment in your park, or in whatever place may please your Excellency, to whom I commend myself with the utmost humility."

Appendix B

Dated Summary of the Later Life of Leonardo

1483. *The Last Supper* begun.

1487. Leonardo is installed as general artificer and architect. He is at work in an atelier in an ancient Visconti palace on the Great Steed, and in the refectory of Santa Maria delle Grazie on mural decorations. We presently find him engaged in irrigation schemes, linking rivers and waterways, and in a vast plan of city reconstruction. He is also employed in decorating the Castello and in portrait-painting. In August he makes a dome for the Consiglio delle Fabbrica del Duomo. On 11th January 1488 he has it back on certain conditions. He was paid for making a second. Bramante also sent in a design for the cupola of Milan Cathedral. The work was assigned to the Milanese architects, Amadeo and Dolcebuono, in April 1490.

1489. Leonardo produces the masque *Il Paradiso* in collaboration with Bernardo Bellincioni for the wedding of the young duke, Gian Galeazzo, with Isabella of Aragon. He devises an arrangement of pulleys and cords for the elevation of the Sacred Nail. He begins a book *Concerning the Human Figure*, and makes notes on the study of Light. Through Piero Alamanni, the Florentine agent at Milan, Lodovico appeals to Lorenzo asking for two sculptors to construct the statue. The agent says : " for though he has entrusted the commission to Leonardo da Vinci, he does not seem to me to have much confidence in his ability to carry it to completion." This seems to refer to the casting.

1490. Leonardo writes down : " On the 23rd of April 1490 I began this book, and recommenced the Horse." He goes to Pavia with Francesco di Giorgio of Siena to advise concerning the proposed Duomo there. Leonardo remains at Pavia studying mathematics and architecture.

1491. Marriage of Lodovico Sforza. Leonardo arranges the tourney of Galeazzo di Sanseverino (January).

1492. Leonardo constructs the " pavilion of the garden of the Duchess of Milan," also " the Bath of the Duchess."

1493. The model of the *Cavallo* is displayed under an arch at the wedding of Bianca Sforza. (According to Pacioli it was twenty-six feet high, and would have required five furnaces to cast it.)

1494-1495. Leonardo is one of a commission appointed to consider the plan of a great Hall of Council in the palace of the Florentine Signoria.

1495. Leonardo probably completes the decoration of the camerini assigned to him in the Castello. His delay caused a year's estrangement from his patron, who tried to obtain the services of Perugino.

1496. Giovanni Ambrogio da Predis and Leonardo da Vinci appeal to the Duke asking him to intervene in a dispute between the petitioners and the monks of the Brotherhood of the Conception in San Francesco concerning the valuation of the altarpiece now known as *The Virgin of the Rocks*. From the document discovered in the archives, it is evident that the monks wanted a gilded and carved ancona, that Leonardo himself did the central picture, that the monks, according to the petitioners, had fixed a price that barely covered expenses, and that there was a higher bidder for the picture. Evidently Leonardo recovered his original picture, which found its way to the possession of the French king, while he partly painted a replica for the monks, which remained in Milan till 1787. Gavin Hamilton then brought it to England. It is now in the National Gallery.

Appendix B

1497. Death of the Duchess Beatrice. Lodovico bids his secretary urge Leonardo the Florentine to complete the work in the Refectory, and to bind him in writing to a date of accomplishment. Leonardo complains that his salary is two years in arrears.

1498. *The Last Supper* is probably finished about this year. Leonardo takes part in a Duello of scholars held in the Castello. He complains that he has maintained six men for fifty-six months, and has of late received only fifty ducats. A vineyard is given him by the Duke. Leonardo visits Mantua, carrying viol and lute strings for Isabella.

[At this point may be inserted the fragments of Leonardo's letter of remonstrance to the Duke, as translated by Mr Edward MacCurdy :

"MY LORD,—Knowing the mind of your Excellency to be occupied . . . to remind your Lordships of my small matters and the arts put to silence . . . that my silence was the cause of making your Lordship despise . . . my life in your service, I hold myself ever ready to obey . . . of the horse I say nothing because I know the times . . . to your Lordship how I was two years in arrears with my salary for the . . . with two skilled workmen whose salary and expenses I had always paid . . . that at last I found I had advanced the said work about 15 lire . . . works of fame by which I could show to those who shall see them that I have been . . . everywhere, but I do not know where I could bestow my work to . . . I having been taken up with gaining a living . . . not being informed how it is, I find myself . . . you remember the commission to paint the Camerini . . . I conveyed to your Lordship only requesting . . ."]

1499. The French occupy Milan under Trivulzio. Lodovico escapes to the Tyrol. Leonardo writes : "The Duke has lost the State, his goods, his liberty, and nothing he has undertaken has been completed."

1500. Battle of Novara. Partial destruction of *Cavallo* by Gascon bowmen. Leonardo with Pacioli proceeds to Venice by way of Mantua.

1501-1514. Leonardo varies between Florence and Milan.

1501. Exhibition of the cartoon of *Saint Anne*. Leonardo studies anatomy at Sta Marie Nuova, and is immersed in mathematics. Isabella of Mantua appeals for work of his through Fra Pietro du Nuvolaria ; Leonardo leaves Florence for the service of Cesare Borgia in July.

1502. Patent of authority issued by Cesare Borgia in August.

1503. Leonardo is in Florence in April, and is sent to the camp at Pisa.

1504. Ser Piero da Vinci dies. Leonardo supports San Gallo in the council of artists held to decide the position of Michelangelo's *David*.

1505. The cartoon for *The Battle of Anghiari* is finished at the end of February, 1505. About this period Leonardo is painting Mona Lisa and Ginevra d'Amerigo Benci.

1506. In May Leonardo goes to study birds at Fiesole. In August he is summoned to Milan by the governor, Charles d'Amboise, and is allowed to go for three months under an agreement. Soderini in October expresses anger at the continued absence of the painter. Charles d'Amboise writes diplomatically, suggesting the wishes of the French king.

1507. Louis intervenes. In April Leonardo's vine-garden is restored to him. In May the King is in Milan. Leonardo is working at hydraulics, and studying anatomy with della Torre. The lawsuit forced on him by the dispute over the will of his uncle Francesco brings him twice to Florence in this year.

1508. He lives in the house of Rusticci, the sculptor, which is part of the dwelling of Piero di Braccio Martelli, the mathematician. Charles d'Amboise, Cardinal Ippolito d'Este, and King Louis implore the termination of the lawsuit.

1509. Triumphal entry of Louis XII. at Milan after the Battle of Agnadel. Leonardo completes his reservoir for the Canal of San Cristoforo. He is granted the right of twelve inches of water.

1510. He is appointed an advisory member of the commission on the construction of the choir-stalls in the Cathedral of Milan.

1511. Charles d'Amboise dies before Correggio. The Holy League is formed.

1512. The Battle of Ravenna. Death of Gaston de Foix. Maximilian Sforza

Appendix B

enters Milan with Swiss troops. In December Leonardo watches the conflagration in the city. In March Giovanni de' Medici becomes Pope Leo X. Leonardo seeks the patronage of his brother, Giuliano.

1513. In September Leonardo leaves Milan with Melzi and Salai. He appears in Rome under Giuliano's protection, passes most of the time in scientific experiments in the Belvedere, in anatomy at the Hospital, and geology in the Campagna.

1515. Giuliano de' Medici goes to Savoy to wed Philiberta, and Louis XII. dies. Leonardo accompanies Giuliano with the Papal armies. Battle of Marignano.

1516. In January Leonardo departs to France with King Francis. Death of Giuliano de' Medici.

1516. Leonardo settles at manor-house of Cloux, as "premier peintre et ingenieur et architecte du Roy, meschanischien d'estat," at a salary of seven hundred crowns.

1517. October 10th. He is visited by the Cardinal d'Aragon.

1518. Leonardo records the Day of Saint John.

1519. 2nd May. Death of Leonardo.

1519. 12th August. Burial of Leonardo in the cloister of the Collegiate Church of Saint Florentin in Amboise. [In this year the Duke Lorenzo and his wife died in Florence : Lucrezia Borgia was buried as a Tertiary of Saint Francis ; the Marquis of Mantua made way for Isabella's adored son Federigo ; and the Emperor Maximilian ceased from troubling.]

Leonardo's will was simple and decorous. To Francesco Melzi he left all his books, instruments, drawings, relative to his art and painter's industry, and the remainder of his pension. His vineyard at Milan was divided between Andrea Salaino, who had already built a house on it, and Battista da Villanis. The waiting-woman Mathurine was given two ducats, a fur-lined cloak and a gown. His brothers had the principal and interest of four hundred crowns left in Florence, and the property at Fiesole. Francesco was directed to distribute money among the poor of the Hôtel-Dieu and of St Lazare, and to carry out the elaborate provision for his funeral.

Chief Italian Artists Contemporary with Leonardo da Vinci

North Italian

Leonardo da Vinci, 1452–1519
Fra Angelico, 1387–1455
Ghiberti, 1378–1455
Andrea del Castagno, 1390–1457
Donatello, 1386–1466
Desiderio da Settignano, 1428–1464
Bernardo Rossellino, 1409–1464
Michelozzo Michelozzi, 1391–1472
Paolo Uccello, 1397–1475
Leo Battista Alberti, 1406–1470
Fra Lippo Lippi, 1406–1469
Agostino di Duccio, 1418–1481
Mino da Fiesole, 1431–1484
Giuliano da Majano, 1432–1490
Luca della Robbia, 1400–1482
Benozzo Gozzoli, 1420–1497
Piero della Francesca, 1415–1492
Ercole Roberti, 1430–1496
Matteo di Giovanni, about 1435–1495
Pietro Torrigiani, 1472–1528
Antonio Pollaiuolo, 1429–1498
Pietro Vannucci (Perugino), 1446–1524
Andrea Mantegna, 1431–1506
Luca Signorelli, 1441-1523
Domenico Ghirlandajo, 1449–1494

Benedetto da Majano, 1442–1497
Alesso Baldovinetti, 1427–1499
Andrea Verrocchio, 1435–1488
Sandro Botticelli, 1444–1510
Piero di Cosimo, 1462–1521
Lorenzo di Credi, 1456–1537
Filippino Lippi, 1457–1504
Pinturricchio, 1454–1513
Giuliano di San Gallo, 1445-1516
Antonio di San Gallo, 1455 (?)–1534
Andrea della Robbia, 1435–1525
Francesco Francia, 1450–1517
Andrea Sansovino, 1455–1529
Mariotto Albertinelli, 1474–1515
Giovan Francesco Rusticci, 1474–1515
Fra Bartolommeo, 1475–1517
Michelangelo Buonarroti, 1475–1564
Sodoma (Giovanni Antonio Bazzi), 1477- 1549
Dosso Dossi, 1479–1541
Raphael, 1483–1520
Correggio, 1494–1534
Andrea del Sarto, 1486–1531
Monetto da Brescia, 1498–1554
Benvenuto Cellini, 1500–1572
Bronzino, 1502–1572

Venetian

Antonello da Messina, 1446–1493
Jacopo Bellini. Active, 1430–1470
Veneziano, 1415-1461
Gentile Bellini, 1426-1507
Giovanni Bellini, 1428-1516

Carlo Crivelli, 1430–1493
Vittore Carpaccio, 1450–1522
Giorgione, 1477–1510
Titian, 1477–1576
Palma Vecchio, 1480–1528

Contemporary Artists

Milanese

(Many of these dates are uncertain)

Vincenzo Foppa, 1427–1532
Bernardo Zenale, 1436–1526
Giovan Antonio Amadeo, 1447–1522
Cristoforo Solari (Il Gobbo), 1450 (?)– 1523
Ambrogio Borgognone, 1450 (?)–1523
Caradosso, 1452–1527
Dolcebuone, 1454–1519
Montorfano, mentioned as at work round 1495
Butinone, 1454–1507
Ambrogio da Predis, 1455–1506

Gian Cristoforo Romano, 1464–1512
Andrea Solario, 1465–1515
Giovan Antonio Boltraffio, 1467–1516
Marco d'Oggione, 1470–1530 (?)
Cesare de Sesto, 1477–1523
Bernardino de' Conti. Active *circa* 1490-1522
Francesco Melzi, d. 1570
Gianpietrino, at work during first decades of sixteenth century
Gaudenzio Ferrari, 1481–1546
Bernardino Luini, 1475–1532

Working in Milan under Lodovico Sforza

Filarete, 1410–1472   Bramante, 1444–1514   Bramantino, 1460–1529 (?)

General Dates from 1452-1519

I

Leonardo da Vinci, 1452–1519
Lorenzo de' Medici, 1449–1492
Giuliano de' Medici (1), 1453–1478
Marsilio Ficino, 1433–1491
Poliziano (Angelo Ambrogini), 1454–1494
Savonarola, 1452–1498
Pico della Mirandola, 1463–1494
Niccolo Machiavelli, 1469–1527
Paolo Toscanelli, 1397–1482
Amerigo Vespucci, 1451–1516
Fall of Constantinople in 1453
Hunyadi at Belgrade, 1456
Death of the Cardinal of Portugal, 1459
Embassy from Egypt to Florence, 1467
Tournament of Lorenzo, 1468
Visit of Galeazzo Maria Sforza to Florence, 1471
Revolt of Volterra, 1472
Foundation of University of Pisa, 1473
Assassination of Galeazzo Maria Sforza, 1475
Lodovico Sforza seizes power in Milan, 1476
Grammar of Lascaris printed in Greek in Milan, 1476
The Pazzi Conspiracy, 1476
Visitation of the Plague, 1478
Wars with Naples and Rome, 1479
Battle of Otranto, 1479
Landino's edition of Dante, 1481

II

Lodovico Sforza, 1451–1499
Aldus Manutius, 1450–1515
Christopher Columbus, 1451-1506
Emperor Maximilian, 1470–1524
Isabella d'Este, 1474–1539
Beatrice d'Este, 1475–1497
Charles VIII. of France, 1470–1498
Copernicus, 1473–1543
Ariosto, 1474–1532
Cesare Borgia, 1476–1507
Baldassare Castiglione, 1478–1529
Giuliano de' Medici (II.), 1479–1516
Giovanni de' Medici (Pope Leo X.), 1475–1521

Louis XII. of France, 1462–1515
Charles d'Amboise, Sieur de Chaumont, Governor of Milan, 1505–1511
Marcantonio della Torre in Milan, 1506–1513
Gaston de Foix, 1489–1512
Le Chevalier Bayard, 1473–1524
Cardinal Bembo, 1470–1542
Francis I. of France, 1494–1547
Marguerite d'Angoulême, 1494–1547
Opening of the Tomb of Julia, 1485
Death of Pope Sixtus IV., 1490
Peace between Milan and Venice, 1490
Savonarola at San Marco, 1491
Alliance of Florence and Lodovico Sforza, 1492
Death of Lorenzo de' Medici, 1492
Accession of Rodrigo Borgia as Pope Alexander VI., 1492
Christopher Columbus reaches San Salvador, 1492
First French Invasion under Charles VIII., 1494
Expulsion of the Medici, 1494
Maximilian expels the Turks from Styria, 1494
Lodovico is proclaimed Duke of Milan, 1494
League of Venice, 1495
Marriage of Lodovico with Beatrice d'Este, 1491
Battle of Fornovo, 1495
Albrecht Dürer in Italy, 1495
Statue of Bartolommeo Colleone unveiled, 1496
Bonfire of the Vanities, 1497
Vasco da Gama rounds the Cape, 1497
Consecration of the Cathedral of Pavia, 1497
Medicean Conspiracy, 1497
Death of the Duchess Beatrice, 1497
Death of Savonarola, 1498
Death of Charles VIII., 1498
Battle of Lepanto, 1499
Expedition of Louis XII. against Milan, 1499
First campaign of Cesare Borgia, 1499
Capture of Lodovico Sforza at Novara, 1500
Jubilee Year at Rome, 1500

General Dates from 1452-1519

Copernicus at Rome, 1500

El Gran Tradimento of the Baglioni, 1500

Columbus arrives chained in Spain, 1500

Return of Amerigo Vespucci, 1500

Second campaign of Cesare Borgia, 1500

Piero Soderini, Gonfaloniere of Florence, 1502

Stratagem of Sinigaglia, 1502

Death of Alexander VI. and election of Pope Julius, II., 1503

Discovery of Apollo Belvedere, 1503

Death of Ascanio Sforza, 1505

Erasmus in Italy, 1506

Dürer in Italy, 1505–1506

Revolt of Genoa, 1507

League of Cambrai, 1509

Battle of Agnadel, 1509

Death of Charles d'Amboise before Correggio, 1511

Battle of Ravenna and death of Gaston de Foix, 1512

Sack of Prato, 1512

Return of the Medici to Florence, 1512

Death of Julius II. and election of Leo X., 1513

Battle of Flodden, 1513

Publication of Aldo's Plato, 1513

Expedition of Francis I., Battle of Marignano, 1515

Conspiracy of the Cardinals, 1517

Luther's theses exhibited in Wittenberg, 1517

Deaths of Emperor Maximilian, Francesco Gonzaga, Lucrezia Borgia, and Leonardo, 1519

Bibliography

It is impossible to give a detailed bibliography within the covers of this volume. I name certain books easily accessible to the general reader. They give supplementary information, and different interpretations. "Etc." means that the author named has written other studies, besides what is mentioned, which may be read with profit. It is to be remembered that a great deal of valuable writing on Leonardo is buried in artistic and scientific periodicals, or in the proceedings of societies. Volumes concerned with philosophy, general discussion of art, Greek history, mediævalism in general, or Renaissance ways in particular, I do not give here.

Accessible Leonardo Manuscripts

(1) Codice A, B, C, D, E, F, G, H, I, K, L, M and the two Ashburnham codices kept in the Library of the Institute of Paris. Reproduced in 6 vols., with a literal transcription, French translation and notes by M. C. Ravaisson Mollien.

(2) Codice Trivulziano, in library of Prince Trivulzio, Milan, reproduced with translation and notes by Luca Beltrami.

(3) Codice Atlantico, with translation and notes by G. Piumati. Issued under care of the Accademia dei Lincei, Rome.

(4) Codice del Volo degli Uccelli, with translation and notes by G. Piumati. Published at the instance of M. Sabachnikoff, Paris.

(5) Part of MSS. in Royal Library at Windsor:
    (1) Fogli A. Dell' Anatomie. Published by Sabacknikoff. Translated by Piumati.
    (2) Fogli B. Also translated by Puimati.
    (3) Manoscritti e disegni inediti di Leonardo al Windsor, al British e al South Kensington Museum. Editi de Rouveyre a Parigi. Sketches and studies, 22 vols.

(6) Manuscript in British Museum (Arundel, 263) (not reproduced).

(7) Three volumes of MSS. in Forster Collection, South Kensington.

(8) Treatise on Weight, Light, and the Motion of Water. (Library of Lord Leicester, Holkham Hall.)

(9) Il Codice di L. da V. della Biblioteca di Lord Leicester in Holkham Hall. Pubblicati . . . da Gêrolamo Calvi.

(10) Del Moto e Misura dell'Acqua. Libri nove ordinati da F. Luigi Maria Arconati. Editi sul codice archetipo Barberiano a cura de E. Carusi, ed. A. Favaro, 1923. (Istituto de Studii Vinciani.)

(11) Problèmes de géometrie et d'hydrauliques. 3 pt. MS. inédits reproduits d'après les originaux conservés à la Forster Library. S.K.M.

(12) Sciences psychico mathématiques, 4 vols. Also from the Forster Library.

(13) Quaderni d'anatomia. Pubblicati da O. C. L. Vaugestein, A. Fonahn, H. Hopstock. Con traduzione inglese e tedesca.

(14) Traité de le Peinture traduit integralement pour la première fois en français, sur le Codex Vaticanus (Urbinas), 1270. (Completed with fragments taken from other MSS.) Arranged and corrected by Péladan.

(15) Textes choisies. Pensées, théories, préceptes, fables et facéties. J. M. Péladan.

(16) The Literary Works of Leonardo. Compiled and edited from the original manuscripts by J. P. Richter, 2 vols.

(17) Leonardo da Vinci's Notebooks. Arranged and rendered into English. With Introduction by Edward MacCurdy.

563

Bibliography

Early Lives and Descriptions of Leonardo

Il Libro di Antonio Billi (Archivio Storico Italiano, Series V., tom. 7).

Paolo Giovio. Leonardi Vincii Vita (Storia della Lett. Ital., tom. vii., part 4).

Anonimo Fiorentino (Gaddiano) (Archivio Storico Italiano, Series V., tom. 12).

Giorgio Vasari. Le Vite. Edited by Milanesi.

Sabba da Castiglione. Ricordi.

Lomazzo (G. P.). Trattato dell'Arte della Pittura, Scultura et Architettura. Idea del Tempio della Pittura.

Benvenuto Cellini. Vita di B. C. da lui medesimo scritta. Trattati di B. C . . . uno dell' Oreficeria, l'altro della Scultura. [Treatises of B. C. on Goldsmithing and Sculpture. Trans. by C. R. Ashbee. Life of B. C. Trans. by John Addington Symonds. Life of Benvenuto Cellini. With notes. Trans. by R. H. Hobart Cust.]

Bandello (Matteo). Novelle. (Vol. 3 of Payne's translation.)

Pacioli (Luca). De Divine Proportione.

English Works on Leonardo

Richter (J. P.). Literary Works of Leonardo (2 vols.). Though not reissued since 1883, this is still an invaluable work.

MacCurdy (E.). Leonardo da Vinci's Notebooks, 1906. Leonardo da Vinci, 1904.

Berenson (B.). Florentine Painters of the Renaissance, 1909. Drawings of the Florentine Painters, 2 vols., 1903. North Italian Painters of the Renaissance, 1907. Study and Criticism of Italian Art, 1901-1902. (Third Series.)

Colvin (S.). Selected Drawings from Old Masters in the University Galleries and the Library at Christchurch, Oxford, 1904.

Horne (H. P.). Life of Leonardo da Vinci. Done into English by H. P. Horne, 1903. (Contains valuable notes.) Some Leonardesque Questions, 1902.

Pater (Walter). Studies in the Renaissance, 1893.

Holmes (Sir C. J.). Leonardo da Vinci (British Academy Lecture).

Marks (A.). The St Anne of Leonardo, 1883.

Brinton (Selwyn). Leonardo at Milan. (Part VII. of *The Renaissance : its Art and Life.*)

Cook (Sir T. A.). Leonardo da Vinci, Sculptor, 1923. Spirals in Nature and Art, 1903.

Cook (H. F.). Reviews and Appreciations, 1912. Catalogue of Pictures of Masters of the Milanese and Allied Schools of Lombardy, 1899.

Hind (C. L.). Drawings of Leonardo da Vinci, 1906.

Ellis (Havelock). The Dance of Life, 1924.

Anderson (N. J.). The Admirable Painter : a Study of Leonardo da Vinci, 1915.

Hart (J. B.). The Mechanical Investigations of Leonardo da Vinci, 1925. Makers of Science, etc., 1923.

Singer (C.). Studies in the History and Method of Science (2 vols.), 1917. Discovery of the Circulation of the Blood, 1922. Chapters in the History of Science, 1922.

Williamson (G. C.). Luini.

[Much interesting work has been done in periodicals. Among those not yet mentioned are Messrs Douglas Freshfield, Montgomery Carmichael, E. R. D. Maclagan, Campbell Dodgson.]

French Works on Leonardo

(*When works in foreign languages have been translated the titles are given in English.*)

Séailles (G. de). Léonard de Vinci, l'artiste et le savant. Essai de biographie psychologique, 1906.

Müntz (Eugène). Leonardo da Vinci, Artist, Thinker and Man of Science, 1898. Histoire de l'art pendant la Renaissance, 1886–1895. Etc.

Bibliography

Dan, Le Pere.   Le Trésor . . . de Fontainebleau.
Clément (C.).   Michel-Ange, Léonard de Vinci, Raphael, 1882.
Bertaux (E.).   Les Arts en Italie, 1916.   Etc., etc.
Mauclair (C.).   La peinture italienne, 1911.
Courajod (L.).   Léonard de Vinci et la statue de Francesco Sforza, 1879.
Barrés (M. E.).   Trois stations de psychothérapie, 1923.
Axenfeld (H.).   Les grands peintres.   Écoles d'Italie.
Valéry (P.).   Introduction à la Methode de Léonard de Vinci, 1919.
Vulliaud (P.).   La pensée ésotèrique de Léonard de Vinci, 1910.
Gautier (I.).   Guide de l'amateur au Musée de Louvre, 1882.   Les dieux et les demi-dieux de la peinture, 1864.
Demonts (L.).   Les dessins de L. de V.
Delaborde (H. F.).   Les Maîtres Florentins du Quinzième Siècle, 1887-1888.
Gauthiez (P.).   Luini, 1906.
Taine (H. A.).   Voyage en Italie, 1806.   Philosophe de l'Art en Italie, 1867.
Suarés (A.)   Voyage du Condottiere vers Venise, 1910.
Michel (E.).   Le Forêt de Fontainebleau, 1909.
Stendhal (Henri Beyle).   Histoire de la Peinture en Italie, 1817.
Houssaye (Arsène).   Histoire de Léonard de Vinci, 1869.
Schure (E.).   Précurseurs et Revoltés, 1904.
Duhem (R.).   Études sur Léonard de Vinci.   Ceux qu'il a lus et ceux qui l'ont lu, 1906.
Piot (E.).   Cabinet de l'Amateur.
Duhousset (E.).   Le cheval dans la nature et dans l'art, 1902.
Lécluze (E. J. de).   Léonard de Vinci, 1841.
Duval (Mathias).   L'anatomie des Maîtres, 1890.
Venturi (G. B.).   Essai sur les ouvrages psycho-mathematiques de L. de V., 1797.
Péladan (J. A.).   La dernière leçon de Léonard de Vinci.   Etc., etc.
Léonard de Vinci 1519–1919.   (Centenary volume of *La Nouvelle Révue d'Italie*.)
[Immense and valuable work has appeared in periodicals, by those already mentioned ; also by Léon Dorez, Paul Errara, H. Geymüller, C. F. Trachsel, Salomon Reinach, R. Bonnamen, Marcel Reymond, Georges Beaume, Louis Coppier, Gustave Moreau, A. Michel, J. L. Vaudroyer, F. H. Grüyer, J. Mesnil, M. Mignon, E. Bouvy, E. Aurel, J. de Beaufort, A. Grüyer.   The *Gazette des Beaux Arts* is peculiarly rich in special studies.]

Italian Works on Leonardo

It is here possible only to pay a tribute to the unremitting diligence of Italian scholars.   The *Raccolta Vinciana*, issuing from the Castello Sforzesco, Milano, and edited by Dottore Ettore Verga, Direttore dell'Archivio Storico Civico, Milano, maintains a complete bibliography of works and articles written on Leonardo.   The Istituto di Studii Vinciani, the Reale Commissione Vinciani, and other bodies, continue to deal with the details of the great Italian's life and work.   It is possible only to mention with respect the names of E. Solmi (who has written a concise *Life of Leonardo*, 1900), Luca Beltrami, who is specially interesting on the architecture of Milan, and writers representing a diversity of interests like Girolamo Calvi, E. Verga, M. Baratta, M. Cermenati, G. Carotta, G. Govi, G. Uzielli, Count Malagazzi-Valeri, A. Mazenta, V. Paoli, A. Schiaparelli, G. B. Toni, A. Venturi, A. Luzio, specialist on Isabella d'Este, M. Cermenati, C. Boito, Isidoro del Lungo, G. Fumigalli, A. Favoro, G. Frizzoni, L. Venturi, the Marchese d'Adda, E. Ridolfi.

The first modern study of Leonardo was Amoretti's *Memorie storiche su la vita gli studii e le opere di Leonardo da Vinci* (Milan, 1804).

Valuable memorial volumes of 1919 are the *Conferenzo Fiorentino*, and the volume issued by the Istituto di Studi Vinciani, Rome, 1920, *Per il IV. centenario della morte di Leonardo da Vinci*, edited by Mario Cermenati.   Uzielli's *Ricerche* are necessary to the student.   A well-illustrated biography is G. Lesca's *Leonardo da Vinci*, 1920.   Papini has a lively essay on Leonardo in *Four and Twenty Minds*.   Benedetto Croce also discusses his work.

Bibliography

German

Goethe (J. W. von).   Observations on Leonardo da Vinci's *Last Supper*.
Mueller-Walde (P.).   Leonardo da Vinci, 1890.
Müther (R.).   Leonardo da Vinci, 1907.   History of Painting (2 vols.), 1907.
Rosenberg (C. A.).   Leonardo da Vinci.   1898.
Freud (S.).   Leonardo da Vinci.
Wölfflin (H.).   The Art of the Italian Renaissance, 1903.
Herzfeld (Marie).   Leonardo da Vinci, der Denker, Forscher, and Poet, 1906.
Bode (W. von).   Studien über Leonardo da Vinci, 1921.   Etc., etc.
Chamberlain (H. S.).   Immanuel Kant, 1914.
Steinmann (E.).   Botticelli.   (Trans. by Campbell Dodgson, 1901.)
Gronau (G.).   Leonardo da Vinci, 1914.
Strzygowski (J.).   Studien zu Leonardo.   Etc.
Mackowsky (Hans.).   Verrocchio, 1901.
Seidlitz (Woldenar von).   Ambrogio da Preda und L. da V., 1883; and other studies published in a specialized way.
[Other writers are M. Holl, G. Klein, A. Springer, A. Förster, P. Kristeller, J. Lange, H. Ludwig.]

Scandinavian

Thüs (J.).   The Florentine Years of Leonardo and Verrocchio.   (English translation, 1913.)
Sirèn (O.).   Leonardo da Vinci, the Artist and the Man.   (English version, 1916.)

Russian

Vuolinski (A. L.).   Leonardo da Vinci, 1909.

General History of the Renaissance, 1452-1519

The literature connected with Renaissance Italy is endless.   I take the *Cambridge Modern History* and the works of Burckhardt and John Addington Symonds for granted.   Beneath are a few of the works referring more particularly to the scenes of Leonardo's career.   "Etc." means that the author has more volumes on the subject.

Reumont (A. von).   Lorenzo de' Medici the Magnificent.
Horsburgh (E. L. S.).   Lorenzo the Magnificent and Florence in her Golden Age.
Armstrong (E.).   Lorenzo de' Medici and Florence in the 15th Century.
Gardner (J. E. G.).   The Story of Florence.   Etc.
Young (C. F.).   The Medici.
Ross (J. A.).   Lives of the Early Medici.   Etc.
Perrens (F. J.).   La Civilisation Florentine.
Biagi (Guido).   Private Life of the Renaissance Florentines.   Men and Manners of Old Florence.   Etc.
Lungo (I. del).   Women of Florence.
Hutton (E.).   Florence and the Cities of Northern Tuscany.   Etc.
Condivi (A.).   Life of Michelangelo.   Done into English by H. P. Horne.
Muntz (E.).   La Renaissance en Italie et en France à l'époque de Charles VIII.   Florence et la Toscane.   Etc.
Villari (P.).   Life and Times of Machiavelli.   Life and Times of Savonarola.   Etc.
Gebhart (E.).   Florence.   Botticelli et son époque.   Etc.
Yashiro (Y.).   Sandro Botticelli.
Colvin (S.).   A Florentine Picture-Chronicle.
Monnier (P.).   Le Quattro-Cento (2 vols.).

Bibliography

Rodocanachi (E.). La Première Renaissance. La Femme Italienne. Etc.
Yriarte (C.). Florence: its History, Letters, etc.
Maurras (Charles). Athinée. D'Athènes à Florence.
Mauclair (C.). Florence.
Heywood (W.). Palio and Ponte. Etc.
Horne (H.). Life of Alessandro Felipepi, commonly called Sandro Botticelli.
Bisticci (Vespasiano da). Vite di uomini illustri del secolo XV. (English translation.)
Reymond (M.). Brunelleschi et l'architecture de la Renaissance.
Landucci (L.). Diario. (English translation.)
Pasolini dell' Onda (Count). Caterina Sforza.
Clausse (G.). Les Sforza et les arts en Milanais. Etc.
Ady (C. M.). A History of Milan under the Sforzas.
Malagazzi-Valeri (F.). Il Corte di Lodovico il Moro. Milano (No. 25 and 26 of Serie 1A *Italia Artistica*). Etc.
Romussi (C.). Milano e suoi monumenti (2 vols.).
Corio (B.). Storia di Milano, 1503.
Noyes (E.). Story of Milan.
Mongeri. L'Arte in Milano, 1872.
Gauthiez (P.). Milan.
Cartwright (J.). Isabella d'Este. Beatrice d'Este, Duchess of Milan (1475–1497).
Bellincioni (B.). Le Rime.
Beltrami (L.). Castello di Milano. Etc., etc., etc.
Gardner (J. E. G.). The King of Court Poets. (Other Works on Ferrara.)
Cesaresco Martinengro (Countess). Lombard Studies.
Hutton (E.). Milan and Lombardy. Cities of Lombardy. Etc., etc.
Warner (Sir G. F.). Miniatures and Borders from the Book of Hours of Bona Sforza.
Castiglione (Baldassare). Book of the Courtier. (Translation and notes by L. E. Opdyke.)
Dennistoun (James). Memoirs of the Dukes of Urbino.
Sizeranne (R. de la). Les masques et les visages: portraits célèbres de la Renaissance Italienne (2 vols.).
Delaborde (H. F.). L'expedition de Charles VIII. en Italie.
Comines (P. de). Mémoires.
Maulde la Clavière (M. R. de). Jean d'Auton's Chroniques de Louis XII. Les femmes de la Renaissance. (English translation.) Jean Perréal. Etc.
Pélissier (L. G.). Notes italiennes de l'histoire de France. Récherches dans les archives italiennes. Louis XII. and Lodovico Sforza. Etc.
Bandello (Matteo). Novelle. (The novels of M. B. done into English prose by John Payne. 6 vols.)
Rodocanachi (E.). La Première Renaissance en Italie. La Femme Italienne.
Molinier (E.). Venise. Etc., etc.
Cook (H. F.). Giorgione.
Woodward (W. H.). Cesare Borgia.
Yriarte (Charles). César Borgia. Autour des Borgia. Venise. Vie d'un patricien de Venise.
Alvisi (E.). Cesare Borgia.
Manturanzio (F.). Chronicles of the City of Perugia, 1492–1503.
Roscoe (L.). Life and Pontificate of Leo X.
Lanciani (R. H.). Golden Days of the Renaissance. Etc., etc.
Ricci (C.). Roma.
Scott (Geoffrey). Architecture of Humanism.
Holroyd (C.). Life of Michelangelo.
Vaughan (H. M.). The Medici Popes.
Rolland (Romain). Vie de Michel Ange.
Symonds (J. A.). Life of Michelangelo.
Burchard (J.). Johannis Burchardi—Diarium. Edited by Louis Thuasne. (See other works by Thuasne.)
Gregorovius (F.). Rome in the Middle Ages (vol. viii.). Lucrezia Borgia.

Bibliography

Condivi. Life of Michelangelo. (Trans. and Edited by H. P. Horne.)

Germain (A.). Les Clouets.

Bouchot (H.). Les femmes de Brantôme. La Peinture en France sous les Valois. Etc.

La Ferrière-Percy (H. de). Marguerite d'Angoulême.

Vitry (P.). Tours et les chateaux de Touraine.

Paris (A. R.). Études sur François Premier.

Bournon (F.). Blois, Chambord et les chateaux du Blésois.

Capefigue (J. B. H. R.). François 1er et la Renaissance.

Bossebœuf (L. A.). La Touraine Historique—Amboise. Etc.

Crue (F. de). Anne de Montmorency. La cour de France au XVIe siècle.

Pattison (E. F. S.) (Lady Dilke). Renaissance of Art in France.

Robinson (A. M. F.) (Madame Duclaux). End of the Middle Ages.

Memoirs of Brantôme, l'Estoile, Fleuranges, le Bourgeois de Paris, Le Loyal Serviteur, etc., etc.

The studies of J. Klackzko, A. E. Picot, C. Enlart, Pierre de Nolhac, Armand Baschet, C. Ephrussi, Maurice Mignon, A. Maurel, H. Hauvette, E. Molinier, J. de Foville, R. L. Douglas, Isodoro del Lungo, G. F. Hill, F. A. Hyett, E. M. Rouard, L. Romier, Alessandro Luzio, are among many others which present interesting details and points of view.

Index

Index

Index

571

Index

Index

Index

Index

575

Index

Index

Index

Index

Index